THIRD
EDITION

Assessing Infants and Preschoolers with Special Needs

Mary McLean
University of Wisconsin–Milwaukee

Mark Wolery
Vanderbilt University

Donald B. Bailey Jr.
University of North Carolina

PEARSON

Merrill
Prentice Hall

Upper Saddle River, New Jersey
Columbus, Ohio

Library of Congress Cataloging in Publication Data

McLean, Mary E.
  Assessing infants and preschoolers with special needs/ Mary Mclean, Mark Wolery, Donald B. Bailey, Jr.—3rd ed.
    p. cm.
  Includes bibliographical references and indexes.
  ISBN 0-13-098662-3
  1. Children with disabilities—Education (Preschool)—Evaluation. 2. Children with disabilities—Identification.
  3. Children with disabilities—Psychological testing. I. Wolery, Mark. II. Bailey, Donald B. III. Title.

  LC4019.2.M45 2004
  371.9'043—dc21   2003042029

Vice President and Executive Publisher: Jeffery W. Johnston
Editor: Allyson P. Sharp
Editorial Assistant: Penny Burleson
Production Editor: Sheryl Glicker Langner
Production Coordination: Carlisle Publishers Services
Design Coordinator: Diane C. Lorenzo
Photo Coordinator: Sandy Schaefer
Cover Designer: Ali Mohrman
Cover art: Superstock
Production Manager: Laura Messerly
Director of Marketing: Ann Castel Davis
Marketing Manager: Amy June
Marketing Coordinator: Tyra Poole

This book was set in New Caledonia by Carlisle Communications, Ltd. It was printed and bound by R. R. Donnelley & Sons Company. The cover was printed by Phoenix Color Corp.

Photo Credits: Scott Cunningham/Merrill, pp. 1, 45, 204, 236; Todd Yarrington/Merrill, pp. 22, 262, 451; Anne Vega/Merrill, pp. 71, 100, 345, 487, 545; Barbara Schwartz/Merrill, p. 123; Beth Langley, pp. 134, 136, 159; Reprinted with permission from Vistech Consultants, Inc., Manufacturer of the Teller Acuity Card Testing System, p. 148; David Grossman/PH College, p. 172; Teresa Golson, pp. 307, 306; Ken Karp/PH College, p. 412; Anthony Magnacca/Merrill, p. 517.

Pearson Education Ltd.
Pearson Education Singapore Pte. Ltd.
Pearson Education Canada, Ltd.
Pearson Education—Japan

Pearson Education Australia Pty. Limited
Pearson Education North Asia Ltd.
Pearson Education de Mexico, S.A. de C.V.
Pearson Education Malaysia Pte. Ltd.

10 9 8 7 6 5 4
ISBN: 0-13-098662-3

This book is dedicated to Mary McEvoy, our friend and colleague, who co-authored Chapter 9 in this text. Mary brought a spirit and energy to our field that touched many lives and will be sorely missed.

PREFACE

The organization of this book is similar to that of the previous edition. The first four chapters provide basic information on the assessment process. Chapter 1 includes information on the legal basis and recommended practices in assessing young children with special needs. Chapter 2 provides the foundation of information on tests and measurement. Chapter 3 reviews procedural considerations in assessment of young children. Chapter 4, written by Eleanor Lynch and Marci Hanson, provides the reader with information on ensuring cultural competence in assessment.

The next five chapters cover special concerns in the assessment of young children. Chapter 5 presents information on Child Find, screening, and tracking. Chapter 6, written by Beth Langley, presents detailed information on assessing sensory processes in young children. Chapter 7 addresses assessment of family concerns, resources, and priorities. Chapter 8 provides information on assessing the environments in which young children function. Chapter 9, written by Mary McEvoy, Shelly Neilsen, and Joe Reichle, is new to this edition and focuses on the functional assessment of behavior.

Chapters 10 through 15 are organized according to developmental domains. Chapter 10, written by Katherine McCormick and Leah Nellis, addresses cognitive development. Chapter 11, written by Martha Cook and Jennifer Kilgo, provides information on assessing motor skills. Chapter 12, written by Elizabeth Crais and Joanne Erwick Roberts, addresses communication skills. Chapter 13, written by Sam Odom, Hannah Schertz, Leslie Munson, and Bill Brown, addresses social interaction skills. Chapter 14, written by Ann Garfinkle, presents information on assessing play skills. Chapter 15, written by Eva Horn and Amy Childre, provides information on assessing adaptive skills.

In Chapter 16, the process of using assessment information to plan instructional programs for infants and young children is addressed. The final chapter of the book, Chapter 17, provides information on assessment for the purpose of monitoring child progress.

As indicated in the preface to the first edition (Bailey & Wolery, 1989), reading this book will not make one competent in the assessment of infants and young children. The instructor who has chosen to use this text is advised to carefully plan field-based experiences for students who are learning to assess children, work with families, and engage in collaborative decision making as a member of an assessment team. There is no substitute for quality field experiences.

We would like to thank the following reviewers: Brent A. Askvig, Minot State University; Cynthia A. Dieterich, Cleveland State University; Helmi Owens, Pacific Lutheran University; and Pam Robinson, Oklahoma Baptist University.

ACKNOWLEDGMENTS

We would like to recognize the contributions of the many individuals who were involved in the preparation of this third edition. We are grateful to the chapter authors who contributed their knowledge and their time to the revision of this book. Its quality is in large part due to the considerable expertise amassed in this group of individuals. We are grateful for their hard work.

We dedicate this book to our spouses and children, and to those professionals and families who work diligently together in assessing young children so that intervention will be of the highest quality for every child and family.

Mary McLean
Mark Wolery
Donald B. Bailey

DISCOVER THE COMPANION WEBSITE ACCOMPANYING THIS BOOK

THE PRENTICE HALL COMPANION WEBSITE: A VIRTUAL LEARNING ENVIRONMENT

Technology is a constantly growing and changing aspect of our field that is creating a need for content and resources. To address this emerging need, Prentice Hall has developed an online learning environment for students and professors alike—Companion Websites—to support our textbooks.

In creating a Companion Website, our goal is to build on and enhance what the textbook already offers. For this reason, the content for each user-friendly website is organized by topic and provides the professor and student with a variety of meaningful resources. Common features of a Companion Website include:

For the Professor—

Every Companion Website integrates **Syllabus Manager™,** an online syllabus creation and management utility.

- **Syllabus Manager™** provides you, the instructor, with an easy, step-by-step process to create and revise syllabi, with direct links into Companion Website and other online content without having to learn HTML.
- Students may log-on to your syllabus during any study session. All they need to know is the web address for the Companion Website and the password you've assigned to your syllabus.
- After you have created a syllabus using **Syllabus Manager™,** students may enter the syllabus for their course section from any point in the Companion Website.

- Clicking on a date, the student is shown the list of activities for the assignment. The activities for each assignment—name of the assignment, instructions, and whether or not it is a one-time or repeating assignment.
- Adding assignments consists of clicking on the desired due date, then filling in the details of the assignment—name of the assignment, instructions, and whether or not it is a one-time or repeating assignment.
- In addition, links to other activities can be created easily. If the activity is online, a URL can be entered in the space provided, and it will be linked automatically in the final syllabus.
- Your completed syllabus is hosted on our servers, allowing convenient updates from any computer on the Internet. Changes you make to your syllabus are immediately available to your students at their next logon.

For the Student—

- **Overview and General Information**— General information about the topic and how it will be covered in the website.
- **Web Links**—A variety of websites related to topic areas.
- **Content Methods and Strategies**— Resources that helps to put theories into practice in the special education classroom.
- **Reflective Questions and Case-Based Activities**—Put concepts into action, participate in activities, examine strategies, and more.
- **National and State Laws**—An online guide to how federal and state laws affect your special education classroom.

- **Behavior Management**—An online guide to help manage behaviors in the special education classroom.
- **Message Board**—Virtual bulletin board to post and respond to questions and comments from a national audience.

To take advantage of these and other resources, please visit the *Assessing Infants and Preschoolers with Special Needs*, Third Edition, Companion Website at

www.prenhall.com/mclean

BRIEF CONTENTS

CONTENTS

········

CHAPTER 7
Assessing Family Resources, Priorities, and Concerns   172
Donald B. Bailey Jr.

········

········

. . . .

CHAPTER 13

Assessing Social Competence   412

Samuel L. Odom, Hannah Schertz,
Leslie Munson, William H. Brown

. . . .

CHAPTER 14

Assessing Play Skills   451

Ann N. Garfinkle

Note: Every effort has been made to provide accurate and current Internet information in this book. However, the Internet and information posted on it are constantly changing, so it is inevitable that some of the Internet addresses listed in this textbook will change.

Assessment and Its Importance in Early Intervention/Early Childhood Special Education

Mary McLean
University of Wisconsin–Milwaukee

Assessment is an important and ongoing responsibility of professionals who serve young children and their families. Assessment provides insight into the course of development for young children. It determines which children have a need for special services, defines the services to be provided, and measures the success of early intervention efforts. Parameters of assessment are determined by federal and state legislation and regulations and are influenced by current thinking relative to best practice. Professionals working in early childhood settings must have a solid understanding of assessment concepts and practices, must have skills in the clinical application of these concepts and practices, and must keep up with new instruments, new regulations, and new trends.

Over the past 35 years, the field of Early Intervention/Early Childhood Special Education (EI/ECSE) has grown dramatically, establishing itself as a discipline related to but also different from parent disciplines of Special Education and Early Childhood Education. The knowledge base for assessment in EI/ECSE is uniquely applied to the population of young children with special needs. The term *young children with special needs,* as it is used in this text, refers to children who have an identified disability or delay in development or who have a condition that puts them at risk of developing a disability or a delay. The focus of this text will be children from birth through age 5. As the field of EI/ECSE has grown, the unique aspects of the population of young children with special needs has become apparent (Guralnick, 1997). At the same time, the settings in which assessment and intervention are provided for these children have become less specialized and separate as the philosophy of serving all children in natural environments has become prevalent.

This textbook is designed to provide information needed by professionals who will be responsible for the assessment of infants, toddlers, and preschoolers with special needs. This chapter provides an overview of the legal basis for assessment, the various functions of assessment, and the special challenges presented in assessing young children with special needs. The chapter also introduces the reader to the unique characteristics of assessment that have evolved to meet those challenges.

THE LEGAL BASIS FOR ASSESSMENT PROCEDURES

As indicated earlier, the field of Early Intervention/Early Childhood Special Education is still relatively young. Laws that govern the assessment of young children with special needs have been passed fairly recently. As shown in Figure 1.1, Public Law (P.L.) 94-142, passed in 1975 and called the Education for All Handicapped Children Act, mandated services for all school-age children with disabilities and facilitated the provision of services for preschool children with disabilities in some states. Under this law, states were allowed to choose whether or not to serve preschool children. P.L. 94-142 and its regulations provided guidelines for the assessment of children receiving special education services from state departments of education.

In 1986, P.L. 99-457 was passed, amending P.L. 94-142 and requiring the states to provide a free and appropriate public education to children with disabilities from age 3 through age 5. The regulations that governed school-age children were then made applicable to the assessment of preschool children. In addition, Part H (later to become Part C) was added to the law, establishing incentives for serving infants and toddlers (children from birth until their third birthday) with special needs. Wording in this law and its subsequent regulations provide a legal basis for the assessment of infants and toddlers.

Later legislation has reauthorized and made some changes in the original legislation governing infant/toddler and preschool programs. In 1990, P.L. 101-476 changed the name of the Education of All Handicapped Children Act to the Individuals with Disabilities Education Act (IDEA), emphasizing "people first" terminology and using the term *disability* rather than *handicap.* In 1991,

1975	Public Law 94-142, the Education of All Handicapped Children Act, established services for all school-age children with disabilities and some preschoolers with disabilities. This law and its regulations provide much guidance for assessment procedures for preschoolers.
1986	Public Law 99-457, amending P.L. 94-142, mandated free and appropriate public education for preschool children (ages 3 through 5 years) with disabilities (Part B, Section 619) and established incentives for serving infants and toddlers (Part H).
1990	Public Law 101-476 reauthorized the Education of All Handicapped Children Act (P.L. 94-142) and renamed it the Individuals with Disabilities Education Act (IDEA).
1991	Public Law 102-119 reauthorized and extended Part H of P.L. 99-457 and amended both Part H and Part B, Section 619.
1997	Public Law 105-17 reauthorized IDEA, changed Part H to Part C, increased expectations for children with disabilities by ensuring their access to the general curriculum, strengthened the role of parents in the education of their children, and increased expectations for accountability.

FIGURE 1.1

Legislation affecting assessment in EI/ECSE

P.L. 102-119 reauthorized and amended both the infant/toddler and the preschool legislation.

In 1997, Public Law 105-17, now known as the 1997 Amendments to IDEA or "IDEA '97", reauthorized IDEA and reformatted Parts A–H into Parts A–D:

- Part A provides general provisions of the law including definitions.
- Part B provides the requirements for providing special education and related services for children 3 years through 21 years of age.
- Part C provides the requirements for providing services for infants and toddlers with disabilities, birth to age 3.
- Part D includes provisions for federal funding for discretionary programs including grants for research, personnel preparation, model demonstration, technical assistance, parent training and information centers, and State Program Improvement Grants.

The changes made to IDEA by the 1997 Amendments were significant and, among other things, ensured the access of children with disabilities to the general curriculum to the greatest extent possible, strengthened the role of parents in decision making and involvement in their child's educational program, and ensured the inclusion of children with disabilities in state and district-wide assessment systems.

As indicated, the legislation and regulations that govern the assessment of infants and toddlers are somewhat different from those that govern the assessment of preschoolers. Specifically, Part C of IDEA and the corresponding regulations developed by the U.S. Office of Education specify procedures to be followed with children under the age of 3. Part B, Section 619 of IDEA and the corresponding regulations specify procedures for children from 3 years to 6 years. In many states, the state agencies responsible for these two programs and, therefore, the state regulations to be followed, are also different. Realization of the confusion caused when families make the transition from infant/toddler services to preschool services led to a call for a "seamless" system, and efforts to legislate this system were included in P.L. 102–119. However, in many states the differences between services under Part B, Section 619 and Part C are still quite apparent.

Although Part C and Part B are similar in intent and serve populations with similar needs, there are substantial differences between the two. Part C does not view children as service recipients apart from their families and, therefore, serves birth through 2-year-old children through a family-centered approach. Part B, Section 619 programs for preschool children have been, for the most part, an extension of school-age programs downward to include children from 3 through 5 years of age. These programs are administered by departments of education in each state and jurisdiction and, therefore, tend to be administered and regulated in a manner similar to school-age programs of special education. The approach tends to be more child-centered, based on the identification of the child's need for uniquely designed instruction. As indicated above, there have been attempts to reduce the discrepancy between infant/toddler and preschool programs; for example, P.L. 102-119 allows the use of an Individualized Family Service Plan rather than an Individualized Education Program for preschool children. However, major differences in the legislation and in regulations still exist. Differences also occur from state to state.

Definitions of Eligibility

Federal law provides a general definition of which children are eligible for EI/ECSE services, but each state and jurisdiction is responsible for the exact definition of eligibility as well as designation of diagnostic instruments or procedures to be used. EI/ECSE professionals must be thoroughly familiar with both the federal law and regulations and state guidelines relative to determination of eligibility to serve as a member of an eligibility team. It is not uncommon for there to be frequent changes in federal law and regulations and in state guidelines. The federal law must be reauthorized every five years and is subject to change during each reauthorization. State guidelines can change even more frequently. Professionals, therefore, must remain current in their knowledge of federal and state laws and regulations.

Figure 1.2 presents the wording from IDEA, Part C, relative to the determination of eligibility

---

The term "infant or toddler with a disability":

(A) means an individual under 3 years of age who needs early intervention services because the individual:
   (i) is experiencing developmental delays, as measured by appropriate diagnostic instruments and procedures in one or more of the areas of cognitive development, physical development, communication development, social or emotional development, and adaptive development; or
   (ii) has a diagnosed physical or mental condition which has a high probability of resulting in developmental delay; and

(B) may also include, at a state's discretion, at-risk infants and toddlers. The term "at-risk infant or toddler" means an individual under 3 years of age who would be at risk of experiencing a substantial developmental delay if early intervention services were not provided to the individual.

FIGURE 1.2

Statutory language pertaining to eligibility definitions—IDEA, Part C

Note: From amendments to the Individuals with Disabilities Education Act (IDEA '97), 20 U.S.C. §632(5)(A), §632(5)(B), and §632(1) (1997).

for early intervention services for children from birth through 2 years of age. As can be seen, three groups of children may be eligible for services:

1. Children who have a measurable developmental delay in one or more of five areas: cognitive development, physical development, communication development, social or emotional development, or adaptive development.
2. Children who have a diagnosed condition that probably will result in developmental delay (even if a delay is not currently present).
3. Children who are at risk of having a delay if early intervention is not provided. This third group will be served only if a state chooses to do so. As of June 2002, only eight states and one jurisdiction (Guam) were serving a group of children in this third category, and the definitions of *at risk* varied greatly among these states (Shackelford, 2002b). This number has decreased from 13 states in 1992 to 8 states in 2002 (Shackelford, 1992). Information on children considered to be at risk is presented in Chapter 5 of this text.

Each state or jurisdiction has established criteria for determining whether a measurable developmental delay (category 1 in previous list) exists. According to Shackelford (2002b), some states use a quantitative measure of developmental delay, for instance 2.0 standard deviations below the mean (a standard deviation is a measure of the degree to which a score deviates from the mean) or a 25% delay in a developmental area. However, the specific criteria vary considerably among states in terms of the type of measure used and also in terms of the level of delay required. Shackelford (2002a) found at least three different types of quantitative definitions in use:

1. The difference between chronological age and actual performance level (as determined through an age-equivalent measure of performance in the specified developmental domains). Example: Oklahoma—50% delay in one area or 25% delay in two or more areas. A child who is 18 months old and has an age-equivalent score of 9 months or less in the area of motor development, for example, has a 50% delay in physical development.
2. Delay expressed as performance at a certain number of months below chronological age. Example: Texas—A child 2 to 12 months old must have a 2-month delay; a child 13 to 24 months old must have a 3-month delay; a child 25 to 36 months old must have a 4-month delay. A child younger than 2 months must have documented atypical behaviors.
3. Delay indicated by standard deviations below the mean (requires a norm-referenced instrument). Example: Oregon—2.0 standard deviations (SD) below the mean in one area or 1.5 SD below the mean in two or more areas. For example, if the mean is 100 and the standard deviation is 15.0, a child would need a score below 70 in one area or scores below 77 in two areas to qualify for services. Standard scores are discussed in Chapter 2.

In addition, some states use only a qualitative definition. For example, in California and Hawaii, a multidisciplinary team consensus is required. No level of standard deviation or percentage delay is specified. This type of eligibility does not require a quantitative measure. Using traditional assessments that yield standard scores or age-equivalent scores has been problematic due to the paucity of reliable and valid instruments for this age group (Benn, 1994; Neisworth & Bagnato, 1992; Shonkoff & Meisels, 1991). In recognition of this difficulty, states are required to ensure that "informed clinical opinion" is used in determining eligibility under Part C (34 C.F.R. 303.322 [c][2]). "Informed clinical opinion" refers to the application of the knowledge and skills of the early intervention multidisciplinary team, including the parents, when making eligibility decisions for infants and toddlers (Shackelford, 2002a) and is discussed in the next section.

(A) The term "child with disability" means a child—
  (i)   with mental retardation, hearing impairments (including deafness), speech or language impairments, visual impairments (including blindness), serious emotional disturbance (hereinafter referred to as "emotional disturbance"), orthopedic impairments, autism, traumatic brain injury, other health impairments, or specific learning disabilities; and
  (ii) who, by reason thereof, needs special education and related services.

(B) Child aged 3 through 9—The term "child with a disability" for a child aged 3 through 9 may, at the discretion of the State and the local educational agency, include a child—
  (i)   experiencing developmental delays, as defined by the State and as measured by appropriate diagnostic instruments and procedures, in one or more of the following areas: physical development, cognitive development, communication development, social or emotional development, or adaptive development; and
  (ii) who, by reason thereof, needs special education and related services.

FIGURE 1.3

Eligibility for preschool children under IDEA, Part B

Note: From amendments to the Individuals with Disabilities Education Act (IDEA '97), 20 U.S.C. §1401(3) (1997).

Figure 1.3 presents the wording from IDEA, Part B, relative to the determination of eligibility for services for preschool children with special needs. As can be seen, children who are 3, 4, or 5 years of age may be eligible according to the categories of disability used with school-age children. The federal definitions of the categories of disability are provided in Figure 1.4. Modifications may be made in a category by the states so that it is a better fit for preschool children. It should be noted that in addition to meeting the criteria for one of these categories, the need for special education services and related services must also be demonstrated, as specified in Figure 1.3.

Since the passage of P.L. 102-119, the states have had the option to develop a special category for preschool children defined by a delay in one or more of five developmental areas. IDEA '97 extended this option through age 9. At state and local discretion, children ages 3 years through 9 years may be found eligible for special education on the basis of having a "developmental delay" in

one or more of five developmental areas: physical development, cognitive development, communication development, social or emotional development, and adaptive development. However, a state education agency (SEA) must define "developmental delay" and must determine the age range of children to whom it will apply before any local district has the option to use it. As when using any of the 13 IDEA categories of disability, in addition to meeting eligibility requirements for developmental delay, the need for special education and related services must also be determined (Walsh, Smith, & Taylor, 2000).

Danaher (2001) analyzed the eligibility classifications and criteria put into place relative to this special category in all 50 states, the District of Columbia, American Samoa, and Guam. Almost all (51) of these 53 states and jurisdictions now have a disability category that is unique to young children. Only two of the states and jurisdictions analyzed do not use a category specific to young children. Danaher (2001) found that 19 states extend the use of a developmental delay

Autism means a developmental disability significantly affecting verbal and nonverbal communication and social interaction, generally evident before age 3, that adversely affects educational performance. Other characteristics often associated with autism are engagement in repetitive activities and stereotyped movements, resistance to environmental change or change in daily routines, and unusual responses to sensory experiences. The term does not apply if a child's educational performance is adversely affected primarily because the child has an emotional disturbance, as defined below. A child who manifests the characteristics of "autism" after age 3 could be diagnosed as having "autism" if the criteria above are satisfied.

Deaf-blindness means concomitant hearing and visual impairments, the combination of which causes such severe communication and other developmental and educational problems that they cannot be accommodated in special education programs solely for children with deafness or children with blindness.

Deafness means a hearing impairment which is so severe that the child is impaired in processing linguistic information through hearing, with or without amplification, that adversely affects educational performance.

Emotional disturbance is a term that means a condition exhibiting one or more of the following characteristics over a long period of time and to a marked degree that adversely affects educational performance:

- An inability to learn which cannot be explained by intellectual, sensory, or health factors;
- An inability to build or maintain satisfactory interpersonal relationships with peers and teachers;
- Inappropriate types of behavior or feelings under normal circumstances;
- A general pervasive mood of unhappiness or depression; or
- A tendency to develop physical symptoms or fears associated with personal or school problems.

The term includes schizophrenia. The term does not apply to children who are socially maladjusted, unless it is determined that they have an emotional disturbance.

Hearing impairment means an impairment in hearing, whether permanent or fluctuating, which adversely affects a child's educational performance but that is not included under the definition of "deafness" in this section.

Mental retardation means significantly subaverage general intellectual functioning existing concurrently with deficits in adaptive behavior and manifested during the developmental period that adversely affects a child's educational performance.

Multiple disabilities means concomitant impairments (such as mental retardation-blindness, mental retardation-orthopedic impairment, etc.), the combination of which causes such severe educational problems that they cannot be accommodated in special education programs solely for one of the impairments. The term does not include deaf-blindness.

Orthopedic impairment means a severe orthopedic impairment which adversely affects a child's educational performance. The term includes impairments caused by congenital anomaly (e.g., clubfoot, absence of some member, etc.), impairments caused by disease (e.g., poliomyelitis, bone tuberculosis, etc.), and impairments from other causes (e.g., cerebral palsy, amputations, and fractures or burns which cause contractures).

FIGURE 1.4
IDEA definitions of disabilities (Part B)
Note: From regulations to IDEA Amendments of 1997, 34 C.F.R. §300.7(c) (1999).

Other health impairments means having limited strength, vitality, or alertness including a heightened alertness to environmental stimuli, that results in limited alertness with respect to the educational environment, that—

(i) is due to chronic or acute health problems such as asthma, attention deficit disorder, attention hyperactivity disorder, diabetes, epilepsy, a heart condition, hemophilia, lead poisoning, leukemia, nephritis, rheumatic fever and sickle cell anemia; and
(ii) adversely affects a child's educational performance.

Specific learning disability means a disorder in one or more of the basic psychological processes involved in understanding or in using language, spoken or written, that may manifest itself in an imperfect ability to listen, think, speak, read, write, spell, or do mathematical calculations. The term includes such conditions as perceptual disabilities, brain injury, minimal brain dysfunction, dyslexia, and developmental aphasia. The term does not apply to children who have learning problems that are primarily the result of visual, hearing, or motor disabilities, of mental retardation, or emotional disturbance, or of environmental, cultural, or economic disadvantage.

Speech or language impairment means a communication disorder such as stuttering, impaired articulation, a language impairment or a voice impairment that adversely affects a child's educational performance.

Traumatic brain injury means an acquired injury to the brain caused by an external physical force, resulting in total or partial functional disability or psychosocial impairment, or both, that adversely affects a child's educational performance. The term applies to open or closed head injuries resulting in impairments in one or more areas, such as cognition; language; memory; attention; reasoning; abstract thinking; judgment; problem-solving; sensory, perceptual, and motor abilities; psychosocial behavior; physical function; information processing; and speech. The term does not apply to brain injuries that are congenital or degenerative, or brain injuries induced by birth trauma.

Visual impairment including blindness means an impairment in vision that, even with correction, adversely affects a child's educational performance. The term includes both partial sight and blindness.

FIGURE 1.4
Continued

category beyond age 5. An additional 10 states reported being engaged in piloting or policy changes relative to extending developmental delay beyond age 5. The term "developmental delay" or a similar term such as "significant development delay" is used in 35 states and Guam. Other states and jurisdictions use a variety of other terms such as "preschool special needs," "noncategorical early childhood," and "early childhood disability" (Danaher, 2001).

The relationship of a developmental delay category to other Part B categories varies. Most states (34) add a new category that is used along with the other IDEA categories. In some states, the developmental delay category is used in place of other categories such as mental retardation, emotional disturbance, or learning disability. While in other states, it takes the place of all of the other categories. Finally, in 10 states, developmental delay is used only for those children who don't qualify according to one of the other categories. Wisconsin is an example of this: significant developmental delay is considered only if the other categories don't apply.

The most commonly used criterion for developmental delay is that used by Montana: 2.0 standard deviations below the mean in one developmental area or 1.5 standard deviation below the mean in two areas. Some states, such as Maryland, use percent of delay as a criterion: 20% to 33% delay criterion are commonly used. So, for example, a child who is 48 months old and has an age-equivalent score of 36 months or less in a developmental area has a 25% delay. Some states' criteria include both a standard deviation and a percent delay criterion so that either could be used. In addition, 13 states allow a team consensus or informed clinical opinion in place of test scores, and 11 allow eligibility to be determined on the basis of a diagnosed condition that typically results in a disability or a delay (Danaher, 2001). Updates on the status of eligibility policies and practices for young children under Part B of IDEA can be found at the National Early Childhood Technical Assistance Center Web site: *http://www.nectac.org.*

Part C Regulations Pertaining to Assessment

Part C regulations that govern services for infants and toddlers make a distinction between evaluation and assessment of the child and also include requirements relating to the assessment of the family's concerns, resources, and priorities. Specifically, the following definitions are provided:

> *Evaluation* means the procedures used by appropriate qualified personnel to determine a child's initial and continuing eligibility under this part consistent with the definition of "infants and toddlers with disabilities," including determining the status of the child in each of the developmental areas: cognitive development, physical development (including vision and hearing), communication

development, social or emotional development, adaptive development.

> *Assessment* means the ongoing procedures used by appropriate qualified personnel throughout the period of a child's eligibility under this part to identify (i) the child's unique strengths and needs and the services appropriate to meet those needs; and (ii) the resources, priorities, and concerns of the family and the supports and services necessary to enhance the family's capacity to meet the developmental needs of their infant or toddler with a disability. (34 C.F.R. 303.322, Federal Register, March 12, 1999)

Under Part C regulations, *evaluation* refers to the procedures used to determine eligibility; *assessment* refers to the procedures that lead to the development and periodic review of the Individualized Family Service Plan (IFSP). The IFSP, which is a written plan for providing early intervention services, must include the following:

1. Information about the child's status, including a statement of the child's present level of physical development, cognitive development, communication development, social or emotional development, and adaptive development.

2. A statement of the family's resources, priorities, and concerns related to enhancing the development of the child.

3. A statement of the major outcomes expected for the child and the family; the criteria, procedures, and timelines used to determine the degree to which progress is being made; and whether modifications or revisions of the outcomes or services are necessary.

4. A statement of the specific early intervention services needed to meet the unique needs of the infant or toddler and the family, including the frequency, intensity, and method of delivering services.

5. A statement of the natural environments in which services will appropriately be provided, including a justification of the extent, if any, to which the services will not be provided in a natural environment.

6. The projected dates for initiation of the services to be provided and the anticipated duration of the services.
7. The identification of the service coordinator who will be responsible for the implementation of the plan and coordination with other agencies.
8. The steps to be taken to support the transition of the toddler with a disability to preschool or other appropriate services.

The IFSP must be reviewed at 6-month intervals or more frequently if needed. Every 12 months the child must be re-evaluated. Under Part C regulations, the evaluation and assessment of a child (including the assessment of family resources, priorities, and concerns) must be completed, and the IFSP meeting with the family must be held within 45 days after the referral is received by the responsible agency. Part C regulations also specify procedures for conducting the assessment of family resources, priorities, and concerns. These procedures are discussed in Chapter 7 of this text.

The federal regulations for Part C specify that evaluation and assessment must be conducted by personnel trained to utilize appropriate methods and procedures and must be based on "informed clinical opinion." Informed clinical opinion is a safeguard against eligibility determinations based upon test scores alone and provides for the consideration of both qualitative and quantitative information when addressing challenging questions regarding the development of an infant or toddler and the need for early intervention services. According to Shackleford (2002a) "appropriate training, previous experience with evaluation and assessment, sensitivity to cultural needs, and the ability to elicit and include family perceptions are all important elements of informed clinical opinion" (p. 3). The reader is referred to Shackleford (2002a) for more information on the concept of informed clinical opinion.

Each agency responsible for administering the Part C program also must ensure that nondiscrim-

inatory procedures are followed in evaluation and assessment. Specifically, each agency must ensure that:

1. Tests and other evaluation materials and procedures are administered in the native language of the parents or other mode of communication unless it is clearly not feasible to do so.
2. Any assessment and evaluation procedures and materials that are used are selected and administered so as not to be racially or culturally discriminatory.
3. No single procedure is used as the sole criterion for determining a child's eligibility.
4. Evaluations and assessments are conducted by qualified personnel (Regulations for IDEA '97, §303.323 1999).

Part B Regulations Pertaining to Assessment

The regulations for preschool children are those that apply to school-age children as well. Assessment procedures for preschool children lead to the determination of eligibility and to the development of the Individualized Education Program (IEP). The major components of the IEP for preschool children include the following:

1. A statement of the child's present level of performance including how the disability affects the child's progress in the general curriculum or, for preschool children, how it affects participation in appropriate activities.
2. A statement of measurable annual goals for the child, including benchmarks or short-term objectives related to meeting the child's needs that result from the disability to enable the child to progress in the regular curriculum and related to meeting other educational needs of the child that result from the disability.
3. A statement of the special education and related services needed and a statement of program modifications or support for school

personnel needed by the child to advance toward attaining the annual goals, to progress in the general curriculum and to be educated with other children with disabilities as well as nondisabled children.

4. An explanation of the extent, if any, to which the child will not participate with nondisabled children.
5. A statement of any individual modifications in the administration of state or district-wide assessments of student achievement (to be discussed later in this chapter).
6. The projected date for the beginning of services or modifications and the anticipated frequency, location, and duration of services and modifications.
7. A statement of how the child's progress toward the annual goals will be measured and how the child's parents will be regularly informed of their child's progress (must be at least as often as parents of nondisabled children).

The IEP must be completed within 30 days of the time the child is determined to be eligible for services. A review of the IEP must occur annually, and a complete re-evaluation of the child must occur every 3 years.

Evaluation procedures for Part B are specified in Section 614 of IDEA '97, which states that the local education agency (LEA) must:

1. Use a variety of assessment tools and strategies to gather relevant functional and developmental information, including information provided by the parent, that may assist in determining whether the child is a child with a disability and the content of the child's individualized education program;
2. Not use any single procedure as the sole criterion for determining whether a child is a child with a disability or determining an appropriate educational program for the child; and
3. Use technically sound instruments that may assess the relative contribution of cognitive and behavioral factors, in addition to physical or developmental factors.

In addition, the LEA must ensure that tests and other evaluation materials used to assess a child:

- Are selected and administered so as not to be discriminatory on a racial or cultural basis; and
- Are provided and administered in the child's native language or other mode of communication, unless it is clearly not feasible to do so.

The LEA must also ensure that any standardized tests that are given to the child:

- Have been validated for the specific purpose for which they are used;
- Are administered by trained and knowledgeable personnel; and
- Are administered in accordance with any instructions provided by the producer of such tests (20 U.S.C. §1414 [b][2–3]).

Additional Legislation

In 1994, amendments to the Elementary and Secondary Education Act (ESEA) required that in order to receive Title 1 compensatory education funds, states must develop accountability programs that measure adequate yearly progress (AYP) so that schools not making adequate progress can be identified. In addition, this legislation required that all students with disabilities participate in these assessment programs. Prior to this time, students with disabilities were being systematically excluded from state and district-wide assessments (McGrew, Thurlow, & Spiegel, 1993). IDEA '97 further supported the inclusion of students with disabilities in state and district-wide assessments by mandating that by July 1, 2000, all students with disabilities must participate in any statewide or district-wide assessments which are established for regular students (20 U.S.C. 1412 [a][17]). For example, if state or district-wide assessments are established for grades 3 through 8, all students with disabilities must also participate in these assessments.

Furthermore, IDEA '97 requires each state to establish goals for the performance of children with disabilities and establish performance indicators the state will use to assess progress toward the goals. As states develop standards and statewide assessments for preschool children, young children with disabilities will be included in these assessments.

Participation in assessments can occur for students with disabilities in one of several ways:

- Children with disabilities can be included in the same assessment as other students.
- Children with disabilities can be included in the same assessment but with accommodations.
- Students with disabilities can be assessed with an alternate assessment.

Accommodations are alterations in the environment or in observed child behaviors that will allow assessment of a skill or concept by minimizing the effect of a disability. Accommodations should not make a behavior or concept developmentally easier to demonstrate. However, in the same way that accommodations in the classroom, such as special lighting, more time, and the use of augmentative communication devices allow for the inclusion of children with disabilities in the activities of the classroom, accommodations allow for their inclusion in assessments for accountability. Any accommodation that is written into a child's IEP may be used in a state or district-wide assessment. According to IDEA '97, each child's IEP team is responsible for determining whether the student will take the general assessment without accommodations, with accommodations, or should complete an alternate assessment. Furthermore, the IEP team determines which accommodations are needed by the student, (20 U.S.C. 1413[d][1][A][v]). IDEA '97 does not require infants and toddlers to be included in state or district-wide assessments.

In addition to the Individuals with Disabilities Education Act, there are other federal laws that are important to the field of Early Intervention/Early Childhood Special Education. Professionals need to be aware of each of these laws and how they might impact young children with special needs.

Head Start   Head Start is a federally funded early education program designed for children from low-income families. In 1972, P.L. 92-424 (the Economic Opportunity Amendments) mandated that Head Start programs also serve children with disabilities. No fewer than 10% of the children enrolled in Head Start must be children with disabilities. On January 21, 1993, 45 CFR Part 1308 was published in the Federal Register. This regulation, which provided specific performance standards, including eligibility criteria, for serving children with disabilities in Head Start, clarifies the relationship between Head Start and IDEA, Part B, and identifies steps that local Head Start programs must take to provide a collaborative relationship with local public school programs.

ADA   The Americans with Disabilities Act (ADA), which was signed into law by President Bush on July 26, 1990, guarantees equal opportunity for individuals with disabilities in public accommodations, employment, transportation, state and local government services, and telecommunications. Title III of the ADA prohibits discrimination against individuals with disabilities in public accommodations, which includes child-care facilities. Under this law, child-care providers cannot legally deny services to a child with a disability unless it is determined that serving the child will result in an undue burden or hardship. While the ADA does not provide guidelines or requirements for assessment for early intervention, it certainly can have an impact on how services are provided.

Section 504 of the Rehabilitation Act
Section 504 of the Rehabilitation Act became law in 1973. Since its passage, it has been enforced primarily in relation to employment for individ-

uals with handicaps. Recently, however, the Office of Civil Rights (OCR), which enforces Section 504, has increasingly focused its requirements on the public education system. Section 504 prohibits discrimination against students with handicaps. The population of children who are considered to be handicapped under Section 504 overlaps with, but is not the same as the population of students who are considered to be disabled under IDEA. All children who are identified as being disabled under IDEA are also protected under Section 504, and by fulfilling responsibilities under IDEA, school districts are also meeting the requirements of Section 504 for these children. However, there are some children who are *not* eligible for IDEA services who do qualify under Section 504. Handicapped students under Section 504 are defined as those having any physical or mental impairment that substantially limits one or more major life activities, including learning. For example, a child with Attention Deficit Hyperactivity Disorder (ADHD) may not meet the criteria for IDEA but perhaps would qualify under Section 504. Similarly, a child with arthritis may not be in need of special education services under IDEA but may be considered handicapped under Section 504. If a school district believes that a child is handicapped according to Section 504 and needs special accommodations or services in the regular educational setting, the child must be evaluated to determine eligibility. If the child is deemed eligible, a plan for the delivery of all needed services must be developed. Section 504 clearly applies to children who are in kindergarten or the elementary grades; however, the relationship of 504 to preschool children is not as clear. Most states do not provide a publicly supported educational program to preschool children. When no public education is provided to any children, it is difficult to substantiate discrimination against children who are handicapped. Therefore, unless a state does provide publicly supported preschool services, Section 504 will probably not apply to preschoolers.

THE FUNCTIONS OF ASSESSMENT

Assessment is a generic term that refers to the process of gathering information for the purpose of making decisions. Several different types of decisions need to be made in working with young children with special needs. The purpose of any assessment endeavor must be clear to all involved because it will determine the questions that are asked and the instruments and procedures that are used. This textbook addresses five distinct functions of assessment: identification (including screening), diagnosis and determination of eligibility for special education services, assessment for program planning and service delivery, monitoring of child progress during intervention, and assessment for accountability. Each of these is described in Table 1.1. *Assessment,* as a general term, may refer to any of these functions and will be used generically throughout this text.

Screening is a procedure used to identify infants and preschoolers who may be in need of a more comprehensive evaluation. Screening is typically one part of a broader process of child identification and is completed in a brief period of time. It usually does not provide comprehensive quantitative information relative to the child's developmental status, but rather indicates whether or not further evaluation is necessary; it facilitates the identification of infants and young children who need intervention so that services may begin as early as possible. In many states, it is part of the process of Child Find, which is mandated by federal legislation and requires states to develop and implement programs for finding and identifying young children with special needs. By kindergarten or first grade, most children are enrolled in a school program from which referral for special services will be possible. However, because the population of children under age 5 is not typically as accessible, programs designed to identify young children who need early intervention must be established. Additional information on Child Find and screening is presented in Chapter 5.

TABLE 1.1
The Functions of Assessment

Assessment: The Process of Gathering Information for the Purpose of Making Decisions

Type of Assessment	Function
Identification for referral (screening)	to determine whether to refer the child for further assessment
Diagnosis/Determination of eligibility	to determine whether the child has a disability or developmental delay that meets the criteria specified by the state to receive special education services
Program planning	to identify the services needed by the child and family, the service delivery format and the outcomes or goals and bench marks/short-term objectives for the Individualized Family Service Plan (IFSP) or Individualized Education Program (IEP)
Program monitoring	to monitor the child's progress toward meeting specified outcomes or goals
Program accountability	to measure the overall effectiveness of school programs

Assessment for *diagnosis and determination of eligibility* is employed to determine the presence of conditions that may qualify a child for early intervention or early childhood special education services. Generally, medical conditions, general developmental functioning, sensory and motor functioning, and adaptive behavior in the child's typical environment are addressed. The outcome of these procedures may lead to a definitive diagnosis, such as cerebral palsy, a sensory impairment, or an identified syndrome. In many cases, however, identifying a specific condition that is the cause of the presenting problems may not be possible. In such cases, the identification of a delay in development or factors that put the child at risk of delay in development may be the outcome. The assessment team must also determine whether the child qualifies for EI/ECSE services according to the eligibility criteria followed by their particular state or jurisdiction. As was discussed earlier, eligibility criteria differ from state to state. A child who does not qualify for EI/ECSE services in a state may qualify for other types of state or federal programs. The result of diagnostic assessment, therefore, should not only be determination of eligibility for EI/ECSE services, but should also include recommendations for other services that

may facilitate the child's development. Results should also provide a solid foundation of information to assist in assessment for program planning.

Assessment for *program planning* refers to those procedures used by the assessment team to develop the IFSP or IEP and to revise these plans as necessary. The outcome of assessment for program planning is the identification of special services needed by the child and the family, the service delivery format that will be used (including location of services), and the delineation of intervention objectives as specified in the IFSP or IEP. Guidelines for conducting assessments for instructional planning are described throughout this text. In addition, Chapter 16 describes procedures and models for using assessment results to plan and implement individualized intervention plans.

Assessment continues to be an important activity for early intervention professionals after the IEP or IFSP is completed. The child's progress toward meeting the specified objectives must be *monitored* on a regular basis. Information collected on an ongoing basis allows the team to determine to what extent progress is being made toward goals and objectives or benchmarks and, as a result, to identify changes that should be made in intervention strategies or objectives. When such data is aggregated across all of the children in a program, it may be possible to measure overall program impact. As discussed earlier, recent federal legislation has increased requirements for statewide assessments of both regular and special education students as a means of evaluating the overall effectiveness of school programs. Methods for monitoring child progress and for evaluating program impact are discussed in Chapters 2 and 17.

ASSESSMENT CHALLENGES IN EI/ECSE

All of the assessment functions delineated in Table 1.1 pose challenges for professionals in early intervention: challenges related to the nature of young children with disabilities, challenges related to the use of appropriate assessment instruments and strategies, and, increasingly, the challenge of assessing young children who are acquiring English as a second language.

The Nature of Young Children with Disabilities

As the field of early intervention has grown over the past two decades, it has become increasingly apparent that effective procedures for assessing young children with disabilities differ considerably from what might be described as traditional assessment approaches. Professionals working with young children, whether a disability is present or not, become very aware of characteristics that make young children poor candidates for assessments that are conducted by unfamiliar adults in unfamiliar settings and that require children to do what the adults ask them to do. Infants and toddlers have limited verbal abilities and limited attention spans; in addition, they may show considerable anxiety when interacting with unfamiliar adults. Preschool children may have more verbal ability and a bit longer attention spans, but may not yet understand the need to follow adults' directions and also may be uncomfortable interacting with

unfamiliar adults. Those charged with the assessment of young children, therefore, must determine how to assess them in ways that yield a true picture of their abilities.

A procedural error made frequently in the past, which unfortunately continues to occur, is reliance on procedures utilized with older children (Neisworth & Bagnato, 2000). The resulting scenario was aptly described by Linder (1993) as she asks the reader to imagine himself or herself as a 3-year-old child who is being evaluated because of suspected developmental delays. Experiencing traditional assessment procedures as a 3-year-old emphasizes the problems inherent in using traditional approaches with young children.

> After a necessary potty break and a few tears, the lady lets you see your Mommy and Daddy. But not for long. Here comes another lady to take you to another little room with another table and chairs and different pictures on the wall. This lady doesn't talk much. She just keeps putting pictures in front of you and asking you what they are. Many of the pictures are things that you have seen, but you just don't know what to call them. So you look down at the floor and up at the pictures on the wall. You pull on your shirt and wiggle a lot. You wish this lady would quit with the pictures. You've seen more than enough pictures. Then the lady gets another suitcase, only it's a different color. She pulls out a couple of toys at a time and tells you what she wants you to do with them. Some of these are neat toys and you'd really like to play with them. Every time you start to do something other than what the lady told you to do, however, she takes the toys away. This lady sure is stingy. You are getting tired, so you put your head down on the table. The lady makes you sit up. Finally, she is through. She takes you back to your Mommy and Daddy and tells them that you were "somewhat resistant." (Linder, 1993, pp. 9–10)

The presence of a disability can greatly complicate the task of assessment. The existence of a sensory or motor impairment, for example, requires a method of interacting with the young child that incorporates accommodations into the assessment. The child with a hearing impairment may utilize an alternative method of communication, such as

American Sign Language, which requires particular skill on the part of the examiner. The child with a visual impairment may also need to use an alternative sensory modality (touch) in exploring assessment materials. The child with a physical impairment may have verbal and motor abilities so limited that it becomes very difficult to find a modality that will allow observation of his or her abilities.

The developmental impact of the disability must also be taken into consideration. The child with the hearing impairment has missed out on the verbal environment which lays the foundation for the development of English. The child with the visual impairment has missed out on the visual experiences that form the basis of many concepts. The child with the physical impairment may have been unable to impact his or her environment in any consistent way, and therefore may have become rather passive. These are examples of secondary effects of disabilities that may affect the development of a young child.

The assessment of young children with disabilities can be likened to the task that faces a detective. There may be little or no previous information on the children. Certainly, there will be gaps in our information. Sometimes it is only through close observation that we become alerted to the presence of less obvious disabilities or delays. Therefore the process is very much one of observing, forming hypotheses, and testing those hypotheses through more observation. In fact, assessment is a never-ending, ongoing process throughout the infant, toddler, and preschool years of early intervention as we gain more and more information on the impact of biological and environmental factors on a child's development.

Measurement Challenges

A major challenge to those responsible for the assessment of young children with special needs is the small number of appropriate instruments for use with this population. A handful of instruments have traditionally been used in assessing young children; their relatively small number has resulted in their use even when they are not appropriate. For example, the Denver II (Frankenburg et al., 1992), formerly the Denver Developmental Screening Test, an instrument that has been available for quite a few years, is a developmental screening tool and is not intended for use in determining eligibility or in developing intervention plans. However, it has been used for both of these purposes. The Bayley Scales of Infant Development (Bayley, 1969; 1993) also has been available for a number of years. The first edition of the Bayley was designed for use with children up to the age of 30 months. However, because few instruments were available that included items for this young population, the Bayley was used (misused) in assessing children who were older than 30 months but who functioned developmentally younger than 30 months. The Developmental Activities Screening Inventory (Fewell & Langley, 1984) is a screening tool, but because it yields developmental age scores, it has also been used for eligibility and program planning. As indicated earlier, laws governing both infant/toddler and preschool services state that a test must be validated for the purpose for which it is used (1997 Amendments to IDEA, 20 U.S.C. §414[b][3][B][i]). However, a recent survey of preschool special education, early childhood education and Head Start teachers found that screening instruments were still being used to develop IEPs and IFSPs (Pretti-Frontczak & Maag, 2001). It is incumbent upon the individual who is administering a test to be sure its use is valid for the child being assessed and for the designated purpose of assessment.

Some instruments used in EI/ECSE have been developed for use in early intervention programs but have not undergone rigorous evaluation procedures. Therefore, no information is available on their reliability or validity. Furthermore, some of them allow the generation of developmental age scores when, in fact, they have never been normed on a representative sample of children (Meisels,

1991). In other words, there is no normative population from which to derive a developmental age score. Frequently these instruments rely on developmental milestones identified by other instruments or research studies to be used as norms. Clearly, the challenges presented in the assessment of young children with special needs requires professionals who have solid clinical skills in assessment and a knowledge base that allows them to judge the quality of assessment instruments critically. Chapter 2 includes information on test construction, reliability, and validity that will help the reader evaluate assessment instruments.

English Language Learners

The population of children and families in the United States whose primary language is not English has been growing and, in all likelihood, will continue to grow in the future. The Findings of Congress at the beginning of the 1997 Amendments to IDEA states, "The limited English proficient population is the fastest growing in our nation" (20 U.S.C. 1400[c][7][F]). Preschool teachers increasingly find themselves teaching children who speak no English or are in the process of acquiring English as a second language. We might refer to these children as non-English speaking and as English Language Learners. For most teachers, assessing the development of children who do not have English as their primary language presents a significant challenge.

Assessing young children who speak no English or who are learning English presents challenges for every function of assessment listed in Table 1.1. We will focus here on the first two functions listed: identification for referral and determination of eligibility.

The number of children in special education who are culturally and linguistically diverse is higher than expected based on population figures. This fact may be reflective of the potential for error in the assessment process when children (and families) are not native English speakers.

Clearly, young children should not be referred for evaluation to determine eligibility for special education services simply because they are not native English speakers. Careful observation of a child's language proficiency in school and also in other environments is necessary in attempting to decide whether a particular child might have a language disability (and therefore should be referred for evaluation) or is simply in the process of acquiring a second language (i.e., English). According to Quinones-Eatman (2001), "The greatest myth that pervades schooling and non-English speaking homes is that all aspects of second language learning for the young child are automatic and easy" (p. 10). Quinones-Eatman goes on to explain that children who are acquiring a second language typically go through a nonverbal period or silent period when they realize their home language isn't working but they aren't proficient and confident enough yet to try to use the new (second) language. Teachers may mistakenly assume that this nonverbal child has a language disability. Table 1.2 presents a checklist of steps that should be taken prior to considering making a referral for special education for a child whose primary language is not English. Note that obtaining some basic information about the child's proficiency (competence) in the dominant language (the primary language) is recommended. Teachers will want to ask a Speech Language Pathologist for help with obtaining this information. Finally, it may be helpful to compare the child's behavior and development to other children of the same age who have a similar language and cultural background. Chapter 4 provides more information on ensuring cultural competence in assessment.

If the decision is made to refer a child for evaluation to determine eligibility for special education, additional consideration must be given to planning assessment strategies that will not penalize the child for being non-English speaking. IDEA '97 requires that assessment be conducted in the child's native language unless it is clearly not feasible to do so (20 U.S.C. §1414[b][5]). Following are suggestions from McLean (1998) relative

TABLE 1.2
Checklist of Information Needed Prior to Referral for Evaluation to Determine Eligibility for Special Education

	Yes	No
1. Adequate information about the language dominance and proficiency of family members has been obtained and, if needed, an interpreter/translator has been identified to facilitate communication with the family.	☐	☐
2. Information about the language dominance and proficiency of other caregivers or children who interact routinely with the child has been identified.	☐	☐
3. The family has been asked to share their impressions of the child's development.	☐	☐
4. With the family's permission, other service providers and caregivers have been asked to share their impressions of the child's development.	☐	☐
5. If needed, a cultural guide has been asked to help interpret the child's behavior.	☐	☐
6. All developmental domains, including hearing and vision, have been screened.	☐	☐
7. Screening for language proficiency and dominance has been completed.	☐	☐
8. The child has been observed both in the early childhood setting and at home.	☐	☐
9. The child has had sufficient time to become accustomed to the linguistic and social environment of the early childhood setting.	☐	☐
10. The child's social, cognitive, and motor skills have been observed in situations where language comprehension is not required.	☐	☐

Note: From "Assessing Young Children for Whom English Is a Second Language," by M. McLean, 1998, *Young Exceptional Children, 1*(2), 2, pp. 20–25. Reprinted with permission of the author.

to assessing young children for whom English is a second language:

- Assessment of language dominance and proficiency should be completed first in order to plan further assessment. Assessment should be conducted in the child's dominant language.
- Informal methods, such as observations, interviews of parents and caregivers, and play-based assessment in a comfortable, familiar setting should be used in addition to or in place of more formal methods.
- Any instrument that might be used should be examined for cultural bias by a person from the child's cultural group. Modifications can be made so items will be culturally appropriate. These modifications, however, will invalidate the scoring of the instrument. In this case, the test can be used as a descriptive measure rather

than for reporting scores, and the team's decision will be based on informed clinical opinion rather than on test scores.

- Testing might be done by a professional who is from or is very knowledgeable about the child's cultural group and who speaks the same language or dialect that is the child's primary language.
- If such a professional is not available, testing might be done with the assistance of an interpreter/translator or a cultural guide who works in conjunction with the assessment team in administering the interpreting assessments.
- The assessment team should seek assistance from a professional who is trained in bilingual education to assist in planning the assessment as well as making an informed decision relative to the child's eligibility for special education and related services.

EMERGING TRENDS

Assessment procedures for young children with special needs have historically been most strongly influenced by the traditions and legislation governing assessment in special education. A strong psychometric tradition has prevailed in special education, and this tradition has also been relatively strong in Early Intervention/Early Childhood Special Education. However, in recent years, several emerging trends have served to change the procedures recommended for assessment of young children with special needs (Neisworth & Bagnato, 2000). These trends are a direct result of years of clinical experience with infants and young children and will be evident throughout the chapters of this book.

One trend is the very high priority now placed on family-centered assessment and intervention. Chapter 3 includes a discussion of the importance placed on family participation in the assessment process. Chapter 7 is devoted to strategies for the assessment of family resources, priorities, and concerns as legislated by IDEA.

A second trend is the emerging emphasis on assessment in the natural environment, or ecologically sound assessment practices (Barnett, Macmann, & Carey, 1992). Originally driven by years of clinical experience and research that demonstrated the shortcomings of formal standardized assessment, this movement has been augmented by the movement toward closer collaboration with early childhood education, a discipline strongly in support of assessment of children's behavior in familiar environments and under typical circumstances (NAEYC, 1986, 1988; NAEYC & NAECS/SDE, 1991). Chapter 3 includes a discussion of the variety of strategies that have evolved as a result of efforts to ensure that assessment is ecologically valid. Each chapter of the text that addresses a particular domain also includes strategies for assessment in the natural environment.

A third trend is the importance that has been placed on interdisciplinary assessment strategies, which have been derived from the realization that development cannot realistically be separated into isolated and separate domains. In the infant and young child, developmental domains are interdependent. There are distinct advantages to assessment that is conducted by a team of professionals representing various disciplines who work closely together rather than independently. Team assessment strategies are discussed in Chapter 3. It should be pointed out that this text does present information on assessment separated into chapters by developmental domains. It is recognized that assessing specific areas of development is an artificial undertaking due to the interrelatedness of the developmental areas. However, collecting information in this manner and then reintegrating it through a team effort allows insight into an individual child's development that can facilitate the assessment process.

The purpose of this book is to provide information needed by professionals to engage in assessment activities for identification, eligibility determination, program planning, and program evaluation relative to serving young children with special needs. We believe it represents best practice at this point in time. However, work should continue in refining and improving assessment strategies. Certainly what is considered best practice now will change as new information is gained.

· · · · · · · ·

SUMMARY OF KEY CONCEPTS

■ Assessment is an important and ongoing responsibility of professionals who work with young children. Assessment activities are necessary in order to locate and identify children who need early intervention services, plan appropriate intervention strategies, and monitor the effectiveness of services provided.

- Federal law provides a general definition of eligibility for services as well as general guidelines for the assessment process for both infant/toddler programs and preschool programs. Each state and territory then is responsible for developing the exact criteria and procedures that will be followed.
- Assessment of young children with special needs can be challenging due to the nature of young children, limitations of the assessment instruments currently available, and increasingly, the challenge of assessing children who are non-English speaking.
- A strong psychometric tradition has been prevalent in the assessment of children with disabilities. This tradition has been affected, however, by current trends toward family-centered assessment, utilizing natural environments, and a collaborative approach by all team members.

· · · · · · · ·

REFERENCES

Barnett, D. W., Macmann, G. M., & Carey, K. T. (1992). Early intervention and the assessment of developmental skills: Challenges and directions. *Topics in Early Childhood Special Education, 12*(1), 21–43.

Bayley, N. (1969). *Bayley Scales of Infant Development.* New York: Psychological Corporation.

Bayley, N. (1993). *Bayley Scales of Infant Development-II.* San Antonio, TX: Psychological Corporation.

Benn, R. (1994). Conceptualizing eligibility for early intervention services. In D. M. Bryant & M. A. Graham (Eds.), Implementing early intervention (pp. 18–45). New York: Guilford Press.

Danaher, J. (2001, October). Eligibility policies and practices for young children under Part B of IDEA. *NECTAC Notes #6 (revised).* Chapel Hill, NC: The National Early Childhood Technical Assistance Center.

Fewell, R., & Langley, M. B. (1984). *DASI-II: Developmental Activities Screening Inventory.* Austin, TX: PRO-ED.

Frankenburg, W. K., Dodds, J., Archer, P., Bresnick, B., Mashka, P., Edelman, N., & Shapiro, H. (1992). *Denver II.* Denver, CO: Denver Developmental Materials, Inc.

Guralnick, M. J. (1997). *The effectiveness of early intervention.* Baltimore, MD: Paul H. Brookes.

Individuals with Disabilities Education Act Amendments of 1997. Retrieved August 15, 2002 from *www.ideapractices.org*

Linder, T. W. (1993). *Transdisciplinary play-based assessment: A functional approach to working with young children.* Baltimore, MD: Paul H. Brookes.

McGrew, K. S., Thurlow, M. L. & Spiegel, A. N. (1993). An investigation of the exclusion of students with disabilities in national data collection programs. *Educational Evaluation and Policy Analysis, 15*(3), 339–352.

McLean, M. (1998). Assessing young children for whom English is a second language. *Young Exceptional Children 1*(2), 20–25.

Meisels, S. (1991). Dimensions of early identification. *Journal of Early Intervention, 15*(1), 26–35.

National Association for the Education of Young Children (NAEYC). (1986). Position statement on developmentally appropriate practice in early childhood programs serving children from birth through age 8. *Young Children, 41*(6), 4–29.

National Association for the Education of Young Children (NAEYC). (1988). Position statement on standardized testing of young children 3 through 8 years of age. *Young Children, 46*(3), 21–38.

National Association for the Education of Young Children (NAEYC) and the National Association of Early Childhood Specialists in State Departments of Education (NAECS/SDE). (1991). Guidelines for appropriate curriculum content and assessment in programs serving children ages 3 through 8. *Young Children, 46*(3), 21–38.

Neisworth, J. T., & Bagnato, S. J. (1992). The case against intelligence testing in early intervention. *Topics in Early Childhood Special Education, 12*(1), 1–20.

Neisworth, J. T., & Bagnato, S. J. (2000). Recommended practices in assessment. In S. Sandall, M. McLean, & B. J. Smith (Eds.). *DEC recommended practices in early intervention/early childhood special education.* Longmont, CO: Sopris West.

Pretti-Frontczak, K. & Maag, N. (2001). Linking assessment, IEPs and curriculum: A national study of preschool teachers. Presentation to Division for Early Childhood International Conference. Boston, MA.

Quinones-Eatman, J. (2001). *Preschool second language acquisition: What we know and how we can effectively communicate with young second language learners.* (CLAS Technical Report #5). Champaign, IL: University of Illinois at Urbana-Champaign, Early Childhood Research Institute on Culturally and Linguistically Appropriate Services.

Shackleford, J. (1992, October). State/jurisdiction eligibility definitions for Part H. *NECTAS Notes, 5.* Chapel Hill, NC: The National Early Childhood Technical Assistance System.

Shackleford, J. (2002a, May). Informed clinical opinion. *NECTAC Notes #4 (Revised).* Chapel Hill, NC. The National Early Childhood Technical Assistance Center.

Shackleford, J. (2002b, June). State and jurisdictional eligibility definitions for infants and toddlers with disabilities under IDEA. *NECTAC Notes #5 (Revised).* Chapel Hill, NC: The National Early Childhood Technical Assistance Center.

Shonkoff, J., & Meisels, S. (1991). Defining eligibility for services under Public Law 99-457. *Journal of Early Intervention, 15*(1), 21–25.

Walsh, S., Smith, B. J., & Taylor, R. C. (2000). *IDEA Requirements for Preschoolers with Disabilities.* Reston, VA: The Council for Exceptional Children.

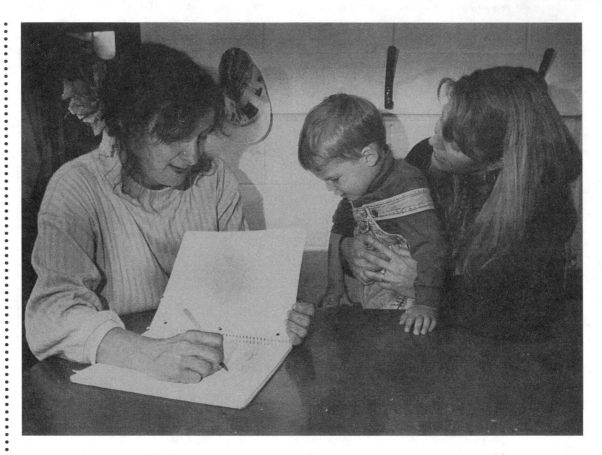

Tests and Test Development

Donald B. Bailey Jr.
University of North Carolina at Chapel Hill

Vignette 1: *A parent calls the preschool special education teacher, distraught following an annual assessment of her child's development. She notes that when a standardized IQ test was given, her child's IQ was lower than it was the previous year. She thought her child had been learning new skills but is now worried that her child may be regressing.*

Vignette 2: *A parent who has just moved from another state enrolls her child for preschool special education services. However, following testing, the school system determines that the child does not meet the state's eligibility requirements for pre-school special education. This has happened because the state from which the parents had moved used 1.5 standard deviations below the mean as the criteria for eligibility, whereas the new state requires development to be 2.0 standard deviations below the mean. The parent wants an explanation of what a standard deviation is.*

Vignette 3: *A student teacher administers the Bayley Scales of Infant Development to a 2-year-old with Down syndrome in order to demonstrate proficiency in developmental assessments. However the resulting score was quite a bit different from the score that the psychologist had obtained in a recent formal assessment. Upon comparing the scores, it was discovered that the two examiners had used different rules for when to start the assessment, resulting in a different set of items being administered.*

These vignettes illustrate but a few of the many challenges preschool special educators and early intervention professionals face when using and interpreting standardized tests or measures of development with children with disabilities. When properly used and interpreted, tests perform important functions. However, early childhood professionals *must* have a basic understanding of how tests are developed, procedures for summarizing test performance, and considerations in evaluating assessment tools. This information is important for at least three reasons. First, early childhood special educators and other professionals should be able to evaluate and select appropriate measures, and they will need to be able to read and understand the technical manual that accompanies most measures. Second, professionals should be aware of the limi-

tations of existing measures so that results may be interpreted accordingly. Finally, all professionals should be able to understand test scores as reported by other members of the interdisciplinary team, to recognize the limitations of the scores, and to explain the scores to parents, as exemplified in the previous vignettes.

TEST STANDARDIZATION

A test is a set of standardized tasks presented to a child. The purpose of testing is to determine how well a child performs on the tasks presented. Standardization includes several components: standard materials, administrative procedures, scoring procedures, and score interpretation. The purpose of standardization is to ensure that all children taking the test receive essentially the same experience, perform the same tasks with the same set of materials, receive the same amount of assistance from the evaluator, and are evaluated according to a standard set of criteria. If the same materials, procedures, or scoring criteria are not used for all children, the results will have limited comparability among children.

For example, assume that an item on a test says "Puts together a three-piece puzzle." If no further instructions were provided, it would be up to each evaluator to decide how to administer and score this item. Some might use a simple snowman puzzle, consisting of three circles of different sizes, whereas others might choose an interlocking puzzle. Some would show the child the puzzle as it should look, disassemble it, and ask the child to put it back together, whereas others would simply place the three pieces in front of the child and ask the child to "Put the puzzle together." Some would impose a 1-minute time limit; others would give the child unlimited time. Obviously, such variations in administrative procedures will influence a child's success with this task.

Standardized procedures are essential if test performance is to be compared across children. In testing a child with disabilities, however, rigid application of standardized procedures may result in erroneous conclusions about that child. For example, a test of cognitive skills may require the child to perform many motor or verbal tasks. A child with cerebral palsy may not be able to perform the motor or verbal components of those tasks, in spite of having the cognitive skills needed to do so. In addition, standardized procedures often are difficult to apply to very young children who are easily distracted and sometimes reluctant to participate in a testing session.

Vignette 3 at the beginning of this chapter illustrates how standardization may present a problem in assessing young children with disabilities. A test like the Bayley Scales will often have guidelines for where to start testing in the sequence of items, usually based on the child's chronological age. The test will also have rules for establishing a *basal* (the level below which items are not administered and assumed to be passed) and a *ceiling* (the level above which items are not administered and assumed to be failed). However, a 2-year-old with Down syndrome may have significant delays and would not pass any items at this level. The psychologist used the child's chronological age as the starting point whereas the student teacher realized that the child would not be able to do any of these items and so started at the child's estimated developmental age. Mayes (1997) showed that where you start can have a significant impact on the child's score, and in fact demonstrated that starting at the chronological age for children with disabilities might result in an inflated test score, the opposite of what might be predicted. Mayes (1997) suggests that those administering developmental assessments to children with disabilities may want to "test the limits" of the basal and ceiling, and certainly should be cautious in interpreting scores from these assessments. However, once a formal score has been obtained, teachers and other professionals who assess young children with disabilities *for instructional purposes* may modify items so that the result is helpful in identifying the supports he or she needs in order to accomplish a task.

TEST CONTENT

A test consists of a set of tasks to which children must respond. How is the content of an assessment tool determined? In part, this is decided by the purpose of the assessment. A screening measure might have different content than would a diagnostic measure. A test of communication skills certainly would differ from a test of self-help skills. At least two approaches may be followed in determining test content: conceptual and statistical. Usually both are incorporated in any item selection process; however, some instruments may weigh one criteria over another, and, in some cases, only one dimension is considered.

Conceptual Criteria

The primary consideration in determining test content is the domain to be tested. For example, if a test developer wanted to create a measure of fine motor skills, several questions would need to be addressed. First, the broad domain of "fine motor" skills would be defined to determine which skills are representative of the domain. For example, *fine motor* might be defined as "any skill involving the use of small muscles." However, this definition might be too broad, since behaviors such as blinking or toe-wiggling all might fit this category. For educational purposes, *fine motor* may be defined as "skills requiring use of the hands or fingers." Regardless of how the domain is conceptualized, it must be defined so that initial decisions can be made regarding the appropriateness of item inclusion.

Second, the developer must consider the major subdomains of the domain to be assessed. For example, fine motor skills would probably include grasping and releasing objects, stacking objects, and using tools such as pencils, scissors, or a spoon. Third, important developmental milestones within each subdomain must be identified. For example, there is a well-defined sequence of milestones in grasping small objects. Finally, the developer may want to attend to functionally important skills within the domain to be assessed. This type of content analysis would focus on fine motor skills likely to be important to the success in home or school environments.

Varying degrees of sophistication and rigor could be applied in the identification of test content. For example, one strategy would be for the developer to include items he or she believed to be important in the domain to be assessed. At a more advanced level, other professionals could be consulted to determine professional consensus as to whether the item was conceptually consistent with the domain under consideration. For example, "experts" in fine motor development could rate a set of items or tasks according to their "fit" within a given domain or subdomain. Other strategies are described in the reliability and validity sections of this chapter.

Statistical Criteria

Once a large pool of potential items has been identified, how are individual items selected? For a criterion-referenced test (one in which a child's performance is compared relative to a body of information), items are selected based on the adequacy with which the items assess the skills in question. A norm-referenced test (one in which a child's performance is compared with that of other children), on the other hand, uses statistical criteria for item inclusion.

For an item to be selected based on statistical criteria, it must develop in a predictable sequence and within a relatively well-defined time frame. Egan and Brown (1986), for example, studied several performance tasks to determine if a predictable developmental sequence emerged. Their data supported use of tasks such as building a tower with 1-inch cubes, copying cube models, copying geometric shapes, and drawing a person in the developmental assessment of children between 18 and 54 months of age. For developmental scales, or those in which a child's age is taken into consideration when deciding where to place items, the most commonly used statistical criteria is to select items passed by 50% of the chil-

dren at a given age level. In the test construction literature this is referred to as "item difficulty level," and often is reported as p = .5, which means that the probability of an individual child of a certain age passing the item is 50%. For example, if approximately half of all children walk by 12 months of age, walking would be an item assigned to the 12-month age level.

Statistical criteria are essential in developing tests to describe a child's developmental status relative to typically developing children. For example, the Bayley Scales of Infant Development (Bayley, 1969) were originally developed to evaluate "a child's developmental status in the first two and one-half years of life" (Bayley, 1969, p. 3). Items initially were selected to "take into account recent theoretical contributions dealing with the nature of early childhood development" (Bayley, 1969, p. 1). Items actually used in the final test were arranged in order of age placement and assigned an age level based on the age at which 50% of sample children passed the item.

In the second edition of the Bayley Scales of Infant Development (Bayley, 1993) the purpose was similar, to assess "the current developmental functioning of infants and children" (p. 1). However, another goal of the BSID-II is to assess children's abilities in order to detect abnormal development and therefore provide information about the "source of the child's delay" (p. 17). Thus, new items are added, administered to a normative group, and statistically analyzed to estimate the developmental status of children with disabilities relative to typically developing children.

Integrating Conceptual and Statistical Criteria

Conceptual and statistical criteria may be used independently or in concert with each other. In an example of combined use, an item pool might be developed based on conceptual criteria and professional validation, and specific items selected from the pool on the basis of statistical criteria. Sometimes items are chosen merely on the basis of statistical criteria with only minor attention to conceptual criteria. For a developer interested only in screening for overall developmental delay, the most important question may be which items best identify children who should be referred for more extensive testing. On the other hand, other test constructors may not be interested in statistical criteria at all in selecting items. For example, if the purpose of an assessment tool is to determine a child's ability to complete certain tasks necessary for success in preschool, then certain items will be included regardless of how they discriminate among children.

Problems in Procedures for Developing Test Content

In evaluating a particular measure, professionals working with children with disabilities should carefully examine the content of the test to determine (a) how the items were derived and (b) whether the content is consistent with programmatic goals for assessment. This information will be critical in deciding whether a particular test will be appropriate for a given purpose. Many instruments currently used by early childhood special educators for instructional purposes provide little in the way of data or description to support the inclusion of items in the measure (Bailey, Jens, & Johnson, 1983).

Professionals should ask questions such as: Who were the specialists who determined test content? What criteria were employed to decide whether an item was important for inclusion? What evidence is given in support of the usefulness of this set of items?

The Battelle Developmental Inventory (Newborg, Stock, Wnek, Guidubaldi, & Svinicki, 1984) incorporated both conceptual and statistical criteria in item selection. Four conceptual criteria were used in the selection of items: "(1) the importance of the behavior in the child's development toward normal functioning in life, (2) the degree of support among professionals and in the literature for identifying the behavior as a milestone in early development, (3) the acceptance of the skill

or behavior among educational practitioners as a critical one for the child to possess or acquire, and (4) the degree to which the behavior is amenable to educational intervention" (Newborg et al., 1984, p. 9). No data are presented, however, to demonstrate how these decisions were made. Bailey, Vandiviere, Dellinger, and Munn (1987) asked 79 teachers who had used the instrument to estimate the percentage of items they considered to be skills that had the potential of being useful now or in the future or were prerequisites for important skills. Overall, the teachers indicated that they considered only about 68% of the items to be good instructional targets. Thus, just because a test developer says the instrument's content is useful for a given purpose does not mean that consumers necessarily agree.

A unique feature of the Battelle Developmental Inventory is the procedure used to select final items. From the pool of items meeting the aforementioned criteria, final items were selected and assigned an age based on statistical criteria. On this particular instrument, the age at which 75% of the children passed an item was the criterion used. Thus it cannot be assumed that every measure will incorporate the 50% criterion.

The point of this section is to encourage professionals to examine closely the procedures used to determine the items included on a particular measure. It is tempting to assume that since the items are part of a published measure, somehow they must be important. However, the items may or may not be consistent with the aims of a local program.

SUMMARIZING TEST PERFORMANCE: NORM-REFERENCED MEASURES

When a test is administered, the child's performance on each item is recorded and assigned a value, referred to as the *item score*. On some tests, the item is simply scored as passed or failed; other tests may allow a range of scores that captures partial or assisted performance. Once an assessment is completed, a *raw score* is derived by summing the item scores. A raw score can usually be computed for subtests as well as for the entire instrument. Although a child's performance on individual items provides important information about specific skills and deficits, raw scores alone are meaningless, except for providing the number of points a child has earned or the number of items passed. For this reason, raw scores are usually converted into some other type of score. The score summary used depends on whether the instrument is a norm-referenced or criterion-referenced measure.

When a single child's performance is compared with a representative sample of children, the result is a *norm-referenced test*. Such instruments are usually developed by administering the measure to a sample of children who are representative of the population to be tested. Examinee's scores can then be compared with the norm group's, allowing an understanding of where the child's performance falls relative to other children his or her age.

The Normative Group

When evaluating the usefulness of a norm-referenced measure, professionals should examine carefully the basis from which norm-referenced scores are derived. Some measures, such as the Learning Accomplishment Profile (Glover, Preminger, & Sanford, 1978; Sanford & Zelman, 1981), the Hawaii Early Learning Profile (Furuno, O'Reilly, Hosaka, Inatsuka, Allman, & Zelsloft, 1979), and the Early Intervention Developmental Profile (Rogers, D'Eugenio, Brown, Donovan, & Lynch, 1981) provide developmental age scores, but the instrument itself was never normed. A developmental age is assigned to each item based on other sources. As Bailey et al. (1987) suggest, this approach can be problematic:

> Since the norms for these measures were gathered in different years and on different populations, their equivalence is uncertain. Furthermore, even if individual item ages may be generally accurate,

the summation of individual item scores to obtain a developmental age is more suspect, since total score analyses were never conducted on the particular reconfiguration of items. (p. 2)

If the test developers administered the instrument to a normative sample, several aspects of that process should be evaluated. First, the year that testing was done should be noted. As society advances, expectations for children change and so too does their typical performance. The older a set of norms, the less likely it is to be representative of children today. To compare a child's performance today with the average 4-year-old of 25 years ago would be misleading. Hanson and Smith (1987), for example, compared current administrations of the Griffiths Scales of Mental Development (Extension) (Griffiths, 1970) with the average scores of children in the normative group that was assessed in 1960 and found that the current sample scored more than 11 points higher than the children in the original standardization sample.

McLean, McCormick, and Baird (1991) suggested that the age equivalents obtained on the Griffiths Scale often overestimate developmental levels for infants. They also reported that "the tendency for Griffiths' scores to be inflated could result in some children not qualifying for services when in fact those services should be made available" (p. 343). Therefore, children with disabilities might not receive necessary services if the Griffiths Scales are used for classifying children as having developmental delays. McLean et al. proposed that the Griffiths Scales should be restandardized for American infants to increase their usefulness in diagnosing children with developmental delays for early intervention.

In addition to the year of testing, characteristics of the normative sample should be inspected. Ideally, the sample should be stratified, with proportionate representation of various cultures, geographic regions, gender, income levels, and urban-rural distribution. If the normative group failed to consider one or more of these variables, its representativeness must be questioned. For example, the Developmental Profile II (Alpern, Boll, &

Shearer, 1980) collected normative data primarily in Indiana and Washington, raising concerns about its general applicability across the United States. Mardell-Czudnowski and Goldenberg (1984) describe the standardization procedures employed with the DIAL-R, a preschool screening test. The original norming population was located only in Illinois and consisted of only 320 children. The restandardization involved 2,447 children, including approximately equal numbers of boys and girls, and data were gathered proportionately from the four major geographic regions in the United States based on 1980 data from the United States Bureau of the Census. Of the total sample, 44.5% was included from diverse cultures in order to create a large and representative subsample.

It should be noted that children with disabilities are rarely included in any normative group. The rationale is that norms should provide an indication of normal developmental sequences and milestones. It is assumed that the purpose of testing is to determine the nature and extent of deviation from the norm. However, there are some valid arguments suggesting that there is some degree of unfairness inherent in comparing the development of a child with a hearing impairment, for example, with that of hearing children.

Norm-Referenced Scores

At least four types of scores can be used to compare a child's performance with that of a normative group: developmental age scores, developmental quotients, standard scores, and percentile ranks.

Developmental Age Scores   A *developmental age score* tells the average age at which 50% of the normative sample achieved a particular raw score. For example, on a given test, 50% of the normative sample may have achieved a raw score of 75 by 36 months of age. Any child with a raw score of 75 could then be said to be functioning at a 36-month developmental level. A developmental age score may be reported for an entire measure or for indi-

vidual subscales. A primary advantage of developmental age scores is that they are easily interpretable by parents and professionals. To say that a child is functioning at a 24-month level has a certain degree of simplicity and face validity. A second advantage of developmental age scores is that they usually do reflect positive change or growth in children (Fewell & Sandall, 1986). If a child has a higher raw score total in the spring than he or she did in the fall, the result will be a higher developmental age. Improvements in raw score performance may not necessarily be reflected by improvements in other types of scores. For parents of children with disabilities who are often informed of their child's slow progress, information provided by developmental age scores may confirm developmental gains where other measures may not.

Salvia and Ysseldyke (1985), however, identified four potential problems when using and interpreting developmental age scores. First, two children with the same developmental age score may have performed completely differently. Since the developmental age score depends solely on the raw score and is a global summary of performance, patterns of performance are obscured. For example, the performance of two children on a set of items from the Battelle Developmental Inventory is displayed in Table 2.1. Both children earned the same number of raw score points and thus would receive the same developmental age score. However, they clearly possess different skills.

A second problem is that most developmental ages are extrapolated scores. This means that children of a particular age may not actually have been tested as part of the normative process. The test developer instead used a statistical procedure to extrapolate such scores. Since development often is uneven (Keogh & Sheehan, 1981), this poses a potential problem. Third, as with all summary scores, to state that a child functions like an average 3-year-old is misleading, since 3-year-olds are quite variable in their abilities. In addition, it must be remembered that by definition, 50% of the population will score below the identified age level and

TABLE 2.1

Example of How Two Children with Different Profiles Can Receive the Same Raw Score

Child A		Child B	
Item Number	Raw Score	Item Number	Raw Score
1	2	1	2
2	2	2	2
3	2	3	1
4	1	4	0
5	2	5	1
6	0	6	2
7	2	7	1
8	0	8	1
9	0	9	1
10	0	10	0
11	0	11	0
12	0	12	0
	Score: 11		Score: 11

50% above. Very few children actually perform precisely at the targeted age level. A developmental age is best interpreted as an estimate within a range of performance. Finally, the differences between developmental ages are not necessarily equal. Consequently, clinicians should be cautious when using developmental age to classify children with disabilities as at-risk or delayed because the unequal intervals between different developmental ages may result in misclassification (Banerji, 1992a). At younger ages, a one-year delay may be more significant than at older ages, when one year is not as great a proportion of the child's total age.

Developmental Quotient Scores A *developmental quotient (DQ)*, or ratio, *score* is computed by dividing a child's developmental age by his or her chronological age and multiplying the result by 100. The average child who is progressing at an average rate would receive a DQ score of 100, as illustrated below:

$$\frac{37 \text{ months (developmental age)}}{37 \text{ months (chronological age)}} \times 100 = 100$$

Because a developmental quotient is a ratio of developmental to chronological age, taking into account the child's age at the time of the test, it is usually a relatively stable score. For this reason, developmental quotients are seen by some as a more desirable unit of measurement than developmental age scores in assessing the effects of intervention. (Snyder-McLean, 1987)

A primary limitation of the developmental quotient is that as children get older, equal increases in developmental age represent smaller proportions of chronological age and thus result in smaller DQ changes. Furthermore, calculating the developmental quotient tells us nothing about the range and standard deviation of scores. Because of this problem, ratio scores are rarely used, since a developmental quotient of 85 at one age is not directly comparable to a DQ of 85 obtained at another age (Bailey & Rosenthal, 1987). However, they are quite common in the early intervention field.

Standard Scores To compensate for problems associated with developmental quotients, most standardized tests now use standard scores for interpreting child performance. A *standard score* is a score that has been transformed to fit a normal curve, with a mean and standard deviation that remain the same across ages. Understanding

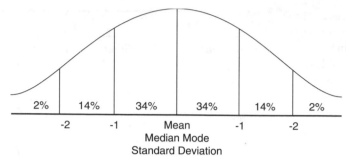

FIGURE 2.1

The normal curve with percentages of the population expected within standard deviation units

standard scores first requires an understanding of the normal curve and the standard deviation.

The normal curve is a theoretical distribution of scores that is the model against which actual performance is interpreted. As displayed in Figure 2.1, the normal curve is bell-shaped. It assumes that on any given variable, most individuals will score at or near the mean. As scores deviate from the mean (either greater than or less than), fewer instances of those scores will be observed. A *standard deviation* is a number that helps in interpreting where any particular score falls within a larger distribution of scores by describing how far a score is from the mean. Within the normal curve model, it is assumed that one standard deviation on either side of the mean encompasses approximately 34% of the individuals in a group, whereas two standard deviations on either side of the mean would encompass 48% of the individuals in a group. A standard deviation is always reported as being above or below the mean. Thus to say that a child's score was 1 standard deviation below the mean would be interpreted to mean that the child's performance was better than 16% of the total population. A score of 1 standard deviation above the mean would be interpreted to mean the child's performance was better than 84% of the population. This type of information is not available when using developmental quotient scores.

Vignette 1 at the beginning of this chapter illustrates the importance of understanding standard deviations. Many states now use standard deviation as the metric for determining whether a student is delayed or not, but the criteria for delay will vary from state to state (Danaher, 2001). Preschool special educators should be aware of the standards for eligibility in their state and be able to interpret for parents the meaning of standard deviation and how it pertains to their child.

For any given test, the mean and standard deviation of standard scores will be defined by the publisher and developed according to specified criteria. Probably the best-known version of the standard score or deviation score has a mean of 100 and a standard deviation of 15, as found in the Bayley Scales of Infant Development and the Battelle Developmental Inventory. Using this scoring system, a child with a score of 85 would be said to have a score that was one standard deviation below the mean (100 − 15). Other instruments, such as the McCarthy Scales of Children's Abilities and the Stanford-Binet Intelligence Test, have a mean of 100 and a standard deviation of 16. Thus from a population perspective, a score of 70 on the Battelle would be interpreted similarly to a score of 68 on the Stanford-Binet, since both scores are 2 standard deviations below the mean.

Occasionally a test may report other versions of standard scores, the most common being a z score or a T score. These scores are interpreted in exactly the same fashion as any other standard score, the only difference being in the defined parameters of the score. A *z score* is a standard score distribution with a mean of zero and a standard deviation of one; a *T score* is a standard score distribution with a mean of 50 and a standard deviation of 10.0. Using the above examples, then, a deviation score of 115, a z score of +1, and a T score of 60 all mean that performance was 1 standard deviation above the mean.

Percentile Ranks A *percentile rank* is another score that provides information regarding an individual's performance relative to the rest of the population. Specifically, percentile ranks tell what percentage of the population performed at or below a given score. Thus, a percentile rank of 50 would be in the average range and is interpreted to mean that the individual's performance exceeded that of 50% of the normative sample.

When the group is divided into fourths, each percentile group is called a *quartile*; when a group is divided into tenths, percentile ranks are called *deciles*. These terms are usually used in a general descriptive fashion, such as "Juan's performance was in the top decile," which means he ranks in the top 10%.

The major limitation of percentile ranks is that they are not on an equal interval scale. The difference between percentile ranks at the extremes is more significant than the difference between percentile ranks closer to the mean, as illustrated by Bailey and Rosenthal (1987). For this reason, percentile ranks should never be used to determine the success of an intervention, nor should they be submitted to any type of data analysis without first converting them to some type of standard score (Sattler, 1982).

Using Extrapolated Scores

When calculating scores for children with disabilities, the examiner often finds the child's raw scores to be too low for the range of scores covered by the specific test. In such cases, two options are available. One is simply to report the child's performance as below the lowest obtainable score on the instrument. For example, a child cannot receive a deviation score below 50 on the Bayley Scales, so many reports would simply state "below 50" as the child's obtained score. A second alternative is to *extrapolate* a score by performing additional calculations. For example, Naglieri (1981) published a table for extrapolating scores on the Bayley Scales down to 28. The Battelle Developmental Inventory provides a formula by which extreme scores may be calculated. The examiner finds the mean and standard deviation for the age level and domain of interest, subtracts the mean from the obtained raw score, and divides the resulting figure by the standard deviation, resulting in a z score. To obtain a deviation score, the z score is multiplied by 15 and then added to 100.

The use of extrapolated scores may be necessary when testing children with disabilities, particularly those with severe disabilities. However, caution should be exercised in interpreting extrapolated scores because they literally are estimates of performance. No children scoring that low were included in the normative sample, and thus the accuracy of extrapolated scores is uncertain. Additionally, extrapolated scores should only be used when a minimum level or score is earned. Wechsler (1974), for example, warned against calculating IQ scores on the Wechsler Intelligence Scale for Children—Revised when the raw scores are not above zero on three verbal and three performance subtests. Bailey et al. (1987) found that when extrapolation procedures were used for children with disabilities assessed with the Battelle Developmental Inventory, 28% of the children in their sample who required score extrapolation received negative deviation quotients, an impossible score. When writing test reports, the examiner should always indicate when scores included in the report were obtained through extrapolation procedures.

Using Norm-Referenced Scores for Evaluating Progress

Professionals in early intervention programs need to be aware that almost all procedures for summarizing child performance have limitations with respect to their use for demonstrating program or intervention effectiveness. While a developmental age score may document improvement, it is difficult to determine what proportion of that improvement is due to maturation. Although developmental quotients may be used to account for the proportion of variance due to maturation, they may not show statistically significant differences between pretest and posttest scores, particularly with older children, because the number of months or years gained becomes a smaller percentage of a child's overall chronological age as he or she gets older. This problem is illustrated in Figure 2.2, which demonstrates how a gain of 6 months in developmental age influences change in the developmental quotient of a child whose developmental age at 12 months was 6 months. As may be seen, as the child gets older, the 6-month gain results in smaller changes in the DQ. Thus two children who gained exactly the same skills and demonstrated the same amount of gain in developmental age would show very different levels of change in DQ scores if they were of different ages.

An example of how different scores can present different pictures of children is evident in a

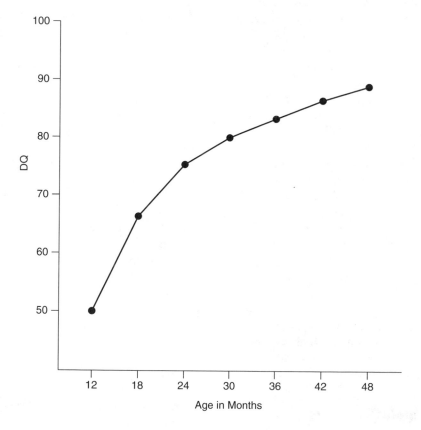

FIGURE 2.2

Effect of a 6-month increase in developmental age scores on the developmental quotient at various ages of a child who at 12 months received an age-equivalent score of 6 months

FIGURE 2.3

Change in developmental quotient scores of 129 preschoolers with disabilities at 4-month intervals

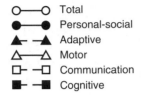

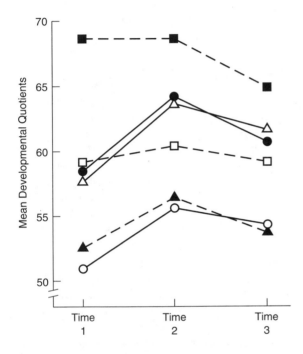

FIGURE 2.4

Change in developmental age scores of 129 preschoolers with disabilities at 4-month intervals

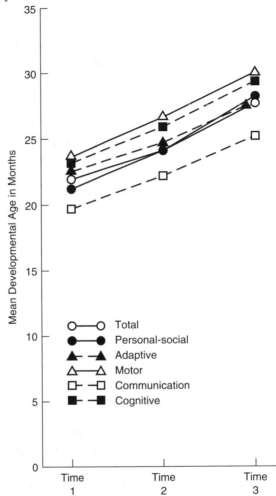

sample of 129 preschoolers with disabilities who were assessed three times (at 4-month intervals) using the Battelle Developmental Inventory. The results of the assessments when developmental quotient scores and developmental age scores were used are displayed in Figure 2.3 and Figure 2.4. As may be seen, developmental age scores displayed a steady growth or increase in total and domain scores across the 8-month period. Deviation scores showed more fluctuation across assessments, but actually remained relatively stable from Time 1 to Time 3 assessments. These data may be interpreted to mean that children in

the sample were not changing their status relative to other children, although they were increasing their ability to perform developmental skills.

A related problem in the use of standardized scores is illustrated in Vignette 2 at the beginning of this chapter. It is a well-documented phenomenon that a child may gain new skills over a period of time and have a higher developmental age score, but yet a lower standard score. This can occur if a child's progress is less than what would be expected with the normative group. For parents, seeing a lower standard score can be discouraging at best and alarming for some if they do not understand that the decline in score does not mean that the child is regressing. Special educators need to be able to explain to parents how this can happen, and should focus on sharing information that shows children's progress on functional skills.

SUMMARIZING TEST PERFORMANCE: CRITERION- AND CURRICULUM-REFERENCED MEASURES

Criterion-referenced measures are tests that measure success or failure to meet some previously determined objective. They are made up of items selected because of their importance to school performance or daily living. Because of their importance, items that are missed typically become teaching targets. Criterion-referenced tests do not provide information about where a child's performance falls relative to his or her peers. Rather, they indicate ability with respect to specific skills.

Criterion-referenced tests attempt to determine the child's strengths and weaknesses without comparing him or her with others and are appropriate whenever a norm-referenced score is not needed. For example, if a preschool teacher is trying to measure progress toward objectives in a center-based program, the criterion-referenced approach offers behavioral, concrete information.

Usually criterion-referenced tests cannot be used alone to make decisions regarding placement or eligibility for services, since those decisions often are based on the nature and extent of the child's developmental delay. However, criterion-referenced tests aid in the understanding of a child's abilities and needs and should be used in placement decisions to complement findings from norm-referenced measures. When determining placement, the primary question should be "Which placement option will best meet a child's needs?" rather than "Which

placement option does the child qualify for according to test scores?" Criterion-referenced measures frequently do a better job of identifying functional needs than do norm-referenced tests. Also, reporting results from criterion-referenced tests often is more desired by parents, since such results can focus on specific strengths and needs rather than emphasizing the child's delay.

A special form of criterion-referenced tests, referred to as *curriculum-referenced testing* or curriculum-based assessment (Neisworth & Bagnato, 1986), involves the assessment of a child's abilities in the context of a predetermined sequence of curriculum objectives. Assessment covers the same materials presented during instruction. Curriculum-referenced tests are, in reality, criterion-referenced tests; however, they differ from other forms of criterion-referenced testing in that a predetermined criterion is not necessarily set and the test is always related to what was taught in the classroom. While the goal of norm-referenced testing is to compare a child with a norm or standard group, and the goal of criterion-referenced testing is to ascertain whether or not a child has acquired a predetermined set of skills, the goal of curriculum-referenced testing is to assess the percentage of material mastered in a given curriculum. Thus, curriculum-referenced tests compare a child's performance with the curriculum.

Curriculum-referenced assessment is a commonly used approach in infant and preschool settings (Bailey, Jens, & Johnson, 1983). Its utility lies in the fact that there is a direct correspondence between assessment procedures and intervention goals. Missed items in the curriculum become subsequent instructional objectives. The primary limitations relate to potential overreliance on the existing curriculum and overly specific interpretation of individual items. Children with disabilities are extraordinarily variable in their individual needs. Early intervention professionals will need to expand upon preset curricula to tailor assessment demands for individual children. In addition, teachers and other professionals must realize that individual curricula items are representative of complex, broad skills. For example, an item such as "puts together a three-piece puzzle" includes cognitive, visual, and motor skills. Instructional activities should not focus merely on putting together a puzzle, but also on relevant functional tasks requiring similar skills.

Criterion-Referenced Scoring

Criterion-referenced and curriculum-referenced tests are scored by first counting the number of items passed. The number itself, equivalent to a raw score, may be the score summary, as in the case of the Evaluation and Programming System for Infants and Young Children (Bailey & Bricker, 1986). The same limitations as described with raw scores for norm-referenced tests, however, pertain to criterion-referenced measures, since the raw score alone is difficult to interpret. The raw score often is converted into a percentage value computed by dividing the raw score by the total possible raw score obtainable. The resulting score is an indication of the percentage of items passed.

With school-age children, performance standards often are set on criterion-referenced tests. A *performance standard* is a specified criterion of performance, such as 8 out of 10 items or 80% of items.

Recently other statistical methods have been applied to selected instruments to generate scores that combine properties of both criterion-referenced and norm-referenced measures. These include the "W-score" as reported in the Woodcock-Johnson II Tests of Cognitive Abilities and in the "Growth Scores" as reported in the Leiter International Performance Scale—Revised (Roid & Miller, 1997). These scores incorporate special statistical methods that show how the child performs relative to a sequence of items and can also be useful in documenting progress over time. As with any test, users of these measures should carefully read the manual accompanying the test and develop an understanding of the precise nature of the particular scores being reported by the test.

Using Criterion-Referenced Scores to Evaluate Progress

Progress on criterion-referenced and curriculum-referenced tests may be described in terms of change in either raw scores or percentage scores. When interpreting criterion-referenced scores, however, professionals should be cautioned that such scores probably are only ordinal in nature, not equal interval. An equal-interval scale is one in which the difficulty level of each item is equivalent; thus, each item requires approximately the same amount of effort to achieve. Equality of item difficulty is rarely documented in criterion-referenced tests, unfortunately, making it difficult to interpret change. For example, one child could achieve several relatively easy items during a period of intervention and demonstrate a sizeable increase in percentage of items passed, whereas another child may achieve only one very difficult item and demonstrate only a small increase in percentage of items passed.

TEST RELIABILITY

In evaluating a particular assessment tool, one concern is the *reliability* of the instrument—the consistency of test performance. If several children were administered the same test and each received a different score, how much of that variability would be attributable to true differences in the children's abilities and how much would be due to what is referred to as "error variance"? If a child took a test over and over again, and no practice effect occurred, what would be the variability in the child's performance? The less error variance in the answer to either of these questions, the greater the test's reliability. Professionals in early intervention should understand the concept of reliability, recognize sources of error in measurement, and be able to read, interpret, and evaluate reliability data.

Sources of Error in Measurement

Measurement error may stem from several sources. The most common are characteristics of the test itself, variation in administrative conditions and child characteristics, and aspects of the examiner.

Test Characteristics A major source of variability is the test itself, which is often the focus of reliability studies. Items on a test should be clear in regard to the materials required and to administrative procedures. If they are not, one examiner might administer an item in one way, and another might use different administrative procedures. In addition, a test should have clear scoring procedures. If not, one examiner might give a child credit for a particular response; another might credit a failure for precisely the same response. Finally, test reliability can be affected by test length; extremely short or extremely long tests are likely to be less reliable.

Administrative and Subject Conditions A second major source of error variance is associated with aspects of the subjects taking the test and the conditions under which the test is administered. Stanley (1971) describes several characteristics of the individual child that might result in score variance on a particular test, including general ability to comprehend instructions, test-taking skills, health, fatigue, motivation, emotional strain, or fluctuations in attention. Performance may also vary by chance associated with "lucky" responses to items. For example, a child may be asked to point to the red block. A child who does not know colors still has a 25% chance of being correct if there are four blocks from which to choose.

Aspects of a particular test administration may also affect a child's performance and result in score variability. For example, the room may be too hot, poorly lit, or stuffy. The child may not interact well with the particular adult administering the test due to unfamiliarity or characteristics of the adult such as personality style, culture, or gender.

The Examiner Finally, the skill of the examiner in administering and scoring the test influences the reliability of administration. A test may have perfectly clear and precise administrative and scoring procedures, but an individual examiner may not have read them all or may have forgotten one or more guidelines. Furthermore, mistakes can be made in score calculations and transformations. The more complex the scoring procedure required and the more calculations that are necessary, the greater the likelihood of error.

Assessing Test Reliability

When examining the reliability of a given test, the professional generally has two sources for information. First, the administrative manual of the particular instrument should provide detailed reliability data. Second, reliability studies of particular measures often are published in the professional literature. This body of information, however, is generally much less accessible to most practicing professionals working with young children with disabilities.

As Stanley (1971) suggests, "there is no single, universal, and absolute reliability for a test" (p. 363). There are many ways to document test reliability, including procedural and scoring reliability, test-retest reliability, alternate forms reliability, the Standard Error of Measurement, and internal consistency reliability. The reliability measure used varies according to the question of interest.

Procedural and Scoring Reliability *Procedural reliability* refers to the extent to which the examiner follows the administrative procedures required by a particular test; scoring reliability refers to the extent to which the score calculations and score summaries are accurate. Both must be assessed by having another individual check the examiner. Procedural reliability could be assessed by having one person observe another administer a test. For each item, the observer notes whether the examiner used the proper materials, placed them in the proper positions, gave the proper directions, and in general followed the test protocol accurately. In this case the reliability measure would be the percentage of items administered correctly. *Scoring reliability* consists of two major aspects. First, did the examiner give the proper credit for the child's response? Generally this will require observation and simultaneous scoring, since testing young children does not generally result in a permanent product such as a written word. Second, did the examiner correctly calculate the child's total score? This question does not require observation. Rather, two individuals must independently score a test. The reliability measure is the extent to which the individuals agree on the final score calculation.

One example of observer reliability was provided by Bailey and Bricker (1986). Two observers independently observed a child participating in routine classroom activities and scored items on the Evaluation and Programming System. A correlation coefficient was used to determine the extent of interobserver agreement. (A correlation coefficient is a statistical measure of how two variables relate to each other. It ranges from −1 to +1, with coefficients near −1 or +1 considered high correlations and coefficients near zero considered low correlations. Generally in reliability studies, one would expect that correlations should be high and positive.) The results of the study indicated that the two observers were much more likely to agree on some domains than on others. For example, the correlations for the Gross Motor (.95), Communication (.85), and Social (.85) domains were much higher than those for the Fine Motor (.64) and Cognitive (.23) domains.

An example of assessing the reliability of score calculations was provided by Bailey et al. (1987). Seventy-nine teachers of 247 preschoolers with disabilities administered the Battelle Development Inventory and sent the results to the authors. Graduate research assistants subsequently checked each protocol for accuracy in score calculation and summaries. Only 11 teachers

(14.5%) and 50 protocols (20.2%) had no scoring errors. The most common problems included simple math errors, failure to establish a basal, and errors in crediting the child for points below the basal.

Test–Retest Reliability A second form of reliability, *test–retest reliability*, requires administering the same test to a group of children on two different occasions and assessing the extent to which their scores are stable over time. For example, Bailey and Bricker (1986), after assessing 28 children, observed and assessed those children again one or two weeks after the initial testing period. The correlation between total test scores in first and second administration was .84. Test–retest reliability for individual subdomains ranged from .46 to .93.

Alternate Forms Reliability Some instrument developers will develop alternate forms of the same measure. *Alternate*, or parallel, *forms reliability* assesses the extent to which a child's performance on one measure is consistent with his or her performance on the other. It requires that the same child be administered both forms of the test. For example, Boehm (1971) developed two forms of the Boehm Test of Basic Concepts. A median alternate form reliability coefficient of .76 is reported in the administrative manual of the instrument. In a sample tryout of the measure, the mean scores on Form A (42.4) and Form B (42.9) were almost equivalent.

Internal Consistency A fourth form of test reliability seeks to determine whether a child's responses on a given administration of a test are *internally consistent*. In other words, was there variability in performance across items or was the child's performance relatively consistent? This type of question can be asked only if an instrument is assumed to assess a single construct; a child's performance across very different domains (e.g., communication and motor) might be expected to vary.

Internal consistency may be assessed using several procedures. One of the simplest is referred to as split-half reliability, a procedure in which the test essentially is divided into two parts (usually odd versus even items). The reliability measure then is the correlation between the two parts. At a more complex level, formulas such as the Kuder-Richardson procedure or Cronbach's Alpha could be used, in which all possible splits are assessed. For example, McLean, McCormick, Bruder, and Burdg (1987) assessed the internal consistency of the Battelle Developmental Inventory using Cronbach's Alpha with data collected on 40 children with disabilities under 30 months of age. Internal consistency was high in all five domains of the measure, ranging from .887 to .963. Similarly, McLean, McCormick, and Baird (1991) analyzed the internal consistency of the Griffiths Scales using Cronbach's Alpha and found high values, ranging from .959 to .97, indicating the performance was consistent across children for each of the scales.

Standard Error of Measurement A final measure of test reliability, the *standard error of measurement* seeks to answer the hypothetical question of how stable a child's performance on a test would be if he or she could take the test over and over again. Assume that this was done, resulting in a large number of scores for the same child on the same test. That set of scores would have a mean and a standard deviation. The standard error of measurement is the standard deviation of that hypothetical distribution and is thus an estimate of that variability. It is reported in units of the test score itself. For example, the administrative manual of the Battelle Development ment Inventory reports that the standard error of measurement for the total BDI score for children in the 6- to 11-month age range is 3.28. This is interpreted to mean that 68% of the time (since, as displayed in Figure 2.1, one standard deviation above and below the mean encompasses 68% of a normal distribution) a child's total raw score would fall within a range of plus or minus 3.28 points.

Summary Comments Regarding Reliability Clearly, test reliability is an important concern in selecting a measure. Although no one score is the "right" reliability, professionals should examine the evidence available for any given measure. Instruments should be selected that have reliability coefficients greater than .80 and preferably greater than .90, and for which there is a small standard error of measurement. Examiners using the test should be familiar with all aspects of test administration and scoring, and periodic checks of both administrative and scoring procedures should be conducted. If a test is known to have low reliability but is still used by a program, results should be interpreted cautiously. For unclear items, a program should adopt local standards for those items and ask each staff person to adhere to them. However, when reports of such administrations are shared with other agencies, any such standards should be fully explained.

TEST VALIDITY

In addition to test reliability, professionals using tests must also be concerned about *test validity*, which refers to the extent to which a test performs the functions for which it was intended. At least four types of validity should be considered: content, instructional, criterion, and construct.

Content Validity

Content validity refers to how well the content of the test represents the domain tested. For example, a test of cognitive skills should cover the major cognitive attainments of young children and should reflect current theories of cognitive development. According to the Standards for Educational and Psychological Tests (American Psychological Association, 1985), "to demonstrate the content validity of a set of test scores, one must show that the behaviors demonstrated in testing constitute a representative sample of behaviors to be exhibited in a desired performance domain . . . . An investigation of content validity requires that the test developer or test user specify his objectives and carefully define the performance domain in light of those objectives" (p. 28).

In evaluating the content validity of a given test, professionals should examine the rationale for item selection as described in the test's technical manual. An initial test of content validity would be the extent to which the test developer convinces you that a thorough and systematic process has occurred in the selection of test content. This should include a discussion of the theoretical basis for item selection, the source of items, and any data to support the extent to which test content reflects the domain assessed. Data supporting content validity typically would consist of the judgment of experts as to the appropriateness of the content. Essentially, content validity is assessed through a logical analysis of the item development process and of the actual items.

Instructional Utility

A second type of validity, one that is closely related to content validity, is *instructional utility*. Here the user would determine the extent to which an instrument provides useful information for planning intervention programs for young children with disabilities.

One way to assess instructional utility is to ask test users to rate the appropriateness of the items for instruction. As described earlier, Bailey et al. (1987) asked teachers to rate the instructional utility of the Battelle Developmental Inventory. They also asked teachers to rate the extent to which standardized adaptations for children with sensory or motor impairments allowed an individual child to demonstrate his or her optimal skills. Bailey and Bricker (1986) asked staff members using the EPS-I to fill out a form regarding the usefulness and appropriateness of items for designing instructional programs. Such information, particularly when provided at the item level, can be useful in revising instruments as well as in evaluating their overall utility.

Criterion Validity

Criterion validity assesses the extent to which a test corresponds to some other independent measure. Two types of criterion validity have been described. *Concurrent validity* refers to the extent to which a test correlates with another measure administered close in time to the first; *predictive validity* refers to the extent to which a test relates to some future measure of performance. An example of concurrent validity was provided by Epstein, Nordness, Nelson and Hertzog (2002), who showed that the Behavioral and Emotional Rating Scale correlated with a number of other measures of behavior and emotion. An example of predictive validity was provided by McCathren, Yoder, and Warren (2000), who showed that children's performance on the Communication and Symbolic Behavior Scale was related to subsequent expressive vocabulary as seen one year later in an unstructured play setting.

Concurrent and predictive validity are particularly important for screening tests. Screening tests that lack concurrent validity are likely to result in children being referred for assessment who will not be diagnosed as delayed. Concurrent validity is also critical in tests used for diagnosis.

Construct Validity

A *construct* is a hypothetical attribute, such as intelligence or creativity, that is designed to account for variability in behavior. The following statements summarize the essence of construct validity: Evidence of construct validity is not found in a single study; rather, judgments of construct validity are based upon an accumulation of research results. In obtaining the information needed to establish construct validity, the investigator begins by formulating hypotheses about the characteristics of those who have high scores on the test in contrast to those who have low scores. Taken together, such hypotheses form at least a tentative theory about the nature of the construct the test is believed to be measuring. In a full investigation, the test may be the dependent variable in some studies and the independent variable in others. Some hypotheses may be "counterhypotheses" suggested by competing interpretations or theories (American Psychological Association, 1985, p. 30).

A test's construct validity is often assessed by determining its *convergent* and *discriminant* validity. A test that has good convergent validity has high positive correlations with other tests measuring the same construct. In contrast, a test that has good discriminant validity has low correlations with tests that measure different constructs. A sample construct validity question would be to ask whether a particular instrument is, in fact, a measure of intelligence. Mahoney (1984) provided an example of testing the construct validity of the Receptive-Expressive Emergent Language Scale with children with mental retardation. In this study, he demonstrated that the instrument provided a developmental sequence of data about children's communicative behavior and that it correlated well with another measure designed to assess the same construct (convergent validity). However, a thorough documentation of construct validity should also show that the measure in question has a low correlation with measures from other domains (discriminant validity). For example, a communication measure should correlate highly with established communication measures and have lower correlations with social and cognitive measures. Although these skills are interrelated, the question is whether the instrument successfully isolates and differentiates these abilities or skills. In test development, the internal consistency of a test is calculated by using a statistical test to evaluate the test's interitem consistency. If the items of a test are positively correlated, then the items are measuring the same construct and the test is thought to have high internal (interitem) consistency. If, however, only clusters of items are correlated with each other, the items are often divided into subtests assessing different constructs. Similar items are often grouped into clusters by experts who have judged the content of the group of items as similar.

Once items have been grouped into subtests, an intercorrelation matrix allows investigation of the relationship among the subtests. When subtests show significant positive correlations with each other they are said to be intercorrelated and therefore measure the same construct. On the other hand, if the intercorrelation matrix shows that subtests are not significantly correlated, each subtest is probably assessing a different construct. An intercorrelation matrix, correlating domains and subdomains (subtests) of the Battelle Developmental Inventory (Newborg et al., 1984), was used when this test was developed to see if the domains and subdomains were significantly intercorrelated. There were high positive correlations among subtests, providing construct validity for the idea that skills on one subtest serve as a basis for predicting similar levels of development on other subtests for typically developing children.

Another statistical method for analyzing a test's construct validity is factor analysis, which is a method for analyzing all the test items to determine which clusters of items are significantly correlated. The results from a factor analysis provide information about whether the content of the items reflects the theory or constructs underlying the test's development. A test's factorial validity is determined in two ways. One method is to correlate scores on the test with scores on other tests that are supposed to measure the same construct(s). The second method is to correlate the scores for all the subtests on a single test, in order to determine what common constructs are measured among the subtests. The latter method is typically used when the test is initially developed.

When a factor analysis is used to assess the relationship between clusters of test items, this method yields a factor matrix, which shows the correlation between factors, representing a cluster of items measuring the same construct and each subtest. If there are high correlations between the subtests and the factors, and if the factors reflect the theoretical constructs that the test is supposed to measure, the test is said to have high construct validity. The researcher is responsible for naming the factors in the factor matrix, based on his or her knowledge of the theoretical constructs assessed by each cluster of items. This type of decision making, in which subjective judgment determines the factors, has been one cause for the criticism of factor analysis.

Banerji (1992b) conducted a factor analysis to determine the factor structure of the Gesell School Readiness Screening Test (Ilg & Ames, 1972; Ilg, Ames, Haines, & Gillespie, 1978), a screening test for children ages 2 to 6 that is often used to determine school readiness. The Gesell has eight subtests assessing skills such as writing, copying shapes, and naming animals. In this factor analysis, the factorial validity of the Gesell was assessed by correlating the eight subtests to see which ones were highly correlated. Results indicated that all the subtests of the Gesell were highly intercorrelated; hence, Banerji concluded that the factor structure of the Gesell could be described by one general factor. Banerji found, however, that it was easier to explain the constructs measured by the Gesell by referring to two factors, visual-motor and language and cognition tasks (Meisels, 1983), even though the test could be described using one general factor. This is an example of how judgment is used to name and choose factors from a factor analysis.

Another problem with factor analysis is that different constructs may describe a child's performance on a test at different ages. For instance, one factor (sensorimotor) may describe a toddler's performance, while several factors (verbal, visual-spatial, cognitive, and motor) may describe a preschooler's performance on the test. Different factor groupings may reflect differences in children's cognitive development at different ages. This may make the age level constructs from factor analyses presented in test manuals inappropriate for children with developmental delays, because their developmental level differs from that of the typically developing children whose scores were used in the original analyses. There-

fore, additional factor analyses for groups of children with different types of developmental disabilities may be necessary to determine what constructs the test measures for children with special needs.

For instance, Snyder and associates (Snyder, Lawson, Thompson, Stricklin, & Sexton, 1993) used factor analysis to evaluate the constructs measured by the Battelle (Newborg et al., 1984) for a sample of children with severe developmental disabilities. The factor matrix indicated that the Battelle measured only three factors for children with severe developmental disabilities. In contrast, the factor matrix for typically developing children presented in the Battelle test manual suggests that this test assesses five factors (called domains). Thus, developmental tests may assess different constructs in children with disabilities, and, if the performance of children with disabilities is interpreted based on factors developed from analyses of the test scores of typically developing children, the clinician will probably draw inaccurate conclusions about the performance of children with disabilities. This error is magnified if the same test is used with a child with a disability over time, because children with disabilities may mature in a way that is qualitatively and quantitatively different from that of their typically developing peers (Snyder et al., 1993).

The factor analysis conducted by Snyder et al. (1993) was a confirmatory factor analysis, which determined whether the factors found for one sample, typically developing children, would be the same for another sample, children with severe developmental disabilities. Bailey, Blasco, and Simeonsson (1992) also conducted a confirmatory factor analysis for mothers' and fathers' responses on the Family Needs Survey to determine whether the needs expressed by mothers and fathers of young children with disabilities were similar. The first factor matrix for a sample of mothers of children with disabilities indicated six factors representing the following needs: family and social support, information, financial, explaining to others, child care, and professional support. The second factor matrix for fathers indicated the Family Needs Survey assessed some similar factors for fathers, but fathers' needs were clustered into a smaller number of factors. Also, the group of test items forming the cluster representing the family and social support factor was different for fathers and mothers. This study provides further support for conducting factor analyses to assess the construct validity for the test for any new group taking a test, because the test may assess different factors for different groups.

Social Validity

A final type of validity that should be mentioned is "social validity." Unfortunately, most standardized tests will not provide information about social validity, as it is not typically a part of the test evaluation process. However, for intervention planning, social validity may be one of the most important considerations in selecting an assessment procedure. Wolf (1978) originally defined social validity as the extent to which consumers or clients find the information from measures or the results of research to be *meaningful* or *relevant*. Myers, McBride, and Peterson (1996) argue that early childhood special educators should make sure that both practitioners and parents are satisfied that the assessment procedures being used provide a true indication of the child's abilities. In a study of children with disabilities, these authors found that parents and professionals rated play-

based assessments as providing more functional information than standardized assessments in a number of areas. Thus, although test manuals are not likely to provide this information, early childhood professionals should, to the greatest extent possible, use assessment instruments and procedures that provide socially useful and valid information as perceived by the users of that information.

Comments About Validity

Questions about validity are of ultimate importance for early childhood special educators and related service personnel because they ask whether an instrument fulfills the function for which it was intended. Validity is both separate from and tied to reliability. Although conceptually they ask very different questions, it is a well-accepted axiom in test development that test validity can be no higher than the test's reliability, and usually is considerably lower. This makes sense, for how could an unreliable or inconsistent measure have any accuracy? However, the fact that a test is reliable does not mean that it has any validity for certain purposes. For example, a screening test may be perfectly reliable but be of no use in planning instructional programs.

Finally, it must be noted that the vast majority of validity studies conducted on norm-referenced measures have failed to examine the validity of these instruments for use with individuals with disabilities (Fuchs, Fuchs, Benowitz, & Barringer, 1987).

· · · · · · · ·

SUMMARY OF KEY CONCEPTS

- Testing is the assessment of children's abilities through the presentation of standardized tasks and application of standardized procedures for interpreting children's performance. It is probably the most widely used, and widely misused, form of assessment, and thus an understanding of the process underlying testing is essential.

- Standardized administration and scoring of tests is important when test scores are used. Standardized procedures may penalize some children with disabilities, however, and results from standardized testing should be interpreted with caution.

- Teachers and other professionals should examine how test content was derived to ensure that content is adequate for the intended purpose.

- Norm-referenced tests compare a child's performance with that of other children, using developmental age scores, developmental quotients, standard scores, or percentile ranks. Each score has advantages and disadvantages. Clinicians should examine the norm group from which these scores were derived, be able to interpret each, and recognize the limitations of each.

- Criterion-referenced measures document children's attainment of predetermined objectives or curriculum items, and generally are more useful than norm-referenced measures for instructional purposes.
- *Reliability* refers to the consistency of test performance. Several factors can influence test reliability.
- *Validity* refers to the extent to which a test performs the functions for which it was intended.

· · · · · · · ·

REFERENCES

Alpern, G. D., Boll, T. J., & Shearer, M. S. (1980). *Developmental Profile II.* Aspen, CO: Psychological Development Publications.

American Psychological Association. (1985). *Standards for educational and psychological tests.* Washington, DC: APA.

Bailey, D. B., Blasco, P. M., & Simeonsson, R. J. (1992). Needs expressed by mothers and fathers of young children with disabilities. *American Journal on Mental Retardation, 97*(1), 1–10.

Bailey, D. B., Jens, K. G., & Johnson, N. (1983). Curricula for handicapped infants. In S. G. Garwood & R. R. Fewell (Eds.), *Educating handicapped infants* (pp. 387–415). Rockville, MD: Aspen.

Bailey, D. B., & Rosenthal, S. L. (1987). Basic principles of measurement and test development. In W. H. Berdine & S. A. Meyer (Eds.), *Assessment in special education.* Boston: Little, Brown.

Bailey, D. B., Vandiviere, P., Dellinger, J., & Munn, D. (1987). The Battelle Developmental Inventory: Teacher perceptions and implementation data. *Journal of Psychoeducational Assessment, 3,* 217–226.

Bailey, E. J., & Bricker, D. (1986). A psychometric study of a criterion-referenced assessment instrument designed for infants and young children. *Journal of the Division for Early Childhood, 10,* 124–134.

Banerji, M. (1992a). An integrated study of the predictive properties of the Gesell School Readiness Screening Test. *Journal of Psychoeducational Assessment, 10,* 240–256.

Banerji, M. (1992b). Factor structure of the Gesell School Readiness Screening Test. *Journal of Psychoeducational Assessment, 10,* 342–354.

Bayley, N. (1969). *Bayley Scales of Infant Development.* New York: The Psychological Corp.

Bayley, N. (1993). *Bayley Scales of Infant Development (2nd ed.)* New York: The Psychological Corp.

Boehm, A. E. (1971). *Boehm Test of Basic Concepts.* New York: The Psychological Corp.

Danaher, J. (2001). *Eligibility policies and practices for young children under Part B of IDEA.* Chapel Hill, NC: National Early Childhood TA Center, FPG Child Development Institute, University of North Carolina at Chapel Hill.

Egan, D. F., & Brown, R. (1986). Developmental assessment: 18 months to 4½ years [Performance test]. *Child: Care, Health, and Development, 12,* 339–349.

Epstein, M., Nordness, P. D., Nelson, J. R., & Hertzog, M. (2002). Convergent validity of the Behavioral and Emotional Rating Scale with primary grade-level students. *Topics in Early Childhood Special Education, 22,* 114–121.

Fewell, R. R., & Sandall, S. R. (1986). Developmental testing of handicapped infants: A measurement dilemma. *Topics in Early Childhood Special Education, 6,* 86–99.

Fuchs, D., Fuchs, L. S., Benowitz, S., & Barringer, K. (1987). Norm-referenced tests: Are they valid for use with handicapped students? *Exceptional Children, 54,* 263–271.

Furuno, S., O'Reilly, A., Hosaka, C. M., Inatsuka, T. T., Allman, T. L., & Zelsloft, B. (1979). *The Hawaii Early Learning Profile.* Palo Alto, CA: VORT.

Glover, M. E., Preminger, J. L., & Sanford, A. R. (1978). *The Early Learning Accomplishment Profile.* Winston-Salem, NC: Kaplan.

Griffiths, R. (1970). *The abilities of young children.* High Wycombe, Great Britain: Cournswood House.

Hanson, R., & Smith, J. A. (1987). Achievements of young children on items of the Griffiths Scales: 1980 compared to 1960. *Child: Care, Health, and Development, 13(3),* 181–195.

Ilg, F. L., & Ames, L. B. (1972). *School readiness.* New York: Harper & Row.

Ilg, F. L., Ames, L. B., Haines, J., & Gillespie, C. (1978). *School readiness.* New York: Harper & Row.

Keogh, B. K., & Sheehan, R. (1981). The use of developmental test data for documenting handicapped children's progress: Problems and recommendations. *Journal of the Division for Early Childhood, 3,* 42–47.

Mahoney, G. (1984). The validity of the Receptive-Expressive Emergent Language Scale with mentally retarded children. *Journal of the Division for Early Childhood, 9,* 86–94.

Mardell-Czudnowski, C., & Goldenberg, D. (1984). Revision and restandardization of a preschool screening test: DIAL becomes DIAL-R. *Journal of the Division for Early Childhood, 8,* 149–156.

Mayes, S. D. (1997). Potential scoring problems using the Bayley Scales of Infant Development-II Mental Scale. *Journal of Early Intervention, 21,* 36–44.

McCathren, R. B., Yoder, P. J., & Warren, S. F. (2000). Testing predictive validity of the Communication Composite of the Communication and Symbolic Behavior Scales. *Journal of Early Intervention, 23,* 36–46.

McLean, M. E., McCormick, K., & Baird, S. M. (1991). Concurrent validity of the Griffiths Mental Development Scales with a population of children under 24 months. *Journal of Early Intervention, 15(4),* 338–344.

McLean, M., McCormick, K., Bruder, M. B., & Burdg, N. B. (1987). An investigation of the validity and reliability of the Battelle Developmental Inventory with a population of children younger than 30 months with identified handicapping conditions. *Journal of the Division for Early Childhood, 11,* 238–246.

Meisels, S. J. (1983). *Developmental screening in early childhood: A guide.* Washington, DC: NAEYC.

Myers, C. L., McBride, S. L., & Peterson, C. A. (1996). Transdisciplinary, play-based assessment in early childhood special education: An examination of social validity. *Topics in Early Childhood Special Education, 16,* 102–126.

Naglieri, J. A. (1981). Extrapolated developmental indices for the Bayley Scales of Infant Development. *American Journal of Mental Deficiency, 85,* 548–550.

Neisworth, J. T., & Bagnato, S. J. (1986). Curriculum-based developmental assessment: Congruence of testing and teaching. *School Psychology Review, 15,* 180–199.

Newborg, J., Stock, J. R., Wnek, L., Guidubaldi, J., & Svinicki, J. (1984). *The Battelle Developmental Inventory.* Allen, TX: DLM/Teaching Resources.

Rogers, S. J., D'Eugenio, D. B., Brown, S. L., Donovan, C. M., & Lynch, E. W. (1981). *Early Intervention Developmental Profile.* Ann Arbor, MI: University of Michigan Press.

Roid, G. H., & Miller, L. J. (1997). *Leiter International Performance Scale–Revised.* Wood Dale, IL: Stoelting.

Salvia, J. & Ysseldyke, J. E. (1985). *Assessment in special and remedial education.* Boston: Houghton Mifflin.

Sanford, A. R., & Zelman, J. G. (1981). *The Learning Accomplishment Profile.* Winston-Salem, NC: Kaplan.

Sattler, J. (1982). *Assessment of children's intelligence and special abilities.* Boston: Allyn & Bacon.

Snyder, P., Lawson, S., Thompson, B., Stricklin, S., & Sexton, D. (1993). Evaluating the psychometric integrity of instruments used in early intervention research: The Battelle Developmental Inventory. *Topics in Early Childhood Special Education, 13(2),* 216–232.

Snyder–McLean, L. (1987). Reporting norm-referenced program evaluation data: Some considerations. *Journal of the Division for Early Childhood, 11,* 254–264.

Stanley, J. C. (1971). Reliability. In R. L. Thorndike (Ed.), *Educational measurement (2nd ed.)* (pp. 356–442). Washington, DC: American Council on Education.

Wechsler, D. (1974). *Manual for Wechsler Intelligence Scale for Children–Revised.* New York: Psychological Corp.

Wolf, M. M. (1978). Social validity: The case for subjective measurement or how applied behavior analysis is finding its heart. *Journal of Applied Behavior Analysis, 11,* 203–214.

Procedural Considerations in Assessing Infants and Preschoolers with Disabilities

Mary McLean
University of Wisconsin–Milwaukee
Elizabeth R. Crais
University of North Carolina at Chapel Hill

Over the past two decades, some consensus has developed in the field as to the assessment procedures that are most effective with children from birth through age 5 with disabilities (Sandall, McLean, & Smith, 2000; Bagnato, Neisworth, & Munson, 1997). This chapter describes the procedures that are recommended for use with these children, organized within discussions of the importance of family and other caregivers' participation in assessment, the importance of cross-disciplinary collaboration, and the importance of assessment in the natural environment.

IMPORTANCE OF FAMILY/ CAREGIVER PARTICIPATION IN ASSESSMENT ACTIVITIES

In recent years, when focusing on the assessment of young children, many professionals have stressed the need to collaborate with family members and other caregivers in planning and implementing the assessment (Bagnato et al., 1997; Crais, 1996, Crais & Belardi, 1999; Sandall et al., 2000; Simeonsson et al., 1996). Traditionally, the involvement of the family included asking child history and developmental questions and, on occasion, having the family complete a family report instrument. In response to legislative and theoretical trends, a number of professionals have attempted additional techniques to encourage family members to take a more active part in assessment. For example, families have been asked to describe the child's daily routine, demonstrate typical interactions with their child, and be physically present during the assessment. Although these efforts may provide professionals with increased information and encourage family members to be more active in the testing sessions, they alone may not facilitate the development of truly collaborative relationships with families in the assessment process. Indeed, despite the fact that recent findings suggest that some programs are adopting more family-centered approaches to

service delivery (Crais & Wilson, 1996; Roberts, Akers, & Behl, 1996; Mahoney & Filer, 1996), many programs continue to offer families few meaningful choices and allow only limited roles in overall decision making (Crais & Belardi, 1999; Lesar Judge, 1997). In addition, the many people who are involved in caring for a young child throughout the day (e.g., childcare providers, teachers, grandparents) may not be considered as important members of the assessment and intervention team. For brevity, the authors have chosen to use the term *caregivers* to represent the primary people (other than the parents or legal guardians) who spend time with the child and who are responsible for some of the child's care. When possible and when desired by the family, all the child's family members and caregivers should be included in the assessment and intervention planning so as to promote shared knowledge· and experiences regarding the child and the early intervention process.

As noted by Bailey et al. (1998), collaborative relationships in early intervention are recognized by several characteristics, including trust, mutual respect, open and clear communication, a collaborative attitude, follow through, and interpersonal skills. If professionals and families seek to be collaborators, they may describe themselves using synonyms commonly substituted for the word *collaborator,* such as *colleague, coworker, copartner,* or *ally* (Crais, 1993). Some professionals suggest that if full collaboration is to be achieved within assessment, families and caregivers must have the opportunity to be active participants *throughout* the entire process rather than just during the actual testing (Boone & Crais, 1999; McLean & McCormick, 1993). Through collaborative efforts, families are provided decision-making opportunities about *all* aspects of the assessment process from the first decision to the last. Ideally, this would include planning the assessment activities; gathering information through interviews, observations, and testing; synthesizing the information; determining whether the gathered information is a fair reflection of a child's abilities and needs; and making decisions based on the shared perceptions of the findings.

Reasons for Building Collaborative Relationships in Assessment

Before discussing strategies to facilitate collaborative efforts by families, caregivers, and other professionals, it is necessary to understand why these types of interactions may be beneficial and desirable. The reasons center around the rights of the family members and the increased family and caregiver satisfaction and empowerment that are made possible by collaborative efforts in assessment.

First, from both theoretical and legislative perspectives, the family is viewed as holding a central position in the child's life and development. If this position is to be maintained, early interventionists must ensure that the family has choices about the roles they play in assessment. One way to ensure that they have such choices is to support and encourage their right to be part of *all* discussions and activities related to the child. When family members are present and feel supported, they may be more likely to take advantage of opportunities to be a part of and shape the entire assessment process.

Because of the family's central position and other caregivers' steady presence in the child's life, these individuals have unique knowledge about the child that is unavailable to many professionals. As suggested by McLean and McCormick (1993), "Parents know their child better than any other member of the assessment team" (p. 65). Indeed, families' concerns about their child's developmental status have been well correlated with the outcome of developmental screening tests (Diamond & Squires, 1993; Glascoe, MacLean, & Stone, 1991; Henderson & Meisels, 1994). Professionals must, therefore, recognize the importance of tapping into the family's knowledge base and gaining the family's and other caregivers' input in the assessment process. Assessment activities must evolve out of the family's (and other caregivers')

concerns and priorities and be responsive to what the family hopes to gain through assessment.

Families and caregivers have also been shown to be reliable in performing activities such as completing screening tools or developmental checklists of the child's behaviors. Moreover, the predictability of the screening process has been shown to increase with the combination of professional administered and parent completed measures (Henderson & Meisels, 1994). Due to their different perspectives, families and professionals should be viewed as independent rather than interchangeable assessors (Suen, Lu, & Neisworth, 1993). Further, family members' participation in observing and rating specific behaviors of their child has led to their increased sensitivity to the development of the child (Dinnebeil & Rule, 1994) and increased contributions in intervention planning and decision making (Brinckerhoff & Vincent, 1987). In addition to assessing the child, family and caregiver participation in identifying areas, contexts, and techniques for assessment can be efficient ways to use these individual's knowledge of the child and can improve the ecological validity of assessments. Moreover, identification of families' priorities for intervention (e.g., whether to intervene, when, where, and in what way) can be accomplished only through collaboration.

Finally, collaborative relationships in assessment are desirable because assessment has a significant impact on current and subsequent feelings and behaviors of both professionals and families (Simeonsson et al., 1996). Most families enter the early intervention system by taking part in some type of assessment of their child, and this experience may set the tone for the interactions that will follow. If professionals take a directive role during assessment, family members may be prompted to take more passive roles. Much has been written in recent years regarding the need to support and strengthen families within early intervention (Dunst, Trivette, & Deal, 1994); however, families and other caregivers may not *feel* supported or empowered in the assessment process. As suggested by Dunst and his colleagues, families (and caregivers) who do not feel empowered are less likely to take an active role or to follow through on actions that are recommended for the child. Professionals may therefore develop incomplete pictures of families and caregivers and may make faulty assumptions based on information gained in less than optimal conditions. Providing opportunities for family and caregiver participation in assessing the child conveys to families and other caregivers that they are important to the assessment process.

Another issue related to the impact of assessment is the level of satisfaction felt by families and caregivers during and following an assessment. In examining this issue, Dunst et al. (1994) suggest that the primary reason for dissatisfaction by families is the failure of professionals to gain consensus with family members on three critical points: (a) the nature of the presenting concern, (b) the need for treatment, and (c) the course of action. They argue that if professionals would focus on gaining consensus on these points, their relationships with families and caregivers would improve, as would the families' and caregivers' satisfaction. Indeed, Beukelman and Mirenda (1992) suggest that a major goal of initial assessment should be the development of a process for long-term consensus building and management.

In sum, collaborative relationships not only recognize the rights of families, they can also improve the efficiency and validity of assessment activities and, ultimately, the satisfaction and ownership felt by families and caregivers. In an attempt to help professionals develop collaborative relationships with families and caregivers, the next section provides an overview of suggested strategies.

Strategies for Building Collaborative Relationships in Assessment

Three primary strategies for developing collaborative relationships within assessment activities include (a) preassessment planning; (b) active family/caregiver participation in assessment; and (c) mutual sharing of assessment results. The focus in all activities is on providing opportunities

for family and caregiver input and decision making and respecting the family's and caregivers' choices and actions.

Preassessment Planning The purpose of preassessment planning is to develop a blueprint for assessment that will be tailored to the individual child and family and will guide the selection of instruments and procedures to be used as well as the schedule of assessment activities (Kjerland & Kovach, 1990; Crais, 1996). The assessment plan should not be developed by one individual. It must be a collaborative effort involving the family, other caregivers, and professionals. Input must be obtained from persons who, because of their expertise and because of their relationship to the child, can observe, gather data, and assess the child's functioning.

The steps involved in planning include:

1. Obtaining background information
2. Determining family goals and participation in the process
3. Identifying other caregivers who should be involved
4. Identifying the contexts for assessment, and
5. Formulating a plan

There are a variety of formats for planning, including face-to-face meetings, forms sent to families and caregivers, telephone discussions, or a combination of formats. In some programs, a service coordinator or family facilitator may meet with the family prior to the assessment to discuss the available options and relay this information to other professionals involved. In other instances, the family may meet with the entire team prior to assessment. Useful forms and questions for preassessment planning appear in Boone and Crais (2000), Crais (1996), and McGonigel, Kaufmann, & Johnson (1991) and typically include questions such as "What questions or concerns do you have about your child?" "How can we be of service to you?" and "What would you like to gain from your interactions with us?" In identifying first the family's concerns about the child and what the family wants or needs from professionals, the collaborators have in essence outlined the direction that the assessment will take. The questions the family has about the child will shape the assessment activities, and professionals can be more responsive to what the family wants from assessment.

For gaining information about family concerns, priorities, and resources (CPRs), various instruments are available, including the Family Information Preference Inventory (Turnbull & Turnbull, 1986), the Family Needs Survey (Bailey & Simeonsson, 1990), and the Family Resource Scale (Leet & Dunst, 1988). In addition to stand-alone instruments, a few child assessment tools now include questionnaires focused on these areas as part of their assessment process. A representative tool is the Hawaii Early Learning Profiles Family Centered Interview (Parks, 1994). This instrument is typically completed by family members, thereby facilitating self-identification of the concerns, priorities, and resources that are most important to the family. In work by Bailey and Blasco (1990), the majority of families reported that instruments such as these were helpful to them; however, they also stressed their strong preference that they be given the option to complete the instruments. In addition, families differed as to whether they preferred the use of a written survey versus more informal and open-ended discussions. Thus, professionals are wise to offer alternatives and to respect families' preferences as to how information is gathered about these issues. Helpful ideas for gathering this type of information with families in face-to-face discussions can be found in Winton (1996) and Winton and Bailey (1993). Chapter 7 of this text presents a comprehensive discussion of assessing family concerns, priorities and resources.

In addition to family CPRs, it is often helpful to gather information from other caregivers who spend a good deal of time with the child. The initial preassessment contact with the family could either directly include other caregivers in planning the assessment or could be a time for the family to identify those caregivers who could either contribute to the assessment process or learn from it. These individuals could then be given an opportunity before or during the assessment to share their perspectives on the child's strengths and needs and their concerns.

A further issue in preassessment is determining the context for assessment—both the location/s and the way in which assessment will take place. Useful questions include "When or where would you like the assessment to take place?" "What are some of the activities you feel are important for letting us see what's typical for your child?" and "Who would you like to be included in the assessment?" The recent focus on providing services to children in their natural environments (Sandall et al., 2000) points to the need to assess these children in those same environments. A sample preassessment planning form developed by Project Dakota (Kjerland & Kovach, 1990) is included in Figure 3.1.

Using a form such as that in Figure 3.1., professionals can gather information about the settings (e.g., home versus daycare), types of activities (e.g., observing the child at play, watching as a family member feeds the child), and persons (e.g., family members, teacher) that the family believes may show the child's strengths and needs. In response to identified areas of concern, the professionals can also suggest a variety of activities that family members and other caregivers may choose to take part in with the child (e.g., completing a developmental checklist, helping administer some test items, engaging the child in social routines). Through this process the professionals, caregivers, and the family begin to identify activities that will be representative of the child's strengths and needs and to identify the desired level of participation by family members and caregivers in each activity.

Active Participation by Family Members and Other Caregivers in Assessment

Traditionally, family participation in child assessment was primarily limited to the provision of background information about the child (e.g., birth history, developmental milestones), brief descriptions of the child's current difficulties, and perhaps observing the child during assessment. In addition, *other caregivers* typically have had few or no opportunities to

1. Questions or concerns others have (e.g., babysitter, clinic, preschool) about my child:
2. Other places you can observe my child:

   Place: Place:

   Contact person: Contact person:

   What to observe: What to observe:
3. I want others to see what my child does when:
4. I prefer the assessment take place:

   _____ at home _____ at another location _____ at the center
5. A time when my child is alert and when working parents can be present is:

   _____ morning _____ afternoon _____ early afternoon
6. People whom I would like to be there other than parents and early intervention staff:
7. My child's favorite toys or activities to help her/him become focused, motivated, and comfortable:
8. During the assessment, I prefer to:

   _____ a. sit beside my child.

   _____ b. help with activities to explore her/his abilities.

   _____ c. offer comfort and support to my child.

   _____ d. exchange ideas with the facilitator.

   _____ e. carry out activities to explore my child's abilities.

   _____ f. permit facilitator to handle and carry out activities.

   _____ g. Other:

FIGURE 3.1

Preassessment planning: The setting (Project Dakota)
Note: From Kjerland, L. & J. Kovach, J. (1990). "Family-Staff Collaboration for Tailored Infant Assessment." In Editors Gibbs, E. and Teti, D., *Interdisciplinary Assessment of Infants: A Guide for Early Intervention Professionals.* Baltimore, MD: Paul H. Brookes Publishing Co. Reprinted with permission.

provide input into the assessment process and yet are expected (as are families) to accept the assessment results and implement the recommendations made. As noted, current efforts to involve families encompass a wider variety of activities, including eliciting particular behaviors from the child, performing some test items, or confirming that the testing was representative of the child. Yet, families and other caregivers continue to be "untapped" resources regarding the child's functioning in natural settings. One assessment activity that is increasingly being encouraged by professionals is that of families assessing their own children. The move toward greater utilization of families as assessors

has been fueled by several factors related to assessment. A primary factor has been the increased recognition that families can be reliable judges of their children's behavior, even in areas in which they were traditionally thought to be unreliable (e.g., developmental level, communication skills). For example, good reliability by families has been seen in determining (a) the child's current level of development (Diamond & Squires, 1993; Bricker and Squires, 1999); (b) whether the child needs referral for testing (Diamond & Squires, 1993; Bricker and Squire, 1999); and (c) the child's current vocabulary and syntax levels (Dale, 1991; Dale, Bates, Reznick, & Morisset, 1989).

Increased reports of family-professional agreement may be partially due to changes in the way children are currently assessed. The use of observational and informal methods to assess children within naturalistic settings has led professionals to do more of what families typically do, namely, to watch children at play and in daily routines. The use of less formal methods may provide increased opportunities for families and professionals to see the child's typical behaviors and come to similar conclusions. In addition, when using more formal methods, families and professionals have often disagreed on "ceiling" levels or those indicating emerging behaviors (Gradel, Thompson, & Sheehan, 1981). However, because families have multiple opportunities to observe their child and because the child is more comfortable with family members, families are probably more likely to see emerging behaviors. Moreover, when observing the child, families often take into account the child's difficulties and can interpret what the child may be able to do with support. As suggested by Gradel and her colleagues (1981), rather than family reliability improving, it may be more a matter of professionals coming closer to what families see and thereby improving their own reliability.

Another factor that may have an impact on reliability is the format of the tools families are asked to use to assess their child's behavior. For most people, performance improves with the use of recognition versus recall questions. As the work of Dale and his colleagues (Dale, 1991; Dale et al., 1989) and Bricker and Squires (1999) has shown, families can be quite reliable when asked to indicate whether their child currently has a particular skill (e.g., uses a pincer grasp, says the word *cookie*). Even mothers who themselves were at risk (e.g., had physically abused or neglected their child, had a history of substance abuse, had not completed high school) have been shown to be reliable in completing developmental questionnaires on their infants (Squires & Bricker, 1991). In addition, the work of Bloch and Seitz (1989) has indicated that families who wish to complete developmental assessments of their children can

be taught to do so with a small amount of professional help.

In regard to tools that utilize family report, there are a variety available that encourage differing levels of family participation. Traditionally, these instruments fall into two categories, those that rely solely on family report and those that utilize family report along with elicitation and observation of child behavior. With most of these instruments, information is typically gathered by the professionals interviewing the family and/or asking about specific behaviors. Example instruments specifically designed to be completed from family report alone include the Vineland Adaptive Behavior Scales (Sparrow, Balla, & Cicchetti, 1984) and the Receptive-Expressive Emergent Language Test (Bzoch & League, 2003). Instruments that combine family report with other information sources (e.g., observation, elicitation) include the Battelle Developmental Inventory (Newborg, Stock, Wnek, Guidubaldi, & Svinicki, 1988), the Sequenced Inventory of Communication Development (Hedrick, Prather, & Tobin, 1984), and the Infant-Toddler Language Scale (Rossetti, 1990).

In recent years, in response to the challenge to include families more directly in assessment and the need to gain greater efficiency and ecological validity, several tools have been designed for completion by families themselves; an example is the Ages and Stages Questionnaires (Bricker & Squires, 1999), formerly the Infant/Child Monitoring Questionnaires (Squires, Bricker, & Potter, 1993). The Ages and Stages Questionnaires are a multidomain developmental measure used to monitor at-risk children. A recently developed family-completed measure of communication skills is the MacArthur Communicative Development Inventories (Fenson et al., 1990). Both of these tools utilize a recognition format in which families indicate whether their child currently has a particular skill. Other tools created for use by non-specialists (e.g., teachers, aides) have also been utilized for completion by families; examples include the Denver Articulation Screening Exam (Drumwright, Van Natta, Camp, Frankenburg, &

Drexler, 1973), used by families to screen their pre-school children's articulation skills (Dopheide & Dallinger, 1976), and the Learning Accomplishment Profile (Sanford & Zelman, 1981). In addition, some standardized assessment tools have been utilized by families who wish to assess their children. Gradel et al. (1981) and Sheehan (1988) have noted the successful completion by families of the Developmental Profile II (Alpern, Boll, & Shearer, 1980) and with modifications (e.g., use of an interview format, simpler vocabulary, and a demonstration of each item), the Bayley Scales of Infant Development (Bayley, 1993) and the McCarthy Scales of Children's Abilities (McCarthy, 1972). To further highlight the collaborative relationship possible between families and professionals, a few instruments have been developed specifically to encourage assessment by families *and* professionals. Example tools are the Family Report instrument from the AEPS (Bricker, 1993) and the Parent/Professional Preschool Performance Profile (Bloch, 1987). Both instruments encourage separate assessment of a child's behaviors by families and professionals and discussion as to what behaviors were seen in one setting (e.g., home, school, clinic) versus another.

An additional area that encourages participation by family members and caregivers is the observation and "assessment" of children in their natural environments and during their daily routines. According to the 2000 OSERS Report to Congress (U.S. Department of Education, 2000), children birth through age 2 primarily receive early intervention services in two locations: their homes and center-based programs, whereas children ages 3 through 5 are primarily served in some type of classroom (e.g., daycare, preschool). As suggested by Hanson and Bruder (2001), early interventionists should use natural environments and view them as opportunities to expand children's and families' learning environments. Because learning occurs throughout the day, professionals need the knowledge and skills to gather information about natural environments and plan collaboratively with all the child's caregivers to implement interven-

tions. Clearly, these interventions should be embedded within the activities that are valued by the child's caregivers (McWilliam, 2000). To find out about the child's routines and the values placed on these routines by family members and caregivers, professionals must take the time to gather this information during assessment.

To identify family and caregiver perspectives on the child's performance in daily routines, several methods are available including the use of an interview format and/or forms to be completed. Within an interview format, common questions include "What kinds of routines does your child take part in during the day?", "Are there times or situations during the day that seem particularly hard for your child?", and "What are the activities your child does with you or others that he/she enjoys?". Using forms for family members or caregivers to complete can also provide perspectives on their concerns about the child, how the child interacts/ performs with them and other children, what strategies they have tried, and what they think the child most needs to learn to be successful across routines or in their setting (e.g., home- or day-care, preschool classroom). Example tools include McWilliam's (1992) Family and Staff Preparation Forms that provide family members and teachers with a list of common home or classroom routines and specific questions about those routines. Example questions include "What does the child usually do during the routine?", "How well does the child fit into the routine?", and "What specific strengths or needs does the child have in this routine?". Developmental checklists such as the HELP (Furuno, et al., 1979) can also provide a format for parents to describe and assess their child's participation in daily routines. This process of gathering information about daily routines can then be part of the overall assessment of the child and help guide the intervention planning efforts to be more ecologically valid and family-centered.

In sum, offering families and caregivers the option to participate in assessing the child has many advantages. It is an efficient use of family, caregiver, and professional time, provides information not available to most professionals, and could improve the ecological validity of the assessment process. Yet, as Sheehan (1988) has suggested regarding family involvement in schools, "parental involvement is not a universal good for all parents, for all children, or for all schools. Rather it is an activity that has benefits for some parents, many children, and most schools" (p. 85). Therefore, professionals must be careful not to judge families or other caregivers who choose not to be active in assessing the child. Indeed, there are numerous other roles that family members and caregivers may choose that facilitate their participation in assessment. The important issue is not whether families and other caregivers choose to participate in assessing the child, but whether they are given the opportunity.

To offer a wider range of roles for families and caregivers in assessment, professionals are increasingly using a variety of new and older assessment instruments. Adapting the work of Bailey, McWilliam, Winton, and Simeonsson (1992), the following section highlights some of the roles possible and provides examples of instruments that may facilitate them. A role that acknowledges families and caregivers as experts on the child is that of *interpreter* of the child's behaviors. For example, for children whose communication attempts are hard to "read", family members and other caregivers may be asked to "interpret" the meanings of these attempts. To elicit families' interpretations of their child's behavior in a more systematic manner, Cardone and Gilkerson (1989) have developed a set of activities based on the Neonatal Behavioral Assessment Scale (Brazelton, 1973) whereby family members serve as interpreters to professionals.

Another role that recognizes the family's and other caregiver's unique relationships with the child is that of *participant*. The recent popularity of arena assessment models, which typically include family members (and sometimes other caregivers) as part of the assessment team, is testimony that professionals believe that family members and caregivers are essential to the assessment process. During an arena assessment, a family member or caregiver may be asked to demonstrate certain skills of the

child (e.g., motor or feeding skills) or to administer some test items. Asking family members to elicit familiar social routines (e.g., peek-a-boo, tickle games) or asking teachers to demonstrate a child's skill in the classroom is one means of facilitating a participant role by families and caregivers. A standardized tool that encourages families or caregivers to be participants in assessment is the Communication and Symbolic Behavior Scales (CSBS) (Wetherby & Prizant, 1993). In the administration of the CSBS, the family member or caregiver is seated on one side of the child, and the examiner is seated on the other. If the child prefers to interact with the family member/caregiver, the examiner guides that person through the administration of the tasks. Family members or caregivers who choose a participant role can provide comfort to and information about the child and can also be actively engaged in interacting with the child.

Another role that family members or caregivers may be encouraged to take is that of *validator* of the assessment activities. This role may be utilized in a variety of ways; first as family members and caregivers help plan the activities, next as the family "coaches" the professionals in favored ways to interact with the child, and later as the family and caregivers reflect on the child's usual behaviors relative to the activities and the results gained. Asking families and caregivers to validate the *planning* and *implementing* of the assessment activities as well as the *results* can provide additional validity and reliability to the entire assessment process. One instrument that formally includes postassessment validation by families is the Communication and Symbolic Behavior Scales (CSBS) by Wetherby and Prizant (1993). Following the administration of this instrument, families are asked to use the "Caregiver Perception Rating" form from the CSBS to rate their child's behavior during the assessment (e.g., less than usual, typical, greater than usual) on several components such as alertness, comfort level, and overall communication. Common validation questions suggested by Boone and Crais (1999) to be used before, during, and after assessment activities can be seen in Figure 3.2.

Possible Validating Questions to Ask Families Prior to Assessment

☐   What kinds of information would be most useful to you?

☐   What kinds of activities or toys would bring out the best in your child?

☐   What have you or others tried that has been helpful to your child?

☐   Will the kinds of activities discussed reflect what your child does at home?

☐   When and where would be the best place/s and time/s to gather information about your child?

Possible Validating Questions to Ask Families During Assessment

☐   Are we getting a representative sample of what your child can do?

☐   Was that a correct interpretation of what your child just said (or did)?

☐   How could we approach this task in a way that would help your child feel more comfortable doing it?

☐   Are there better ways we should be working/playing with your child?

Possible Validating Questions to Ask Families After Assessment

☐   Did we address your primary concerns?

☐   How do you feel about the overall process and the results?

☐   Were the behaviors displayed by your child typical for your child?

☐   What other skills or behaviors does your child do that we were not able to see today?

☐   What could we have done differently?

FIGURE 3.2

Questions to use for validating the assessment process

Note: From "Strategies for Achieving Family Driven Assessment and Intervention Planning," by H. Boone & E. Crais, 1999 *Young Exceptional Children*, 3(1), 2–12. Copyright 1999 by Division for Early Childhood of the Council for Exceptional Children. Reprinted with permission.

Finally, in response to identified areas of concern, professionals can offer various levels of *participation* to families and caregivers in assessment. Professionals can first describe possible assessment activities and the typical role that may be associated with an activity (e.g., family member/caregiver helps elicit child behaviors, family/caregiver completes observations of child at home/preschool). They can then ask families and caregivers to indicate both the type of activities and the role they prefer. As suggested by Crais (1996), the activities and family/caregiver roles selected will depend on (a) the family's priorities regarding the type of information they seek (e.g., developmental levels, ideas for intervention); (b) the system requirements for assessment (e.g., eligibility requirements); (c) the family's and caregiver's ideas and preferences for how information about the child is gathered; and (d) the type of tools or activities that will provide the information desired. As suggested by Sheehan (1988), there may also be a minimum level of interest and skill exhibited by families that may influence their participation in assessment. However, as noted by Diamond and Squires (1993), this hypothesized minimum level may vary with the content of the questions and the way information is gathered (e.g., interview format versus having the family complete a form). Therefore, in seeking family and caregiver participation in assessment, professionals may wish to offer a variety of available activities and roles and encourage each family member and caregiver to choose the one/s they prefer.

Mutual Sharing of Assessment Results

A final strategy for building collaborative relationships between professionals, families, and other caregivers in assessment is to focus on the sharing of assessment results and to determine ways that families and caregivers may actively participate. Traditionally, assessment results have been shared at the end of the process, and professionals have often taken the lead and played the largest role. In recent years, professionals have begun to develop alternative strategies such as beginning the discussion by (a) asking family members and caregivers to give their impressions of the assessment; (b) addressing the family's major concerns first in the sharing session; and/or (c) asking family members and caregivers what they currently view as the child's strengths or needs. In addition, a number of professionals have suggested ways that family members and caregivers can not only take part in the sharing meeting, but can also play a prominent role (Crais, 1996; Kjerland & Kovach, 1990).

One important idea in helping families and other caregivers take a greater part in sharing meetings is to recognize that generally, the more active families and caregivers are *during* the assessment planning and implementation, the more likely they are to take an active part during the sharing of the results and the intervention planning. Brinckerhoff and Vincent (1987) demonstrated this principle by asking several families before their child's IEP meetings to complete a family profile and a developmental assessment of their child, to provide an overview of their daily routines, and to meet with a liaison person to prepare for the meeting. The families in the control group were contacted in the usual way about the meetings, but were not asked to perform any special activities prior to the meeting. Brinckerhoff and Vincent reported significant differences between the two groups of families in their participation in the IEP meetings. The families who had been more active in the process before the meeting made more contributions, generated more goals, and made more programming decisions during the meeting. In addition, the professionals in the meetings made more home programming suggestions for the families in the experimental group and made more decisions for the control group. Brinckerhoff and Vincent (1987) also noted that the premeeting activities helped the families in the experimental group match their information on the child with the school personnel's information and helped them pinpoint their child's abilities and needs.

Whether or not family members and caregivers participate directly in assessment, they may be offered additional options that could help them prepare for the sharing session. For example, they may be encouraged to think about or write down characteristics of the child, their observations of when and under what conditions the child performs best/least well, what they would like the child to achieve in the next month or year, and what possible ways they see to help the child achieve in these areas. In addition, when there is time between the assessment and the discussion of results (even several minutes), some professionals suggest providing families and caregivers with a list of questions they may want to consider before the discussion (Crais, 1996). Useful questions could include: "What were your overall impressions of the assessment today?", "What were the activities that (the child's name) seemed to do well?", "What were the activities that seemed difficult for (the child's name)?", "What kinds of skills do you think your child needs help with?", and "What area would you like to discuss first?"

Another successful strategy that may facilitate family, caregiver, and professional collaboration is the sharing of assessment information in an ongoing manner. Rather than save all the assessment results until the end, some professionals, families, and caregivers have found it useful to discuss the information at discrete points throughout the assessment. For example, as each task, tool, or series of tasks is completed, the families, caregivers, and professional(s) may relate their observations and/or findings. In addition, this ongoing sharing may lead families, caregivers, and assessment professionals to work together throughout the assessment to develop and try various modifications or interventions. By discussing the assessment information in an ongoing way, professionals, families, and caregivers can reduce the amount of information to be shared at any one time and can integrate intervention planning in earlier phases of the assessment.

Whether information is shared during or after the assessment, it is important that the sharing be performed in a way that is useful to families and caregivers in decision making, that promotes feelings of competence and self-worth, and that facilitates ownership of the decisions by family members and caregivers. It is often useful at the end of the assessment process for professionals to ask families and caregivers if their concerns were addressed and what, if anything, they still need from professionals. Reviewing any preassessment or information-gathering forms that were utilized earlier may help to identify new or continuing concerns and the need for support or further information. After the sharing meeting, some families may also appreciate the option of having a follow-up meeting to review the information with others important to the child's development. In addition, some professionals find it helpful to offer families (and caregivers, if families agree) the option of reviewing a draft of the follow-up report in case they wish to add or change information before the report is finalized. In these ways, professionals ensure that families are receiving the services and information that are most useful to them.

In summary, it is clear that assessment activities are extremely important in setting the tone and expectations for subsequent interactions. When families, caregivers, and professionals are partners in assessment, they work together to achieve commonly agreed on goals and outcomes, they develop relationships built on trust and respect, and they seek to strengthen the child's, family's, and caregiver's feelings of self-worth. As families, caregivers, and other professionals determine

together the assessment content, activities, and results, they are shaping the future for what will happen for the child and the family.

IMPORTANCE OF CROSS-DISCIPLINARY COLLABORATION

The need for building collaborative relationships in assessment is not limited to the relationship between families and professionals. Collaborative relationships must also be forged among the various disciplines and agencies involved. Both Part B and Part C require that assessment be a multidisciplinary effort. According to the law, *multidisciplinary* means "the involvement of two or more disciplines or professions in the provision of integrated and coordinated services, including evaluation and assessment activities" (34 C.F.R. Sec. 303.17). The disciplines that may be involved in assessing young children with special needs include audiology, early childhood education, early childhood special education, family therapy, medicine, nursing, nutrition, occupational therapy, orientation and mobility, physical therapy, psychology, social work, and speech-language pathology. Not all of these disciplines will necessarily be involved in the assessment of a particular child, although the family should always be central to the assessment team, as discussed above. The manner in which the various individuals involved in assessment organize themselves and relate to one another is critical in the assessment of young children. The importance of collaborative relationships extends, of course, to intervention as well and includes not only individuals but also agencies (Bruder & Bologna, 1993; Guralnick, 2000; Jesien, 1996).

Models of Team Functioning

Typically, three models of team organization are described in relation to assessment: multidisciplinary, interdisciplinary, and transdisciplinary

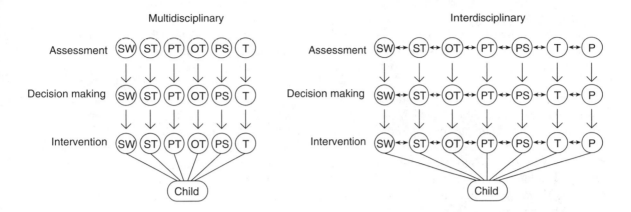

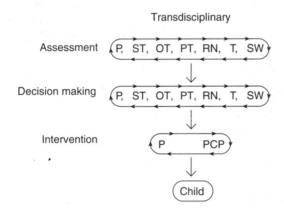

FIGURE 3.3

Models of assessment team organization
Note: From *Project KAI Training Packet*, by G. Woodruff and C. Hanson, 1987. Unpublished manuscript. Reprinted with permission.

(Bruder, 1996; Foley, 1990; McGonigel, Woodruff, & Roszmann-Millican, 1994; Tuchman, 1996). A diagram representing each of these team organizations is presented in Figure 3.3.

Members of a *multidisciplinary team* work independently, using instruments or procedures representative of their disciplines. Assessment results are reported separately to the family, who must then try to integrate the information and suggestions given them by different professionals. According to Bagnato and Neisworth (1991), it is not accurate to refer to this approach as a model of team functioning, since the professionals involved do not in fact operate as a team but rather as individuals. This approach is often not family-friendly and can create a burden and confusion for the family.

As Figure 3.3 demonstrates, in the *interdisciplinary team,* a premium is placed on communication among team members so that the outcome of assessment and program planning is more unified. In this model, professionals may work individually during the assessment or may work together in subgroups, but there is a definite attempt to communicate. However, McGonigel et al. (1994) point out that communication problems frequently remain within an interdisciplinary model, since team members may not fully understand the training and expertise of their teammates. In addition, team members working separately may find discrepancies in their assessment results. The reader will notice that the family is considered to be a part of the team in this model.

The *transdisciplinary team* model is an attempt to maximize communication and collaboration among team members by crossing disciplinary boundaries. According to Bruder and Bologna (1993), the family is also more central on transdisciplinary teams than in the interdisciplinary model. Families are involved to whatever extent they choose in assessment and program planning, and family choices predominate. All team members share responsibility for assessment and development of the intervention plan, but the plan will be carried out by the family and one team member who serves as the primary service provider (McGonigel et al., 1994). The transdisciplinary approach has been identified as being especially appropriate for Part C programs due to its emphasis on the family and on cross-disciplinary work. However, it has also been applied in school-age settings (Rainforth, York, & MacDonald, 1992) and in serving preschool children with disabilities in typical early childhood settings (Bruder, 1994).

McGonigel et al. (1994) suggest that these three models of team functioning are not mutually exclusive, but that they actually represent points on a continuum moving from less to more interaction among the disciplines. Tuchman (1996) points out that many teams combine elements of one or more of the three basic models in relation to the needs of children and families and the resources available.

Developing a transdisciplinary team approach may not be possible for every assessment team. Central to becoming transdisciplinary is the process of *role release,* which allows individual team members to carry out activities that would normally be the responsibility of another discipline. McGonigel et al. (1994) provide a description of the components of this process and warn that successful role release requires continuous attention to team building and team maintenance, which will require staff training, time, and support from administrators. Activities that facilitate role release, as described by McGonigel et al (1994) are listed in Figure 3.4.

One component of the transdisciplinary team approach that has been adopted by many assessment teams is the arena approach. *Arena assessment* is the simultaneous evaluation of the child by multiple professionals of differing disciplines (Foley, 1990; Linder, 1993; McGonigel et al., 1994). Instead of each professional working with the child separately, the team of professionals works together with the child, allowing a common sample of behavior and immediate sharing of expertise and information. The rationale for arena assessment is based on the relative difficulty of separating physical, cognitive, and sensory domains of development in the young child. When implemented correctly, the advantages of this approach extend to everyone involved—the child, the family, and the professionals. Since all professionals are working together, the amount of actual time spent in assessment by the child and the family is reduced. Family members can provide information once rather than being asked the same questions by each professional in turn. Professionals have the advantage of immediate access to the skills and knowledge of their teammates. In addition, consensus building is facilitated since a common sampling of behavior has been the basis of evaluation for all team members. Figure 3.5 presents a sequence of events that might be

Role Release Component	Activities
Role Extension	*Read new articles and books within your discipline or about your child's condition.
	*Attend conferences, seminars, and lectures.
	*Join a professional organization in your field or a family-to-family network.
	*Explore resources at libraries or media centers.
Role Enrichment	*Listen to parents discuss their child's strengths and needs.
	*Ask for explanations of unfamiliar technical language or jargon.
	*Do an appraisal of what you wish you knew more about and what you could teach others.
Role Expansion	*Watch someone from another discipline work with a child, and check your perception of what you observe.
	*Attend a workshop in another field that includes some "hands-on" practicum experience.
	*Rotate the role of transdisciplinary arena assessment facilitator among all service providers on the team.
Role Exchange	*Allow yourself to be videotaped practicing a technique from another discipline; invite a team member from that discipline to review and critique the videotape with you.
	*Work side-by-side in the center-based program, demonstrating interventions to families and staff.
	*Suggest strategies for achieving an Individualized Family Service Plan (IFSP) outcome outside your own discipline; check your accuracy with other team members.
Role Release	*Do a self-appraisal: List new skills within your intervention repertoire that other team members have taught you.
	*Monitor the performance of the service providers on your child's IFSP team.
	*Present on the "whole" child at a clinical conference.
	*Accept responsibility for implementing, with the family, an entire IFSP.
Role Support	*Ask for help when you feel "stuck."
	*Offer help when you see a team member struggling with a complex intervention.
	*Provide any intervention that only you can provide, but share the child's progress and any related interventions with the primary service provider and the family.

FIGURE 3.4

Activities to promote role release for families and professionals on transdisciplinary teams
Note: From McGonigel, M. J., Woodruff, G., and Roszmann-Millican, M. (1994). "The Transdisciplinary Team: A model for Family-Centered Early Intervention." In Editors Johnson, L. J. et al, *Meeting Early Intervention Challenges: Issues from Birth to Three* (2nd ed.). Baltimore: Paul H. Brookes Publishing Co. Reprinted with permission.

Greeting and Warm-Up (Family and team members visit, child is allowed to explore and get to know team members.)

Formal Task-Centered Sequence (The main assessment instrument is administered by the primary facilitator. Other team members observe and may score discipline-specific instruments or make clinical notes.)

Snack Break and Refueling (Snack and bathroom break provides an opportunity to observe self-help skills and parent-child interaction.)

Story Time or Teaching Samples (A story-time format may be used to expand the language sample, or a brief teaching sequence might be used to observe how the child processes new information and generalizes learning to new materials.)

Free Play (The child's spontaneous movement and interaction with toys will be observed. With older children, bringing in a peer at this point may allow observation of social interaction skills as well.)

Brief Staffing and Feedback (The team members take a minute to formulate impressions while the parent facilitator collects the parents' comments about the session. Parents and other team members will then come together to share initial impressions so the parents have some closure and do not go away with undue anxiety. A formal staffing of the evaluation will be held at a later time.)

FIGURE 3.5

Possible sequence for an arena evaluation
Note: From "Portrait of the Arena Evaluation: Assessment in the Transdisciplinary Approach" by G. Md. Foley, 1990, in E. Gibbs & D. Teti (Eds.) *Interdisciplinary Assessment of Infants: A Guide for Early Intervention.* Copyright 1994 by Paul H. Brookes. Adapted with permission.

followed during an arena assessment as described by Foley (1990).

The organization of an arena assessment is based on the concept of a primary facilitator. One member of the team is designated to serve as primary facilitator by interacting with the parent and child and eliciting the main sample of structured behavior. This does not mean that other team members are forbidden to interact with the child; for example, the physical therapist may need to lay hands on the child to assess muscle tone even though another team member is the primary facilitator. It does mean, however, that if there is an instrument or instruments that serve as the more structured part of the evaluation, all team members may need to become proficient at administration. The primary facilitator may be designated as such because the needs of the child best match his or her discipline, because of a relationship established with the child or the family, or because of other considerations that may arise. A family facilitator may also be designated to record

family members' input and answer their questions throughout the evaluation (Linder, 1993). Some teams also choose one member to be the coach for the arena assessment. The coach serves as a resource to the facilitator by observing the process and reminding the facilitator of planned assessment strategies or items that may be overlooked as the assessment proceeds. Figure 3.6 is a drawing that depicts an arena assessment.

The arena assessment incorporates preassessment planning (described earlier) as an important component of the assessment process. The family may be a part of the planning meeting if they choose; they are also present or invited to be present at all meetings in which assessment results are discussed. As noted in Figure 3.5, assessment results may be shared with the family, at least informally, immediately after the assessment.

McGonigel et al. (1994) describe a meeting of the team for the purpose of team maintenance that takes place after the arena assessment and does not

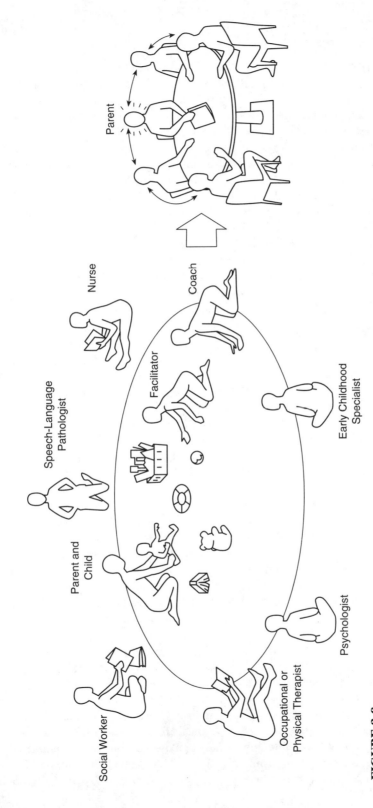

FIGURE 3.6

Example of an arena assessment

Note: From McGonigel, M. J., Woodruff, G., and Roszmann-Millican, M. (1994). "The Transdisciplinary Team: A Model for Family-Centered Early Intervention." In Editors Johnson, L. J. et al. *Meeting Early Intervention Challenges: Issues From Birth to Three* (2nd ed.). Baltimore: Paul H. Brookes Publishing Co. Reprinted with permission.

include the family. The purpose of this meeting is to evaluate the team process and how it went during the assessment. Even though an additional meeting could be costly in terms of the professionals' time, McGonigel and her colleagues stress the importance of this procedure for team functioning.

The arena format has been identified as especially appropriate for the assessment of young children (Foley, 1990; Linder, 1993; McGonigel et al., 1994). However, McGonigel and her colleagues caution that it will not be best for all children and all families. Therefore, assessment teams must be willing to change their methods of assessing young children to fit the needs of individual children and families.

Collaborative Decision Making

Inherent in the transdisciplinary team model described above is attention to team building and team maintenance activities that will facilitate the process of decision making by team members. The EI/ECSE professional may work consistently with the same group of people in doing assessments, but it is more likely that he or she will work with at least several if not many different groups. A group of individuals will not necessarily work together as a team without some conscious effort being put toward team building. Maddux (1988) has identified differences between groups and teams. According to Maddux, a group of people become a team when they are working from a common philosophy with shared goals. In addition, team members need to develop the skills necessary to maintain open and honest communication and to resolve conflicts that may arise as part of the decision-making process. Unfortunately, preservice training programs for professionals who will be serving young children frequently do not include preparation in the skills needed to become an effective team member (Bailey, Palsha, & Huntington, 1990; Crais & Leonard, 1990).

Members of early childhood assessment teams must be aware of the extent to which their group is actually functioning as a team in carrying out the responsibilities of assessment and decision making. Olson and Murphy (1999) have developed a team self-assessment that can be used by teams to evaluate how they are doing as a team. Also, the latest version of the Division for Early Childhood Recommended Practices includes a strand of practices on interdisciplinary models (McWilliam 2000). The identified practices, which focus on intervention as well as assessment, are included in a program assessment (Hemmeter, Joseph, Smith & Sandall, 2001) that can also be used to assess team functioning. Requests for support in the form of in-service training on team building or additional time that may be necessary for team maintenance should be made to administrators as needed.

An instrument which includes guidelines for team assessment and decision making as well as a framework for the integration of data from multiple data sources is the Infant-Toddler Developmental Assessment (IDA; Provence, Erikson, Vater & Palmeri, 1995). The IDA is a family-centered, clinical assessment process which is designed as a team assessment and includes six phases: referral and pre-interview data gathering, initial parent interview, health review, developmental observation and assessment, integration and synthesis, and sharing findings and report (Erikson, 2001). Collaborative decision making is clearly central to quality assessment of young children. It will not, however, automatically occur but must be nurtured. The IDA facilitates team assessment by the way it has been designed.

The System to Plan Early Childhood Services (SPECS) (Bagnato & Neisworth, 1990), a team decision-making format that links cross-disciplinary assessment, was derived to facilitate the process of decision making by teams of professionals representing various disciplines (Bagnato & Neisworth, 1991). It uses structured clinical judgment ratings to evaluate the competencies of children from 24 to 72 months of age in six domains. SPECS is composed of three components: Developmental Specs, Team Specs, and Program Specs. Developmental Specs uses five-point Likert rating scales to record the judgments of the family and professional team members about the child's developmental and behavioral capabilities and needs. Team Specs enables the team to determine a consensus rating of each developmental area, which is then cross-referenced with 10 therapy options (physical therapy, speech/language therapy, etc.). Program Specs assists the team in making decisions about the content and strategies to be designated in the intervention plan. Bagnato et al. (1997) refer to the model that underlies the SPECS system as a convergent assessment model:

> Convergent assessments are generated when a team of professionals and parents collaborates to construct and use an individualized assessment battery for a child. The resultant battery comprises several methods of assessment that blend qualitative and quantitative information about a child, his or her physical and social environment (e.g., home, preschool), and the family. (p 18)

An assessment "battery" which includes multiple measures and multiple sources of information across multiple settings on multiple occasions, as described by Bagnato et al. (1997), will yield assessment results that can be used by the team with greater confidence.

IMPORTANCE OF ASSESSMENT IN THE NATURAL ENVIRONMENT

A quote from Urie Bronfenbrenner (1977) about developmental psychology has recently been applied to describe the assessment of young children: "The science of the strange behavior of children in strange situations with strange adults for the briefest possible period of time" (p. 513). This quote communicates our seemingly increasing dissatisfaction with traditional assessment strategies that perhaps rely too much on highly structured practices and unfamiliar settings. The danger is that test scores that result from such practices will be used to make eligibility and programmatic decisions without consideration of whether such results adequately characterize the child's typical behavior.

According to Bracken (1991), "test behavior should never be interpreted unconditionally as representative of a child's typical behavior in any other setting" (p. 42). It is customary to end an assessment session by asking the family whether their child's behavior was representative of his or her typical behavior. Even a positive response to this question, however, should not result in reliance on the outcome of direct testing as the sole basis upon which eligibility or program planning decisions are made. While tests or assessment instruments certainly may be a part of the evaluation and assessment process, particularly if state regulations do require a quantitative score for determining eligibility, it is also fair to say that the assessment of young children does not need to be test-based or limited to the use of tests (Bagnato et al., 1997; Wolery, 1994). In addition to traditional assessment instruments or tests, the assessment team has a variety of assessment strategies available that will allow the team to sample behavior in a way that is representative of the child's typical functioning.

The 1997 Amendments to IDEA demonstrate a strong preference for serving infants and toddlers with disabilities in the natural environment to the extent appropriate for the child (Walsh, Rous, & Lutzer, 2000). IDEA Part C regulations define "natural environments" as settings that are natural or normal for the child's age peers who have no disabilities (34 C.F.R. §303.18). Similarly, for preschool children, there is a clear preference for educating children with disabilities with their non-disabled peers in typical early care and education settings. Assessment for program planning, therefore, must assess children in their typical environments or natural environments in order to develop an appropriate intervention plan. For both the eligibility function and the program planning function of assessment, assessment in the natural environment will be important.

As indicated earlier, the preassessment planning process will identify the questions that will guide the assessment, the strategies and instruments to be used, and the times and places for carrying out the planned strategies. This procedure will allow the team to plan assessment strategies that will gather information in a way that is most reflective of the child's typical behavior in typical settings.

A variety of assessment formats can be used in assessing young children. Norm-referenced, criterion-referenced, and curriculum-referenced instruments have traditionally been part of assessment and are discussed in Chapter 2. A *norm-referenced* instrument compares a measure of the child's development to norms derived from a population of children. Norm-referenced instruments commonly utilize rather structured procedures for assessment; however, some, for example the Battelle Developmental Inventory (Newborg et al., 1988), also allow the use of observation and family report. If a quantitative score is required as an outcome of assessment, the team will probably decide to utilize a norm-referenced instrument that then can be supplemented with other procedures that require less structure. *Criterion-referenced* instruments measure success or failure in meeting some previously determined objectives. Items are selected for inclusion on a criterion-referenced instrument because of their importance to the child's daily functioning. *Curriculum-referenced* instruments, which compare a child's developmental attainments with a pre-existing curriculum, facilitate the process of program planning, since intervention targets might then be suggested by the curriculum. Norm-referenced, criterion-referenced, and curriculum-referenced instruments are certainly important tools for determining eligibility for services and program planning and can also be used to monitor child progress. There are, however, additional formats that might be used by the team to ensure that assessment results are representative of the child's typical behavior. These include judgment-based assessment, systematic observation, anecdotal recording, play-based assessment, ecological assessment, interactive assessment, and authentic assessment. Each of these will be discussed next.

Judgment-based instruments ask professionals or caregivers to record their perceptions of the child's functioning. Usually in the form of a checklist or a rating scale, these instruments provide information from family members, caregivers, and/or professionals based on their observation of the child. This can be done through *in situ* observation, meaning that the rater observes the child for a period of time and then records his or her impressions, or it can be done based on impressions over time. The Behavior Rating Scale, which is part of the revised Bayley Scales of Infant Development (Bayley, 1993), uses judgment-based assessment by asking the examiner to judge the child's behavior following administration of the Bayley. The System to Plan Early Childhood Services (SPECS) (Bagnato & Neisworth, 1990), which was discussed earlier, uses judgment-based assessment to facilitate team decision making regarding program eligibility and the level and scope of intervention services needed. Judgment-based assessment provides a mechanism for getting input from a variety of individuals who are familiar with the child.

Systematic observation can be carried out in the home or in preschool settings, allowing measurement of behavior occurring in any environment. It involves structured observation and recording of child behavior and yields quantifiable data. It has been utilized traditionally in applied behavior analysis research. As indicated above, observation can be carried out in natural settings *(in vivo)* or through a staged or structured situation in order to elicit particular behaviors (Neisworth & Bagnato, 1988). Systematic observation differs from judgment-based assessment in that it is designed to yield an objective reporting of observed behavior rather than a judgment or an impression of behavior. As described in Chapter 13, systematic observation typically includes the use of time-sampling and interval-recording procedures to record observed behavior.

Anecdotal recording is a written description of a child's behavior in a particular situation. Anecdotal records can be kept by caregivers, teachers, and therapists as part of initial assessment or to monitor child progress. In making an anecdotal record, the individual attempts to describe the behavior as completely as possible. Anecdotal recording may be objective (facts) or may include impressions or judgments as long as this is clearly indicated. Frequently, circumstances or events in the environment that preceded or followed the child's behavior will also be recorded. A running record is a form of anecdotal recording that typically is planned in advance and continues for a longer period of time. The communication-sampling strategy that is described in Chapter 12 is an example of a running record.

It is common for early childhood professionals to keep a record of children's behavior in a log or journal. Sometimes the adult will record anecdotally while observing the child; at other times, information or observations may be recorded at the end of the day or during a period of free time (Bentzen, 2000). Such logs or journals can be very helpful in adding information from the natural environment to the assessment of a child with special needs.

Play-based assessment utilizes play as the medium for observing child behavior. Since this type of assessment is done rather informally in a play setting, the behavior observed is considered to be more typical of the child's behavior in the natural environment than in a structured assessment. The work of Linder (1993) has been instrumental in demonstrating how play can be used as the basis for assessment. A typical assessment using Linder's system includes free-play and also semistructured play, during which the facilitator attempts to elicit particular behaviors from the child. It includes an opportunity for observation of parent-child interaction and also of the child's interaction with peers. Linder's system utilizes a transdisciplinary team approach, as described earlier, and covers all areas of development. The work of Bricker and her colleagues on the Assessment, Evaluation, and Programming System (Bricker, 2002) also utilizes play as a medium for curriculum-based assessment and, in addition, describes strategies for setting up play centers within a classroom to facilitate the assessment process.

Ecological assessment provides information on the physical and social features of the child's typical environments, both at home and in child-care or preschool settings. Ecological assessment is exemplified by instruments such as the Early Childhood Environment Rating Scale (Harms & Clifford, 1980), which is designed to give an overall picture of surroundings for children and adults in preschool settings. Ecological assessment has also been applied to the preparation of children for other environments through the use of the ecological inventory (Noonan & McCormick, 1993; McCormick & Noonan, 2002), which evaluates the skills required in other current or future environments as a basis for program planning. Carl Dunst and his colleagues have developed ecological assessment strategies that facilitate the identification of the wealth of learning opportunities that exist for children in their home and community environments (Dunst et al, 2001; Dunst, Herter & Shields, 2000; Dunst, 2001; Dunst, Bruder, Trivette, Raab, & McLean, 2001). Dunst's procedures include both identifying opportunities for preferred activities within the community (community mapping; Dunst, Herter, Shields, & Bennis, 2001) and "everyday activity mapping" for family routines and activities.

Interactive assessment is actually a component of ecological assessment that focuses on the social interactions that take place between children and family members or between children and peers. Interactive measures may take the form of rating scales, checklists, or coded observation of interactions. For example, the Parent Behavior Progression (Bromwich, 1981) is a checklist that measures the initial status and subsequent changes in parenting behavior. It is the result of observation of parent-child interactions and is completed as part of an infant intervention program that focuses on the parent-child dyad. Another measure of parent-child interaction that is accomplished through systematic observation is the Infant-Parent Social Interaction Code (Baird, Haas, McCormick, Carruth, & Turner, 1992), which utilizes a videotaped sample of parent-child interaction as a basis for coding various infant and parent behaviors.

Authentic assessment refers to assessment based on student efforts in actual performance situations completing real-life tasks rather than on the results of group tests such as achievement tests (Losardo & Notari-Syverson, 2001). One approach to authentic assessment is the collection in a *portfolio* of examples of a child's work that illustrates efforts, progress, and achievements over time. A child's portfolio is typically composed of work samples that might include the child's writing, drawings, pages of journals, photos of the child's constructions, tape recordings, or video recordings (Meisels & Steele, 1991). Portfolios are designed to demonstrate the child's emerging abilities over a period of time; they provide an opportunity for the child to be involved in selecting and judging his or her own work. The Work Sampling System (Meisels, 1992) is an example of an authentic assessment system; it includes developmental checklists, portfolios, and summary reports. It is designed for children from age 3

to grade 3. Meisels is also developing an authentic performance assessment for infants and toddlers called *The Ounce of Prevention Scale* (Meisels, Dombro, Marsden, Weston, & Jewkes, in preparation) which will allow continual developmental monitoring of child development for the purpose of program planning and implementation (Meisels, 2001).

For young children who do not yet write or draw, the use of photographs and audio- or videotapes might be the most feasible way to demonstrate progress in developmental areas. Anecdotal notes and running records such as a language sample might also be included. Family members might also want to contribute to their child's portfolio.

The assessment team has many options for gathering information for the purpose of making decisions about young children with special needs. To obtain a truly representative picture of child functioning, the team must strive to obtain information from multiple sources and multiple settings.

• • • • • • • •

SUMMARY OF KEY CONCEPTS

- Recommended practices for assessing infants and preschoolers include providing the opportunity for family participation, cross-disciplinary collaboration, and assessment in the natural environment.

- Establishing a truly collaborative relationship with families during assessment means providing them the opportunity to be active participants throughout the entire process, including planning the assessment, gathering information, and making decisions as a result of the assessment.

- A plan for assessment can be developed by the family/professional team that will determine the goals for assessment and the strategies/instruments to be used.

- Families can be offered the opportunity to participate in the assessment in a variety of roles,

including being interpreters of their child's behavior, participants in the assessment, and validators of the assessment activities.

- Typical models of team functioning include the multidisciplinary, interdisciplinary, and transdisciplinary approaches. Arena assessment, the simultaneous assessment of the child by multiple professionals, is one component of the transdisciplinary team model.

- Assessment of infants and preschoolers does not need to be limited to the use of tests. Other strategies that allow for the gathering of information from natural environments include judgment-based assessment, systematic observation, narrative descriptions, play-based assessment, ecological inventories, interactive assessment, and authentic assessment.

· · · · · · · ·
REFERENCES

Alpern, G., Boll, T., & Shearer, M. (1980). *Developmental Profile II*. Aspen, CO: Psychological Development Publications.

Bagnato, S. J., & Neisworth, J. T. (1990). *System to plan early childhood services*. Circle Pines, MN: American Guidance Service.

Bagnato, S. J., & Neisworth, J. T. (1991). *Assessment for early intervention: Best practices for professionals*. New York: Guilford Press.

Bagnato, S. J., Neisworth, J. T., & Munson, S. M. (1997). *LINKing: Assessment and early intervention*. Baltimore, MD: Paul II. Brookes.

Bailey, D., & Blasco, P. (1990). Parents' perspectives on a written survey of family needs. *Journal of Early Intervention, 14*(3), 196–203.

Bailey, D., McWilliam, R., Aytch Darkes, L., Hebbeler, K., Simeonsson, R., Spiker, D., & Wagner, M. (1998). Family outcomes in early intervention: A framework for program evaluation and efficacy research. *Exceptional Children, 64*(3), 313–328.

Bailey, D., McWilliam, P., Winton, P., & Simeonsson, R. (1992). *Implementing family-centered services in early intervention: A team-based model for change*. Cambridge, MA: Brookline Books.

Bailey, D., Palsha, S., & Huntington, G. (1990). Preservice preparation of special educators to serve infants with handicaps and their families: Current status and training needs. *Journal of Early Intervention, 14*(1), 43–54.

Bailey, D., & Simeonsson, R. (1990). *Family Needs Survey—Revised*. Chapel Hill, NC: Frank Porter Graham Child Development Center.

Baird, S. M., Haas, L. M., McCormick, K., Carruth, C., & Turner, K. (1992). Approaching an objective system for observation and measurement: Infant-parent social interaction code. *Topics in Early Childhood Special Education, 12*(4), 544–571.

Bayley, N. (1993). *Bayley Scales of Infant Development* (2nd ed.). San Antonio, TX: The Psychological Corp.

Bentzen, W. R. (2000). *Seeing young children: A guide to observing and recording behavior* (4th ed.). Albany, NY: Delmar Publishers.

Beukelman, D. & Mirenda, P. (1992). *Augmentative and alternative communication: Management of severe communication disorders in children and adults*. Baltimore, MD: Paul H. Brookes.

Bloch, J. (1987). *Parent/Professional Preschool Performance Profile*. Syosset, NY: Variety Pre-Schoolers' Workshop.

Bloch, J., & Seitz, M. (1989). Parents as assessors of children: A collaborative approach to helping. *Social Work in Education, 11*(4), 226–244.

Boone, H., & Crais, E. (1999). Strategies for family-driven assessment and intervention planning. *Young Exceptional Children, 3*(1), 2–12.

Bracken, B. (1991). The clinical observation of preschool assessment behavior. In B. Bracken (Ed.), *The psychoeducational assessment of preschool children* (2nd ed.) (pp. 40–52). Boston: Allyn and Bacon.

Brazelton, T. (1973). *Neonatal Behavioral Assessment Scale*. Philadelphia: J. B. Lippincott.

Bricker, D. (2002). *Assessment, evaluation, and programming system for infants and children* (2nd ed.). Baltimore: Paul H. Brookes.

Bricker, D., & Squires, J. (1999). *Ages and Stages Questionnaires* (ASQ) (2nd ed.). Baltimore, MD: Paul H. Brookes.

Brinckerhoff, J., & Vincent, L. (1987). Increasing parental decision making at the individualized educational program meeting. *Journal of the Division for Early Childhood, 11*, 46–48.

Bromwich, R. (1981). *Working with parents and infants*. Baltimore: University Park Press.

Bronfenbrenner, U. (1977). Toward an experimental ecology of human development. *American Psychologist, 32*(7), 513–531.

Bruder, M. B. (1994). Working with members of other disciplines: Collaboration for success. In M. Wolery & J. S. Wilbers (Eds.), *Including children with special needs in early childhood programs* (pp. 45–70). Washington, DC: National Association for the Education of Young Children.

Bruder, M. B. (1996). Interdisciplinary collaboration in service delivery. In R. A. McWilliam (Ed.), *Rethinking pull-out services in early intervention*. Baltimore: Paul H. Brookes, 27–48.

Bruder, M. B., & Bologna, T. (1993). Collaboration and service coordination for effective early intervention. In W. Brown, S. K. Thurman, & L. F. Pearl (Eds.), *Family-centered early intervention with infants and toddlers* (pp. 103–128). Baltimore: Paul H. Brookes.

Bzoch, K. & League, R. (1991). *Redeptive-Expressive Emergent Language Scale–2*. Austin, TX: PRO-ED.

Cardone, I., & Gilkerson, L. (1989). Family administered neonatal activities: An innovative component of family-centered care. *Zero to Three, 10*(1), 23–28.

Crais, E. (1993). Families and professionals as collaborators in assessment. *Topics in Language Disorders, 14*(1), 29–40.

Crais, E. (1996). Applying family-centered principles to child assessment. In P. McWilliam, P. Winton, & E. Crais (Eds.), *Practical strategies for family-centered early intervention* (pp. 69–96). Baltimore: Paul H. Brookes.

Crais, E. & Belardi, C. (1999). Family participation in child assessment: Perceptions of families and professionals. *Infant-Toddler Intervention, 9*(3), 209–238.

Crais, E. & Leonard, R. (1990). P.L. 99–457: Are speech-language pathologists prepared for the challenge? *ASHA, 32*(April), 57–61.

Crais, E. & Wilson, L. (1996). The role of parents in child assessment: Self-perception of practicing professionals. *Infant-Toddler Intervention, 6*(2), 125–143.

Dale, P. (1991). The validity of a parent report measure of vocabulary and syntax at 24 months. *Journal of Speech and Hearing Research, 34,* 565–571.

Dale, P., Bates, E., Reznick, S., & Morisset, C. (1989). The validity of a parent report instrument on child language at twenty months. *Journal of Child Language, 16,* 239–249.

Diamond, K., & Squires, J. (1993). The role of parental report in the screening and assessment of young children. *Journal of Early Intervention, 17*(2), 107–115.

Dinnebeil, L. & Rule, S. (1994). Congruence between parents' and professionals' judgments about the development of young children with disabilities: A review of the literature. *Topics in Early Childhood Special Education, 14*(1), 1–25.

Dopheide, W., & Dallinger, J. (1976). Preschool articulation screening by parents. *Language, Speech, and Hearing in the Schools, 7,* 124–127.

Drumwright, A., Van Natta, P., Camp, B., Frankenburg, W., & Drexler, H. (1973). The Denver Articulation Screening Exam. *Journal of Speech and Hearing Disorders, 38,* 3–14.

Dunst, C. J. (2001). Participation of young children with disabilities in community learning activities. In M. J. Guralnick (Ed.), *Early childhood inclusion: Focus on change* (pp. 307–333). Baltimore: Paul H. Brookes.

Dunst, C. J., Bruder, M. B., Trivette, C., Hamby, D., Raab, M. & McLean, M. (2001). Characteristics and consequences of everyday natural learning opportunities. *Topics in Early Childhood Special Education, 21*(2), 68–92.

Dunst, C. J., Bruder, M. B., Trivette, C., Raab, M., & McLean, M. (2001). Natural learning opportunities for infants, toddlers and preschoolers. *Young Exceptional Children, 4*(3), 18–25.

Dunst, C. J., Herter, S., & Shields, H. (2000). Interest-based natural learning opportunities. In S. Sandall & M. Ostrosky (Eds.), *Young Exceptional Children Monograph Series No. 2: Natural Environments and inclusion.* Longmont, CO: Sopris West.

Dunst, C. J., Herter, S., Shields, H. & Bennis, L. (2001). Mapping community-based natural learning opportunities. *Young Exceptional Children, 4*(4), 16–24.

Dunst, C., Trivette, C., & Deal, A. (1994). *Supporting and strengthening families: vol. 1: Methods, strategies, and practices.* Cambridge, MA: Brookline Books.

Erikson, J. (2001). From demonstration model into the real world: Some experiences with IDA. *Zero to Three, 21*(4), 20–28.

Fenson, L., Dale, P., Reznick, S., Thal, D., Bates, E., Hartung, J., Pethick, S., & Reilly, J. (1990). *MacArthur Communicative Development Inventories.* San Diego, CA: Center for Research in Language.

Foley, G. M. (1990). Portrait of the arena evaluation: Assessment in the transdisciplinary approach. In E. Gibbs & D. Teti (Eds.), *Interdisciplinary assessment of infants: A guide for early intervention* (pp. 271–286). Baltimore, MD: Paul H. Brookes.

Furuno, S., O'Reilly, K. A., Hosaka, C. M., Inatsuka, T. T., Allman, T. L., & Zeisloft, B. (1979). *Hawaii Early Learning Profile.* Palo Alto, CA: Vort.

Glascoe, F., MacLean, W., & Stone, W. (1991). The importance of parents' concerns about their child's behavior. *Clinical Pediatrics, 30,* 8–11.

Gradel, K., Thompson, M., & Sheehan, R. (1981). Parental and professional agreement in early childhood assessment. *Topics in Early Childhood Special Education, 1,* 31–39.

Guralnick, J. J. (2000). Interdisciplinary team assessment for young children: Purposes and practices. In M. J. Guralnick (Ed.), *Interdisciplinary clinical assessment of young children with developmental disabilities.* Baltimore: Paul H. Brookes, 3–15.

Hanson, M. & Bruder, M. (2001). Early intervention: Promises to keep. *Infants and Young Children, 13* (3), 47–58.

Harms, T., & Clifford, R. M. (1980). *Early Childhood Environment Rating Scale.* New York: Teachers College Press.

Hedrick, D., Prather, E., & Tobin, A. (1984). *Sequenced Inventory of Communication Development (Rev. ed.).* Seattle, WA: University of Washington Press.

Hemmeter, M. L., Joseph, G. E., Smith, B. J., & Sandall, S. (2001). *DEC recommended practices program assessment: Improving practices for young children with special needs and their families.* Longmont, CO: Sopris West.

Henderson, L., & Meisels, S. (1994). Parental involvement in the developmental screening of their young child: A multiple source perspective. *Journal of Early Intervention, 18*(2), 141–154.

Individuals with Disabilities Education Act Amendments of 1997. *www.ideapractices.org*

Jesien, G. S. (1996). Interagency collaboration: What, why and with whom? In P. Rosin, A. Whitehead, L. I. Tuchman, G. S. Jesien, A. L. Begun, & L. Irwin (Eds.), *Partnership in family-centered care: A guide to collaborative early intervention.* Baltimore: Paul H. Brookes.

Kjerland, L., & Kovach, J. (1990). Family-staff collaboration for tailored infant assessment. In E. Gibbs & D. Teti (Eds.), *Interdisciplinary assessment of infants: A guide for early intervention professionals* (pp. 287–298). Baltimore: Paul H. Brookes.

Leet, H., & Dunst, C. (1988). *Family Resource Scale.* In C. Dunst, C. Trivette, & A. Deal (Eds.), *Enabling and empowering families* (p. 141). Cambridge, MA: Brookline Books.

Lesar Judge, S. (1997). Parental expectations of helpgiving practices and control appraisals in early intervention programs. *Topics in Early Childhood Special Education, 17*(4), 457–476.

Linder, T. (1993). *Transdisciplinary play-based assessment: A functional approach to working with young children* (Rev. ed.). Baltimore, MD: Paul H. Brookes.

Losardo, A. & Notari-Syverson, A. (2001). *Alternative approaches to assessing young children.* Baltimore: Paul H. Brookes.

Maddux, R. E. (1988). *Team building: An exercise in leadership.* Los Altos, CA: Crisp Publications.

Mahoney, G., & Filer, J. (1996). How responsive is early intervention to the priorities and needs of families? *Topics in Early Childhood Special Education, 16*(4), 437–457.

McCarthy, D. (1972). *McCarthy Scales of Children's Abilities.* New York: The Psychological Corp.

McCormick, L. & Noonan, M. J. (2002). Ecological assessment and planning. In M. Ostrosky & E. Horn (Eds.), *Young Exceptional Children Monograph Series No. 4: Assessment: Gathering Meaningful Information.*

McGonigel, M., Kaufmann, R., & Johnson, B. (1991). *Guidelines and recommended practices for the individualized family service plan* (2nd ed.). Bethesda, MD: Association for the Care of Children's Health.

McGonigel, M. J., Woodruff, G., & Roszmann-Millican, M. (1994). The transdisciplinary team: A model for family-centered early intervention. In L. J. Johnson, R. J. Gallagher, M. J. LaMontagne, J. B. Jordan, J. J. Gallagher, P. L. Hutinger, & M. B. Karnes (Eds.), *Meeting early intervention challenges* (pp. 95–131). Baltimore: Paul H. Brookes.

McLean, M., & McCormick, K. (1993). Assessment and evaluation in early intervention. In W. Brown, S. Thurman, & L. Pearl (Eds.), *Family-centered early intervention with infants and toddlers* (pp. 43–79). Baltimore: Paul H. Brookes.

McWilliam, R. (1992). *Family-centered intervention planning: A routines-based approach.* Tucson, AZ: Communication Skill Builders.

McWilliam, R. (2000). Recommended practices in interdisciplinary models. In S. Sandall, M. McLean & B. Smith (Eds.), *DEC recommended practices in early intervention/early childhood special education.* Longmont, CO: Sopris West.

McWilliam, R. A. (2000). It's only natural . . . to have early intervention in the environments where it's needed. In S. Sandall & M. Ostrosky (Eds.), *Young Exceptional Children Monograph Series No. 2: Natural Environments and Inclusion* (pp. 17–26). Denver, CO: The Division for Early Childhood of the Council for Exceptional Children.

Meisels, S. (1992). *The work sampling system: An overview.* Ann Arbor, MI: University of Michigan.

Meisels, S. J. (2001). Fusing assessment and intervention: Changing parents' and providers' views of young children. *Zero to Three, 21*(4), 4–10.

Meisels, S. J., Dombro, A. L., Marsden, D. B., Weston, D. R. & Jewkes, A. (In preparation). *The Ounce of Prevention Scale.* Ann Arbor, MI: University of Michigan, School of Education.

Meisels, S., & Steele, D. (1991). *The early childhood portfolio collection process.* Ann Arbor, MI: University of Michigan Center for Human Growth and Development.

Neisworth, J. T., & Bagnato, S. J. (1988). Assessment in early childhood special education: A typology of dependent measures. In S. L. Odom & M. L. Karnes (Eds.), *Early intervention for infants and children with handicaps* (pp. 23–44). Baltimore: Paul H. Brookes.

Newborg, J., Stock, J. R., Wnek, L., Guidubaldi, J., & Svinicki, J. (1988). *The Battelle Developmental Inventory.* Dallas, TX: DLM Teaching Resources.

Noonan, M. J., & McCormick, L. (1993). *Early intervention in natural environments: Methods and procedures.* Pacific Grove, CA: Brooks/Cole Publishing Company.

Olson, J. & Murphy, C. L. (1999). Self-assessment: A key process of successful team development. *Young Exceptional Children, 2*(3), 2–8.

Parks, S. (1994). HELP Family Centered Interview. Palo Alto, CA: Vort Corporation.

Provence, S. Erikson, J., Vater, S., & Palmeri, S. (1995). *Infant-Toddler Developmental Assessment: IDA.* Chicago, IL: Riverside Publishing Company.

Rainforth, B., York, J., & MacDonald, C. (1992). *Collaborative teams for students with severe disabilities: Integrating therapy and educational services.* Baltimore: Paul H. Brookes.

Roberts, R., Akers, A., & Behl, D. (1996). Family-level service coordination within home visiting programs. *Topics in Early Childhood Special Education, 16*(3), 279–301.

Rossetti, L. (1990). *Infant-Toddler Language Scale.* East Moline, IL: Linguisystems.

Sandall, S., McLean, M., & Smith, B. (2000). *DEC recommended practices in early intervention/early childhood special education.* Longmont, CO: Sopris West.

Sanford, A., & Zelman, J. (1981). *The Learning Accomplishment Profile.* Winston-Salem, NC: Kaplan.

Sheehan, R. (1988). Involvement of parents in early childhood assessment. In R. Sheehan & T. Wachs (Eds.), *Assessment of young developmentally disabled children* (pp. 75–90). New York: Plenum.

Simeonsson, R., Huntington, G., Sturtz-McMillen, J., Haugh-Dodds, A., Halperin, D., & Zipper, I. (1996). Services for young children and families: Evaluating intervention cycles. *Infants and Young Children, 9*(2), 31–42.

Sparrow, S., Balla, D., & Cicchetti, D. (1984). *Vineland Adaptive Behavior Scales.* Circle Pines, MN: American Guidance Service.

Squires, J., & Bricker, D. (1991). Impact of completing infant developmental questionnaires on at-risk mothers. *Journal of Early Intervention, 15,* 162–172.

Squires J., Bricker, D., & Potter, L. (1993). *Infant/child monitoring questionnaires: Procedures manual.* Eugene, OR: University of Oregon Center on Human Development.

Suen, H. K., Lu, C. H., & Neisworth, J. T. (1993). Measurement of team decision-making through generalizability theory. *Journal of Psychoeducational Assessment, 11,* 120–132.

Tuchman, L. I. (1996). The team and models of teaming. In P. Rosin, A. Whitehead, L. I. Tuchman, G. S. Jesien, A. L. Begun, & L. Irwin (Eds.), *Partnership in family-centered care: A guide to collaborative early intervention.* Baltimore: Paul H. Brookes.

Turnbull, A., & Turnbull, H. (1986). *Family Information Preference Inventory.* In A. Turnbull & H. Turnbull (Eds.), *Families, professionals, and exceptionality: A special partnership* (pp. 368–373). Upper Saddle River, NJ: Merrill/Prentice Hall.

U.S. Department of Education. (2000). *Twenty-second annual report to Congress on the implementation of the Individuals with Disabilities Education Act. http://www.ed.gov/offices/OSERS/OSEP.*

Walsh, S., Rous, B., & Lutzer, C. (2000). The federal IDEA natural environments provisions. In S. Sandall & M. Ostrosky (Eds.), *Young Exceptional Children Monograph Series No. 2: Natural Environments and Inclusion.* Longmont, CO: Sopris West.

Wetherby, A., & Prizant, B. (1993). *Communication and Symbolic Behavior Scale* (1st ed.). Chicago: Riverside Publishing Company.

Winton, P. (1996). Understanding family concerns, priorities, and resources. In P. McWilliam, P. Winton, & E. Crais (Eds.), *Practical strategies for family-centered early intervention* (pp. 31–53). Baltimore: Paul H. Brookes.

Winton, P., & Bailey, D. (1993). Communicating with families: Examining practices and facilitating change. In J. Paul & R. Simeonsson (Eds.), *Children with special needs: Family, culture and society* (pp. 210–230). Orlando, FL: Harcourt Brace Jovanovich.

Wolery, M. (1994). Assessing children with special needs. In M. Wolery & J. S. Wilbers (Eds.), *Including children with special needs in early childhood programs* (pp. 71–96). Washington, DC: National Association for the Education of Young Children.

Family Diversity, Assessment, and Cultural Competence

Eleanor W. Lynch
San Diego State University
Marci J. Hanson
San Francisco State University

Note: The examples used throughout the narrative are hypothetical, although many draw upon actual events and experiences or composites.

71

• • • • • • • •

*There never were, in the world, two opinions
alike, no more than two hairs, or two grains;
the most universal quality is diversity.*

Montaigne, *Essays* (1580–88)

• • • • • • • •

Families, like the faces and fingerprints of the
individuals who comprise them, are all different.
Opinions, values, beliefs, goals, resources, languages,
styles of interaction, and modes of communication
vary from family to family, just as they vary among
individuals within each family. Yet, service providers
who work with young children and their families
are required to follow consistent procedures that
conform to agency policies while, at the same time,
delivering these services in an individualized manner
that is responsive and sensitive to the diversity of the
families being served. In the area of assessment,
balancing family diversity and the requirements for
data gathering is particularly challenging (McLean,
2000). This chapter focuses on the rationale for
increasing cultural competence in the assessment
process and strategies for improving practice.

The notion of culturally nonbiased assessment is
not new. Service providers in the education, social
services, and health fields have grappled with the
issues surrounding the provision of "appropriate,"
culturally nonbiased, multi-and-interdisciplinary
assessments of young children for many years.
However, assessment in early childhood remains
a complex and sometimes controversial topic. No
single method or instrument is capable of detecting
and/or predicting which children need intervention
or evaluating the effects of the intervention
regimen. The introduction and implementation of
the Individualized Family Service Plan (IFSP)
through Public Law 99-457 in 1986 (now retitled
the Individuals with Disabilities Education Act, or
IDEA, Public Law 105-17 of 1997) created the
additional challenges. Service systems had to
develop methods to ensure family input and participation in the IFSP process and, with the family's

permission, assess family strengths and needs in
ways that are culturally appropriate and respectful
of family diversity (Banks, 2001). The caution
offered by Colarusso and Kana (1991) over a
decade ago, remains equally true today:

> Differences in variables, such as socioeconomic
> status, marital status, cultural background,
> geographic location, family values, attitudes,
> interests, desires, and coping strategies for
> dealing with this potentially stressful situation,
> leave policy makers the potential to design rules
> applicable and appropriate for some families
> and not others. (p. 9)

These challenges emphasize the need to examine the methods used in assessing the child as well
as assessing family concerns, priorities, resources,
and needs. The implications of varying family characteristics on planning assessments, deciding upon
assessment strategies, gathering information, and
sharing assessment data with families are raised in
light of the changing demographics in the United
States. This is followed by a discussion of strategies
that can be used to increase cross-cultural competence in the assessment process and guidelines for
improving assessment practice with families from
culturally and linguistically diverse backgrounds.
Strategies for working effectively with interpreters
are addressed followed by a comprehensive discussion of the components of the assessment
process. Each component is examined and analyzed with examples that illustrate practices that
are culturally insensitive followed by strategies for
improving practice and procedures. The chapter
concludes with a restatement of key concepts.

RATIONALE FOR EXAMINING ASSESSMENT MODELS AND PRACTICES

Assessment models and practices used with
young children and their families have evolved
over the past 40 years (Fewell, 2000;
McConnell, 2000). Although there have been
many changes in the models used today versus

those used in the past, changes in demographics, family constellation, and overall diversity have outpaced the changes in the models. As a result, it is time to re-examine what we do and how we do it in relation to the diversity of the children and families being served.

Changing Demographics and Increasing Family Diversity

Families vary on a multitude of dimensions. Education, religion, ethnicity, race, culture, values, beliefs, socioeconomic status, opportunity, geographic location, primary language, and sources of affiliation all contribute to the variability that is characteristic of families in the United States and elsewhere. Each of these dimensions, and many that are not mentioned, contributes to a family's perspective on the assessment of their son or daughter. Several of the most salient areas of variability are discussed in the sections that follow. As you read them, consider your own experiences and the effect that those experiences might have on your views of assessment.

Ethnic, Cultural, and Linguistic Diversity

The United States is no longer considered a melting-pot nation comprised of individuals from a wide range of cultural and ethnic backgrounds who share a common language and cultural value system. Although a greater sense of unity emerged in late 2001, the nation reflects a wide range of groups who retain strong ties with their native heritage. While most of those in the United States do participate and share in aspects of so-called "American" culture, terms such as *cultural diversity, cultural pluralism,* and *multiculturalism* more clearly characterize the society as it exists today.

As of April 1, 2000, the United States had a total population of 281,421,906 (U.S. Census Bureau, undated A). Of that number, approximately one-third (31%) identified themselves as Hispanic or Latino; African American or Black; American Indian or Native Alaskan; Asian; Native Hawaiian or Other Pacific Islander; or

multiracial (U.S. Census Bureau, undated B). These totals do not, however, present the full picture. In many states, population diversity is more evenly distributed making the term *majority population* meaningless in many communities. Because many localities have no single group that represents 50% or more of the population, numeric minorities do not exist. In California, for example, no cultural or ethnic group is in the majority, with a state population of nearly 47% white non-Latino, 32% Latino, 11% Asian and Pacific Islander, 6% African American, and approximately 1% Native American or Alaskan Native ("Diverse, Yet Distinct," 2001). More even population distributions cannot, however, be claimed in terms of education, opportunity, socioeconomic status, health care, and a host of other indicators that are associated with developmental outcomes. According to the Children's Defense Fund (2000), "if recent patterns persist, one out of every three children born in 2000 will have spent at least a year in poverty by his or her 18th birthday" (p. 1).

The linguistic diversity within the United States is also important to note. U.S. Census Bureau data from the 2000 census are not yet available; however, in 1990, nearly 1.5 million individuals over age 5 were reported to be English-language learners. Another 3 million had limited English-language skills (U.S. Census Bureau, 1990). Because language is foundational to family participation in the assessment process as well as determining a child's performance, it is evident that the nation's language diversity can no longer be ignored.

According to a report titled *America's Children 1999* (ChildStats.gov, 1999) the number of white, non-Latino children has decreased from 74% in 1980 to 65% in 1998. During the same time frame, the percent of black, non-Latino and American Indian/Alaska Native children has been stable while the percent of Asian/Pacific Islander and Latino children has increased. Most significant is the increase in the percentage of Latino children. Latinos are the largest-growing group in the

United States with an increase in the child population from 9% in 1980 to 15% in 1998. By 2020, projections suggest that 1 in 5 children in the United States will be Latino.

Socioeconomic Status and the Effects of Poverty

A family's socioeconomic status is likely to exercise a profound effect on the family's resources and ability to mobilize resources. The Children's Defense Fund (2000) reported that in 1998 the number of children living in poverty decreased for the fifth consecutive year. However, nearly 20% of children in the United States still live below the poverty line as defined by family size and income. In fact, the gap between rich and poor families is at its highest in the 52 years that these data have been collected. These figures are particularly alarming in that poor children are getting poorer. In 1998, 26% of children living in poverty lived in families whose incomes were below *half* of the poverty line (Children's Defense Fund, 2000).

According to the Children's Defense Fund (2000), "Every 40 seconds a baby is born into poverty" (p. xxviii). In 1998 the distribution of impoverished children varied by race and ethnicity with 10.6% of non-Latino, white children; 18% of Asian and Pacific Islander children; 34.4% of Latino children of any race, and 36.7% of African American children identified as living in poverty (Children's Defense Fund, 2000).

Families living in poverty may be deeply and negatively affected by their socioeconomic situation, and situations created by poverty may create or interact with other risk factors. For example, studies have revealed a strong relationship between poverty and outcomes such as poor health, high infant mortality, lack of child care, homelessness, poor educational outcomes, and crime (reviewed in Hanson & Lynch, 1992). It is unrealistic to expect families who are grappling with the effects of poverty and struggling to survive to wholeheartedly and willingly embrace and participate in assessment and educational services for their young children.

Family Structure

In recent years family structures have changed. In 1998, 68% of the children in the United States lived with two parents, down from 77% in 1980 (ChildStats.gov, 1999). Almost a quarter (23%) of children lived with only their mothers while 4% lived with only their fathers. Another 4% lived with neither their mother or their father. These percentages are, however, somewhat misleading. Many of these households include more than a single parent. Grandparents, same-sex partners, and unmarried heterosexual partners are not included. According to Riche (2000) 14% of the children who would officially be counted as living in a single-parent family in 1990 were actually living with a cohabiting couple who had chosen not to marry or could not legally marry because they were of the same sex.

Families of today are characterized by great variation in terms of size and composition and include those with two parents, a single parent, teen parents, gay/lesbian parents; divorced, blended, extended, adoptive, foster; and couples without children. Descriptors such as *traditional family* and *nuclear family* have little meaning.

Family Characteristics

Just as dramatic changes have occurred in recent decades in the structure of families, other characteristics of families have also changed. Increased life expectancy and smaller families have resulted in fewer years devoted to childrearing and in multi-generational families (Riche, 2000). However, fertility rates differ across ethnic and cultural groups (ChildStats.gov, 1999), and various families may define *family* differently, with some including only members with blood or legal ties, while others include a wider range of members (Lynch & Hanson, 1998). Thus, the overall trends may not be true for any given family.

After a sharp rise, the number of births per thousand to teens between 15 and 19 years old stabilized at approximately 44 per 1000 (Children's Defense Fund, 2000). Being born to a teenage mother continues to put children at risk. Lack of education, limited earning power, and the demands of single parenting are associated with poverty, which in turn does not promote optimal outcomes.

Religion   Because of our national perspective on separating issues of church and state, defining families in terms of religious orientation is often not addressed in discussions of assessment and intervention. However, families' religious beliefs and practices may greatly influence their choices, preferences, goals, and resources. The population of the United States varies greatly with respect to religious beliefs. In a study of American religious affiliation Kosmin, Mayer, and Keysar (2001) found that although the percentage of American adults reporting affiliation with one or another religion had declined from 90% in 1990, 81% of those polled in 2001 did identify with a religious group. The largest percentage identify with one of the many Christian denominations; however, the percent who identify themselves as Christians has decreased and the number who identify with other faiths (e.g., Jewish, Muslim, Buddhist, Hindu, Unitarian) has increased. Although a family's religious or spiritual orientation may not initially seem to be important to the assessment process, it may influence their goals for their child, the way in which they describe their family's priorities, and the extent to which they choose to become involved in intervention programs and services.

Implications of Diversity on the Child and Family Assessment Process

Almost daily a story of a potential cultural clash emerges in the communities in which the authors live and work—from failing to work through a trained interpreter, to asking questions that the family considered to be intrusive, to basing assessments on skills that are not part of a child's daily life. Such situations highlight the need for a range of information-gathering options that truly reflect the diversity of family preferences and backgrounds.

Even in the most well-intentioned service systems, cultural clashes between service providers and the children and families with whom they work can occur because of differences in beliefs, values, behaviors, and language. In addition to the obvious problems that occur when interpreters/translators are not present or not trained when family members are deaf or speak a language different from the service providers, there are more subtle differences related to linguistic diversity. In an article from 1984, Dale and Hoshino describe misunderstandings that led to communication barriers in a neonatal intensive care unit and relate examples of confusion and difficulties with terminology. One such example is the translation of the word *surgery,* which translates to "butchery" in the Hmong language. Another example of a cultural clash between a service provider and a family is provided by Joe and Malach (1998). A Native American family traveled from the reservation to meet with an early interventionist. She suggested that they eat lunch at the local Owl Cafe. The suggestion was inappropriate because in the family's culture, owls are considered a bad omen. As these illustrations point out, merely translating terms or discussing procedures with families is not enough. Apart from these potential difficulties are examples that range from cases of inappropriate referral for child abuse when "bruises" found on children were really birthmarks or had been created by native medical/health practices, to failure of families to participate in services due to misunderstanding of terms and procedures.

Other illustrations of difficulties in the assessment process focus on the materials or methods used. As one parent from an upper-middle-class background recently observed, her young child did not know what an ironing board was because she had so rarely seen one! Other less humorous examples of evaluating children's developmental knowledge and skills abound. For instance, children may be unable to identify or manipulate items in a standard testing kit because they have never had the opportunity in their homes to see these items (most of which are based on materials available in middle-class households). Repeatedly, we are reminded that assessment and intervention services for young children and their families must be delivered in a culturally competent way by individuals sensitive to, respectful of, and knowledgeable about the families' sociocultural practices, values, and folkways.

Summary

These factors represent a few of the many dimensions on which families vary. An examination of population trends indicates increasing diversity in the years to come and also serves to identify some shifts in the population, such as deepening poverty among some households and the diversity of family membership, that will require new approaches and new skills.

A review of the changing demographics highlights the need for service providers to develop flexibility, openness, respect, sensitivity, new knowledge, and an appreciation of the many facets of family life. Because this may be complicated by the fact that many of the current service providers are from ethnic and cultural groups that differ from the family groups with whom they work, there continue to be needs in the areas of personnel training, recruitment, hiring, and retention of individuals from groups that have previously been underrepresented in the population of service providers (Lynch & Hanson, 1998).

DEVELOPING COMPETENCE IN WORKING ACROSS CULTURES

Defining Cross-Cultural Competence

As our country's citizenry has become increasingly diverse, attention has been directed toward examining the "how" of providing services to persons whose perspectives may differ, sometimes even

radically, from those of the service providers. This is often termed "developing cross-cultural competence." A definition of this concept is provided by Green (1982), who described "ethnic competence" as the ability "to conduct one's professional work in a way that is congruent with the behavior and expectations that members of a distinctive culture recognize as appropriate among themselves" (p. 52).

It is important to remember, however, that an individual's culture is not a prescribed script for behavior. It does nevertheless represent a framework that "must be viewed as a set of tendencies or possibilities from which to choose" (Anderson & Fenichel, 1989, p. 8). The cultural identification that children and their families hold exercises a profound influence on all aspects of their lifeways.

This ability to work with children and families whose cultural practices differ from one's own perspective, requires a commitment to gaining new information and becoming aware of the ways in which one thinks and behaves. Though offered several decades ago, the analysis made by Green (1982) still today provides a succinct account of the personal attributes of individual service providers and the types of support that should be provided by their organizations if one is to demonstrate ethnic competence. These attributes include (1) awareness of one's own cultural limitations; (2) one's openness to cultural differences; (3) the adoption of a learning style that is client-oriented, interactive, and flexible; (4) the ability to help someone recognize and use resources; and (5) the recognition of the integrity of all cultures. These characteristics provide undergirding for the development of cultural competence.

Strategies for Enhancing Cross-Cultural Competence

The topic of attaining cultural competence is not new (Lynch & Hanson, 1993). Business and government organizations have long recognized the need for training their workers who are employed overseas or who interact in today's global economy. A number of training models has been used and most share some common characteristics. Lynch and Hanson (1993) suggest that these characteristics can be applied to personnel preparation for individuals employed in the service professions in the United States who may be called upon to work with families from a variety of ethnic, cultural, and linguistic backgrounds. They outline three training components that are essential in the quest to attain cross-cultural competence. These components are (1) clarifying one's own values; (2) gaining cultural-specific information; and (3) applying and practicing the methods and information acquired through self-examination and information gathering. These components are similar to the four steps in developing a "posture of reciprocity" described by Harry, Kalyanpur, and Day (1999, p. 7). The four steps include (1) identifying one's own values and assumptions; (2) ascertaining the family's perspective; (3) acknowledging the family's perspective and explaining one's own perspective (examining the potential contradictions and ways in which these perspectives overlap); and (4) determining a strategy that incorporates both perspectives. These steps are examined in the discussion that follows.

Self-Examination Culture is a part of all of us. We may or may not be aware of how our beliefs and values affect the ways in which we conduct our lives. It is not until we are aware of this influence and are clear about our own cultural perspectives that we can truly recognize and appreciate the cultural perspectives of others. Without this clarification and appreciation of differences in ways of conducting daily living, the potential for cultural clashes exists between service providers and children and their families participating in the services. Self-examination is much more difficult than it sounds at first glance. It involves a determined effort to identify one's own family structures, family parables and proverbs, family rituals, celebrations, the style of

interaction among family members, and family values, to name just a few considerations. Our own values and beliefs and our "own culture" is often so subtle that we are unaware of it. But it is a powerful force in shaping who we are as individuals and how we conduct ourselves in all human interactions. (For additional information on this topic see Harry, 1992c).

Knowledge Acquisition Cross-cultural competence is facilitated by the acquisition of culture-specific information. This means gaining knowledge about cultures other than our own with which we are familiar. Such information can be acquired through a variety of activities including reading (both fiction and nonfiction), the arts (e.g., movies, paintings, theater), cultural festivals, travel, sampling foods from other cultures, and so on. One way to acquire this information is through personal and professional contacts with individuals who bridge cultures—in other words, individuals who understand and are able to operate in several cultures. These "cultural guides" who provide a perspective that may be new and unfamiliar are invaluable in the process of designing and implementing appropriate services. Such guides can be located through participation in community events, personal contacts, suggestions from client families, and state and local professional networks and organizations designed for this purpose. As can be seen, the knowledge of information regarding cultural practices in cultures beyond our own can be gleaned through both indirect (e.g., reading, viewing movies, observing) and direct (e.g., interaction and participation) means. The important step is embarking on the journey. The quest for this information and the opportunities to learn new ways never has to have an ending. It is not a product but rather a continuing process.

Reflective Service Delivery The third component in attaining cross-cultural competence involves applying the knowledge and information in service delivery practices (Lynch & Hanson, 1993). The application of this new knowledge may require organizational change and certainly support for efforts to make service systems more responsive to a wide range of children and families. It also requires the efforts of individuals to seek coaches and guides in the process. Methods for obtaining feedback and continually updating knowledge are essential as well. In addition to developing sensitivity to and appreciation for differences in families' values on such issues as child independence, early education and treatment, family participation, and health care, practitioners must acquire and apply skills related to effective communication. Communication styles may vary radically from child to child and family to family. For some, informal contacts may be the norm; for others, highly formalized interactions may be appropriate. Some may benefit from the use of a direct communication approach, but in other cases a more indirect method of communicating may be warranted.

Perhaps the most important step in applying this knowledge in assessment and service delivery settings, is the use of *reflective practices*. This step involves the clear recognition on the part of the assessor/service provider of her or his own values and beliefs about what is important in the assessment/intervention process and how that process should be conducted. These personal preferences then must be considered side-by-side with the perspectives presented by the family members as to their concerns, their priorities, their style of decision making, their interactional patterns and so forth. This ability to respect behaviors and preferences that may be unfamiliar or different is essential to establishing effective practices and in avoiding or minimizing potential difficulties (Barrera, 2000; Harry, Kalyanpur, & Day, 1999).

Barrera (2000) describes three important dimensions to be considered in "recognizing the pervasive influence of culture and cultural dynamics" (p. 17) in work with young children

and their families. First, the *communicative-linguistic dimension* acknowledges potential differences in the languages(s) used and communication styles and preferences of families and their service providers. For example, individuals place different value on the use of verbal and nonverbal means of communication. This recognition is crucial in order to prevent misunderstandings when differences in meaning are encountered. The second dimension is the *sensory-cognitive dimension*. This dimension refers to the potential for differences in priorities (e.g., goals for children in social abilities vs. cognitive abilities), strategies for acquiring new information (e.g., verbal vs. nonverbal), and strategies for gleaning and understanding information and making decisions (e.g., interpersonal, linear, individual, communal). Families and service providers may differ on primary goals or on the focus for children. Third, on the *personal-social dimension* families and service providers may differ in their degree of acculturation to one another's culture and to the professional service culture. They also may be challenged to understand differing perspectives related to family structure, power, and social position and roles.

The acknowledgement of multiple perspectives—one's own goals and perspectives and also the family's goals and perspective—is crucial to enhancing reciprocal decision making. This ability to "walk in another's shoes" or view an event through another lens, is a crucial step toward the provision of services that are culturally respectful, and ultimately, more effective.

Attaining cross-cultural competence, thus, requires a tremendous openness, sensitivity, and commitment to learning about and respecting the lifeways of groups whose values may be unfamiliar or different from one's own. It also involves a commitment to taking the time to learn and reflect, as well as a willingness to conduct one's professional activities in a new way that may feel uncomfortable but that will broaden one's reach and opportunities.

Guidelines and Cultural Considerations in Data Gathering

Cultural considerations may play a significant role in family views of children and childrearing practices, family roles and structures, disability and causation, health and healing practices, and views toward change and intervention, as well as in communication styles and methods (Hanson, Lynch, & Wayman, 1990). For the practitioner involved in the assessment of young children and their families, these considerations can be overwhelming. Wayman, Lynch, & Hanson (1991) suggest a series of thought-provoking questions that are designed to provide guidance to the assessor or interventionist who is called on to work with families from various cultures. The questions are not meant to be used as an assessment of the families or as a checklist for evaluating families; they merely highlight issues that may be encountered in the process of working closely with families of young children in gathering information (see Figure 4.1).

Caveats

As noted earlier, cultural orientation is only one dimension on which children and families may vary. It is essential that practitioners make no assumptions about needs and goals based on the families' ethnic and/or cultural perspective. First, family members may differ both across cultural groups and within cultural groups (even within the family itself) in terms of the degree to which they identify with a given cultural perspective or practice. Some individuals wholly adopt their native perspective and customs, while other individuals pick and choose from their primary or native customs and practices as well as from those of the culture in which they now live. Second, life circumstances and historical events may also affect this degree of identification, such as children entering the public schools, divorce or death or remarriage, change in employment, change in living arrangements or

location of home, and changes in the political climate between the native country and the adoptive country. Practitioners must be aware that these shifts may occur and they must be able to adapt their behavior and style during interactions with families in order to be responsive to family needs and concerns.

Other factors also interact with or override the influence of culture at any given time. For example, a family living in poverty or in homeless conditions may have very different needs and motivation to seek assessment and intervention services from those of another family whose members are from the same cultural group but who have adequate income and a roof over their heads. Issues of socioeconomic status, wellness/sickness, education, job opportunities, immigration circumstances, age, gender, and language proficiency, for instance, all may exert a profound influence over families' concerns, priorities, and resources. In many instances these issues define the family's concerns to a much greater extent than does the cultural or ethnic label. The term "culture of poverty," for example, alludes to the degree to which living under impoverished conditions affects all aspects of the family's life. Therefore, while identifying customs, rituals, and tendencies that are associated with particular cultural groups can be useful in establishing communication and designing assessment and intervention practices to fit the children's and family's needs, cultural stereotyping must be steadfastly avoided. Many other factors also exert a tremendous influence over the goals, priorities, and resources of families.

Summary

As Lynch and Hanson (1993) stated: "Many of the early intervention programs of today and all of the early intervention programs of tomorrow require staff members who are able to work respectfully and effectively with families whose values, beliefs, behaviors, and language differ from their own" (p. 54). These abilities are of

Part I—Family Structure and Child-Rearing Practices

• **Family Structure**

  • **Family Composition**

    • Who are the members of the family system?

    • Who are the key decision makers?

    • Is decision making related to specific situations?

    • Is decision making individual or group-oriented?

    • Do family members all live in the same household?

    • What is the relationship of friends to the family system?

    • What is the hierarchy within the family? Is status related to gender and/or age?

  • **Primary Caregiver(s)**

    • Who is the primary caregiver?

    • Who else participates in the caregiving?

    • What is the amount of care given by mother vs. others?

    • How much time does the infant spend away from the primary caregiver?

    • Is there conflict between (among) caregivers regarding appropriate practices?

    • What ecological/environmental issues impinge upon general care-giving (e.g., housing, jobs)?

• **Child-rearing Practices**

  • **Family Feeding Practices**

    • What are the family feeding practices?

    • What are the beliefs regarding breast-feeding and weaning?

    • What are the beliefs regarding bottle feeding?

    • What are the family practices when transitioning to solid food?

    • Which family member(s) prepare food?

    • Is food purchased or homemade?

    • Which family member(s) feed the child?

    • What is the configuration of the family mealtime?

    • What are the family's views on independent feeding?

    • Is there a discrepancy among family members regarding the beliefs and practices related to feeding the infant/toddler?

  • **Family Sleeping Patterns**

    • Does the infant sleep in the same room/bed as the parents?

    • At what age is the infant moved away from close proximity to the mother?

FIGURE 4.1

Guidelines for the home visitor

Source: From "Home-Based Early Childhood Services: Cultural Sensitivity in a Family Systems Approach" by K. I. Wayman, E. W. Lynch, & M. J. Hanson, 1991, *Topics in Early Childhood Special Education, 10*(4), pp. 56–75. Copyright 1991 by PRO-ED, Inc. Adapted by permission.

- Is there an established bedtime?
- What is the family response to an infant when he/she awakes at night?
- What practices surround daytime napping?
- **Family's Response to Disobedience and Aggression**
  - What are the parameters of acceptable child behavior?
  - What form does the discipline take?
  - Who metes out the disciplinary action?
- **Family's Response to a Crying Infant**
  - Temporal qualities—How long before the caregiver picks up a crying infant?
  - How does the caregiver calm an upset infant?

Part II—Family Perceptions and Attitudes

- **Family Perception of Child's Disability**
  - Are there cultural or religious factors that would shape family perceptions?
  - To what/where/whom does the family assign responsibility for their child's disability?
  - How does the family view the role of fate in their lives?
  - How does the family view their role in intervening with their child?
  - Do they feel they can make a difference or do they consider it hopeless?
- **Family's Perception of Health and Healing**
  - **What is the family's approach to medical needs?**
    - Do they rely solely on Western medical services?
    - Do they rely solely on holistic approaches?
    - Do they utilize a combination of these approaches?
  - **Who is the primary medical provider or conveyer of medical information?**
    - Family members? Elders? Friends? Folk healers? Family doctor? Medical specialists?
  - **Do all members of the family agree on approaches to medical needs?**
- **Family's Perception of Help-Seeking and Intervention**
  - Who does the family seek help from—family members or outside agencies/individuals?
  - Does the family seek help directly or indirectly?
  - What are the general feelings of family when seeking assistance—ashamed, angry, demand as a right, view as unnecessary?
  - With which community systems does the family interact? (educational/medical/social)?
  - How are these interactions completed (face to face, telephone, letter)?
  - Which family member interacts with other systems?
  - Does that family member feel comfortable when interacting with other systems?

Ensuring Cultural Competence in Assessment

Part III: Language and Communication Styles

• **Language**
  • **To what degree:**
    • Is the home visitor proficient in the family's native language?
    • Is the family proficient in English?
  • **If an interpreter is used:**
    • With which culture is the interpreter primarily affiliated?
    • Is the interpreter familiar with the colloquialisms of the family members' country/region of origin?
    • Is the family member comfortable with the interpreter? (Would the family member feel more comfortable with an interpreter of the same sex?)
  • **If written materials are used, are they in the family's native language?**
• **Interaction Styles**
  • Does the family communicate with each other in a direct or indirect way?
  • Do family members share feelings when discussing emotional issues?
  • Does the family ask the home visitor direct questions?
  • Does the family value a lengthy social time at each home visit unrelated to the early childhood services program goals?
  • Is it important for the family to know about the home visitor's extended family? Is the home visitor comfortable sharing that information?

FIGURE 4.1
Continued

particular importance in the assessment process. The remainder of this chapter outlines strategies and steps toward becoming culturally competent in each phase or component of the assessment process.

STRATEGIES FOR WORKING EFFECTIVELY WITH INTERPRETERS AND TRANSLATORS

Given the tremendous diversity in terms of ethnicity, culture, languages, and dialects spoken by families served through educational, social, and health care agencies, translators and interpreters often play a key role. Frequently, service providers and the families they serve do not share the same primary language and cultural experience. Given the shortages in professionally trained personnel from diverse cultural and linguistic backgrounds and the lack of attention in the past to issues of culture in personnel preparation, this is not surprising (Chen, McLean, Corso, & Bruns, 2001). Therefore, most practitioners will be called upon to work extensively with and through translators and interpreters. As the following section illustrates, speaking the language is not enough. For translations to reliably communicate the message, the translator as well as the early childhood practitioner must be familiar with the family's culture and the meaning of terms and actions in that culture.

Skills of the Interpreter

To be effective, interpreters should be proficient in the family's language and dialect as well as the language of the interventionist. However, language proficiency alone is not enough. Interpreters must also be aware of the cultural rules that govern each person's interactions and be able to interpret subtle nuances with tact and sensitivity (Lynch, 1998; Ohtake, Fowler, & Santos, 2001).

Interpreters also need to be trained in the dynamics and principles of interpretation and understand their role, including its requirements and its boundaries (Chen, Chan, Brekken, & Valverde, 2000). Knowledge of the specific field in which they are doing the interpretation is important because interpreting in a court of law requires different skills and vocabulary from interpreting in a program for young children with disabilities and their families. Although advanced training in the areas of early childhood, disability, and assessment is unlikely, interpreters should at least have a basic understanding of some of the concepts and terminology so that they can convey information accurately. Although context rather than literal, word-for-word translations is the goal, interpreters should avoid glossing over information, inserting their own opinion and advice, or omitting, adding or paraphrasing in ways that alter the intent or content of the information (Langdon, Siegel, Halog, & Sánchez-Boyce, 1994).

Interpreters can contribute significantly to facilitating communication by helping the interventionist establish a comfortable pace and watching for cues that reflect the family's acceptance and understanding of the information being presented. Like all professionals, interpreters are bound by the rules of confidentiality and neutrality, and their manner and dress should convey respect for the family.

The Needs of the Interpreter

From the preceding paragraphs it is evident that the role of the interpreter is complex. It requires a wide range of cross-cultural, language, content knowledge, and interpersonal skills. It is not surprising therefore that interpreting can be stressful. Because of the shortage of qualified interpreters, those who are well trained are often overused and overworked. Few service systems have as many qualified interpreters as they need, resulting in increased workloads, inadequate time to prepare for interactions, and inadequate time to debrief. Interpreters may contribute to their own exhaustion because they see themselves as the family's "life raft" and the only person who can help the family negotiate the system. The emotional demands brought about by the content of the information may also cause stress. As interpreters watch families struggle with difficult information and limited options, they may over-identify with the family and take on some of the burden that they assume the family is feeling. This may be further complicated because in some settings the interpreter may not meet with the family again and, therefore, not have the opportunity to see the resolutions to problems or the resilience that many families exhibit.

Professionals who work with interpreters may add to the stress. They too are often overworked and have little time for preparing the interpreter for the next interaction. Some of their frustration may result in impatience, which makes it more difficult for the interpreter to do his or her job well. Over two decades ago Benhamida (1988) identified a problem that continues to exist; bilingual staff in agencies are often asked to serve as interpreters without compensation or without relief from their other day-to-day responsibilities. This dual role and the guilt associated with not doing either job as they would like adds further pressure to the lives of many interpreters.

Although interpreting will always be demanding, those who work with interpreters can help to reduce the most stressful aspects. Planning ahead, allowing adequate time, and regarding the interpreter as an essential member of the team will benefit families, interpreters, and interventionists.

Confidentiality and Interpreted Interactions

Families have both legal and moral rights to privacy. Adding a third party to the interactions makes it even more important to constantly monitor these rights and ensure that they are being respected. Anyone acting as an interpreter should be trained in confidentiality issues, and families should be given choices for interpretation (Ohtake, Fowler, & Santos, 2001). For example, families and interpreters who live in the same neighborhood or see each other socially may not be an appropriate match. Likewise, interpreters and families who share the same language but not the same cultural background or country of origin may not work together effectively. Differences in social class, recency of arrival, gender, cultural affiliation, and educational level may also affect a family's trust and level of comfort with an interpreter. And, like everyone else, interpreters bring different communication styles and levels of interpersonal skills, credibility, and competence to interactions with families that can enhance or interfere with family/professional relationships.

Friends and Family Members as Interpreters

Because the demand for fully qualified interpreters is typically greater than the supply, interventionists often find themselves relying on family friends or family members to translate and interpret. Although this may seem to be the only alternative, it is often unsatisfactory. The relationships of family members and friends often interfere with accurate interpretation. To save the family from difficult news, a friend serving as an interpreter may soften the message in ways that are not accurate and do not convey the essential information. Families may also feel that the confidentiality of the information is compromised when friends become interpreters, especially if the friend is known to gossip. In some instances,

families may feel that the information that is being exchanged is extremely personal and should not be shared outside the family.

Using family members as interpreters is also fraught with difficulty. Because the older children of recent immigrants are often more skilled in English than their parents, it often falls to them to interpret for the parents and grandparents. Because such a role reversal can lead to mutual resentment, discomfort for all family members, and a manipulation of information that is detrimental to family functioning, using children or teens to interpret should be avoided (Lynch, 1998).

Preparing for Interpreted Interactions

Interpreters and interventionists need time together to prepare for interactions with families. The interpreter should be made aware of the purpose of the meeting, the content that is of greatest importance, issues that may be sensitive, any technical words or terms that may be used, and the role that s/he is being asked to take in any data collection (Langdon, Siegel, Halog, & Sánchez-Boyce, 1994). If written documents are to be shared, the interpreter should be given the opportunity to review them prior to the interaction. The interpreter may also want to meet with the family prior to the three-way interaction to establish rapport and to learn their patterns of communication and language sophistication.

Guidelines for Working with an Interpreter

Several authors (e.g., Ohtake, Fowler, & Santos, 2001; Chen, Chan, Brekken, & Valverde, 2000; & Lynch, 1998) have suggested guidelines for working more effectively with interpreters. Strategies include learning some words and phrases in the family's language; addressing all words and remarks to the family, not the interpreter; avoiding verbal and nonverbal language that could be culturally offensive to the family; speaking somewhat more slowly and clearly but not more loudly; and limiting the amount of information communicated to a few sentences before translation.

The importance of trained, skillful interpreters cannot be underestimated in human service agencies where many professionals do not share the language or the culture of the families whom they serve. Training, supporting, and incorporating interpreters on the team is a prerequisite to effective service in many areas of the country.

CULTURAL COMPETENCE AND THE ASSESSMENT PROCESS

The Individuals with Disabilities Education Act, or IDEA (Public Law 105-117 of 1997), affirms the importance of family diversity in the assessment process. Regulations require that assessments be nondiscriminatory, that they be conducted in the family's native language or other preferred mode of communication unless it is clearly not feasible, and that procedures and materials used in the assessment do not discriminate based on culture or race. These regulations are intended to implement the spirit and intent of the law, but broadly stated regulations must be transformed into strategies that can be implemented at the programmatic level to ensure that the regulations are put into practice. The remaining sections of this chapter highlight some of the issues that assessors encounter when working with families from diverse cultural, ethnic, linguistic, and socioeconomic backgrounds. Strategies are suggested to make assessment more responsive to diversity considerations. Although the issues focus on child assessment, many can also be applied to gathering information about families' concerns, priorities, and resources.

As the previous sections of this chapter have described, ensuring that assessment is culturally competent begins long before assessing a child or gathering information about the family's concerns, priorities, and resources. It begins with the philosophy and approach of the program or

service system, the interpretation of administrative requirements related to assessment practices, and the individual values, beliefs, and biases of each staff member. In other words, the stage for culturally competent assessment is set long before members of the assessment team ever meet the child and family.

Culture exerts an impact on development, and culture exerts an impact on the assessment process. Barrera (1996) states that "culturally responsive assessment requires a sensitivity to the ways children and their families perceive, believe, evaluate, and behave, as well as to the ways assessors perceive, believe, evaluate, and behave" (p. 71). She describes the need for mediation, or in other words, the attention to the transfer of information in meaningful ways across cultural contexts. Given that assessors and service providers are often challenged to perform assessments with children and families whose perspectives differ from their own, attention to maximizing this exchange of information between service providers and families is warranted.

The role of family members in the assessment process is paramount. The Zero to Three Work Group on Developmental Assessment (Greenspan & Meisels, 1996) identifies principles that reflect appropriate assessment procedures for young children. These principles underscore the integral part families play in this process. Understanding young children within the context of their families is a central feature of a developmentally appropriate assessment. Parents and other familiar adults are the individuals most able to describe the child's capabilities and challenges, and the child's developmental history. Further, they are the individuals best able to interact with the child and elicit the child's optimal level of functioning. Observations of young children within the context of interactions with their caregivers is typically the optimal assessment situation in order to ensure the child's sense of security and comfort, and enhance the child's active engagement. It is evident, therefore, that practitioners and assessment personnel must be able to establish a collaborative alliance with the child's family members in order to conduct an appropriate and meaningful assessment.

Establishing alliances between assessors and family members, reciprocal information exchange, and joint decision making between service providers and families can be accomplished only through culturally responsive practices. At each step in the assessment process cultural concerns can arise.

The multiple steps within the assessment process (McLoughlin & Lewis, 2001) may be described in different terms by different people, but the assessment process in early childhood typically includes identification and screening, assessment planning, active assessment, interpretation of assessment findings, and decision making regarding intervention. In the sections that follow, each of these steps is described briefly, the issues related to cultural competence are presented, and guidelines are recommended for addressing the issues. Additional discussion and suggestions for providing culturally responsive assessments are available in Barrera (1996).

Identification and Screening

Identification and screening procedures are typically designed to determine which children require more formalized and comprehensive assessment procedures. Assessments used for screening purposes are always designed with balance in mind—balance between over-identifying and under-identifying children who may need further assessment and services. Over-identification results in referring too many children without developmental problems for costly and potentially anxiety-producing assessments. Under-identification results in missing some children with developmental difficulties who need more comprehensive assessments that lead to recommendations for services. However, when identification and screening programs are designed to include children from diverse cultural, ethnic, socioeconomic, and linguistic backgrounds, achieving the

balance between over-identification and under-identification is more complex. The complexity arises because of differences in experience, language, and child-rearing practices that may influence a child's performance as well as from the paucity of adequate measures and the inherent problems of measuring the skills and abilities of very young children.

Screening procedures for infants, toddlers, and preschoolers include multiple measures, such as families' descriptions of the child's capabilities and developmental history, observations, and measures of developmental status, general health, sensory system functioning, and behavioral characteristics. Past practice tended to consider the child's performance to be directly related to innate characteristics. However, as the literature on risk factors versus opportunity factors grows, it is clear that all of the variables that provide the context for the life of the child and family contribute to the child's performance (Dunst, 1993; Meisels & Fenichel, 1996; Rhodes & Brown, 1991). Culture and language are certainly contextual variables, as are the family's length of time in the United States and their socioeconomic status. These factors may also determine whether or not a family participates in screening activities. Factors related to diversity also interact with procedures that are used for screening and identification. Therefore, as practices and procedures are developed, the following issues may arise. Each issue is presented with a short description, an example that might be encountered in practice, and guidelines for assessors.

Issue: Family Participation Encouraging families from diverse cultural and language groups to participate in screening opportunities is one of the first issues that assessors may encounter. There are multiple opportunities in the United States for families to have their young children screened. Neighborhood clinics, health fairs at hospitals and shopping centers, and screening clinics sponsored by health and education agencies are frequent occurrences in most communities. Typically they are free and are held at places that are thought to be easily accessible to families. However, not all families choose to participate. Consider these examples.

The Estrella family has recently come to Florida from El Salvador. Although they are fully documented, they have temporarily moved in with relatives who fled El Salvador in fear of political reprisals. These relatives were originally given political asylum in the United States, but they no longer are eligible for that status. Although Mr. and Mrs. Estrella are concerned about their daughter Oralia, they are afraid to get involved with any organization that might ask questions that would expose their undocumented relatives.

The Woo family has lived in San Francisco's Chinatown for several generations. Despite their long-time residence in the United States, they have maintained many of the traditional practices that their ancestors brought from Mainland China. For health care they use a wide range of herbal medicines. Except for the immunizations and vaccinations that are required to enter their children in school, they have never become involved in Western medicine. Recently they have noticed that their youngest son is developing very slowly compared with his older brothers and sisters. Although they have seen posters advertising a community health fair that includes developmental screening, it is not something that they have considered. Such a public event using Western medicine is not a part of their experience, nor is the idea that one should "look for trouble."

These are just two examples of families who may choose not to participate in screening and identification efforts. Other families may not because they do not understand the language in which the events are publicized, because they do not have transportation to get to screening programs, or because they are not familiar with the reasons for screening.

Guidelines for encouraging families to utilize identification and screening programs. To encourage families to participate, screening efforts should be embedded in the natural events and activities of the community. The best way to learn about what

is natural for the community is to ask cultural guides or mediators who live in or are familiar with the community and its residents (Chan, 1990; Lynch & Hanson, 1998; Yonemitsu & Cleveland, 1992). If particular holidays or celebrations, political activities, or religious ceremonies traditionally bring people together, they may be the venue for screening efforts and may also provide opportunities for community leaders to talk with families about the importance of screening and early intervention. The importance of anything is related to its value to each individual; therefore, the Anglo-European view of the importance of finding problems and working to resolve them early may be quite contrary to the position that problems and their resolution are God's will (Lynch & Hanson, 1998). The value of services for children who have developmental difficulties may best be explained from the perspective of another member of the same cultural or ethnic group who can work from the same frame of reference to personalize the discussion (Harry, 1992a).

Even families who are eager to participate cannot become involved if the information advertising the screening or the information that they are given as a result of screening is not presented in a language that they can understand. Communicating with families requires that printed materials be available in the family's language, that there be nonprint methods available for sharing information with those who have limited literacy, and that trained personnel be available who are both bilingual and bicultural.

Procedures that are designed to look for problems are threatening by nature. Most individuals are anxious when they are being evaluated. Families who are not familiar with screening and assessment and who are not from cultures or families in which evaluation is commonplace may feel considerable discomfort with the idea of screening and the procedures that are used. Linking screening to events and activities that are accepted by individuals within the community and devising procedures that emphasize strengths and include incentives such as free diapers, a gift certificate at a neighborhood store, or a toy for the child may encourage families to participate.

Issue: Selecting Appropriate Screening Procedures Procedures used in the screening and identification of young children typically compare the child's performance with the performance of others of the same chronological age. Although the achievement of developmental milestones is often thought to be universal, different families, and sometimes different cultures, place different emphases on various behaviors and developmental milestones (Lynch & Hanson, 1998). Just as different families have different expectations for their children, so too may families from diverse cultures. The following example illustrates such differences.

> *When the mobile screening van came into their neighborhood, her parents eagerly took 3-year-old Sharma. They were surprised when the assessors expressed concerns about toilet training, her limited use of expressive language, and her willingness to interact so comfortably with strangers. Now Sharma's parents are confused and worried. Toilet training is not a family priority; Sharma's six older brothers and sisters are very attentive to her, and she never has to ask for anything. Sharma is also part of a large, extended family that includes grandparents, aunts, uncles, and cousins. She has become used to lots of people who play with and care for her. Why do the assessors think she should be toilet trained so early, talking more, and unfriendly to people? Is Sharma really behind?*

Family priorities, children's opportunities to practice, and the families' culture all can influence when children attain developmental skills and milestones. In cultures in which individuation and independence are considered less important than interdependence, young children may demonstrate different developmental patterns. For example, in many Middle Eastern and Latino families, the emphasis is upon attachment and parent-child bonding (Sharifzadeh, 1998; Zuniga, 1998); toddlers and preschoolers may not be pushed toward independence in eating, dressing, sleeping, or toilet training. As a result, screening

instruments that rely on norms for Anglo-European children from middle-income homes may inappropriately identify some children as not meeting developmental expectations though these children come from families who hold different expectations for their children.

Children who come from homes in which English is not spoken or homes in which more than one language is spoken may also be over-identified in screening programs (Gollnick & Chinn, 1990). Although children from families who speak languages other than English often learn one or more languages, their initial vocabularies may be smaller in each language; they may mix grammar and syntax in their early years of language learning. In a screening assessment, these children's language may differ from the norm.

Guidelines for selecting appropriate screening measures. Several strategies can help ensure that assessors do not over-select or under-select children from various cultural groups in their screening programs. The first is to have professionals and parents from the cultural community review the instruments prior to selection. They may find that specific items are not appropriate or occur at different times for children in their community. For example, young children who are learning to use chopsticks rather than a knife and fork might fail some self-help items simply because they have not had opportunities to practice. Likewise, young children who are carried all the time and not allowed to play on the floor may appear to be somewhat behind their age peers in motor development. By having professionals and family members from the groups to be screened examine the screening instruments and procedures prior to their use, a great deal of misunderstanding can be avoided.

Some communities may decide that norms on the existing screening instruments are not appropriate for them. Examples are independent toileting, self-feeding, or sleeping alone in a baby bed. One option is to develop community-based norms that compare children with others of the same background in the same area. However, community-based norms can be a double-edged sword. Although they do not over-identify, they can provide a false sense of well-being and cause later inequities when children within a particular community have limited opportunities to learn the behaviors and skills that are expected in school. For example, young children with and without disabilities in affluent homes are typically exposed to lots of books, toys, and the kinds of communicative patterns that are used in preschool and school environments. Young children in less affluent settings may not have the same opportunities to interact with materials and language, and their skills in these areas may be less well developed when they enter preschool or school. Because community-based norms would not identify children if they were not different from others within their immediate community, young children who might profit from added opportunities would not be identified.

A final strategy for selecting appropriate screening procedures is to integrally involve parents and other knowledgeable family members in the screening process. Several open-ended questions that ask parents or primary caregivers what they see as the child's strengths or whether or not they have any concerns can contribute significantly to accurate screening. The accuracy of parents' perceptions has been confirmed by the literature (Hayes, 1990; Sexton, Thompson, Perez, & Rheams, 1990).

Assessment Planning

When a child has been referred for more comprehensive assessment, the first step in the process is planning. Family-centered planning is a joint effort among professionals, family members, and any other individuals whom the family selects (Dunst, Trivette, & Deal, 1988; McGonigel, Kaufman, & Hurth, 1991; Meisels & Fenichel, 1996; StevensDominguez, Beam, & Thomas, 1989). For families who do not speak English well or who have had little exposure to special education

practices in the United States, participating in the assessment planning process may be especially difficult. They may be unfamiliar with the assessment process, have different expectations and beliefs about parental and professional roles, and be unable to communicate in the language of the assessors.

Issue: Collaborating with Families Who View Professionals as Experts In many cultural groups, teachers and others related to education are viewed as experts. Members of these families may consider sharing information or expressing their concerns, or even making eye contact with professionals, to be inappropriate. To these families, speaking out may be considered rude or offensive. The example that follows illustrates one family's experience as they were encouraged to participate in planning the assessment for their child.

> *Tuyet's parents are recent immigrants from Vietnam. They were brought up to respect teachers, and in their village teachers held positions of high esteem. Tuyet has Down syndrome, and their physician suggested that they contact the local early intervention program. After much discussion within the family and assistance from an agency that works with new immigrants, they made the contact. The early intervention team asked to assess Tuyet and invited her parents to pose questions, provide information, and be involved in all aspects of the planning process. Tuyet's parents were very confused. To ask a question of a teacher or other person who is highly respected would be an insult. It would mean that the person had not explained things well enough. To point that out by questioning would cause that person to lose face. Tuyet's parents certainly wouldn't want to be responsible for all of those professionals losing face. And besides, what did they know? Professionals are supposed to know what to do. Why were they asking them, her parents? Could it be that they really don't know how to do their job? If that is so, then they don't want them working with Tuyet.*

Regardless of the professionals' desire and eager attempts to get Tuyet's family to express their concerns and priorities, the family felt confused and constrained. The assessment team members were working with a cultural perception that was different from their own.

Guidelines for encouraging family participation in assessment planning. Long-standing beliefs are not changed overnight. Some families may need extended periods of time in the system before they openly express their concerns or question professionals. Others may elect to adapt to the ways of the new systems that they encounter fairly quickly. Still others may never comfortably exchange information with professionals. Regardless of where the family is on this continuum, family-centered services make it imperative for professionals to determine the family's level of comfort with these procedures and develop ways in which to incorporate family input.

As in many of the transactions that occur between service providers and families whose culture, ethnicity, language, or socioeconomic status differ, a bilingual/bicultural mediator can play an important role in gathering information about the family's concerns, priorities, and resources. In less formal conversations, mediators can talk with appropriate family members and learn about the child and the family context. With the family's permission, this information can be shared with the team. When members of the assessment team meet with the family, the mediator may be the family's voice describing the child's strengths, the family's major concerns, and the best way to approach the child.

Some families who are not comfortable talking about their child's problems may be willing to complete short checklists that pinpoint the child's development or list areas in which families typically have concerns. If written forms are used, it is, of course, equally important to provide them in the family's preferred language and to determine whether or not written materials are appropriate to the family members' literacy levels. Some families may choose not to respond to written materials. For them, the bilingual/bicultural guide may be especially important.

In some instances, families may elect not to participate in the assessment planning process at all. If this occurs, interventionists need not feel that they have failed; however, they may want to continue to invite family participation in the process and continually review their practices to ensure that families are truly welcomed.

Selection of Assessment Instruments and Strategies

Determining what instruments and strategies are to be used is an issue in any assessment; however, selecting those that are culturally and linguistically appropriate adds another dimension that assessors must consider. The first concern is language. Is the instrument available in the family's/child's preferred language? If it is, are there norms that are appropriate for comparisons or has the instrument simply been translated? Although assessors may decide that a translated instrument will provide more information than they can gather in any other way, it is important to view the results with caution. Finally, if the instrument is available in the child's and family's language and determined to be appropriate for the child, is there a trained assessor who can administer the test?

The use of observations, play assessments, and family interviews conducted by trained personnel who are culturally sensitive and knowledgeable are likely to provide more developmentally appropriate and informative assessment results than are formal instruments in any event (Meisels & Fenichel, 1996). The example that follows provides an illustration of the difficulties that can occur when instruments are not culturally and linguistically appropriate.

The da Silva family just moved to the United States from Brazil, and they have come to the local school district to inquire about special education support services for their son Jarvis, who has muscular dystrophy. Jarvis's parents are fluent in both Portuguese and English, but Jarvis's only language is Portuguese. Unsure about how to proceed, one assessor suggested that an instrument available in Spanish be used for the assessment, assuming that everyone in

South America speaks Spanish. Another assessor suggested that Jarvis's parents be asked to translate the questions from a standardized instrument used to measure general information into Portuguese to get Jarvis's response. But as the test went on, it became clear that many of the items dealt with information specific to growing up in the United States, such as the names and values of various coins. After a frustrating experience for everyone involved, it was obvious that the team needed another strategy.

Another aspect of instrument and strategy selection relates to the child's experiences and opportunities. Children who have been carried for their first year of life and never been put on the floor to play or explore may be less motorically competent than their age peers who have been encouraged to move around their environments. Children who have not had toys to play with or other objects to manipulate may not show the same interest in or competence with objects. They may, however, show considerable interest in people and interpersonal interactions. Children whose families put considerable emphasis on nurturing and do not push for early independence may lack some of the self-help skills displayed by their age peers. Children who have been very ill or malnourished, or those who have had very limited or uneven nurturing may show deficits in cognitive abilities as well as in social interactions. Delays in any of these areas are important to determine, but the child's experiential base must be considered before the information is used for diagnosis or intervention planning.

Guidelines for selecting appropriate assessment instruments and strategies. Before selecting any assessment strategy or procedure, members of the assessment team may wish to consider alternative ways to gather the same information. If a child has severe multiple disabilities, observation and family report typically yield the most useful information regardless of culture and language. Even for children with less severe disabilities, observation and report are preferred to

results of a standardized instrument that may be invalid and unreliable.

It is not uncommon for cultural taboos to arise during an assessment. For example, shaking a rattle found in the home of a Native American infant to check hearing is not considered appropriate. The way in which a child is handled during an assessment is equally important in some cultures. Patting a Muslim child on the head is incorrect. Washing off pollen or dyes on Native American or East Indian children is not appropriate; offering enthusiastic compliments and praise may cause Latino families to fear that attention has been unduly called to the child, putting him or her in danger (Lynch, 1993). When selecting assessment strategies, check with a cultural mediator who can provide insight into beliefs that the family may have that could lead to discomfort or embarrassment in an assessment.

Assessors typically try to determine when and where the assessment should take place in order to interact with the child in optimal circumstances. In addition to the considerations that are a part of that decision for any child, it may be important to ensure that the time meets the family's cultural preferences. For example, some families may depend upon astrologers to determine auspicious times for important life events. Although one day may be like any other to the professional members of the assessment team, for the family, one may be associated with better luck than another. An additional consideration has to do with various holidays and religious celebrations that may be important to the family but unfamiliar to the assessors. Learning more about each of the cultures, religions, and practices in one's own community can prevent discomfort caused by conflicts in families' and professionals' priorities.

Finally, part of the planning process is determining what is needed during the assessment. Interpreter services may need to be arranged. Materials that are familiar to the child may need to be gathered and procedures and instruction materials may need to be translated.

Conducting the Assessment

Family members and assessors need to feel as comfortable as possible with one another. Assessment is not easy for any family, but when everything in the setting is unfamiliar, it is even more difficult. Thinking through the procedures and the process and considering the setting from the family's perspective may help increase everyone's comfort. The following issues may need to be considered to make the assessment go smoothly.

Issue: Supporting Communication and Understanding Exemplary child assessment requires a set of highly technical skills as well as the ability to be flexible and attend to the responses and reactions of children and their family members. All of the skills and behaviors that assessors look for when a child is being assessed are not intuitively obvious. For example, for someone unfamiliar with what can be learned from a specific task, putting forms in a formboard does not appear to provide much information about the child's performance or ability. However, the assessor may use formboards to assess the child's grasp, reach, motor planning skills, problem solving strategies, and attention, and to screen for tremors. Although a wealth of information can be gained by observing children perform specific tasks for which the demands are well known, what is being observed and learned needs to be made explicit.

> *Jennifer's parents were concerned about her development, so they requested that she be assessed by the school district's transdisciplinary team. The team members requested that they conduct the assessment in the family's home. When they arrived, one person, who had brought a bag of toys, played with Jennifer, another talked to her parents, and the third observed and listened. Jennifer's parents thought that Jennifer was going to be assessed. Why were the professionals just playing and asking questions? Why didn't they do something?*

Standardized assessments are not the only types of assessment about which families may

have questions. As play-based assessment has become more common (Linder, 1990), many parents inquire about what assessors are learning from play.

Guidelines for supporting communication and understanding. When assessors explain what they are observing and why it is important, assessment tasks and procedures make more sense. Assessors can support communication and understanding with families by describing what they will be doing in an assessment, how they will be doing it, and why it is important. When assessment is demystified, it can increase everyone's comfort in the situation.

Another component to support communication and understanding is to ask for the parents' or family members' perspectives on the child's performance in the assessment situation. Assessments conducted outside of the child's natural environment by an unfamiliar assessor may not yield results that accurately reflect the child's skills and abilities. If an assessment must occur in such a situation, parents should be asked to comment on how they judged the performance. Was it similar to or different from the child's typical responses? Were any materials used that are unfamiliar to the child? How did they think the child responded to the assessor?

Issue: Creating a Secure and Nonthreatening Environment For both the child and the family, a secure and nonthreatening assessment environment is optimal. All individuals have settings and situations in which they are comfortable and those in which they are not. For many people, assessments and evaluations—whether they relate to one's health, financial status, or job performance—are situations that create anxiety. This anxiety is heightened when the assessment involves your own child or someone who is very close to you, especially if the assessment might result in bad news. Creating an assessment environment that is as comfortable as possible for all involved will ease some of this anxiety. Consider the following scenario.

> *Latanya was born in her mother's seventh month of pregnancy. At birth she weighed under 1500 grams, and she spent the first three months of her life in the neonatal intensive care unit. At 15 months of age, she was scheduled to be assessed at a follow-up clinic connected to the NICU where she was born. Latanya's mother, Myrene, dreaded this assessment, but she knew that it was important to learn more about how Latanya was doing. When she arrived at the clinic, she was told that the assessors were running a little late and that she would have to wait for about 45 minutes before they would see her and Latanya. As they waited, Latanya became tired and fussy. When it was finally their turn, Myrene explained to the assessors that Latanya was not at her best. They brushed off her comments, took Latanya from her, and proceeded with the assessment. Several times Myrene tried to tell them that Latanya wasn't doing things for them that she did at home, but they didn't seem to be listening. Following the assessment, they said that they had some concerns but didn't share what they were. They told Myrene that they'd have to go write their report and that they'd ask her to come back in a couple of weeks. Before she had time to ask any questions, they were gone. Myrene left the clinic full of fear. What were their concerns? Why didn't they talk with her about them? Was there something so seriously wrong that they were afraid to tell her? How could she possibly wait two weeks to know what they were thinking?*

It may seem that Myrene's experience is too bad to be true, but things like that do happen. Instead of making assessment procedures less threatening, some settings actually raise anxiety. Although it is not possible to eliminate all concerns, the guidelines that follow suggest ways in which thoughtful planning can reduce the threat of assessment.

Guidelines for creating a nonthreatening environment. Developmentally appropriate assessments are built around collaborative alliances with the child's family. This alliance must be built through contact and communication with the child's parents and caregivers. This alliance can help reduce the threat posed by the assessment process. Knowing who will be working with the child and what they will be doing enables parents to feel more comfortable with the process.

Conducting the assessment in surroundings that are familiar to the child and the family may also help to reduce anxiety. Most children and families are more comfortable in their own homes than in a clinic. When assessments are conducted in the home, families from some cultural groups may serve food to their guests. For some families, sharing food and drink is an important custom that demonstrates the family's generosity and signifies respect for the visitors. The guests' acceptance and enjoyment of what is offered is an important part of the ritual.

For those who prefer not to have the assessment take place in their home, making the assessment setting as comfortable as possible is important. One way to do this may be to create a setting that is professional yet friendly in appearance by providing, for example, chairs that are comfortable for adults; toys for children; extra diapers; attractive pictures, posters, or children's art; and juice, tea, coffee, soft drinks, and snacks for adults and children. The point is not that the setting has to be expensively decorated or extensively furnished, but it should be a welcoming environment that invites families in.

Even more important than the message that the physical space sends is the message that the assessors communicate. The message should be one of respect, equality, support, and expertise. Although families come to professionals to seek their expertise, the professionals should not assume that they are the only experts. Each family brings a wealth of knowledge about their child's temperament, behavior, likes, dislikes, skills, and abilities. Knowledge of such factors informs the assessment and is extremely valuable for adequately assessing the child's needs and the family's concerns, priorities, resources, and preferences.

Knowledge of family and culture-specific information may assist assessors to reduce the threat in assessment settings. Some families may prefer a very direct approach; others may want to spend time talking with the assessor and socializing before the assessment is conducted. Some will want to begin over a cup of tea and seemingly unrelated conversation; others will want to maximize the child's time with the assessor. No family wants to feel rushed or pushed or that the assessors are not doing a thorough job.

Exchanging information about the assessment findings immediately after its conclusion can help to allay fears. Instead of sending families away to wait for results, discussing what was observed and how the child performed can mitigate concerns. Of equal importance is getting the family members' perceptions of how the child performed. Was it a good day for the child or a bad day? Was the performance typical or atypical? Ensuring that families know that assessment is an ongoing process and that there will be other opportunities to gather information can also make the situation less threatening. Finally, allowing time for questions and explanations and making it clear that families can contact the team member with whom they are most familiar if they have questions also reduces the threat of assessment.

Interpreting and Presenting Assessment Findings

Assessment is technical. It requires considerable training in measurement, the areas being assessed, specific instruments and strategies, and typical and atypical child development. Information gathered in assessments is often associated with technical language or jargon. One of the responsibilities of the assessment team is to make the information clear to those who have not been technically trained. Making assessment information clear is even more difficult when family members and assessors do not share the same language and must work through interpreters and translators.

Issue: Sharing Information Clearly and in a Caring Manner In addition to making information clear, assessors are responsible for making it as understandable and acceptable as

possible. Because assessments do not always result in findings that families are hoping to hear, it is important to consider how the information will be received and to use strategies that make it as easy as possible to hear.

> *Gavin's parents felt that he should be assessed prior to entry into a neighborhood preschool because of their concerns over his behavior. He spoke very little, spent hours spinning toys, and had tantrums whenever his routine was changed. After a comprehensive assessment, the team members sat down with Gavin's parents to discuss their findings. Several read their reports, which were full of acronyms, columns of standard scores, and paragraphs that detailed his difficult behavior during the assessments. After each of the assessors had presented this information, the chair of the group said, "Well, Mr. and Mrs. Carson, it seems clear that Gavin is autistic." Gavin is now 23 years old, and his parents still describe that experience in preschool as one of the worst moments of their lives.*

There is no good way to deliver bad news, but some ways are kinder and more caring than others. The treatment of Gavin's parents was neither kind nor caring.

Guidelines for sharing information clearly and in a caring manner. An important guideline for making information clear is to present it in the language the family uses. If this involves an interpreter, the guidelines presented earlier in this chapter can be used to increase the likelihood that families and professionals will have a positive experience. A critical factor when working with an interpreter is to allow enough time for the interaction to take place. Interpreting takes double the usual time needed, and it is a process that cannot be rushed.

For families who share the same primary language as the assessors, there may still be communication problems because of technical terms. The goal is for the family to understand exactly what is being said, not to impress them with fancy language. A rule of thumb is to present information as if you were presenting it to a friend who is bright but knows nothing about assessment, child development, or disability.

In addition to language considerations, some families from diverse cultural groups may have different understandings of the words that are used in relation to children with special needs (Harry, 1992b). To avoid confusion, a cultural guide is particularly important to help the assessment team and family members reach a common understanding of what each is saying.

A final guideline applies across all cultures and languages. Because no parents want to hear that their child is having problems with learning, behavior, or development, it is important to find the most sensitive way to present the information. Emphasizing the child's strengths while being realistic about the areas of need; allowing time for family members to process the information; letting silences occur; listening; supporting; accepting parents' anger or frustration; and demonstrating one's own caring and concern for the child and the family make the process more humane. These practices are more natural and sincere if the bearer of bad news has taken time to establish relationships with the family prior to the assessment process.

Family-Professional Decision Making

A final step in the assessment process is making decisions about intervention services. Decisions should be made collaboratively by family members and professionals, with each bringing his or her expertise to the table. However, it is not always easy. Professionals have to view family members as having knowledge and preferences that are important to the decision. Likewise, family members must view themselves as having expertise that is important to the decision-making process. Reaching this understanding is sometimes complicated by differences in language, communication style, and culture.

Issue: Determining What Families Want
When languages, culturally determined expectations, and styles of communication differ, it is especially challenging to engage in joint decision making. The following example illustrates one of the problems that can occur.

> *Depak was assessed six months ago and it was jointly decided by his parents and the professionals on the assessment team that he should be enrolled in a preschool program where the staff would receive support and consultation from one of the preschool resource teachers. In addition, Depak's parents, who had recently arrived from India, would receive home visits to help them understand more about Depak's development and the range of community services that would be available to them. At the time, the parents seemed quite pleased with the decisions that were made at the meeting. They nodded in apparent agreement and signed all of the forms. However, Depak has attended the preschool program only a few days over the past six months, and his parents have never been available when the home visitor arrives at the time they have scheduled for the visit. The resource teacher and the home visitor are provoked about the family's lack of follow-through, and they have begun to question how much they care about helping Depak. On the other hand, Depak's parents can't believe that the teachers wanted to enroll Depak in a regular preschool program where there would be children without disabilities. They also can't imagine having someone come into their home to discuss community services for Depak's needs. Why do they insist on calling attention to Depak's disability? Of course they agreed to what was suggested and signed the papers, but they were just being polite.*

It is often difficult for professionals to determine what families want. Different values, beliefs, experiences, and styles of communicating result in clashes even when both parties are trying to understand and work with each other.

Guidelines for determining what families want. Perhaps the best way to determine what any family wants is to listen to what they say (or sometimes don't say). Even small interchanges can provide valuable information that will enable professionals to make suggestions that are consistent with family concerns, priorities, and preferences. In addition, a cultural guide who understands the cultural implications of various decisions can be a valuable resource in the decision-making process.

Professionals should be aware of culture- and family-specific information that will help them determine who the real decision makers are. In some families, grandparents may play that role. In others, elders or chiefs may need to be involved in all decisions related to the family's welfare. In some cultures, decisions are not made by the mother and father, but are brought to others because of their wisdom or role in the larger community.

A final caveat relates to differences in communication patterns and styles that may interfere with understanding. When families from diverse cultures nod in apparent agreement, sign the forms, or smile as decisions are being made, it does not necessarily mean that they are in agreement with what is occurring or that they intend to act on the decisions that are being made. Instead, they are showing their politeness and deference to presumed authority. When families do not do what professionals expect, it is often because professionals had inaccurate expectations.

SUMMARY OF KEY CONCEPTS

- Families and children who are served by early intervention and early childhood special education programs are characterized by their diversity in culture, ethnicity, race, language, family structure, composition, values, and socioeconomic status. Because this diversity among families is often greater than the diversity among service providers, it is important to examine professional and program practices to ensure that they are sensitive to families' preferences and backgrounds.

- Family diversity requires that professionals strive to increase their competence in cross-cultural interactions. A lifelong process, increasing cross-cultural competence includes three components: clarifying one's own values; learning about cultures, values, beliefs, and behaviors that differ from one's own; and applying the information acquired through self-examination and information gathering to professionals' practice.

- Working with and through interpreters and translators requires time and skill. All interactions that are mediated by translation require thoughtful planning, additional time to conduct, and debriefing of all concerned.

- Culture influences child-rearing practices, and these influences must be considered when gathering data. Developmental milestones are not universal and may differ, depending on the family's views of infancy and early childhood.

- Cultural, ethnic, linguistic, and sociocultural diversity affect every aspect of the assessment process. Assessors can work with families and cultural mediators to develop guidelines for culturally competent assessment practices that respect families' backgrounds and preferences and ensure that the information gathered is accurate and useful to both the interventionist and the family.

REFERENCES

Anderson, P. P., & Fenichel, E. S. (1989). *Serving culturally diverse families of infants and toddlers with disabilities.* Washington, DC: NCCIP.

Banks, R. A. (2001). *Sensitivity to cultural and linguistic diversity in early intervention family information gathering* (CLAS Technical Report #9).

Champaign, IL: University of Illinois at Urbana-Champaign, Early Childhood Research Institute on Culturally and Linguistically Appropriate Services.

Barrera, I. (2000). Honoring differences: Essential features of appropriate ECSE services for young children from diverse sociocultural environments. *Young Exceptional Children, 3,* 17–24.

Barrera, I. (1996). Thoughts on the assessment of young children whose sociocultural background is unfamiliar to the assessor. In S. J. Meisels & E. Fenichel (Eds.), *New visions for the developmental assessment of infants and young children* (pp. 69–84). Washington DC: Zero to Three–National Center for Infants, Toddlers, and Families.

Benhamida, L. (1988). *Interpreting in mental health settings for refugees and others: A guide for the professional interpreter.* Minneapolis, MN: University of Minnesota Refugee Assistance Program, Mental Health Technical Assistance Center.

Chan, S. (1990). Early intervention with culturally diverse families of infants and toddlers with disabilities. *Infants and Young Children, 3*(2), 78–87.

Chen, D., Chan, S., Brekken, L., & Valverde, A. (Producers), (2000). *Conversations for three: Communicating through interpreters* [Videotape]. Baltimore: Paul H. Brookes.

Chen, D., McLean, M., Corso, R., & Bruns, D. (2001). *Working together in early childhood intervention: Cultural considerations in helping relationships and service utilization* (CLAS Technical Report #11). Champaign, IL: University of Illinois at Urbana-Champaign, Early Childhood Research Institute on Culturally and Linguistically Appropriate Services.

Children's Defense Fund. (2000). *Yearbook 2000: The state of America's children.* Washington, DC: Author.

ChildStats.gov. (1999). *America's children 1999.* Retrieved January 20, 2002, from *http://www.childstats.gov/ac1999/poptxt.asp*

Colarusso, R. P., & Kana, T. G. (1991). Public Law 99-457, Part H, Infant and toddler programs: Status and implications. *Focus on Exceptional Children, 23*(8), 1–12.

Dale, M. L., & Hoshino, L. B. (1984). Belief systems of Hispanic and pan-Asian populations in California: Implications for the delivery of care in the neonatal intensive care unit. *Journal of the California Perinatal Association, 4*(2), 21–25.

Diverse, yet distinct. (2001, April 1). *The Union Tribune,* p. A21.

Dunst, C. J. (1993). Implications of risk and opportunity factors for assessment and intervention practices. *Topics in Early Childhood Special Education, 13,* 143–153.

Dunst, C. J., Trivette, C., & Deal, A. (1988). *Enabling and empowering families: Principles and guidelines for practice.* Cambridge, MA: Brookline Books.

Fewell, R. R. (2000). Assessment of young children with special needs: Foundation for tomorrow. *Topics in Early Childhood Special Education, 20*(1), 38–42.

Gollnick, D. M., & Chinn, P. C. (1990). *Multicultural education in a pluralistic society.* Upper Saddle River, NJ: Merrill/Prentice Hall.

Green, J. W. (1982). *Cultural awareness in the human services.* Upper Saddle River, NJ: Prentice Hall.

Greenspan, S. I., & Meisels, S. J. (1996). Toward a new vision for the developmental assessment of infants and young children. In S. J. Meisels & E. Fenichel (Eds.), *New visions for the developmental assessment of infants and young children* (pp. 11–26). Washington DC: Zero to Three–National Center for Infants, Toddlers, and Families.

Hanson, M. J., & Lynch, E. W. (1992). Family diversity: Implications for policy and practice. *Topics in Early Childhood Special Education, 12*(3), 283–306.

Hanson, M. J., Lynch, E. W., & Wayman, K. I. (1990). Honoring the cultural diversity of families when gathering data. *Topics in Early Childhood Special Education, 10*(1), 112–131.

Harry, B. (1992a). Restructuring the participation of African-American parents in special education. *Exceptional Children, 59,* 123–131.

Harry, B. (1992b). *Cultural diversity, families, and the special education system: Communication and empowerment.* New York: Teachers College Press.

Harry, B. (1992c). Developing cultural self-awareness: The first step in values clarification for early interventionists. *Topics in Early Childhood Special Education, 12,* 333–350.

Harry, B., Kalyanpur, M., & Day, M. (1999). *Building cultural reciprocity with families: Case studies in special education.* Baltimore: Paul H. Brookes.

Hayes, A. (1990). The context and future of judgment-based assessment. *Topics in Early Childhood Special Education, 10*(3), 1–12.

Joe, J. R., & Malach, R. S. (1998). Families with Native American roots. In E. W. Lynch & M. J. Hanson (Eds.), *Developing cross-cultural competence: A guide for working with children and their families* (2nd ed.) (pp. 127–162). Baltimore: Paul H. Brookes.

Kosmin, B. A., Mayer, E., & Keysar, A. (2001). *American religious identification survey.* Retrieved January 20,

2002, from The Graduate Center of the City University of New York Web site: *http://www.gc.cuny.edu/studies/key_findings.htm*

Langdon, H. W., Siegel, V., Halog, L., & Sánchez-Boyce, M. (1994). *The interpreter translator process in the educational setting.* (Available from Resources in Special Education, WestEd, 429 J Street, Sacramento, CA 95814.)

Linder, T. W. (1990). *Transdisciplinary play-based assessment.* Baltimore: Paul H. Brookes.

Lynch, E. W. (1998). Developing cross-cultural competence. In E. W. Lynch & M. J. Hanson, *Developing cross-cultural competence: A guide for working with children and their families* (2nd ed.) (pp. 47–86). Baltimore: Paul H. Brookes.

Lynch, E. W. (1993, June). *Cross-cultural competence: From surprise to sensitivity to success.* Paper presented at the 28th Annual Meeting of the Association for the Care of Children's Health, Chicago.

Lynch, E. W., & Hanson, M. J. (Eds.). (1998). *Developing cross-cultural competence: A guide for working with children and families* (2nd ed.). Baltimore: Paul H. Brookes.

Lynch, E. W., & Hanson, M. J. (1993). Changing demographics: Implications for training in early intervention. *Infants and Young Children, 6*(1), 50–55.

McConnell, S. R. (2000). Assessment in early intervention and early childhood special education: Building on the past to project into our future. *Topics in Early Childhood Special Education, 20*(1), 43–48.

McGonigel, M. J., Kaufman, R. K., & Hurth, J. L. (1991). The IFSP sequence. In M. J. McGonigel, R. K. Kaufman, & B. H. Johnson (Eds.), *Guidelines and recommended practices for the individualized family service plan* (2nd ed.) (pp. 15–28). Washington, DC: Association for the Care of Children's Health.

McLean, M. (2000). *Conducting child assessments* (CLAS Technical Report #2). Champaign, IL: University of Illinois at Urbana-Champaign, Early Childhood Research Institute on Culturally and Linguistically Appropriate Services.

McLoughlin, J. A., & Lewis, R. B. (2001). *Assessing special students* (5th ed.). Upper Saddle River, NJ: Merrill/Prentice Hall.

Meisels, S. J., & Fenichel, E., (Eds.) (1996). *New visions for the developmental assessment of infants and young children.* Washington DC: Zero to Three–National Center for Infants, Toddlers, and Families.

Montaigne, M. de. (1580). *Les essais.* Bordeaus, France: Simon Millanges.

Ohtake, Y., Fowler, S. A., & Santos, R. M. (2001). *Working with interpreters to plan early childhood services with limited-English-proficient families* (CLAS Technical Report #12). Champaign, IL: University of Illinois at Urbana-Champaign, Early Childhood Research Institute on Culturally and Linguistically Appropriate Services.

Rhodes, W., & Brown, W. (Eds.). (1991). *Why some children succeed despite the odds.* New York: Praeger.

Riche, M. F. (2000). America's diversity and growth: Signposts for the 21st century. *Population Bulletin, 55*(2). Washington, DC: Population Reference Bureau.

Sexton, D., Thompson, B., Perez, J., & Rheams, T. (1990). Maternal versus professional estimates of developmental status for young children with handicaps: An ecological approach. *Topics in Early Childhood Special Education, 10*(3), 80–95.

Sharifzadeh, V.-S. (1998). Families with Middle Eastern roots. In E. W. Lynch & M. J. Hanson (Eds.), *Developing cross-cultural competence: A guide for working with children and their families* (pp. 441–482). Baltimore: Paul H. Brookes.

StevensDominguez, M., Beam, G., & Thomas, P. (1989). *Guide for family-centered services.* Albuquerque, NM: University of New Mexico Press.

U.S. Census Bureau. (1990). Detailed language spoken at home and ability to speak English for persons 5 years and over—50 languages with greatest number or speakers. Retrieved January 20, 2002, from *http://www.census.gov/population/socdemo/language/table5.txt*

U.S. Census Bureau. (n.d. A). *Profile of general demographic characteristics: 2000.* Retrieved January 17, 2002, from *http://factfinder.census.gov/servlet/BasicFactsServlet*

U.S. Census Bureau (n.d. B). *Profile of general demographic characteristics: 2000.* Retrieved January 17, 2002, from *http://factfinder.census.gov/servlet/QTTable?ds_name=DEC_2000_SF1_U&geo_id=01000US&qr_name=DEC_2000_SF1_U_DP1*

Wayman, K. I., Lynch, E. W., & Hanson, M. J. (1991). Home-based early childhood services: Cultural sensitivity in a family systems approach. *Topics in Early Childhood Special Education, 10*(4), 56–75.

Yonemitsu, D. M., & Cleveland, J. O. (1992). *Culturally competent service delivery: A training manual for bilingual/bicultural case managers.* (Available from Southeast Asian Developmental Disabilities Project of the San Diego Imperial Counties Developmental Services, Inc., 4355 Ruffin Road, San Diego, CA 92123.)

Zuniga, M. E. (1998). Families with Latino roots. In E. W. Lynch & M. J. Hanson (Eds.). *Developing cross-cultural competence: A guide for working with children and their families* (pp. 209–250). Baltimore: Paul H. Brookes.

Identification and Referral

Mary McLean

University of Wisconsin–Milwaukee

Vignette 1: Maria is a child-care provider who has recently started her first job in a large urban child care center. She is concerned about one of her children, who at 15 months still isn't walking and does not produce any words. Maria knows this is late but she also was taught that not all children are the same in their patterns of development. The child's parents have not expressed any concerns. Maria has heard about a state program for young children with disabilities but she's not sure this child has a disability and she doesn't know how to contact that program.

Vignette 2: Yvonne gave birth to Carlos when she was 16. She was able to finish high school and now has a job. But she is worried about Carlos. At 32 months of age, he doesn't talk much at all except to repeat a few phrases he heard on TV. He can walk and even runs. However, when they are with Yvonne's sisters and her young children, Carlos just seems to be very different. He doesn't play with the other children but instead plays with the same toy over and over. Yvonne's mother, who watches Carlos while Yvonne works, explains his behavior as "just Carlos." Yvonne doesn't know who to ask for help.

Finding those children who are in need of early intervention services is part of the assessment process in early intervention. Unlike school-age children, infants, toddlers, and preschoolers in most states are not required to participate in publicly supported educational programs. Having a program available for young children with special needs does not ensure that the children who need such services will find their way to the program. Similarly, as seen in the vignette above, parents frequently report that it takes much time and effort to discover how to access assessment and intervention services for a child with special needs. To address these problems, Child Find programs have been established in each state and territory. This chapter will present information relative to Child Find programs and to assessment instruments which are used to assist in the identification and referral process.

RATIONALE AND DEFINITIONS

The rationale for establishing a system of child identification and referral is based on the importance of intervening as early as possible, the need to support families of young children with special needs, and the legal mandates for child identification with which states must comply. Without such a system, many young children will go without needed services until they are of school age. It has been generally established that early intervention programs are effective (Guralnick, 1997). In fact Public Law 105-17, the 1997 Amendments to the Individuals with Disabilities Education Act (IDEA) states that there is a need for early intervention (birth to age 3) programs in order to reduce costs by minimizing the need for special education and related services when infants and toddlers reach school age (20 USC 1431 [a]). To the extent that children are not identified early, services may be more costly.

Another reason for establishing a system of child identification is to assist families in their initial search for assistance with their child. At a time when the family is dealing with the difficulties inherent in suspecting or learning about their child's disability, the resulting stress can be lessened if access to information about services is readily available to them. Unfortunately, many families have stories about the frustration they faced in finding out what services might be available for their child. Professionals in education, medicine, social services, and child care can help by being knowledgeable about early intervention services in their state and community.

Finally, there are legal mandates for child identification with which states must comply. Both Part B and Part C of IDEA require Child Find procedures, as do other programs serving young children. The legal basis for Child Find is described below.

Child Find is a systematic process of identifying infants and young children who are eligible or potentially eligible for enrollment in intervention programs. Child Find efforts are designed to inform the general public, both professionals and nonprofessionals, about typical and atypical child development as well as referral procedures if assessment or intervention is thought to be necessary for a particular child. Children with readily identified and diagnosed disabilities are typically the easiest for medical, educational, or social service professionals to identify. Child Find activities for this group consist of ensuring appropriate referral as soon as the disability is suspected or diagnosed. However, the diagnosis of a disability is not readily accomplished with many young children. Some children may be "at risk" for developing a disability because of environmental or biological factors. Others may be suspected of having a disability by parents or caregivers in the absence of a readily identifiable disability and in the absence of any risk factors. For these young children, screening and child monitoring systems can help to identify the need for services as early as possible.

Screening is an assessment process, the purpose of which is to identify children who may need further evaluation in order to determine whether early intervention should be provided (Meisels & Provence, 1989). Screening tests are generally quickly administered and inexpensive and yield only a determination of whether or not further evaluation is needed.

Child monitoring or *tracking* is a system for providing continuous monitoring of the developmental progress of children who are thought to be at risk of manifesting developmental difficulties. Sometimes referred to as a "high-risk registry" or "follow-up services," a tracking system can also provide data that are useful to agencies for program planning purposes.

CHILD FIND

Legal Basis of Child Find

IDEA requires the establishment of a Child Find program in each state for children from birth through age 21. Part C of the 1997 Amendments to IDEA also requires a comprehensive Child Find system. The lead agency for infant/toddler services in each state, with the assistance of the governor-appointed Interagency Coordinating Council, must ensure coordination of the Child Find system with all other state efforts to identify children for various education, health, and social service programs, including (a) Part B of the Individuals with Disabilities Education Act (IDEA), (b) Maternal and Child Health programs under Title V of the Social Security Act, (c) the Early and Periodic Screening, Diagnosis, and Treatment (EPSDT) program under Title XIX of the Social Security Act, (d) programs under the Developmental Disabilities Act, (e) Head Start, and (f) the Supplemental Security Income program under Title XVI of the Social Security Act (34 C.F.R. 303.321). Coordination with these programs must ensure that there will not be duplication of efforts and that the Child Find system will be implemented effectively within the state by making use of existing resources of the state. In many states, the Interagency Coordinating Council established under Part C serves in an advisory capacity for infant, toddler, and preschool programs in the state, thus helping to coordinate Child Find efforts for children from birth through age 5.

The Child Find system that is developed within a state must also include procedures to be used by primary referral sources when referring a child for evaluation and assessment or for intervention. Primary referral sources are specified as hospitals, physicians, parents, daycare programs, local education agencies, public health facilities, social service agencies, and other health care providers. Specifically, for infants and toddlers, the system must ensure that referrals for evaluation and assessment or intervention are made no more than two working days after a child has been identified by a referral source.

Components of Child Find Programs

Bourland and Harbin (1987) suggested that Child Find should be broadly defined and should include at least ten components, which are

---

Component Description

Definition of target population The population to be identified must be defined and described.

Coordination Coordination of Child Find activities across agencies must occur to ensure efficient use of resources.

Financial resources The limited financial resources available for child services must be reviewed to ensure efficient use.

Public awareness Information about services and how to access them is described through the mass media and other communication mechanisms.

Referrals A mechanism must exist for different agencies and professionals to be informed about making appropriate referrals to other agencies.

Screening and prescreening Procedures should exist for informal screening information being disseminated to the public (e.g., listing of developmental skills on a brochure) and formal screening available to individuals and groups.

Data management, registries and tracking systems A means of tracking children, ensuring follow-up, and maintaining records must be established.

Case management Some person or agency must be responsible for maintaining contact with identified children and ensuring that they obtain necessary services.

Diagnostic assessment Services must be available for conducting diagnostic assessments and for identifying the intervention services needed.

Trained personnel Personnel must be trained to implement the Child Find program.

FIGURE 5.1

Components of comprehensive child find programs
Note: Based on information from *START Resource Packet: Child Find,* by B. Bourland and G. Harbin, 1987, Chapel Hill, NC: Frank Porter Graham Child Development Center, University of North Carolina.

described in Figure 5.1. In any state, and even in a particular community, responsibility for these components may certainly cut across agencies and service programs. Coordination is essential so that duplication of efforts can be reduced and gaps in services can be identified. Formalized interagency agreements have been developed in many states to assist in the coordination of child identification efforts. The realization that every community is unique also has prompted many states to establish local coordinating groups and even formalized local agreements to assist in coordination.

Public Awareness Program

IDEA also specifies that each state must implement a public awareness program focusing on the early identification of children who are eligible for services. The lead agency for Part C must make available to all primary referral sources (specified earlier) information to be given to parents on the availability of early intervention services. In addition, the public must be informed about the state's early intervention program, the Child Find system (including how to make referrals and how to gain access to evaluation and intervention services), and the state central directory, which includes information on early intervention services, resources, and experts available in the state. The law suggests that methods used to inform the public might include television, radio, and newspaper releases, pamphlets and posters in locations such as hospitals and doctors' offices, and the use of a toll-free telephone service (34 C.F.R. 303.320).

CHILD MONITORING

As part of the Child Find program, many states have implemented a system for monitoring or tracking infants and young children who are considered to be at risk due to identified biological or environmental factors. By monitoring the development of these children frequently throughout infancy and the preschool years, a program can help to ensure that children who are in need of early intervention will receive services as soon as possible. Under Part C, states are required to have a system for compiling data on the number of eligible infants and toddlers who are in need of early intervention services, the number actually served, and the types of services provided. The development of a monitoring program can ensure compliance with this requirement of Part C as well and can thus also serve an important planning function for states and communities. The potential for monitoring programs to serve a role in the prevention of disability has also become apparent. In order to understand these potential benefits of a monitoring system, it is important to first understand the concepts of *prevention* and *at risk* as they relate to early intervention.

Prevention

Prevention efforts, as discussed in the public health literature, are frequently identified as occurring at three levels (Sameroff & Fiese, 1990; Simeonsson, 1991). *Primary prevention* is practiced prior to the onset of the disease (or disability) and has the effect of reducing or removing factors that contribute to the condition, thereby preventing the occurrence of the condition. *Secondary prevention* is practiced after the condition has been identified but before it has caused disability, thereby reducing the occurrence of disability. *Tertiary prevention* occurs after the disability has been experienced, with the goal of reducing other problems that might occur directly or indirectly as a result of the disability.

Providing early intervention services to children who are at risk is a form of primary prevention. The definition of *at risk* will be discussed further in the following section. Intervention in this case is provided before symptoms (problems or delays in development) are apparent. Under Part C, states may choose whether to provide intervention services to infants and toddlers who are at risk. In some states, children who are at risk but do not qualify for early intervention services are provided with a monitoring service, which is a form of secondary prevention. A tracking or monitoring system facilitates the early identification of problems and thereby provides the opportunity to intervene early and reduce or eliminate the problem in development. An example of this would be an infant with chronic ear infections. Monitoring this child's development would allow the early identification of hearing problems or a speech and language delay. The earliest intervention might then prevent the need for special education services for this child at a later time.

Meisels (1991) suggests that the Child Find and public awareness requirements of IDEA may, in fact, lead to primary prevention activities. For example, if, as a result of public awareness activities, a woman abstains from drinking alcohol during her pregnancy, public awareness efforts have served a primary prevention role.

Determination of eligibility for special education services has traditionally followed a treatment approach in which eligibility is contingent on some predetermined criterion, usually the identification of a disability (Simeonsson, 1991). Only after a condition has become manifest is treatment offered. This is an example of tertiary prevention in that intervention here might reduce other problems that directly or indirectly occur as a result of the disability. For example, intervention services for a child with cerebral palsy may prevent the development of muscle contractures (shortened muscles) and thus also may prevent the occurrence of joint deformities. The child will still have cerebral palsy but may have increased capacity to move in his environment as a result of early intervention.

Viewing intervention from a primary, secondary, and tertiary prevention perspective may result in a more inclusionary and thus more effective approach to reducing the incidence of developmental delay and disability in the population of infants and young children. As indicated earlier, Part C allows the provision of services to children who are at risk before a disability or delay is evident. States that do not choose to provide intervention services to this group may decide to provide monitoring services so that problems can be identified as soon as possible, and the impact on the child can be minimized through early intervention. The 1997 Amendments to IDEA allow any state that does not provide services to at-risk infants and toddlers to identify, evaluate and refer at-risk infants and toddlers and conduct periodic follow-up on each child referred to determine if the condition of the child has changed relative to eligibility (20 U.S.C. §1438[4]).

Determination of Risk

As explained above and in Chapter 1, according to the federal definition of eligibility for services under Part C (see Figure 5.2), there is a category of children designated as at risk who may receive early intervention services at a state's discretion (in other words, the state is not required to serve these children but may use federal money to do so). Discussions of risk factors in children have traditionally been based on three categories identified by Tjossem (1976) as the following:

Established risk: diagnosed medical disorders of known etiology bearing relatively well-known expectancies for developmental outcome within specified ranges of developmental delay (p. 5).

Biological risk: a history of prenatal, perinatal, neonatal, and early development events suggestive of biological insult(s) to the developing central nervous system and which, either singly or collectively, increase the probability of later appearing aberrant development (p. 5).

Environmental risk: biologically sound infants for whom early life experiences including maternal and family care, health care, opportunities for expression of adaptive behaviors, and patterns of physical and social stimulation are sufficiently limiting

---

The term "infant or toddler with a disability":

(A) means an individual under 3 years of age who needs early intervention services because the individual:

    (i) is experiencing developmental delays, as measured by appropriate diagnostic instruments and procedures in one or more of the areas of cognitive development, physical development, communication development, social or emotional development, and adaptive development; or

    (ii) has a diagnosed physical or mental condition which has a high probability of resulting in developmental delay; and

(B) may also include, at a state's discretion, at-risk infants and toddlers. The term "at-risk infant or toddler" means an individual under 3 years of age who would be at risk of experiencing a substantial developmental delay if early intervention services were not provided to the individual.

FIGURE 5.2

Statutory language pertaining to eligibility definitions—IDEA, Part C

Note: From amendments to the Individuals with Disabilities Education Act (IDEA '97), 20 U.S.C. §632(5)(A), §632(5)(B), and §632(1) (1997).

to the extent that, without corrective intervention, they impart high probability for delayed development (p. 5).

Biological risk conditions include such factors as low birth weight, intraventricular hemorrhage (brain bleeds) at birth, and preterm birth. The presence of one or more biological risk conditions does not necessarily mean that a child will eventually demonstrate a disability or a delay in development.

Environmental risk conditions include such factors as poverty, young parental age, child abuse or neglect, and the presence of developmental disability in the parents. Again, such factors may place a child at risk but will not automatically ensure that the child will develop a disability or delay in development.

Established risk corresponds to the second category of eligibility listed in Figure 5.2, (Aii) children with a diagnosed condition that has a high probability of resulting in developmental delay. As defined in the law, examples of conditions that fit into this category include:

> chromosomal abnormalities; genetic or congenital disorders; severe sensory impairments, including hearing and vision; inborn errors of metabolism; disorders reflecting disturbance of the development of the nervous system; congenital infections; disorders secondary to exposure to toxic substances, including fetal alcohol syndrome; and severe attachment disorders (Note 1, 34 C.F.R. 303.16).

Children in this category are automatically eligible for services under Part C. There are, however, differences among the states concerning which conditions qualify a child for services. Unless a state's definition of this category is very clear, there also may be differences in eligibility practices among early intervention programs within a state.

The category of *at risk* in the federal law (see B in Figure 5.2) pertains primarily to biological and environmental risk as defined above. As indicated earlier, a state may decide to provide early intervention services to children who are at risk, but it is not required to do so. According to Harbin, Danaher,

and Derrick (1994), 27 states originally indicated an intent to serve children who are at risk. A review of state and jurisdictional eligibility definitions by Shackelford (2002), however, found only 8 states and Guam reported serving a population of at-risk infants and toddlers. A state that decides to serve this group must develop guidelines for determining which children will be eligible for services under this category; these guidelines vary considerably. According to Shackelford (2002), one state includes biological risk factors only, while the others who are serving at-risk children include some combination of biological and environmental factors. The factors specified by the states differ, and the number of factors required differ, ranging from one to five factors.

Monitoring Systems

As indicated above, some states have developed systems to follow children who are at risk for developmental delay or disability but do not qualify for early intervention services. Shackelford (2002) identified 11 states and three jurisdictions that report keeping track of children who are at risk and monitoring the need for referral through periodic follow up.

Typically, referral for such monitoring systems can be made by medical, social service, or education professionals, or by parents or family members. In some states, a system of registry is tied to the birth certificate process. Under a *birth review* system, information about the newborn's birth can make the child eligible for tracking. The parents then are offered this service if they desire.

Monitoring systems evaluate the development of children on a regular basis. In some states, monitoring instruments are sent to parents, who fill them out and return them by mail. In other states, professionals administer an instrument either through home visits or at a clinic. Sensitivity to cultural variations and differences among families is critical for a successful program whether services are home-based or provided at a distance. Chapter 4 provides information on cultural considerations in assessment. As in the provision of early intervention services, it may be necessary to provide several options for participation in a monitoring program in order to best meet families' diverse needs.

In most states, monitoring or tracking programs are an interagency effort even if administratively they are housed with one agency. Some states provide services for infants and toddlers only; others extend monitoring up to the point of entry into kindergarten.

Example of a Monitoring Instrument

An instrument that was developed specifically for monitoring child development at a distance is the Ages and Stages Questionnaires (ASQ) (Bricker & Squires, 1999), formerly called the Infant/Child Monitoring Questionnaire (ICMQ). The ASQ includes 11 questionnaires to be given when the child is 4, 6, 8, 12, 16, 18, 20, 24, 30, 36, and 48 months of age. The questionnaires are mailed to the family one week before the child reaches each designated age.

Each questionnaire contains 30 questions divided into five sections: gross motor, fine motor, communication, problem solving, and personal-social development. Many of the items include small illustrations to assist the parents in evaluating their child's behavior. An example from the 48 month questionnaire is provided in Figure 5.3. The parents are instructed to try each item with their child before scoring it. Scoring is done by checking the appropriate box: "yes," "sometimes," or "not yet."

The returned questionnaire is scored by staff by assigning a value of 10 to "yes" answers, 5 to "sometimes" answers, and 0 to "not yet" answers. The score for each domain is then computed and compared with cutoff scores in the manual. If the child's score falls at or below the cutoff score in any area, arrangements are made to refer him or her for further evaluation. The cutoff score can be set at 1, 1.5, or 2 standard deviations below the mean. Of course, using the 1 or 1.5 standard deviation cutoff scores will increase the number of children who are referred.

The Ages and Stages Questionnaires can also be used as an interview tool with families either in person or over the telephone as long as the parent has a copy of the instrument to refer to during the interview. They are available in English, Spanish, French, and Korean and are being developed in Mandarin, Russian, and Arabic. The ASQ user's guide (Squires, Potter, & Bricker, 2002) includes procedures to be used by a program in establishing a monitoring system, for example, establishing children's files and implementing a "tickler" system to prompt the mailing of questionnaires to families at appropriate times. A companion to the ASQ, the ASQ:SE (Ages and Stages Questionnaires: Social Emotional) (Squires, Bricker & Twombly, 2002) will be discussed later in this chapter.

SCREENING
Definition and Rationale

Screening is defined by Meisels and Provence (1989) as "a brief assessment procedure designed to identify children who should receive more intensive diagnosis or assessment" (p. 58).

Screening large numbers of children for possible sensory, behavioral, or developmental problems should allow the early detection of such problems. Early intervention may then serve to prevent the development of a disability or at least may lessen the impact on child development. A number of different programs and professionals are either required or encouraged to screen young children for the purpose of early identification of problems. For example, Head Start and Early Head Start regulations require that each child must undergo screening of hearing, vision, behavior, and developmental areas within 45 days of the child's entry into the program. Public health nurses and programs such as the Early and Periodic, Screening, Diagnosis, and Treatment (EPSDT) program under Title XIX of the Social Security Act provide screening. Many public and private child-care programs offer screening as a service to their families. The American Academy of Pediatrics

FINE MOTOR   *Be sure to try each activity with your child.*

1. Does your child put together a six-piece interlocking puzzle? (If one is not available, take a full-page picture from a magazine or catalog and cut it into six pieces. Does your child put it back together correctly?)   ❑   ❑   ❑   ____

2. Using child-safe scissors, does your child cut a paper in half on a more or less straight line, making the blades go up and down? (Carefully watch your child's use of scissors for safety reasons.)   ❑   ❑   ❑   ____

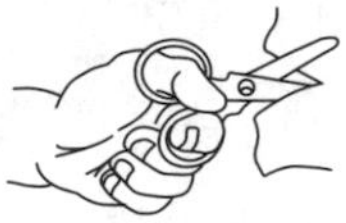

3. Using the shapes below to look at, does your child copy at least three shapes onto a large piece of paper using a pencil or crayon, without tracing? Your child's drawings should look similar to the design of the shapes below, but they may be different in size.   ❑   ❑   ❑   ____

L + I O

4. Does your child unbutton one or more buttons? Your child may use his own clothing or a doll's clothing.   ❑   ❑   ❑   ____

5. Does your child draw pictures of people that have at least three of the following features: head, eyes, nose, mouth, neck, hair, trunk, arms, hands, legs, or feet?   ❑   ❑   ❑   ____

6. Does your child color mostly within the lines in a coloring book? Your child should not go more than 1/4 inch outside the lines on most of the picture.   ❑   ❑   ❑   ____

FINE MOTOR TOTAL   ____

FIGURE 5.3

Sample of items from the 48 month ages and stages questionnaire
Note: From D. Bricker, and J. Squires (1999). *Ages and Stages Questionnaires: A Parent-Completed Child Monitoring System.* Baltimore: Paul H. Brookes Publishing Company. Reprinted with permission.

Committee on Children with Disabilities recently issued a statement on "developmental surveillance" and screening (American Academy of Pediatrics (AAP) Committee on Children with Disabilities, 2001). In this statement, pediatricians are encouraged to use developmental surveillance (identified as a continuous process of attending to parent concerns and making informative observations of children) as well as periodic use of standardized developmental screening tools to identify children who may need further evaluation. This statement by the AAP encourages pediatricians to

1. Screening and assessment should be viewed as services—as part of the intervention process and not only as means of identification and measurement.
2. Processes, procedures, and instruments intended for screening and assessment should only be used for their specified purposes.
3. Multiple sources of information should be included in screening and assessment.
4. Developmental screening should take place on a recurrent or periodic basis. It is inappropriate to screen young children only once during their early years. Similarly, provisions should be made for reevaluation or reassessment after services have been initiated.
5. Developmental screening should be viewed as only one path to more in-depth assessment. Failure to qualify for services based on a single source of screening information should not become a barrier to further evaluation for intervention services if other risk factors (e.g., environmental, medical, familial) are present.
6. Screening and assessment procedures should be reliable and valid.
7. Family members should be an integral part of the screening and assessment process. Information provided by family members is critically important for determining whether or not to initiate more in-depth assessment and for designing appropriate intervention strategies. Parents should be accorded complete informed consent at all stages of the screening and assessment process.
8. During screening or assessment of developmental strengths and problems, the more relevant and familiar the tasks and setting are to the child and the child's family, the more likely it is that the results will be valid.
9. All tests, procedures, and processes intended for screening or assessment must be culturally sensitive.
10. Extensive and comprehensive training is needed by those who screen and assess very young children.

FIGURE 5.4
Guidelines for screening and assessment
Note: From *Screening and Assessment: Guidelines for Identifying Young Disabled and Developmentally Vulnerable Children and Their Families,* by S. Meisels and S. Provence, 1989, Arlington, VA: *Zero to Three.* Reprinted with permission.

coordinate their efforts with early identification services in the community mandated by IDEA.

Recommended Guidelines for the Screening Process

A document published by the National Center for Clinical Infant Programs (Meisels & Provence, 1989) provides recommended guidelines for screening and assessment, which are listed in Figure 5.4. The following discussion will focus on several aspects of the identification and referral process: the use of multiple sources of information, the involvement of family members, and the

evaluation of screening programs. The reader is referred to Chapter 4 of this text for an in-depth discussion of cultural competence in assessment, including screening.

Multivariate Screening A comprehensive screening program should include information from a variety of sources. According to Meisels and Wasik (1990), "early identification requires that data be obtained from multiple sources; that it combine caregiving and environmental information with data about the child's biological status" (p. 624). It has been standard practice for screening efforts to include developmental, behavioral, and sensory screening as well as screening of health factors. Developmental and behavioral instruments will be discussed later in this chapter. Screening for hearing and vision problems is discussed in Chapter 6. As the knowledge base increases relative to the factors that best predict the later occurrence of developmental delay or disability, there is increased emphasis on screening environmental and caregiving factors as well. Henderson and Meisels (1994) combined results from a parent questionnaire with results from an individually administered developmental screener and found increased accuracy in determining which children did not need further evaluation. In a study of adolescents both with and without disabilities, Kochanek, Kabacoff, and Lipsitt (1990) found that characteristics of the family, such as maternal education, were more predictive of child status at adolescence than characteristics of the child from birth to age 3. Based on this research, the authors suggest that family factors, not just attributes of the child, must be considered in any determination of the need or potential need for early intervention services. The *Family Psychosocial Screening* (Kemper & Kelleher, 1996) is an example of an instrument used by pediatricians that screens for psychosocial risk factors in the family which are associated with developmental problems (American Academy of Pediatrics Committee on Children with Disabilities, 2001). Included in this screening instrument are items related to parental history of abuse as a child, parental substance abuse, and maternal depression.

Family-Centered Screening Procedures
In Chapter 3, a rationale for the provision of family-centered evaluation and assessment services is provided. A family-centered philosophy should also be the basis for identification and screening programs, and several of the recommendations for screening and assessment listed in Figure 5.4 relate to such an approach. To be consistent, screening should be viewed as part of interven-

tion. Meisels and Provence (1989) remind us that screening is often the family's first experience with the educational or human service system and is "potentially a short-term therapeutic experience in itself" (p. 23).

The seventh recommendation listed in Figure 5.4 is that family members should be an integral part of the screening process. Chapter 3 provides a strong rationale for the inclusion of information from family members in the screening process. Parents and caregivers should be informed about the entire process in advance; they should be told about the purpose and the potential outcomes, the procedures to be followed, and the qualifications of the professionals involved. The parents should be given the option to participate in the screening process where possible. Perhaps most importantly, the parents should receive the results of the screening immediately and in jargon-free terminology.

There has been increased interest recently in using parent report instruments as screening tools rather than direct assessment of the child. Research has shown that parental report can be used reliably in identifying young children who need further evaluation (Bricker & Squires, 1989; Glascoe, 1997; Glascoe & Dworkin, 1995). Furthermore, Glascoe, Foster and Wolraich (1997) conducted a cost-benefit analysis of developmental screening procedures which concluded that parent report was the least costly among procedures used by pediatricians. According to the American Academy of Pediatrics, parent report screeners such as *The Child Development Inventory Screeners* (Ireton, 1987; 1988; 1994a; 1994b) the *Ages and Stages Questionnaires* (Bricker & Squires, 1999) and the *Parents' Evaluation of Developmental Status* (PEDS) (Glascoe, 1998) have been found through research to have good psychometric properties (American Academy of Pediatrics, 2001).

Evaluation of Screening Programs
Because screening programs should be evaluated on a regular basis to ensure effectiveness, several types of data will need to be collected and analyzed.

The following evaluation questions might guide evaluation efforts:

- Are there children who passed the screening and later are found to need special education services?
- Are there children referred for evaluation who are found to not be eligible for services?
- Are the families who participate in screening satisfied with the experience?
- Is evaluation being completed in a timely fashion for those children who are referred for evaluation as a result of screening?

The first two questions can be answered by completing a follow-up of the children who have been screened and comparing these data with the children who eventually are identified as needing special services. There may be children identified as needing special education during the elementary years who were never screened during their early years. Follow-up can assist in determining if this is happening and why, so that steps can be taken to correct the problem. Ideally, a screening program would identify for evaluation only those children who are later found to be eligible for early intervention or special education services. Because children either are or are not in need of special services (as determined by the eligibility criteria that guide admission into early intervention or special education programs), and children either are or are not referred for evaluation to

determine this eligibility as a result of the screening program, four potential outcomes are possible, as indicated in Figure 5.5.

A *false positive* refers to a situation in which a child is referred for evaluation based on the results of a screening, but is not found to be in need of special services. In other words, the screening incorrectly identifies the child as being in need of special services. A *false negative* refers to a situation in which a child passes the screening and is not referred for evaluation, but later is identified as being in need of special services. Both false positives and false negatives indicate situations in which an error has been made. False positives can unnecessarily cause anxiety in families and can be costly in terms of evaluation expenses. False negatives, however, create even more serious consequences for the children who may have benefitted from early intervention but did not receive it due to errors in the screening process. Generally, it is preferable to err on the side of false positives than to fail to identify children who are in need of services.

Families should be given the opportunity to evaluate their experience with the screening program. This can be done by survey either immediately following the screening, through a mailed questionnaire, or by telephone contact. A follow-up of each child who is screened can also determine how quickly evaluation is completed after screening so that time lags can be identified and corrected if possible.

	Referred for Evaluation	Not Referred for Evaluation
Eligible for Special Services		False Negative
Not Eligible for Special Services	False Positive	

FIGURE 5.5
Potential outcomes for screening

In addition to these areas of evaluation, the reliability and validity of the screening instruments used should be considered. The following section includes information on reliability and validity.

Selection of Screening Instruments

According to Meisels and Wasik (1990), developmental screening instruments should be "brief, norm-referenced, inexpensive, standardized in administration, objectively scored, broadly focused across all areas of development, reliable and valid" (p. 613). Meisels and Wasik add to this that screeners should be "sensitive to the sample of children who are developmentally at risk and specific to the portion of the screening population that is not at risk" (p. 613).

Reliability of Screening Tools and Procedures   Reliability, as described in Chapter 2, is a critical dimension of tests and other measurement activities. It refers to the consistency and stability of measurement. Screening measures are usually norm-referenced tests for which reliability estimates can be obtained. When establishing a screening program, interventionists should read the test manual carefully and review research articles that have assessed the reliability of the measure in question. However, the presence of acceptable reliability estimates and studies by the test author or other researchers is only the beginning in ensuring that screening procedures are reliably implemented. Procedural reliability and scoring reliability, as described in Chapter 2, are also critical in screening. To ensure that instruments are appropriately administered and scored, all members of the screening team should be fully trained in test administration and scoring. Periodically conducting procedural and scoring reliability checks as described in Chapter 2 can also serve to ensure reliability in screening.

Validity of Screening Tools and Procedures   As also noted in Chapter 2, validity is a critical dimension of tests and deals with the extent to which measures can be used for specific purposes. Two types of criterion validity are important for screening measures: concurrent validity and predictive validity. *Concurrent validity,* as it relates to screening measures, refers to the extent to which the screening test agrees with more thorough measures (usually diagnostic tests) at about the same point in time. Because the focus of screening frequently is development, the screening tests should have high agreement with more thorough developmental measures that would be administered within a few days. *Predictive validity,* as it relates to screening measures, refers to the extent to which the screening test agrees with children's performance on outcome measures later in time. For example, predictive validity is seen when a screening measure given to 4-year-old children accurately predicts performance on an instrument administered in first grade. The validity of commonly used screening tests is addressed later in this chapter.

To be valid, screening measures should also be free from bias due to age, gender, geographic factors, economic background, and racial or ethnic status. Interventionists should carefully evaluate the test manuals and the research that has been conducted on various measures to determine whether the standardization population included children from the ages to be screened, an equal distribution of males and females, children of different racial and ethnic groups, and families from a variety of economic backgrounds, and that it sampled geographic regions similar to those for which the measures are being considered.

Sensitivity and Specificity   Of particular importance in selecting a screening instrument is the degree of sensitivity and specificity reported (Lichtenstein & Ireton, 1991). *Sensitivity* refers to the ability of the test to identify a high proportion of the children who are indeed developmentally delayed or have a disability. *Specificity* refers to the ability of the test to not identify children who do not have a disability or developmental delays. In other words, the test should sort those who should and should not be referred to evaluation for eligibility. Evaluating sensitivity and specificity is important in determining the cutoff score for making referrals. Screening programs can adjust the cutoff score for screening instruments in order to increase the sensitivity and specificity of the instrument in relation to the community of children with whom it is being used. For example, the Battelle Developmental Inventory Screening Test (Newborg, Stock, Wnek, Guidubaldi, & Svinicki, 1988) allows the examiner to choose a cutoff score that is equivalent to 1, 1.5, or 2 standard deviations below the mean. The DIAL-3 (Mardell-Czudnowski & Goldenberg, 1998) test results can be interpreted using a cutoff score at 1, 1.3, 1.5, 1.7 or 2 standard deviations below the mean.

Information on Selected Screening Instruments

The following section provides information on seven currently used developmental screening instruments and two behavioral instruments. Information on sensory screening procedures is presented in Chapter 6. Additional information on behavioral screeners is provided in Chapter 13.

AGS Early Screening Profiles The AGS Early Screening Profiles (Harrison et al., 1990), published by the American Guidance Service (AGS), is norm-referenced and consists of seven parts: Cognitive/Language Profile, Motor Profile, Self-Help/Social Profile, Articulation Survey, Home Survey, Health History Survey, and Behavior Survey. Each component can be used independently or in combination with other components. The Cognitive/Language Profile was developed by the authors of the Kaufman Assessment Battery for Children (Kaufman & Kaufman, 1983); the Motor Profile was developed by the author of the Bruininks-Oseretsky Test of Motor Proficiency (Bruininks, 1978); the Self-Help/Social Profile was developed by two of the authors of the Vineland Adaptive Behavior Scales (Sparrow, Balla, & Cicchetti, 1984).

The AGS Early Screening Profiles is an individually administered screening instrument for children from 2 years 0 months through 6 years 11 months. Development is screened in multiple domains (cognitive/language, motor, self-help/social) and includes information obtained from multiple sources—parents, teachers or day-care providers, and examiners. The Cognitive/Language Profile consists of four subtests—verbal concepts, visual discrimination, logical relations, and basic school skills. The Motor Profile includes a gross motor subtest and a fine motor subtest; the Self-Help/Social Profile includes both parent and teacher reports on communication, daily living skills, and socialization and motor skills domains. The Articulation Survey uses direct testing to measure articulation of single words and intelligibility during continuous speech. The Home Survey and Health History Survey are 12-item questionnaires to be completed by the parents. The Behavior Survey is completed by the examiner following administration of the Cognitive/Language and Motor Profiles.

The Early Screening Profiles can be administered to large numbers of children using a station format, where children move from place to place. The authors suggest that a screening coordinator be responsible for developing and implementing the screening program and training other examiners. Administration time for the three profiles is estimated to be between 15 and 40 minutes, and time estimated for completion of the surveys is 15 minutes.

The AGS Early Screening Profiles provide a choice of two levels of scoring. Level I scores yield Screening Indexes, which can be obtained quickly. They range from 1 to 6; 1 and 2 are below average performance and 5 and 6 are above average. Screening Indexes can be obtained for the Cognitive/Language Profile, the Motor Profile, the Self-Help/Social Profile: Parent, and the Self-Help/Social Profile: Teacher. In addition, a Total Screening Index can be obtained and the Cognitive/Language Profile can yield a Cognitive Index and a Language Index.

Level II scoring yields standard scores, normal curve equivalents, percentiles, stanines, and age equivalents for the three profiles and the Total Screening score. For the surveys, Level II provides a descriptive outcome: above average, average, and below average.

The AGS Early Screening Profiles were standardized on 1,149 children. The population was stratified according to the 1990 census estimates on sex, race/ethnic group, region of the United States, size of school district, and parental level of education.

The manual for the AGS Early Screening Profiles includes a good deal of information on reliability and validity. Internal consistency reliability is reported to range from .41 to .95 for each component. Test-retest reliability ranged from .66 to .91. Interrater reliability was measured for the Motor Profile and ranged from .83 to .99.

The manual also includes considerable evidence of concurrent validity measured as comparisons with numerous other instruments. Short-term (two years) evidence of predictive validity is also provided. The authors addressed construct validity by demonstrating that the profiles effectively identified both at-risk and gifted children.

Battelle Developmental Inventory Screening Test

The Battelle Developmental Screening Test (Newborg et al., 1988) consists of 96 items taken from the 341 items of the Battelle Developmental Inventory (BDI), which is described in Chapter 10. The BDI Screening Test is a norm-referenced, individually administered screener that covers the five domains assessed with the full BDI: personal-social, adaptive, motor, communication, and cognition. The same age range is covered: birth to age 8. Administration and item scoring procedures for the BDI screener are the same as for the full BDI. Three different procedures may be used: direct testing, observation, and interview. Cutoff scores may be chosen from three probability levels that correspond to 1, 1.5, or 2 standard deviations (SDs) below the mean.

The BDI was standardized on a sample of 800 children selected on the basis of geographical region, race, gender, and urban or rural residence. The manual reports administration to a "clinical" sample that included children with disabilities, but little information is provided about this group. The original manual, which was published in 1984, included norms that were inaccurate. A new manual with "recalibrated" norms was published in 1988.

The BDI manual provides no information on reliability of the screener, but reports that it correlates highly with the full BDI. McLean, McCormick, Baird, and Mayfield (1987) found the correlations to be less than those reported by the manual. Perhaps more importantly, however, this study also found that the specificity of the BDI was poor. Use of this instrument with a population of 30 children resulted in considerable overreferral. The BDI is now published by Riverside Publishing Company and is currently being revised. A new edition is expected to be available by 2005.

Brigance Screens

Four screening instruments have been developed by Albert Brigance for young children:

- Infant and Toddler Screen, ages 0–11 + 12–23 months (Brigance, 2002)
- Early Preschool Screen, ages 2 & 2½ (Brigance, 1998a)
- Preschool Screen, ages 3 & 4 (Brigance, 1998b)
- K & 1 Screen, grades K & 1 (Brigance, 1997)

The Brigance Screens are administered individually and can be completed in 10–20 minutes. The Infant & Toddler Screen can be completed by direct elicitation of skills or by parent report while the three older screens are administered by direct elicitation. For these three (Early Preschool Screen, Preschool Screen, and K & 1 Screen), additional forms for recording the examiner's observations, teacher's rating and parent rating are also available for use but not required. The Infant & Toddler Screen also has additional forms for examiner and teacher observations as well as a parent-child interaction rating form.

The original Brigance Screens included the Early Preschool Screen, the Preschool Screen, and the K & 1 Screen. These three screens consisted of items selected from the Brigance Diagnostic Inventory of Early Development (IED) (Brigance, 1979). The IED was standardized on 1,156 children ranging in age from one year to more than six years stratified by gender, race, urban/rural/suburban, and geographic location. In 1995, these three screens were restandardized on a total of 408 children stratified for geographic region, income level of families and educational experience of the child. The Infant & Toddler Screen was developed later and standardized on 411 children between birth and 2 years of age.

The standardization of the screens resulted in suggested cutoff scores which should be able to identify 75% of the children who do need further assessment and 82% of the children who do not need further assessment (Glascoe, 2002). In addition, the Brigance screens now yield criterion-referenced and norm-referenced scores as well as growth indicator scores which can be obtained as a measure of progress during the school year. The technical report for the Brigance screens (Glascoe, 2002) includes additional information on the content validity, concurrent validity, internal consistency reliability, and standard error of measurement of the screens.

Denver II   The Denver II (Frankenburg et al., 1992) is the latest revision of the Denver Developmental Screening Test, which was originally published in 1975. It is norm-referenced and is individually administered. The Denver II can be administered to children between birth and 6 years of age and covers four domains of child development: personal-social, fine motor-adaptive, language, and gross motor. Figure 5.6 illustrates the protocol for the Denver II. The materials needed for administration are provided in a test kit that is small and very portable.

The Denver II includes 125 items across the four domains. However, only the items that lie closest to the age line that is drawn on the protocol are typically administered (see Figure 5.6). Items that run through and to the left of the age line are administered to determine whether the child needs further assessment for possible developmental delay. If time permits, items to the right of the age line may be administered to determine relative strengths of the child. The latest version of the Denver has added five ratings of the child's behavior during testing, which are recorded in the bottom left-hand corner of the protocol.

Four possible scores may be recorded for the items: pass, fail, no opportunity, and refusal. Based on the position of failed or refused items relative to the age line, the overall outcome for the screener may be interpreted as normal, suspect, or untestable. A suspect or untestable outcome warrants rescreening in 1–2 weeks to rule out the possibility that fatigue or illness effected the score. If the rescreening also results in an outcome of suspect or untestable, the decision of whether or not to refer for a full evaluation is made by the supervising professional (Frankenburg et al., 1992).

The Denver II provides printed training materials in the training manual (Frankenburg et al., 1992), and training videotapes are available. The manual also provides a proficiency test that can be self-administered and scored in order to determine readiness for administration of the instrument. A technical manual is available that includes information about the standardization process and studies involving the Denver (Frankenburg et al., 1996).

The Denver II was standardized on 2,096 children in Colorado, stratified according to maternal education, ethnic group, and rural or urban residence. Marking and shading on each item on the protocol provides information on the average age at which 25%, 50%, 75%, and 90% of the population passed each item. This information is also in table form in the training manual.

The Denver II test forms are available in English and Spanish. A supplement to the training manual is also available in Spanish. Two videotapes are available for training. One is an introduction and the other details administration

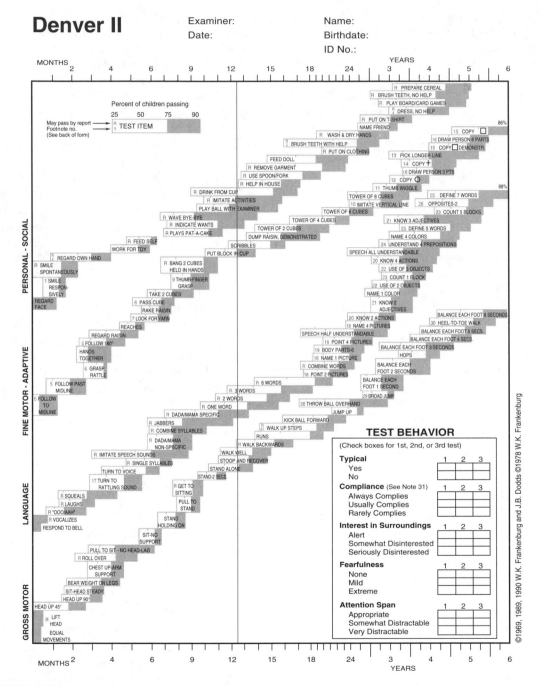

FIGURE 5.6

Protocol for the Denver II with age line drawn at 12 months, 15 days

Note: From *Denver II Training Manual* by W. K. Frankenburg and J. B. Dodds, 1992, Denver, CO: Denver Developmental Materials. Reprinted with permission.

of each item. The technical manual includes norms for the Denver II items divided into subgroups according to maternal education and also race (Anglo, Hispanic, Black).

Developmental Indicators for the Assessment of Learning–Third Edition (DIAL-3)

Developmental Indicators for the Assessment of Learning (Mardell & Goldenberg, 1975) was first published in 1975. The first revision, DIAL-R, was published in 1983 and was updated in 1990. The current edition (DIAL-3) (Mardell-Czudnowski & Goldenberg, 1998) has been modified considerably from the first two editions. The DIAL-3 is a norm-referenced instrument that now includes five screening areas-motor, concepts, language, self-help development and social development. Children between the ages of 3 years and 6 years, 11 months can be screened with the DIAL-3, and the estimated time of administration is 20 to 30 minutes. A new feature of the DIAL-3 is the Speed DIAL, a subset of items from motor, concepts, and language areas that can be administered in 15 to 20 minutes. The DIAL-3 and Speed DIAL are available in English and Spanish.

Most of the materials needed for testing are available in the DIAL-3 materials kit. The test uses a station format with children rotating through the stations individually. Adults administer the items in the motor, concept, and language areas, and one adult serves as the coordinator for the overall process. Scores for self-help development and social development are obtained from a parent questionnaire. Volunteers may also be used to play with children who are waiting or to accompany some children through the stations. Six to nine children can be screened in an hour.

The DIAL-3 also includes a training video in English and Spanish, the parent questionnaire in both English and Spanish, and parent/child activity forms in both English and Spanish that provide suggestions to parents to facilitate their child's

development. A software program is available to assist in scoring and in producing a parent report.

Two results are possible from the scores of the DIAL-3: "potential delay" (requires further assessment) and "ok" (developing satisfactorily). Cutoff scores can be selected from one of five levels: 1.0 SD, 1.3 SD, 1.5 SD, 1.7 SD and 2.0 SD below the mean.

The norms that are used in the DIAL-3 were obtained from a standardization process that took place between 1995 and 1997 and included 1,560 English speaking and 605 Spanish speaking children. The sample was stratified according to age, gender, geographic region, SES/parent education, and race based on the 1994 census.

The DIAL-3 manual reports test-retest and internal consistency reliabilities. The test-retest reliabilities range from .67 to .88. Internal consistency reliabilities for the five area scores range from .66 to .85. The manual also addresses content and concurrent validity.

FirstSTEP: Screening Test for Evaluating Preschoolers

FirstSTEP (Miller, 1993) is an individually administered, norm-referenced screening test for children from 2 years, 9 months, to 6 years, 2 months. It is designed to be a companion to the Miller Assessment for Preschoolers (MAP) (Miller, 1988). FirstSTEP covers the five developmental domains specified by IDEA: cognition, communication, motor, social-emotional, and adaptive behavior.

FirstSTEP includes 12 subtests in game format; they are divided into cognitive, communication, and motor domains (four subtests in each of the three domains). The results on these three domains make up the Composite Score for the test. In addition, a Social-Emotional Scale and an Adaptive Behavior Checklist cover the two additional domains specified by IDEA. A third and optional scale, The Parent/Teacher Scale, has also been developed to add information about the child's typical behavior at home or at school in addition to the behavior observed during the screening.

The item pool for FirstSTEP was developed from examination of the tryout edition items from the Miller Assessment for Preschoolers. Two pilot editions and a tryout edition were tested and reviewed by subject matter experts prior to standardization of the instrument. The standardization population consisted of 1,433 children across seven age groups. Approximately equal numbers of boys and girls were included. The sample was spread across nine geographic regions of the United States and paralleled the 1988 census data in terms of geographical location and race/ethnicity. The sample included the same proportion of Whites, African Americans, Hispanics, Asian Americans, and Native Americans as delineated in the 1988 census. In addition, parent education was also a stratification variable.

Each domain has a mean of 10 and a standard deviation of 3.0. The composite score has a mean of 50 and a standard deviation of 10.0. Within each domain, a scaled score of 7 or 13 represents 1.0 standard deviation below or above the mean. Scaled scores of 4 or 16 represent 2.0 standard deviations below or above the mean. A color-coded system is used to indicate whether the child's score is in the normal or delayed range; green indicates that the score is within acceptable limits, red indicates performance is below acceptable limits and further testing is necessary. A score in the yellow area can be considered borderline, and clinical judgment plus information from the developmental history and parent/teacher input should be used to determine whether to refer the child for evaluation.

The FirstSTEP manual presents split-half reliability coefficients for the domain scores and internal consistency scores (using coefficient alpha) for the adaptive behavior checklist, social-emotional scale, and parent/teacher scale. Standard Errors of Measurement are also provided. Reliability coefficients ranged from .65 to .95. Test-retest reliability was also assessed for a group of 86 children randomly selected from the standardization group. Decision consistency as assessed for this group ranged from .85 to .93. Stability coefficients of the domain and composite scores ranged from .82 to .93. Interrater agreement also was assessed on 43 cases from the standardization group. The correlation coefficients obtained from the resulting scaled scores of two raters ranged from .77 to .96.

The FirstSTEP manual presents the results of a number of concurrent validity studies, including correlations with the Miller Assessment for Preschoolers, the Wechsler Preschool and Primary Scale of Intelligence–Revised, the Bruininks-Oseretsky Test of Motor Proficiency, the Test of Language Development Primary–Second Edition, the Walker Problem Behavior Identification Checklist–Revised, and the Vineland Scale of Adaptive Behavior. Evidence of both convergent validity (high correlations between scales that measure the same thing) and discriminant validity (lower correlations with measures of different constructs) is provided.

Child Development Inventory Screeners

The Child Development Inventory screeners have evolved from the original Minnesota Child Development Inventory (MCDI) (Ireton & Thwing, 1972) which was scored based on parent response to 320 specific questions about their child's behavior and development. Four screeners have been developed:

Infant Development Inventory, birth
    to 18 months (Ireton, 1994b)
Early Child Development Inventory,
    15 months to 3 years (Ireton, 1988)
Preschool Development Inventory, 3 years
    to kindergarten (Ireton, 1987)
Child Development Review, 18 months
    to 5 years (Ireton, 1994a)

The first three screeners measure development in social, self-help, gross motor, fine motor and language development. These instruments each include 60 yes–no questions about the child's development, which can be mailed to families, answered by interview or through observation or direct testing of the child. Parents are also asked to describe their child, to report any special problems or concerns and to indicate how they are doing as parents. Developmental age norms have been established for the child development items from earlier forms of the MCDI. The outcome of each scale is the need for further evaluation. The Child Development Review also includes a problems checklist covering health, growth, vision, hearing, motor, language, sleep, eating, toileting, and behavior problems. The author of these screeners, Harold Ireton, recommends the use of the Infant Development Inventory, birth to 18 months, followed by the Child Development Review, 18 months to 5 years, for pediatricians providing well-child care (Ireton, 1996) and also for health and educational agencies involved in developmental screening (personal communication). The instruments, which combine information from parents with the observations of professionals, can be used by professionals from a variety of disciplines who are responsible for identification and referral of young children who may need early intervention. The CDI screeners are also available in Spanish.

Screening Behavior

Increasingly, service providers have been required to screen young children in the area of social-emotional development or behavior. Two instruments which have been designed to screen a young child's behavior for problems which warrant follow up are described below. Additional information on screening behavior can be found in Chapter 13.

The Temperament and Atypical Behavior Scale (TABS)
The Temperament and Atypical Behavior Scale (TABS) (Neisworth, Bagnato, Salvia & Hunt, 1999) includes both a screener and an assessment tool for children from 11–71 months of age. The assessment tool includes 55 items arranged into four subtests: detached, hyper-sensitive/active, underreactive, dysregulated. The screener includes 15 items taken from the assessment tool. The TABS can be completed by the parent or by a professional who knows the child well (obtaining parent responses is preferred). Each item identifies a problem behavior (i.e. "has wild temper tantrums") to which the respondent indicates "yes" (if it's a current problem) or "no" (if it's not a problem). The screener is scored by adding all of the items marked *yes*. Follow-up with the complete 55 item assessment tool is recommended if one or more items are marked *yes*.

The TABS was normed on a population of 621 children between 11 and 71 months of age. The authors report 2.4% false negatives and 14.5% false positives in a comparison of the outcomes from the screener with the outcomes from the assessment tool (Neisworth et al., 1999).

Ages and Stages Questionnaires: Social-Emotional
The Ages and Stages Questionnaires: Social-Emotional (ASQ:SE) (Squires, Bricker & Twombly, 2002) follows the same format as the ASQ (described earlier) using parent-completed forms periodically between 6 months and 60 months to identify children who should receive further assessment. Questionnaires have been developed for 6, 12, 18, 24, 30, 36, 48, and 60 months and contain 22–36 questions addressing the following areas: self-regulation, compliance, communication, adaptive functioning, autonomy, affect, and interaction with people. Parents answer *most of the time, sometimes,* or *rarely or never* to each item. In addition, parents can indicate for each behavior whether or not it is a concern. An information summary sheet completed by professionals provides a numerical equivalent for each parent response, which are added to get a total score. This total score is then compared to a cutoff score to determine whether the child should be referred for further evaluation. Programs can maintain the results of each questionnaire over time, thus providing for periodic screening. Like the ASQ, the ASQ:SE is also available in Spanish.

· · · · · · · ·
SUMMARY OF KEY CONCEPTS

- Child Find is a systematic process of identifying infants and preschoolers who are potentially eligible for early intervention services. Each state is required to establish a system of Child Find for children from birth to age 21.
- Screening is an assessment process designed to identify children who may need further evaluation in order to determine whether early intervention should be provided.
- Child monitoring or tracking is a system for providing continuous monitoring of the developmental progress of children who are thought to be at risk for developmental problems.

- Prevention efforts can be described as primary, secondary, or tertiary prevention. Monitoring systems are an example of secondary prevention.
- Risk factors in children have been described as established risk, biological risk, and environmental risk.
- Screening programs for young children should include information from a variety of sources, should include family members in the screening process, and should be evaluated on a regular basis to determine effectiveness.
- In selecting screening instruments, early intervention personnel should consider reliability, validity, sensitivity, and specificity.

· · · · · · · ·
REFERENCES

American Academy of Pediatrics Committee on Children with Disabilities (2001). Developmental surveillance and screening of infants and young children. *Pediatrics, 108*(1), 192–196.

Bourland, B., & Harbin, G. (1987). *START resource packet: Child Find.* Chapel Hill, NC: Frank Porter Graham Child Development Center, University of North Carolina.

Bricker, D. & Squires, J. (1989). The effectiveness of parental screening of at-risk infants: The infant monitoring questionnaires. *Topics in Early Childhood Special Education, 9*(3), 67–85.

Bricker, D., & Squires, J. (1999). *Ages and Stages Questionnaires (ASQ): A parent-completed child-monitoring system* (2nd ed.). Baltimore: Paul H. Brookes.

Brigance, A. H. (1979). *Brigance Diagnostic Inventory of Early Development.* Billerica, MA: Curriculum Associates.

Brigance, A. H. (1997). *K & 1 Screen.* Billerica, MA: Curriculum Associates.

Brigance, A. H. (1998a). *Early Preschool Screen.* Billerica, MA: Curriculum Associates.

Brigance, A. H. (1998b). *Preschool Screen.* Billerica, MA: Curriculum Associates.

Brigance, A. H. (2002). *Infant & Toddler Screen.* Billerica, MA: Curriculum Associates.

Bruininks, R. H. (1978). *Bruininks-Oseretsky Test of Motor Proficiency.* Circle Pines, MN: American Guidance Service.

Frankenburg, W. K., Dodds, J., Archer, P., Bresnick, B., Maschka, P., Edelman, N. & Shapiro, H. (1992). *Denver II training manual.* Denver, CO: Denver Developmental Materials.

Frankenburg, W. K., Dodds, J., Archer, P., Bresnick, B., Maschka, P., Edelman, N., & Shapiro, H. (1996). *Denver II technical manual.* Denver, CO: Denver Developmental Materials.

Glascoe, F. P. (1997). Parents' concerns about children's development: Prescreening technique or screening test? *Pediatrics, 99,* 552–528.

Glascoe, F. P. (1998). *Collaborating with parents: Using parents' evaluation of developmental status to detect and address developmental and behavioral problems.* Nashville, TN: Ellsworth & Vanderneer Press.

Glascoe, F. P. (2002). A validation study and the psychometric properties of the Brigance Screens. North Billerica, MA: Curriculum Associates.

Glascoe, F. P. & Dworkin, P. H. (1995). The role of parents in the detection of developmental and behavioral problems. *Pediatrics, 95,* 829–836.

Glascoe, F. P., Foster, E. M., Wolraich, M. L. (1997). An economic analysis of developmental detection methods. *Pediatrics, 99,* 830–837.

Guralnick, M. J. (1997). Second generation research in the field of early intervention. In M. J. Guralnick (Ed.), *The effectiveness of early intervention.* Baltimore: Paul H. Brookes.

Harbin, G., Danaher, J., & Derrick, T. (1994). Comparison of eligibility policies for infant/toddler programs and preschool special education programs. *Topics in Early Childhood Special Education, 14*(4), 455–471.

Harrison, P. L., Kaufman, A. S., Kaufman, N. L., Bruininks, P. H., Rynders, J., Ilmer, S., Sparrow, S. S., & Cicchetti, D. V. (1990). *AGS Early Screening Profiles.* Circle Pines, MN: American Guidance Service.

Henderson, L. W., & Meisels, S. (1994). Parental involvement in the developmental screening of their young children: A multiple-source perspective. *Journal of Early Intervention, 18*(2), 141–154.

Individuals with Disabilities Education Act Amendments of 1997. www.ideapractices.org

Ireton, H. R. (1987). *Preschool Development Inventory Manual.* Minneapolis, MN: Behavior Science Systems.

Ireton, H. R. (1988). *Early Child Development Inventory Manual.* Minneapolis, MN: Behavior Science Systems.

Ireton, H. R. (1994a). *Child Development Review Manual.* Minneapolis, MN: Behavior Science Systems.

Ireton, H. R. (1994b). *Infant Development Inventory.* Minneapolis, MN: Behavior Science Systems.

Ireton, H. R. (1996). The Child Development Review: Monitoring children's development using parents and pediatricians' observations. *Infants and Young Children, 9*(1), 42–52.

Ireton, H. R. & Thwing, E. (1972). *Minnesota Child Development Inventory.* Minneapolis, MN: Behavior Science Systems.

Kaufman, A. S., & Kaufman, N. L. (1983). *Kaufman Assessment Battery for Children.* Circle Pines, MN: American Guidance Service.

Kemper, K. J. & Kelleher, K. J. (1996). Family psychosocial screening: Instruments and techniques. *Ambulatory Child Health, 4,* 325–339.

Kochanek, T. K., Kabacoff, R. I., & Lipsitt, L. P. (1990). Early identification of developmentally disabled and at-risk preschool children. *Exceptional Children, 56*(6), 528–538.

Lichtenstein, R., & Ireton, H. (1991). Preschool screening for developmental and educational problems. In B. A. Bracken (Ed.), *The psychoeducational assessment of preschool children* (pp. 486–513). Boston: Allyn & Bacon.

Mardell, C., & Goldenberg, D. (1975). *Developmental Indicators for the Assessment of Learning.* Edison, NJ: Childcraft Education Corporation.

Mardell-Czudnowski, C., & Goldenberg, D. (1998). *Developmental Indicators for the Assessment of Learning* (3rd ed.) *(DIAL-3).* Circle Pines, MN: American Guidance Service.

McLean, M., McCormick, K., Baird, S., & Mayfield, P. (1987). A study of the concurrent validity of the Battelle Developmental Inventory Screening Test. *Diagnostique, 13*(1), 10–20.

Meisels, S. (1991). Dimensions of early identification. *Journal of Early Intervention, 15*(1), 26–35.

Meisels, S. J., & Provence, S. (1989). *Screening and assessment: Guidelines for identifying young disabled and developmentally vulnerable children and their families.* Washington, DC: National Center for Clinical Infant Programs.

Meisels, S. J., & Wasik, B. A. (1990). Who should be served? Identifying children in need of early intervention. In S. J. Meisels & J. P. Shonkoff (Eds.), *Handbook of early childhood intervention* (pp. 605–632). New York: Cambridge University Press.

Miller, L. J. (1988). *Miller Assessment for Preschoolers (MAP).* San Antonio, TX: The Psychological Corp.

Miller, L. J. (1993). *FirstSTEP Screening Test for Evaluating Preschoolers.* San Antonio, TX: The Psychological Corp.

Neisworth, J. T., Bagnato, S. J., Salvia, J. & Hunt, F. M. (1999). *Temperament and Atypical Behavior Scale: Early Childhood Indicators of Developmental Dysfunction.* Baltimore: Paul H. Brookes.

Newborg, J., Stock, J. R., Wnek, L., Guidubaldi, J., & Svinicki, J. (1988). *Battelle Developmental Inventory.* Itasca, IL: Riverside Publishing.

Sameroff, A. J., & Fiese, B. H. (1990). Transactional regulation and early intervention. In S. J. Meisels & J. P. Shonkoff (Eds.), *Handbook of early childhood intervention* (pp. 119–149). New York: Cambridge University Press.

Shackleford, J. (2002). State and jurisdictional eligibility definitions for infants and toddlers with disabilities under IDEA: NECTAC Notes #5 (Revised). Chapel Hill, N.C.: National Early Childhood Technical Assistance Center.

Simeonsson, R. (1991). Primary, secondary and tertiary prevention in early intervention. *Journal of Early Intervention, 15*(2), 124–134.

Sparrow, S. S., Balla, D. A., & Cicchetti, D. V. (1984). *Vineland Adaptive Behavior Scale.* Circle Pines, MN: American Guidance Service.

Squires, J., Bricker, D. & Twombly, E. (2002). *Ages and Stages Questionnaires: Social Emotional.* Baltimore: Paul H. Brookes.

Squires, J., Potter, L. & Bricker, D. (2002). *Ages and Stages Questionnaires user's guide* (2nd ed.). Baltimore: Paul H. Brookes.

Tjossem, T. D. (1976). Early intervention: Issues and approaches. In T. D. Tjossem (Ed.), *Intervention strategies for high risk infants and young children* (pp. 3–33). Baltimore: University Park Press.

Screening and Assessment of Sensory Functions

M. Beth Langley

*Prekindergarten Handicapped Assessment Team, Pinellas
County Schools, Largo, FL*

Increased survival rates of preterm infants have contributed to a significant rise in major disabling conditions among those infants, with approximately 20% of premature infants manifesting cerebral palsy, mental retardation, hydrocephalus, or visual and/or hearing impairments. Many of these infants may also manifest immature, disorganized, and/or dysfunctional proximal sensory systems that interfere with the perception, integration, modulation, and application of sensory information from the auditory and visual channels. Nationwide, professionals in early intervention have reported significant increases in the population of young children identified as having a regulatory disorder (Neisworth, Bagnato, & Salvia, 1995) and dysfunction of sensory integration. Presenting sensory symptomology associated with these latter two disorders often are difficult to differentiate from characteristics associated with autism and further complicate both diagnosis and decisions regarding appropriate intervention models and strategies. The Individuals with Disabilities Education Act (IDEA) requires states to identify young children with disabilities through use of at-risk criteria and appropriate screening techniques and expediently evaluate them for eligibility for intervention models that will mitigate or at least minimize the effects of the sensory impairment on all aspects of development. The earlier the nature of the sensory deficit(s) or dysfunction can be discerned, the more quickly intervention strategies can be implemented to facilitate competencies and compensations needed for exploring, playing, learning, communicating, and adapting to day-to-day routines and interactions. The child's general developmental level, behavioral state, response topography, and attentional and motivational factors must be considered when selecting assessment strategies and eliciting stimuli for the screening and assessment of sensory functions. Regardless of age, the child's ability to attend to, receive, process, modulate, and respond to incoming sensory experiences will be governed by the integrity and organizational capacity of his or her central nervous system.

This chapter will address principles, strategies, technology, and both formal and informal tools related to the screening and assessment of auditory, visual, and proximal sensory systems.

SCREENING AND ASSESSMENT OF AUDITORY FUNCTIONING

Incidence of Hearing Impairment Among Young Children with Disabilities

The number of children born with some degree of deafness has been projected to exceed one in one thousand live births (Stein, 1999) and Fortnum, Summerfield, Marshall, Davis, and Bamford (2001) estimated that 50% to 90% more children are diagnosed with hearing impairment by the age of 9 years, increasing the prevalence figures to 1.33/1000 among children of 5 years and older. The incidence of congenital severe and profound hearing loss has been estimated to occur in 4 to 11 per 10,000 newborns (Tomaski & Grundfast, 1999) and Stein (1999) reported a prevalence of sensorineural loss in 5.7/1000 of the universal population. Eavey and Bertero (1995) indicated incidence of handicapping sensorineural hearing loss among survivors of the neonatal intensive care unit (NICU) to range from 2% to 4%, approximately 20 to 50 times the frequency expected for normal newborns. Approximately half of all congenital hearing loss discovered during childhood is associated with genetic abnormalities (Tran & Grundfast, 1997; Tomaski & Grundfast, 1999) and the Joint Committee on Infant Hearing (JCIH) (2000) proposed that 30% to 40% of children with hearing loss manifest additional disabilities that will further compromise communication and development. The 2000 JCIH report further delineated prevalences of hearing loss of 11.7% in infants with syndromes associated with hearing loss, including Down syndrome; 6.6% of a familial etiology, 5.5% due to meningitis, and 4.7% in infants with craniofascial anomalies. Additionally, the committee reported on the discovery of DFNB1, a gene responsible for recessive, non-syndromic, sensorineural hearing loss which is responsible for approximately 15% of all infant hearing loss. Both children with Down syndrome and with cerebral palsy have a high incidence of hearing impairment, and Saenz (1999) reported that children with Down syndrome are more likely to have otitis media because of midfacial malformations that prevent optimal drainage of eustachian tubes and sinuses. Chen (2000) found that over 75 percent of children with Down syndrome have a hearing loss and that over 35 percent of children with hearing loss have an additional disability.

Effects of Hearing Loss: Rationale for Early Detection

Permanent childhood hearing impairment during the first three years of life can significantly interfere with communication competency, literacy development, academic attainment, social and emotional well-being, and overall optimal development and quality of life (Diefendorf, 1997; Fortnum et al., 2001). Diefendorf (1997) pointed out that the effects of the hearing loss will depend on both the stage of development present at the advent of the loss as well as the degree of loss. Downs and Yoshinaga-Itano (1999) underscored the importance of early detection of hearing impairment, noting that the inner ear and eighth cranial nerve achieve greatest maturation from the fifth month of gestation to between 18 and 28 months and are at optimal readiness for the shaping of auditory ability from environmental sounds. A child with congenital loss of hearing is at greater disadvantage for the development of oral language than the child who experienced normal hearing prior to the onset of hearing loss. The greater the hearing loss, the less the availability of acoustic cues for the child. Moderate to profound hearing loss impedes the development of both receptive and expressive speech and language and may lead to profound speech delays (Bess & Paradise, 1994; Leung & Kao, 1999). Shriberg, Friel-Patti, Flipsen, and Brown (2000) reported that 33% of children who demonstrated greater than 20 dB average hearing levels at 12 to 18 months presented with speech delay and low language outcomes at 3 years of age. Children whose hearing loss was identified and who received intervention prior to 6 months of age had significantly better speech and language and personal-social skills over children whose loss was detected after 6 months of age. Downs and Yoshinaga-Itano (1999) reported that children with normal cognitive development achieved normal language scores when provided intervention prior to 6 months of age, regardless of whether their sensorineural loss was mild or profound. Hoover (2000) cited studies indicating that infants whose hearing loss was detected and treated prior to 6 months of age maintained language development commensurate with their cognitive abilities through the age of 5 years.

The newest consideration on the forefront of early detection and intervention of hearing loss is the prospect of *cochlear implants*. The JCIH (2000) proposed that cochlear implants may be an option for children 12 months and older with profound hearing loss who show limited benefit from conventional amplifications. Grote (2000) cited evidence that deaf children who have not learned to speak should have a cochlear implant as soon as possible. Electrophysiological measures including an auditory brain-stem response (ABR) (a meaure of the responsiveness of the auditory nerve to sound) and electrocochleography (a measure of cochlear function) are used to confirm permanent childhood hearing impairment (PCHI) and to select candidates for cochlear implants. Richardson and Williamson (1998) emphasized the importance of early detection of hearing loss associated with meningitis, informing us that within a few months of meningitis the cochlear duct may be obliterated by new bone formation, making implantation ineffective or even impossible.

Initial Identification of Hearing Impairment

The 2000 JCIH has endorsed universal newborn hearing screening (UNHS) with the goal of using a physiological measure to screen the hearing of infants at birth or of referring infants for screening prior to 1 month of age. This committee proposed that the detection of a hearing loss should lead to medical evaluation and confirmation by 3 months of age and to the implementation of intervention services prior to 6 months of age. Kennedy, Kimm, Thornton, and Davis (2000) presented evidence of the effectiveness of universal neonatal screening in detecting hearing loss prior to the age of 6 months and minimizing the effects of the loss on speech and language development. Additionally recommended was that all infants who pass the newborn screen but who manifest risk indicators associated with hearing loss, auditory neural conduction disorders, and/or brain-stem auditory pathway dysfunction be followed audiologically as well as medically for 3 years at 6 month intervals (JCIH, 2000). Further, the committee proposed that all infants who demonstrate delayed auditory and/or communication skills receive an audiological evaluation to rule out hearing loss. While profound hearing losses are typically identified between 9 and 12 months, Diefendorf (1997) and Fortnum et al. (2001) noted that the median age of confirmation of congenital hearing loss exceeds 18 months of age. Grote (2000) surmised that approximately 10% to 20% of PCHI is progressive loss that begins later in life. Unilateral loss may go undetected until 5 or 6 years of age since most hearing screenings conducted during infancy and early childhood are conducted in sound fields and an interaural (difference in hearing thresholds between the two ears) loss may not be found (Auslander, Lewis, Schulte, & Stelmachowicz et al., 1991; Grote, 2000). The 2000 JCIH high-risk criteria for identifying neonates, infants, and preschoolers at risk for hearing loss is presented in Figure 6.1.

Parents are typically the first to suspect that something is wrong with their infant's hearing when the infant doesn't respond to household noises such as the vacuum cleaner or to the parent's voice. Particularly, when the child fails to develop speech and language skills commensurate with peers, a hearing loss is often thought to be responsible for the delays in speech and language. Signs that a physical problem with the ear or an associated hearing loss may exist include the following:

- Discharges from the ear canal
- Mouth breathing
- The child tugs or pulls at his or her ears
- Decreased or abnormal quality of vocalization
- Failure to respond to sudden, loud sounds
- Failure to orient to parents' voices
- Heightened visual awareness during play and social interactions
- A look of surprise and/or smiling as the parent picks up the child even though the parent has been engaged in conversation with the child at near distances
- Musical or other auditory toys are held against a preferred ear
- The child tends to orient his or her head so that the better ear is toward sound sources
- The child omits voiceless sounds when speaking
- The child has difficulty discriminating similar sounds (e.g., tongue/thumb; goat/coat; gum/done)

Tomaski and Grundfast (1999) cautioned that hereditary hearing impairment (HHI) may be indicated when a family history includes the presence of hearing loss prior to the age of 30, a white forelock of hair, premature graying, different colored eyes, kidney abnormalities, night blindness, early childhood cardiac arrhythmias or a sibling with sudden cardiac death.

Dimensions of Determining and Classifying a Hearing Impairment

Hearing in children is considered normal when the lowest level of sound that elicits a response 50% of the time (threshold) is less than 15 decibels (dB).

Infants from birth through 28 days where Universal Neonatal Hearing Screening is unavailable:

- An illness or condition requiring admission of 48 hours or greater to the NICU
- Stigmata or other findings associated with a syndrome known to include a sensorineural and/or conductive hearing loss
- Family history of permanent childhood sensorineural hearing loss
- Craniofacial anomalies, including those with morphologic abnormalities of the pinna and ear canal
- In-utero infection such as cytomegalovirus, herpes, toxoplasmosis, or rubella

Infants from 29 days through 2 years at risk for progressive or delayed-onset sensorineural and/or conductive hearing loss:

- Caregiver concern regarding hearing, speech, language, or developmental delay
- Family history of permanent childhood hearing loss
- Stigmata or other findings associated with a syndrome known to include sensorineural hearing loss or Eustachian tube dysfunction
- Postnatal infections associated with sensorineural hearing loss including bacterial meningitis
- In-utero infections such as cytomegalovirus, herpes, rubella, syphilis, and toxoplasmosis
- Neonatal indicators, specifically hyperbilirubinemia at a serum level requiring exchange transfusion, persistent pulmonary hypertension of the newborn associated with mechanical ventilation, and conditions requiring the use of extracorporeal membrane oxygenation (ECMO)
- Syndromes associated with progressive hearing loss such as neurofibromatosis, osteopetrosis, and Ushers syndrome
- Neurodegenerative disorders such as Hunter syndrome, or sensory motor neuropathies, such as Friedreich's ataxia and Charcot-Marie-Tooth syndrome
- Head trauma
- Recurrent or persistent otitis media with effusion for at least 3 months

Hearing should be screened and/or monitored in older preschoolers and young children when:

- Caregivers have concerns regarding hearing, speech, language, or learning abilities
- There is family history of late or delayed onset hereditary loss
- Otitis media with effusion recurs or persists for at least 3 months
- There are skull or facial abnormalities, especially those that can cause changes to the structure of the pinna and ear canal
- Characteristics or other findings occur that are associated with a syndrome known to include hearing loss
- Head trauma occurs with loss of consciousness
- There is a reported exposure to potentially damaging noise levels or to drugs that frequently cause hearing loss

FIGURE 6.1

Hearing risk indicators from birth through the preschool years

Note: From "Year 2000 Position Statement: Principles and Guidelines for Early Hearing Detection and Intervention Programs," by Joint Committee on Infant Hearing, 2000, *Pediatrics, 106*, p. 798–817, copyright American Academy of Pediatrics, 2000, and from "Universal Newborn Hearing Screening," by D. C. Thompson, H. McPhillips, R. L. Davis, T. L. Lieu, C. J. Homer, & M. Helfand, 2001, *Journal of the American Medical Association, 286* (16), 2000–2010, copyright American Medical Association, 2001. Adapted with permission.

Ideally, a hearing threshold is obtained by assessing hearing within a specially sound-treated room designed to provide an optimal acoustic environment. A variety of sounds (pure tones, warble tones, white noise, and speech) are generated and delivered through headphones or speakers within the testing area (also referred to as sound-field) with an audiometer The child's responses are plotted on an *audiogram,* a graph of hearing as a function of the frequency (pitch) of a sound (Abdala, 1999). The threshold is obtained for each frequency, measured in vibrations per second or Hertz (Hz) from 250 Hz to 8000 Hz. Frequency is plotted on the horizontal axis of the audiogram from left to right and the level of sound from 0 dB to 110 dB is plotted on the vertical axis. A whisper is estimated to be 30 dB, conversational level speech 45 dB to 50 dB, and loud music 100 dB. Low-frequency sounds range between 250 Hz to 2000 Hz while sounds within the 3000 Hz to 8000 Hz range are considered high-frequency sounds. The child's performance at ranges between 500 Hz to 2000 Hz is particularly important because these frequencies are critical to speech. Threshold sensitivity is plotted on the audiogram with an O for the right ear and with an X for the left ear. It is common practice to use the average audiometric air conduction threshold across the middle three frequencies (500, 1000, and 2000 Hz) to classify level of hearing (Gatty, 1996). Bone conduction thresholds are obtained by delivering sound to the cochlea through the vibration of an appliance that is placed against the mastoid bone. Sounds are transmitted via the skull bones rather than through the conductive pathway. Comparison of air and bone conduction thresholds allows the audiologist to determine whether the hearing loss is conductive or sensorineural. An air-bone gap, with better bone conduction than air conduction thresholds, indicates that the loss is conductive.

Hearing loss is defined by the location of the impairment, the degree of severity of loss, and whether the loss is unilateral or bilateral. Hearing impairments may be conductive, sensorineural, mixed, or central in nature depending on the site

of the dysfunction or impairment. Figure 6.2 depicts anatomy of the external and middle ear system. A *conductive hearing loss* occurs when there is any interference in the conduction of sound between the external auditory canal and the inner ear (cochlea) due to malformation of the outer ear (such as atresia or stenosis), the presence of excessive cerumen (ear wax), a perforated eardrum, or middle ear fluid (Gatty, 1996). Conductive hearing losses are usually temporary and can usually be corrected through medical or surgical intervention. They are most frequently associated with middle ear effusion (fluid) subsequent to repeated otitis media (Rovers, Ingels, Van der Wilt, Zielhuis, & Van den Broek, 2001). Generally, such losses are managed through a regimen of antibiotics and decongestants to open the eustachian tube but frequently insertion of tympanostomy tubes (ventilation tubes) to restore hearing to a normal level and minimize language delays is required. Gatty (1996) cautioned that some conductive losses may require amplification. Kogan, Overpeck, Hoffman, & Casselbrant (2000) reported that when bilateral effusion has persisted for more than 3 months with bilateral hearing deficits resulting in a 20 dB threshold level or worse in the better ear, insertion of tympanostomy tubes is warranted. The most frequent risk factors for otitis media include lack of breast feeding, exposure to tobacco smoke, and day care.

A *sensorineural loss* results from damage to the sensory end organs (cochlear hair cells), the cochlea (the organ within the ear that converts vibrations into nerve impulses), or the auditory nerve and is generally irreversible. Sensorineural losses primarily involve the higher frequencies and clarity of auditory perceptions (discrimination of one sound from another) is diminished even after speech is made sufficiently loud. Sensorineural losses are often associated with intrauterine infection, kernicterus, ototoxic drugs, bacterial meningitis, hypoxia, intracranial hemorrhage, certain syndromes (Waardenburg, Goldenhar, Treacher-Collins), and chromosomal abnormalities (Leung &

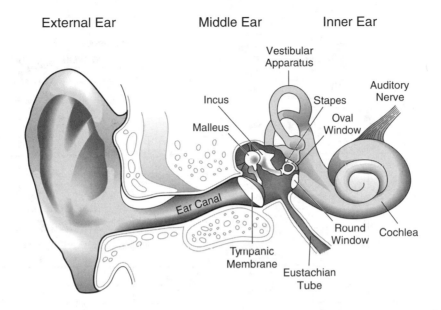

External Ear   Middle Ear   Inner Ear

FIGURE 6.2

Structure of the ear

Note: From *Children with Disabilities: A Medical Primer* (5th ed.), by M. L. Batshaw (2002). Baltimore: Paul H. Brookes. Reprinted with permission.

Kao, 1999). Richardson & Williamson (1998) cautioned that sensorineural loss is often a serious complication of childhood bacterial meningitis with approximately 10% of survivors sustaining hearing loss.

A *mixed-hearing loss* occurs when both a conductive and a sensorineural component are present. Such a loss is detected on the audiogram when there is a significant gap (space) between the threshold levels obtained by air conduction and by bone conduction. In a mixed loss, the sensorineural component is the more severe and the hearing will improve only as much as the conductive loss can be ameliorated.

A *central auditory processing disorder* (CAPD) is commonly associated with developmentally delayed children, particularly those with diagnosed or suspected neurological impairment and with autism. Children diagnosed with CAPD perceive sound but have difficulty responding on a cortical level (processing and interpreting sound). They demonstrate inconsistent responses to speech, sudden sounds, and simultaneous noises and may not localize to sound although the peripheral auditory system is intact. Although hearing sensitivity may be normal, the child often functions as if he or she were deaf. Audiograms depicting each of the primary hearing losses are presented in Figure 6.3, while the parameters of the different levels of hearing loss and related communication and educational relevance as described by Gatty (1996) are delineated in Table 6.1.

Audiological Screening: Procedural Considerations

The audiologist is most often the individual responsible for the screening and assessment of hearing of infants and toddlers, although within hospitals and clinical settings nurses may also be trained to use screening measures. While the same basic procedures are used for both screening and diagnostic assessment, Diefendorf (1997)

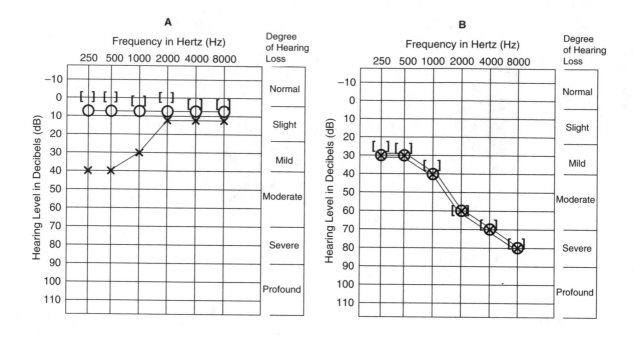

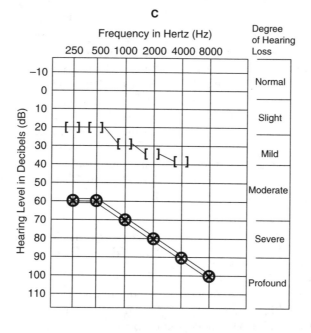

Key: [= R ear, bone conduction

] = L ear, bone conduction

O = R ear, air conduction

X = L ear, air conduction

FIGURE 6.3

Sample audiograms depicting three types of hearing loss. (A) depicts a unilateral conductive loss in the left ear; (B) represents a bilateral sensorineural loss; and (C) indicates a mixed hearing loss.

TABLE 6.1

Characteristics and Educational Relevance of a Hearing Loss

Degree of Hearing Loss	Classification	Hearing Competence	Educational Needs
15 to 30 dB	Mild	Perceive conversational speech; near normal speech and language development	Hearing needs monitored; educated within the main-stream; may benefit from an FM (frequency modulation) system
31-60 dB	Moderate	High probability that with hearing aids, speech and language skills will evolve spontaneously	Typically educated within the mainstream; may benefit from an FM system
61-90 dB	Severe	Perceive speech when provided with hearing aids and auditory training; may speak on phone; articulation typically intelligible	With sufficient support services, educated in the mainstream
91-120 dB	Profound	Hearing potential and competence vary; May be able to perceive rhythm and tone of speech with aided hearing; may recognize vowel; differentiate some consonants	May require extensive support services; may require some or all of educational needs addressed within special classes for children with hearing impairments
Greater than 120 dB	Totally deaf	May perceive speech through sense of touch; May depend on lip reading to understand speech; typically cannot benefit from hearing aids; may learn to recognize environmental sounds (telephone, door closing)	May benefit from vibratotactile or frequency transposition aids; may be candidates for cochlear implants

Note: From "Early Intervention and Management of Hearing in Infants and Toddlers," by Gatty (1996), *Infants and Young Children: Interdisciplinary Journal of Special Care Practices* 9(1), pp. 6–7. Copyright 1996 by Aspen Publishers, Inc. Adapted with permission.

stated that the goals of screening include accurate detection of those infants and children for risk classification and the timely transition between detection, diagnosis, and intervention. Speech and language therapists, early childhood specialists, special education teachers, teachers of the deaf and hard of hearing, nurses, and even well-trained volunteers are called upon to screen hearing through observations of behavior and use of the audiometer when screening preschoolers.

Early interventionists may be called upon to screen the hearing of children referred for or served in early intervention programs to rule out hearing concerns. Downs' (1984) HEAR Kit system provides a variety of calibrated noisemakers intended for use in screening the hearing of young children. Chen (1999) provided a series of questions for guiding observations of a child's hearing within structured situations in addition to a form for systematic recording of responses to sounds and speech within functional contexts.

Screening procedures for newborns and infants are physiological in nature and include some form of otoacoustic emissions (OAEs) (measure of cochlear status based on stimulation of the hair cells within the middle ear) or auditory brain-stem response (ABR) (Thompson, McPhillips, Davis, Lieu, Homer, & Helfand, 2001). The Joint Commission on Infant Hearing recommended a two-stage screening protocol using objective physiological measures for the universal screening of newborns. Infants are initially screened with OAEs and subsequently with ABR technology if they fail the OAE. For the purpose of the universal newborn hearing screen, hearing loss was defined as a permanent bilateral or unilateral, sensory or conductive hearing loss averaging 30 dB to 40 dB or more in the 500–4000 Hz frequency range.

The most common screening procedure conducted in offices of audiologists, pediatricians, and/or otolaryngologists and at community infant-toddler and preschool screenings is immittance or impedance testing to rule out a conductive loss. Initially, the physician or the audiologist uses an otoscope to examine the ear canal and tympanic membrane (eardrum) to detect indications of an infection or the presence of fluid. Drainage from the ear or excess cerumen may preclude objective testing such as immittance audiometry. Immittance tests evaluate the status of the middle ear system and may include tympanometry, acoustic reflex, and static acoustic testing. Tympanometry produces a graph which depicts the compliance (movement) of the tympanic membrane (eardrum) in response to changes in pressure introduced within the ear canal. As depicted in Figure 6.4 a normal functioning middle ear system will result in a type A tympanogram but a dysfunctional system will reflect a "flat" or "negative" tympanogram. Acoustic reflexes provide diagnostic information relative to hearing sensitivity based on the contraction of tiny ear muscles in response to sound. Static acoustic impedance, a measure of the physical volume of air in the ear canal, can detect the presence of a perforated ear drum and whether ventilation tubes remain patent (open). Acoustic reflexes are absent in the presence of a moderate or greater hearing loss (Abdala, 1999). Acoustic immittance measures are especially valuable for young children with special needs because they require no intentional responses on behalf of the child. The principle disadvantage associated with immittance procedures is that the test battery cannot be completed during vocalizations, crying, or yelling, and any movement will influence the accuracy of the acoustic reflex. Figure 6.5 demonstrates the use of immittance with an infant as he is held by his mother.

Pure tone screening with an audiometer is used to determine risk of hearing impairment in preschoolers. Pure-tone screening is most reliable with children functioning at a developmental level of 3 years and older. During a screening, the frequencies of 500, 1000, 2000, and 4000 Hz are each tested at the intensity level of 20 dB HL and the child is instructed to raise a hand, release a block into a can, or perform some other simple motor task when he or she hears the tone. If the ambient

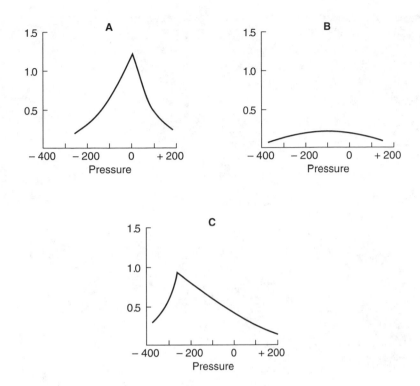

FIGURE 6.4

The three major types of tympanograms. Type A shows normal functioning; Type B shows fluid in the middle ear or an open pressure equalizing tube; Type C shows negative middle ear pressure.

noise of the screening setting is too great, a level of 25 dB is used and/or the frequency of 500 Hz omitted. Lack of response to any one frequency level in either ear screened at the criterion level is considered a failure.

Audiological Assessment: Representative Methods

Audiologists, experts in identification, evaluation, and auditory habilitation of children who are hard of hearing and deaf, are responsible for the selection, design and administration of an audiological test battery. The audiological assessment should provide information regarding the integrity of the auditory system, estimate hearing thresholds (or sensitivity), provide some idea of the functional application of hearing in day-to-day situations, and identify intervention options. Additionally, the assessment should include a visual inspection of the outer ear for any malformations or signs indicative of a possible hearing loss. The JCIH recommends that audiological assessment should include both physiological measures, such as OAEs, ABRs, and pure tone audiometry, and developmentally appropriate behavioral strategies. An accurate and reliable assessment of hearing in young children is best obtained when the procedures selected accommodate the child's developmental level and response capability. Regardless of age and/or developmental level, ear specific estimates of type, degree, and configuration of hearing loss should be obtained.

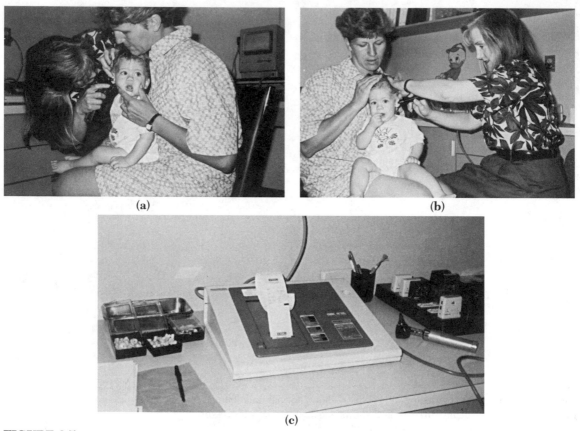

(a)

(b)

(c)

FIGURE 6.5

Figure 6.5 (a) shows a pediatric audiologist inspecting the ear canal of an infant prior to conducting impedance (or immittance) audiometry. In Figure 6.5 (b), an infant's middle ear functioning is assessed with impedance audiometry. Figure 6.5 (c) depicts the impedance unit with the printout of the tympanogram.

Behavioral Approaches to Hearing Assessment

An estimate of hearing sensitivity may be obtained through behavioral audiometric procedures when pure-tone hearing thresholds cannot be achieved due to age, developmental level, or other child variables. The selection of the most appropriate behavioral approach is governed primarily by the developmental age of the child, but other factors such as the presence of a physical and/or sensory impairment also should be considered. *Behavioral observation audiometry* (BOA) is most typically used with children below the age of 5 or 6 months.

BOA is the least cognitively demanding auditory approach as it relies on the infant's or child's spontaneous responses to sounds of a variety of intensities and frequencies presented within a structured context. Warble tones, noisemakers, white noise, speech, music, and the parent/caregiver's and/or audiologist's voice are presented in sound-field and the child's responses noted. Behavioral responses include reflexive reactions, such as a startle response or crying; alerting and arousal behaviors, such as an increase or a decrease in respiration or activity levels, eye widening, blinking, eyebrow arching, arousal from sleep; and localization responses such as orienting, looking, pointing, or reaching toward the sound source. Regardless of the response, the key to the effectiveness of BOA is the consistency of the identified behavior in response to sound. Abdala (1999, p. 255) advised that "If the infant startles appropriately at 65 dB HL, has a speech awareness threshold (SAT) of 40 dB HL, responds to both low- and high-frequency noisemakers at moderate levels of sound, and the parent reports the infant shows normal responding and interest in sounds at home, it is likely that the infant has normal hearing in at least one ear." The primary disadvantage associated with behavioral audiometric procedures that utilize a sound-field milieu is that a hearing loss in at least one ear cannot be ruled out as both ears are tested simultaneously. The more critical aspect of behavioral testing, however, is the expertise of the audiologist relative to the range and quality of normal auditory responses characteristic of each developmental stage in the sequence of hearing maturation. The child's minimal response level to each calibrated tone or noise stimuli is plotted on an audiogram with the symbol S (indicating sound-field). The BOA audiogram, however, represents only overall overt responses to sound from the child's better hearing ear. Folsom and Diefendorf (1999) cautioned that behavioral observation audiometry is a poor predictor of auditory sensitivity and is not recommended for assessing frequency specific threshold sensitivity in newborns, infants, or young children. Nevertheless, BOA provides a quick, simple, and inexpensive means of estimating hearing sensitivity, facilitates decisions regarding which formal test procedures may be most effective, and suggests the level and quality of responses that can be expected. Additionally, it is a valid and effective procedure for identifying hearing loss in children with disabilities when auditory responses are judged in relation to the child's developmental level (Abdala, 1999; Folsom & Diefendorf, 1999).

Techniques that use operant reinforcement principles to develop reliable responses to auditory input include *visual reinforcement audiometry* (VRA), *tangible reinforcement operant*

conditioning audiometry (TROCA), and *conditioned play audiometry* (CPA). VRA is most effectively used with children between 6 months and 2 years of age. The child's natural inclination to turn his head in search of a sound source is reinforced with a visual reinforcement that typically consists of flashing lights and the activation of mechanical toys or computer-generated video clips. Sound is introduced through one of two or more speakers and, once the child is conditioned to turn toward the correct speaker, the sound is gradually lowered to detect the child's VRA threshold (the lowest sound that reliably elicits the head turning response). Abdala (1999) found that children as young as 5 to 9 months of age can be conditioned to respond to VRA. Reinforcement with tangible rewards for responses to sound stimuli, TROCA requires the child to press a button or lever at the presentation of auditory stimuli in order to receive edibles such as Fruit Loops or small trinkets. TROCA procedures may be used either in sound-fields or under earphones and is an effective alternative behavioral audiometric approach for use with children who are visually impaired. Figure 6.6 portrays the use of TROCA with a visually impaired child.

Children as young as 18 months may be conditioned to respond through conditioned play audiometry (CPA) to pure-tone auditory signals produced either in a sound-field or through earphones. During CPA, developmentally appropriate play tasks such as placing a ring on a stacking cone, inserting or removing a peg in a pegboard, or releasing a block or other small toy into a container are used to condition the child to respond when the signal is perceived. Carefully timed and delivered social praise serves as the reinforcement for CPA. Encouraging the child to hold the manipulative item (stacking ring, peg, block, etc.) next to the earphone on the same side of the body as the ear being tested helps the child wait for the signal and provides a clear beginning and end to each stimulus. Gradually, the tone signals are decreased as the central frequencies (between

FIGURE 6.6

Tangible reinforcement operant conditioning audiometry (TROCA) being used with a child with multiple impairments. Each time the child presses the touch pad in response to an auditory signal, he is rewarded with cereal delivered through the tray of the reinforcement unit.

500 Hz and 2000 to 4000 Hz) are swept through at 20 dB. The primary advantage of play audiometry is that ear-specific, true auditory thresholds can be obtained. Northern and Downs (1991) recommend that the criteria for referral for further audiometric testing be failure to respond to a 20 dB signal at any frequency during pure-tone screening although Downs & Yoshinaga-Itano (1999) proposed that awareness or localization of stimuli at 45 dB HL may be considered to constitute a passing response for children with developmental delays.

Physiological Measures

When a child cannot reliably respond to behavioral observation audiological techniques for age, sensory, cognitive, physical, or behavioral reasons, objective physiological measures such as *otoacoustic emissions* (OAEs) and *auditory brain-stem responses* may be employed. These measures do not require volitional responses and subsequently, do not measure functional hearing. However, as Abdala (1999) points out, these tests are very useful because they "correlate with hearing in a systematic way" and are predictive of hearing status.

Evoked otoacoustic emissions evaluate cochlear status through the noninvasive use of a small microphone placed within the infant's or child's ear canal. Thompson et al. (2001) explained that otoacoustic emissions are inaudible sounds from the cochlea in response to audible stimulation. The outer hair cells of an intact cochlea vibrate, which emits an echo back through the middle ear (Diefendorf, 1997). When OAEs are present, hearing is normal or there may be a mild loss but their absence signals a moderate to profound hearing loss. Transient-evoked otoacoustic emissions (TEOAE) are elicited by clicks, while distortion product OAEs (DPOAE) are evoked with tones, and each represent different frequencies. OAEs can be efficiently administered and are sensitive to blockage in the outer ear canal, middle ear fluid, and damage to the outer hair cells of the cochlea but cannot be used to obtain hearing thresholds, detect neural dysfunction, or distinguish between cochlear and conductive losses (JCIH, 2000; Richardson & Williamson, 1998; and Thompson, 2001).

A measure of how the auditory nerve responds to sound as it travels from the inner ear along the auditory brain-stem pathways to the brain, the auditory brain-stem response (ABR) is considered the gold standard of physiological audiological testing. Electrodes, devices that record neural activity below the skin, are placed on the infant's or child's scalp and brain-wave activity in response to a click stimulus is recorded. The ABR can be elicited from premies of 27 weeks of age, and an infant is considered to pass an ABR screen when responses are obtained at 30 dB to 40 dB HL. The ABR detects primarily high frequency sounds (2000 Hz to 6000 Hz) and has limited ability for frequency specificity. The use of automated ABR technology is preferred for screening. Each ear can be screened at 35 dB HL within a few minutes and can be administered by trained nonprofessionals (Eavey & Bertero, 1995). Folsom and Diefendorf (1999) explained that a normal OAE in combination with an abnormal ABR represents the hallmark sign of some form of auditory nerve pathology, brain-stem neuropathy, or brain-stem conduction defect. The primary disadvantages of the ABR are the expense of the procedure and the fact that most children between 6 months and 4 years of age must be sedated for the duration of the procedure. Abdala (1999) and Northern and Downs (1991) also warn that ABRs may not yield valid data on children with severe neurological impairments, since such damage interferes with registration of the signal at the brain level and, consequently, recorded responses may be more a reflection of the central nervous system impairment than of the perception of sound. Folsom and Diefendorf (1999) further advised that the use of OAEs and ABRs indicate only auditory function while behavioral approaches can estimate levels of hearing. Table 6.2 describes audiometric procedures, their purpose, intended population, results, and limitations.

Speech Audiometry

The child's awareness of and sensitivity to speech is measured by obtaining *speech awareness thresholds* (SAT) or *speech reception thresholds* (SRT). Instead of pure tones, the audiologist introduces speech through the headphones or speakers within the sound-treated testing room. Speech awareness thresholds can be measured in infants as well as in children who may not yet be able to imitate words. Depending on the age of the child, the audiologist may vocalize "buh buh buh," "bye bye," "oh-oh!" or "peek-a-boo!" "touch your nose," "Where's mama?" or other age-relevant phrases.

Speech reception thresholds (SRT) may be established in many 2- and 3-year-old children in sound-field conditions and in 3- and 4-year-old children under earphones. Typically, toys or pictures, depending on the age and developmental

level of the child, are selected to represent spondaics (two-syllable words that are pronounced with equal stress on each syllable (e.g., pancake, airplane, hot dog), and the child is asked to point to the stimulus item or repeat the stimulus word. The words are presented in gradually decreasing intensity increments until a speech reception threshold (SRT) is established. While there are standardized speech reception tests, the two most frequently used with children aged 3 years and older are the Northwestern University Children's Perception of Speech Test (NU-CHIPS) (Elliot & Katz, 1980) and the Pediatric Speech Intelligibility Test (PSI) (Jerger, Lewis, & Hawkins, 1980).

The Role of Early Childhood Personnel in the Assessment of Auditory Functioning

Instructional personnel who work with the child on a daily basis may be the first to detect the possibility of a hearing loss and to make the initial referrals for remediation or amplification. Audiological assessments conducted in unfamiliar settings may not provide an accurate account of how the child uses hearing in day-to-day situations. Early childhood personnel are able to observe the child's reactions to common environmental sounds such as garbage trucks, emergency vehicles, and telephones. Attention to the types of noisemakers the child chooses during music time and to the nature of his or her responses and attention during group instructional settings often yields valuable data regarding both frequencies and intensities of sound that influence the child's hearing during routine activities and in familiar settings. The child with a hearing loss may fail to respond to directions or to the announcement of exciting or preferred activities if he or she is not looking at the teacher. During group activities, the child may be inattentive or may fail to monitor his or her loudness during quiet activities such as watching a movie or during story or nap time. Frequent requests for repeated directions or responses of "huh?" even

TABLE 6.2

A Comparison of Pediatric Audiometric Procedures

Test	Age	Purpose	Procedure	Results	Limitations
Behavioral Observation Audiometry (BOA)	Birth through 7 months	Assesses hearing acuity using unconditioned responses to sound, e.g., reflexive and orienting behaviors	The infant is observed for changes in behavior after presentation of an acoustic stimulus in the sound-field (through speakers) or with Hear-Kit Noisemakers.	This screening test provides information about age-appropriateness of an infant's response to suprathreshold sound. Can rule out significant hearing loss.	This method relies solely on the audiologist's observations to determine when a response to sound has occurred. Cannot be used to define auditory thresholds.
Visual Reinforcement Audiometry (VRA)	7 through 30 months	Assesses hearing acuity using conditioned responses to sound, e.g., head turning	The child is conditioned to provide a specific response to an acoustic stimulus. For example, a head turn in the direction of the sound source is rewarded by lighting and/or activating an animated toy. Once the child is conditioned to respond to the sound, the intensity of the signal is reduced to determine threshold of hearing.	This procedure can be used to determine threshold of hearing.	Because signals are typically presented through a loudspeaker, thresholds obtained indicate acuity of the "better hearing ear."
Conditioned Play Audiometry	30 months through 5 years	Assesses hearing acuity using conditioned responses to sound by engaging in play-oriented activities	The child is conditioned to perform a play activity (e.g., dropping a block in a bucket) whenever s/he hears a sound. Once the child is conditioned, threshold of hearing can be determined by decreasing signal intensity. Speech reception threshold (SRT) testing may also be completed.	This test is usually performed under earphones to obtain ear- and frequency-specific information about hearing acuity. Results define the nature and degree of hearing impairment.	Results obtained may depend on the child's developmental level.

Test Method	Age Range	Assesses	Description	Comments
Conventional Behavioral Audiologic Assessment	School-age through adulthood	Assesses hearing acuity by requiring a specific response to an acoustic stimulus, such as hand-raising or button push	The patient is asked to raise his/her hand or press a button each time s/he hears a sound. Basic audiologic assessment also includes speech reception threshold (SRT) testing and word recognition measures. Comprehensive assessment includes tympanometry, acoustic reflex and acoustic reflex decay testing in addition to the above.	This test is performed by air and bone conduction to obtain ear- and frequency-specific information. Results define the nature and degree of hearing impairment.
Tympanometry	4 months through adulthood	Assesses the status of the middle ear system	A probe tone is introduced into the ear. The amount of sound reflected by the tympanic membrane is measured by a probe in the ear canal as the pressure in the ear canal is varied.	Provides information about the status of the tympanic membrane and middle ear system (e.g., effusion, negative pressure).
Otoacoustic Emissions (OAE)	Birth through adulthood	Assesses auditory function through the level of the cochlea	Acoustic emissions generated by the outer hair cells in the cochlea are elicited by direct acoustic stimulation and are recorded by a small microphone placed in the ear canal.	Presence of evoked otoacoustic emissions is correlated with hearing thresholds of 30 dB or better. Specialized equipment is required for accurate assessment of infants under 4 months of age. Because measurement of emissions relies on reverse transduction of sound through the middle ear, presence of middle ear pathology will preclude recording.
Brain-stem Auditory Evoked Response (BAER) or Auditory Brain-stem Response (ABR)	Birth through adulthood	Assesses auditory function through the level of the brain-stem	The auditory system is stimulated by a brief acoustic signal via air or bone conduction. The resulting neuroelectric activity is recorded by surface electrodes placed on the head. The response is assessed based on the identification of component waves, their morphology and the measurement of absolute and interwave latencies.	Provides ear-specific information and some frequency-specific information about hearing acuity within 5-10 dB of behavioral thresholds. Can also detect retrocochlear pathologies. Requires infant to be in sleep state. Can assess infants in natural sleep up to about 4 months of age. Older infants and young children require sedation.

Note: From "Test Methods Summary Chart", by University of Michigan Child Hearing Information, (n.d.). Copyright University of Michigan. Reprinted with permission.

when the child is looking may indicate a hearing loss. The teacher should pay particular attention to the auditory attentiveness and articulation patterns of children who sustain frequent ear infections. Chen (1999) emphasized "there is a significant difference between the amount of hearing required to detect the presence of sound and the amount of hearing required to discriminate and comprehend sound" (p. 234).

Educators of children with hearing impairment should collaborate closely with the family, audiologist, and teacher of hearing impaired in the selection of sensory aids (hearing aids, FM systems, vibrotactile aids, cochlear implants), language approach (auditory-verbal, auditory-oral, cued speech, total communication, American sign language, or bilingual-bicultural), and environmental arrangements to ensure consistency and multiple opportunities for optimal use of hearing (Gatty, 1996). A comprehensive discussion of the variables to consider in selection and management of hearing aids is detailed by Hoover (2000). The goal of early intervention includes provision of amplification (when appropriate), facilitation of developmentally appropriate language skills, enhancing the family's understanding of the child's strengths and needs, and promotion of the family's competence in advocating for their child (JCIH, 2000). Matkin and Wilcox (1999, p. 145) emphasized the importance of serving children with a continuum of hearing loss within the educational system, not just those children with the most significant losses. They offered the following guidelines for educationally significant hearing loss as set forth by the Colorado Department of Education:

- An average pure-tone loss in the speech range of 20 dB HL or greater, not reversible within a reasonable amount of time
- An average high-frequency, pure-tone loss of 35 dB HL or greater in the better ear at two or more of the following frequencies: 2000, 3000, 5000, and 6000 Hz
- A permanent unilateral hearing loss of 35 dB HL or greater in the speech range

- Any hearing impairment that significantly affects communication with others and in which the child requires supplemental assistance or modification of instructional methods to achieve optimum performance

In conclusion, whether a hearing impairment is detected through informal observation, through formal screening measures, or through sophisticated procedures and instruments, early identification leads to intervention services that can promote optimal development of hearing for speech and language development and minimize the effects of the hearing loss on all developmental processes.

SCREENING AND ASSESSMENT OF VISUAL FUNCTIONING

The first three months of a child's life are the most critical to the development of the visual system; even a few days of monocular deprivation during this time can permanently alter the visual system. The sense of vision plays a primary role in the integration of perceptions from other sensory modalities and Lewis and Allman (2000) reported that between 90% and 95% of learning occurs through the visual channel. Significantly low vision, chronic fluctuating vision, and blindness can have deleterious and pervasive effects on the rate, quality, and patterns of development in the young child and can severely impede the development of independence, communication, and social interactions (Ferrell, 1998; Hatton, Bailey, Burchinal, & Ferrell, 1997; Langley, 1998; Lewis & Allman, 2000; and Teplin, 1995).

Incidence of Visual Impairment in Children with Disabilities

Childhood blindness and severe visual impairment occurs in approximately 2 to 10 per 10,000 births and acquired visual impairment during childhood is approximately one fifth as prevalent, with approximately half of congenital and later-onset blindness having a hereditary basis (Jan, Skyanda, & Groenveld, 1990; Teplin, 1995). Deitz and Ferrell (1993) reported that of this number of children, approximately 25% are totally blind. Hatton (2001) found that childhood blindness accounts for approximately 4% of those who are considered to be blind within the general world-wide population. Data accrued during the first year of the Model Registry of Early Childhood Visual Impairment Consortium revealed that of 406 children from birth to 3 years of age who demonstrated visual impairment, 22% were found to have developmental delays and 33% to have one or more disabilities (Hatton, 2001). Estimates of multiple disabilities among children who are visually impaired have ranged from 40% to 70% (Deitz & Ferrell, 1993; Wesson & Maino, 1995; Teplin, 1995). Jan et al. (1990) found visual impairment in approximately 23% of children with mental retardation, 8% of children with hearing impairment, 13% of children with a seizure disorder, and 14% of children with heart defects. High degrees of myopia (nearsightedness) have been reported in children with Down syndrome although Wesson and Maino (1995) observed that 88% of children with Down syndrome below the age of 25 months presented with approximately two degrees of hyperopia (farsightedness). However, these authors' experiences led them to conclude that the children with myopia demonstrated more severely impaired vision. Additional visual impairments associated with Down syndrome include astigmatism, strabismus, cataracts, and nystagmus. Langley (1998) and Wesson and Maino (1995) reported that refractive errors are present in 21% to 76% of children with cerebral palsy, 60% of whom demonstrated significant hyperopia, myopia, or astigmatism. Hyperopia is three times more prevalent in children with postural tone deficits than in the general population. In addition to refractive errors, cortical visual impairment, fixation deficits, field limitations, convergence insufficiency, nystagmus, and optic atrophy are commonly associated with neuromo-

tor disorders. Gaze limitations, intermittent strabismus, and abnormal retinal function have been reported in children with autism (Wesson & Maino, 1995).

The most common cause of blindness in infants is retinopathy of prematurity (ROP), occurring at a rate of 75% in infants weighing less than 1,000 grams at birth but affecting only 4% (the majority of active ROP cases resolve spontaneously with few sequelae) (Glass, 1993). Other visual problems associated with prematurity include congenital cataracts, high myopia, strabismus, and amblyopia. Glass (1993) also reports that cortical visual impairment occurs with extreme prematurity and is most often associated with severe central nervous system damage. More recently, Hatton (2001) participated in a study that revealed the most prevalent forms of significant visual impairment in children under three included cortical visual impairment, retinopathy of prematurity, and optic nerve hypoplasia (refer to Table 6.3 for a description of common vision impairments associated with young children). Teplin (1995) identified the causes of acquired blindness as including genetic abnormalities, infections such as meningitis, tumors, brain injuries, and eye injuries.

Dimensions and Classification of Visual Impairment

A child's level of acuity and/or extent of visual fields are considered in the diagnosis of a severe visual impairment. A function of macular integrity, visual acuity was described by Orel-Bixler (1999) as "a threshold measure of the eye's ability to detect fine detail or fine resolution." In children who can respond in some manner to letters, shapes, and symbols, acuity is evaluated with standard optotype cards or charts. Linear arrangements of stimuli are felt to yield a more accurate estimate of acuity than are cards with a single optotype (shape, symbols, letter) because resolution of linear figures is influenced by the presence of the surrounding figures and place greater demands on the visual system. However, older toddlers and children with multiple impairments often can respond successfully to single optotypes when they cannot be assessed through more traditional measures. A visual acuity of 20/20 represents normal vision. The numerator indicates the distance from the eye to the visual target, while the denominator indicates the smallest visual stimulus that the child can correctly and consistently identify. A child whose acuity is 20/70 or worse in the better eye with best correction is considered to be partially sighted, the minimum level of vision required to receive public school vision services under Part C early intervention and IDEA mandates in most states. When a child presents with an acuity of 20/200 or worse in the better eye with best correction, he is considered to be legally blind. Deitz and Ferrell (1993) argued that the current definition of visual impairment does not consider fluctuating visual abilities as seen in cortically visually impaired children, environmental factors that affect vision in specific situations, or deteriorating visual loss. Two children with the same acuity may use their vision very differently because of personal and environmental factors. Regardless of the level of acuity, personal factors such as neuromotor integrity, cognitive functioning, attention and organizational behaviors, and experience will influence how and what a child actually sees. Romano (1990) posited that an acuity of 20/200 was sufficient and adequate visual ability for the tasks and activities expected of preschool children. A child with an acuity of 20/200 can identify and discriminate details in 2-inch pictures when held close to the eyes and can typically visualize simple, colorful 5 to 7 inch pictures at 3 to 5 feet.

The normal visual field, the entire area of physical space visible to the eye without shifting gaze, approaches adult levels by 18 months of age although 4 to 6 month olds readily respond to peripheral information. The visual field of an adult when looking straight ahead is approximately 65 degrees nasally, 95 degrees temporally, 50 degrees superiorly, and 70 degrees inferiorly (Atkinson &

Van Hof-van Duin, 1993). A visual field of 20 degrees or less, regardless of acuity, falls within the classification of legal blindness.

The classification of vision problems in children with disabilities may be organized by their effects on the visual system. Common childhood visual defects can be grouped according to (1) structural abnormality or disease of the visual system, such as conjunctivitis, aniridia, and cataracts; (2) impaired visual acuity, such as nearsightedness (myopia), farsightedness (hyperopia), or amblyopia; (3) impaired ocular movements, such as nystagmus, strabismus, and paresis; and (4) impaired visual awareness due to constricted visual fields or cortical impairment (Jan, Skyanda, Groenveld, & Hoyt, 1987). While they typically do not render a child partially sighted or legally blind, two of the most prevalent visual problems in young children are amblyopia and strabismus.

Amblyopia, the most common cause of visual loss in children under 6 years of age is the reduction of acuity in one eye due to insufficient stimulation of the brain's visual pathways when no apparent pathological aberration exists in either the eye or the visual pathways (Teplin, 1995). The primary etiology of amblyopia is visual confusion that occurs with the loss of equal binocular input and the presence of dissimilar visual images at the retinal level. In an attempt to resolve the visual confusion, the child subconsciously "turns off" the vision in the weaker eye and the stronger eye becomes dominant. Conditions that place children at risk for amblyopia include strabismus, a significant difference in refractive error between the two eyes, ptosis (drooping of the upper eyelid), congenital nystagmus, optic nerve hypoplasia, convergence insufficiency, and prolonged occlusion of one eye (Cibis & Fitzgerald, 1993; Teplin, 1995). Amblyopia is easily treatable if it is the primary cause of low vision and is diagnosed prior to 4 years of age, however Teplin cautions that success in restoring complete vision diminishes between 4 and 9 years of age. Patching is the first line of defense in the remediation of amblyopia. The patch is placed over the good or stronger eye in an effort to force the child to use, and subsequently improve, the vision in the weaker eye. The regime of patching depends on the age of the child, the severity of the amblyopia, and the time of initial detection. Romano (1990) urged the detection and remediation of amblyopia as early as possible, since the general rule is one month of treatment for each year of age at the time of diagnosis.

When one eye deviates in any direction from its normal alignment, *strabismus* is the resulting sequelae. Strabismus is found in 5% of preschool children and can result from impaired motor function, impaired sensory functioning, and refractive errors. Infants often give the appearance of strabismus because of prominent epicanthal folds and reduced interpupillary distance although the eyes are straight. This condition is referred to as pseudostrabismus and resolves with growth. Esotropia (turning in or adduction of eyes from midline) and exotropia (turning out or abduction of eyes from midline) are forms of strabismus. Intermittent turning in or out of an eye in a child of 2 months or less is considered normal, however Teplin (1995) advised that persistent misalignment after this period indicates the need for an ophthalmological referral. Depending on the nature of the strabismus and the age of onset, it is managed through patching, the prescription of corrective lenses, or surgery on the extraocular muscles. Strabismus is often associated with neurological impairments such as hydrocephalus and cerebral palsy and with intrauterine infections, especially toxoplasmosis and cytomegalic inclusion (CMV) disease, as well as with prematurity. Additional visual conditions common to young children with disabilities and associated visual effects are described in Table 6.3.

Screening and Assessment of Visual Function

Vision screening at birth and within the first 6 months of age is essential to the detection of any abnormality that precludes good binocular vision. According to Orel-Bixler (1999), the American Academy of Optometry and the American Academy of Ophthalmology recommend complete eye examinations by a medical eye care specialist for all infants at 6 to 8 months of age and again at 30 months. Premature infants are evaluated and followed postnatally by an ophthalmologist due to their high risk of retinopathy of prematurity and other visual problems associated with prematurity. Crouch, E.R. and Kennedy, R.A. (1993) advised that the primary physician or pediatrician should additionally screen a child's vision at birth and prior to entering kindergarten. Parents are generally the first to recognize that a vision concern exists in an otherwise "normal" infant when they observe visual inattention, inconsistent or lack of responses to familiar faces, failure to fixate and follow objects or faces, or the presence of gross abnormalities such as nystagmus, wandering eye movements, or a persistent strabismus. Additional behaviors indicative of a vision problem have been suggested by Teplin (1995, p. 22) and include:

- Lack of eye contact by 3 months of age
- Lack of visual fixation or following by 3 months of age
- Lack of accurate reaching for objects by 6 months
- Persistent lack of coordinated eye movements or sustained crossing of one eye after 4 to 6 months
- Frequent horizontal or vertical "jerky" eye movements
- Lack of a clear, black pupil
- Persistent tearing when not crying
- Significant sensitivity to bright light
- Drooping of an eyelid sufficient to obscure the pupil
- Any asymmetry of pupillary size
- Any obvious abnormality of the shape or structure of the eyes

Observation of any of these symptoms warrants evaluation by a medical eye-care specialist. Romano (1990) stressed the importance of listening to parents' concerns regarding their child's vision and insightfully advised, "parents are rarely wrong

TABLE 6.3
Common Childhood Visual Conditions

Visual Condition	Nature of Condition	Effects on Vision
Albinism	Congenital absence of eye pigment caused by an enzyme insufficiency	Acuity of 20/200 or better; photophobia, refractive errors, loss of central vision nystagmus; poor depth
Amblyopia	Reduced vision in the absence of structural damage; results from a difference in acuity between the eyes or from a lack of alignment	Often referred to as "lazy eye," if uncorrected within a critical time period, vision in the weaker eye is "turned off" by the brain and the dominant eye takes over; results in impairment of depth and fusion in addition to diminished acuity
Cataracts	Opacity of any size or degree in the crystalline lens	Acuity of 20/50 to 20/200; possible photophobia; if the lens is removed, accommodation power is lost; strabismus may develop
Congenital Amaurosis of Leber (CAL)	Congenital tapetoretinal degeneration beginning in utero	Profound visual loss at birth, nystagmus, poorly reactive pupils, extinguished ERG, light perception may be present, high incidence of hyperopia
Color Blindness	Congenital dysfunction of the cones, nerves of the retina	Blue/yellow vision lost initially with retinal diseases; red/green loss first associated with optic nerve lesions
Congenital Glaucoma	Congenital condition caused by an increase in intraocular pressure	Photophobia, bulging or hazy cornea, excess tearing, optic nerve damage, early onset blindness may be present; later developing glaucoma may reduce acuity to 20/50; amblyopia

Cortical Visual Impairment	Lack of visual attention and awareness with a normal ocular evaluation and the absence of nystagmus	Aware of flashing lights, movement, and bright colors; peripheral fields often most functional; tactile exploration substituted for visual; reaches with face turned to the side; vision fluctuates over time
Nystagmus	Congenital or acquired condition that results in rhythmic eye oscillations that are either equal in amplitude or greater in one direction	Acuity may be diminished; compensatory head turn may evolve
Optic Atrophy	Degeneration of the optic nerve that can be either congenital or acquired and may result from postinflammatory infection of compressed optic nerve or may be part of a multisystem disorder affecting the CNS	Depending on the form, acuity 20/30 to 20/200; sluggish pupillary response; visual field deficits; color vision loss; nystagmus
Optic Nerve Hypoplasia	Nonprogressive, congenital disorder of the optic nerve; diminished number of optic nerve fibers in the optic nerve	Minimal vision impairment to total blindness; bitemporal field defects; diminished pupillary reaction; associated with midline defects and growth hormone deficiency
Retinopathy of Prematurity	Congenital condition of the retinal vascular system associated with prematurity in which there is extraretinal vascular proliferation which may lead to tractional retinal detachment	Depending on the progress of the fibrovascular process, minimal to no effects in Grade 1 to high myopia loss of central vision, glaucoma, and strabismus in Grade III to total retinal detachment and blindness in Plus disease
Strabismus	Deviation in the alignment of eyes either inward (esotropia) or outward (exotropia)	Loss of fusion, depth; if uncorrected, amblyopia may occur; child may adopt a compensatory head posture

Note: From *Decision Making in Pediatric Ophthalmology,* by G. W. Cibis, A. C. Tongue, and M. L. Stass-Isern (Eds.), 1993, St. Louis, MO: Mosby-Year Book, Inc.; *The Eye in Infancy* by S. J. Isenberg (Ed.), 1989, Chicago, IL: Year Book Medical Publisher; "Pediatric Neuro-ophthalmology," by L. J. Martyn, 1983, *The Pediatric Clinics of North America, 42*(8), 103–1121.

when they think that there is a problem with their child's eyes or vision" (p. 361).

Clinical Evaluation of Vision

Facets of a comprehensive assessment of vision by an optometrist or ophthalmologist have been delineated by Orel-Bixler (1999) and include the following (pp. 111–112):

- A medical history of the medical and ocular health of both the child and his family
- Use of confrontation tests to evaluate fixation and eye movement behaviors

- An evaluation for refractive or focusing errors
- An evaluation of visual fields (central and peripheral)
- An evaluation of the health of the anterior and posterior eye structures (Figure 6.7 depicts the general anatomy of the healthy eye)
- Provision of qualitative and quantitative estimates of visual acuity and functional use of vision
- Measures of contrast sensitivity and color vision
- Referrals for additional diagnostic tests needed to assess or confirm vision problems related to health and integrity of the eyes and/or central nervous system

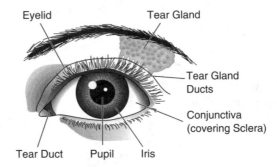

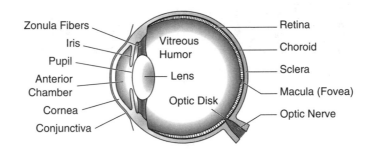

FIGURE 6.7

Diagrams of the external surface of the eye and its surrounding structures (top) and of a lateral view of the posterior segment of the eye and optic nerve (bottom). The posterior segment of the eye and any related anomalies may be viewed only through indirect ophthalmoscopy whereas the superficial structures of the eye can be observed with the naked eye.

Note: From *Children with Disabilities: A Medical Primer* (5th ed.), by M. L. Batshaw (2002). Baltimore: Paul H. Brookes. Reprinted with permission.

- counseling with family and caregivers regarding findings or diagnosis and intervention options and referral to early intervention services when warranted.

Observation of the child's external structures may immediately yield evidence of a vision concern. A drooping lid (ptosis), keyhole shaped pupil or irregularly shaped iris (coloboma), unequal pupils, or lack of symmetry between the eyes all signal vision concerns which may significantly impede binocular vision. One of the most common means of initially ascertaining (and ruling out) the presence of strabismus is the Hirschberg test, which uses the beam from a penlight or other light source to determine whether the reflection of light is centrally located in each pupil. The anterior eye structures are observed with the biomicroscope (slit lamp) and include assessment of the clarity of the cornea and lens and the detection of cataracts. The child's ability to fixate and follow visual stimuli, monocularly and binocularly, provides information relative to acuity, field losses, the integrity of the six extraocular muscles, the function of the cranial nerves III, IV, and VI, and of brain structures other than motor neurons that control eye movements (Orel-Bixler, 1999). In addition to observing eye movements as a variety of developmentally appropriate stimuli are used to elicit gaze and following behaviors, cover tests and use of prisms are used to evaluate the integrity of extraocular muscles and cranial nerves. The direct and indirect ophthalmoscope are used to evaluate the posterior structures of the eyes and provide views of the optic nerve, retina, macula, and retinal vasculature. Orel-Bixler (1999) noted that the advantage of the direct ophthalmoscope is that dilation of the child's eyes is not required although the indirect ophthalmoscope provides for optimal view of the extreme peripheral retina. An objective measure of focusing (refractive) errors, especially in preverbal children, may be obtained with the retinoscope, which allows the evaluator to observe the movements of a light reflex generated in the child's eye. Hyperopia is detected when the light reflex moves in the same direction of the evaluator's light while the light reflex moves in the opposite direction of the evaluator's light when myopia is present. Orel-Bixler (1999) explains that the nature of prescriptive lenses is determined by holding different powers of lenses in front of the eye until the light reflex no longer moves.

The cornerstone of a vision assessment is the evaluation of *visual acuity*. When appropriate and possible, both near-point acuity (vision within 16 inches [40 cm] from the face) and far-point acuity (vision at and beyond 10 feet [3 meters]) should be measured. Often only gross estimates of visual function can be measured in children under 5 and those with additional disabilities due to the attentional, cognitive, motoric, verbal, and perceptual organization constraints associated with this population of children. The acuity of young children can be estimated by a combination of behavioral and electrophysiological techniques including optokinetic nystagmus, visual evoked potentials, preferential looking strategies, and photoscreening. Optokinetic nystagmus (OKN) can be induced with stripes of graded degrees printed on either a rotating drum or a cloth flag. When the stripes are moved across the visual field, involuntary oscillations of the eyes, referred to as nystagmus, are elicited. Acuity is determined by the smallest width of stripe that triggers the nystagmus.

Preferential looking (FPL) techniques such as the Teller Acuity Cards (Teller, 1979), portrayed in Figure 6.8, and modifications of this approach for clinical administration, the acuity-card procedure (Teller, McDonald, & Preston, 1986), are dependent on the child's visual fixation to various widths of alternating black and white stripes contrasted with a gray background.

The Teller Acuity Cards are a set of 17 cards that are gray with a black and white grating to one side of a central peephole that allows an observer to determine whether the child has fixated the stripes. The cards can be presented either through

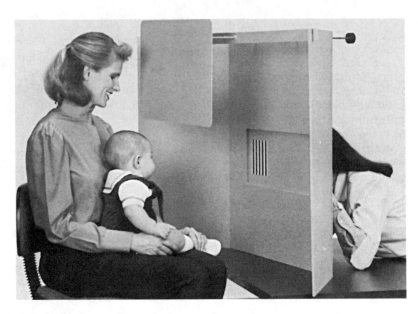

FIGURE 6.8
Preferential Looking (PL) assessment with the Teller Acuity Cards
Note: Reprinted with permission from Vistech Consultants, Inc., manufacturer of the Teller Acuity Card Testing System.

the standard stage-like frame apparatus or through a more practical "en face presentation" (Hartmann, 1996). Successively smaller stripes are presented to the child until the observer determines that the child's behavior suggests that he no longer perceives the stripes. The smallest stripe pattern detected by the child represents his visual threshold. The acuity card procedure can measure both binocular and monocular acuities and is most effective with children 8 months of age and younger, as older children tend to lose interest more quickly. Several clinicians have adapted the procedure for office use, and preferential looking techniques have been used effectively to determine acuity levels in neurologically impaired and cortically visually impaired children (Adams & Courage, 1990; Birch & Bane, 1991; Cibis, 1993). An adaptation of the preferential looking strategy was devised by Hyvarinen (1992) and consists of a series of single paddles, each of which has black-and-white striped patterns of varying widths. The same principle for establishing a visual threshold is

employed with the paddles as for the acuity card procedure. Orel-Bixler (1999) warns that preferential looking derived acuities may be only conservative estimates.

Visual functioning in infants, children with low vision, and children with developmental disabilities often is evaluated through electrophysiological measures such as *visual evoked potential* (VEP). This technique measures vision at the cortical level and assesses the integrity of the visual pathway from the retina to the visual cortex by recording brain wave activity elicited through visual stimuli including flashes of light or patterns (Hartmann, 1996). While a VEP can provide estimates of visual acuity and determine whether a visual problem is due to a retinal or more central visual dysfunction, it does not assess the degree of functional vision available.

Photoscreening has been used successfully with infants and with children with special needs to detect risk factors for amblyopia including high refractive errors, anisometropia (differences in refractive errors between the two eyes), media opacities, and strabismus (Enzenauer, Freeman, Larson, & Williams, 2000). Photoscreening involves the use of special camera equipment that records light reflected from the cornea and is designed particularly for use with preverbal and nonverbal children for whom conventional screening methods may not be successful. Advantages include portability, successful use by volunteers, and effectiveness with younger children. The primary disadvantages are that the procedure, while a quantifiable objective measure, currently only detects risk factors rather than amblyopia itself and the photograph must be interpreted by qualified, skilled professionals (Hartmann et al., 2000). Additionally, photoscreening is reliable only if the child accurately fixates on the camera lens center or visual target long enough for the picture to be taken.

Methods for Estimating Acuity

When a child is cognitively able to discriminate, match, or label symbols, more traditional optotype acuity measures can be administered. Recently the Preschool Vision Screening Task Force of the American Academy of Pediatrics (Hartmann et al., 2000) suggested use of the HOTV letters (Lippmann, 1969), the Lea SYMBOLS (Hyvarinen, 1992), and the Tumbling E for screening the acuity of preschoolers between the ages of 36 to 59 months because they can be administered to each eye separately.

Although the Snellen E Charts (among them the Tumbling E) and the Allen Cards (Preschool Vision Test) (Allen, 1957) are frequently used for screening by pediatricians and eye-care specialists working with children, these measures have not been effective with preschool children with disabilities because of their perceptual demands for discrimination of spatial orientation and visual closure. Symbol sets that have been used more successfully with preschool children include the New York Flashcard Test of Vision (Faye, 1968), the Lea SYMBOLS (Hyvarinen, 1992), the Massachusetts Visual Acuity Test (Mayer & Moore, n.d.), and the Bailey-Hall Cereal Test (Bailey & Hall, 1983).

A test distance of 10 feet (3 meters) is consistently proposed when testing acuities of preschool children to better maintain attention to task. Testing at this distance usually necessitates adjustment of the obtained acuity to reflect 20/20 thresholds. Good lighting is essential, both eyes should be tested, and administration of the tests should be adjusted to accommodate the physical, visual, communication, and attention needs of the child. When the child is verbal, any consistent label applied to the symbols should be accepted. While alternative strategies may be necessary, near vision, in addition to distance vision, should be assessed due to the high frequency of farsightedness (difficulty seeing up close) reported in children with disabilities. The following procedures have the potential for meeting all of these criteria.

The New York Flashcards are comprised of three symbols: an apple, a house, and an umbrella. A single symbol is printed on each card, representing Snellen acuities from 10/15 to 20/200. The child may be given the 20/200 symbols and asked to point to the one that matches the stimulus flashcard. If the child is severely physically limited, two symbols may be presented simultaneously at distance and the child asked to look at the one specified by the examiner. The Lea SYMBOLS are a comprehensive system for assessing the vision of young children and are comprised of a variety of test stimuli, including grating paddles, Hiding Heidi faces, symbols, and numbers. The hallmark symbols consist of a house, an apple/heart, a circle, and a square. The primary advantage of the Lea SYMBOLS is that they are equally sensitive to blur and equally difficult to distinguish. The stimuli sets most useful with children with disabilities are the Single Symbol book and flash cards (Fern, n.d.). Each of these techniques presents only a single symbol (circle, square, heart/apple, house) on each stimulus card. The only difference between the sets is that one is bound in a booklet and the other is comprised of individual flash cards. The Massachusetts Visual Acuity Test (Mayer & Moore, n.d.) uses the Lea SYMBOLS to screen both near and distance vision in children ages 2½ to 6 years. Eight individual rectangular flash cards are used to screen both left and right eyes for distance acuity levels between 20/20 and 20/80 at ten-foot distances. Five Lea SYMBOLS are printed on each card, only one of which is repeated (heart/apple, circle, square, house, circle, etc.). Near vision is tested with a single card with multiple lines printed in two columns, one for each eye, which screens acuities between 20/10 and 20/200. Each series of symbols is separated into individual boxes to assist the child in remaining focused on the same line. Bailey and Hall (1983) devised an ingenious means of estimating acuity in which the child discriminates between single pictures of a Chex-type cereal and a Cheerios-type cereal of gradually diminishing sizes. Because most children have had experiences with Cheerios, the symbol is readily recognized by and motivating to them. This measure is effectively used with children who can indicate their choice only through eye gaze by holding each of the two cards side by side and asking the child to find the Cheerio (or the name of the cereal with which they are most familiar) and randomly alternating the position of the target stimulus until the visual threshold is reached. The following acuity guidelines for referring a child to a medical eye-care specialist have been proposed by the Preschool Vision Screening Task Force of the American Academy of Pediatrics (Hartmann et al., 2000) and by Teplin (1995) based on test distances of ten feet (3 meters):

Age	Referral Criteria
24 months	less than 20/50 in one or both eyes
36 to 47 months:	less than 20/40 in one or both eyes
48 to 59 months:	less than 20/30 in one or both eyes
any age	a two-line difference between the eyes

When formal acuity measures are not feasible, the general level of acuity may be estimated through interviewing parents and caregivers about the child's use of near and distance vision during daily activities and through observations of the child's attention to items in the environment and of the distance between the child and the stimulus when he detects it. Another means of obtaining gross acuities entails enticing the child to pick up or point to small items such as bits of crackers, threads, tiny toys and candies, and cake decorating beads (Langley, 1998; Schlange & Maino, 1995; Sonksen, 1983; Wesson & Maino, 1995). A number of charts available for assisting the evaluator assign estimates of acuity when using the clinical measures described have been developed by Jose (1983), Sonksen (1983), Sonksen, Petrie, & Drew (1991) and Wesson & Maino (1995). While clinical measures of visual acuity provide only rough estimates of what the child can see, they are essential when attempting to determine visual capacity in children who cannot perform on formal measures. Assessment of acuity in infants and preschoolers should yield an estimate of both the size of stimuli and of viewing distances that are optimal for the demands of the contexts in which the children must function. A summary of the techniques used to determine acuity in infants and young children has been prepared by Teplin (1995) and is presented in Table 6.4.

Color and Contrast Vision

Color vision defects may be either hereditary or acquired. Hereditary color vision defects are typically red-green in nature. Congenital color vision defects occur because of impaired cone photopigments and are prevalent in 8% to 10% of the male population and less than .05% of the female population. Orel-Bixler (1999) suggested that family history of color vision defects may reveal initial information about the probability of an inherited form of color blindness. Blue-yellow vision deficits are much more rare and most often coincide with eye diseases, particularly with significant retinopathy of prematurity. Orel-Bixler (1999) advised that acquired color vision deficits (red-green or

TABLE 6.4
A Comparison of Pediatric Acuity Techniques

Method	Description	Advantages	Disadvantages
Optokinetic nystagmus (OKN)	Black & white grating (on a cloth strip or on a rotating drum) is moved in one direction across child's visual field; acuity estimates based on finest grating that elicits nystagmus.	Useful to detect whether child has any vision at all. Minimum equipment needed.	Looking at a moving target may not be using the same brain circuits as those used for vision of stationary objects. Examiner's judgments of child's eye movements are sometimes difficult. Not widely used for acuity measurement.
Preferential looking (PL) tests (e.g., Teller Acuity Cards)	Infant is shown series of paired stimuli; one with grating stripes of certain width, the other a gray target of equal luminance. Infant prefers looking at stripes as long as he or she can discriminate them. Discrimination of narrower stripes implies better acuity. Acuity is based on subjective decision by tester as to infant's overall looking behavior over many pairs of stimuli.	Stimuli are stationary (vs OKN moving stripes). Test distance and amount of visual field covered by stimuli are constant. Infant's looking behavior is easier for observer to judge than in OKN. Tester can interact with infant in between presentations, which strengthens visual attention to test. Modified "low-vision" cards have been successful in obtaining acuities in visually impaired young children. Can be successful in assessing vision of retarded and multihandicapped children.	Possibility of tester bias. Limited durability of the cards (e.g., worn spots attracting infant's attention). Hazardous to equate PL acuities with Snellen equivalents. PL acuities in strabismic amblyopia may be overestimated.

TABLE 6.4 Continued

Method	Description	Advantages	Disadvantages
Visually evoked potential (VEP)	Recording (from electroencephalogramt-ype sensors on child's scalp) an electrical signal from occipital region of brain following visual stimulation. The most informative stimuli are patterns (e.g., checkerboard, stripes) rather than flashes of light. Computer averages out "background" brain signals.	Does not rely on motor response of infant (thus potentially useful in cerebral palsy). Better reproducibility than OKN or PL. Facilitated by active, social engagement of child by examiner.	Equipment is very expensive. Extensive training of tester is mandatory. Hazardous to equate VEP acuities with Snellen equivalents. Validation studies are very difficult to carry out. Not yet widely used for routine acuity measurements.
Observation of child's spontaneous visual fixation & following	Using different-sized objects of varying contrast and at different distances from face, examiner observes child's eye movements and child's attempts to reach for object.	Practical. Correlates closely with functional vision. Crudely quantifiable by distance and size of target object.	Lacks precision. Variable reproducibility. Difficult to express as a "Snellen" equivalent (i.e., 20/200). Dependent on infant's visual attention and awake/alert state. Limited usefulness in children with neurologic impairment of eye or limb movements (e.g., some forms of cerebral palsy).
Picture cards (e.g., Allen figures, symbol test)	Child either names picture on distant eye chart or simply points to matching picture on a card he or she is holding. Self-illuminated chart is best.	Avoid confusion related to unfamiliarity with letters (e.g., Snellen). Allow at least some quantitation of distance acuity.	Require attention and cooperation of child. Require appropriate and standardized illumination of target pictures. Are not equivalent to Snellen acuities.

Snellen "Illiterate" E	Child is shown series of "E" shapes in different directional orientations. Child is asked to show with his hand which way the "legs" are pointing. For children 3 years of age or older.	Retains nearly all of the accuracy of true Snellen letters. Does not require any verbal response.	Requires child's attention and cooperation. Relatively uninteresting visual target. Children who are developmentally below 4 years may not be mature enough to reliably indicate direction. Use of isolated "E" targets may overestimate acuity by eliminating the normal "crowding effect" inherent when symbols are surrounded by other symbols.
Matching letter tests (e.g., Sheridan's STYCAR, Lippman's HOTV)	Child views letters on distant eye chart and simply points to matching letter on a card he or she is holding. Self-illuminated chart is best. Intended for the 2–3-year-old who cannot yet respond to Snellen Illiterate E test.	Usually enjoyable for children. Brief. Simple. Does not require any verbal response.	Use of isolated letter targets may overestimate acuity by eliminating the normal "crowding effect" inherent when symbols are surrounded by other symbols. Not as accurate as Snellen Illiterate E test.

Note: From "Visual Impairment in Infants and Young Children," by S. W. Teplin, 1995, *Infants and Young Children: An Interdisciplinary Journal of Special Care Practices, 8*(1), pp. 18–51. Copyright 1995 by Aspen Publishers, Inc. Reprinted with permission.

blue-yellow) are associated with optic nerve disorders, retinal disorders, and pathology of the central nervous system and that changes in color perception could signal a decrease in visual acuity or visual fields or the presence of disease. Fischer (1996) advised that many pharmaceutical agents such as antibiotics, analgesics, and anticonvulsants may change color perception, either temporarily or permanently. The goals of color vision testing are to detect any color confusion that may be present and to discern how it may affect daily life. Most color vision tests require that the child identify a number, shape, form, or traceable path of one color or set of colors embedded in a different color. However, Fischer (1996) noted that most test manufacturers suggest that an acuity of better than 20/200 is needed to see the figures because of the low contrast between the foreground and the background of such tests. Preschool teachers are often the first to question color vision when the child has difficulty consistently naming and identifying colors. While most color vision tests are too difficult for preschool children, Color Vision Testing Made Easy (CVTME) (Waggoner, 1994) was developed for use with children from 3 to 6 years of age. Designed to detect red-green color deficiencies, the CVTME consists of 14 plates that use simple forms (circle, star, square) and pictures (boat, balloon, dog, car). The CVTME has been found valid for use with 3-year-olds (Cotter, Lee, & French, 1999) and with individuals who are mentally handicapped (Erickson & Block, 1999). Orel-Bixler (1999) reported that behavioral tests for color vision using faces in a forced preferential looking paradigm are currently under development.

Perception of color and detail may be affected by the child's contrast sensitivity, the ability to discriminate differences in brightness or shades of gray created by degree of reflected light. Orel-Bixler (1999) suggested that contrast sensitivity does not reach adult levels until 1 to 2 years of age in most children. Hyvarinen's Hiding Heidi cards assess contrast sensitivity in children who can point or eye gaze to indicate what they can see. Cards with a single image of the Hiding Heidi face which gradually decreases in contrast are presented one at a time simultaneously with a blank card. The two cards are presented as one with the blank card on top of the Hiding Heidi image. At the time of presentation, the cards are quickly separated and it is anticipated that the child will direct her gaze toward the Hiding Heidi image. The cards are presented in this manner until the child's behavior signals he no longer perceives a difference between the image and the blank card. Children who can label or match may be administered Hyvarinen's Lea SYMBOLS Low Contrast Test, which uses the Lea SYMBOLS presented in a linear manner. Each line of symbols successively decreases in contrast from the background. The child's level of contrast sensitivity is indicated by the last line of symbols most consistently identified.

Dimensions of a Functional Vision Assessment

The most important data for a parent, a teacher, other caregivers, and service providers to have is knowledge of what the child can see and predictions of how he may respond to items encountered in different environments. Jose, Smith, and Shane (1980) emphasized that "the numbers attached to a diagnosis are not as important as the information that the child can see a half-inch block at three feet" (p. 4). A pioneer in the field of visual learning and assessment, Barraga (1976) coined the term visual efficiency to refer to each child's unique ability to use his vision functionally to process, accommodate, and adapt to his visual environment. Sonksen et al., (1991) included in an assessment of functional vision the child's visual reactions in natural contexts, such as visual awareness of silent objects of different sizes, color, and luminance available at various distances and in different fields of vision. A valid and reliable assessment of vision is dependent on the interventionist's knowledge of the components of visual function, on an appreciation of the type and quality of responses expected at different developmental levels, and on the nature of stimuli critical to eliciting specific visual behaviors. Observations of how the child spontaneously uses vision in the natural environment will yield valuable information regarding how functional vision is for carrying out daily life functions as well as the conditions that appear to facilitate efficient use of vision. While a functional vision assessment is typically conducted by a teacher of the visually impaired, impressions of parents and caregivers regarding what, how, where, and when the child uses vision should be an integral part of the assessment.

In addition to acuity, the precise measurement of visual fields, depth, color, and contrast is often difficult if not impossible in young children with delays. An estimate of the child's visual fields may be achieved with the use of two equally attractive mechanical, illuminated, or motion toys. The child's attention is held at the midline with one of the toys while the second toy is moved systematically around the face of an imaginary clock 13 to 18 inches away from the child. With the child's attention held at midline, the second toy is activated at each clock position and observations of the positions that elicit the child's gaze shift are recorded. Alternatively, the child's attention may be held at midline by one observer while another interventionist introduces stimuli from behind the child into peripheral fields. Positions in which the child fails to orient may be reassessed to determine whether the lack of orientation is due to lack of attention or to a true absence of vision in that field. Attention to where the child looks (or fails to look) may provide the best indication of his fields. A child may be noted consistently to color on only one side of the page, to point to pictures at only the top half of pages in a book, or to consistently fail to note obstacles on one side of the body when playing outdoors.

Color perception may be assessed by observing whether the child tends to gravitate to toys of only a specific color or to gather toys of a specific color from others as he plays. Matching and sorting activities should require the child to simultaneously discriminate among toys of browns, reds, and greens, and between blues and yellows to rule out the two primary color deficiencies. Problems with contrast sensitivity may be present when the child cannot locate a beige cup on a natural wood counter, find a white bar of soap that has fallen into a white sink, or locate a favorite truck in a bin of vehicles of a similar color. The child who seems overwhelmed and disorganized when trying to play on visually busy playmats designed for use in daycare and preschool settings should be further observed for other contrast and perceptual difficulties. The child's ability to perceive depth may be noted as he or she moves across various textures, descends or ascends different levels of height, and reaches into deep containers to obtain chips or cookies. The child who overreaches or underreaches when taking items off surfaces or placing items in small holes, on stacking posts, or in containers, and who avoids stairs, curbs, and crossing from the tile to the carpet may have some form of depth perception impairment. In addition to describing the range of the child's visual behaviors, variables that appear to support the use of vision, and barriers that interfere with the use of vision, the functional vision assessment should also document if, how, and when the child's vision impedes developmental and educational progress. Additional outcomes expected from an assessment of functional vision are delineated in Figure 6.9.

Among commercially available assessments of functional vision, the Screening Tests for Young Children and Retardates (STYCAR) (Sheridan, 1973) is one of the most creative, practical, and functional tools. Despite its unfortunate title, the STYCAR is an easily administered, comprehensive assessment, using miniature toys and graduated sizes of styrofoam balls to estimate acuity, visual fields, and visual processing abilities. Children from the age of 6 months are easily motivated to participate in this assessment because of the nature of the manipulatives. Sonksen has enriched the field of functional vision assessment by providing several critical articles that detail both the assessment of and programming for visual development in young children with visual impairments

VISION CHARACTERISTICS

- Nature of stimuli to which the child most consistently responds (light, movement, objects, people, etc.)
- Optimal size of toys and objects needed for efficient access at both near and far point
- Optimal distances, relative to the task and objects involved
- Optimal placement of stimuli relative to the child's position
- Efficiency of eye movements for localization, fixation, shift of gaze, and scanning
- Compensations noted that signal misalignment, field deficits, diminished acuity and/or postural limitations
- Quality of eye-hand coordination
- Apparent effectiveness of prescribed lenses or aids
- Quality of visual responses
  1) during self-imposed movement,
  2) in response to postural shifts imposed by others, and
  3) when moving on riding toys, with mobility aids, and in self- or motor-powered wheel chairs
- Stability of vision over time
- Perceptual abilities including color, depth, and figure-ground discrimination

CHILD VARIABLES INFLUENCING USE OF VISION

- Effects of medications
- Optimal attending time
- Typical processing, response, and fatigue latencies
- Postural limitations
- Cognitive function
- Pacing and interaction style needs
- Positioning and handling needs that affect the visual system

CONTEXT VARIABLES

- Contexts in which the child is most motivated to use vision
- Effects of sound and noise on the use of vision
- Quality of foreground and background illumination needed
- Quality of contrast needed between foreground and background
- Nature and quality of stimuli that most consistently elicit use of vision
  1) size
  2) quality (light, motion, sound elements)
  3) proximity of stimuli to one another
  4) position relative to the child

FIGURE 6.9

Expected outcomes of an assessment of functional vision

- Nature of cues, prompts, and reinforcers needed to elicit and maintain visual attention
- Task components that require vision
- Positioning equipment needed to facilitate vision
- Temperament and motivational factors

ELIGIBILITY VARIABLES

- Description of whether and how the child's vision impedes mobility, daily living, play, communication, social, and/or developmental and educational skills and progress
- Description of the supports needed to facilitate the child's use of vision (contexts, strategies, materials, equipment, pacing, time frame, intervention personnel, etc.)
- Description of the service delivery model needed to address vision concerns
- Proposed draft of goals and benchmarks in which strategies for managing vision needs are embedded within and across instructional areas

FIGURE 6.9
Continued

and multiple disabilities (Sonksen, 1983; Sonksen & Macrae, 1987; Sonksen, Petrie, & Drew, 1991). Comprehensive strategies for conducting a functional vision assessment with young children with multiple disabilities and severe handicapping conditions have been developed by Langley (1998) and Topor (1999).

The most recent contribution to the field, the Individualized, Systematic Assessment of Visual Efficiency (ISAVE) is a comprehensive process for screening and assessing visual behaviors of children with severe disabilities functioning within the birth to 5 year developmental range (Langley, 1998). ISAVE provides strategies for assessing environmental, sensory, perceptual, and physical influences related to the use of vision but is designed to allow the evaluator to select the components of the instrument that are most relevant to the needs of the child being assessed. Unique features of the ISAVE include (1) an ecological assessment of visual behaviors; (2) a component that addresses critical postural, movement, and transitional behaviors that support and contribute to the development of specific visual skills; (3) a component that ascertains whether the child displays the hallmark characteristics associated with

cortical visual impairment; and (4) a component that assists in evaluating and managing the vision in children whose vision is believed to be no greater than light perception. An additional component, the Baby Screen, screens eight areas of visual functioning in infants from prematurity through 12 months of age, three of which may be found in Figure 6.10.

In addition to Response to Light, Fixation, and Following, the other five domains encompass the assessment of Visual Acuity, Visual Fields, Binocularity, Social Gaze, and Visual Perception.

The Role of Early Childhood Personnel in the Assessment of Visual Functioning

Early childhood personnel may be the first to engage the toddler and young child in activities requiring focusing at near point for extended amounts of time. Initially, play activities consist of general gross motor exploration and play with large, colorful toys, and refined visual abilities are generally not required. Once in an instructional setting, however, the child is more likely to experience more time in close investigation of his world

Response to Light	
P	Pupils respond slowly
P	Pupil size very small
P	Incubated infant may not turn toward light
B–6wk	Turns to diffuse light
B–6wk	Minimal pupil response
B–6wk	Eyes orient light source
6wk–4mos	Brisk response to light
8–12mos	Creeps toward light
8–12mos	Uncovers light
Comments	
P Passed	
F Failed	

Fixation	
P	Eyes open, no fixation
P	Fixation fleeting
B–6wk	Brief fixation light
B–6wk	Regards colorful object
6wk–4mo	Sustained fixation
6wk–4mo	Shift: Stuck one object
6wk–4mo	Preoccupied human face
4–8mos	Attends object 5–10 sec
4–8mos	Fixates image in mirror
4–8mos	Fixates object in room
Comments	
P Passed	
F Failed	

Following	
B–6wk	Unstable, brief
B–6wk	Head/eyes together
B–6wk	Jerky: direction of moving target
B–6wk	Follow object to mid-line, <90 degrees
B–6wk	Central pursuit 90
6wk–4mo	Follows upward 30
6wk–4mo	Follows downward
6wk–4mo	Central pursuit 180
6wk–4mo	Eyes follow all planes of gaze
6wk–4mo	Eyes more mobile
Comments	
P Passed	
F Failed	

FIGURE 6.10

Three scales of visual functioning

Note: From "Three Scales of Visual Functioning," in *Individualized, Systematic Assessment of Visual Efficiency: Baby Screen,* by M. B. Langley (1998), Louisville, KY: American Printing House for the Blind. Reprinted with permission from the American Printing House for the Blind.

and increased visual demands may reveal visual difficulties. Observations of the infant shown in Figure 6.11 as he interacted with the interventionist and with toys revealed difficulties in attending to moving toys and objects, visual attention in different postures, and eye-hand coordination. The interventionist may notice that the child consistently moves closer to see books and pictures or that the child's eyes are red and watery after prolonged attention to art work, picture books, and fine motor activities. The child may be observed to tilt his or her head when focusing on something in the distance or when trying to string beads or cut. The child may be observed consistently to label items according to their general configuration rather than to more specific details (e.g., labeling a

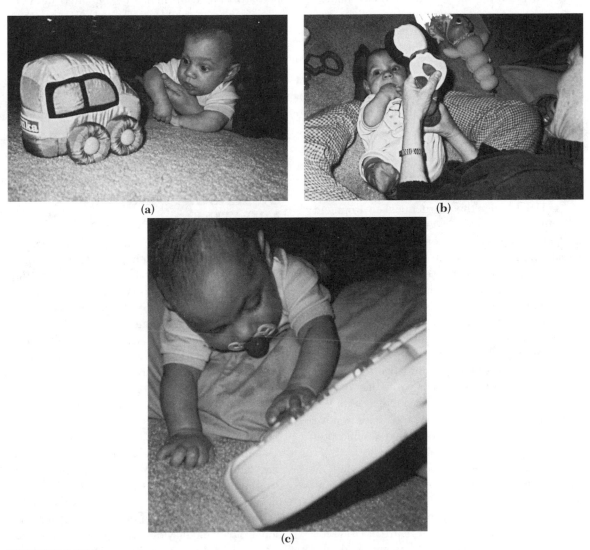

(a)

(b)

(c)

FIGURE 6.11
Screening vision of an infant. The screening of (a) fixation, (b) following behaviors, and (c) eye-hand coordination in an infant suspected of having a visual impairment.

shovel as a spoon). During play in various activity centers, the child may be noted to consistently ignore items on one side of his or her body or, when engaged in matching or lotto games, fail to scan the same general area each time. The interventionist should be particularly concerned about the child who may be extremely sensitive to changes in lighting or who may lack awareness of surface changes when moving from one area to another. Children who are drawn to light, who prefer to light gaze rather than play with toys, to flick their fingers before their eyes in the direction of a light source, who appear suddenly to lack awareness of objects around them, or who have difficulty distinguishing details and complain of headaches should be referred immediately to a medical eye-care specialist for formal evaluation of vision.

The early interventionist working with a visually impaired infant or preschooler must communicate frequently and work closely with the child's parents, teacher of the visually impaired, and therapists (1) to arrange the instructional environment and support the child's posture so as to facilitate optimal use of residual vision in contingent learning situations; (2) to monitor and adjust illumination, contrast, and working distances to minimize fatigue factors; and (3) to select, design, and modify learning materials to enhance the child's visual attention and organizational processes. As the case manager for children with significant physical and communication limitations, the early interventionist may need to take the initiative for seeking the assistance of the teacher of the visually impaired as well as the child's therapists to determine range of visual behaviors and needs relative to the use of an augmentative communication device or a power wheel chair.

Regardless of the specific instrument or process selected for the screening and assessment of visual behaviors, the ultimate goal is to determine the nature and quality of conditions and contexts that best support the child's use of vision for movement within the environment and for dynamic participation in daily living, play, social, and learning contexts.

Although hearing and vision are addressed in most well-baby clinics and in early childhood screening programs, tactile, vestibular, and proprioceptive sensory systems are typically not screened unless an insightful pediatrician or parent suspects problems in these areas. However, because of the importance of these underlying sensory modalities in the development of compensatory behaviors in hearing impaired and visually impaired children, knowledge of their intactness and integration with other sensory channels is essential. In addition, young children who demonstrate significant difficulty organizing themselves and responding appropriately to social interactions and sensory information from the environment may be manifesting some form of dysfunction of sensory integration (DSI).

SCREENING AND ASSESSMENT OF SENSORY PROCESSING ABILITIES

While the senses of vision and hearing are considered distal (or environmental) sensory modalities along with taste and smell, the vestibular, tactile, and proprioceptive sensory receptors comprise the cluster of proximal (or body) sensory modalities (Williamson, Anzalone, & Hanft, 2000). Integration of all these basic sensory processes forms the foundation for emotional stability and organized learning behaviors. Whenever a deficit occurs in one sensory modality, the quality of input to the central nervous system from other sensory channels is compromised. Dysfunction in sensory processing abilities can affect sensorimotor development, learning, and behavior related to day-to-day activities in a number of different ways, depending on the etiology, type, and degree of impairment dysfunction. Problems with sensory processing may lead to sensation seeking or sensation avoidance behaviors, poor registration and/or hyperactivity and distractibility depending on the child's neurological threshold and the nature and demands of the task he must respond to and environment in which he functions at any point in time (Dunn, 1997).

Children at Risk for Sensory Processing Dysfunction

Infants with extreme prematurity are significantly at risk for both proximal and distal sensory disorders and disorganization due to multiple life-saving interventions that lead to impaired sensory mechanisms, multiple negative sensory experiences, and lack of or insufficient nurturing pressure touch sensations. The premature child may be either hyporesponsive to sensory information or hyperaroused and easily overwhelmed by sensory stimuli. Visually impaired infants often manifest proximal sensory deficits in the forms of tactile defensiveness, gravitational insecurity, and poor feeding behaviors. Hearing impaired children with a sensorineural loss may experience poor balance and coordination due to the damage to the vestibular nerve. Poor tactile-kinesthetic awareness and bilateral integration may interfere with the planning, organization, and formation of manual signs. Children who exhibit self-injurious behaviors or cravings for intense forms of sensory input from one or all of the proximal sensory receptors are often found to have seriously disturbed, disorganized, or poorly integrated sensory systems. Children with movement disorders such as cerebral palsy and spinal cord damage experience a vast array of sensory perception difficulties and the quality of their movement is often a direct reflection of their ability to perceive incoming sensory information critical to body schema and awareness of position in space. Williamson et al. (2000) noted that children with autistic spectrum disorders have sensory modulation problems. DeGangi and Greenspan (1989) espoused that infants unable to process sensory experiences normally might not avail themselves of the spectrum of sensory experiences critical for responding to and assimilating new learning opportunities. At greater risk for being able to organize themselves in order to attend to, process, and learn from experiences are children labeled as *regulatory disordered*. DeGangi (1991) explained that a regulatory disorder is "defined by persistent symptoms that interfere with adaptive functioning" (p. 3). Regulatory disordered infants have been found to be at high risk for later perceptual, language, sensory integrative, and behavioral difficulties during the preschool years (DeGangi, 1991). DeGangi detailed the primary identifying characteristics of a child with regulatory disorders:

- Sleep disorders that result from high states of arousal that inhibit the ability to sleep;
- Extreme difficulties self-consoling and severe temper tantrums;
- Significant feeding problems;
- Hyperarousal that leads to disorganization during transitions from one activity to the next, distractibility, attention to extraneous details in the environment, and easy sensory overloading; and
- "Fussiness, irritability, an unhappy mood state, and a tendency to quickly escalate from contentment to distress" (p. 4)

All of these developmental problems depict dysfunction in sensory processing that has a direct effect on how well a child copes with and adapts to daily life requirements.

Dimensions of an Assessment of Sensory Processing Abilities

An assessment of sensory processing should ascertain both the child's ability to modulate sensory information (register, orient, and initiate a response) and to perceive and discriminate sensory information from each modality (Williamson et al., 2000). The child's ability to integrate sensory modalities, including the ability to filter out extraneous information and to attend to relevant sensory data, should be analyzed. The child's general developmental level must be considered in determining the appropriateness of behavioral responses, and assessment should focus on how the child processes sensory information in response to environmental challenges (Williamson et al., 2000, and Dunn, 1999). The most appropriate and effective means of assessing sensory processing are through caregiver interview and through observations of the child within functional contexts such as structured and unstructured social interactions and play, mealtimes, grooming activities, interactions with family members, and during transitions between activities and settings. Best practices suggest the necessity of multiple observations of the child over time to address the variability of his performance because of the influence emotional status, environmental factors (e.g., noise, lighting, and number of people present), accumulated sensory build-up, availability of supports (e.g., people, routines, and contexts), and general coping skills (Williamson et al., 2000). Additionally, Williamson and his colleagues suggest that the nature of the child's responses to any sensory input is influenced by his self-regulation of arousal, attention, affect, and action. Guidelines suggested by Williamson et al. (2000) for structuring observations of sensory processing abilities are provided in Figure 6.12.

The first component of the assessment, the child's ability to regulate sensory processes, should address the child's sensory threshold, which indicates the amount of stimuli needed for the nervous system to react to stimuli (Dunn, 1997). A low threshold may result in hyperactivity or sensory defensiveness. A high threshold can lead to hyporeactivity, decreased arousal, and passivity. Behaviors associated with each of these states are described by Dunn (1997) and Williamson et al. (2000).

An assessment of the discrimination ability of primary perceptual functions entails the second component of an assessment of sensory processes. Assessment of vestibular function should include observations regarding the child's quality of postural tone and postural reactions, the ability to assume and maintain supine flexion and prone extension patterns, reactions to imposed movement and to antigravity movement, and observations of behaviors such as self-imposed spinning,

spinning of objects, stereotypic rocking behaviors, and excessive and disorganized movement (e.g., hyperactivity). The presence and length of nystagmus in response to controlled spinning or of nystagmus in the absence of visual impairment will provide insight regarding the integrity of the vestibular system.

The *tactile system* is responsible for perception of touch, pressure, temperature, and pain. The sense of touch or tactile sensation is comprised of an early protective system that becomes integrated into a more mature discriminative system that interprets tactile input for cognitive functions. Children who tend to be tactually defensive have failed to fully integrate the early protective touch system. Sears (1994) explained that dysfunction in the tactile system may result in aversive responses such as pain, fear, and discomfort. *Tactile defensiveness* is neurologically based and a component of a larger constellation of aversive reactions in response to stimulation across one or more sensory modalities that results in irrational-appearing behaviors (Sears, 1994). Determining whether a tactile response is indicative of a defensive system or a reaction to novelty and unfamiliarity will depend on the context in which the response is elicited and on how quickly the child adapts to the stimulus. A child's resistance to imposed demands may mistakenly be perceived as tactile defensiveness. Observing the child as he explores a set of novel materials will facilitate decisions regarding the integrity of the tactile system. If he willingly explores items such as slinkies, Koosh balls, stuffed animals, and playdough but refuses to cooperate when directed to play with an item that may be above his competency level, tactile defensiveness may be ruled out. The child's awareness of both light and firm touch should be explored in addition to requiring him to identify or match objects placed in his hand without the assistance of vision. This ability to discriminate tactile properties of objects is referred to as stereognosis. The child's responsiveness to texture and temperature as well as his ability to localize and discriminate single and dual touch points (two-point

Arousal

- What is the child's state of alertness and how does it change in response to different sensory experiences?
- Is the child able to transition smoothly between different states of alertness?
- Is the child able to sustain levels of energy and activity that support successful task engagement?
- Does the child have a narrow or wide range of optimal arousal?
- Does the child have a range of coping strategies that enable him to modulate sensory reactivity and arousal?

Attention

- Is the child able to maintain selective focus on relevant stimuli?
- Is the child able to shift attention between two or more targets or modalities?
- Is the duration of the child's attention span comparable to other children of the same age?
- Does the child prefer or avoid certain sensory modalities?

Affect

- Does the child have an organized range of emotional expression?
- Is there a predominant emotional tone in the child (e.g., fearfulness, anxiety, defiance, or withdrawal)?
- Is the child available for social interaction with peers and adults?
- Will the child interact socially with peers and adults?
- Does the child have a playful disposition that reflects ease in the situation and supports learning and engagement?

Action

- Is the child able to formulate goals for play behavior that are appropriate to his or her developmental skills and environmental opportunities?
- Is the child able to solve problems encountered during exploration or play with creativity, flexibility, and persistence?
- Is the child's behavior characterized by consistent approach or avoidance of specific materials or tasks?
- Does the child have adequate motor planning and coordination for age appropriate tasks?

Context

- What sensory input characterizes the physical and social environments?
- What are the sensory properties of the identified sensory systems (rate, intensity, duration)?
- Does the environment require the child to form a response by organizing information simultaneously from different sensory systems?

FIGURE 6.12

Guidelines to structure observations of sensory processing

Note: From "Assessment of Sensory Processing, Praxis, and Motor Performance," by G. G. Williamson, M. E. Anzalone, and B. E. Hanft, 2000, *ICDL Clinical Practice Guidelines*, pp. 161–162. Copyright 2000 by The Interdisciplinary Council on Developmental & Learning Disorders. Reprinted with permission. Available from *www.icdl.com*

- What is the quality of the physical environment in terms of temperature, lighting, noise, space, and related properties?
- What are the social characteristics of the situation?
- What are the specific environments, situations, or individuals that are particularly organizing for the child?
- Does the environment provide a routine that is reasonably predictable, consistent, and structured?

FIGURE 6.12

Continued

discrimination) should also be assessed. Royeen (1986; 1987) developed strategies for assessing the tactile ability of young children and for determining the presence of tactile defensive behaviors.

Receptors within the joints, tendons, and muscles that govern awareness of the position of body parts and of the body's position in space, both at rest and during movement, are referred to as the *proprioceptive system.* Kinesthesia is the conscious awareness of joint motion. Somatosensory perception is the integration of vestibular, tactile, and proprioceptive modalities and is critical for development of body scheme and for the organization, planning, and initiation of movement. Tasks traditionally administered to assess proprioceptive awareness and function include identification and localization of body parts, imitation of postures, and maintenance of imposed postures, both with and without vision (vision occluded). Although children with developmental disabilities may experience difficulty in complying with tasks designed to assess proprioceptive function, postural and movement behaviors and reactions to firm or deep pressure indicate the level of intactness. Porter (1984) suggests that proprioceptive dysfunction may be suspected if an extremity lags behind during movement transitions or if the child fails to appropriately position extremities during transitions, weight-bearing, or resting postures. Observing the child's reactions to vibration, traction, and approximation of joints, ability to grade strength and rhythm of movement, and ability to

accommodate to size, shape, and weight of objects will also provide some indication of proprioceptive function.

Assessment Procedures: Representational Methods

Traditionally, the assessment of sensorimotor functions is addressed by occupational and physical therapists; however, developmental specialists, early intervention specialists, teachers of the visually impaired and hearing impaired, and nurses are often responsible for the screening and assessment of basic sensory processes. In addition to observations of the child within natural contexts and interviews of caregivers, assessment procedures may include formal instruments designed to assess sensory processes and carefully selected items contained within developmental scales that address specific sensory processes. The Miller Assessment for Preschoolers (MAP) (Miller, 1982) is a standardized screening tool designed to identify children with "moderate preacademic problems" (manual, p. 1) that place a child developmentally at risk. The MAP consists of 27 items that address critical skills in the areas of Sensory and Motor, Cognitive, and Combined Abilities. The Sensory Motor section is divided into a Foundations Index and a Coordination Index. The Foundations Index includes items that address sensory integrative and neurodevelopmental parameters of sensory functioning such as (1) sense of position and movement, (2) sense of touch, and (3) basic components of movement. A Supplemental Observations section provides subjective but qualitative information regarding a child's performance. Miller explains that "certain children, although scoring within acceptable limits on these items, must use unusual compensatory methods to do so. It might be suspected that if increasingly complex demands were made of these children, these unusual methods, requiring increased effort, would no longer be adequate to compensate for the underlying problems" (p. 175).

A criterion-referenced test of sensory processing and reactivity in infants from 4 to 18 months, the Test of Sensory Function in Infants (TSFI) (DeGangi & Greenspan, 1989), assesses 24 items across five subdomains, which include reactivity to tactile deep pressure, adaptive motor functions, visual tactile integration, ocular motor control, and reactivity to vestibular stimulation. Individual items were selected based on their ability to indicate sensory integrative dysfunction in children and to identify children at risk for learning disability. DeGangi and Greenspan (1989) suggested that the TSFI should be used in conjunction with other standardized assessment measures. DeGangi, Poisson, Sickel, and Weiner (1995) developed The Infant Toddler Symptom Checklist, a series of checklists for caregivers of children from 7 to 30 months of age, to screen for sensory processing and regulatory concerns. The Infant Toddler Symptom Checklist assesses self-regulation, attention, movement, emotional status, vision, language, and the child's reactions and behaviors in response to bathing, eating, and sleeping. More recently, DeGangi and Balzer-Martin (2000) have developed strategies for assessing the sensory processing abilities of preschoolers. The Sensorimotor History Questionnaire for Preschoolers (DeGangi & Balzer-Martin, 2000) was validated on 3-and 4-year-olds but the authors proposed it is also appropriate for 5-year-olds. The questionnaire consists of a series of checklists divided into the areas of Self-Regulation, Sensory Processing of Touch,

Sensory Processing of Movement, Emotional Maturity, and Motor Maturity. Completion of the questionnaire indicates whether the child exhibits normal or at-risk behaviors within the assessed areas.

Based on a caregiver's perceptions of how a child responds to various sensory experiences within typical daily life events, the Sensory Profile (Dunn, 1999) is a standardized measure of sensory processing for children from 3 to 10 years of age. The Sensory Profile is based on the influence of the interaction between neurological thresholds and behavioral responses (Dunn, 1997) and was designed to "gather information about children's sensory processing abilities that support and/or interfere with functional performance" (Dunn, 1999, p. 3) The Sensory Profile examines sensory processing, modulation, and behavioral and emotional responses and the child's performance is characterized as being typical, as reflecting a probable difference, or as reflecting a definite difference in sensory processing. Dunn (1999) reported that 43 items on the Caregiver Questionnaire clustered into three factors (sensory seeking, emotionally reactive, and inattention/distractibility) that appeared consistent with behaviors characteristic of children with ADHD. The short form of the Sensory Profile contains 38 items selected from the original 125 and addresses tactile, taste/smell, movement sensitivity, and visual/auditory sensitivity; auditory filtering; and additionally assesses for low energy and weakness. The Infant/Toddler Sensory Profile (Dunn & Daniels 2000) is a 58-item checklist that assesses general, auditory, visual, tactile, and vestibular processing in infants between the ages of birth and 3 years. The child's performance is rated either as typical or at-risk.

Zeitlin, Williamson, and Szczepanski (1988) developed the Early Coping Inventory for children ages from 4 to 36 months to assess sensorimotor organization, reactivity, and self-initiation within the contexts of coping with day-to-day activities. The Temperament and Atypical

Behavior Scale (TABS) (Bagnato, Neisworth, Salvia, & Hunt, 1999) was designed for use with children from 11 to 71 months to assess for the presence of atypical self-regulatory behavior. The TABS consists of both a standardized screening checklist of 15 items and a more comprehensive assessment checklist of 55 items that is completed by the child's primary caregivers. Behaviors assessed fall within four different categories of potential concern: Detached, Hyper-sensitive/Active, Underreactive, and Dysregulated, and the child's pattern of behaviors results in a Temperament and Regulatory Index (TRI). The authors found that TRI scores from 5 to 9 indicate a child is at risk for atypical temperament and/or self-regulation while scores of 10 or greater signal serious difficulties in these areas. Additionally, the authors proposed that the TABS scores are "useful in meeting criteria for early intervention program eligibility and for wraparound mental health behavioral support." A major advantage of the TABS is that the manual provides multiple intervention suggestions to address the behaviors caregivers indicate are a problem.

Developmental scales with subtests that address regulatory/organizational processes and tactile, vestibular, and/or proprioceptive functions include the Hawaii Early Learning Profile: HELP (birth–3) (Parks, Furuno, O'Reilly, Inatsuka, & Hoska, et al. 1994); Hawaii Early Learning Profile for Preschoolers: HELP (3–6) (Vort Corporation, 1995); the Psychoeducational Profile, Revised (Schopler, Reichler, Bashford, Lansing, & Marcus, 1990); the Carolina Curriculum for Infants and Toddlers with Special Needs, second edition (Johnson-Martin, Jens, Attermeier, & Hacker, 1991); the Carolina Curriculum for Preschoolers with Special Needs (Johnson-Martin, Attermeier, & Hacker, 1990); and the Vulpe Assessment Battery (Vulpe, 1994). In addition, the second edition of the Bayley Scales of Infant Development (Bayley, 1993) incorporated specific items to assist in the diagnosis of children with sensory integration dysfunction.

The Role of Early Intervention Personnel in the Assessment of Sensory Perception and Integration

When an infant or toddler is difficult to console, irritable, and easily disorganized, even in the context of routine and familiarity, early childhood personnel should suspect a regulatory disorder or dysfunctional sensory integration processes. The caregiver may note that the child avoids direct gaze, prefers not to be held and cuddled, and may persist in rocking behaviors and head banging behaviors beyond the expected time frame or engage in these behaviors to an excessive degree and to the exclusion of other, adaptive behaviors. This infant may crave firm, deep pressure and seek out vibratory sources such as stereo speakers and the washing machine.

Behaviors in the classroom that may be indicative of sensory integration dysfunction encompass difficulties in changing response modes and in performing simultaneous actions, such as listening to a story and stringing beads, and a desire to play away from other children and in enclosed spaces. The instructor may notice that the child frequently leaves a group setting for a short period of time but returns spontaneously, appearing calmer and more organized. In contrast, he or she may lack appropriate strategies for social interaction, aggressing toward children by pushing and grabbing rather than seeking attention or requesting toys in more socially acceptable ways. He or she may avoid specific art activities, food textures, and the dress-up center. During sensory activities, he or she may not be able to identify objects held in the hand when vision is occluded and may be overly sensitive to smells. During group activities, the child may not want to be touched or held. Patting him or her on the back during rest time may result in explosive tantrums. The early interventionist should also be concerned when a child sustains a severe injury but reacts with minimal awareness or pain. A child with spina bifida should be checked frequently for abrasions and monitored carefully for deficiencies in perception because injuries may be exacerbated due to a lack of sensitivity and subsequent lack of awareness. When observations and impressions of reactions to various types of sensory experiences culminate in a profile of abnormal behaviors and responses such as those previously mentioned, early childhood personnel should refer the child for a comprehensive assessment by a pediatric occupational therapist.

The integration of sensory processes is essential to the development of adaptive cognitive and motoric abilities. Determining specific sensory processing strengths, weaknesses, and needs will identify a child's primary learning channels as well as critical compensatory strategies needed to support optimal developmental functioning in a range of environments. An understanding of the child's unique sensory abilities and needs will also facilitate selection of appropriate learning materials, instructional pacing, and specific handling techniques that will enable the child to function comfortably and efficiently in response to daily demands.

········
SUMMARY OF KEY CONCEPTS

- Universal newborn screenings for vision and hearing are essential for the detection of concerns within the first month of life and referral for intervention, if needed, prior to six months of age to minimize the effects of vision and hearing loss on learning and development.

- There is a high incidence of hearing loss, vision impairment, and regulatory disorders associated with prematurity; the earlier they are detected and intervention provided, the less at risk the child may be for developmental delays associated with the specific impairment.

- Screening for acuity only, either for vision or for hearing purposes, is insufficient in detecting how information is perceived and used and may be misleading relative to the pursual of intervention services as more central and global processing deficits may not be accounted for.

- Observations of the caregivers who most frequently come into contact with young children may offer the most valuable information relative to how the child uses sensory information on a day-to-day basis to function within a variety of environments.

- Accurate screening information may be obtained when the measures are developmentally relevant, match the child's response topography, and complement observations of functioning within typical and natural environments.

- Classification of hearing loss depends on the location of the impairment, the degree and severity of loss, and whether the loss is unilateral or bilateral. The Joint Commission on Infant Hearing recommends a two-stage screening protocol for universal screening of newborns using objective physiological measures. Hearing in children is considered normal when sounds are detected at less than 15 dB HL.

- Classification of vision loss is based on levels of acuity, degree of visual fields, and whether the visual impairment is progressive. Normal vision in a preschool child ranges from 20/20 to 20/40. The vision of children with disabilities can be assessed through a variety of nonverbal measures that encompass preferential looking procedures, behavioral techniques, and the use of tests specially designed for use with populations of young, disabled children.

- The proximal sensory systems include vestibular, tactile, and proprioceptive modalities and serve as the foundation for emotional stability and organized learning behaviors. There are a variety of standardized sensory checklists that may be used with infants as well as preschoolers to determine whether a child is at risk for or displays significant sensory dysfunction.

- Children who display difficulty with the integration of information from several sensory systems, who are easily disorganized, and who have difficulty regulating or modulating their behavior may be manifesting a regulatory disorder or dysfunction of sensory integration which should be treated as early as possible through occupational therapy services.

········

REFERENCES

Abdala, C. (1999). Pediatric audiology: Evaluating infants. In D. Chen (Ed.), *Essential elements in early intervention: Visual impairment and multiple disabilities* (pp. 246–284). New York: AFB Press.

Adams, R. J., & Courage, M. L. (1990). Assessment of visual acuity in children with severe neurological impairments. *Journal of Pediatric Ophthalmology and Strabismus, 27,* 57–62.

Allen, H. F. (1957). Testing visual acuity in preschool children: Norms, variables, and a new picture test. *Pediatrics, 19,* 1093–1100.

Atkinson, J., & Van Hof-van Duin, J. (1993). Visual assessment during the first years of life. In A. R. Fielder, A. B. Best, & M.C.O. Bax (Eds.), "The management of visual impairment in childhood." *Clinics in Developmental Medicine, 128* (9–29). London: MacKeith Press.

Auslander, M. C., Lewis, D. E., Schulte, L., & Stelmachowicz, P. G. (1991). Localization ability in infants with simulated unilateral hearing loss. *Ear and Hearing, 12*(6), 371–376.

Bailey, I. L., & Hall, A. (1983). *Bailey-Hall Cereal Test for the Measurement of Acuity in Children.* Berkeley, CA: Multimedia Center, School of Optometry, University of California.

Barraga, N. C. (1976). *Visual handicaps and learning: A developmental approach.* Belmont, CA: Wadsworth.

Batshaw, M. L. (2002). *Children with disabilities: A medical primer.* Baltimore: Paul H. Brookes.

Bayley, N. (1993). *Bayley Scales of Infant Development* (2nd ed.). San Antonio: The Psychological Corp.: A Harcourt Assessment Co.

Bess, F. H., & Paradise, J. L. (1994). Universal screening for infant hearing impairment; not simple, not risk-free, not necessarily beneficial, and not presently justified. *Pediatrics, 93*(2), 330–334.

Birch, E. E., & Bane, M. C. (1991). Forced-choice preferential looking acuity of children with cortical visual impairment. *Developmental Medicine and Child Neurology, 33,* 722–729.

Chen, D. (2000). Identifying vision and hearing problems in infants with disabilities. *IDA News, 27*(3), 1–3.

Chen, D. (1999). Understanding hearing loss: Implications for early intervention. In D. Chen (Ed.), *Essential elements in early intervention: Visual impairment and multiple disabilities* (pp. 207–245). New York: AFB Press.

Cibis, G. W. (1993). Vision testing in infants and children. In G. W. Cibis, A. C. Tongue, & M. L. Stass-Isern (Eds.), *Decision making in pediatric ophthalmology* (pp. 304–305). St. Louis, MO: Mosby Year Book.

Cibis, G. W., & Fitzgerald, K. (1993). Electrophysiologic acuity testing. In G. W. Cibis, A. C. Tongue, & M. L. Stass-Isern (Eds.), *Decision making in pediatric ophthalmology* (pp. 298–299). St. Louis, MO: Mosby Year Book.

Cotter, S. A., Lee, D. Y., & French, A. L. (1999). Evaluation of a new color vision test: "Color Vision Testing Made Easy." *Journal of American Academy of Optometry, 76*(9), 631–636.

Crouch, E.R., & Kennedy, R.A. (1993). Vision screening guidelines. In G.W. Cibis, A.C. Tongue, & M.L. Stass-Isern (Eds.). *Decision making in pediatric ophthalmology* (pp. 196–197). St. Louis, MO: Mosby Year Book.

DeGangi, G. A. (1991). Assessment of sensory, emotional, and attentional problems in regulatory disordered infants: Part 1. *Infants and Young Children: An Interdisciplinary Journal of Special Care Practices, 3*(3), 1–8.

DeGangi, G. A. & Balzer-Martin, L. A. (2000). The sensorimotor history questionnaire for preschoolers. In G. Williamson, M. Anzalone and B. Hanft (Eds.) *ICDL Clinical Practice Guidelines.* Bethesda, MD: Interdisciplinary Council on Developmental and Learning Disorders.

DeGangi, G. A., & Greenspan, S. I. (1989). *Test of Sensory Function in Infants.* Los Angeles, CA: Western Psychological Services.

DeGangi, G. A., Poisson, S., Sickel, R. Z., & Weiner, A. S. (1995). *Infant/Toddler Symptom Checklist: A screening tool for parents.* San Antonio, TX: Therapy Skill Builders, a division of Psychological Corp.: A Harcourt Assessment Co.

Diefendorf, A.O. (1997). Screening for hearing loss in infants. *Volta Review, 99*(5). 43–63.

Deitz, S. J., & Ferrell, K. A. (1993). Early services for young children with visual impairment: From diagnosis to comprehensive services. *Infants and Young Children: An Interdisciplinary Journal of Special Care Practices, 6*(1), 68–76.

Downs, M. P. (1984). *The HEAR Kit System.* Englewood, CO: Bam World Markets.

Downs, M. P., & Yoshinaga-Itano, C. (1999). The efficacy of early identification for children with hearing impairment. In N. J. Roizen & A. O. Diefendorf (Eds.), *The Pediatric Clinics of North America, 46*(1), 79–87.

Dunn, W. (1999). *Sensory Profile: User's Manual.* San Antonio, TX: Psychological Corp. A Harcourt Assessment Co.

Dunn, W. (1997). The impact of sensory processing abilities on the daily lives of young children and their families: A conceptual model. *Infants and Young Children: An Interdisciplinary Journal of Special Care Practices, 9*(4), 23–35.

Dunn, W., & Daniels, D. B. (2000). *Infant/Toddler Sensory Profile.* San Antonio, TX: The Psychological Corp.: A Harcourt Assessment Co.

Eavey R. D., and Bertero Mdo.C., Thornton A.R., Herrmann, B.S., Joseph, J.M., Gliklich, R.E., Krishnamoorthy, K.S., & Todres, I.D. (1995). Failure to clinically predict NICU hearing loss. *Clinical Pediatrics, 34*(3), 138–145.

Elliot, L., & Katz, D. (1980). Development of a new children's test of speech discrimination. St. Louis, MO: Auditec.

Enzenauer, R. W., Freeman, H. L., Larson, M. R., & Williams, T. L. (2000). Photoscreening for amblyogenic factors by public health personnel: the Eyecor Camera System. *Ophthalmic Epidemiology, 7*(1), 1–12.

Erickson, G. B., & Block, S. S. (1999). Testability of a color vision screening test in a population with mental retardation. *Journal of the American Optometric Association, 70*(12), 758–763.

Faye, E. E. (1968). An acuity test for preschool children with subnormal vision. *Journal of Pediatric Ophthalmology, 5,* 210–212.

Fern, K. (n.d.). Lea SYMBOLS®: Single presentation flash cards. LaSalle, IL: Precision Vision.

Ferrell, K. A. (1998). Project PRISM: A longitudinal study of the developmental patterns of children who are visually impaired. Final Report. CFDA 84.0203C [field-initiated research HO23C10188]. Greeley, CO: University of Northern Colorado.

Fischer, M. L. (1996). Clinical implications of color vision deficiencies. In B. P. Rosenthal and R. G. Cole (Eds.), *Functional assessment of low vision* (pp. 105–127). St. Louis: Mosby.

Folsom, R. C. & Diefendorf, A. O. (1999). Physiologic and behavioral approaches to pediatric hearing assessment. In N. J. Roizen & A. O. Diefendorf (Eds.), *The Pediatric Clinics of North America, 46*(1), 107–117.

Fortnum, H. M., Summerfield, A. Q., Marshall, D. H., Davis, A. C., & Bamford, J. M. (2001). Prevalence of permanent childhood hearing impairment in the United Kingdom and implications for universal neonatal hearing screening: Questionnaire-based ascertainment study. *British Medical Journal, 323*(7312), 536–538.

Gatty, J. C. (1996). Early intervention and management of hearing in infants and toddlers. *Infants and Young Children: An Interdisciplinary Journal of Special Care Practices, 9*(1), 1–15.

Glass, P. (1993). Development of visual function in preterm infants: Implications for early intervention. *Infants and Young Children: An Interdisciplinary Journal of Special Care Practices, 6*(1), 11–20.

Grote, J. J. (2000). Neonatal screening for hearing impairment. *Lancet, 355*(9203), 513–514.

Hartmann, E. E. (1996). Functional vision assessment of infants. In B. P. Rosenthal and R. G. Cole (Eds.), *Functional assessment of low vision* (pp. 45–62). St. Louis: Mosby.

Hartmann, E. E., Dobson, V., Hainline, L., Marsh-Tootle, W., Quinn, G. E., & Ruttum, M. S., et al. (2000). Preschool vision screening: Summary of a task force report. *Pediatrics, 106*(5), 1105–1116.

Hatton, D. D. (2001). Model registry of early childhood visual impairment: First-Year results. *Journal of Visual Impairment and Blindness, 95*(7), pp. 418–433.

Hatton, D. D., Bailey, D. B., Burchinal, M. R., & Ferrell, K. A. (1997). Developmental growth curves of preschool children with vision impairments, *Child Development, 68,* 788–806.

Hoover, B. M. (2000). Hearing aid fitting in infants. *Volta Review, 102*(2), pp. 57–74.

Hyvarinen, L . (1992). The Lea SYMBOLS® System. LaSalle, IL: Precision Vision.

Jan, J. E., Skyanda, A., & Groenveld, M. (1990). Habilitation and rehabilitation of visually impaired and blind children. *Pediatrician, 17,* 202–207.

Jan, J. E., Skyanda, A., Groenveld, M., & Hoyt, C. S. (1987). Behavioural characteristics of children with permanent cortical visual impairment. *Developmental Medicine and Child Neurology, 29,* 571–576.

Jerger, S., Lewis, S., & Hawkins, J. (1980). Pediatric speech intelligibility test: I. Generation of test materials. *International Journal of Pediatric Otolalryngology, 2,* 217–230.

Johnson-Martin, N., Attermeier, S. M., & Hacker, B. J. (1990). *The Carolina Curriculum for Preschoolers with Special Needs.* Baltimore: Paul H. Brookes.

Johnson-Martin, N., Jens, K. G., Attermeier, S. M., & Hacker, B. J. (1991). *The Carolina Curriculum for Infants and Toddlers with Special Needs* (2nd ed.). Baltimore: Paul H. Brookes.

Joint Commission on Infant Hearing (2000). Year 2000 position statement: Principles and guidelines for early hearing detection and intervention programs. *Pediatrics, 106*(4), 798–818.

Jose, R. T. (1983). The eye and functional vision. In R. T. Jose (Ed.), *Understanding low vision* (pp. 3–42). New York: American Foundation for the Blind.

Jose, R. T., Smith, A. J., & Shane, K. G. (1980). Evaluating and stimulating vision in the multiply impaired. *Journal of Visual Impairment and Blindness, 74,* 2–8.

Kennedy, C., Kimm, L., Thornton, R., & Davis, A. (2000). False positives in universal neonatal screening for permanent childhood hearing impairment. *Lancet, 356*(9245), 1903–1904.

Kogan, M. D., Overpeck, M. D., Hoffman, H. J., & Cassellbrant, M. L. (2000). Factors associated with tympanostomy tube insertion among preschool-aged children in the United States. *American Journal of Public Health, 90*(2), 245–250.

Langley, M. B. (1998). Individualized, systematic assessment of visual efficiency (ISAVE). Louisville, KY: American Printing House for the Blind.

Leung, A. K. C. & Kao, C. P. (1999). Management of the child with speech delay. *American Family Physician, 59*(11), 3121–3129.

Lewis, S., and Allman, C. B. (2000). *Seeing eye to eye: An administrator's guide to students with low vision.* New York: American Foundation for the Blind Press.

Lippmann, O. (1969). Vision of young children. *Archives of Ophthalmology, 81,* 763–775.

Matkin, N. D., & Wilcox, A. M. (1999). Considerations in the education of children with hearing loss. In N. J. Roizen & A. O. Diefendorf (Eds.), *The Pediatric Clinics of North America, 46*(1), 143–152.

Mayer, L., & Moore, B. (n.d). *Massachusetts Visual Acuity Test.* LaSalle, IL: Precision Vision.

Miller, L. J. (1982). *Miller Assessment for Preschoolers.* San Antonio, TX: Psychological Corp.: A Harcourt Assessment Co.

Neisworth, J. T., Bagnato, S. J., & Salvia, J. (1995). Neurobehavioral markers for early regulatory disorders. *Infants and Young Children: An Interdisciplinary Journal of Special Care Practices, 8*(1), 8–17.

Neisworth, J. T., Bagnato, S. J., Salvia, J., & Hunt, F. M. (1999). *Temperament and Atypical Behavior Scale: Early Childhood Indicators of Developmental Dysfunction.* Baltimore: Paul H. Brookes.

Northern, J. L., & Downs, M. P. (1991). *Hearing in children* (4th ed.). Baltimore: Williams and Wilkins.

Orel-Bixler, D. (1999). Clinical vision assessments for infants. In D. Chen (Ed.), *Essential elements in early intervention: Visual impairment and multiple disabilities* (pp. 107–156). New York: AFB Press.

Parks, S., Furuno, S., O'Reilly, K., Inatsuka, T., Hoska, C. M., & Zeisloft-Falbey, B. (1994). *Hawaii Early Learning Profile (HELP) Birth to 3.* Palo Alto, CA: VORT Corp.

Porter, R. (1984). Sensory considerations in handling techniques. In B. H. Connolly & P. C. Montgomery (Eds.), *Therapeutic exercise in developmental disabilities* (pp. 43–53). Chattanooga, TN: Chattanooga Corp.

Richardson, M. P. & Williamson, T. J. (1998). Otoacoustic emissions as a screening test for hearing impairment in children recovering from acute bacterial meningitis. *Pediatrics, 102*(6), 1364–1368.

Romano, P. E. (1990). Vision/eye screening: Test twice and refer once. *Pediatric Annals, 19,* 359–367.

Rovers, M. M., Ingels, K., Van der Wilt, G. J., Zielhuis, G. A., & Van den Broek, P. (2001). Otitis media with effusion in infants: Is screening and treatment with ventilation tubes necessary? *Canadian Medical Association Journal, 165*(8), 1055–1056.

Royeen, C. B. (1986). Development of a touch scale for measuring tactile defensiveness in children. *American Journal of Occupational Therapy, 40*(6), 414–419.

Royeen, C. B. (1987). TIP-Touch inventory for preschoolers: A pilot study. *Physical and Occupational Therapy in Pediatrics, 7*(1), 29–41.

Saenz, R. B. (1999). Primary care of infants and young children with Down syndrome. *American Family Physician, 59*(2), 381–390.

Schlange, D. G., & Maino, D. M. (1995). Clinical behavioral objectives: Assessment techniques for special populations. In D. M. Maino (Ed.), *Diagnosis and management of special populations* (pp. 151–185). St. Louis, MO: Mosby.

Schopler, E., Reichler, R. J., Bashford, A., Lansing, M. D., & Marcus, L. M. (1990). *Psychoeducational Profile, Revised* (PEP-R). Austin, TX: PRO-ED.

Sears, C. J. (1994). Recognizing and coping with tactile defensiveness in young children. *Infants and Young Children: An Interdisciplinary Journal of Special Care Practices, 6*, 47–53.

Sheridan, M. (1973). *The Stycar Test of Vision.* Windsor, Berks, England: NFER Publishing Co., Ltd.

Shriberg, L. D., Friel-Patti, S., Flipsen Jr., P., and Brown, R. L. (2000). Otitis media, fluctuant hearing loss, and speech-language outcomes: A preliminary structural equation model. *Journal of Speech, Language, and Hearing Research, 43*(1), 100–120.

Sonksen, P. (1983). The assessment of vision for development in severely visually handicapped babies. *Acta Ophthalmologica (Copenhagen) 157,* 82–90.

Sonksen, P. M., & Macrae, A. J. (1987). Vision for colored pictures at different acuities: The Sonksen picture guide to visual function. *Developmental Medicine and Child Neurology, 29,* 337–347.

Sonksen, P. M., Petrie, A., & Drew, K. J. (1991). Promotion of visual development of severely visually impaired babies: Evaluation of a developmentally based programme. *Developmental Medicine and Child Neurology, 33,* 320–335.

Stein, L. K. (1999). Factors influencing the efficacy of universal newborn hearing screening. In N. J. Roizen & A. O. Diefendorf (Eds.), *The Pediatric Clinics of North America, 46*(1), 95–105.

Teller, D. Y. (1979). The forced choice preferential looking procedure: A psychophysical technique for use with human infants. *Infant Behavior and Development, 2,* 135–153.

Teller, D. Y., McDonald, M. A., & Preston, K. (1986). Assessment of visual acuity in infants and children: The acuity card procedure, *Developmental Medicine and Child Neurology, 28,* 779–789.

Teplin, S. W. (1995). Visual impairment in infants and young children. *Infants and Young Children: An Interdisciplinary Journal of Special Care Practices, 8*(1), 18–51.

Thompson, D. C., McPhillips, H., Davis, R. L., Lieu, T. L., Homer, C. J., & Helfand, M. (2001). Universal newborn hearing screening. *Journal of the American Medical Association, 286*(16), 2000–2010.

Tomaski, S. M. & Grundfast, K. M. (1999). A stepwise approach to the diagnosis and treatment of hereditary hearing loss. In N. J. Roizen, & A. O. Diefendorf (Eds.), *The Pediatric Clinics of North America, 46*(1), 35–47.

Topor, I. (1999). Functional vision assessments and early interventions. In D. Chen (Ed.), *Essential elements in early intervention: Visual impairment and multiple disabilities* (pp. 157–206). New York: AFB Press.

Tran, L. A. P., & Grundfast, K. M. (1997). Hereditary hearing loss. *Volta Review, 99*(5), 63–69.

VORT Corporation. (1995). *Hawaii Early Learning Profile (HELP): HELP for Preschoolers (3–6).* Palo Alto, CA: VORT Corp.

Vulpe, S. G. (1994). *Vulpe Assessment Battery-Revised.* East Aurora, NY: Slosson Educational Publications.

Waggoner, T. L. (1994). *Color vision testing made easy.* Gulf Breeze, FL: Home Vision Care.

Wesson, M. D, & Maino, D. M. (1995). Oculovisual findings in children with Down syndrome, cerebral palsy, and mental retardation without specific etiology. In D. M. Maino (Ed.), *Diagnosis and management of special populations* (pp. 17–54). St. Louis, MO: Mosby Year Book.

Williamson, G. G., Anzalone, M. E., & Hanft, B. (2000). Assessment of sensory processing, praxis, and motor performance. *ICDL Clinical Practice Guidelines,* 155–184. Bethesda, MD: Interdisciplinary Council on Developmental and Learning Disorders.

Zeitlin, S., Williamson, G. G., & Szczepanski, M. (1988). *The Early Coping Inventory.* Bensonville, IL: Scholastic Testing Service

Assessing Family Resources, Priorities, and Concerns

Donald B. Bailey, Jr.
University of North Carolina at Chapel Hill

Assessment in early childhood special education typically involves gathering information about the child with a disability. Child assessment still occupies a major part of a professional's time, and a wide range of appropriate methods and procedures are available. However, expectations for a comprehensive assessment have expanded significantly and now include a documentation of family resources, priorities, and concerns (Krauss, 2000). Although current federal regulations require family assessments only when the child is an infant or toddler under 36 months of age, many early intervention and preschool programs are rethinking their relationships with families and altering services so that they are responsive to both child and family needs. This chapter provides a rationale for family assessment in early intervention, identifies dimensions and procedural considerations, describes representative measures, and discusses strategies for translating family assessment information into goals and services.

RATIONALE

In this chapter, we define *family assessment* as "the ongoing and interactive process by which professionals gather information in order to determine family priorities for goals and services" (Bailey, 1991, p. 27). Why should we gather this information? In the context of early intervention, at least five reasons can be identified: legislative requirements; the need to individualize services; the need to establish a trusting, open, and collaborative relationship between parents and professionals; theoretical bases; and the need to expand program evaluation activities.

Legislative Requirements for Family Assessment

Public Law 99-457 (now the Individuals with Disabilities Education Act) was far-reaching in its mandates to expand the availability of early intervention services to infants, toddlers, and preschool-

ers with disabilities. It also served as one vehicle for promoting substantial changes in the nature and focus of early intervention. By establishing the *Individualized Family Service Program* (IFSP) as the vehicle by which services are provided for infants and toddlers, the law acknowledges that family support and children's services are inextricably linked components that must be provided as part of any comprehensive early intervention effort. To develop an IFSP, the law stipulates that programs must be able to conduct an assessment of family resources, priorities, and concerns related to enhancing their child's development. The regulations accompanying the legislation stipulate that family assessment is to be a voluntary activity for families, conducted only if the parents feel that such an assessment would be appropriate and helpful. In addition, any family assessment activities must be conducted by personnel trained to use appropriate methods and procedures, based at least in part on information provided by the family through a personal interview, and should incorporate the family's own description of its resources, priorities, and concerns. As we shall see shortly, these legislative requirements may be interpreted in a variety of ways and have resulted in considerable debate among professionals as to the best strategies for implementing this mandate. Clearly, however, programs must be prepared to offer these services, and most are now engaged in a variety of family assessment activities.

Federal legislation allows but does not require states to use the IFSP for children over 36 months of age, and most states have chosen to use the more traditional Individualized Education Plan (IEP) for preschoolers. However, for other nonlegal reasons, especially in the context of family assessment as defined in this chapter, family assessment is likely to be important regardless of the child's age.

Individualizing Services

Early intervention professionals spend hundreds of hours every year assessing children and interpreting the results of that process. Although some assessments are conducted to determine eligibility for services, most assessment activities are designed to determine each child's abilities and needs so that an individualized program of services can be provided. A fundamental tenet of all special education endeavors is that each child is unique. Because no one curriculum can meet the diverse needs of children with disabilities, the operational definition of *appropriate* education rests heavily on the extent to which the particular goals established and services provided meet the needs of the individual child. The vehicle by which a child's goals and services are determined is the assessment process.

This reasoning can be extended logically to the provision of services for families. Families differ widely in many respects, including the meaning they attach to their child's disability, the way the family is organized, the goals they have for their children, their views of service providers and public systems of family assistance, and the ways in which they want to be involved in making decisions and providing services for their child. Research in recent years has sought to explain this variability in family adaptation, focusing on such factors as child characteristics (e.g., severity, temperament, maladaptive behavior), caregiver characteristics (e.g., parent IQ, psychological well-being, socioeconomic status), formal and informal sources of support, belief systems (including religion), appraisal systems, styles of coping, ethnicity, and culture (Shapiro, Blacher, & Lopez, 1998). Each of these variables has been shown to be related to some extent to family functioning, but not in a way that is always applicable to every family.

Making assumptions about any of these dimensions for a particular family could easily result in faulty conclusions and the provision of a service plan that is not consistent with an individual family's needs and priorities. Thus a second rationale for family assessment is to ensure that family services are individualized.

Building Relationships

An early intervention endeavor is rarely accomplished in a neutral and distant fashion. Most of the time it rests on a relationship or set of relationships that families establish with professionals. There is often a close bond between parent and professional, but the relationship may become strained or even adversarial. A third goal of family assessment is to promote positive relationships between parents and professionals by communicating, in a positive fashion, that professionals generally are aware that raising a child with a disability imposes unique challenges for a family, are interested in listening to the family's concerns and priorities, and are willing, given the resources that are available, to individualize child and family services accordingly. McWilliam, Tocci, and Harbin (1998) found that relationships are essential to what is considered family-centered practice, and key components of these relationships include positiveness, responsiveness, orientation to the whole family, friendliness, and sensitivity.

It should be noted that while family assessment has the potential for achieving these goals, it also has the potential for standing in the way of positive relationships, especially if families view the process as intrusive or not relevant to their child's needs. Thus caution must be exercised in the way family assessment is conceptualized and implemented.

Theoretical Rationale

The rationale for family assessment also has an important theoretical basis. Several decades ago, the prevailing view was that the relationship between parent and child, especially between parent and infant, was unidirectional. That is, most effort was expended in understanding how the parent influenced the child. Bell (1968) argued that, in fact, this relationship is bidirectional; although the parent certainly influences the child, it is clear that parental behavior is in turn altered by the child's behavior. Sameroff and his colleagues (Sameroff & Chandler, 1975; Sameroff & Fiese, 2000) have expanded this concept to a transactional model, arguing that not only is the interaction bidirectional, but also, children and caregivers continue to influence each other in repeated transactions over time. Bronfenbrenner (1977) proposed an ecological model that expands the sphere of influence beyond parent and child to include broader neighborhood and community systems. In fact, family life might be best characterized as a series of evolving accommodations to a range of life experiences over time (Gallimore et al., 1996). Although our field continues to discuss alternative models, it is widely agreed that some sort of general systems model is needed to understand families and how they function (Cox & Paley, 1997). According to *systems theory,* families function as organizational units—they struggle to achieve balance, they become increasingly complex over time, and family members continually affect and are influenced by each other (Steinglass, 1984).

These theories have helped us realize several important facts (Bailey & Simeonsson, 1988b). First, a child with a disability inevitably has an effect on a family—usually a range of effects, some positive and some challenging. Thus family support becomes an important goal of early intervention. Second, any intervention with the child almost certainly will have an influence on the family. Furthermore, any intervention or support with one family member is likely to affect the child with a disability as well as other family members. Finally, families live in a broader community that includes their culture, neighborhoods, extended family members, friends, and religious organizations. Family assessment ought to help professionals understand and appreciate the complex ecology in which families live so that services can be provided in a way that builds on natural ecological supports and fits with what Bernheimer, Gallimore, and Weisner (1990) refer to as the family's "ecological niche." They argue that each family constructs a view of itself that is consistent with their culture and circumstances. Family assessment can help professionals understand both the objective aspects of this ecology

(e.g., family living conditions) as well as how family members perceive their ecology.

Evaluating Quality of Services and Outcomes for Families

Early intervention programs are accountable to the children and families they serve, to the local community, and to the state and federal agencies that provide much of the funding for early intervention services. Historically this accountability has rested almost exclusively on the quality of services for children with disabilities. Today, however, early intervention programs must also be accountable for services to families. This poses significant challenges to any evaluator. Although it is relatively easy to document child changes in basic areas of development (e.g., cognitive, language, motor), behavioral and social skills, and engagement, the effects of programs on families can be more difficult to document. This does not reduce the importance of this concept, however, and thus a final reason for engaging in family assessment is to document whether the program has been responsive to family needs and the decision to be involved.

Bailey (2001) suggests that early intervention and preschool have three levels of accountability and should be evaluated accordingly. The first is whether the program has provided the family with all of the services to which they are entitled. The second is whether the program has provided services that are of high quality. A final question is whether families have achieved important outcomes for themselves (in addition to their children) as a result of early intervention. Each level is complicated and comes with its own set of assessment considerations, such as how to define and measure quality. With respect to family outcomes, several authors have suggested frameworks for conceptualizing family outcomes (Bailey et al., 1998; Early Childhood Research Institute on Measuring Growth and Development, 1998; Roberts, Innocenti, & Goetze, 1999; Turnbull, Turbiville, & Turnbull, 2000). Much similarity exists across these models, and three commonly agreed upon domains are (a) family satisfaction with services, the family's knowledge of child development, and their ability to provide a developmentally supportive environment and advocate for their child's needs, and (c) the overall quality of the family's life and the changes that are needed in order to meet their child's needs (Bailey, 2001).

DIMENSIONS OF FAMILY ASSESSMENT

Although family assessment is a relatively recent phenomenon in early intervention, the process of gathering information about families has a much more extensive history. Understanding the historical context and roots is important as we seek to construct a framework for assessment that is meaningful in the context of early intervention. This framework then provides the basis for determining the various dimensions of family assessment.

Traditions in Family Assessment

Professionals from a variety of disciplines have engaged in family assessment for years. These efforts have yielded a large number of instruments and procedures. Which of them have relevance for early intervention? This question is best answered by examining the measures in the context of three related but distinct historical traditions: research, clinical, and support (Bailey & Henderson, 1993). In the research tradition, investigators have used assessment instruments in order to understand the general nature of families, how they function, and how they develop. As described by Simeonsson (1988), researchers have focused on structural aspects of the family (who is in the family and how they interact with each other), developmental aspects (how the family grows and changes over time), and functional aspects (what tasks the family needs to accomplish, what stresses they experience, and what strategies they use to meet demands and adapt to stressful events). In the clinical tradition, assessment instruments have been developed to help family therapists, psycho-

logists, and social workers counsel families who are experiencing problems in some aspect of family relationships. A variety of assessment techniques have been developed to pinpoint specific areas of difficulty, and some are used to classify families into typologies (e.g., Beavers & Voeller, 1983; McCubbin & Thompson, 1987b).

The research and clinical traditions differ in a number of ways. In the research tradition the goal is to develop a generalized understanding about the nature of families, whereas the goal of clinical assessment is to gain a better understanding of a particular family. Scientists who gather data in the research tradition rarely meet the families they study; clinicians often know the most intimate and personal details about a particular family. Assessments in the research tradition do not usually benefit families directly; clinical assessment is designed to aid directly through the process of therapeutic counseling.

These frameworks are presented in order to emphasize that a fundamental criterion for evaluating the appropriateness of a given family assessment procedure is whether its purpose and format are consistent with the goals of the context in which it is being used. Although many of the instruments developed in the research and clinical traditions have excellent psychometric properties and have yielded important information about families, this does not necessarily mean that the measures will be especially useful in the context of early intervention, which is neither necessarily clinically nor research-based in its orientation.

Family assessment strategies for early intervention have emerged out of a third tradition, the support tradition (Bailey & Henderson, 1993). Zigler and Black (1989) have suggested that family support programs have as their ultimate goal enabling families to be independent by promoting their own informal support network. The support tradition differs from the clinical tradition in that it does not assume that there is something inherently wrong or problematic within the family. Rather it starts with the assumption that each family is competent and like any other family, the primary difference being that this family happens to have a child with a disability. In recognition of the difficulties that often arise in raising a child with a disability, the support tradition attempts to provide services to alleviate any perceived caregiving burden, make available to families an array of resources and services, and facilitate easy access to these services, hopefully helping families feel competent to deal with present and future challenges. Family assessment strategies evolving from the support tradition are designed to determine a family's resources and supports and how the family perceives those resources relative to their concerns and priorities. The overall goal is to gather sufficient information so that the early intervention professional can provide an array of supportive services that are consistent with each family's values and concerns.

Recognizing that family assessment in early intervention emanates from the support tradition has direct implications for early intervention professionals. For example, an assessment of marital satisfaction would be highly consistent with the research on clinical traditions (depending on the particular problem under study or treatment). However, it is highly unlikely that such a measure would be used in the support tradition. Although perceived support by a spouse has been shown to be important for many individuals (e.g., McKinney & Peterson, 1987), improving marital relations is not likely to be an early intervention goal; furthermore, asking questions about marital relations is likely to be viewed as intrusive by many families and thus prevent the development of a trusting and collaborative relationship between parents and professionals. On the other hand, family members who express concern about marital relationships should be supported in finding services to address that concern.

Domains of Family Assessment

What, then, are the domains of family assessment? This would be a relatively easy question to answer if we were talking about children; most professionals would identify such critical areas of development as motor, communication, cognitive, adaptive, and social skills. But in the case of family assessment, the answer is not so clear. A review of the existing literature reveals many potential domains that could be assessed: stress, coping styles, teaching skills, parent-child interaction, the home environment, locus of control, support systems, and stages of grief, to name but a few. However, the discussion of traditions in family assessment suggests that most of these domains are not likely to be appropriate for family assessment conducted for the purpose of providing support.

According to federal legislation, the appropriate domains for assessment are family resources, priorities, and concerns related to the care of the child with a disability. This means that family assessments ought to be designed to determine the family's perception of the child, of his or her needs, and of the family's desires for services or other kinds of support from professionals. This still is very general, however. In order to provide a more functional framework for family assessment, it might be useful to organize the assessment model around key questions, the answers to which would help professionals provide services in a more family-centered fashion (Bailey & Henderson, 1993). Three questions are likely to be essential in this process: (1) What roles does the family want to play in the process of making decisions about their child and in providing educational or therapeutic interventions? (2) What does this family want from the service system? (3) How do family members perceive the service system and what constitutes an acceptable relationship between parents and service providers? Each of these questions likely will result in a series of related questions that provide important supplementary information.

How does this family want to be involved in planning and providing services? Families vary considerably in the extent to which they want to be involved in assessment, team meetings, decision making, and service delivery. Some families want to play a major leadership role in determining the assessment information to be gathered, participating in the team meeting, and making decisions about goals and services for the child and the family. At the other end of the continuum, some families would prefer that professionals take the leadership in these roles. In fact, the range of possible roles family members could fill is very wide. Four considerations are important in the context of this domain.

First, a family-centered approach does not force families to be at any particular point in the continuum of involvement in planning. Turning over the leadership of a team meeting, for example, might be very positive and supportive for some families, but might be quite threatening for others. Because such wide variability exists in desired parental roles, an individualized assessment of these preferences is essential.

Second, it should be recognized that family preferences for involvement may vary depending on the nature of the activity. For example, there are many domains in which parents could potentially be involved: decisions about the goals and nature of the child assessment process, the extent to which they want to be involved in child assessment, participation in team meetings and decision making, involvement in the child's intervention activities, and participation in case management activities. One parent may want to participate actively in the team meeting but would prefer that professionals make all decisions related to the child's assessment. A second parent may prefer a professional case manager but want to be actively involved in her child's treatment. A third parent may want to play leadership roles in all areas. Therefore, any assessment of the parents' wishes to be involved in the process of making decisions and providing services should not be a general assessment, but rather should seek to ascertain preferred roles in a variety of different contexts.

Third, it is also important to recognize that family preferences could easily change over time. For example, one parent might initially feel insecure and very uncomfortable in trying to play a leadership role when surrounded by a team of highly trained professionals. But after almost a year of early intervention services and frequent interactions with professionals, he feels more comfortable and confident in his own opinions and skills and gradually begins to exert more influence and play more extensive roles. Another parent, however, may initially not trust professionals and therefore play a very active role in the initial processes. After a year of participating in early intervention, however, she gradually relinquishes some of those roles as she takes on her own professional responsibilities and feels more comfortable with allowing the professionals to make decisions without her constant input. These two examples demonstrate the changes in role preference that quite likely will occur during the period of time a professional has the opportunity to provide services to a child and family. Thus it becomes important for professionals not to assume continuity of role preferences and to provide regular opportunities for parents to express their desired roles.

Finally, professionals should also realize that some families may want or need assistance so that they can participate fully in various program activities. For example, Brinckerhoff and Vincent (1986), prior to the IEP meeting, gave parents a brief assessment inventory for them to describe their child's typical skills at home and then met with the parents individually to help them anticipate what would happen in the team meeting. They found that parents who participated in these activities were more likely to make comments and suggestions during the actual team meeting. Likewise, Goldstein and Turnbull (1982) found that an informal individual meeting with parents served to increase active parent participation in the subsequent IEP meeting. These data suggest that for some parents lack of participation reflects an insecurity about the process or a perceived lack of skills. Thus it would be a good idea to make options available for parents on an ongoing basis that recognize the concerns parents might have and provide opportunities for building both confidence and skills.

What does this family want from the service system? The second major focus of family assessment is determining family goals and desires for services. Historically, of course, the primary service most parents want is therapeutic and specialized educational interventions for their child with a disability, and this remains true today. As professionals, we would never have the chance to interact with a particular family if that family did not have a child with a disability, and it is the disability itself that is likely to be of concern to most parents. Thus one essential aspect of family assessment is determining the goals families have for their children, the settings in which they would like their child to spend time, and the services they feel would best help their child achieve his or her goals.

For some families, a focus on the child's needs is sufficient. However, many families have additional concerns, sometimes temporary and sometimes long-term, with which early intervention professionals could be of help. Many early intervention programs have made assumptions about the kind of support services families would like, offering such activities as parent support groups, parent training sessions, or sibling support groups. However, we have come to realize that a standard program of services is likely to meet the needs of only some families. Thus an assessment of individual priorities and concerns is important.

A primary consideration in this aspect of family assessment is recognizing that the likely range of concerns families might have is considerable. One of the needs most frequently expressed by parents is for more information about their child and his or her disability, suggestions for teaching the child or handling behavior problems, and information regarding services available for their child both now and in the future (Bailey, Blasco, & Simeonsson, 1992; Cooper & Allred, 1992). Other families may have needs related to family and social support (e.g., someone to talk with about

concerns), finances (ranging from basic expenses to the costs of special equipment), ideas for explaining their child's condition to other people or helping nuclear or extended family members cope with the disability, child care (e.g., babysitters, respite care providers, day-care), professional and community support (e.g., a counselor, an understanding physician, or a parents' support group), or case management services to help locate and gain access to a variety of community resources and coordinate efforts across agencies. This short list provides some indication of the expanded roles now expected of early intervention programs and professionals. Obviously, early intervention and preschool programs will not be able to provide all of these services directly; however, professionals should be aware of other community resources that could be helpful and provide support and assistance for families. For example, if a family wants their child placed in a regular day-care center near the office where one of the parents is employed, an early intervention professional might work with the staff of the child-care program so that they can appropriately support the child's learning and therapeutic goals.

It should also be recognized that family needs and concerns are likely to change over time. Families may have more needs for support when they are experiencing or anticipating an event of some significance (Wikler, 1981). Some of these events are directly related to the child with a disability. For example, when parents are first told about their child's disability or when they gain new and unexpected information at a later time (e.g., a preschooler begins to experience mild seizures), they may want repeated opportunities to speak with a professional to discuss the meaning or implications of this information (Cunningham, Morgan, & McGucken, 1984). A transition from one program to another is also a stressful event (Hanson et al., 2000). During the early childhood period, at least four such transitions are potentially challenging: (1) from the hospital to home (especially if the hospital is where the initial diagnosis occurred or if the stay in the hospital was extended due to complications, illness, or sur- gery); (2) first-time entry into the early interven- tion service delivery systems; (3) the transition into some type of center-based program with other children; and (4) entry into kindergarten. Prior to these transitions, parents may want infor- mation and support in making decisions regarding the transition placement decision, the child may need to be prepared for the transition in some way, and an early intervention professional may need to be available during the transition period to ensure that things go smoothly. Often this involves signifi- cant parent involvement, several meetings, and interagency cooperation (Noonan & Kilgo, 1987; Rosenkoetter, Hains, & Fowler, 1994). Of special importance to families is the availability of a range of acceptable options for their child's next place- ment (Hanson et al., 2000). In recognition of the special challenges associated with changes in programs and agencies, IDEA even requires that a formal transition plan be developed prior to the child's third birthday to ensure a smooth transition from infant to preschool programs.

How do family members perceive the service system? A third domain of family assessment is determining each family's perception of the service system. Such information is important as professionals seek to establish and build relation- ships with families. It is also an important part of any program evaluation effort.

At the outset it must be recognized that family perceptions of the service system are often deeply rooted in cultural or family group values about what constitutes an appropriate relationship between families and professionals (Applequist & Bailey, 2000; Bailey, Skinner, Rodriguez, Gut, & Correa, 1999; Chen & McCollum, 2001). In some cultures going to a professional or public agency for services and support is a completely logical and acceptable course of action. In other cultures, professionals and persons who are not members of the cultural group may be viewed with distrust, or dealing with such professionals may simply be viewed as an inappropriate thing to do (see Chapter 4). Even within cultures there is likely to

be great variability in families' willingness to seek outside help. Thus an important goal of family assessment, especially when professionals are just getting to know a family, is to ascertain the family's view of service providers. Such infor- mation is critical in determining how fast to move with a family and will be essential in formu- lating an approach that is sensitive to the family's expectations for appropriate behavior.

A related goal in this domain is the documenta- tion of parent satisfaction with services and the interactions they have had with professionals. Assessment of satisfaction should be multifaceted rather than generic, because families may be satisfied with some aspects of the program but not others. Simeonsson (1988) recommends that the assessment of satisfaction should cover communi- cation patterns between parents and profes- sionals, the quality of service provided to both child and family, and the extent to which par- ents consider the early intervention team to be competent, sensitive, and empathetic.

GENERAL PROCEDURAL CONSIDERATIONS IN FAMILY ASSESSMENT

Family assessment, when conducted appropri- ately, can expand traditional child-focused assess- ment models and help early intervention programs be consistent with a family-centered approach to services. Many professionals and parents, however, experience a negative reaction when they hear the term *family assessment*, probably because they associate it with more formal testing with its standardized procedures and scores that are often interpreted in comparison with some normative sample. Because of the potentially sensitive nature of family assessment for both parent and profes- sional, this section draws heavily on two previous publications (Bailey, 1991; Bailey & Henderson, 1993) to discuss six considerations: multimethod approaches, assessment as intervention, timing of assessment, whose job family assessment is, variations in family and professional perceptions, and evaluation of family assessment instruments and procedures.

Multimethod Approaches

At the beginning of this chapter family assessment was defined as the process of gathering information in order to determine family priorities for goals and services. From this framework, one could view every interaction a professional has with a family as a form of family assessment. It is well known from the family therapy literature that an effective therapist takes the opportunity to learn about a family or a family member in the context of all interactions. This requires starting out with a set of questions (e.g., How do these parents want to participate in the decision-making process?), gathering information related to those questions, forming and reformulating hypotheses over the context of repeated interactions with families, and maintaining an open and noncritical stance throughout this process (Selvini, Boscolo, Cecchin, & Prata, 1980). Early intervention professionals should take advantage of the information that is inherent in phone calls, notes, and informal exchanges during arrival and departure in order to learn about family resources, priorities, and concerns. Typically this information is available from the verbal and nonverbal exchanges that occur between parents and professionals.

In addition to using effective communication skills in informal contexts, at least three other general strategies are available. The *focused interview* (Winton, 1988b; Winton & Bailey, 1988) is a somewhat more structured interaction in which the professional identifies in advance topics to be discussed and plans a series of questions likely to develop a positive relationship with the family members participating in the interview and elicit the desired information. Paper-and-pencil measures primarily exist in the form of questionnaires and rating scales. Some families prefer paper-and-pencil strategies for sharing information, either because it is a more comfortable format for them or because the items on the survey (e.g., a list of possible family needs or program services) provide a set of definite options from which to choose as compared with an open-ended interview (Bailey & Blasco, 1990). Finally, direct observation procedures can be used to describe such dimensions as parent-child interactions or the home environment.

Each of the procedures will be described in greater detail later in this chapter. The message in this section is that family assessment can involve an array of strategies, all of which should be taken advantage of as professionals seek to ascertain family perceptions and desires.

Assessment as Intervention

A second general point is that the assessment process itself is rarely a neutral event, and in fact may have the effect of an intervention, sometimes with intended effects but perhaps more often resulting in unintended consequences. Tomm (1987), speaking from the context of family therapy, suggests that anything a therapist does is possibly significant because it might either affirm or challenge something the family or an individual family member says or does. This is likely to be true in early intervention as well. Despite all of our efforts to enable and empower families so that they feel competent as caregivers and as decision makers (Dunst, Trivette, & Deal, 1988), most parents view professionals as having a great deal of valuable expertise as well as being in control of resources. Because parents often want access to both information and services, professionals are seen as authority figures and gatekeepers, providing or denying access to services. Professional views of both the child and the family are thus of great importance to families and, as Tomm (1987) suggests, all professional activities may take on great meaning for many families.

Given this possibility, professionals should recognize that the very act of conducting family assessment is likely to affect the relationship between parents and professionals as well as the parents' views of themselves. The nature of this influence will vary depending on the assessment activity and the parents' perception of it. For example, informally asking how a sibling reacted to recent surgery for a brother or sister with Down syndrome might be viewed as prying by some families and as caring by others. Providing families with the opportunity to complete a survey of family needs might be viewed as meaningless paperwork by some fathers and as a good vehicle for identifying needed support services by others. An assessment of the quality of parent-child interactions might be viewed as a helpful attempt to deal with behavior problems by one mother and as a judgmental effort to determine adequacy of parenting styles by another. These examples show that it is important for professionals to recognize that family assessment activities ought to improve the relationships between families and professionals and should help identify needs for services. However, sometimes the assessment process can have negative effects and thus great care must be taken to ensure that the extent, nature, and methodology of family assessment is consistent with each individual family's preferences and views.

Timing of Family Assessments

When in the process of becoming acquainted with families should assessments be conducted? Some professionals argue that assessment is too personal to do when one is just beginning to know a family. Others have argued that an early assessment of family resources, priorities, and concerns is essential to good planning. Consistent with earlier points in this chapter, two guidelines are important. First, if one takes the broad definition of family assessment as any activity in which the professional gains new information about the family's perception of resources, priorities, and concerns, then the question is meaningless. A professional engages in family assessment from the first interaction. Thus the question becomes not one of if and when family assessments are done, but rather

one of the nature and formality of the assessment activities. Second, regardless of the nature and timing of the assessment, it is important that the professional communicate, very early in the acquaintance process, a willingness to listen to family concerns and to respond to an array of family requests for services. How this is done will vary from family to family, but the family support component of early intervention should not be viewed as something that is put off until the professional has had a chance to focus on the child's needs and the family has had time to develop a relationship with professionals. It is in the context of those very processes that the most important family assessment activities are conducted.

Assigning Responsibility for Family Assessment

Whose job is it to conduct family assessments? The regulations accompanying federal early intervention legislation state that such assessments must be conducted by individuals who have received appropriate training. What does this mean? One interpretation is that only social workers, nurses, or psychologists should conduct family assessments, since they are the professionals most likely to have received extensive training in working with families (Bailey, Simeonsson, Yoder, & Huntington, 1990). If one takes the definition of family assessment offered in this chapter, however, it is every professional's responsibility to engage in assessment activities. Every professional who interacts with a family and their child has the opportunity to learn more about the nature and extent of family preferences for services, roles, and relationships with professionals, by paying attention to the questions, comments, and behavioral responses observed in the context of those interactions.

This diffuse responsibility does not reduce the need for specialized training, however. Research has documented that professionals in special education and the allied health professions often receive only minimal training in working with families (Bailey et al., 1990). Furthermore, they report that their family skills and the extent to which they value family roles are less than that reported by social workers and nurses (Bailey, Palsha, & Simeonsson, 1991). These data, coupled with findings across multiple settings indicating discrepancies between typical and desired practices in working with families (Bailey, Buysse, Edmondson, & Smith, 1992; Brown & Ritchie, 1990; Mahoney & O'Sullivan, 1990; Rushton, 1990), suggest that more training is needed so the professionals who interact most frequently with children and families have the skills needed to assess family resources, priorities, and concerns. Probably the most important of these skills is the ability to communicate effectively with families and to establish a trusting and collaborative relationship. Beyond that, specific training is certainly needed for particular assessment procedures, especially those such as measures of parent-child interaction that require reliable observational techniques.

Professional versus Family Perceptions

A frequently raised concern among early intervention professionals is the discrepancy that is sometimes observed between parent and professional perceptions of needs for the child and the family (Bailey, 1991). This concern gets to a more basic issue in the context of assessment, namely the difference between objective and subjective perceptions of reality. Historically, child assessment procedures have had the goal of obtaining an objective view of the child, one that is not biased by the tester's own values or experiences, a view that is applied and interpreted in similar ways across all children tested. Thus children are presented a standard set of materials, in a standard format, with standard directions, and standard criteria for scoring responses. Each item has an agreed-upon correct answer, and the quality of the child's performance is evaluated against this standard.

In family assessment, however, it is the subjective and personal view of families that is essential. Research across a number of fields of inquiry has documented that perception of events is a powerful determinant of the way in which an individual or a family responds to that event (McCubbin & Patterson, 1983). Families and professionals are quite likely to disagree on several perceptual dimensions. For example, when discussing the cause and meaning of disability, professionals are likely to focus on biomedical, genetic, and experiential aspects of causation. Although families are interested in these aspects, they are also likely to address questions of meaning: Why did this happen to me or my child, and what is the meaning of this event? Research indicates that culture is a powerful determinant of a family's interpretive frameworks, resulting in a continuum of beliefs ranging from biomedical to folk to religious. Perceived needs of the child and the family constitute a second arena in which the perceptions of parents may be different from that of professionals. For example, the physical therapist may feel strongly that the most important service for a child relates to positioning and adaptive equipment, but a parent might feel that integration with typically developing children is of utmost importance. A third area of possible disagreement is one's perception of the need for and usefulness of particular services. For example, a professional may feel that a parent support group would be very helpful for a father, but the father is not at all interested in participating in such an activity.

These examples are presented to support the argument that subjective views of family resources, priorities, and concerns constitute the primary basis of family assessment. This point of view is reflected in federal legislation, which states that the results of family assessment must be based on the family's own description of its resources, priorities, and concerns. Rarely will there be a "correct" answer in family assessment that is comparable to the "correct" answer in child assessment. Professionals must, for the most part, accept the family's view as the legitimate assessment at a particular point in time. This ensures that the resulting information is useful in designing services that meet individual family perceptions of needs. Of what use is a program of services that by professional standards is outstanding but is not perceived by family members as useful or responsive?

Evaluating Assessment Methods and Procedures

Throughout this text we have discussed the importance of evaluating the reliability and validity of instruments for assessing children's behavior and development. In some instances, these same standards apply to family assessment procedures. This is especially true for measures that have norms and standardized scoring procedures such as the Parenting Stress Index (Abidin, 1990) or observational measures requiring precise coding of parent or child behaviors, such as the Nursing Child Assessment Feeding Scale (Barnard, 1978a). McGrew, Gilman, and Johnson (1992) reviewed a variety of scales designed to assess family needs and rated them on various dimensions of reliability and validity. Many of the measures fell short of the usual expectations for such information, and the authors called for more research to document psychometric properties of family assessment measures.

However, in many cases traditional measures of the quality of an instrument may not be sufficient for family assessment procedures (Henderson, Aydlett, & Bailey, 1993). Consider, for example, an interview with a father, the purpose of which is to discuss his feelings about his child's transition from preschool to kindergarten. No score emerges from this process and the father's responses are not compared with some norm group. His feelings may be time-limited, changing with home circumstances and in accordance with his perceptions of the quality of program for his child. Or take the example of a written survey of family needs. Should this measure have internal consistency or test-retest reliability? What is the criterion against which such

responses should be validated? Furthermore, what if one argues that the only way to get a comprehensive view of family resources, priorities, and concerns is to use multiple methods for assessment? If this is the case, does it make sense to evaluate one piece of the assessment process as an isolated measure, or should the evaluation address the overall process? In many ways, this is not too different from assessments conducted to establish goals for children. For example, in identifying the factors that are related to high levels of children's engagement, direct observation with a reliable and valid code may be helpful; however, informal observations, anecdotal records, and the general perceptions of caregivers may be used to obtain rich information about the toys, activities, and contexts that excite, motivate, and captivate children's attention and interaction. To ignore such "subjective" measures would mean that critical information would be lost.

Clearly, family assessment strategies should be evaluated rigorously with regard to their effects and usefulness. When appropriate, the traditional standards of reliability and validity should be applied, and the measurement procedures judged accordingly. However, as Henderson et al. (1993) suggest, two criteria are of fundamental importance. Does the assessment procedure result in useful information? Is the process acceptable to families? With regard to the first criterion, professionals should ask whether the process is helpful in developing an IEP or IFSP that is functional for the child or the family. Too often, assessments are conducted and the results are filed away with little attempt to use the data in a meaningful way for intervention purposes. Families naturally feel frustrated when asked to provide information that is not subsequently used to individualize services (Bailey & Blasco, 1990). The likelihood of this happening is reduced if the process provides information that is truly helpful and of direct relevance for planning purposes. With regard to the second criterion, it may be helpful to ask families to provide feedback on the extent to which they believe certain assessment procedures would provide them appropriate and acceptable avenues for conveying information about resources, priorities, and concerns. Examples of gathering information about family perceptions of the acceptability of different procedures have been provided by Bailey and Blasco (1990), Sexton, Snyder, Rheams, Barron-Sharp, and Perez (1991), and Summers et al. (1990). In general, this research shows that families have definite opinions about the content, timing, and format of family assessment procedures. Their opinions vary, however, and while it may be useful to get group information, an individualized approach will be needed. For example, Bailey and Blasco (1990) asked parents if they would prefer sharing information in a written format or through face-to-face discussions with a professional. About 60% of the mothers preferred personal discussions, but 40% preferred a written survey. The opposite findings were obtained from fathers. Clearly, different parents have different preferences. A family-centered approach to assessment not only allows families to decide whether or not they want to participate in family assessment activities, but also provides reasonable alternatives for strategies for sharing this information.

REPRESENTATIVE METHODS AND PROCEDURES

As we have already discussed, family assessment can take many forms, ranging from informal to very structured. In this section we review and discuss four types of family assessment strategies: informal communication, semistructured interviews, surveys and rating scales, and direct observation procedures.

Informal Communication

Probably the most frequently used form of family assessment (although often not recognized as family assessment) is the informal communication that occurs in the context of daily routines and interactions between families and professionals. Telephone calls, arrival and departure times, notes, and chance interactions that occur in the community all provide occasions for learning more about family resources, priorities, and concerns. The key strategy is for professionals to take advantage of these opportunities and to use the information gained to help answer three ongoing questions: (1) How does this family want to be involved in decision making and service provision? (2) What does this family want from the service system? and (3) How do family members perceive the service system and our relationship with them?

Of fundamental importance in informal contexts is the professional's use of good communication skills. Winton (1988a), in a synthesis of research findings, suggests that there are four critical communication skills: listening, asking questions, responding, and integrating.

Listening One of the most frequent complaints of parents is that professionals have not heard what parents are trying to say to them (Turnbull & Turnbull, 1990). Being a good listener sounds easy, but in fact it is a skill that must be developed and used in an active rather than a passive fashion. According to Winton (1988a), listening requires the professional to show interest in what the parent has to say by attending and responding in both verbal (e.g., responding to comments) and nonverbal (e.g., nodding, appropriate eye contact) ways. A good listener hears what the parent is saying and also pays attention to the nonverbal cues that parents send. Maintaining an accepting attitude is important; judgmental comments, too much suggestion-giving, and preaching are sure ways to cut a communicative interchange short. Among the most frequently observed errors in communicating are interrupting, making irrelevant responses, and using communication styles that seem awkward or unnatural (Matarazzo, Phillips, Wiens, & Saslow, 1965). A good listener allows the communicative partner time to speak, pays attention to the verbal and nonverbal components of communication, and responds in a relevant and noncritical fashion. A good listener also recognizes individual variation in communication styles and preferences, which are likely to vary as a function of culture, education, personality, and experience and comfort in interacting with professionals.

Asking Questions A second key communication skill is the ability to ask questions in an appropriate fashion. Asking questions is one way of showing interest in the person with whom you are communicating and is an important way to elicit information that might not otherwise be provided. However, questions can create problems if they are viewed as intrusive or prying or if they are asked in a way that limits responses or communicates judgment. Professionals need to be aware of various ways in which questions can be asked and the advantages and disadvantages of each.

Winton and Bailey (1993) compare and contrast three dimensions of question asking. The first dimension addresses the focus and specificity of questions, with a distinction usually being drawn between closed-ended and open-ended questions. A closed-ended question is one that has a specific answer, either a yes/no response or a specific fact. Examples of closed-ended questions include "How old is Yolanda?" and "Does Marcus have a regular bedtime?" Closed-ended questions are very appropriate if facts are essential. However, it should be recognized that closed-ended questions usually result in short conversations and provide only the information asked for. Open-ended questions are asked in such a way as to allow for a range of responses. For example, instead of asking whether or not Marcus has a regular bedtime, one could ask "What are bedtimes like with Marcus?" This question gives the respondent an opportunity to share a range of things about bedtime and to describe feelings about that experience as well. More importantly, it allows the respondent to focus on what is of importance to him or her rather than on what is of importance to the person asking the question.

A second dimension of question asking is the nature of the question being asked and the message it sends. Some questions appear investigatory in nature and may send a message of blaming the respondent. For example, on a Friday morning drop-off at the child-care center a parent may comment to the therapist that she had not been able to do much with her daughter's physical therapy activities this week. A follow-up question to this comment could be asked in two different ways: "These activities are really important for Maria; why didn't you do them?" or "I know you have other children at home and you are really busy. Is there anything else going on that I should know about that could be of help to us?" The first question places blame on the parent and conveys judgment about the parent's decision not to do therapy. The second conveys a sensitivity to the complicated demands of family life.

A third dimension of questioning addresses the extent to which a question should offer explicit suggestions for solving a problem, and a distinction has been drawn in the literature between strategic and reflexive questions (Tomm, 1987). The suggestion emanating from this literature is that professionals should ask questions in ways that help families develop solutions on their own rather than making specific suggestions. For example, a father might call to let the social worker know that he and his wife will not be attending a parent meeting because they cannot find a babysitter. A *strategic question* like "Why don't you call the local respite care program?" suggests a specific strategy and either places the parent in a position of having to justify why this was not done or perhaps makes them feel incompetent (Why didn't I think of that?). An alternative question would be "Can you think of ways in the future that you could participate in the meeting and still feel comfortable with child care?"—a *reflexive question* that prompts the father to think about the situation and reflect on alternative solutions. This is not to suggest that strategic questions should never be used, but rather that alternatives should be considered whenever possible to help families feel competent as decision makers and problem solvers.

Responding A third communication skill is the ability to respond appropriately to parents' comments and questions, and two considerations are important here. First, responses should be related to both the content and the feelings expressed by parents (Winton, 1988a). A conversation is an interaction between two or more individuals in which there is a logic to the flow and in which each participant responds to the messages sent by the other. Messages usually have information about both objective and subjective reality, providing facts as well as telling how the participant feels about the situation. One way to be an effective communicator is to acknowledge and reflect on what you think are both the content ("So you're saying that you would like Diane to be placed in the Tiny Tots Day-Care Center") and the feelings contained in a particular message ("So you're saying that although you are worried about whether Diane will have access to all of the special services you need, placement in her sister's daycare center is more important to you at this time"). This conveys an interest in what the communicator says, states what you have heard or felt, and allows the communicator to verify or alter your interpretation of the messages.

Second, responses should attempt to be neutral as opposed to overly supportive or critical (Selvini et al., 1980). The reason for this suggestion relates back to the whole concept of enabling and empowering parents and supporting them in their decision making. The professional's criticism or praise of a parent's decision can create an artificial level of permission and support that may not be helpful for some families. Ultimately, the criteria for evaluating a decision should be whether it accomplishes the goals established and whether parents are satisfied. Although it is certainly acceptable and sometimes an ethical imperative for professionals to give feedback on choices that parents make, it is important to recognize that too

much dependency on professional opinion is probably not a good situation.

Integrating Finally, a good communicator is able to conduct a communicative interchange in as natural a fashion as possible and to integrate the information received in that context with other knowledge in order to gain from this assessment opportunity. It is important that parents feel that they have engaged in a conversation with a caring professional, not that they have just seen a therapist who was using professional therapeutic tactics to uncover hidden concerns or meanings. These conversations occur in the context of normal daily routines and as such should feel comfortable and helpful for parents. This increases the likelihood that they will use the opportunities again in the future to share information and feelings. After such interchanges, professionals should reflect on the three fundamental questions described earlier regarding the domains of family assessment and ask whether the interaction changed the nature of the information available regarding family resources, priorities, and concerns.

Semistructured Interviews/Discussions

A second family assessment procedure is the use of *semistructured interviews* or discussions. These procedures rely heavily on the use of the communication skills described in the preceding section; in fact, face-to-face verbal communication is the essence of both contexts. In contrast to informal communication exchanges, however, which are rarely planned, semistructured interviews or discussions are usually planned and conducted in order to achieve one or more goals. The goal may be very specific, such as determining family preferences for their child's placement next year, or very global, such as discussing hopes and aspirations for the child and the family. These interactions may be initiated by either the parent or the professional.

Given the goal-oriented nature of these interviews and discussions, a structure is needed to ensure that the intended goals are achieved. It is important, however, for this structure to be flexible enough that the interview or discussion is comfortable for both parents and professionals and that it can adjust itself according to the interactions that occur rather than strictly following a preset agenda. Winton (1988b) and Winton and Bailey (1988) suggest that five phases be considered in these interactions: preliminary preparations, introduction, inventory, summarizing, and closure.

Preliminary Preparation   The first step is to prepare for the meeting. Typically this would involve clarifying the goals of the meeting and gathering any data that would facilitate the discussion and decision making. For example, if the discussion were to focus on placements for next year, it would be helpful to have information about essential characteristics of the placement options that exist. If the purpose of the meeting is more global, it may sometimes be helpful to have families complete or at least look at a survey of family needs (described in the next section) or a list of potential program services so that they have an idea of what is possible for the program to provide. In any case, the professional should take time prior to the meeting to review any existing information, gather pertinent new information, and anticipate possible concerns or requests that might emerge in the meeting.

Introduction   One of the first things that should be done at the beginning of the interview is to review the purpose of the meeting. This could be done either by the parent or by the professional, but it is important that each participant has an understanding of what is intended to be accomplished. This does not mean that other goals might not emerge; in fact, they often will. But it sets out an agreed-upon expectation that at least provides a beginning point for discussion. This time can also be used to confirm the time allotted for the

meeting, to reaffirm confidentiality, and to assess whether the initial goals are indeed the ones the parents want to address or if other more pressing concerns have emerged.

Inventory   This phase essentially is a review of the facts and feelings as perceived by all relevant parties so that an informed decision can be made. Of essential importance is to assess the family's perceptions. For example, in the context of placement decisions, the professional may have the facts about different options, but the parents will have preferences that are influenced by their perceptions of their child's needs and abilities, proximity to home, ease of access, perceived fit, cost, and other factors that would be impossible for the professional to know. This phase is important because full disclosure and discussion of all relevant information is essential for effective decision making.

Summarizing   When all of the information has been discussed, it should be reviewed and the costs and benefits of various options weighed. The professional can play an important role in summarizing this information and reflecting both the content of the information and the feelings shared by parents or other caregivers. Parents then need to have the opportunity to make decisions that are consistent with their resources, priorities, and concerns. These can often be elicited through effective use of the reflexive questioning strategies as described above; additional examples of these strategies are provided by Winton and Bailey (1993). Included in this discussion must be the feasibility of the goals and the extent to which the services desired can be provided by the early intervention program or if they must be sought through other agencies and programs. Supportive case management from the early intervention program can help families gain access to these additional services and is thus an important early intervention service in and of itself.

Closure   The final phase of the interview or discussion is a summary of the events that have transpired, an expression of appreciation on the part of the professional for the family's time and willingness to share, and a final opportunity to make changes or reflect on the process itself. It is important for the meeting to have some closure to it and ideally it should not be ended until everyone, but especially the family members, feels that the goals originally established have been met or at least addressed in a satisfactory fashion.

Caregiver-Completed Surveys and Rating Scales

A third type of family assessment procedure is the use of *surveys* and *rating scales* that are completed by the caregiver. Typically these measures fall into two categories. The first consists of nonstandardized instruments designed primarily to give parents an opportunity to indicate perceived needs for services that could be provided by the early intervention program or that the early intervention program could help access. The second consists of standardized measures designed to assess a variety of domains such as parenting stress, child temperament, or parental locus of control.

Nonstandardized Surveys/Rating Scales

Since the mid-1980s several nonstandardized surveys or rating scales have been developed to assist caregivers and early intervention professionals in identifying family needs for services. Some characteristics of four such measures are displayed in Table 7.1, and a copy of one such instrument is displayed in Figure 7.1. Each consists of a list of needs commonly expressed by families of young children with disabilities. Some are needs for services that might be provided directly by the early intervention program, such as information about their child's disability or more time to talk with their child's teacher or therapist. Others are needs that could best be provided by other agencies, but for which the early intervention program could be helpful in terms of identifying relevant agencies, facilitating initial contacts, and providing supportive coordination of services. Although the surveys

differ to some extent in terms of content, there is considerable overlap and it is probably safe to say that each provides a relatively comprehensive listing of reasonable needs and services. Each also has a way for parents or other caregivers to indicate the extent to which they perceive each item to be a need or the extent to which they would like services. However, the nature of these response formats varies considerably. For example, the Family Needs Scale (Dunst, Cooper, Weeldreyer, Snyder, & Chase, 1988) asks parents to rate the frequency of each need on a scale from 1 (almost never) to 5 (almost always), whereas the Family Needs Survey (Bailey & Simeonsson, 1990), simply asks parents to indicate if this is a topic they would like to discuss further with a staff member. A final characteristic of these instruments is that they were designed primarily as practical aids for professionals and family members as they seek to develop individualized family support programs. Thus the use of summary scores or the comparison of responses to a norm group are not characteristic of these instruments. Although some have been used for research purposes, with summary scores used for various analyses (e.g., Bailey et al., 1992), their primary use is a straightforward interpretation of responses to individual items.

Research in recent years has provided important information about the nature and usefulness of these measures. First, both parents and professionals have reported that measures such as these are potentially useful ways for parents to share perspectives with professionals. For example, Bailey and Blasco (1990) found that most mothers and fathers in a multistate study rated the Family Needs Survey as likely to be helpful for them and for professionals and stated that they would feel comfortable in sharing this information. Sexton et al. (1991) found that although mothers made some distinctions among measures, they rated three different measures as positive and helpful. Interestingly, mothers' ratings of the potential usefulness of the surveys was higher than the ratings of professionals. Both the Bailey and Blasco study and the Sexton et al. study found that, if given

TABLE 7.1
Characteristics of Some Commonly Used Surveys of Family Needs

Instrument	Number of Items	Domains	Response Format	Sample Item
Family Needs Survey (Bailey & Simeonsson, 1990)	35	Information Family and Social Support Financial Explaining to Others Child Care Professional Support Community Services	Would you like to discuss this topic with a staff person from our program? No Not sure Yes	Locating a day-care program or preschool for my child
Family Needs Scale (Dunst et al., 1988)	41	Items not grouped by domain	To what extent do you feel the need for any of the following types of help or assistance? NA Not applicable 1. Almost never 2. Seldom 3. Sometimes 4. Often 5. Almost always	Having medical and dental care for my child
Parent Needs Survey (Seligman & Darling, 1989)	26	Items are not grouped by domain	Please check the space that best describes your need or desire for help in each area ____ I really need some help in this area. ____ I would like some help, but my need is not that great. ____ I don't need any help in this area.	More information about how I can help my child
How Can We Help? (Child Development Resources, 1989)	39	Information Child Care Community Services Medical and Dental Care Talking About Our Child Planning for the Future	____ We have enough. ____ We would like more. ____ Not sure.	Determining the best setting for our child

Child's Name: _____   Person Completing Survey: _____
Date Completed: ___/___/___   Relationship to Child: _____

Dear Parent:

   Many families of young children have needs for information or support. If you wish, our staff are very willing to discuss these needs with you and work with you to identify resources that might be helpful.

   Listed below are some needs commonly expressed by families. It would be helpful to us if you would check in the columns on the right any topics you would like to discuss. At the end there is a place for you to describe other topics not included in the list.

   If you choose to complete this form, the information you provide will be kept confidential. If you would prefer not to complete the survey at this time, you may keep it for your records.

TOPICS	Would you like to discuss this topic with a staff person from our program?		
	No	Not Sure	Yes
Information			
1. How children grow and develop			
2. How to play or talk with my child			
3. How to teach my child			
4. How to handle my child's behavior			
5. Information about any condition or disability my child might have			
6. Information about services that are presently available for my child			
7. Information about the services my child might receive in the future			
Family & Social Support			
1. Talking with someone in my family about concerns			
2. Having friends to talk to			
3. Finding more time for myself			
4. Helping my spouse accept any condition our child might have			
5. Helping our family discuss problems and reach solutions			
6. Helping our family support each other during difficult times			
7. Deciding who will do household chores, child care, and other family tasks			
8. Deciding on and doing family recreational activities			
Financial			
1. Paying for expenses such as food, housing, medical care, clothing, or transportation			
2. Getting any special equipment my child needs			
3. Paying for therapy, day care, or other services my child needs			
4. Counselling or help in getting a job			
5. Paying for babysitting or respite care			
6. Paying for toys that my child needs			

FIGURE 7.1

Family needs survey (Revised 1990)

Note: From D. B. Bailey and M. Wolery, 1992, *Teaching Infants and Preschoolers with Disabilities,* p. 66. New York: Merrill/MacMillan. Used with permission.

	Would you like to discuss this topic with a staff person from our program?		
TOPICS	**No**	**Not Sure**	**Yes**
Explaining to Others			
1. Explaining my child's condition to my parents or my spouse's parents			
2. Explaining my child's condition to his or her siblings			
3. Knowing how to respond when friends, neighbors, or strangers ask questions about my child			
4. Explaining my child's condition to other children			
5. Finding reading material about other families who have a child like mine			
Child Care			
1. Locating babysitters or respite care providers who are willing and able to care for my child			
2. Locating a daycare program or preschool for my child			
3. Getting appropriate care for my child in a church or synagogue during religious services			
Professional Support			
1. Meeting with a minister, priest, or rabbi			
2. Meeting with a counselor (psychologist, social worker, psychiatrist)			
3. More time to talk to my child's teacher or therapist			
Community Services			
1. Meeting and talking with other parents who have a child like mine			
2. Locating a doctor who understands me and my child's needs			
3. Locating a dentist who will see my child			

Other: Please list other topics or provide any other information that you feel would be helpful to discuss.

_____

_____

_____

Is there a particular person with whom you would prefer to meet?

_____

_____

_____

Thank you for your time.
We hope this form will be helpful to you in identifying the services that you feel are important.

FIGURE 7.1

Continued

a choice, nearly half of the mothers actually preferred sharing this information through written rather than verbal means. Both studies also showed that parent ratings did not vary as a function of ethnic background or family income.

A second finding that has emerged from the research literature is that if asked, families will indeed express needs for support in a variety of areas. A consistent finding across several studies is the high frequency of expressed needs for information (Bailey et al., 1992; Bailey & Simeonsson, 1988a; Cooper & Allred, 1992; Garshelis & McConnell, 1993). Beyond informational needs, quite a bit of variability has been observed, but it is safe to say that in every study published thus far, all items are endorsed by at least some families. This suggests that families of young children with disabilities are highly individualized in their needs and are willing to express their individual needs in a survey format. Of course, this has implications for early intervention programs because it shows that programs must be prepared to respond to a wide variety of needs.

A third finding is that although the surveys include a wide array of family concerns, it is clear that a professionally generated list is insufficient to capture all of the concerns a family may want to express. Open-ended questions on the survey (Bailey & Simeonsson, 1988a) and follow-up interviews (Winton & Bailey, 1988) have both been shown to be important additions for comprehensive information gathering and clarification of survey responses.

Fourth, professionals need to realize that families are very sensitive about both the wording and the format of material that is sent to them. For example, Bailey and Blasco (1990) found that parents did not like the original wording of a response for the Family Needs Survey (*Definitely need help*) because it made it seem that they were desperate and really had a problem. If a written survey is used, it would probably be a good idea to ask some parents to review it to determine its acceptability and perceived usefulness and to make changes if necessary.

Finally, asking parents to complete a survey sends an explicit message that the program is willing to tailor services in accordance with caregiver responses. Families are understandably frustrated when they are asked to complete forms that they perceive as meaningless or that they perceive as meaningful but for which there is no follow-up. Professionals should be aware of the expectations such a survey establishes and be prepared to either provide services or help families locate services in accordance with expressions for desired assistance.

It should be noted that other measures have been developed in the past five years that tap areas in addition to family needs for services. Dunst and his colleagues have developed a number of these; they are described in Dunst, Trivette, and Deal (1988). Perhaps the most frequently used of the Dunst measures is the Family Support Scale (Dunst, Jenkins, & Trivette, 1988), which consists of a list of 18 people and groups that families may use as sources of support. Respondents are asked to rate on a scale from 1 (not at all helpful) to 5 (extremely helpful) how helpful the sources have been to their family over the past 3 to 6 months. Research with this measure (e.g., Dunst, 1985) as well as research in other contexts provides clear evidence that perceived support is critical to family coping and adaptation. Knowledge of family resources is a key aspect of family assessment, and scales such as the Family Support Scale, used in conjunction with interviews and informal discussions with parents, can provide information that would be useful in working with families to identify areas in which additional support is needed or areas of special strength (e.g., an extended family that lives nearby) that could be drawn on to meet particular needs (e.g., child care during parent meetings).

Standardized Parent-Completed Measures
The types of scales mentioned in the previous section were developed by researchers and practitioners working with early intervention programs in need of a practical means to identify family

concerns. Other measures have been developed using more traditional instrument development procedures and have been recommended for different purposes. In general, such measures are not likely to be used globally with all families in the context of a program's family assessment efforts, but only occasionally depending on the assessment needs of a particular context. They are similar to the measures described in the previous section in that they rely almost exclusively on the parent's or other caregiver's response to a particular item. The major differences have to do with the way data are summarized and interpreted. Measures in this category typically result in scores that are interpreted in reference to a normative group or relative to a cut-off score that indicates that an individual or a family is at risk for some type of problem.

Stress measures constitute one such assessment. One of the original stress measures that has been widely used in the research literature and clinical practice is the Questionnaire on Resources and Stress (QRS) (Holroyd, 1974, 1986). The instrument consists of 285 items grouped into three scales: Personal Problems, Family Problems, and Problems of Index Case (limitations and needs of the family member with a disability). Each item consists of a problem statement (e.g., "As the time passes I think it will take more and more to care for____," which the respondent marks as true or false. A 66-item short form was developed by the author and a 52-item short version was empirically developed and reported by Friedrich, Greenberg, and Crnic (1983). Another example of a stress measure is the Parenting Stress Index (PSI) (Abidin, 1990). Whereas the QRS is designed for all ages, the PSI focuses on families with children up to 12 years of age. The PSI has 101 items organized into two domains (child domain and parent domain) and 16 scales. Each item consists of a statement (e.g., "Since having this child I have been unable to do new and different things"). The respondents use a scale from 1 (strongly agree) to 5 (strongly disagree) to indicate the extent to which the statement is true for them. Both the PSI and the QRS can be interpreted relative to normative groups and have cut-off scores that suggest the need for referral to specialized services. Thus the measures might best be used as a screening procedure for subsequent referral.

Literally hundreds of studies have used these two measures and generally have found them to be useful indicators of stress and predictive of families in need of additional support. For example, research on the PSI has shown that stress can vary as a function of child characteristics (e.g., Bendell, Stone, Field, & Goldstein, 1989) and that the scale can be used to evaluate the impact of a family support program (Telleen, Herzog, & Kilbane, 1989) or predict maternal responsiveness (Wilfong, Saylor, & Elksnin, 1991).

Other measures have been developed for documenting other aspects of family functioning in a normative fashion. For example, McCubbin and Thompson (1987a) describe a wide variety of measures developed by the Family Stress Coping and Health Project. Among the most well known of these are the Family Inventory of Life Events and Changes (McCubbin, Patterson, & Wilson, 1983) (an indicator of life events likely to cause stress in families), the Family Inventory of Resources for Management (McCubbin, Comeau, & Harkins, 1981) (a documentation of the resources families feel they have available to them in everyday life), and the Family Crisis Oriented Personal Evaluation Scales (McCubbin, Olson, & Larsen, 1981) (a measure of problem-solving strategies used by families). As with the PSI and the QRS, all of these measures emanate from a strong research tradition, and their usefulness in the context of research and clinical work has been well documented.

Despite this considerable research and the well-documented usefulness of these measures, early intervention professionals should exercise caution in using them. Recalling our discussion at the beginning of this chapter, these measures come from the research and clinical traditions and usually do not have direct relevance for early intervention professionals. They were designed primarily for use by psychologists and family therapists; most early intervention professionals do not have the training needed to interpret the results accurately or to follow up except through referral (Slentz & Bricker, 1992). In addition, some families may view use of measures such as these as an intrusion on their personal lives, especially if they have not approached the early intervention professional with concerns in these areas.

Standardized Measures and Rating Scales Completed by Professionals

A final category of family assessment procedures is the use of standardized measures and rating scales completed by professionals. As in the previous two categories, these measures can be relatively informal, with a straightforward interpretation resting primarily on responses to each item, or normative, with interpretation based on external norms or criteria. The primary differentiating feature is that these instruments are completed by professionals rather than by parents, and thus constitute a situation in which a person who is not a family member is making a judgment about some aspects of the family. Although such information can be useful, early intervention professionals should be aware that some families may find such ratings judgmental and, if done improperly, offensive. Thus care should be exercised in the use of these measures. Professionals should discuss them with parents and make sure that the assessment is consistent with the family's view of what they want from the early intervention services system.

One set of measures that fall in this category consists of instruments to assess the amount and quality of the interaction between parents and children. The use of parent-child interaction measures is typically justified for two reasons. The first reason is the well-documented finding that the quality of parent-child interactions significantly shapes the child's language, cognitive, social, and emotional development (e.g., Hart & Risley, 1992). Early intervention professionals see children with disabilities for only a short time.

Parents spend much more time with their children and thus it is argued that by helping the family improve the amount and quality of parent-child interactions the professional extends the benefits of early intervention in a powerful and enduring fashion. The second reason is that there have been a large number of studies that have documented inadequacies in one or more aspects of the interactions between parents and their children with disabilities (e.g., McGhee & Eckerman, 1983; Yoder, 1987). In part this has been attributed to characteristics of the child with a disability (e.g., being difficult to "read") and in part to what some have described as an overcompensation on the part of the parent to ensure that their child succeeds and learns. Thus the literature argues that parent-child interaction is critical to a child's development and provides some evidence that the quality of interactions between parents and children with disabilities sometimes appears to be inadequate. Parent-child interaction measures are designed to help professionals document whether or not there is a problem and, if so, to describe its nature and the context in which it occurs.

A number of parent-child interaction measures are described by Comfort (1988) and Grotevant and Carlson (1989). Two of the better-known measures are in the Nursing Child Assessment Satellite Training (NCAST) tools: the Nursing Child Assessment Feeding Scale (NCAFS) (Barnard, 1978a) and the Nursing Child Assessment Teaching Scale (NCATS) (Barnard, 1978b), both of which are used to rate the extent to which parents and children interact in a mutually effective and synchronous fashion. The NCAFS, used during the first year of life, employs 76 items in four domains (sensitivity to cues, response to distress, social-emotional growth fostering, and cognitive growth fostering) rated as yes or no in the context of a feeding experience. The NCATS, used from birth to 3 years, uses 73 items to rate the same four domains when the parent is asked to try to teach the child something. Huber (1991) summarizes the research on the NCAST scales and finds them to have adequate reliability and validity. They are efficient, requiring only a short administration time, and can provide useful clinical information about the quality of interaction. Another example of a parent-child interaction scale is the Maternal Behavior Rating Scale (Mahoney, Finger, & Powell, 1985). This scale uses a 10-minute sample of free-play between parent and child to assess parent's expressiveness, warmth, sensitivity to child state, achievement orientation, social stimulation, effectiveness, directiveness, child's activity level, attention span, enjoyment, and expressiveness. Other measures, such as the Social Interaction Assessment/Intervention measure (McCollum & Stayton, 1985), the Parent Behavior Progression (Bromwich, 1981), and the Teaching Skills Inventory (Rosenberg, Robinson, & Beckman, 1984), have different formats but assess similarly overlapping dimensions of parent-child interaction.

In addition to measures of parent-child interaction, another example of a professionally completed measure is a rating of the child's home environment. By far the best known of these measures is the Home Observation for the Measurement of the Environment (HOME) (Caldwell, 1972). Two versions of this instrument exist, one for infants from birth to 3 years and one for preschoolers ages 3 to 6 years. The measures are divided into subscales such as emotional and verbal responsivity of the mother, avoidance of restriction and punishment, organization of physical and temporal environment, provision of appropriate play materials, maternal involvement with the child, and opportunities for variety in daily stimulation. Each item is rated true or false by the professionals after a home visit. Research has clearly documented relationships between the HOME ratings and children's language and cognitive development (e.g., Piper & Ramsay, 1980).

Measures of parent-child interaction and the home environment share similar assumptions. They both assume that the home environment and the quality of parent-child interactions are critical to the child's development. However, they constitute a professional judgment about the competence of a parent or the quality of a home, two dimensions of family life that are fundamental to a family's identity and pride and represent dimensions of family life that may differ across cultures. Because most measures of the quality of parent-child interactions and the home environment are based on a white, middle-class conception of quality, professionals should be aware of two essential aspects of this type of assessment. First, the process of conducting such assessments can be threatening to parents because it addresses the very heart of parent competence. Second, the process may incorporate criteria for quality with which some families do not agree. Professionals need to be very careful in the ways such measures are used. Ideally their use should grow out of parents' initiatives and concerns so that the professional is not put in the role of critic or evaluator, but rather the role of consultant and supporter.

STRATEGIES FOR TRANSLATING FAMILY ASSESSMENT INFORMATION INTO GOALS AND SERVICES

The family assessment process has as its ultimate goal the identification of family resources, priorities, and concerns so that early intervention and preschool programs can be tailored to individual family needs and desires for services. In striving to achieve this goal, the strategies by which family assessment information is gathered ought to foster a trusting relationship between parents and professionals and help families feel confident in their roles as team members and parents. Ample research suggests that programs are not providing the full array of family services, that parents want such services (DeGangi, Royeen, & Wietlisbach, 1992; Mahoney, O'Sullivan, & Dennebaum, 1990), and that parents are frustrated when services are provided in a way that ignores the other demands of family life or fails to consider how intervention efforts fit into family routines and environments (Brotherson & Goldstein, 1992). Family assessment can identify the kinds of services or resources parents want so that programs can become more responsive.

This chapter concludes with several recommendations about the assessment process and the translation of assessment information into goals and services. These recommendations address the collaborative nature of this process, the values and perspectives of each team member, and the identification of goals and services.

The Collaborative Process

Virtually every publication that addresses the process of family assessment and goal planning emphasizes the importance of making this a collaborative process (e.g., Turnbull & Turnbull, 1990). The variability across families and across cultures and the goal of promoting the role of families as full team members necessitate a collaborative endeavor (Lynch & Hanson, 1992). Duwa, Wells, and Lalinde (1993) suggest that a family-centered approach to the identification of concerns, priorities, and resources ought to encompass the following characteristics: (1) all concerns evolve from the family based on their culture, values, and lifestyle; (2) concerns encompass the entire family unit and their lifestyle, culture, values, etc.; (3) priorities are based on what the family wishes to focus their energy on; (4) formal and/or informal resources will be utilized as selected by the family; (5) families identify what resources are acceptable from a complete list of what is available; (6) families are encouraged to visualize needs and assess family strengths and weaknesses themselves; and (7) families use their emotions to sort out their strengths, weaknesses, concerns, priorities, and resources (pp. 108–109).

These recommendations are consistent with those offered by other groups (e.g., McGonigel, Kaufmann, & Johnson, 1991), emphasizing the nature of this process as a collaborative one that involves open and ongoing communication between parents and professionals, a recognition of family diversity, and a heavy reliance on family priorities for services and the ways in which this process occurs.

Throughout this process, professionals must work hard to promote family participation and family choice. Kaiser and Hemmeter (1989) argue that many decisions involved in early intervention reflect value-grounded assumptions about what is best for a child or a family. As Bailey (1987) has shown, in many cases the values of professionals and the values of parents differ. Garshelis and McConnell (1993), in a comparison of professional and parent perceptions of family needs, found that only 47% of the professionals' responses matched those of families. These findings emphasize that the perspective of families must form the basis for determining goals and deciding on services as a result of family assessment activities.

Identifying Family Goals and Responding to Expressed Needs

What goals are likely to emerge from this process? For many families, the goals on the IFSP or the IEP will address only the child's needs. If family assessment is conducted properly, part of its focus is on the family's goals and aspirations for their child. Since the child is the reason that professionals have a chance to interact with families, it is entirely appropriate that a child-focused plan be the result of this process for many families. Professionals should not feel disappointed if family assessment does not result in goals other than child goals. The key is for families to be involved in the assessment and planning process, and for them to feel that their opinions have been valued and their concerns heard.

For other families, the goals that emerge from this process may address a variety of other areas in addition to developmental or behavioral goals for the child. As suggested by Bailey, Winton, Rouse, and Turnbull (1990) and Beckman and Bristol

(1991), family goals range on a continuum from child proximal to child distal. Child proximal goals are family goals that relate directly to the child with a disability and often involve activities such as home-based instruction by parents or the search for more information about their child's disability. Child distal goals are family goals related to broader family needs, some of which are related to their child's disability (e.g., family support or participation in community services beyond those provided by the school or early intervention program, such as community recreational programs) and some of which relate to the family's ability to access basic resources such as transportation, food stamps, or housing.

Research suggests that in most cases IFSPs are far more likely to address child goals or child proximal goals. For example, Mahoney et al. (1990) found that families received services in a wide variety of areas, but they were more likely to receive services related to information about their child, engagement with the service system (e.g., laws, advocacy, transition planning, etc.), and family instructional activities (e.g., teaching the family how to perform a teaching or therapeutic activity with the child), and were less likely to receive services related to personal and family assistance (e.g., counseling, stress management, parent support groups) or resource assistance (e.g., transportation, community services). All areas of support were rated by families as highly desired, with the exception of personal and family assistance, which was endorsed by only one third of the families. These data suggest that, despite the concerns of some professionals that family assessments will result in massive changes in the types of services provided, most families request support in areas that are directly related to their child or access to community services. They also suggest, however, that professionals may find it easier to write child goals; when family goals are written, they are most likely to focus on family implementation of therapy and instruction, a finding also reported by Bailey et al. (1990). An exception to this finding is a study by Espe-Sherwindt (1991),

who examined a number of IFSPs written with parents with mental retardation or other special needs. She found that the majority of outcome statements could be categorized as basic family needs, family enrichment, and support or counseling services. This finding most likely reflects the unique needs of this group of parents; however, it may also reflect the author's systematic use of strategies for promoting problem-solving opportunities for parents with mental retardation (Espe-Sherwindt & Crable, 1993). Regardless, it is clear that the nature and content of the IFSP can (and should) vary depending on the individual family.

Ample research (e.g., Bailey et al., 1992; Garshelis & McConnell, 1993) demonstrates that if asked, many families will express a wide variety of needs, some of which are related to the child and some to broader family support. Thus early interventionists should be prepared to expand the nature and format of services offered or to refer parents to other agencies and professionals when requested services are not directly available through the early intervention program. Raab, Davis, and Trepanier (1993) argue that planning goals in the area of family support should focus away from the provision of services (assistance drawn from existing services offered in a relatively inflexible fashion) and toward the provision of resources (assistance in the form of a range of supports that can be drawn on and adapted in a flexible fashion). This suggestion is consistent with the broader goals of the family assessment process, and emphasizes the need for a flexible support system that is driven by the needs and desires of the family rather than by the extent to which a particular service is currently in existence.

Writing goals and developing a service or resource plan for family support may be different from the process of writing specific objectives for children. Perhaps instead of talking about objectives it may be more useful to refer to goals or outcomes. Drawing on a series of ethnographic interviews with families, Able-Boone, Sandall,

Loughry, and Frederick (1990) found that families preferred that IFSP outcomes be stated in the form of suggestions rather than in the usual objective format. Thus the emphasis should be on stating the goal or outcome using the family's terms and then developing a resource implementation plan that is consistent with the way they would like the need to be met.

· · · · · · · ·
SUMMARY OF KEY CONCEPTS

- Family assessment is a process by which information is gathered to determine family priorities for goals and services.
- Family assessment is justified because of legislative requirements to individualize services, to establish positive relationships, for theoretical reasons, and to evaluate the quality of services.
- Family assessment is best conducted in an informal fashion, using a variety of procedures over time.
- Family assessment should be designed to determine (a) the family's goals for their child; (b) the family's desires for family support; and (c) the family's view of the service system and service providers.
- When conducting assessments with families, professionals should (a) use multimethod approaches; (b) recognize that assessment activities are potential interventions; (c) consider carefully the timing of assessment activities; (d) define with the family their roles in assessment; (e) seek families' perceptions; and (f) evaluate the measures and procedures that are used.
- Potential assessment strategies include informal communication, semistructured interviews, surveys and rating scales, and direct observations.
- When translating assessment information into goals and services, professionals should engage in a collaborative process with families, recognize the values and perspectives of each team member, and develop supportive and individualized goals and services.

· · · · · · · ·
REFERENCES

Abidin, R. R. (1990). *Parenting Stress Index* (3rd ed.). Charlottesville, VA: Pediatric Psychology Press.

Able-Boone, H., Sandall, S. R., Loughry, A., & Frederick, L. L. (1990). An informed, family-centered approach to Public Law 99-457: Parental views. *Topics in Early Childhood Special Education, 10*(1), 100–111.

Applequist, K. L., & Bailey, D. B. (2000). Navajo caregivers' perceptions of early intervention services. *Journal of Early Intervention, 23,* 47–61.

Bailey, D. B. (1987). Collaborative goal-setting with families: Resolving differences in values and priorities for services. *Topics in Early Childhood Special Education, 7*(2), 59–71.

Bailey, D. B. (2001). Evaluating parent involvement and family support in early intervention and preschool programs. *Journal of Early Intervention, 24,* 1–14.

Bailey, D. B. (1991). Issues and perspectives on family assessment. *Infants and Young Children, 4*(1), 26–34.

Bailey, D. B., & Blasco, P. M. (1990). Parents' perspectives on a written survey of family needs. *Journal of Early Intervention, 14,* 196–203.

Bailey, D. B., Blasco, P. M., & Simeonsson, R. J. (1992). Needs expressed by mothers and fathers of young children with disabilities. *American Journal on Mental Retardation, 97,* 1–10.

Bailey, D. B., Buysse, V., Edmondson, R., & Smith, T. M. (1992). Creating family-centered services in early intervention: Perceptions of professionals in four states. *Exceptional Children, 58,* 298–309.

Bailey, D. B., & Henderson, L. (1993). Traditions in family assessment: Toward a reflective, inquiry-oriented approach. In D. M. Bryant & M. Graham (Eds.), *Implementing early intervention: From research to best practice* (pp. 124–147). New York: Guilford Press.

Bailey, D. B., McWilliam, R. A., Darkes, L. A., Hebbeler, K., Simeonsson, R. J., Spiker, D., & Wagner, M. (1998). Family outcomes in early intervention: A framework for program evaluation and efficacy research. *Exceptional Children, 64*, 313–328.

Bailey, D. B., Palsha, S. A., & Simeonsson, R. J. (1991). Professional concerns, skills, and perceived importance of work with families in early intervention. *Exceptional Children, 58*, 156–165.

Bailey, D. B., & Simeonsson, R. J. (1988a). Assessing needs of families with handicapped infants. *Journal of Special Education, 22*, 117–127.

Bailey, D. B., & Simeonsson, R. J. (Eds.) (1988b). *Family assessment in early intervention.* Upper Saddle River, NJ: Merrill/Prentice Hall.

Bailey, D. B., & Simeonsson, R. J. (1990). *Family needs survey.* Chapel Hill, NC: Frank Porter Graham Child Development Center, University of North Carolina.

Bailey, D. B., Simeonsson, R. J., Yoder, D. E., & Huntington, G. S. (1990). Preparing professionals to serve infants and toddlers with handicaps and their families: An integrative analysis across eight disciplines. *Exceptional Children, 57*, 26–35.

Bailey, D.B., Skinner, D., Rodriguez, P., Gut, D., & Correa, V. (1999). Awareness, use, and satisfaction with services for Latino parents of young children with disabilities. *Exceptional Children, 65*, 367–381.

Bailey, D. B., Winton, P. J., Rouse, L., & Turnbull, A. P. (1990). Family goals in infant intervention: Analysis and issues. *Journal of Early Intervention, 14*, 15–26.

Barnard, K. E. (1978a). *Nursing Child Assessment Feeding Scale.* Seattle: University of Washington.

Barnard, K. E. (1978b). *Nursing Child Assessment Teaching Scale.* Seattle: University of Washington.

Beavers, W. R., & Voeller, M. N. (1983). Family models: Comparing and contrasting the Olson model with the Beavers systems model. *Family Process, 22*, 85–98.

Beckman, P. J., & Bristol, M. M. (1991). Issues in developing the IFSP: A framework for establishing family outcomes. *Topics in Early Childhood Special Education, 11*(3), 19–31.

Bell, R. Q. (1968). A reinterpretation of the direction of effects in studies of socialization. *Psychological Review, 75*, 81–95.

Bendell, R. D., Stone, W. L., Field, T. M., & Goldstein, S. (1989). Children's effects on parenting stress in a low income, minority population. *Topics in Early Childhood Special Education, 8*, 58–71.

Bernheimer, L. P., Gallimore, R., & Weisner, T. S. (1990). Ecocultural theory as a context for the Individual Family Service Plan. *Journal of Early Intervention, 14*, 219–233.

Brinckerhoff, J. L., & Vincent, L. J. (1986). Increasing parental decision-making at the Individualized Educational Program meeting. *Journal of the Division for Early Childhood, 11*, 46–58.

Bromwich, R. (1981). *Working with parents and infants: An interactional approach.* Baltimore: University Park Press.

Bronfenbrenner, U. (1977). Toward an experimental ecology of human development. *American Psychologist, 32*, 513–531.

Brotherson, M. J., & Goldstein, B. L. (1992). Time as a resource and constraint for parents of young children with disabilities: Implications for early intervention services. *Topics in Early Childhood Special Education, 12*, 508–527.

Brown, J., & Ritchie, J. A. (1990). Nurses' perceptions of parent and nurse roles in caring for hospitalized children. *Children's Health Care, 19*, 28–36.

Caldwell, B. (1972). *HOME Inventory.* Little Rock, AR: University of Arkansas.

Chen, Y., & McCollum, J. A. (2001). Taiwanese mothers' perspectives of parent-infant interaction with children with Down syndrome. *Journal of Early Intervention, 24*, 252–265.

Child Development Resources. (1989). *How Can We Help?* Lightfoot, VA: Child Development Resources.

Comfort, M. (1988). Assessing parent-child interaction. In D. Bailey & R. Simeonsson (Eds.), *Family assessment in early intervention* (pp. 65–94). Upper Saddle River, NJ: Merrill/Prentice Hall.

Cooper, C. S., & Allred, K. W. (1992). A comparison of mothers' versus fathers' needs for support in caring for a young child with special needs. *Infant-Toddler Intervention, 2*(3), 205–221.

Cox, M., & Paley, B. (1997). Families as systems. *Annual Review of Psychology, 48*, 243–267.

Cunningham, C. C., Morgan, P. A., & McGucken, R. B. (1984). Down's syndrome: Is dissatisfaction with disclosure of diagnosis inevitable? *Developmental Medicine and Child Neurology, 26,* 33–39.

DeGangi, C., Royeen, C. B., & Wietlisbach, S. (1992). How to examine the individualized family service planning process: Preliminary findings and a procedural guide. *Infants and Young Children, 5*(2), 42–56.

Dunst, C. J. (1985). Rethinking early intervention. *Analysis and Intervention in Developmental Disabilities, 5,* 165–201.

Dunst, C. J., Cooper, C. S., Weeldreyer, J. C., Snyder, K. D., & Chase, J. H. (1988). Family needs scale. In C. J. Dunst, C. M. Trivette, & A. G. Deal (Eds.), *Enabling and empowering families: Principles and guidelines for practice* (p. 151). Cambridge, MA: Brookline Books.

Dunst, C. J., Jenkins, V., & Trivette, C. (1988). Family support scale. In C. J. Dunst, C. M. Trivette, & A. G. Deal (Eds.), *Enabling and empowering families: Principles and guidelines for practice.* Cambridge, MA: Brookline Books.

Dunst, C. J., Trivette, C. M., & Deal, A. G. (Eds.). (1988). *Enabling and empowering families: Principles and guidelines for practice.* Cambridge, MA: Brookline Books.

Duwa, S. M., Wells, C., & Lalinde, P. (1993). Creating family centered programs and policies. In D. M. Bryant & M. A. Graham (Eds.), *Implementing early intervention: From research to effective practices* (pp. 92–123). New York: Guilford Press.

Early Childhood Research Institute on Measuring Growth and Development (1998). *Family outcomes in a growth and development model* (Tech. Rep. No. 7). Minneapolis, MN: Center for Early Education and Development, University of Minnesota.

Espe-Sherwindt, M. (1991). The IFSP and parents with special needs/mental retardation. *Topics in Early Childhood Special Education, 11*(3), 107–120.

Espe-Sherwindt, M., & Crable, S. (1993). Parents with mental retardation: Moving beyond the myths. *Topics in Early Childhood Special Education, 13,* 154–174.

Friedrich, W. N., Greenberg, M. T., & Crnic, K. (1983). A short form of the questionnaire on resources and stress. *American Journal of Mental Deficiency, 88,* 41–48.

Gallimore, R., Coots, J., Weisner, T., Garner, H., & Guthrie, D. (1996). Family responses to children with early developmental delays II: Accommodation intensity and activity in early and middle childhood. *American Journal on Mental Retardation, 101,* 215–232.

Garshelis, J. A., & McConnell, S. R. (1993). Comparison of family needs assessed by mothers, individual professionals, and interdisciplinary teams. *Journal of Early Intervention, 16,* 36–49.

Goldstein, S., & Turnbull, A. P. (1982). The use of two strategies to increase parent participation in IEP conferences. *Exceptional Children, 48,* 360–361.

Grotevant, H. D., & Carlson, C. I. (1989). *Family assessment: A guide to methods and measures.* New York: Guilford Press.

Hanson, M. J., Beckman, P. J., Horn, E., Marquart, J., Sandall, S. R., & Greig, D., et al. (2000). Entering preschool: Family and professional experiences in this transition process. *Journal of Early Intervention, 23,* 279–293.

Hart, B., & Risley, T. R. (1992). American parenting of language learning children: Persisting differences in family-child interactions observed in natural home environments. *Developmental Psychology, 28,* 1096–1105.

Henderson, L. W., Aydlett, L. A., & Bailey, D. B. (1993). Evaluating family needs surveys: Do standard measures of reliability and validity tell us what we want to know? *Journal of Psychoeducational Assessment, 11,* 208–219.

Holroyd, J. (1974). The questionnaire on resources and stress: An instrument to measure family response to a handicapped member. *Journal of Community Psychology, 2,* 92–94.

Holroyd, J. (1986). *Questionnaire on resources and stress for families with a chronically ill or handicapped member: Manual.* Brandon, VT: Clinical Psychology Publishing.

Huber, C. J. (1991). Documenting quality of parent-child interaction: Use of the NCAST Scales. *Infants and Young Children, 4*(2), 63–75.

Kaiser, A. P., & Hemmeter, M. L. (1989). Value-based approaches to early intervention. *Topics in Early Childhood Special Education, 8*(4), 72–86.

Krauss, M. W. (2000). Family assessment within early intervention programs. In J. P. Shonkoff & S. J. Meisels (Eds.), *Handbook of early childhood intervention* (2nd ed., pp. 290–308). Cambridge, MA: Cambridge University Press.

Lynch, E. W., & Hanson, M. J. (Eds.) (1992). *Developing cross-cultural competence.* Baltimore: Paul H. Brookes.

Mahoney, G., Finger, I., & Powell, A. (1985). Relationship of maternal behavioral style to the development of organically impaired mentally retarded infants. *American Journal of Mental Deficiency, 90,* 296–302.

Mahoney, G., & O'Sullivan, P. (1990). Early intervention practices with families of children with handicaps. *Mental Retardation, 28,* 169–176.

Mahoney, G., O'Sullivan, P., & Dennebaum, J. (1990). A national study of mothers' perceptions of family-focused intervention. *Journal of Early Intervention, 14,* 133–146.

Matarazzo, R., Phillips, J., Wiens, A., & Saslow, G. (1965). Learning the art of interviewing: A study of what beginning students do and their patterns of change. *Psychotherapy: Theory, Research and Practice, 2,* 49–60.

McCollum, J. A., & Stayton, V. D. (1985). Infant/parent interaction: Studies and intervention guidelines based on the SIAI model. *Journal of the Division for Early Childhood, 9*(2), 125–135.

McCubbin, H. I., Comeau, J. K., & Harkins, J. A. (1981). *Family Inventory of Resources for Management.* Madison, WI: Family Stress Coping and Health Project.

McCubbin, H. L., Olson, D. H., & Larsen, A. S. (1981). *Family Crisis Oriented Personal Scales.* Madison, WI: Family Stress Coping and Health Project.

McCubbin, H. I., & Patterson, J. M. (1983). Family transitions: Adaptation to stress. In H. McCubbin & C. Figley (Eds.), *Stress and the family: Vol. 1. Coping with normative transitions* (pp. 5–25). New York: Brunner/Mazel.

McCubbin, H. I., Patterson, J. M., & Wilson, L. R. (1983). *Family Inventory of Life Events and Changes.* Madison, WI: Family Stress Coping and Health Project.

McCubbin, H. I., & Thompson, A. I. (1987a). *Family assessment inventories for research and practice.* Madison, WI: University of Wisconsin–Madison.

McCubbin, H. I., & Thompson, A. I. (1987b). Family typologies and family assessment. In H. I. McCubbin & A. I. Thompson (Eds.), *Family assessment inventories for research and practice* (pp. 35–62). Madison, WI: University of Wisconsin–Madison.

McGhee, L. J., & Eckerman, C. O. (1983). The preterm infant as a social partner: Responsive but not readable. *Infant Behavior and Development, 6,* 461–470.

McGonigel, M. J., Kaufmann, R. K., & Johnson, B. H. (Eds.). (1991). *Guidelines and recommended practices for the Individualized Family Service Plan* (2nd ed.). Bethesda, MD: Association for the Care of Children's Health.

McGrew, K. S., Gilman, C. J., & Johnson, S. (1992). A review of scales to assess family needs. *Journal of Psychoeducational Assessment, 10,* 4–25.

McKinney, B., & Peterson, R. A. (1987). Predictors of stress in parents of developmentally disabled children. *Journal of Pediatric Psychology, 12,* 133–150.

McWilliam R. A., Tocci, L., & Harbin, G. (1998). Family-centered services: Service providers' discourse and behavior. *Topics in Early Childhood Special Education, 18,* 206–221.

Noonan, M. J., & Kilgo, J. L. (1987). Transition services for early age individuals with severe mental retardation. In R. N. Ianacone & R. A. Stodder (Eds.), *Transition issues and directions* (pp. 25–37). Reston, VA: Council for Exceptional Children.

Piper, M. C., & Ramsay, M. K. (1980). Effects of early home environment on the mental development of Down syndrome infants. *American Journal of Mental Deficiency, 85,* 39–44.

Raab, M. M., Davis, M. S., & Trepanier, A. M. (1993). Resources vs. services: Changing the focus of intervention for infants and young children. *Infants and Young Children, 5*(3), 1–11.

Roberts, R. N., Innocenti, M.S., & Goetze, L. D. (1999). Emerging issues from state level evaluations of early intervention programs. *Journal of Early Intervention, 22,* 152–163.

Rosenberg, S., Robinson, C., & Beckman, P. (1984). Teaching skills inventory: A measure of parent performance. *Journal of the Division for Early Childhood, 8,* 107–113.

Rosenkoetter, S. E., Hains, A. H., & Fowler, S. A. (1994). *Bridging early services for children with special needs and their families: A practical guide for transition planning.* Baltimore: Paul H. Brookes.

Rushton, C. H. (1990). Family-centered care in the critical care setting: Myth or reality? *Children's Health Care, 19*(2), 68–77.

Sameroff, A. J., & Chandler, M. J. (1975). Reproductive risk and the continuum of care-taking casualty. In F. D. Horowitz, M. Hetherington, S. Scarr-Salapatek, & G. Siegel (Eds.), *Review of child development research* (Vol. 4) (pp. 187–244). Chicago: University of Chicago Press.

Sameroff, A. J., & Fiese, B. (2000). Transactional regulation: The developmental ecology of early intervention. In J. P. Shonkoff & S. J. Meisels (Eds.), *Handbook of early childhood intervention* (2nd ed., pp. 135–159). Cambridge, MA: Cambridge University Press.

Seligman, M., & Darling, R. B. (1989). *Ordinary families, special children: A systems approach to childhood disability.* New York: Guilford.

Selvini, M. P., Boscolo, L., Cecchin, G., & Prata, G. (1980). Hypothesizing–circularity–neutrality: Three guidelines for the conductor of the session. *Family Process, 19,* 3–12.

Sexton, D., Snyder, P., Rheams, T., Barron-Sharp, B., & Perez, J. (1991). Considerations in using written surveys to identify family strengths and needs during the IFSP process. *Topics in Early Childhood Special Education, 11,* 81–91.

Shapiro, J., Blacher, J., & Lopez, S. R. (1998). Maternal reactions to children with mental retardation. In J. A. Burack, R. M. Hodapp, & E. Zigler (Eds.), *Handbook of mental retardation and development* (pp. 606–636). Cambridge, UK: Cambridge University Press.

Simeonsson, R. J. (1988). Unique characteristics of families with young handicapped children. In D. B. Bailey & R. J. Simeonsson (Eds.), *Family assessment in early intervention* (pp. 27–43). Upper Saddle River, NJ: Merrill/Prentice Hall.

Slentz, K. L., & Bricker, D. (1992). Family-guided assessment for IFSP development: Jumping off the family assessment bandwagon. *Journal of Early Intervention, 16,* 11–19.

Steinglass, P. (1984). Family systems theory and therapy: A clinical application of general systems theory. *Psychiatric Annals, 14*(8), 582–586.

Summers, J. A., Dell'Oliver, C., Turnbull, A. P., Benson, H. A., Santelli, E., & Campbell, M., et al. (1990). Examining the Individualized Family Service Plan process: What are family and practitioner preferences? *Topics in Early Childhood Special Education, 10,* 78–99.

Telleen, S., Herzog, A., & Kilbane, T. L. (1989). Impact of a family support program on mothers' social support and parenting stress. *American Journal of Orthopsychiatry, 59,* 410–419.

Tomm, K. (1987). Interventive interviewing: Part 1. Strategizing as a fourth guideline for the therapist. *Family Process, 26,* 3–13.

Turnbull, A. P., & Turnbull, H. R. (1990). *Families, professionals, and exceptionality: A special partnership* (2nd ed.). Upper Saddle River, NJ: Merrill/Prentice Hall.

Turnbull, A. P., Turbiville, V., & Turnbull, H. R. (2000). Evolution of family-professional models: Collective empowerment as the model for the early 21st century. In J. P. Shonkoff & S. J. Meisels (Eds.), *Handbook of early childhood intervention* (2nd ed., pp. 630–650). Cambridge, MA: Cambridge University Press.

Wikler, L. (1981). Chronic stresses of families of mentally retarded children. *Family Relations, 30,* 281–288.

Wilfong, E. W., Saylor, C., & Elksnin, N. (1991). Influences on responsiveness: Interactions between mothers and their premature infants. *Infant Mental Health Journal, 12,* 31–39.

Winton, P. J. (1988a). Effective communication between parents and professionals. In D. Bailey & R. Simeonsson (Eds.), *Family assessment in early intervention* (pp. 207–228). Upper Saddle River, NJ: Merrill/Prentice Hall.

Winton, P. J. (1988b). The family-focused interview: An assessment measure and goal-setting mechanism. In D. B. Bailey & R. J. Simeonsson (Eds.), *Family assessment in early intervention* (pp. 185–206). Upper Saddle River, NJ: Merrill/Prentice Hall.

Winton, P. J., & Bailey, D. B. (1988). The family-focused interview: A mechanism for collaborative goal-setting with families. *Journal of the Division for Early Childhood, 12,* 195–207.

Winton, P. J., & Bailey, D. B. (1993). Communicating with families: Examining practices and facilitating change. In J. Paul & R. J. Simeonsson (Eds.), *Children with special needs: Family, culture, and society* (pp. 210–230). Orlando, FL: Harcourt Brace Jovanovich.

Yoder, P. (1987). Relationship between degree of infant handicap and clarity of infant cues. *American Journal of Mental Deficiency, 91,* 639–641.

Zigler, E., & Black, K. (1989). America's family support movement: Strengths and limitations. *American Journal of Orthopsychiatry, 59,* 6–19.

Assessing Children's Environments

Mark Wolery
Vanderbilt University

Most of this text is devoted to methods for assessing children. All children, however, live in environments, and those environments have a great deal to do with children's abilities, how well they learn, when they use particular skills, and how competent they are perceived to be. Further, intervention and educational programs are manipulations of children's environments; thus, understanding those environments is central to making decisions about using assessment results in planning children's individualized intervention programs. In this chapter, environments are defined and theoretical perspectives for understanding children's environments are noted. The rationale for measuring children's environments is then discussed, followed by a description of methods for assessing environments.

DEFINITIONS AND THEORETICAL PERSPECTIVES OF ENVIRONMENTS

A dictionary definition of *environment* is "the circumstances, objects, or conditions by which one is surrounded" and a second meaning is "the aggregate of the social and cultural conditions that influence the life of an individual or community" (*Webster's Ninth New Collegiate Dictionary*, 1988, p. 416). These two meanings capture many of the concepts that form the foundations for the measures discussed in this chapter. However, to put these meanings in context, the contributions of general systems theory and ecological psychology are important. From "this perspective, individuals, families, organizations, and agencies are not viewed as independently functioning units but rather as components of an 'organized whole.' This 'whole' is a hierarchical and orderly system of interrelated and interdependent components" (Bailey & Wolery, 1992, p. 64). The "whole" changes over time as individuals, entities, and components within it interact and adapt to influences from within and external to the system. Some key concepts in the ecological perspective are (a) systems are hierarchical, having different levels of organization which are nested within each other and have proximal to distal influences on the individual, (b) changes in one part or level of the system influence other parts or levels, (c) individuals and their environments are interrelated—influencing and being influenced by another through their actions and perceptions, and (d) children's immediate environments include physical (inanimate) components and social (animate) components (Bailey & Wolery, 1992; Thurman, 1997; Bronfenbrenner, 1992).

Bronfenbrenner's (1977, 1979, 1992) ecological theory of human development is perhaps the most widely known and understood ecological theory in developmental psychology and early intervention. He proposed that the ecology had different levels and represented those levels as concentric circles with the child in the middle. An example, related to early intervention is shown in Figure 8.1. Bronfenbrenner's levels are the microsystem, mesosystem, exosystem, and macrosystem. The microsystem represents the immediate settings in which the child spends time. Examples, as shown in Figure 8.1, are the home, the classroom program, or other places where the child interacts with the social and physical components of a setting. The mesosystem are the relationships between microsystems and the people in them. This includes the interactions and relationships between the child's parents and teachers, parents and service coordinator or home visitor, and the interactions and relationships between the professional members of the child's team. The exosystem are the societal structures that influence the mesosystem and microsystem but of which the child is not a direct participant. This includes formal intervention and social services as well as more informal organizations and agencies. Events and characteristics in the exosystem can put children at risk for developmental problems (e.g., lack of community resources) or can be an opportunity or enhancing factor for children's developmental progress (e.g., multiple, varied, and safe community resources) (Dunst, 1993; Garbarino & Ganzel, 2000). The macrosystem are the beliefs and values of the culture or subculture

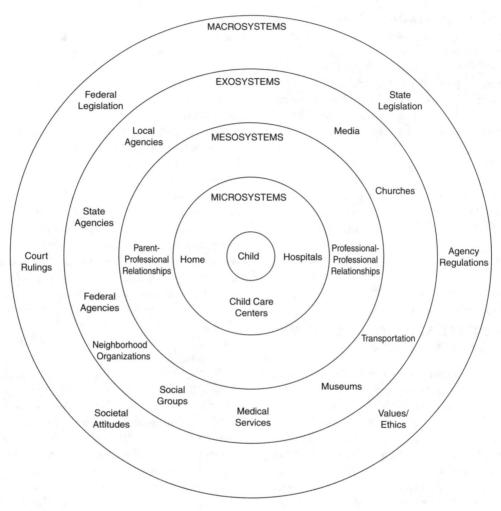

FIGURE 8.1
Depiction of four levels of the environment as it relates to early intervention for young children with disabilities.
Note: Based on Bronfenbrenner's theory taken from D. B. Bailey and M. Wolery (1992). *Teaching Infants and Preschoolers with Disabilities* (p. 66). New York: Merrill/Macmillan. Used with permission.

as well as policies of governmental agencies forming the context in which the other systems operate. This model has been quite useful in planning and carrying out intervention services as well as recognizing the multiple factors that influence family well-being and functioning and children's learning and development (Bailey, Farel, O'Donnell, Simeonsson, & Miller, 1986; Dunst, 2000; Thurman, 1997).

Horowitz proposes another ecological systems theory (Horowitz, 1987; Horowitz & Haritos, 1998). In this model the ecology is seen as a system with different levels of environmental inputs and influences on children's learning. The different levels also are seen as concentric circles with the child in the center and the inputs and influences most proximal to the child are the innermost circles. The four levels of Horowitz's model are: (1) "environment as stimulus array—amount, intensity, pattern, variety," (2) "environment as variation in learning opportunity," (3) "environment as social system," and (4) "environment as cultural context" (Horowitz & Haritos, 1998, p. 34). The first two levels (environment as stimulus array and as learning opportunities) allow for definition and measurement of the nature and quality of settings in which children spend time. This includes social as well as physical stimulus arrays, and physical (with toys and materials) and social learning opportunities (interactions with peers, siblings, adults). The third level (social system) is similar to Bronfenbrenner's exosystem and may include risk and opportunity factors that reside in the family and in the communities in which children live. The fourth level (cultural context) is similar to Bronfenbrenner's macrosystem.

Another theoretical perspective of the environment is Thurman's (1977, 1997) ecological congruence model. Thurman proposed three dimensions for his model, each of which occur on a continuum. The dimensions are (a) the degree of deviance (difference) of the child's behavior for a given context or setting, (b) the degree of child competence in doing functional tasks in that context or setting, and (c) the degree of tolerance for difference by the child and by adults—the adult's tolerance of the child's difference, and the child's tolerance for aspects of the setting, including adult behavior. The continuum for each dimension ranges from high to low. In this model, deviance and tolerance for difference are socially constructed notions and may be context specific, and competence is defined by the situation—the extent to which the child performs tasks specific to the setting competently. A central foundation of this approach is the concept of adaptive fit, which "results from mutual acceptance between the individual and the environment" (Thurman, 1997, p. 12). Intervention in this model is designed to build or promote adaptive fit between children and their environments. This model is often depicted as a cube with each of the three dimensions being a different edge of that cube.

Individuals, of course, live and act in settings, which are locations that have physical properties (such as space, furnishings, and materials) and social properties such as the behaviors, attitudes, and perceptions of other individuals who share that space. Settings are characterized in Bronfenbrenner's model as the microsystems, in Horowitz's model as the stimulus array and variations in learning opportunities, and in Thurman's model as the context. In all of these models, attention is given to the usual events and routines that occur within children's current environments. The assumption is that the events, activities, and routines of daily life constitute the situation (context) in which children's experiences interact with their characteristics to produce learning and thus development. This has led Dunst and colleagues (Dunst, Bruder, et al., 2001; Dunst, Hamby, Trivette, Raab, & Bruder, 2000; Dunst, Trivette, Humphries, Raab, & Roper, 2001) to study the influences of these factors on children's behavior and learning. They use the term "activity settings" to refer to these everyday events and define activity settings "as a situation-specific experience, opportunity, or event that involves a child's interaction with people, the physical environment, or both, and provides a context for a child to learn about his or her own abilities and capabilities as well as the propensities of others" (Dunst, Bruder, et al., 2001, p. 70). We observe children in natural contexts and interview their families and caregivers to understand how they function in those activity settings, and we gather information about the activity settings and the broader contexts to understand how to provide experiences that will lead to greater child competence and fit.

RATIONALE FOR ASSESSING CHILDREN'S ENVIRONMENTS

There are at least three major reasons or purposes for assessing children's environments: ensuring children's safety, improving the quality of children's environments, and assisting in planning and carrying out interventions. Each of these is described in the following sections.

Ensuring Child Safety

The primary reason for assessing the safety of children's environments is to prevent (reduce or eliminate) child death and injury. For the United States, the National Center for Injury Prevention and Control of the Centers for Disease Control and Prevention (*www.cdc.gov/ncipc/wisqars*, 2002) reports that in 1999 unintentional injury (accidents) was the leading cause of death in children 1 to 5 years of age, with a total of 2,193 deaths. Excluding the fourth leading cause of death, which was homicide (541 deaths), the number of children (1–5 years of age) who died by unintentional injury was greater than the sum of deaths by the other ten leading causes—all of which were disease related. Of the deaths by unintentional injury, 31.5% were due to motor vehicle traffic accidents, 24.1% to drowning, 16.2% to fire or burns, 8.2% to suffocation, 5.2% to events while being a pedestrian, 2.7% to falls, and the remainder to a variety of other events. For infants (children less than 1 year of age) in 1999, unintentional injury was the seventh leading cause of death, with 845 deaths. Of these deaths, 55.9% were due to suffocation (not sudden infant death syndrome), 21.2% to traffic accidents, 8% to drowning, and 5.2% to fire and burns.

In terms of nonfatal unintentional injuries, the ten leading causes of injury and the estimated number of children injured are shown in Table 8.1. These injuries are for 2000 and include only those involving an emergency room visit other than visits due to illness. As indicated, falling and being struck by or crushed against something other than a motor vehicle or machinery are the two leading causes of nonfatal injuries across the three age levels reported (i.e., less than 1 year, 1 to 4 years, and 5 to 9 years). Surveys of preschool teachers and families of preschool children confirm falling as a major cause of injuries (Huber, Marchand-Martella, Martella, & Wood,

1996). For deaths and nonfatal unintentional injuries, the assumption is that the causes are preventable. While many reasons children are injured are tied to specific factors in the situation (presence of unsafe materials, lack of supervision), the incidence of unintended injury to children is higher in impoverished communities (Reading, Langford, Haynes, & Lovett, 1999). Thus, an important reason for assessing children's environments is to identify any conditions, events, or situations that may lead to unintentional child injury or death.

Improving the Quality of Children's Environments

Although there is tremendous variability, many young children, including those with developmental delays and disabilities, have a primary home environment, and they may spend time in nonparental and/or out-of-home care (Shonkoff & Phillips, 2000). For example, in 2001, 52% of the infants and toddlers (birth through age 2) were in nonparental care with many of those receiving care in a home (their own or in someone else's home) and 17% were in center-based care (i.e., childcare programs, Head Start, prekindergarten classes, nursery schools, and other early childhood programs); and 76% of the preschoolers (3 to 6 years of age and not yet in kindergarten) were in nonparental care with 56% being in center-based care (Federal Interagency Forum on Child and Family Statistics, 2002). Also, many children have multiple care arrangements simultaneously; for example, a home environment, a morning intervention class, and relative or family day-care in the afternoon until a parent returns from work. Many children also will have two home environments when their parents are separated and have joint custody of the child. For most young children, their relevant environments will change over the preschool years with more class attendance likely as they become preschoolers. Thus, most children will have multiple environments when they are in early intervention.

TABLE 8.1
Estimated Number of Children with Nonfatal Unintentional Injuries by Cause and Child Age

Rank	Child Age in Years					
	Less than 1 year		**1 to 4 years**		**5 to 9 years**	
	Cause	*# of children*	*Cause*	*# of children*	*Cause*	*# of children*
1	Falls	135,251	Falls	900,850	Falls	688,942
2	Struck by or against[a]	39,452	Struck by or Against[a]	440,984	Struck by or against[a]	496,279
3	Fire/burn	17,704	Bite or sting[b]	146,945	Pedal cyclist[c]	152,483
4	Foreign body[d]	14,604	Foreign body[d]	121,077	Cut or pierce	140,719
5	MV occupant[e]	10,315	Cut or pierce	98,800	Bite or sting[b]	110,223
6	Bite or sting[b]	9,947	Poisoning[f]	80,447	MV occupant[e]	88,296
7	Poisoning[f]	7,091	Overexertion[g]	65,234	Overexertion[g]	78,717
8	Cut or pierce	6,368	MV occupant[e]	63,234	Dog bite	60,923
9	Inhalation or suffocation[h]	95,857	Fire or burn	62,595	Foreign body[d]	56,681
10	Unknown or unspecified	4,583	Unknown or unspecified	43,328	Unknown or unspecified	52,472

[a]Injury resulting from being hit or crushed by a human, animal, or inanimate object other than a motor vehicle or machinery
[b]Injury from poisonous or nonpoisonous bite or sting other than a dog bite
[c]Injury to a pedal cycle rider from collision, loss of control, or crash
[d]Injury resulting from entrance of a foreign body into or through the eye or other natural body opening that does not block an airway
[e]Injury caused by a motor vehicle collision, rollover, crash, or some other event involving another vehicle, an object, or a pedestrian
[f]Injury caused by ingestion, inhalation, absorption through the skin, or injection of a drug, toxin, or other chemical
[g]Injury caused by working the body or a body part too hard, causing damage to a muscle, tendon, ligament, cartilage, joint, or periphery nerve (strains, sprains, twisted ankle)
[h]Injury caused by inhalation, aspiration, or ingestion of food or other object that blocks the airway or causes suffocation

Note: Based on data from the National Center for Injury Prevention and Control, Centers for Disease Control and Prevention (2002). *www.cdc.gov/ncipc/wisqars*

Over the last thirty years, a great deal of effort has been devoted to understanding the home and classroom conditions and characteristics that are associated with high and low quality. Clear research evidence exists that the quality of the home environment (in association with many other factors) is related to children's outcomes on a range of important measures (e.g., Bradley, 1994). Further, the quality of early childhood programs is related to children's outcomes. The National Research Council's report on pedagogy in the early years concluded the quality of early

childhood programs was critical to children's outcomes (Bowman, Donovan, & Burns, 2001). While it is unclear from current research what proportion of young children spend time in low-quality homes and low-quality nonparental care, many young children who live in impoverished communities, in overstressed families, and in families with minimal supports and resources are in homes characterized as being of low quality. For child-care programs, a majority of the studied programs were found to have mediocre to low quality (Cost, Quality, and Child Outcomes Study

Team, 1995). Further, Bowman et al. (2001) state, "it can be safely concluded that most early education and care programs in the United States do not approach ideal levels of quality and that programs designed to reduce the gap between rich and poor in early childhood educational opportunity are far from optimal" (p. 181). Fortunately, many of the factors and issues that constitute low quality in homes and in programs can be addressed and changed. As a result, a primary reason for measuring children's environments is to assess the quality of those settings and thereby devise and carry out plans to improve that quality, when appropriate.

Planning Children's Individualized Intervention Plans

Each infant and toddler who had developmental delays and disabilities should have an Individualized Family Service Plan (IFSP), and each preschooler with developmental delays and disabilities should have an individualized educational program (IEP). Much of this text is devoted to assessing children to identify goals for those individualized plans and for identifying strategies for helping children acquire and use the skills identified in the outcomes and goals. An important part of developing those plans is making sure the identified goals are (a) needed in children's current environments (or immediate future environments) and (b) identifying any additional goals children need in their current environments. Assessing the expectations, demands, and arrangements of children's environments is a method for determining whether the goals are functional in children's environments and for determining whether additional goals should be established. Thus, we assess children's environments, including children in the context of those settings, to identify goals. In addition to identifying goals, we need to understand which practices are used in children's current settings, the demands on adults in those settings that may interfere with or support use of the recommended intervention practices, and the modifications needed in those environ-

ments to increase the feasibility of using recommended practices. Thus, two additional reasons for assessing environments are to identify goals for children and to plan how to implement recommended practices for addressing those goals.

Summary

Children's environments, both homes and classrooms, should be assessed to promote safety and thereby prevent unintentional child death and injury. Another reason for assessing environments is to increase the quality of their home and classroom environments and thereby increase the likelihood of desirable child outcomes. Finally, environments should be assessed to identify unique goals needed in children's current settings and to plan how relevant intervention strategies and practices can be used in those environments; such assessment should result in better learning as well as better adaptive fit of children in their environments.

REPRESENTATIVE MEASURES FOR ASSESSING CHILDREN'S HOME AND CLASSROOM ENVIRONMENTS

Some measures for assessing children's environments are well established, well studied, used broadly, and consistently predictive of children's outcomes. Other measures are less well developed, have not been studied extensively, and may be in the process of being refined. In this section, both types of measures are described. This section is organized around the major reasons for assessing children's environments: promoting safety, increasing quality, and planning interventions. Across these sections, attention is given to two important environments: homes and classroom programs (including playgrounds). However, homes should not be restricted to the home in which the child resides; for example, if a child spends every day with grandparents or another adult in those persons' homes, the assessment of such home environments may be as relevant as assessing the home in which the child and his or her parents reside.

ASSESSING THE SAFETY OF CHILDREN'S ENVIRONMENTS

Assessing Safety in Homes

As noted previously, a large number of children have unintentional injuries each year, and many of these could be prevented. Thus, the goals of assessing the safety of children's homes are to prevent child injury and death and to assist families in protecting their young children.

Inventories of Home Safety A measure for assessing the home safety is the *Home Inventory of Dangers and Safety Precautions–2* (HIDSP–2) (Tymchuk, Lang, Dolyniuk, Berney-Ficklin, & Spitz, 1999). This measure is based on the assumption that injury prevention has at least two major components: identification and removal of dangers, and the use of precautions to prevent injury (Tymchuk et al., 1999). For example, removal of a fire hazard (e.g., accessible matches or lighters) is an identification and removal of a danger, and the purchase of a fire extinguisher is a precautionary action. The HIDSP–2 originated from earlier tools (Tymchuk, 1991) and was designed to combine measures and reduce administration time and effort. The HIDSP–2 has 14 categories of dangers and precautions, and is administered through parental interview in the family's home, followed by direct observation of the home environment. The categories of dangers and precautions are (a) fire, (b) electrical, (c) suffocation by an ingested object (e.g., food), (d) suffocation by a mechanical object (plastic bags, curtain cords), (e) fire arms and weapons, (f) solid and liquid poisons, (g) heavy objects (e.g., a large object that could fall on the child), (h) sharp and pointed objects, (i) clutter, (j) inappropriate edi-

bles (e.g., garbage storage, alcohol), (k) dangerous animals and toys, (l) cooking practices and environment, (m) yard and outdoors, and (n) general (e.g., windows and doors have working locks). For each of these categories, the HIDSP–2 has interview questions and items for observation. Also, each category has an assessment of both dangers and precautions. The interview requires 30–60 minutes with more time being taken when the space is large and the parents deliberate and provide long answers to the interview questions.

In terms of technical adequacy, the test/retest reliability with one week between assessments produced high levels of reliability (i.e., above 90%) for dangers and precautions. Alpha estimates on the pretest indicated suitable levels for dangers and precautions but not for the individual categories within each of these two domains (Tymchuk et al., 1999). The measure appears to have high content validity—given it is based directly on epidemiological data about the causes of injuries. Further, the validity of the measure appears to be high in terms of guiding individualized parent education programs about dangers and precautions to be taken. When used before and after an individualized parent education program, reductions occurred in identified dangers, and increases occurred in parental precautionary practices (Tymchuk et al., 1999).

Another measure is the *Home Accident Prevention Inventory–Revised* (HAPI–R) (Mandel, Bigelow, & Lutzker, 1998; Metchikian, Mink, Bigelow, Lutzker, & Doctor, 1999). This inventory is completed by direct observation of home environments by trained observers. The scale includes seven types of dangers: "(a) poisoning by solids and liquids, (b) fire and electrical hazards, (c) suffocation by mechanical objects, (d) ingestible small objects, (e) sharp objects, (f) firearms, (g) falling hazards, and (h) drowning hazards" (Metchikian et al., 1999, pp. 26–27). It was developed with input from experts in injury prevention. Inter-rater agreement of trained observers has been high in studies using the scale (Mandel et al., 1998; Metchikian et al., 1999). The scale has been used with families reported for abuse and neglect to assist them in reducing the safety hazards in their homes. The scale is available in *Reducing Child Maltreatment* (Lutzker & Bigelow, 2001).

Checklists of Home Safety In addition to these two measures, a large number of checklists and abundant information on safety are readily available to families and professionals. These checklists often are designed to help parents assess or check the safety of their homes, toys, child-related equipment (e.g., car seats, cribs), and other potential hazards. Because the intended audience is parents, not professionals, the checklists frequently are written in plain language and easily read by the general public. Many are available in both English and Spanish. Three useful Web sites for this information and these checklists are the U.S. Consumer Product Safety Commission (*www.cpsc.gov*), American Academy of Pediatrics (*www.aap.org*), and the National Safety Council (*www.nsc.org*).

The U.S. Consumer Product Safety Commission (CPSC) has a number of safety checklists available on its Web site. Examples are the *Poison Lookout Checklist* (CPSC, Document #383), which is a series of binary questions about potential poisons (including medications) in the kitchen, bathroom, and garage or storage area of the home; the *Soft Contained Play Equipment Safety Checklist* (CPSC, Document #328), which is a list of statements about things to check with soft play equipment and includes a rationale for why each should be checked; and the *Home Playground Safety Checklist* (CPSC Document #323), which is a list of statements about how to install and check the safety of home playgrounds. In addition, the CPSC provides notices on the safe use of some products; for example, CPSC Document #5119 instructs parents and early childhood personnel to avoid putting plastic climbing equipment on hard wooden or carpeted floors and concrete or asphalt surfaces. Besides checklists and bulletins on safety, the CPSC also provides notices of recalls of toys, equipment, and clothing that pose safety

risks. Early childhood programs and individuals can subscribe at their Web site to receive electronic notices of news related to safety, including recall notices. The CPSC, of course, has a much broader mission than child safety; however, much of its information is related to child safety and is easily used by families and early childhood personnel.

The American Academy of Pediatrics (*www.aap.org*) also has a number of resources related to child safety, including checklists. Its Web site has information for parents, teachers, and pediatricians. It has a program titled, The Injury Prevention Program (TIPP), which includes information to guide pediatricians in talking with parents about safety. TIPP has fact sheets and questionnaires for families related to safety, which are age-based with separate sheets for birth to 6 months, 6 to 12 months, 1 to 2 years, 2 to 4 years, and 5 years of age. The questionnaires and fact sheets target particular risks related to a given age. Their Web site also includes links to other safety related websites. The National Safety Council (*www.nsc.org*) is dedicated to influencing the public to engage in safe practices in home, work, and recreation. They have a library of resources related to safety issues, and they provide training, consulting, and advocacy related to safety as well as a directory of training events related to safety. They have a checklist on family preparedness for emergencies. This is a binary list of questions about preparations for potential dangers such as fires, flooding, weather-related disasters, and so forth.

Although the technical adequacy (reliability and validity) of these checklists is essentially unknown, The Home Inventory of Dangers and Safety Precautions–2 (Tymchuk et al., 1999) and the Home Accident Prevention Inventory–Revised (Metchikian et al., 1999) have been used reliability to evaluate the safety of home environments. The less well-studied checklists and these two inventories provide early intervention professionals with information and tools for assessing home environments to prevent child injury.

Using Home-Safety Assessments

Professionals can use these inventories and check-lists in at least three different ways. First, professionals can use them to provide information to families about potential safety risks and the precautions needed to prevent unintentional injury. Although many factors influence the likelihood of unintentional child injury, a major factor is the lack of parental knowledge about the potential dangers and risks (Greaves, Glik, Kronenfeld, & Jackson, 1994). Thus, providing information on home safety is an appropriate role for early interventionists.

Second, professionals can distribute selected checklists to families and encourage them to use the checklists to evaluate their home environments. When distributing checklists, professionals should be careful not to imply families are uncaring or unsafe with their children or that their home is inadequate. Rather, information about injury prevention and the checklists of home safety should be distributed as part of usual information on child rearing. Professionals also should be familiar with the content of the checklists distributed to families and be prepared to respond to questions stimulated by their use. Prevention of some unintentional injury can occur by removing or securing dangerous items (e.g., ensuring unsafe cleaning products are in childproofed cabinets), restricting access to dangerous places (putting gates at the top of stairs when toddlers are present), or using specific precautions (e.g., having a fire escape plan); other prevention occurs by having rules about child behavior (e.g., not climbing on furniture, not running with scissors). Children's knowledge of home safety rules, however, is not associated with reductions in the frequency of injuries, but children's actual compliance with those rules and parental supervision of that compliance are more likely to be associated with injury prevention (Morrongiello, Midgett, & Shields, 2001). Thus, early interventionists can assist families in setting rules and in teaching compliance with those rules. A number of studies have focused on helping children engage in safe behaviors, par-

ticularly around abduction by strangers and prevention of sexual abuse (Bevill & Gast, 1998).

Third, professionals can help families use the checklists to evaluate their homes or use the more well-developed inventories in home visits. This help may come in the form of jointly completing the home safety checklists or inventories during home visits, providing them with information, problem-solving ways to reduce risks, helping families establish reasonable limits and rules for child behavior, encouraging parental supervision, and helping families find resources for making repairs or purchase needed fixtures (e.g., cabinet locks) to improve home safety. Because professionals may be involved with a given family for 2 or 3 years, helping families recognize the changing safety risks for children as they grow older is an important issue. For example, when a child learns to move from place to place (e.g., by crawling or walking), the potential increases for many injuries that did not exist previously. Similarly, when children begin to pull up on furniture or begin to play outside, new safety risks are likely. Thus, ensuring home safety is an issue that should be revisited throughout the early childhood years. Families who are less likely to obtain and use information generally available to the public (e.g., parents who are young, parents with mental retardation, those who are confirmed cases of neglect) may be important candidates for direct assistance from professionals related to home safety (Lutzker & Bigelow, 2001; Tymchuk et al., 1999).

Finally, a note on child abuse and neglect is relevant. Some injuries of young children are directly from physical assaults by their caregivers and some are from persistent lack of attention to and supervision of children. In 2000, about 12.2 per 1,000 children were victims of reported and confirmed maltreatment (physical abuse, neglect, psychological abuse, and sexual abuse), however, the rate was greater for younger children—15.7 per 1,000 for children under the age of 3 (National Clearinghouse on Child Abuse and Neglect Information, 2002). Instances of death from abuse and neglect was 1.71 per 100,000 children, and those under the age of 6 accounted for 85% of the deaths (National Clearinghouse on Child Abuse and Neglect Information, 2002). Although a large number of factors increase children's risk for abuse—including spousal abuse (McKibben, DeVos, & Newberger, 1989), the presence of a disability appears to be associated with increased risk for abuse (Randall & Parrila, 2001). The National Clearinghouse on Child Abuse and Neglect Information provides a good deal of resources related to abuse and neglect at its Web site (*www.calib.com/nccanch*). Early intervention professionals may be in contact with children and families in which abuse is occurring or is likely, and they have three roles related to abuse. First, there are specific obligations under the law to report suspected cases of child abuse and neglect to the appropriate authorities. All early intervention professionals should be aware of those obligations and know how and to whom suspected cases should be reported. Second, despite suspected or confirmed cases of abuse or neglect, early intervention professionals are obligated to assist the family in promoting the development, learning, and well-being of the child and to support the family in getting the help and resources they need. However, in fulfilling this role, they should be aware of their professional boundaries. Most early intervention professionals do not have formal preparation as social workers or as mental health professionals; therefore, our role is not that of providing counseling and therapy. Third, making home safety and the prevention of child injury a part of early intervention professionals' usual activities with families may well emphasize the need for and importance of child safety. This emphasis may assist parents who are at risk for abusing their children to refrain from such actions.

Assessing Center-Based (Classroom) Safety

Although some measures of early childhood classroom quality (e.g., *Early Childhood Environment Rating Scale–Revised*, Harms, Clifford, & Cryer, 1998) include safety issues as part of the behav-

ioral anchors for some items or have one or two items on safety, these scales do not have subscales or checklists to evaluate classroom or playground safety specifically and in detail. Most licensing and regulatory agencies focus part of their evaluations of classroom programs on safety issues, and may focus more on safety than on the use of developmentally appropriate practices (Gallagher, Rooney, & Campbell, 1999). However, the CPSC (1999) conducted a study of 220 licensed childcare programs across the nation–including General Services Administration childcare centers, non-profit centers, for-profit centers, and in-home settings (family day-care). The study focused on eight safety issues: safety of cribs, use of soft bedding, playground surfaces, playground maintenance, child safety gates, window blind cords, child clothing with drawstrings, and presence of recalled products. This study resulted in two major findings. First, nearly two-thirds of the programs (all of which were licensed) had at least one safety hazard in the areas they studied. Second, a subsequent review of state licensing requirements found most of the hazards evaluated in the study were not adequately covered in the state licensing requirements and regulations. An outcome of the study was the development of the checklist presented in Table 8.2. In addition, the CPSC (Document #325) published a detailed handbook that has information on the layout of playgrounds, installation and maintenance of playground equipment, general playground hazards, and drawings with dimensions related to construction and safety of playground equipment. In that document, the *Public Playground Safety Checklist* (CPSC, Document #327) is included; this checklist is presented in Table 8.3

Although there is a dearth of well-developed, well-studied inventories and checklists of classroom and playground safety, considerable information about safety practices is available. Some of this information is in the form of standards against which classroom programs can assess themselves. For example, the National Association for the Education of Young Children (NAEYC) (1998)

TABLE 8.2

U. S. Consumer Product Safety Commission's Child Care Safety Checklist for Parents and Child-Care Providers

1. **CRIBS**: Make sure cribs meet current national safety standards and are in good condition. Look for a certification safety seal. Older cribs may not meet current standards. Cribs slats should be no more than 2 ⅜" apart, and mattresses should fit snuggly.
   This can prevent strangulation and suffocation associated with older cribs and mattresses that are too small.

2. **SOFT BEDDING**: Be sure that no pillows, soft bedding, or comforters are used when you put babies to sleep. Babies should be put to sleep on their backs in a crib with a firm, flat mattress.
   This can help reduce Sudden Infant Death Syndrome (SIDS) and suffocation related to soft bedding.

3. **PLAYGROUND SURFACING**: Look for safe surfacing on outdoor playgrounds—at least 12 inches of wood chips, mulch, sand or pea gravel, or mats made of safety-tested rubber or rubber-like materials.
   This helps protect against injuries from falls, especially head injuries.

4. **PLAYGROUND MAINTENANCE**: Check playground surfacing and equipment regularly to make sure they are maintained in good condition.
   This can help prevent injuries, especially from falls.

5. **SAFETY GATES**: Be sure that safety gates are used to keep children away from potentially dangerous areas, especially stairs.
   Safety gates can protect against many hazards, especially falls.

6. **WINDOW BLIND AND CURTAIN CORDS**: Be sure miniblinds and venetian blinds do not have looped cords. Check that vertical blinds, continuous looped blinds, drapery cords have tension or tie-down devices to hold the cords tight.
   These safety devices can prevent strangulation in the loops of window blind and curtain cords.

7. **CLOTHING DRAWSTRINGS**: Be sure there are no drawstrings around the hood and neck of children's outerwear clothing. Other types of clothing fasteners, like snaps, zippers, or hook and loop fasteners (such as Velcro), should be used.
   Drawstrings can catch on playground and other equipment and can strangle young children.

8. **RECALLED PRODUCTS**: Check that no recalled products are being used and that a current list of recalled children's products is readily visible.
   Recalled products pose a threat of injury or death. Displaying a list of recalled products will remind caretakers and parents to remove or repair potentially dangerous children's toys and products.

Note: Taken from U.S. Consumer Product Safety Commission (no date). *Be Sure Your Child Care Setting Is as Safe as It Can Be.* Document # 242. *www.cpsc.gov.*

accreditation standards include two sections related to safety; these are the health and safety standards and the food preparation standards. Perhaps the most comprehensive treatment of the issue is the performance standards guidelines published jointly by the American Academy of Pediatrics, American Public Health Association, and National Resource Center for Health and Safety in Child Care (2002). This document contains a great deal of practical information on topics such as staff health, promoting and protecting child health, issues related to nutrition, food safety, control of infectious diseases, use of equipment and maintenance of equipment and

TABLE 8.3
U.S. Consumer Product Safety Commission's *Public Playground Safety Checklist*

Here are 10 important tips for parents and community groups to keep in mind to help ensure playground safety.

1. Makes sure **surfaces** around playground equipment have at least 12 inches of wood chips, mulch, or pea gravel, or are mats made of safety-tested rubber or rubber-like materials.
2. Check that protective **surfacing extends** at least 6 feet in all directions from play equipment. For swings, be sure surfacing extends, in back and front, twice the height of the suspending bar.
3. Make sure play structures more than 30 inches high are **spaced** at least 9 feet apart.
4. Check for **dangerous hardware,** like open "S" hooks or protruding bolt ends.
5. Make sure **spaces** that could trap children, such as openings in guardrails or between ladder rungs, measure less than 3.5 inches or more than 9 inches.
6. Check for **sharp points or edges** in equipment.
7. Look out for **tripping hazards,** like exposed concrete footings, tree stumps, and rocks.
8. Make sure elevated surfaces, like platforms and ramps, have **guardrails** to prevent falls.
9. Check **playgrounds regularly** to see that equipment and surfacing are in good condition.
10. **Carefully supervise children** on playgrounds to make sure they're safe.

Note: Taken from U.S. Consumer Product Safety Commission (no date). *Public Playground Safety Checklist.* Document # 325. *www.cpsc.gov.*

playgrounds, and many other topics. The information is easy to read, practical, and reasonable. In addition, the National Resource Center for Health and Safety in Child Care maintains a Web site with information on promoting children's health and safety in classrooms and centers (*nrc.uchsc.edu*).

Using Classroom Safety Assessments

As with assessing the safety of homes, the purposes are to identify dangers and eliminate or reduce them and determine whether classroom staff members are engaging in precautions that will prevent injuries. To accomplish these purposes, professionals should educate themselves about potential dangers as well as practices that promote safety. Such education can occur by reviewing licensing requirements related to health and safety. Some programs (e.g., public school classes) may not be required to undergo formal licensing. In such cases, professionals can secure licensing requirements for their states

and compare their settings to those standards. The National Resource Center for Health and Safety in Child Care maintains a description of each state's licensing requirements for different types of programs on its Web site. In addition to educating themselves, teachers and other professionals should periodically evaluate the safety of their classrooms and playgrounds using the checklists or standards. From these periodic evaluations, actions should be taken to correct any deficiencies.

ASSESSING THE QUALITY OF CHILDREN'S ENVIRONMENTS

Among the many factors influencing children's development and learning are children's experiences in the environment. A fundamental assumption is that children will have more growth-promoting experiences and positive interactions in high- as compared to low-quality environments. As a result, effort has been devoted to identifying the dimensions of quality and then assessing them in children's environments. In this section, procedures for assessing home quality and classroom or group-care quality are discussed.

Assessing the Quality of Home Environments

Home Observation and Measurement of the Environment Caldwell and Bradley at the University of Arkansas at Little Rock developed the most well known and widely used measures of the home environment: The *Home Observational and Measurement of the Environment* (HOME) (Caldwell & Bradley, 1984;). The HOME is actually four scales each for a different age group: the Infant/Toddler HOME (birth to 3 years of age), Early Childhood HOME (3 to 6 years of age), Middle Childhood HOME (6 to 10 years of age), and the Early Adolescent HOME (10 to 15 years of age). A short form of each scale is available (Bradley, Corwyn, McAdoo, & Coll, 2001). Only the Infant/Toddler and Early Childhood HOME scales are described here.

The HOME scales were developed to assess "the quality and quantity of stimulation and support available to a child in the home environment" (Bradley, 1994, p. 242). The scales are designed to identify "inputs from objects, events, and transactions occurring in the family surroundings" for the child (Bradley, 1994, p. 242). Importantly, the HOME scales assess the social as well as the physical aspects of the environment. The Infant/Toddler HOME (Caldwell & Bradley, 1984) has six subscales: (a) parental responsivity, (b) acceptance of the child, (c) organization of the environment, (d) learning materials, (e) parental involvement, and (f) variety in experience. The six subscales have a total of 45 items. The Early Childhood HOME (Bradley & Caldwell, 1976) has eight subscales: (a) learning materials, (b) language stimulation, (c) physical environment, (d) parental responsivity, (e) learning stimulation, (f) modeling of social maturity, (g) variety in experi-

rience, and (h) acceptance of the child. A total of 55 items are assessed across these eight subscales.

With both the Infant/Toddler and Early Childhood scales, the items are in the form of binary (yes/no) questions. The scales are administered during a home visit of approximately 1 to 1.5 hours. The interviewer, however, does not ask the questions in a yes/no format, but uses a conversational style to elicit information from the parent for answering the questions. Thus, a semi-structured interview format is used to solicit information and put families at ease. The interviewer also scores items based on his or her observations while on the home visit (Bradley, 1994). The scores for the scales are the number of questions answered as "yes."

The HOME scales have been used with the major racial groups in the United States (Bradley et al. 2001). The scales also have been used in different countries throughout the world (Bradley, Corwyn, & Whiteside-Mansell, 1997). They have been used extensively with young children living in poverty, children at risk for developmental problems due to low birth weight, children with disabilities, and children who have or are at risk for health problems (Bradley, 1994). The major use of the scales has been in research to identify the influences of home environments on children's development, the effects of factors such as poverty on children's environments and thus their development, and to evaluate the effects of intervention programs and policy initiatives. Recently, the HOME scales have been used to describe the similarity and differences in the home environments of families from different racial groups and of different levels of socio-economic status (Bradley et al., 2001). Comprehensive bibliographies and completed analyses on specific research questions are available at the University of Arkansas Web site (*www.ualr.edu/~HOME*).

The reliability of the HOME scales has been assessed in several studies and generally found adequate. For the total score, internal consistency estimates are greater than .80, but those estimates are often lower for the subscale scores (Bradley,

1994). Inter-rater agreement also is often at or above acceptable levels (e.g., 85% agreement or greater). Acceptable inter-rater estimates also were found when chance agreements were controlled. Thus, trained observers can use the measures reliably.

Other Scales of Home Environments
Although the HOME scales are widely known and used, other scales are available. Wachs has developed two other scales that deserve mention. The *Purdue Home Stimulation Inventory* (PHSI, Wachs, 1979) is used to assess the physical dimensions of home environments of infants. The inventory is completed through observation and interviews, and focuses on the toys available, people in the environment, how crowded the environment is, and what occurs in the environment. The measure appears to be associated with children's cognitive development. Subsequent research with the PHSI documents the influence of the physical environment on young children's development (Wachs, Francis, & McQuiston, 1979; Wachs, Morrow, & Slabach, 1990). Another measure, the *Confusion, Hubbub, and Order Scale* (CHAOS, Matheny, Wachs, Ludwig, & Phillips, 1995) is an observational measure of home environments of young children. This scale appears to capture processes that occur related to the predictability, order, and consistency within the home. These measures have adequate reliability and are useful research tools.

Using Assessment Information of Home Environments

As noted, the HOME scales, PHSI, and CHAOS have been used primarily as research tools with the HOME scales also being used to evaluate the effects of intervention programs and policy initiatives. However, these measures also have clinical applications, because they appear to provide useful information about the quality of children's home environments. In terms of helping families provide their children with improved home envir-

onments, professionals should examine the scales at the subscale rather than item level. For example, if several items in the parental responsivity section are judged to be "no"s, then attention should be given to helping parents be more responsive to and with their children. Single items should not be selected as potential areas of focus or goals. Similarly, if items on the PHSI show crowding in the home and lack of age-appropriate privacy or stimulus shelter for the child, then attention to these general concerns rather than to the specific items is warranted. Further, when setting goals with families, professionals should remember their role is to assist families in making their own decisions rather than making decisions for the family. Another use of these scales is to identify home/family environments in which more or less attention should be given to providing social support. In this sense, the scales may provide professionals with a rational process for making decisions about how to distribute their efforts in a large caseload.

In administering these scales and using the results with families, professionals should remember that the manner in which they interact with families may be as important as the content or focus of those interactions (Dunst, 2000). In addition, professionals should keep in mind that these scales are one picture of children's home lives, and other impressions they get from the family (positive and negative) should be considered in developing plans of action with families. When professionals and families come from different social, economic, and racial groups, professionals have a special obligation to understand their own biases, beliefs, and unspoken assumptions about what is good for children and what constitutes adequate home environments (see Chapter 4).

Assessing the Quality of Classroom Environments

As noted in the beginning of this chapter, an ecological perspective assumes any setting (e.g., classroom) operates in the context of broader systems and forces (e.g., the interactions between providers, service system, federal and state laws and regulations, societal beliefs). Thus, the quality of a classroom can be influenced by a number of factors outside it. In Figure 8.2, a model is provided for focusing the assessment of classroom quality at a proximal level. In this model, the interactions of the child with peers and teachers (often in activities and with materials) are placed in the center. These interactions are often referred to in the literature as *process quality*—the nature of interactions that influence the quality of children's experiences and thus their learning. The second level of the classroom ecology is the classroom features, which includes the curriculum being used, the instructional practices of the adults, the nature of activities and routines in the class, the scheduling of activities, and the nature and quantity of the materials with which the child interacts. The classroom features also include elements of process quality. The third level of the classroom ecology includes the staff characteristics and the class structures. The staff characteristics include their formal preparation, experience, and views about their roles and the goals they have related to teaching. The class structure includes factors such as the number of children in the class (group size); the adult-to-child ratios; the size of the space and its arrangement; the nature of the equipment and furnishings; and the number of hours per day, days per week, and months per year the class operates. The staff characteristics and class structures are often referred to as *regulatory quality* or *structural quality*, because these issues are easily quantified and therefore regulated by governing bodies. The final level of the class ecology is the administrative characteristics of the program of which the class is a member. The philosophy of the program and its goals, the administrative structure (e.g, policies, compensation for staff), the context of the program (e.g., funding, connection to other agencies), and supports for staff (e.g., specialists for consultation related to children with disabilities, planning time, staff development programs) all influence how the other levels of the ecology

function. Theoretically, aspects of quality can be measured at each level of the classroom ecology shown in Figure 8.2. The measures described below assess specific aspects of the ecology.

Environmental Rating Scales   Several instruments are available for evaluating the quality of group-care arrangements. Harms, Clifford, Cryer, and their colleagues at the Frank Porter Graham Child Development Institute of the University of North Carolina have devoted several years of systematic work to developing scales for measuring the quality of children's classroom and other group care environments. These measures include *Early Childhood Environment Rating Scales–Revised* (ECERS-R, Harms et al., 1998), *Infant/Toddler Environment Rating Scale–Revised* (ITERS–R, Harms, Cryer, & Clifford, in press), and *Family Day Care Rating Scale* (FDCRS, Harms, & Clifford, 1989). A similar measure is the *School-Age Care Environment Rating Scale* (Harms, Jacobs, & White, 1996) to assess the quality of before and after school care for elementary-age children; this measure is not described. The developers of these measures maintain a Web site (*www.fpg.unc.edu*) related to these measures. In addition to descriptions of the scales and bibliographies of the scales' use, the Web site has notices of training institutes for using the scales, notes about recommended modifications and clarifications of the items or indicators, and a listing of the languages into which the scales have been translated. Videotapes are available for learning to use the scales. These scales were designed for assessing the quality of classrooms for children without disabilities, and are consistent with the guidelines for developmentally appropriate practices. They include some mention of children with disabilities, but the scales were not constructed to be consistent with recommended practices related to children with disabilities.

The ECERS–R (Harms et al., 1998) is a revision of the Early Childhood Environment Rating Scale (Harms & Clifford, 1980). The ECERS–R is designed to evaluate the quality of classes of children who range in age from 2.5 through 5

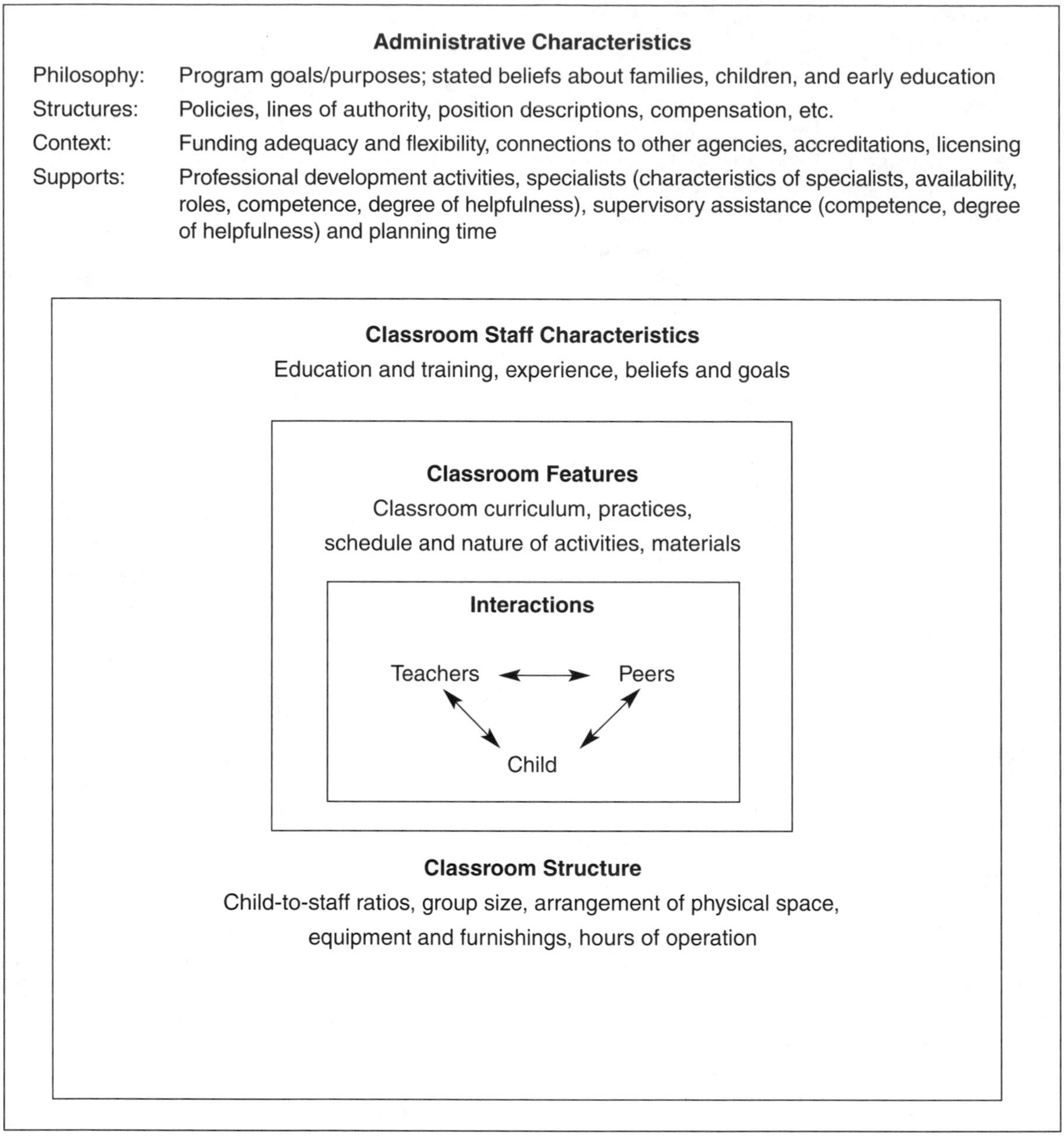

Administrative Characteristics

Philosophy: Program goals/purposes; stated beliefs about families, children, and early education

Structures: Policies, lines of authority, position descriptions, compensation, etc.

Context: Funding adequacy and flexibility, connections to other agencies, accreditations, licensing

Supports: Professional development activities, specialists (characteristics of specialists, availability, roles, competence, degree of helpfulness), supervisory assistance (competence, degree of helpfulness) and planning time

Classroom Staff Characteristics

Education and training, experience, beliefs and goals

Classroom Features

Classroom curriculum, practices, schedule and nature of activities, materials

Interactions

Teachers ←——→ Peers

Child

Classroom Structure

Child-to-staff ratios, group size, arrangement of physical space, equipment and furnishings, hours of operation

FIGURE 8.2

Ecology of the classroom—identifying factors that may influence teachers' behavior and children's learning. Based on a model presented by J. J. Carta (2002, July). *Measuring Program Quality: Early Childhood.* OSEP Research Project Directors' Conference. Washington, DC. Used with permission.

years. It provides an index of a single classroom's quality on a number of dimensions as well as a summary estimate of global classroom quality. The measure is intended to be used as a research tool and to identify areas or program weaknesses and then to monitor program improvement. The ECERS–R has 43 items in seven scales: (a) space and furnishings (8 items), (b) personal care routines (6 items), (c) language-reasoning (4 items), (d) activities (10 items), (e) interaction (5 items), (f) program structure (4 items—including one item on provisions for children with disabilities), and (g) parents and staff (6 items).

As with the first edition, the ECERS–R is completed by direct observation of the classroom being evaluated. A minimum of 2 hours of observation is needed, but additional time may provide greater opportunities to observe important aspects. Interviews of about 20 minutes can be used after the observation to obtain information for scoring items that could not be rated during the observation. The manual includes specific directions about how to conduct the observations, and a score sheet is provided for use during the observation. Selected terms used in the rating scale are defined. The ECERS–R uses a 7-point rating scale for each item. The odd numbered ratings (i.e., 1, 3, 5, and 7) have behavioral anchors or indicators, and the odd numbered items have a global characterization (1 is inadequate, 3 is minimal, 5 is good, and 7 is excellent). For most items in the ECERS–R, there are two or more indicators for each odd-numbered rating. In addition, most items have "notes for clarification" that make the specific anchors clearer and provide more definition to the indicators. Many items have questions to ask that can be used during interviews to score difficult to observe practices or qualities. The observer can mark each indicator as a yes or no (not applicable is allowed on some items), and this provides more precision in understanding why a given rating was given for an item. However, if each indicator is scored, the manual indicates a longer observation (e.g., 3.5 to 4 hours) may be necessary, and a longer interview (e.g., 45 minutes) will likely be needed. A sample item is presented in Table 8.4. Precise administration procedures are described in the manual. Observers should score the indicators as a yes or no, starting with the indicators under the 1 (inadequate) column. Rules are provided about assigning the numerical rating for an item. For example, "A rating of 1 must be given if any indicator under 1 is scored Yes" and "A rating of 2 is given when all indicators under 1 are scored No and at least half of the indicators under 3 are scored Yes" (Harms et al., 1998, p. 8). Ratings can be summarized across items for each subscale, and an average score for each subscale can be calculated. Also, an average score across subscales can be calculated. The ECERS–R Profile is a single sheet that provides a summary of each rating for each item by subscale. This can be used as an easy reference for discussing scores with classroom staff.

The inter-rater reliability for the ECERS–R, as described in the manual, is acceptable (i.e., 86.1% for the total scale). Item level agreement was lower; however, this is to be expected given that each indicator carries a relatively large number of percentage points—thus one or two disagreements could lower the percentage of agreement. The internal consistency of the total scale was good (i.e., .92) and was somewhat lower for the subscales (i.e., low of .71 for parents and staff, and high of .88 for activities), suggesting the total scores and the subscale scores may be useful for analysis and reporting. The content validity of the measure is high given it is based on the original version and advances in what is considered quality early education.

The ECERS and the ECERS–R have been used extensively for a number of purposes. The scales have been used as research tools in dozens of studies on program quality as well as the effects of quality on children's learning and development (e.g., Burchinal, Cryer, Clifford, & Howes, 2002). The scale also is useful in program evaluations such as identifying areas of staff development and then evaluating the effects of efforts to address

TABLE 8.4
Sample Item (# 23—Sand/Water) from the *Early Childhood Environment Rating Scale—Revised Edition*

Inadequate		Minimal		Good		Excellent
1	2	3	4	5	6	7
1.1 No provision for sand or water play, outdoors or indoors		3.1 Some provision for sand or water play accessible either outdoors or indoors		5.1 Provision for sand and water play (either outdoors or indoors)		7.1 Provision for sand and water play, both indoors and outdoors (weather permitting)
1.2 No toys to use for sand or water play		3.2 Some sand/water toys accessible		5.2 Variety of toys accessible for play (e.g., containers, spoons, funnels, scoops, shovels, pots and pans, molds, toy people, animals, and trucks)		7.2 Different activities done with sand and water (e.g., bubbles added to water, material in sand table changed, e.g., rice substituted for sand)
				5.3 Sand or water play available to children for at least 1 hour daily		

Notes for clarification

Materials that can easily be poured, such as rice, lentils, bird seed, and cornmeal may be substituted for sand. Sand or sand substitute must be available in sufficient quantity so children can dig in it, fill containers, and pour.

"Provision" for sand and water requires action on the part of staff to provide appropriate materials for such play. Allowing children to play in puddles or dig in the dirt on the playground does not meet the requirements for this item.

Each room does not have to have its own sand and water table, but must be able to use a sand and water table regularly if it is shared with another room.

Questions

(3.1) Do you use sand or water with the children? How is this handled? About how often? Where is this available?

(3.2) Are there any toys for children to use with sand or water play? Please describe them.

(7.2) Do you change the activities children do with sand and water?

Note: Taken from T. Harms, R. M. Clifford, and D. Cryer (1998). *Early Childhood Environment Rating Scale –Revised.* New York: Teachers College Press. Used with permission.

weaknesses (Sheridan, 2001). The ECERS also has been used to evaluate the impact of policy initiatives on the quality of child care (Bryant, Maxwell, & Burchinal, 1999). The scale also has been used to compare the quality of inclusive and noninclusive classes (La Paro, Sexton, & Snyder, 1998). In some states, regulatory bodies are using the ECERS–R scores as part of the information used to make decisions about child-care licensing, or about the level of license a program receives (in states with multilevel licensing structures).

The ITERS–R is a revision of the Infant/Toddler Environment Rating Scale (Harms, Cryer, & Clifford, 1990). The ITERS–R is currently in press, but the structure and development work on the revision is completed and reflected in the following comments. The ITERS–R has 39 items across seven subscales: (a) space and furnishings (5 items), (b) personal care routines (6 items), (c) listening and talking (3 items), (d) activities (10 items), (e) interaction (4 items), and (f) program structure (4 items), (g) parents and staff (7 items). The ITERS–is designed for assessing the quality of a single class or group of children who are 2.5 years old (30 months) or younger. It is completed by direct observation and supplemented by a follow-up interview. The authors recommend a minimum of 3 hours of observation and about 20 to 30 minutes for the interview. As with the ECERS–R, a score sheet is provided to record observations and ratings, including, marking each indicator. A profile also is included to summarize ratings across items, subscales, and total scale. The items of the ITERS–R are structured in the same format as the ECERS–R. A 7-point rating system is used with odd-numbered items having anchors with specific indicators. Notes for clarification are included as are questions for use in interviews. The scoring procedures are similar to the ECERS–R.

Inter-rater agreement on the ITERS–R appears to be quite good. At the indicator level, across all indicators the average agreement for trained observers exceeded 90%, and only one indicator was below 80% agreement. Acceptable inter-rater agreement percentages also occurred at the item level, when agreement was defined as the raters being within 1 point of one another. In terms of internal consistency, alphas for the total scale and subscales were calculated. For the total scale, the alpha was .93. In terms of the subscales, all had alphas in the acceptable levels except for two subscales: space and furnishings and personal care routines. Thus, scores for these subscales may be suspect. The uses of the ITERS–R are likely to be similar to those of the ECERS–R, but for classrooms of younger children.

The FDCRS (Harms & Clifford, 1989) is designed to rate the quality of family day-care settings from infancy through kindergarten. The FDCRS has 32 items in six scales: (a) space and furnishings (six items), (b) basic care (seven items), (c) language and reasoning (four items—two of which have separate parts for infants and toddlers and preschoolers), (d) learning activities (9 items), (e) social development (3 items), and (f) adult needs (3 items). A seventh scale, described as supplementary items, is titled, "provisions for exceptional children" and includes eight items. The FDCRS uses the same rating structure as the ECERS–R and ITERS–R with a 7-point scale and behavioral anchors for the odd-numbered ratings. In addition, the items of the FDCRS are designed to evaluate the six broad competency areas of the Child Development Associate program, which is an on-the-job training program for non-degreed early childhood personnel (Phillips, 1994). In addition to the evaluation of staff, the FDCRS has the same functions as the ECERS–R; that is, it can be used as a research and program evaluation tool and as a means for helping assign graded licensure to programs. Although the reliability of the FDCRS appears acceptable, no reliability data were reported for the supplemental items related to children with disabilities.

In addition to the above measures by Clifford and Harms and their colleagues, other researchers also have developed instruments for measuring the quality of classroom environments. A measure designed to assess the extent to which classrooms conform to the guidelines for developmentally appropriate practices is the *Classroom Practices Inventory* (CPI) (Hyson, Hirsh-Pasek, & Rescorla, 1990). The CPI has 26 items, 20 of which focus on the program and activity focus of the classroom, and six of which focus on the emotional climate of the classroom. Each item is rated on a 5-point Likert-type scale with 1 being "not at all like this classroom" and 5 being "very much like this classroom" (Hyson et al., 1990, p. 493). Ten of the items in the program and activity focus section of the scale are indicative of developmentally appropriate practice, and 10 are indicative of developmentally inappropriate practice. In the emotional climate section, four items are indicative of positive emotional climate, and two are indicative of negative climate. The CPI has high internal consistency, but exact interobserver agreement is only in acceptable ranges when agreements are scored within 1 point. The CPI was not specifically designed to measure inclusive classrooms and was based on the original set of guidelines on developmental appropriateness (i.e., Bredekamp, 1987).

The *Preschool Assessment of the Classroom Environment Scale–Revised* (PACE–R) (Raab, Dunst, Whaley, LeGrand, & Taylor, 1997) is another scale for evaluating the quality of a classroom and the program in which it is based. The PACE–R has seven subscales; each has five items, and each item is rated on a 5-point scale. The odd-numbered ratings are behaviorally anchored. The subscales were empirically derived and are (a) program foundation and philosophy, (b) management and training (of staff), (c) environmental organization, (d) staffing patterns, (e) instructional context, (f) instructional techniques, and (g) program evaluation. The PACE–R is administered using three measurement strategies: observation, interviews, and document reviews. A 2 to 4 hour observation is needed and is used to complete four of the seven subscales (i.e., environmental organization, staffing patterns, instructional context, and instructional techniques). In terms of reliability, the subscales each have acceptable to high inter-rater agreement estimates, and the intra-observer agreement was

also high (i.e., observer scores the same program on two different occasions). The internal consistency of the PACE–R is acceptable with coefficient alphas for each subscale being above .70. The subscales of environmental organization and instructional context were highly related to children's outcomes in terms of their social engagement, engagement with the physical environment, social responsiveness, and cognitive style. The instructional techniques were strongly correlated with children's social engagement and cognitive style, whereas staffing patterns were related to children's engagement with the physical environment, their social responsiveness, and cognitive style (personal communication, Raab, 8/20/02). The items are highly appropriate for inclusive classrooms and are consistent with the recommended practices for young children with disabilities as well as those without disabilities.

The *Assessment of Practices in Early Elementary Classrooms* (APEEC), Hemmeter, Maxwell, Ault, & Schuster, 2001) is another scale for evaluating classroom quality, and specifically the extent to which classrooms conform to guidelines related to developmentally appropriate practices. It is useful for kindergarten through grade three classrooms. The APEEC has three domains that were derived through expert review and field testing: (a) physical environment (four items), (b) instructional context (six items), and (c) social context (six items). The APEEC uses a 7-point rating structure similar to the ECERS–R; odd-numbered ratings are anchored with indicators that can each be scored. A summary sheet is provided to show the results for each item, domain, and total scale. The inter-rater agreement is acceptable at the item level. The ratings on the APEEC are correlated positively with the amount of children's observed engagement in classroom activities (Symons, Clark, Roberts, & Bailey, 2001).

Measures of Teacher Behavior and Practice
Although the above measures include items assessing teachers' interactions with children, they also address a number of other issues related to class-

room quality. Other measures are more circumscribed and focus specifically on teachers' interactions and behavior with children.

The *Arnett Scale of Caregiver Behavior* (Arnett, 1989) is a direct assessment of teacher or caregiver behavior. It contains 30 items describing potential behaviors or characteristics of adults in classrooms, such as "speaks warmly to the children (e.g., positive tone of voice, body language)" and "seems enthusiastic about the children's activities and efforts (e.g., congratulates children, states appreciation for their efforts)." Based on an observation of the classroom, an observer rates each item on a 4-point scale related to the frequency with which that item is observed (i.e., "not at all," "somewhat," "quite a bit," and "very much"). The scale is often used with the ECERS–R or ITERS in assessing quality and appears to capture some process quality that apparently is not assessed by those measures.

Another measure of teachers' interactions and behavior with children is the *Teaching Style Rating Scale* (TSRS) (McWilliam, Scarborough, Bagby, & Sweeney, 1996). This scale includes two sections: a teaching behavior section evaluating seven teaching behaviors (redirects, introduces, elaborates, follows, informs, acknowledges, praises), and the other is an affective section with 14 affective items. The teaching behaviors are rated for frequency on a 7-point Likert scale (1 = never, 3 = occasionally, 5 = often, and 7 = most of the time). The affective items include such things as activity level, tone, physical responsiveness, expansion, and interactive quality. These items are rated on a 5-point scale with the odd-numbered items behaviorally anchored. The measure is completed by observation of the class over the course of a couple hours, making notes about specific teacher behavior and interactions, and then completing the rating scale after the observation while consulting notes collected during the observation (de Kruif, McWilliam, Ridley, & Wakely, 2000). In the de Kruif et al. study, the affective items had a high internal consistency with a Cronbach's alpha of 0.89. The TSRS can be used to classify teachers by their styles of interaction, which appear to hold specific implications for training those teachers to provide high-quality experiences for children.

Alternative Approaches The ITERS–R, ECERS–R, PACE–R, and CPI are measures of classroom quality; as such, the unit of measurement and description is the classroom. In any classroom, however, children may have different experiences, which vary on dimensions of quality (Carta, Sainato, & Greenwood, 1988). Thus, a given classroom may produce high-quality experiences for most children but not for one or two children in the class. This is a concern especially in inclusive classrooms where the quality may be high for children without disabilities but not for the child with disabilities. The *Quality of Inclusive Experiences Measure* (QIEM) (Wolery, Pauca, Brashers, & Grant, 2000) was developed to assess an individual child's experiences in an inclusive classroom rather than the experiences of most children in the class. The QIEM is designed to assess different levels of the classroom ecology as presented in Figure 8.2 with particular attention on children's interactions at the center of the model. The QIEM has seven subscales (a) program goals and purposes, (b) staff supports and perceptions, (c) accessibility and adequacy of the physical environment, (d) individualized intervention use, (e) participation and engagement, (f) adult–child contacts and relationships, and (g) child–child contacts and interactions. The first two subscales focus on the program, all remaining scales focus on the individual child. Each subscale has several rating items that are summed to calculate the subscale scores. Interviews, document reviews, and questionnaires are used for the first two subscales (i.e., goals and purposes, staff supports), and the others are completed primarily through observation supplemented with questionnaires and document reviews for the individualizing instruction subscale. Although trained observers can complete the measure with relatively high inter-rater agreement, the measure takes 2 to 3 days (2 to 3 hours per day) to complete.

Little development research has been completed with the measure. The QIEM was designed as a program improvement measure to increase the quality of inclusion for individual children, although it may be used as a research or program evaluation tool as well. Because the QIEM focuses on an individual child in the class, it cannot be used to evaluate whether a classroom would be a suitable inclusive option prior to placement.

Another approach for assessing the quality of classroom environments is to assess whether and to what extent recommended practices are being used or the extent to which classrooms conform to standards of practice. The NAEYC (1998) accreditation standards—standards used to assess programs for accreditation—can be used to determine the extent to which programs are complying with the developmentally appropriate practice guidelines (Bredekamp & Copple, 1997). The American Academy of Pediatrics, American Public Health Association, and National Resource Center for Health and Safety in Child Care (2002) document also has standards against which classroom quality can be evaluated. These documents contain information on structural quality (e.g., child–staff ratios, space, group size, staff preparation) and on process quality.

Similarly, the Division for Early Childhood (DEC) has established a set of practice recommendations related to assessment, child-focused interventions, family-based practices, interdisciplinary practices, and practices in technology applications (Sandall, McLean, & Smith, 2000). To accompany these practice recommendations, DEC has published an assessment process to determine the extent to which classrooms and programs use the recommended practices (Hemmeter, Joseph, Smith, & Sandall, 2001). This assessment process can be used for program improvement, to identify staff development needs, to evaluate the effects of initiatives (e.g., staff development programs) to improve quality, and as a research tool. Observation, interviews, and staff ratings are methods by which data could be gathered during the assessment process. When assessing a classroom or program, one of five ratings (i.e., not applicable, not implemented, partially implemented, fully implemented, and don't know) is assigned for each of the recommended practices being assessed. Summary forms, graphs for depicting the percentage of scores for each area of practice, and sample action plan forms for improving use of recommended practices are provided (Hemmeter, Joseph, et al., 2001). Although no information is given about the reliability of this process, the validity of the recommended practices is high. Specifically, they were developed from a comprehensive process involving a review of the literature, the opinions of experts, and multiple phases of review.

Finally, one measure, *Child Care Plus+ Floor Plan Analysis* (Mulligan, Harper-Whalen, & Morris, 2002) is an assessment of how space is being used. Specifically, it examines the number of square feet used by a program, the movement in the space, and the amount of space children have in each of 13 key areas (i.e., greeting, block play, reading, active play, private play, dramatic play, sensory play, construction play, art, fine motor/manipulative, private storage, bathroom, and eating). The *Floor Plan Analysis* involves actually measuring the room dimensions, making a scale drawing of the space, taking photos of the room from different vantage points, calculating the space used by children by key area, noting children's movement patterns on the scale drawing of the space, and calculating the usable square feet per child. The results are useful in making decisions about room arrangement and adjustments to take better advantage of the space available.

Using Information from Assessments of Classroom Quality

Two fundamental assumptions about classroom quality are worth noting. First, higher-quality classrooms are associated with more positive and desirable child outcomes (Bowman et al., 2001). Second, inclusion of children with disabilities should occur in high-quality as compared to low-quality classrooms (Horn, Lieber, Sandall,

Schwartz, & Wolery, 2002; McWilliam, Wolery, & Odom, 2001; Odom & Bailey, 2001). Assessing the quality of classroom environments is done for a number of reasons: (a) identifying areas and issues for classroom and program improvement, (b) evaluating program improvement efforts, (b) monitoring the quality of the classrooms, (c) evaluating the suitability of classrooms for placing children with disabilities, (d) identifying staff training needs, (e) conducting staff performance evaluations, (f) assessing quality to make decisions about levels of program licensure, and (g) research. None of these measures is appropriate for all of these purposes, but as a group these measures provide teachers, administrators, and intervention teams with options for each purpose. Some of these measures focus on broad dimensions of the classroom environment (e.g., ECERS–R, Harms et al., 1998; PACE–R, Raab et al., 1997); on specific issues such as space (e.g., *Floor Plan Analysis*, Mulligan et al., 2002); on the use of recommended practices (e.g., Hemmeter, Joseph, et al., 2001); on the teachers' behavior (e.g., TSRS, McWilliam et al., 1996), and on the effects of the environment on individual children with disabilities (e.g., QIEM, Wolery et al., 2000). Thus, as with other measures, the environmental assessment tools should be used for the purposes for which they were intended.

Although their purposes may be different, teachers and teacher supervisors, intervention teams, administrators, program evaluators, and individuals in regulatory agencies can use these measures. For example, teachers and teacher supervisors could use the environmental measures in designing their classrooms, in monitoring their operation at the broad level as well as at the practice level, and in making decisions about needed training and consultation. Use of these measures for such purposes, of course, should be accompanied by reflection about the classroom, individual children and their needs, and the program's resources. Most of the measures are not designed to evaluate the effects of environments on individual children's experiences; rather the measures assess the classroom as a unit and as such chil-

dren's experiences on average. Thus, understanding the effects of the environment on individual children requires careful monitoring of those children.

Administrators and teacher supervisors can use the measures to identify staff training needs, to document program quality and initiate program improvement activities, to describe the quality of their programs to the public and governmental agencies, to obtain information for use in staff performance evaluations, and to examine broad program issues. Some of the measures examine program issues outside of the classroom, such as program philosophy (e.g., PACE–R, Raab et al., 1997). When using the measures in staff performance evaluations, it is important to take note of the effects of the ecology in which the class operates (e.g., Figure 8.2). For example, if the classroom personnel have no supports from specialists, large class sizes, limited space, and minimal materials and equipment, then their performance on the above measures is likely to be influenced negatively. In some cases, the scales assess factors that may be influenced by the quality of intervention teams rather than just classroom staff. Thus, despite the appeal and utility of using these measures in staff performance evaluation, the factors influencing classroom staff members' performance must be considered. Also, process quality is a dynamic rather than static construct; thus, an assessment of acceptable or high quality at one point may not reflect later assessment of quality. The quality of classrooms and programs can deteriorate or can increase with time. Nonetheless, these measures provide early childhood personnel with a large number of ways to analyze their efforts and make judgments about needed actions.

ASSESSING ENVIRONMENTS TO PLAN CHILDREN'S PROGRAMS

Children's behavior occurs in context—that is, in their environments such as home, class, and community settings. Their behavior is influenced by the factors in those environments and they influence those environments (Thurman, 1997). Thus, understanding children's environments is an important element in using assessment information to plan children's individualized intervention programs (see Chapter 16). In this section, procedures are described for considering environment issues when planning intervention programs.

Assessing Environments to Identify Goals

Many years ago, Brown, Branston, Hamre-Nietupski, Pumpian, Certo, and Gruenewald (1979) argued that developmental assessments were of limited utility with older individuals (e.g., adolescents) with significant disabilities for setting intervention goals. They reasoned that an ecological perspective held more utility. They recommended identifying children's environments and subenvironments, the activities that occurred within those subenvironments, and then assessing individual's competence related to those activities. The activities in which individuals were not competent would then be adapted to promote partici-

pation, or goals would be established to teach competence in those activities. Thurman and Widerstrom (1990) used a similar logic and a somewhat different ecological perspective (i.e., ecological congruence) and identified a number of steps for identifying children's goals. These are presented in Table 8.5. As shown, these steps involve identifying the situations in which children spend time as well as the tasks required in those settings. These tasks may be in the form of routines such as eating meals, transitions from a home or classroom to a car for transportation within the community, diapering and toileting routines, dressing/undressing routines, and others. The tasks may come in the form of interacting with siblings and classmates during play, participating in an art activity, and many others. The key is that the tasks important in each environment are identified. Identification of environments and tasks are done primarily through interviews and observation. The child's competence is then compared against those tasks, and children's motivation to complete those tasks is assessed. Judgments also are made about children's tolerance for events and stimuli in the environment. Assessment of these

TABLE 8.5
Steps for Planning Interventions Using Thurman's Ecological Model

1. Identify the major environmental settings that are important to the child's life.
2. Develop an inventory of critical tasks in those settings (i.e., those that make the setting function).
3. Assess the child's competence to perform those tasks.
4. Assess motivational variables (i.e., contingency structures) and other factors that affect the child's ability to perform tasks.
5. Assess the child's tolerance of the environment.
6. Determine which of the child's behaviors and characteristics are outside the level of tolerance of the system. (These behaviors and characteristics may be those labeled as deviant, or they may be the result of insufficient development of the child to perform necessary tasks.)
7. Identify objectives for each component of the ecology (i.e., child and system) that, when accomplished, will lead to increased ecological congruence.
8. Identify strategies for accomplishment of the objectives.
9. Establish a means by which interventions are to be monitored and their effectiveness assessed.

Note: Taken from Thurman K. S. and Widerstrom A. H. (1990). *Infants and Young Children with Special Needs: A Developmental and Ecological Approach* (2nd ed, p. 212). Baltimore: Paul H. Brookes, Publishing Co. Used with permission.

factors is made through observation of the child attempting the tasks. Task-analyzing the routines and tasks to assess children's performance of each step is recommended, as is noting the levels of assistance children need to complete each step. Judgments—based on observation and interviews and team discussion—are used to identify and determine which child behaviors are outside of the environment's tolerance. Objectives for adapting the environment or goals for teaching the child functional tasks are written and addressed in intervention.

A variation on this process is McWilliam's (1992) routines-based process for working with families of young children with disabilities. This involves a number of checklists and interviews designed to assist families in identifying routines in which children need assistance and thereby identifying goals for intervention. This can also be accomplished by conducting an interview with families about their child's day, beginning with when the child awakes and progressing through bedtime routines. These processes help identify situations in which goals should be set for adapting routines, for promoting the child's abilities, and for which families need assistance.

Another variation, based on Thurman's (1997) ecological congruence theory, is the ecological congruence assessment process for use in early childhood classrooms. This process uses the form shown in Figure 8.3 (Wolery, Brashers, Grant, & Pauca, 2000). With this process, the team observes the child in each activity and routine of the classroom, including arrival time, free play, diapering and toileting routines, snack and meals, circle time, outdoor play, structured play routines, transitions within the classroom, and transitions from the classroom to playground or other destinations, and any other activities or routines that occur on a regular basis in the classroom. During each activity and routine, the team or teacher observes and records judgments about whether the child is doing the same thing as his or her classmates. If the child is doing different things, then the team determines whether that difference is acceptable.

If it is not, then this may be an area for which a goal should be established. After determining whether the child is doing the same thing as his or her classmates, the team determines whether the child needs more help than his/her classmates in each activity or routine. If more help is needed, then the nature of the help is identified (i.e., help getting started, help staying engaged, help doing the requisite skills, and/or help dealing with peers). More than one type of help may be relevant for the child in any given routine or activity. This information also assists in identifying goals. For example, if the child has difficulty staying engaged in several activities, then a goal could be set for promoting engagement. The procedures for collecting assessment information with this process and for analyzing the collected information and using it to plan or adjust children's programs have been described (Wolery, Brashers, & Neitzel, 2002).

Assessing Environments to Implement Interventions

In addition to setting goals based on an analysis of children's competence in activities and routines in the natural environment, the team should also consider environmental factors when identifying learning opportunities and selecting or devising intervention practices. The ecological congruence assessment practice (Wolery et al., 2002) has been used to identify adjustments of intervention practices as well as the need for new interventions. Teams should attempt to match intervention practices to the constraints of and demands on caregivers' behavior and energy, whether those caregivers are family members or teachers in classrooms. For example, encouraging parents to work on dressing skills during wake-up time may be appropriate for some families but inappropriate for others. If a family has multiple children to get up, dressed, fed, and off to school and work, then it may not be reasonable to focus on teaching dressing at that time. Similarly, if a child is particularly fussy after waking up, then delaying instructional

Activity Time	Children's Participation	Helping Issues	Notes
	Is child doing the same thing as peers? Yes No If no, what is child doing? What are peers doing?	Does child require more help than peers? Yes No If yes, for what is the help given? a. needs help getting engaged b. needs help staying engaged c. needs help dealing with peers d. doesn't have skills to do activity	
	Is child doing the same thing as peers? Yes No If no, what is child doing? What are peers doing?	Does child require more help than peers? Yes No If yes, for what is the help given? a. needs help getting engaged b. needs help staying engaged c. needs help dealing with peers d. doesn't have skills to do activity	
	Is child doing the same thing as peers? Yes No If no, what is child doing? What are peers doing?	Does child require more help than peers? Yes No If yes, for what is the help given? a. needs help getting engaged b. needs help staying engaged c. needs help dealing with peers d. doesn't have skills to do activity	

Teacher: _____ Child with Disabilities: _____ Date: _____

Classroom: _____

FIGURE 8.3

Ecological congruence assessment process to identify goals and potential changes in intervention practices for young children with disabilities in inclusive early childhood classrooms.

Note: This form was developed by the staff of the Individualizing Inclusion in Child Care project (Grant No. H0324980207). Wolery, M., Brashers, M. S., Grant, S., & Pauca, T. (2000). *Ecological Congruence Assessment for Classroom Activities and Routines in Childcare.* Chapel Hill, NC: Frank Porter Graham Child Development Center.

interactions requiring the child to expend effort may be wise.

Four general guidelines are offered to assist in planning interventions for children. First, *skills should be taught in context, but other factors should also be considered when identifying times for learning opportunities.* Although instruction

should be provided in context, some times when skills are needed are not appropriate times for instruction. For example, if the child is very hungry, then teaching self-feeding skills may not be indicated until the child's hunger has been addressed. Thus, considering the child's temperament and receptivity to instruction at any given time is relevant. Similarly, other skills such as communication, social, and motor skills should be taught in context (i.e., when needed), but they should be taught when adults can be attentive and responsive to the child and when intervention practices can be used with fidelity. Understanding usual adult–child interaction patterns in given situations, and the adults' responsibilities (e.g., classroom maintenance, supervision of children) in those contexts is central to identifying intervention practices that are likely to be used. Further, particular teaching styles are likely to call for specific types of training if children are to benefit maximally from ongoing interactions with those teachers (de Kruif et al., 2000). Assessing the teacher's interaction styles with the TSRS and using that information to provide training as well as select interventions is advised.

Second, *identify routines, activities, and events based on children's interests and engagement should be selected as learning opportunities* (Dunst, Bruder, et al., 2001; Dunst et al., 2000). Activities designed based on children's interests are likely to provide children with learning opportunities for important skills. Thus, assessing children's interests and preferences (see Chapter 16) is important in deciding when and how to intervene. The ecological congruence assessment process (Wolery et al., 2002) also is useful for identifying opportunities when the child is engaged and likely to be receptive to interventions.

Third, *consider adapting the context and task as well as the child's competence.* Ecological assessment can identify usual tasks, activities, and routines for which the child lacks the competence to be independent. In some cases, teaching the child the needed skills is relevant, and in other cases, adapting the task or activity is relevant. For example, if a child cannot fasten clothing, using clothing that does not require fasteners is an appropriate adaptation. These adaptations can include changing materials, getting other materials, shortening activities, simplifying the demands of the activity, adjusting the physical space, and many others.

Fourth, *monitor whether the interventions are actually being integrated into children's activities and routines.* As discussed in Chapter 17, some interventions are not effective when they are used infrequently or with low fidelity (Peterson & McConnell, 1996; Holcombe, Wolery, & Snyder, 1994). Monitoring the fidelity and frequency with which interventions are used is necessary. The individualization subscale of the QIEM is designed to assess the extent to which intervention practices are individualized and actually implemented. Other issues to consider in monitoring implementation are discussed in Chapter 17.

········

SUMMARY OF KEY CONCEPTS

- A number of theorists have devised models of children's environments, and the power of the proximal and distal environment on children's learning and development are well known. There are three primary reasons for assessing children's environments: to prevent injury and death, to increase the quality of children's environments, and to devise intervention goals and procedures. A number of measures for doing these things are available to intervention teams.

- The settings in which children participate are influenced by the environmental forces outside of that setting, and each setting exists within broader ecological systems.

- Children's home and classroom environments should be assessed to identify potential hazards that could lead to injury or death and for adults use of precautionary practices.

- The quality of children's home and classroom environments influences their learning and development.

- Assessing the quality of children's environments can be used to promote higher quality.
- Children's environments should be assessed to identify goals for intervention and intervention practices.

- A large number of tools are available for assessing the safety and quality of children's environments, including checklists and rating scales.

········

REFERENCES

American Academy of Pediatrics, American Public Health Association, & National Resource Center for Health and Safety in Child Care. (2002). *Caring for our children—national health and safety performance standards: Guidelines for out-of-home child care programs* (2nd ed.). Elk Grove Village, IL: American Academy of Pediatrics.

Arnett, J. (1989). Caregivers in day-care centers: Does training matter? *Journal of Applied Developmental Psychology, 10,* 541–552.

Bailey, D. B., Farel, A. M., O'Donnell, K. J., Simeonsson, R. J., & Miller, C. A. (1986). Preparing infant interventionists: Interdepartmental training in special education and maternal and child health. *Journal of the Division for Early Childhood, 11,* 67–77.

Bailey, D. B., & Wolery, M. (1992). *Teaching infants and preschoolers with disabilities* (2nd ed.). Columbus, OH: Macmillan.

Bevill, A. R., & Gast, D. L. (1998). Social safety for young children: A review of the literature on safety skills instruction. *Topics in Early Childhood Special Education, 18,* 222–234.

Bowman, B. T., Donovan, M. S., & Burns, M. S. (2001). *Eager to learn: Educating our preschoolers.* Washington, DC: National Academy Press.

Bradley, R. H. (1994). The HOME inventory: Review and reflections. In H. W. Reese (Ed.), *Advances in child development and behavior* (Vol. 24, pp. 241–288). San Diego, CA: Academic Press.

Bradley, R. H., & Caldwell, B. M. (1976). The relationship of infants' home environments to mental test performance at fifty-four months: A follow-up study. *Child Development, 47,* 1172–1174.

Bradley, R. H., Corwyn, R. F., McAdoo, H. P., Coll, C. G. (2001). The home environment of children in the United States Part I: Variations by age, ethnicity, and poverty status. *Child Development, 72,* 1844–1867.

Bradley, R. H., Corwyn, R. F., & Whiteside-Mansell, L. (1997). Life at home: same time, different places. An examination of the HOME Inventory in different cultures. *Early Development and Parenting, 6,* 1–19.

Bredekamp, S. (1987). *Developmentally appropriate practice in early childhood programs serving children from birth through age 8.* Washington, DC: National Association for the Education of Young Children.

Bredekamp S., & Copple, C. (Eds.) (1997). *Developmentally appropriate practice in early childhood programs* (Rev. ed.). Washington, DC: National Association for the Education of Young Children.

Bronfenbrenner, U. (1977). Toward an experimental ecology of human development. *American Psychologist, 32,* 513–531.

Bronfenbrenner, U. (1979). *The ecology of human development: Experiments by nature and design.* Cambridge, MA: Harvard University Press.

Bronfenbrenner, U. (1992). *Ecological systems theory.* London: Jessica Kingsley Publishers.

Brown, L., Branston, M. B., Hamre-Nietupski, S., Pumpian, I., Certo, N., & Gruenewald, L. (1979). A strategy for developing chronologically-age-appropriate and functional curricular content for severely handicapped adolescents and young adults. *Journal of Special Education, 13,* 81–90.

Bryant, D. M., Maxwell, K. L., & Burchinal, M. (1999). Effects of a community initiative on the quality of child care. *Early Childhood Research Quarterly, 14,* 449–464.

Burchinal, M. R., Cryer, D., Clifford, R. M., & Howes, C. (2002). Caregiver training and classroom quality in child care centers. *Applied Developmental Science, 6,* 2–11.

Caldwell, B., & Bradley, R. H. (1984). *Home observation for measurement of the environment.* Little Rock, AR: University of Arkansas at Little Rock.

Carta, J. J., Sainato, D. M., & Greenwood, C. R. (1988). Advances in the ecological assessment of classroom instruction for young children with handicaps. In S. L. Odom & M. B. Karnes (Eds.), *Early intervention for infants and children with handicaps: An empirical base.* (pp. 217–239). Baltimore: Paul H. Brookes.

Consumer Product Safety Commission. (n.d.). *Handbook for public playground safety.* (Document #325). Washington, DC: U.S. Consumer Product Safety Commission. (*www.cpsc.gov*).

Consumer Product Safety Commission. (n.d.). *Home playground safety checklist.* (CPSC Document #323). Washington, DC: U.S. Consumer Product Safety Commission. (*www.cpsc.gov*).

Consumer Product Safety Commission. (n.d.). *Never put children's climbing gyms on hard surfaces, indoors or outdoors.* (Document #5119). Washington, DC: U.S. Consumer Product Safety Commission. (*www.cpsc.gov*).

Consumer Product Safety Commission. (n.d.). *Poison lookout checklist.* (Document #383). Washington, DC: U.S. Consumer Product Safety Commission. (*www.cpsc.gov*).

Consumer Product Safety Commission. (n.d.). *Public playground safety checklist.* (Document #327). Washington, DC: U.S. Consumer Product Safety Commission. (*www.cpsc.gov*).

Consumer Product Safety Commission. (n.d). *Soft contained play equipment safety checklist.* (Document #328). Washington, DC: U.S. Consumer Product Safety Commission. (*www.cpsc.gov*).

Consumer Product Safety Commission. (1999). *Safety hazards in child care settings.* Washington, DC: U.S. Consumer Product Safety Commission.

Cost, Quality, and Child Outcomes Study Team (1995). *Cost, quality, and child outcomes in child care centers.* Denver, CO: Department of Economics, University of Colorado at Denver.

de Kruif, R. E. L., McWilliam, R. A., Ridley, S. M., & Wakely, M. B. (2000). Classification of teachers' interaction behaviors in early childhood classrooms. *Early Childhood Research Quarterly, 15,* 247–268.

Dunst, C. J., (1993). Implications of risk and opportunity for assessment and intervention practice. *Topics in Early Childhood Special Education, 13,* 143–153.

Dunst, C. J. (2000). Revisiting "rethinking early intervention." *Topics in Early Childhood Special Education, 20,* 95–104.

Dunst, C. J., Bruder, M. B., Trivette, C. M., Hamby, D., Raab, M., & McLean, M. E. (2001). Characteristics and consequences of everyday natural learning opportunities. *Topics in Early Childhood Special Education, 21,* 68–92.

Dunst, C. J., Hamby, D., Trivette, C. M., Raab, M., & Bruder, M. B. (2000). Everyday family and community life and children's naturally occurring learning opportunities. *Journal of Early Intervention, 23,* 151–164.

Dunst, C. J., Trivette, C. M., Humphries, T., Raab, M., & Roper, N. (2001). Contrasting approaches to natural learning environments interventions. *Infants and Young Children, 14*(2), 48–63.

Federal Interagency Forum on Child and Family Statistics. (2002). *American's children: Key national indicators of well-being, 2002.* Pittsburgh, PA: U.S. Government Printing Office. *www.childstats.gov*

Gallagher, J. J., Rooney, R., & Campbell, S. (1999). Child care licensing regulations and child care quality in four states. *Early Childhood Research Quarterly, 14,* 313–333.

Garbarino, J., & Ganzel, B. (2000). The human ecology of early risk. In J. P. Shonkoff & S. J. Meisels (Eds.), *Handbook of early childhood intervention* (2nd ed., pp. 76–93). New York: Cambridge University Press.

Greaves, P., Glik, D. C., Kronenfeld, J. J., & Jackson, K. (1994). Determinants of controllable in-home child safety hazards. *Health Education Research, 9,* 307–315.

Harms, T., & Clifford, R. M. (1980). *Early Childhood Environment Rating Scale.* New York: Teachers College Press.

Harms, T., & Clifford, R. M. (1989). *Family Day Care Environment Rating Scale.* New York: Teachers College Press.

Harms, T., Clifford, R. M., & Cryer, D. (1998). *Early Childhood Environment Rating Scale* (Rev ed.). New York: Teachers College Press.

Harms, T., Cryer, D., & Clifford, R. M. (1990). *Infant-Toddler Environment Rating Scale.* New York: Teachers College Press.

Harms, T., Cryer, D., & Clifford, R. M. (in press). *Infant-Toddler Environment Rating Scale—Revised Edition.* New York: Teachers College Press.

Harms, T., Jacobs, D. & White, E. (1996). *School-Age Care Environment Rating Scale.* New York: Teachers College Press.

Hemmeter, M. L., Joseph, G. E., Smith, B. J., & Sandall, S. (2001). *DEC recommended practices program assessment: Improving practices for young children with special needs and their families.* Longmont, CO: Sopris West.

Hemmeter, M. L., Maxwell, K. L., Ault, M. J., & Schuster, J. W. (2001). *Assessment of Practices in Early Elementary Classrooms.* New York: Teachers College Press.

Holcombe, A., Wolery, M., & Snyder, E. (1994). Effects of two levels of procedural fidelity with constant time delay on children's learning. *Journal of Behavioral Education, 4,* 49–73.

Horn, E., Lieber, J., Sandall, S. R., Schwartz, I. S., & Wolery, R. A. (2002). Classroom models for individualized instruction. In S. L. Odom (Ed.), *Widening the circle: Including children with disabilities in preschool programs* (pp. 46–60). New York: Teachers College Press.

Horowitz, F. D. (1987). *Exploring developmental theories: Toward a structural/behavioral model of development.* Hillsdale, NJ: Lawrence Erlbaum.

Horowitz, F. D., & Haritos, C. (1998). The organism and the environment: Implications for understanding mental retardation. In J. A. Burack, R. M. Hodapp, & E. Zigler (Eds.), *Handbook of mental retardation and development* (pp. 20–40). New York: Cambridge University Press.

Huber, G., Marchand-Martella, N. E., Martella, R. C., & Wood, W. S. (1996). A survey of the frequency of accidents' injuries for preschoolers enrolled in an inner-city Head Start program. *Education and Treatment of Children, 19,* 46–54.

Hyson, M. C., Hirsh-Pasek, K., & Rescorla, L. (1990). The classroom practices inventory: An observation instrument based on NAEYC's guidelines for developmentally appropriate practices for 4-and 5-year-old children. *Early Childhood Research Quarterly, 5,* 475–494.

La Paro, K. M., Sexton, D., & Snyder, P. (1998). Program quality characteristics in segregated and inclusive early childhood settings. *Early Childhood Research Quarterly, 13,* 151–167.

Lutzker, J. R., & Bigelow, K. M. (2001). *Reducing child maltreatment.* New York: Guilford Press.

Mandel, U., Bigelow, K. M., & Lutzker, J. R. (1998). Using video to reduce home safety hazards with parents reported for child abuse and neglect. *Journal of Family Violence, 13,* 147–162.

Matheny, A. P., Wachs, T. D., Ludwig, J. L., & Phillips, K. (1995). Bringing order out of chaos: Psychometric characteristics of the confusion, hubbub, and order scale. *Journal of Applied Developmental Psychology, 16,* 429–444.

McKibben L, DeVos E, & Newberger E. (1989). Victimization of mothers of abused children: A controlled study. *Pediatrics, 84,* 531–535.

McWilliam, R. A. (1992). *Family-centered intervention planning: A routines-based approach.* Tucson, AZ: Communication Skill Builders.

McWilliam, R. A., Scarborough, A. A., Bagby, J. H., & Sweeney, A. L. (1996). *Teaching Styles Rating Scale.* Chapel Hill, NC: Frank Porter Graham Child Development Institute, University of North Carolina.

McWilliam, R. A., Wolery, M., & Odom, S. L. (2001). Instructional perspectives in inclusive preschool classrooms. In M. J. Guralnick (Ed.), *Early childhood inclusion: Focus on change* (pp. 503–527). Baltimore: Paul H. Brookes.

Metchikian, K. L., Mink, J. M., Bigelow, K. M., Lutzker, J. R., & Doctor, R. M. (1999). Reducing home safety hazards in the homes of parents reported for neglect. *Child and Family Behavior Therapy, 21*(3), 23–34.

Morrongiello, B. A., Midgett, C., & Shields, R. (2001). Don't run with scissors: Young children's knowledge of home safety rules. *Journal of Pediatric Psychology, 26,* 105–115.

Mulligan, S., Harper-Whalen, S., & Morris, S. (2002). *Child Care Plus+ Floor Plan Analysis for Early Childhood Programs.* Missoula, MT: University of Montana.

National Association for the Education of Young Children (NAEYC). (1998). *Accreditation criteria and procedures of the National Association for the Education of Young Children.* Washington, DC: Author.

National Center for Injury Prevention and Control, Centers for Disease Control and Prevention (2002). *www.cdc.gov/ncipc/wisqars*

National Clearinghouse on Child Abuse and Neglect Information (2002). *National child abuse and neglect data system (NCANDS): Summary of key findings from calendar year 2000.* Washington, DC: Children's Bureau, Administration on Children, Youth, and Families.

Odom, S. L., & Bailey, D. B. (2001). Inclusive preschool programs: Classroom ecology and child outcomes. In M. J. Guralnick (Ed.), *Early childhood inclusion:*

Focus on change. (pp. 253–276). Baltimore: Paul H. Brookes.

Peterson, C. A., & McConnell, S. R. (1996). Factors related to intervention integrity and child outcome in social skills interventions. *Journal of Early Intervention, 20,* 146–164.

Phillips, C. B. (1994). At the core: What every early childhood professional should know. In J. Johnson, & J. B. McCracken (Eds.), *The early childhood career lattice: Perspectives on professional development* (pp. 57–59). Washington, DC: National Association for the Education of Young Children.

Raab, M., Dunst, C. J., Whaley, K. T., LeGrand, C. D., & Taylor, M. (1997). *Preschool Assessment of the Classroom Environment Scale* (Rev.). Unpublished Scale. Orelena Hawks Puckett Institute, Asheville, NC.

Randall, W., & Parrila, R. (2001). Ethnicity, disability, and risk for abuse. *Developmental Disabilities Bulletin, 29,* 60–80.

Reading, R., Langford, I. H., Haynes, R., & Lovett, A. (1999). Accidents to preschool children: Comparing family and neighbourhood risk factors. *Social Science and Medicine, 48,* 321–330.

Sandall, S., McLean, M. E., & Smith, B. J. (2000). *DEC recommended practices in early intervention/early childhood special education.* Longmont, CO: Sopris West.

Sheridan, S. (2001). Quality evaluation and quality enhancement in preschool: A model of competence development. *Early Child Development and Care, 166,* 7–27.

Shonkoff, J. P., & Phillips, D. A. (2000). *From neurons to neighborhoods: The science of early childhood development.* Washington, DC: National Academy Press.

Symons, F. J., Clark, R. D., Roberts, J. P., & Bailey, D. B. (2001). Classroom behavior of elementary school-age boys with fragile X syndrome. *Journal of Special Education, 34,* 194–202.

Thurman, S. K. (1977). The congruence of behavioral ecologies: A model for special education programming. *Journal of Special Education, 11,* 329–333.

Thurman, S. K. (1997). Systems, ecologies, and the context of early intervention. In S. K. Thurman, J. R.

Cornwell, & S. R. Gottwald (Eds.), *Contexts of early intervention: Systems and settings* (pp. 3–17). Baltimore: Paul H. Brookes.

Thurman, K. S., & Widerstrom, A. H. (1990). *Infants and young children with special needs: A developmental and ecological approach* (2nd ed.). Baltimore: Paul H. Brookes.

Tymchuk, A. (1991). Instruments for the assessment of safety with parents and others who are mentally handicapped. *Mental Handicap, 19,* 4–10.

Tymchuk, A. J., Lang, C. M., Dolyniuk, C. A., Berncy-Ficklin, K., & Spitz, R. (1999). The Home Inventory of Dangers and Safety Precautions–2: Addressing critical needs for prescriptive assessment devices in child maltreatment and in healthcare. *Child Abuse and Neglect, 23,* 1–14.

Wachs, T. D. (1979). Proximal experience and early cognitive-intellectual development: The physical environment. *Merrill Palmer Quarterly, 25,* 3–41.

Wachs, T. D., Francis, J., & McQuiston, S. (1979). Psychological dimensions of the infant's physical environment. *Infant Behavior and Development, 2,* 155–161.

Wachs, T. D., Morrow, J., & Slabach, E. H. (1990). Intra-individual variability in infant visual recognition memory performance: Temperamental and environmental correlates. *Infant Behavior and Development, 13,* 397–403.

Webster's Ninth New Collegiate Dictionary. (1988). Springfield, MA: Merriam-Webster.

Wolery, M., Brashers, M. S., Grant, S., & Pauca, T. (2000). *Ecological congruence assessment for classroom activities and routines in childcare.* Chapel Hill, NC: Frank Porter Graham Child Development Center.

Wolery, M., Brashers, M. S., & Neitzel, J. C. (2002). Ecological congruence assessment for classroom activities and routines: Identifying goals and intervention practices in childcare. *Topics in Early Childhood Special Education, 22,* 131–142.

Wolery, M., Pauca, T., Brashers, M. S., & Grant, S. (2000). *Quality of Inclusive Experiences Measure.* Chapel Hill, NC: Frank Porter Graham Child Development Institute, University of North Carolina.

Functional Behavioral Assessment in Early Education Settings

Mary A. McEvoy
University of Minnesota
Shelley Neilsen
Minneapolis Public Schools
Joe Reichle
University of Minnesota

Preparation of this chapter was supported in part by
Grants No. HO24D40006 and HO24P10017 from the
U.S. Department of Education to Drs. McEvoy and
Reichle. The authors wish to thank the members of
the Minnesota Behavioral Support Project for
contributions to previous versions of this chapter.
A Web site on preschool challenging behavior is
available at www.ici2.umn.edu/preschoolbehavior.

INTRODUCTION

Early childhood educators report that a primary issue they face on a day-to-day basis is the increase in young children's challenging behavior (Buscemi, Bennett, Thomas, & Deluca, 1995; Feil & Becker, 1993; Sinclair, Del'Homme, & Gonzalez, 1993). In some instances, these behaviors may be developmentally appropriate. For example, all children go through periods where they exhibit behaviors that may be frustrating to adults. These behavior challenges respond in most instances to either environmental interventions or adult feedback. However, for some children, the intensity and duration of challenging behaviors require additional, specific interventions. These behaviors might range from developmentally inappropriate aggression, self-injury, property destruction, and other disruptive behaviors to isolation and withdrawal. These behaviors directly impact the relationships that the child has with other children and adults and may put the child at risk for a restrictive educational setting (Horner & Carr, 1997).

The issue of challenging behaviors has received a great deal of attention in both the popular and academic press. In addition, policy makers at the national, state, and local levels have addressed challenging behavior through legislative means. When Congress reauthorized the Individuals with Disabilities Education Act (IDEA '97), the discipline provisions of this legislation were the most contentious (Office of Special Education Programs, 1997). Congress and advocates debated extensively with both the definition of challenging behavior as well as the effective procedures needed to manage them. One result of the deliberation was a number of provisions directing schools to not only determine the form of a challenging behavior, but also to address specifically the underlying function of the behavior using Functional Behavioral Assessment.

Functional Behavioral Assessment (FBA) has both a legal and a best-practices imperative. From a legal perspective, the reauthorized Individuals with Disabilities Education Act included several amendments that specifically addressed discipline. These amendments had three major themes. The first theme reaffirmed the right of all children to be educated in a safe, well-disciplined environment. Second, it was noted that educators should use effective techniques and proactive methods to prevent and respond to challenging behavior. Finally, the law required that IEPs contain behavioral interventions that will result in a decrease in discipline problems (Katsiyannis & Maag, 1998).

To implement these themes, the IDEA discipline provision requires that an FBA must be conducted prior to suspension or change in placement. The rationale behind this mandate is that, with an FBA, educators are less likely to rely on reactive interventions (i.e., expulsion) and focus on implementing effective techniques and positive methods to teach more appropriate behavior (Axelrod, 1987; Durand, 1982). Functional Behavioral Assessment provides critical best-practice information about the context of the behavior. The assessment procedures identify what the behavior looks like, when it is most likely and least likely to occur, and why the child is engaging in the challenging behavior. Once these events are identified, interventions are designed that focus on altering the environment to prevent problem behaviors and teach new, socially appropriate behaviors (Carr, Horner, & Turnbull, 1999). The subsequent strategies focus on helping children change undesirable patterns of behavior and expand on their growing repertoire of skills (Dunlap & Fox, 1996). By arranging the environment and altering the antecedent of challenging behavior, adults can prevent the behavior. By teaching children new skills, they can learn to better manage interactions with peers and adults (Dunlap & Fox, 1996).

Because the information from an FBA allows educators to design interventions that are proactive, positive, and teach new skills (DEC position paper, 1998), it is considered best practice when assessing children with challenging behavior. Without this information early educators may rely on interventions that are ineffective, counterproductive, and reactive. The purpose of this chapter is to assist early educators in conducting a Functional Behavioral Assessment (FBA). We will begin by defining the terms affiliated with an FBA. We will then describe the benefits of conducting an FBA, the types of information that are needed and ways to collect it. Finally, we will discuss ways to link the information obtained from an FBA to effective, antecedent-based interventions for young children.

FUNCTIONAL BEHAVIORAL ASSESSMENT

Professionals in early childhood report an increasing number of children with challenging behavior in special education classrooms, Head Start classrooms, child-care centers, and community settings (Buscemi, et al., 1995; Feil & Becker, 1993; Sinclair, et al., 1993). In addition, there is an increasing number of children who have disabilities being served in natural settings, and this has heightened the need for practical strategies for intervening with the challenging behavior of all children (Hemmeter, 1999). Furthermore, challenging behavior has been reported to be the greatest barrier in providing services in the natural setting (Reichle, Davis, Freeman, & Horner, 1999). Consider, for example, the following scenarios.

> Scene 1: *During group time, Julia screams and runs away from the group. Sometimes she hides under a table or in the toy box and sometimes she just runs.*
>
> Scene 2: *During group time, Chris screams and runs away from the teacher. When the teacher attempts to help him to group, he hits, slaps, and even spits at the teacher.*

In both of these scenarios, the early childhood educator is probably asking two important questions: *What do I do when this behavior occurs? (How/or should I respond?)* and *How do I prevent this behavior from occurring tomorrow?* The answers to these questions do not always come easily.

Children who engage in chronic, frequent, and high intensity challenging behavior, like in the examples above, require systematic intervention efforts. While it is not always obvious what appropriate management techniques are needed for these children, it is clear that information from a Functional Behavioral Assessment will provide answers to the questions raised above.

Functional Behavioral Assessment is a well-defined process that educators and families undertake in order to determine when and why a child might be engaging in challenging behavior. The form or topography of the behavior is operationalized, defined in a way that is observable and measurable. The events that immediately precede (*antecedents*) and follow (*reinforcers*) the behavior are recorded. This information allows us to determine times of the day that the behavior is likely to occur, the conditions that are present that may trigger the behavior, and the consequences that follow and maintain challenging behavior. Thus, educators and families have more information about the challenging behavior to help them choose more effective interventions (Chandler & Dahlquist, 2002; Strain et al., 1992; Sugai, Lewis-Palmer, & Hagan, 1998).

What Is a Functional Behavioral Assessment?

Functional Behavioral Assessment is a method for identifying the variables that consistently predict and maintain challenging behavior (Horner & Carr, 1997). This assists in identifying people, events, or activities that trigger challenging behavior, making predictions about when those behaviors are likely to occur, and identifying possible reinforcement contingencies (Strain, et al., 1992). Before the specific components of an FBA are described, several underlying assumptions of Functional Behavioral Assessment need to be discussed.

The first assumption is that behavior occurs for a reason and serves a specific function for the child (Horner, 1994). For some children, challenging behavior becomes the most effective and efficient way to communicate their wants and needs. Although the behaviors may be considered "challenging" by others, from the child's perspective they are reasonable and effective responses to events that have been reinforced over a period of time. For example, Casey pushes a peer during free time and gets the toy that the peer has. In this case, though the behavior is not appropriate or safe, Casey has learned that it is an effective way to obtain something that she wants. Obtaining the toy positively reinforces Casey's challenging behavior.

The second assumption is that behavior can change (e.g., increase and decrease) as a result of the presentation of a task and the response to the challenging behavior. Consider Pat. He screams "No!" and throws toys when asked to put them away. If the teacher walks away and allows Pat to continue to play she could be reinforcing the screaming behavior and inadvertently increasing his challenging behavior. However, she could alter the way transitions are presented to Pat and provide a transition cue, (e.g., *In one minute, it's time to clean up*), a clear signal to indicate time to clean up (e.g., music starts, lights are turned off). In addition, if she uses verbal or physical reinforcement (e.g., stamp on the hand for coming to the next activity, social praise) to reinforce Pat for following directions, she may increase the likelihood that he will make the transition successfully.

A third assumption is that effective interventions are based on assessment of the relationship between environment and behavior. Using the example above with Casey, by examining the timing and the result of hitting, her teachers are better prepared to design an intervention. For example, implementing a social skills curriculum that promotes sharing might be an effective intervention.

Domains and Dimensions

One common theme of the assumptions described previously is that ongoing, careful data collection and analysis are essential. The purpose of a Functional Behavioral Assessment is to identify the variables that consistently predict and maintain challenging behavior (Horner & Carr, 1997). This is accomplished by determining an observable and measurable *description* of the target behaviors, *predicting* when and under what conditions the behaviors occur, and assessing the *function* of the behaviors. This information is then used to design an *intervention* to decrease the undesirable behavior while at the same time teaching an alternative desirable behavior. These components are described in the sections that follow.

Description of the Target Behavior(s)

Challenging behavior can be defined as any action produced by the child that results in self-injury or injury to others, causes damage to the physical environment, interferes with learning new skills, and/or socially isolates the child (Doss & Reichle, 1991). While challenging behavior can be defined generically, as in the previous sentence, one of the first steps in conducting a Functional Behavioral Assessment is to define the typography of the challenging behavior for a particular child.

The FBA process begins with clearly defining the behavior of concern, or the *form* of the challenging behavior. Challenging behaviors may take many forms. These may include:

1. **Self-injurious behaviors,** such as scratching, biting, head banging, punching, face slapping, pinching, eye gouging, ear pulling, hand mouthing, arm biting, and self-choking;
2. **Aggression,** such as hitting, scratching, kicking, biting, and pinching others and knocking over objects;
3. **Tantrums,** such as persistent crying, loud vocalizations, screaming, and whining;
4. **Property destruction,** such as breaking materials, toys, destroying class projects, and throwing materials;
5. **Social avoidance,** such as looking away and leaving group activities;
6. **Self-stimulatory behaviors,** such as body rocking, hand flapping, mouthing, and body posturing.

It is evident from this list that challenging behaviors may range in severity from those that are relatively harmless (e.g., whining, crying, screaming) to actions that actually pose danger to the individual or others (e.g., aggression, self-inflicted injuries). It is important that everyone associated with the child agree about the specific topography of the behavior. For example, a teacher may see a child crying and say the child is sad. A parent might see the same child and think the child is hurt. In both instances, regardless of why the behavior is occurring, the form of the behavior is crying.

The form of the behavior is defined by making it observable, measurable, and discrete. If you can see it, hear it, feel it, or smell it, it's observable. If you can count it or measure it, it's measurable. If it has a beginning and end, it's discrete. It's important to define the form of the behavior for several reasons. First, the definition provides focus on an observable action. This allows for more precision and accuracy when conducting an FBA. Second, by defining the behavior, the focus is on the behavior, not on the child. For example instead of saying the child is "angry," early educators can report specifically what the child did, such as shoved five times in line, or was out of his seat twenty times during group. Focusing on observable behavior, lessens value-laden communication and the potential for misunderstanding.

In most instances, once a form of a behavior has been identified, educators and families begin the process of intervention selection. Interventions are often selected because they have been effective in addressing a particular form of behavior or because they are easy to implement. Unfortunately, the intervention itself may actually reinforce rather than decrease the challenging behavior. Consider the following scenario:

Hannah, a 4-year-old child, begins to cry and hit other children during group time. As a result of this behavior, the teacher sends Hannah away from the group, telling her that she can return as soon as she has calmed himself. Once Hannah is quiet, the teacher invites her to return to the group, commenting about how she is welcome to join them and how much they enjoy her partici-

pation when she is calm. Unfortunately, the teacher reports that Hannah's outbursts in the circle time have not decreased. She is perplexed that "time out," an effective intervention at other times, is not working in this situation.

There are two important things to consider in this scenario. First, it is likely that Hannah does not want to participate in the group and has learned that a quick and predictable way to get released from the activity is to engage in challenging behavior. Second, Hannah has learned over time that she will be allowed to "escape" an activity or situation by engaging in challenging behavior. By allowing the child to escape, the teacher is actually reinforcing, rather than decreasing, the challenging behavior. She is increasing the chances that Hannah will repeat the behavior. Operationalizing the form of challenging behavior is an important first step in conducting a Functional Behavioral Assessment. This will allow the teacher to determine what the behavior is and begin to examine when and why the child is engaging in the challenging behavior. Knowing both the *what* (form) and *why* (function) will allow educators and families to design more effective interventions.

Prediction of When and Under What Conditions Behaviors Occur

In the example above, what the teacher did *after* the behavior (the consequence) influenced the child's behavior. Similarly, specific things that occur *before* a behavior (the antecedents) also influence behavior change. The antecedent is referred to technically as the discriminative stimulus and is defined as the variable that sets the occasion for the behavior (Alberto & Troutman, 1999). In addition to a single discriminative stimulus, the antecedent might include a chain of discriminative stimuli (Mace, Lalli, & Lalli, 1991). Researchers have demonstrated that variables such as diverting attention, denying access to tangibles, and presenting task demands accurately predict the occurrence of challenging behavior (Carr, Newsom, & Binkoff,

1976; Gunter, Shores, Jack, Denny, & DePaepe, 1994; Kern, Childs, Dunlap, Clarke, & Falk, 1994; Vaughn & Horner, 1995). For example, Asmus and colleagues (1999) examined the effects of task demand on three preschool children with mental retardation using different types of tasks and therapists. The study was conducted in the families' homes; the mothers and experimenters served as the therapists. The results showed that each child's challenging behavior occurred only when task demands were presented. The researchers concluded that it was the task demand itself that occasioned aberrant behavior and that the specific task, specific setting, and therapist were usually irrelevant (Asmus et al., 1999).

A number of researchers have studied the effects of various antecedent events in the form of curricular revisions on the on-task and challenging behavior of students in school settings. For example, Dunlap, Kern-Dunlap, Clarke, and Robbins (1991) examined the effects of various curricular revisions, such as shortening the duration of the task, interspersing fine motor and gross motor tasks, and choice making on the challenging behavior of an individual with developmental disabilities. The results indicated that altering these variables eliminated severely disruptive behavior and increased on-task responding. In addition to curricular revisions, a variety of studies have examined related instructional variables such as high probability requests (Davis, Brady, Williams, & Hamilton, 1992) and reducing task difficulty (Carr & Durand, 1985).

Like curricular revisions for adolescents, curricular revisions with preschool children alter the way tasks are presented. A major task for preschoolers is play. Consequently the availability of toys may have a significant impact on problem behavior. Blair, Umbreit, and Eck, (2000) examined the impact of the availability of toys on a 4-year-old child's challenging behavior in a child-care setting. The authors hypothesized that the instances of challenging behavior were sensitive to the ratio of toys to peers during free-play time. The results showed that when there were few toys

and many peers, challenging behavior occurred at a higher rate than when there were enough toys for each child. A different study examined the impact of preferred and nonpreferred activities with and without choice on a 4-year-old in a child-care setting. The results indicated that, regardless of choice, the child engaged in less challenging behavior when he was given preferred activities (Umbreit & Blair, 1997).

The aforementioned studies show how various antecedent events influence challenging behavior. By identifying the antecedent events for a particular child, teachers and parents can predict when challenging behavior is likely to occur. Once these antecedents are identified, then teachers and parents can alter or eliminate the antecedent variable. Umbreit and Blair (1997) used preferred activities (identified during assessment) to improve the likelihood of appropriate behavior. The FBA determined that transition from outside play to indoor activity was one of the problematic activities. Further, the request to begin the transition was the antecedent, or predictor, of the problem behavior. The authors chose an activity the child enjoyed, helping staff members, and presented that offer to the child simultaneous with the instruction to begin the transition. Thus, the antecedent was altered to decrease the likelihood of challenging behavior.

The Functions of Behavior

O'Neill et al. (1991, 1997) have delineated a number of functions that challenging behaviors might serve. Most children engage in challenging behavior in order to **obtain desired outcomes** or to **escape undesired outcomes**. Figure 9.1 expands on these two categories by illustrating that challenging behaviors emitted to obtain or to escape can be either socially motivated or nonsocially motivated.

The functions of challenging behavior are determined by identifying the relation between the occurrence of a target behavior (e.g., hitting peers) and the outcome of or response to that

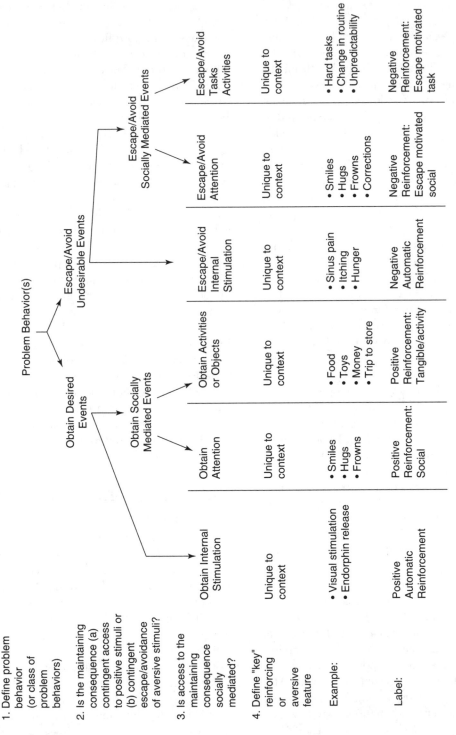

FIGURE 9.1

Potential socially motivated or nonsocially motivated functions of challenging behaviors emitted to obtain or to escape

Note. From *Functional Assessment and Program Development for Problem Behavior: A Practical Handbook,* 2nd edition, by R. E. O'Neil, R. H. Horner, R. W. Albin, J. R. Sprague, K. Storey, J. Newton. c. 1997. Reprinted with permission of Wadsworth, an imprint of the Wadsworth Group, a division of Thomson Learning. Fax 800-730-2215.

behavior (e.g., obtaining attention). Functions of problem behavior fall into two broad categories: those maintained by positive reinforcement (e.g., to obtain) and those maintained by negative reinforcement (e.g., to escape or avoid aversive stimuli) (Carr, Robinson, & Palumbo, 1990; Carr, Taylor, & Robinson, 1991; Iwata, Dorsey, Slifer, Bauman, & Richman, 1982; Repp, Felce, & Barton, 1988). These categories can be further delineated into the social functions of "to obtain attention, tangibles, or tasks/activities" and "to escape attention, tangibles, or tasks/activities." There is also a nonsocial category that involves automatic reinforcement and biological reinforcement. Each of the maintaining consequences will be discussed next.

Attention Any form of adult or peer attention provided contingent on the occurrence of a problem behavior has been shown to reinforce challenging behaviors (Lalli & Goh, 1993; Taylor, 1994). A child may engage in challenging behavior when there is a deprivation of attention, when an adult's attention has been diverted, and when the child needs assistance. In addition, it's important to consider the form of attention. Attention may take the form of a verbal reprimand or redirection, adult proximity, or physical touch.

The effect of teacher attention on behavior has been the topic of research for several decades. Lovaas, Freitag, Gold, and Kassorla (1965) conducted one of the earliest and most influential studies examining the role of attention with a young child with self-injurious behaviors. The results showed that when attention, in the form of empathetic statements, was presented contingent on challenging behavior, self-injurious behavior increased. Thomas, Becker, and Armstrong (1968) examined the effect of teacher attention across a classroom of first-grade students. They altered rates of teacher approval and disapproval statements. The authors found that when the teacher provided attention contingent on challenging behavior, the rates of challenging behavior increased. Moreover, when the teacher provided

attention contingent on appropriate behavior, rates of appropriate behavior increased. In more recent years a variety of studies have examined attention as a function of challenging behavior. Lalli, Browder, Mace, & Brown (1993) conducted a functional analysis with three elementary-aged students with developmental disabilities and challenging behaviors (i.e., head banging, aggression, and self-scratching). For 2 of the 3 participants, the descriptive data indicated that challenging behavior was positively reinforced in the form of staff attention. To further analyze their hypothesis, the researchers examined the results of three different conditions: a) differential reinforcement of alternative behavior (the teacher provided praise on a fixed-interval schedule that was increased from 30 seconds to 90 seconds), b) contingent attention to challenging behavior (on a variable schedule), and c) adaptive skills training (e.g., waving arm and giving teacher a toy to initiate social interaction). Following baseline, the differential attention to alternate behavior (DRA) condition was presented and self-injurious behavior (SIB) dropped to near zero levels. When the contingent attention condition was presented, SIB returned to near baseline levels. When the children were taught to request attention appropriately, challenging behavior again dropped to near zero rates and the targeted adaptive behaviors increased (Lalli et al., 1993). The results of this study support the authors' hypothesis that challenging behavior was maintained by teacher attention.

Tangible Items Tangible items, such as toys, food, games, and other activities, provided contingent on challenging behavior have also been shown to reinforce challenging behavior. Lalli and Goh (1993) identified the following three situations during which children engage in challenging behavior to obtain a tangible item. These include when the child has been denied access, when the item has been removed, and when the child has been asked to wait for the item. Piazza and colleagues (1997) conducted a study on the function and treatment of elopement for three children with developmental disabilities. *Elopement* is defined as leaving or running away from the activity. The authors hypothesized that access to tangibles maintained the challenging behavior for two of the three children participating in the study. For both children attention, task demand, and tangible items were provided contingent on elopement. The authors reported that elopement occurred at higher rates during the tangibles condition and concluded that the children's challenging behavior was maintained by access to tangibles (Piazza et al., 1997).

Escape   Escape or avoidance of an unpleasant, nonpreferred or aversive stimulus has also been found to maintain challenging behavior. A variety of research has shown that escape from task-related demands has been found to negatively reinforce SIB (Iwata et al., 1982; Iwata et al., 1994), self-stimulation (Durand & Carr, 1987), and aggression and disruption (Dunlap et al., 1991; Umbreit & Blair, 1997). A child may engage in challenging behavior to delay, reduce, or end the unpleasant or nonpreferred tasks or activities.

Iwata and colleagues have studied the function of SIB for over two decades and have specifically examined the role of negative reinforcement in the maintenance and treatment of SIB. Iwata, Pace, Kalsher, Cowdery, and Cataldo (1990) examined the function of SIB for seven students (age range 4 to 16). The students were exposed to the following conditions: attention, demand, medical, alone, and play. Each condition was presented during 15-minute sessions. Attention and escape were provided contingent on SIB. The results showed that six of the seven students engaged in SIB more frequently in the demand condition than any other condition. The authors suggested that the task demand was considered an aversive event and the contingent removal or postponement served as negative reinforcement. Furthermore, in a summary of 152 single-case analyses of the function of SIB, negative reinforcement accounted for the largest percent of cases (38%) (Iwata et al., 1994).

Multiple Functions   The research described above supports the hypothesis that certain antecedents predict challenging behavior and certain consequences maintain challenging behavior. In addition, a single behavior may be maintained by multiple functions. For example, Durand (1982) examined how different stimulus conditions (task demand and vibration) influenced self-injurious behavior. He found that one type of SIB, flicks to the nose, decreased under the easy-demand conditions, but hits to the head remained high throughout both easy and difficult conditions. Only when vibration was added to the easy condition did hits to the head decrease. Based on the results of this study, Durand concluded that SIB might serve more than one function. In another example, Haring and Kennedy (1990) demonstrated that a single form of challenging behavior, self-stimulation, served an escape function in one setting and a self-stimulation function in another. Day, Horner, and O'Neill (1994) supported the multiple-function hypothesis in a study with three individuals exhibiting SIB and aggression. A reversal design was used to compare easy and hard tasks, presence or absence of preferred items, and the efficiency of SIB or aggression to obtain reinforcement. The results showed that individuals engaged in the same form of challenging behavior to escape a difficult task and to obtain a preferred item. Based on the studies reviewed above, it appears that challenging behavior needs to be assessed in a variety of contexts so that the existence of multiple controlling contingencies may be identified (Day et al., 1994). It is probable that different interventions are needed to address each of the functions of the problem behavior.

Identifying Nonsocial Consequences   The research above has described challenging behavior that is reinforced through some type of social consequence (e.g., attention or escape from difficult or undesirable task). However, some children, albeit a smaller number, engage in challenging behavior that serves a nonsocial function.

Sometimes referred to as biological and automatic reinforcement, this behavior is maintained by nonsocial consequences that occur independent of the social environment (Iwata, Vollmer, & Zarcone, 1990). Research in this area is limited. The behavior may take the form of self-injurious or self-stimulatory behavior. It appears that automatic reinforcement generates sensory reinforcers based on visual, auditory, tactile, and even gustatory stimulation (Horner & Carr, 1997). In these instances, children engage in challenging behavior to obtain either internal (e.g., vestibular stimulation or kinesthetic feedback) or external (e.g., visual or auditory feedback) sensory stimulation (Lalli & Goh, 1993).

A Functional Behavioral Assessment can help educators determine if the behavior is socially or nonsocially reinforced. It is important to rule out a social function of behavior, even when the form may appear to be sensory motivated (McEvoy & Reichle, 2002). For example, children with poor communication repertoires may bite themselves in order to obtain adult attention or to be left alone.

How to Conduct a Functional Behavioral Assessment

Figure 9.2 represents the steps that are part of the Functional Behavioral Assessment process. The steps include three major categories of assessment: indirect assessments, direct observation assessments and environmental manipulations (functional analysis). Figure 9.2 also provides examples of assessments that might be used at each step.

Indirect Assessments   These include existing written documents, interviews, checklists, rating scales, and questionnaires that are designed to obtain information regarding the perceived function of a challenging behavior, as well as the factors that predict or maintain the behavior. In some cases, an indirect assessment will be the only source of Functional Behavioral Assessment information. However, it is more likely to be used as the initial step of a more thorough assessment process.

Existing Written Documents   There are several different indirect assessment methods that can be used to obtain functional assessment information. Reviewing existing written documents entails closely examining written reports in order to obtain information relevant to the child's engagement in challenging behaviors. Existing written documents may include an Individualized Family Service Plan (IFSP), Individualized Educational Plan (IEP), and related service personnel reports (e.g., occupational therapist, physical therapist, speech/language therapist, psychologist, social worker, family counselor). These documents provide important information, as does documentation from other child-care providers (e.g., day-care provider, bus driver, preschool teacher) and information from other assessments that have been conducted or information regarding outcomes from previous interventions.

It is important to review existing written documents early on in the functional assessment process. Information from written documents may enable the early educators to rule out physical or medical conditions that may be causing the child to engage in challenging behavior. They may also provide important information regarding events that may have occurred in the past, such as multiple home placements or the loss of a parent or sibling. In addition, reviewing existing written documents may provide information regarding interventions implemented previously and whether or not these interventions were successful in decreasing or eliminating challenging behaviors.

There are several advantages and disadvantages with this method. The information obtained may be helpful in determining the child's history of challenging behavior in multiple settings. However, caution must be taken not to over-interpret the record review information. For example, variables that influence behavior in certain settings may not be present or acceptable in the setting of concern. In addition, the documented challenging behavior may have served an alternate function in the past. Finally, the information may not have been obtained initially by a reliable source.

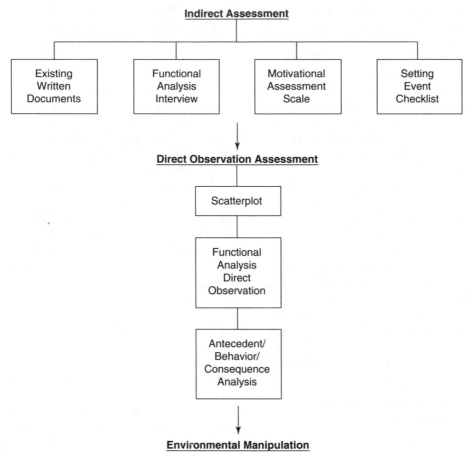

FIGURE 9.2

Major categories of the Functional Behavioral Assessment Process

The Motivation Assessment Scale (MAS) The MAS (Durand & Crimmins, 1990) is a questionnaire containing 16 questions designed to pinpoint the function(s) of a challenging behavior. Durand and Crimmins (1990) have noted that the MAS serves two primary purposes: to identify situations in which the child is likely to engage in challenging behavior and to obtain important information about the perceived function of challenging behavior.

The MAS helps to determine the extent to which significant adults in the child's life think that the challenging behavior serves the function of obtaining attention, escaping or avoiding non-preferred activities, obtaining preferred items or activities, or providing sensory stimulation. The following four types of questions address each of the four function categories (i.e., attention, escape, obtain tangible reinforcers, and sensory).

1. *Does the behavior occur when you stop attending to this person?* (This question probes a possible attention function.)
2. *Does the behavior occur when any requests are made of this person?* (This question involves an escape or avoidance function.)

3. *Does the behavior stop occurring shortly after you give this person the toy, food, or activity that she or he has requested?* (This question determines whether access to tangibles maintains challenging behavior.)
4. *Does it appear to you that this person enjoys performing the behavior?* (It feels, tastes, looks, smells, and/or sounds pleasing.) (This question addresses a sensory function.)

The benefits of the MAS are that it can be completed quickly and the instructions are easily interpreted by parents and staff allowing for independent completion and analysis of the rating scale. The MAS can also assist in identifying potential function(s) that the challenging behavior may be serving for the child.

The drawbacks include the fact that the MAS does not provide information regarding setting events or environmental influences that may be associated with challenging behavior. Nor does it provide information regarding the frequency or consequences of the behavior or information about prior intervention efforts and their outcomes. Finally, the reliability of responses may be questionable. For example, different interviewees familiar with the same child may respond differently to the same set of questions.

Setting Event Checklists A setting event checklist helps the interventionist identify variables in the child's previous or present environment that may influence whether or not challenging behavior occurs. These variables are defined as *"setting events"* and can be:

- Temporally distant from the occurrence of challenging behavior (e.g., the child has an altercation with her sibling 2 hours before engaging in challenging behavior);
- In close proximity to the occurrence of challenging behavior (e.g., the child had a favorite toy taken away 5 minutes before engaging in the challenging behavior); or
- May be an ongoing situation or state (e.g., the child is extremely fatigued due to interrupted

sleep, or a nonpreferred person is present in the environment)

Setting events may include a child's *physical state* (e.g., medical condition, illness, side effects of medication, fatigue, hunger, thirst), *social state* (e.g., adverse social interactions, change in caregiver, anticipated event canceled or postponed), or information about the child's *environment* (e.g., crowded, noisy, unstructured). When a child's behavior pattern is unpredictable and clear antecedents are not determined, it is helpful to collect information regarding the categories of setting events described above. This information can be derived via the development and consistent completion of a setting event checklist similar to that found in Figure 9.3. In this example, the family and the teaching team complete and share information with one another. The top part, "Today's News," is completed by the teaching team at the end of the day and provides information for the family about their child's day. The bottom part, "Happenings from Home" is completed by the family and given to the teaching team at the beginning of the child's day. Once the team obtains this information, possible changes can be made in the child's day. It is important to note that setting event checklists should be developed with the individual child in mind.

Data obtained from a setting events checklist allows the observer to identify events that may influence whether or not a challenging behavior will occur. In addition, when used in conjunction with a direct observation system, the checklist provides information on which setting events are most predictive of the challenging behavior.

Unfortunately, there are a number of limitations with this type of assessment. First, it does not provide information regarding possible functions of the challenging behavior(s). Second, there is no information about prior intervention efforts and their outcomes.

The Functional Analysis Interview The goal of the Functional Analysis Interview (FAI) is to gather information regarding the context surrounding the

TODAYS NEWS.......   DATE_____

Your child was:

Great Mood!   Good   So-So   Unhappy

Concerns:

Special treat today was:

Speech   Gym   OT   PT   Fine Motor

Tomorrow we will need:

HAPPENINGS FROM HOME........

Great Mood!   Good   So-So   Unhappy

Slept All Night   1/2 Night   1/4 Night   Less Than_____

Ate Supper   Ate Breakfast

TV Interrupted_____

Was Refused an Object/Activity_____

Time Out in His/Her Room_____

Today's Outings: OT   PT   Speech   Shopping

Other:

Alternative Care Giver:

Feelin' Good   Tired/Lethargic   Just Gettin' Over It

Concerns:

ANYTHING ELSE SPECIAL ABOUT YOUR CHILD TODAY?

FIGURE 9.3
Setting events checklist

challenging behavior from individuals closest to the child. These individuals may include family members, teachers, child-care providers, educational assistants, and related service providers. A consultant, case-manager, or program administrator can facilitate the interviews in a one-to-one format or as a team. The purpose of the interview is to describe the problem behavior, identify physical and environmental factors that reliably result in the occurrence of the behavior, and determine the potential functions of the behavior and the consequences that maintain it (O'Neill et al., 1990). Information from each of these areas can assist in developing hypotheses regarding the function(s) of the challenging behavior(s). The FAI can also aid in identifying variables that can be targeted through direct observation and/or environmental arrangements. This information can be helpful in designing interventions to decrease the probability that the child will engage in the challenging behavior.

The Functional Analysis Interview should be conducted during the initial stages of the functional assessment process. This will help to rule out any medical or physical issues that may be causing the child to engage in challenging behavior. The information from the interview will help target times of the day where the challenging behavior is and is not likely to occur. It will also identify variables (e.g., antecedents, hypothesized functions, and consequences) that are likely to occur while the child is observed. This will help in targeting the key times and activities for later direct observation.

The advantages of the FAI are that it assists in obtaining information regarding the potential function of the challenging behavior. It provides information about the setting events, antecedents, and consequences of challenging behavior. This information, in turn, allows one to hypothesize a function of the challenging behavior. The interview also provides information about the efficiency of the child's challenging behavior (e.g., rate, quality) and immediacy of reinforcement delivered contingent on the occurrence of the behavior

Due to the length of the Functional Assessment Interview, it can be time-consuming to complete and it may be difficult to determine which events are related to specific challenging behaviors. In addition, information reported by staff during an interview may not be objective and reliable. Staff may tend to provide opinions rather than facts, and different staff familiar with the

same child may respond differently to the same set of interview questions.

Direct Observation Assessments Direct observation assessments are another important component of functional assessment. The child is observed directly in the context of his or her natural environment and the form of the challenging behavior, and its antecedents and consequences, are recorded.

There are arrays of direct observation procedures. These vary in the type of information that they provide and the extent to which the information assists in developing hypotheses about the factors that predict and maintain a behavior. These include (a) Scatterplot, (b) Antecedent/Behavior/Consequence (ABC) Analysis, and (c) the Functional Analysis Direct Observation.

The *Scatterplot* (Touchette, MacDonald & Langer, 1985) is an interval recording method that provides general information concerning the distribution of occurrences of challenging behaviors across a day (see Figure 9.4). Initially, the Scatterplot observation system can be used to verify information obtained through the interview process. At this point, it may be conducted in order to isolate activities or times of the day that warrant more elaborate systems of direct observation (e.g., ABC Analysis or Functional Analysis Direct Observation). The Scatterplot observation system may also be utilized throughout the entire functional assessment process. It may be useful to verify times of the day when the behavior is and is not likely to occur. Additionally, the Scatterplot can easily be used by parents and/or educators, thus allowing for observation to be conducted in the absence of an outside observer. The following step-by-step directions describe how to complete the Scatterplot.

1. Define the target behavior. This information can be gathered from the interview information.
2. Complete the "key." There are several ways to use the key, which is a benefit of the Scatterplot. For example: When observing one behavior put a

Scatterplot

Name:_____

Description of behavior(s) of interest:_____

_____

Directions: At the end of each time interval, fill in the square indicating the appropriate time and date
on the chart using the code given below.

_____ ☐   _____ ☐   _____ ☐   _____ ☐

Time

Date																			

FIGURE 9.4

Distribution of occurrences of challenging behaviors across a day
Note: Reprinted with permission from Touchette, P. E., MacDonald, R. F., & Langer, S. N. (1985). A Scatterplot for Identifying
Stimulus Control of Problem Behavior. *Journal of Applied Behavior Analysis, 18,* 343–351.

slash in the box when the behavior occurs ◰. For two behaviors cross the slash so it becomes an X ⊠. Color in the entire box when all three behaviors occur ■.

3. Complete the time intervals. To get the most accurate data the intervals should be relatively small (10 to 20 minutes).

4. Complete the date at the bottom of the form. Several days of data can be collected on one form.

After completing these steps, the Scatterplot is ready to use. When the child engages in the defined challenging behavior it is recorded in the specific time interval using the appropriate code as described in the key. After several days of data are collected, a visble pattern should emerge.

The Scatterplot is relatively easy to use and interpret, thus allowing the observer to pinpoint the time periods during the day in which the identified challenging behavior is highly likely and highly unlikely to occur. This can then be followed up with a more detailed assessment during specific time periods.

However, the Scatterplot does not provide information regarding setting events, immediate antecedents, or consequences that may be associated with the challenging behavior. It also does not provide information regarding the antecedents or consequences that precede or follow the child's engagement in challenging behavior.

The antecedent/behavior/consequence analysis (ABC) is a method of direct observation that involves the use of narrative to record the immediate antecedents and consequences present each time the behavior(s) of interest are emitted by the child (Sulzer-Azaroff & Mayer, 1986) (see Figure 9.5). In addition to identifying the frequency with which a particular challenging behavior occurred, the ABC analysis allows further defining and delineating of the events, activities, and contingencies that are in place when challenging behaviors occur.

The ABC Analysis may be conducted once it has been determined where and when the child is likely to engage in challenging behaviors. This

information may be obtained via the interview process and later confirmed through the use of a Scatterplot observation system. The information obtained from the ABC analysis may assist in identifying the behaviors and the environmental events that require further analysis. Additionally, this method of direct observation may enable the observer to refine an objective definition of the challenging behavior, as well as suggest additional factors maintaining and controlling the behavior that were not identified during indirect methods of assessment. The following steps describe how to complete an ABC analysis.

1. The first step is to define the target behavior. While the ABC analysis may help you pin down the specific challenging behavior, prior to collecting data it is helpful to have a general definition of the target behavior(s).

2. Next, observe and record the behavior. An ABC log can be completed by an observer or completed by any member of the teaching team or family. For each instance of target behavior record what happened right before the behavior (the antecedent), record the behavior, and record what happened immediately following the behavior (the consequence). It is also helpful to record the date and time the behavior occurred and any additional comments that are necessary.

3. The last step in completing the ABC analysis is summarizing the data. To do this, the teacher examines each column. For example, the teacher would look at the antecedent column for patterns, such as behaviors occurring more frequently during a particular activity, with a particular peer, with a particular teacher, when the teacher is working with another child, during a transition, or when the child is asked to stop playing with a toy. Additionally, the teacher would look at the consequence column for patterns such as, is the child getting out of the activity, is he/she getting teacher attention, or does he/she get more time with a toy? As patterns emerge, the team has more information regarding antecedents and function.

ABC Analysis

Name:_____

Description of behavior(s) of interest: _____

_____

_____

Date	Time	Antecedent	Behavior	Consequence	Comments

FIGURE 9.5

Record of the immediate antecedents and consequences of challenging behavior

Note: Reprinted with permission from Reichle, J., & Johnston, S. (1993). Replacing Challenging Behavior: The Role of Communication Intervention. *Topics in Language Disorders, 13,* 61–76. Copyright © 1993, Aspen Publishers, Inc., www.aspenpub.com.

The ABC analysis, while relatively time-consuming, provides specific information about the antecedents and consequences that surround challenging behavior. It also confirms information obtained during the interview process.

Functional Analysis Direct Observation (O'Neill et al., 1990; 1997) is a system that appears to combine many of the advantages of the previously discussed direct observation systems. This form shown in Figure 9.6 is similar to the Scatterplot format in that the grid allows the observer to record the occurrence of challenging behavior relative to the time of day (vertical axis). It is also similar to the ABC data collection system in that it also includes information about the occurrence of challenging behavior relative to specific setting events, antecedents, and consequences. The form also allows the observer to identify patterns of occurrence and nonoccurrence of the challenging behavior(s), identify relationships between and among different challenging behaviors, and speculate on the possible function of each occurrence of challenging behavior. In addition, this assessment is capable of collecting frequency data on the number of occurrences of behavior when behaviors are discrete.

The Functional Analysis Direct Observation should be conducted just following the functional analysis interview. This will enable the observer to retrieve pertinent information from the interview and place it on the direct observation form. Conducting the Functional Analysis Direct Observation following the interview process enables the observer to identify the most relevant times of the day in which the child should be observed. On some occasions a completed Functional Analysis Direct Observation form will be easily interpreted. Clear patterns may emerge that may help in determining the function of challenging behavior. At other times, a more systematic look at the patterns of challenging behavior using an environmental manipulation (or functional analysis) procedure may be necessary. The following provides step-by-step directions on how to complete the Functional Analysis Direct Observation.

1. Information from the interview, Scatterplot, and ABC analysis is used to complete the target behaviors section. List the five behaviors that occur the most frequently or are the highest priority.

2. The "Predictors" section is partially completed and additionally predictors can be added as information emerges from the indirect measures.

3. The "Perceived Functions" section is divided into two major categories—to obtain and to escape. In addition there are two blank columns as well as an "other/don't know" column and two "actual consequences" columns. These blank columns can be completed using the information from other indirect and direct measures.

4. The time intervals are recorded in the far left column. Like with the Scatterplot, smaller increments (approximately 20 minutes) are recommended.

5. When the top and far left column are completed, the form is ready to use. To record instances of challenging behavior, antecedents, and consequences a numerical system is used. For the first instance of challenging behavior, record a 1 in the column below that target behavior and in the appropriate time interval row. Next, go across to the predictor section and record a 1 in the same time interval row and under the specific predictor. Finally, record a 1 in the same row under the specific consequence column. For the next instance of problem behavior, record a 2 in the target behavior column and in the appropriate time interval row and across the predictors and consequences sections. Continue collecting additional data in this way. Each new instance of behavior is a new number.

6. After using #1 to record that specific behavior, cross out #1 at the bottom of the page in the row titled events.

The advantages of using the Functional Analysis Direct Observation form are many. It can assist in identifying and/or verifying potential antecedents/setting events, potential functions that the challenging behavior may serve for the child, and consequences that are typically

Name:

Starting Date: Ending Date:

Functional Analysis Direct Observation Form

	Behaviors					Predictors									Perceived Functions: Get/Obtain				Perceived Functions: Escape/Avoid						Actual Conseq.	
Time						DemandRequest	Difficult Task	Transition	Interruption	Alone (no attention)					Attention	Desired Item/Activity	Self-Stimulation		Demand/Request	Activity ( )	Person		Other/Don't Know			Comments (if nothing happened in period, write initials.)
Totals																										

Events: 1 2 3 4 5 6 7 8 9 10 11 12 13 14 15 16 17 18 19 20 21 22 23 24 25

Date:

FIGURE 9.6

Record of challenging behavior, antecedents and consequences, and potential function(s).

Note. From *Functional Assessment and Program Development for Problem Behavior: A Practical Handbook*, 2nd edition, by R. E. O'Neil, R. H. Horner, R. W. Albin, J. R. Sprague, K. Storey, J. Newton. c. 1997. Reprinted with permission of Wadsworth, an imprint of the Wadsworth Group, a division of Thomson Learning. Fax 800-730-2215.

provided when the challenging behavior occurs. It provides a frequency count of each of the challenging behaviors being observed. In addition, it helps identify a possible connection between antecedents and consequences and a particular challenging behavior. One disadvantage is that the use of the form requires training that can be time-consuming.

In summary, there are a number of direct observation strategies available for use in the functional assessment of challenging behaviors. Each of these strategies provides a different breadth and/or depth of information. Therefore, prior to selecting any particular strategy or combination of strategies, the observer must consider the relative advantages and disadvantages. Factors to consider include: (a) frequency of behavior (high versus low), (b) breadth of data necessary (the need to identify times when behavior is likely to occur versus the need to conduct an in-depth analysis of variables that predict or maintain the challenging behavior), and (c) resources available to implement the assessment strategy (e.g., staff availability)(Cone & Foster, 1982).

It is also important to recognize that all direct observation data is correlational and not causal (Iwata et al., 1990; Mace et al., 1991; Pyles & Bailey, 1990; Sasso et al., 1992). Therefore, it is not possible to infer causation based on direct observation. Further analysis is necessary to ascertain the actual variables that are responsible for challenging behavior.

In some instances, direct observations in natural environments may not be sufficient. This is because it may be difficult to isolate the specific variables that are associated with challenging behavior. When direct observation is insufficient, an environmental manipulation (also known as a functional analysis) may be necessary.

Environmental Manipulation
In an environmental manipulation, or functional analysis, the hypothesis of interest is verified directly through manipulation and replication (Iwata et al., 1990). Therefore, it provides the greatest possible precision and confidence in building an understanding of when, where, and why problem behaviors occur (O'Neill et al., 1997). The basic idea of an environmental manipulation is to observe incidents of challenging behavior during at least two analogue conditions. In one condition (usually considered the experimental condition) the variable predicted to produce or maintain challenging behavior is presented, and in the other condition (the control condition) the variable is absent. All other variables remain constant throughout the conditions. The goal is to demonstrate differential effects and then to reveal consistent patterns in the data (Iwata et al., 1990).

A number of investigators have discussed the use of environmental manipulation assessments as an adjunct to direct observations and/or indirect assessments (Reichle & Johnston, 1993; Durand, 1990; O'Neill et al., 1990, 1997). During antecedent environmental manipulations, a specific variable (for instance, attention) is manipulated before challenging behavior has occurred. For example, consider an environmental manipulation implemented to confirm that a child's challenging behavior is sensitive to rates of adult attention. In one condition of the assessment, a teacher may provide a child with constant attention as the child completes a task. In another condition of the assessment, the teacher may provide the child with minimal attention during the same task. The presentation of the two conditions (i.e., constant and minimal attention) is noncontingent upon any behavior that the child emits. If the child's behavior were sensitive to rates of teacher attention, then one would expect the challenging behavior to *increase* under the condition where the teacher attention is minimal.

During consequence environmental manipulations, several variables are examined sequentially. For example, the educator may be considering attention and escape as possible functions of challenging behavior. To confirm the function, a minimum of three different conditions would be tested: attention, escape, and play. In the first condition, the teacher delivers attention following any instance of the challenging behavior. In the second condition, the teacher removes the task when challenging behavior occurs. In the third condition, the child is given free access to preferred items and attention (regardless of the occurrence or nonoccurrence of challenging behavior) while task demands are minimal. In this way, the occurrence of challenging behavior is influenced through antecedent and consequence manipulations, and compared across conditions. If challenging behavior occurs more often in one particular condition than the others, this would indicate the potential function of the challenging behavior.

Environmental manipulation assessments are a helpful means of testing hypotheses of the function or functions that challenging behavior serves. These hypotheses are generated after obtaining other functional assessment information (e.g., MAS, Functional Analysis Interview, ABC Analysis, Scatterplots, Functional Analysis Direct Observation) that can help narrow the variables that influence the occurrence and nonoccurrence of the challenging behavior. When the hypothesized functions cannot be confirmed adequately, an environmental manipulation becomes useful. Environmental manipulations can be most useful with behaviors that are not dangerous or life threatening, and that occur frequently (several times per day), at predictable times of day, or during predictable activities. Due to the risk of provoking challenging behavior, it is important that the interventionist is well trained and has the resources necessary to keep all participants of an environmental manipulation safe.

O'Neill et al (1990) outlined a number of factors that should be examined prior to implementing environmental manipulations. Environmental manipulations should (a) only be used when it is possible for the interventionist to manipulate the potentially relevant variables, (b) weighed against the potential risks to the individual, as well as other involved people, and (c) only be implemented after receiving the required consent for its implementation. The potential benefits of this procedure should be balanced against the safety of the individual, the interventionist, and others in the environment.

DESIGNING INTERVENTION PROGRAMS

Functional Behavioral Assessment procedures were designed to promote the development of positive, proactive interventions (Dunlap et al., 1993). With information about both the form and the function of the challenging behavior, interventions can be selected that focus on the antecedents as well as the consequences of the behavior. This can be accomplished by (a) altering the antecedents that predict challenging behavior, (b) establishing or strengthening the response–reinforce relationship for a more appropriate behavior, and (c) weakening the maintaining response–reinforcer relationship (Dunlap et al., 1991; Neilsen, 2001).

Recently, the Division for Early Childhood (DEC) developed a position statement on challenging behavior (DEC, 1998). In the statement, the organization specifically noted there are numerous services that can be added to a child's natural environment to promote appropriate behavior while decreasing challenging behavior. In addition, DEC points out that families must play a critical role in designing and carrying out interventions for challenging behavior if they are to be effective. Thus the role of the educator is to work with the family to select interventions that have been proven effective. These may include curricular revisions, environmental adaptations, or specific behavioral interventions focused on the child that address both form and function.

One goal of any intervention should be to teach children behaviors that, to the greatest extent possible, honor the function of the behavior but are socially appropriate (i.e., incompatible with challenging behavior). Thus, the new behaviors must be both **functionally equiva-**

lent to and **more efficient** than the challenging behaviors. A functionally equivalent behavior serves the same purpose as the challenging behavior. An efficient behavior is one that the child can produce with ease. Thus, the new socially acceptable behavior must be easier to produce than the challenging behavior while recruiting the desired outcome (or function) within a short period of time. For example, if David engages in tantrum behavior (i.e., crying, lying on floor, stomping feet, throwing objects) in order to escape a nonpreferred activity, it is reasonable to conclude that teaching him to touch a symbol that indicates *I want to take a break* would require less effort than the challenging behavior. The use of this new response would also make it possible for David to escape the task sooner than the demonstration of the old behaviors.

When replacing socially motivated challenging behaviors with communicative alternatives, the educator or parent must decide whether or not to "honor," or reinforce, the function of the child's challenging behavior. For example, in some situations it is entirely appropriate to honor a function. Consider Clare, who acts aggressively on the playground because she wants to participate in a game with her peers. In this situation, Clare may be taught to request access to the group (e.g., teach her to sign *Play please*), and it is likely that she will be reinforced (i.e., provided with an opportunity to play with her peers) each time she uses this communicative function. In other situations, it may be acceptable for the child's communicative function to be honored, but on a temporary basis only. For example, Christina may engage in tantrum behavior in order to gain access to soda pop at mealtimes. Initially, her parents may choose to teach her an appropriate means of requesting this preferred beverage at mealtimes and for a short time will provide her with soda pop each time she asks appropriately. However, over the course of time, they plan to have Christina choose a more nutritious beverage to drink with her meal.

There are, however, situations where educators and families are unable to honor a child's communicative intent because it may be harmful to his health or well-being. For example, Franco screams and hits when asked to take his seizure medication. In this situation, it is not appropriate for him to avoid the medication. As a result, it is important to consider carefully whether or not Franco's communicative function will be reinforced prior to choosing a communicative replacement as an intervention strategy.

SUMMARY

The available literature suggests that determining the *function* of a challenging behavior and subsequently designing an intervention based on it results in a decrease in the challenging behavior. The process that has been used to obtain information regarding the function of a challenging behavior is referred to as a **Functional Behavioral Assessment** (Durand, 1990; Horner et al., 1990). A functional assessment is a process of determining the relationship between events in a person's environment and the occurrence of challenging behaviors. A number of methods have been discussed for collecting functional assessment information. These functional assessment methods can be divided into the categories of indirect assessments, direct observation assessments, and environmental manipulations. The decision regarding which method or combination of methods of functional assessment and subsequent intervention to implement will depend upon factors such as the frequency of the behavior, the information needed to meet the goals of a functional assessment, and the resources (e.g., staff time) available (Neilsen, Olive, Donovan, & McEvoy, 1999). Considering both the form and function of behavior will assist in designing effective positive interventions that teach children more effective and efficient ways to communicate, while at the same time eliminating challenging behavior.

· · · · · · · ·
SUMMARY OF KEY CONCEPTS

- Most challenging behavior is reinforced by the consequences that follow it.
- For some children, challenging behavior becomes an effective and efficient way to communicate their wants and needs.
- The most effective way to assess challenging behavior is by conducting a Functional Behavioral Assessment.
- A Functional Behavioral Assessment is mandated through state and federal special education laws.
- A Functional Behavioral Assessment provides information about what the challenging behav-

ior looks like (form) and why the child is engaging in the behavior (function).
- The primary functions of challenging behavior are to obtain something (e.g., attention, toy) or escape something (e.g., difficult task, teacher attention). Occasionally, challenging behavior may serve a sensory function.
- A Functional Behavioral Assessment includes interviews, observations, and other types of data collection. In addition, if the function is not clear, an environmental manipulation may be necessary.
- The most effective interventions are those that address both the form and function of behavior.

· · · · · · · ·
REFERENCES

Alberto, P. A. & Troutman, A. C. (1999). *Applied behavior analysis for teachers* (5th ed.). Upper Saddle River, NJ: Simon & Schuster.

Asmus, J. M., Wacker, D. P., Harding, J., Berg, W., Derby, K. M., & Kocis, E. (1999). Evaluation of antecedent stimulus parameters for the treatment of escape-maintained aberrant behavior. *Journal of Applied Behavior Analysis, 32,* 495–513.

Axelrod, S. (1987). Functional and structural analysis of behavior: Approaches leading to reduced use of punishment procedures. *Research in Developmental Disabilities, 8,* 165–178.

Blair, K., Umbreit, J. & Eck, S. (2000). Analysis of multiple variables related to a young child's aggressive behavior. *Journal of Positive Behavior Interventions, 2,* 33–39.

Buscemi, L., Bennett, T., Thomas, D., & Deluca, D. A. (1995). Head Start: Challenges and training needs. *Journal of Early Intervention, 20*(1), 1–13.

Carr, E. G. & Durand, V. M. (1985). Reducing behavior problems through functional communication training. *Journal of Applied Behavior Analysis, 18*(2), 111–126.

Carr, E. G., Horner, R. H., Turnbull, A. P. (1999). *Positive behavioral support for people with developmental disabilities.* Washington, DC: American Association on Mental Retardation.

Carr, E. G., Newsom, C. D., & Binkoff, J. A. (1976). Stimulus control of self-destructive behavior in a psychotic child. *Journal of Abnormal Child Psychology, 4*(2), 139–153.

Carr, E. G., Robinson, S. & Palumbo, L. W. (1990). The wrong issue: Aversive versus nonaversive treatment. The right issue: Functional versus nonfunctional treatment. In A. C. Repp, & N. N Singh (Eds.), *Perspectives in the use of nonaversive and aversive interventions for persons with developmental disabilities* (pp. 361–379). Chicago: Sycamore.

Carr, E. G., Taylor, J. C., & Robinson, S. (1991). The effects of severe behavior problems in children on the teaching behavior of adults. *Journal of Applied Behavior Analysis, 24*(3), 523–535.

Chandler, L. K, & Dahlquist, C. M. (2002). *Functional assessment: Strategies to prevent and remediate challenging behavior in school settings.* Upper Saddle River, NJ: Merrill/Prentice Hall.

Cone, J. D., & Foster, S. L. (1982). Direct observation in clinical psychology. In P. L.. Kendall & J. N. Butcher (Eds.), *Handbook of research methods in clinical psychology.* New York: Wiley.

Davis, C. A., Brady, M. P., Williams, R. E., & Hamilton, R. (1992). Effects of high-probability requests on the acquisition and generalization of responses to requests in young children with behavior disorders. *Journal of Applied Behavior Analysis, 25*(4), 905–916.

Day, H. M., Horner, R. H., & O'Neill, R. E. (1994). Multiple functions of problem behaviors: Assessment and intervention. *Journal of Applied Behavior Analysis, 27*(2), 279–289.

Division for Early Childhood (DEC) (1998, April). Division for Early Childhood (DEC) Position statement on interventions for challenging behavior. Denver, CO: Author. (www.dec-sped.org).

Doss, L. S., & Reichle, J. (1991). Replacing excess behavior with an initial communicative repertoire. In J. Reichle, J. York, & J. Sigafoos (Eds.), *Implementing augmentative and alternative communication: Strategies for learners with severe disabilities.* Baltimore: Paul H. Brookes.

Dunlap, G. & Fox, L. (1996). Early intervention and serious problem behaviors: A comprehensive approach. In L. Kern-Dunlap, R. Koegel, & G. Dunlap (Eds.), *Positive behavioral support: Including people with difficult behaviors in the community* (pp. 31–50). Baltimore: Paul H. Brookes.

Dunlap, G., Kern-Dunlap, L., Clarke, S., & Robbins, F. (1991). Functional assessment, curricular revision, and severe behavior problems. *Journal of Applied Behavior Analysis, 24*(2), 387–397.

Dunlap, G., Kern, L., dePerczel, M., Clarke, S., Wilson, D., Childs, K., E., et al. (1993). Functional analysis of classroom variables for students with emotional and behavioral disorders. *Behavioral Disorders, 18*(4), 275–291.

Durand, V. M. (1982). Analysis and intervention of self-injurious behavior. *Journal for the Association of Severe Handicaps, 7* (Winter), 44–53.

Durand, V. M. (1990). *Severe behavior problems: A functional communication training approach.* New York: Guilford Press.

Durand, V. M., & Carr, E. G. (1987). Social influences on "self-stimulatory" behavior: Analysis and treatment application. *Journal of Applied Behavior Analysis, 20*(2), 119–132.

Durand, V. M., & Crimmins D. B. (1990). Assessment. In V. M. Durand (Ed.), *Severe behavior problems: A functional communication training approach* (pp. 31–82). New York: Guilford.

Feil, E. & Becker, W. (1993). Investigation of a multiple-gated screening system for preschool behavior problems. *Behavior Disorders, 19*(1), 44–53.

Gunter, P. L., Shores., R. E., Jack, S. L., Denny, R. K., & DePaepe, P. A. (1994). A case study of the effects of altering instructional interactions on the disruptive behavior of a child identified with severe behavior disorders. *Education and Treatment of Children, 17*(3), 435–444.

Haring, T. G. & Kennedy, C. H. (1990). Contextual control of problem behavior in students with severe disabilities. *Journal of Applied Behavior Analysis, 23*(2), 235–243.

Hemmeter, M. L. (1999). Introduction: Practical ideas for addressing challenging behavior. In S. Sandall and M. Ostrosky (Eds.), *Practical ideas for addressing challenging behavior* (pp.1–2). Denver: Sopris West.

Horner, R. H. (1994). Functional Behavioral Assessment: Contributions and future directions. *Journal of Applied Behavior Analysis, 27*(1), 401–404.

Horner, R. H. & Carr, E. G. (1997). Behavioral support for students with severe disabilities: Functional Behavioral Assessment and comprehensive intervention. *The Journal of Special Education, 31*(1), 84–104.

Iwata, B. A., Dorsey, M. F., Slifer, K. J., Bauman, K. E., & Richman, G. S. (1982). Toward a functional analysis of self-injury. *Analysis and Intervention in Developmental Disabilities, 2,* 3–20.

Iwata, B., Pace, G. M., Dorsey, M. F., Zarcone, J. R., Vollmer, T. R., Smith, R. G., et al. (1994). The function of self-injurious behavior: An experimental-epidemiological analysis. *Journal of Applied Behavior Analysis, 27*(2), 215–240.

Iwata, B. A., Pace, G. M., Kalsher, M. J., Cowdery, G. E., & Cataldo, M. F. (1990). Experimental analysis and extinction of self-injurious escape behavior. *Journal of Applied Behavior Analysis, 23*(1), 11–27.

Iwata, B. A., Vollmer, T. R., & Zarcone, J. R. (1990). The experimental (functional) analysis of behavior disorders: Methodology, applications, and limitations. In A. C. Repp, & N. N. Singh (Eds.), *Perspectives on the use of nonaversive and aversive interventions for persons with developmental disabilities* (pp. 301–330). Chicago: Sycamore.

Katsiyannis, A. & Maag, J. (1998). Disciplining students with disabilities: Issues and considerations for implementing IDEA '97. *Behavioral Disorders, 23*(4), 276–289.

Kern, L., Childs, K. E., Dunlap, G., Clarke, S., & Falk, G. (1994). Using assessment-based curricular interventions to improve the classroom behavior of a student with emotional and behavioral challenges. *Journal of Applied Behavior Analysis, 27*(1), 7–19.

Lalli, J. S., Browder, D., Mace, F. C. & Brown, D. K. (1993). Teacher use of descriptive analysis data to implement interventions to decrease students' problem behaviors. *Journal of Applied Behavior Analysis, 26*(2), 227–238.

Lalli, J. S. & Goh. H. (1993). Naturalistic observations in community settings. In R. Reichle, & D. Wacker (Eds.), *Communicative alternatives to challenging behavior: Integrating functional assessment and intervention strategies* (Vol. 3, pp. 11–39). Baltimore: Paul H. Brookes.

Lovaas, O.I, Freitag, G., Gold, V. J., Kassorla, I. C. (1965). Experimental studies in childhood schizophrenia: Analysis of self-destructive behavior. *Journal of Experimental Child Psychology, 2,* 67–84.

Mace, F. C. (1994). The significance and future of functional analysis methodologies. *Journal of Applied Behavior Analysis, 27*(2), 385–392.

Mace, F. C., Lalli, J. S., & Lalli, E. P. (1991). Functional analysis and treatment of aberrant behavior. *Research in Developmental Disabilities, 12,* 155–180.

McEvoy, M. A. & Reichle, J. (2002). Further consideration of the role of the environment on stereotypic and self-injurious behavior. *Journal of Early Intervention, 23,* 22–23.

Neilsen, S. L, (2001). M. A., Extending positive behavioral support to young children with challenging behavior. Unpublished doctoral dissertation. University of Minnesota, Minneapolis.

Neilsen, S., Olive, M. L., Donovan, A. & McEvoy, M. A. (1999). Challenging behaviors in your classroom? Don't react—teach instead! In S. Sandall and M. Ostrosky (Eds.), *Practical ideas for addressing challenging behavior* (pp 5–15). Denver: Sopris West.

Office of Special Education Programs (1997). *Memorandum 97–7. Initial disciplinary guidance related to removal of children with disabilities from their current educational placement for 10 school days or less.* U.S. Department of Education.

O'Neill, R. E., Horner, R. H., Albin, R., Sprague, K., Storey, K., & Newton, J. (1991). *Functional Behavioral Assessment and program development for problem behaviors.* Pacific Grove: Brooks/Cole.

O'Neill, R. E., Horner, R. H., Albin, R., Sprague, K., Storey, K., & Newton, J. (1997). *Functional Behavioral Assessment and program development for*

problem behaviors: A practical handbook. Pacific Grove: Brooks/Cole.

Piazza, C. C., Hanley, G. P., Bowman, L. G., Ruyter, J. M., Lindauer, S. E., & Saionta, D. M. (1997). Functional analysis and treatment of elopement. *Journal of Applied Behavior Analysis, 30*(4), 653–672.

Pyles, D. A. M., & Bailey, J. S. (1990). Diagnosing severe behavior problems. In A. Repp, & N. N. Singh (Eds.), *Perspectives on the use of nonaversive and aversive intervention for persons with developmental disabilities* (pp. 381–401). Chicago: Sycamore.

Reichle, J., Davis, C., Freeman, R., & Horner, R. (1999). Effective behavioral support for socially maintained problem behavior. In N. Wieseler and R. Hanson (Eds.), *Challenging behavior of persons with mental health disorders and severe developmental disabilities* (pp. 237–260). Reston, VA: AAMR Books.

Reichle, J., & Johnston, S. J. (1993). Replacing challenging behavior: The role of communication intervention. *Topics in Language Disorders,* 13(3), 61–76.

Repp, A. C., Felce, D., & Barton, L. E. (1988). Basing the treatment of stereotypic and self-injurious behaviors on hypotheses of their causes. *Journal of Applied Behavior Analysis, 21*(3), 281–289.

Sasso, G. M., Reimers, T. M., Cooper, L. J., Wacker, D., Berg, W., Steege, M., Kelly, L., & Allaire, A. (1992). Use of descriptive and experimental analyses to identify the functional properties of aberrant behavior in school settings. *Journal of Applied Behavior Analysis, 25*(4), 809–821.

Sinclair, E., Del'Homme, M. & Gonzalez, M. (1993). Systematic screening for preschool behavioral disorders. *Behavioral Disorders, 18*(3), 177–188.

Strain, P. S., McConnell, S. R., Carta, J. J., Fowler, S. A., Neisworth, J. T., & Wolery, M. (1992). Behaviorism in early intervention. *Topics in Early Childhood Special Education, 12*(1), 121–141.

Sugai, G., Lewis-Palmer, T. & Hagan, S. (1998). Using functional assessments to develop behavior support plans. *Preventing School Failure, 43*(1), 6–13.

Sulzer-Azaroff, B. C., & Mayer, G. R. (1986). *Achieving educational excellence using behavioral strategies.* New York: Rinehart & Winston.

Taylor, J. C. (1994). Functional assessment and functionally-derived treatment for child behavior problems. *Special Services in the Schools, 9*(1), 39–67.

Thomas, D. R., Becker, W. C., & Armstrong, M. (1968). Production and elimination of disruptive classroom behavior by systematically varying teachers' behavior. *Journal of Applied Behavior Analysis, 1*(1), 35–45.

Touchette, P. E., MacDonald, R. F., & Langer, S. N. (1985). A Scatterplot for identifying stimulus control of problem behavior. *Journal of Applied Behavior Analysis, 18*(4), 343–351.

Umbreit, J. & Blair, K. (1997). Using structural analysis to facilitate treatment of aggression and noncompliance in a young child at-risk for behavioral disorders. *Behavioral Disorders, 22*(2), 75–86.

Vaughn, B. & Horner, R. H. (1995). Effects of concrete versus verbal choice systems on problem behavior. *Augmentative and Alternative Communication, 11,* 89–92.

Assessing Cognitive Development

Katherine McCormick
Leah Nellis
University of Kentucky

RATIONALE

The assessment of cognition or intelligence has a long history in the fields of psychology and education. As early as 1869 Sir Francis Galton began work in measuring and quantifying mental characteristics, yet at the turn of the millennium many researchers and practitioners are still occupied with this task. Recent attention and advances in the cognitive sciences have expanded and broadened the concept of learning, and advances in measurement have increased the ability of science to interpret the complex phenomena of intelligence (Pelligrino, Chudowsky, & Glaser, 2001). The National Academy of Science released *From Neurons to Neighborhoods: The Science of Early Childhood Development* (Shonkoff & Phillips, 2000) to provide a synthesis of contemporary thought about early experience, development of the brain, and intelligence to the public and scientific communities. These scientists sought answers to some of the same questions asked by Galton and his colleagues. Why has so much thought and energy been expended toward the understanding and measurement of cognition? Three explanations are plausible. First, intelligence is highly valued as a human characteristic or capability. Second, cognition or intelligence is a multifaceted phenomenon confounded with many other domains of human behavior, thereby complicating its own identification. Finally, in order to arrive at an accurate measure of intelligence, the scientific community—educators, psychologists, developmental specialists—must agree on a common definition.

Defining intelligence is not an easy task. During a famous symposium in 1921, 13 eminent psychologists were asked to share their definitions of intelligence, which resulted in 13 different definitions. Science, however, has since made some progress toward consensus. In 1990, when asked to rate what they believed to be important elements of intelligence, 1,020 experts in psychology, sociology, education, and genetics rated three behavioral descriptions with greater than 96% agreement; the three descriptions were abstract thinking or reasoning, the capacity to acquire knowledge, and problem-solving ability (Sattler, 1990). Contemporary theories of learning and knowing focus on the way knowledge is "represented, organized and processed in the mind" (Pelligrino et al., p. 3). Current theories also emphasize the social dimensions of learning. Contemporary measurement theory and practice have benefited from advances in computer technology, statistical modeling, and analyses (Fewell, 2000). This chapter provides a brief historical perspective regarding the development of the concept of intelligence and cognition and the accompanying efforts to measure and validate this phenomenon.

Theoretical Perspectives on Cognitive Development

Cognitive Stage/Piagetian In 1952 Jean Piaget wrote, "It is indisputable that (traditional) tests of mental age have, on the whole, lived up to what was expected of them: a rapid and convenient estimate of an individual's general level. But it is no less obvious that they simply measure a 'yield' without reaching constructive operation themselves" (Hoy & Gregg, 1994, p. 230). Piaget was interested in two types of problem solving: logico-mathematical and physical knowledge. He hypothesized that reasoning and problem solving develop through sequential stages. Organization and adaptation, two basic processes important to Piaget, result from the use and practice of *schemas* and through the processes of *assimilation* and *accommodation*. An infant possesses very immature sensorimotor organizational systems, or schemas; as he or she interacts with objects, people, and environments, these schemas change and mature. The acquisition of new information is termed *assimilation;* the use of information to modify existing organizational structures is called *accommodation*. *Adaptation* is the process of assimilating new information and accommodating old information to make sense of both the new and the old.

Piaget hypothesized that the presentation of new information that did not fit with the old would cause the individual some mental discomfort, or what Piaget termed "disequilibration." He proposed that disequilibration is a motivating process that drives an individual to make things fit or establish equilibrium. Therefore, a need to understand the world and fit the new with the old is seen as cognitive maturity and development.

Piaget classified cognitive behaviors into four stages of development: sensorimotor, preoperational, concrete operational, and formal operational. The first stage, *sensorimotor,* encompasses approximately the first 2 years and consists of six substages. The second stage, *preoperational,* is usually observed in typically developing children between the ages of 2 and 7. The hallmark of this stage is symbolic representation—the understanding that a symbol represents an object. The child is also able to think and talk about objects and people not physically present.

Piagetian approaches to cognitive development attempt to measure qualitative differences in a child's reasoning rather than quantitative differences. Tests are constructed according to age levels, with item clusters that attempt to measure multiple aspects of cognition such as seriation, conservation, number and spatial concepts, object permanence, deductive and inductive logic, classification, and decentration. The use of these assessments requires a broad understanding of Piagetian theory for accurate interpretation and administration; however, the richness of the information obtained is worth the effort. This approach holds particular utility for the assessment of children with disabilities, especially those with severe impairments. The most commonly used Piagetian assessment tool for the sensorimotor period (birth to 24 months) was developed by Uzgiris and Hunt (1975) and expanded by Dunst (1980).

Information Processing   Information processing models of intelligence have been greatly influenced by the Russian psychologists Vygotsky and Luria (Hoy & Gregg, 1994). Vygotsky suggests that memory, attention, and conceptualizations are the products of the child's organization of object and social interactions. Vygotsky and Luria believe in the concept of mediated learning, especially when used by parents in early concept acquisition. Parents guide and mark or signal certain activities and objects for their child's attention. Therefore, intelligence is seen as the result of social learning experiences. Cognition develops through the child's internalization of social interactions and experiences (Hoy & Gregg).

A second example of an information processing model is provided by the work of Campione and Brown (1978), who developed their theory of intelligence using two basic components: an architectural system (the structural component) and an executive system (the control component). The architectural system acts as a scaffold comprised of capacity, durability (retention), and efficiency (speed of information encoded); the executive operates as the learned components, including knowledge, schemes, control processes, and metacognition (Sattler, 1990). The use of schemas appears again in this theory and is used to describe the active construction of the rules of thinking. The architectural system may be considered as the biologically/genetically based component of intelligence; the executive system refers to environmentally based components. The information processing approach is currently enjoying attention by the scientific community, especially the areas of metacognition and memory (Pelligrino et al., 2001). Current theorists are investigating the importance of the cognitive architecture including short- and long-term memory. Estimates of how people organize and retrieve information are of critical interest in understanding "what people know; how they know it; and how they are able to use that knowledge to answer questions, solve problems, and engage in additional learning" (Pelligrino et al., p. 3). For more information about contemporary theories and issues in the measurement of cognition and general knowledge, the reader is encouraged to review Pelligrino et al. (2001).

Social Learning Vygotsky and Luria conceptualized cognitive development in a social context. The concept of a "proximal zone of development" suggests that there is a zone that "reflects the distance between the actual developmental level as determined by independent problem solving and the level of potential development as determined through problem solving under adult guidance or in collaboration with more capable peers" (Vygotsky, 1978, p. 86). In other words, development occurs when a problem is presented that is just beyond the child's ability, and an adult or peer is able to mediate the experience to move the child to a new level of understanding (Anastasiow, 1986). Losardo and Notari-Syverson (2001) suggest that development occurs when children move from "other-regulation" to "self-regulation" (p. 7). Bandura (1978) also describes development through a social learning model termed *reciprocal determinism,* in which learning develops through the interaction of socialization, developmental status, environmental factors, and the child's motivation. In other words, the characteristics and properties of the environment in interaction with one another and with the child's thinking and judgment about his behavior account for the learning of new behavior and understanding of past and present behavior (Gage & Berliner, 1991).

Maturational/Developmental A major effort to establish developmental markers during the preschool years was undertaken in 1925 at the Yale Clinic for Child Development under the leadership of Arnold Gesell. Gesell and his fellow researchers postulated that development and growth were biologically predetermined. This maturational perspective hypothesized a time-bound developmental model in which qualitative change occurred in the young child at the "appropriate time." As children age and mature, their capabilities, behaviors, and cognitive development change. To document this maturational model, Gesell and his colleagues identified 150 items in four areas (motor, language, adaptive, and personal–social) and presented them as developmental schedules for 10 age levels (birth and 4, 6, 9, 12, 18, 24, 36, 48, and 60 months) (Kelly & Surbeck, 2000).

Functional The functional model of development owes its origin to operant learning theory from the field of psychology, typically referred to as behaviorism. In this model, all behavior is considered as learned behavior. All living organisms repeat behavior that is satisfying and avoid behavior that is not. Learning occurs as children practice a new behavior, find it functional, and experience reinforcing consequences (Peterson, 1987). The functional model is derived from the notion that the most critical and functional behaviors for the developing child are those that produce pleasing and positive interactions with people, objects, and environments. This model has as its major assumption that behavior is determined by the interaction of people and their environment. The most important principle associated with this approach is *reinforcement,* defined as an event that follows a response and that changes the probability of a response occurring again. For example, Skinner's explanation of learning is based on the premise that the consequences of behavior determine the probability that the behavior will occur again (Lefrancois, 1995).

Brain-Behavior Relationship Brain development is the process whereby specific brain regions reorganize and change allowing for the development of particular abilities, including cognition (Johnson, 1999). Scientific advances have resulted in both an increased understanding of and interest in the study of neuroscience and cognitive development in young children over recent years. A review of the research is beyond the scope of this chapter. Interested readers are directed to resources such as Kolb and Fantie (1997) and Johnson (1997) for a comprehensive discussion. Reflecting current research, a National Research Council and Institute of Medicine report authored by Shonkoff and Phillips (2000) articulates core concepts of human development to guide the efforts of parents, caregivers, and policy makers. Shonkoff and Phillips regard human development as a lifelong process of dynamic interactions between biology and one's cultural environment, in which children are active participants. The process of development is characterized by a series of significant transitions making individual differences likely and difficult to distinguish from more long-term disabilities. Effective early intervention is conceptualized as practices that enhance protective factors during a time when a vulnerability to risk continues but can potentially be diminished. The growing body of knowledge about brain-behavior relationships has the potential for impacting the practices of parenting, child care, and education. However, as Bailey, Bruer, Symons, and Lichtman (2001) point out, it is critical that such research be integrated and interpreted correctly by the public and political communities which shape policy, programs, and services in early childhood education.

Conclusions Witt, Elliott, Kramer, and Gresham (1994) suggest that in a general sense, cognition includes a broad spectrum of mental abilities that are often referred to as intelligence. In practice, however, it is the subsets of cognition, such as attention, memory, comprehension, and reasoning, that are of concern to educators and psychologists. This is not to say that our focus should remain on these component skills. Instead, contemporary theories seek to encompass the more complex aspects of learning and knowing (Pelligrino et al., 2001). Regardless of one's theoretical foundation, the assessment of cognition in young children is important for planning and for describing children's current developmental repertoire. Assessments may be used to determine program eligibility, to plan interventions, to identify environments and techniques by which development is facilitated, and to evaluate progress. By determining the abilities and information children possess and in what environments they are most likely to demonstrate these abilities, the most effective interventions can be designed, using the most efficient methods in the most natural environ-

ments. To attempt to provide intervention without an understanding of a child's present level of functioning would waste both resources and time. Because the cognitive development of young children is closely enmeshed with motor and communication behavior, the reader is directed to Chapters 11 and 12 to more fully understand this important area of development.

DIMENSIONS OF ASSESSMENT

Behaviors Typically Sampled by Cognitive Assessments

Discrimination, generalization, motor behavior, general information, vocabulary, comprehension, sequencing, analogies, abstract reasoning, and paired-associate learning are some of the behaviors typically sampled by cognitive assessments. Test developers must meet a level of adequacy in behaviors sampled while dealing with the attentional constraints of young children and examiners. As children age, the number of items must increase to measure more stable traits. Behavior sampling for infants and toddlers may include behaviors that require motor and sensory awareness and integration. During the early months, these motor and sensory behaviors are indicative of cognitive development. As children age and their behavioral repertoire expands, cognitive skills may be measured by a broader spectrum of behaviors, such as language, problem-solving tasks, vocabulary usage, and memory items.

Measurement Scales

There are four scales of measurements typically used in assessment: nominal, ordinal, ratio, and equal interval. *Nominal scales* use names or numbers to represent the variables; they use numbers without an inherent relationship to one another to name people or objects (Salvia & Ysseldyke, 2001). *Ordinal scales* order or rank objects, persons, or events. Numbers that are adjacent indicate higher or lower value;

however, the value is not always equivalent. For example, children can be ranked from first to last based on their ability to name the days of the week, but the difference in the rank between the first child and the second child may not be equal to the difference between the second and third children. The first child may have named all seven days, the second child only six, and the third child only two.

The magnitude of the difference between two adjacent values on *ratio scales* is equivalent. Weight is measured on a ratio scale; the difference between 15 and 16 pounds is the same as the difference between 150 and 151 pounds. Ratio scales have a second important attribute; they have an absolute zero (Salvia & Ysseldyke, 2001). A ratio scale without the absolute zero is an *interval scale*. The important characteristic of this scale is that ratios cannot be derived from an interval scale. Since intelligence is typically measured with an *equal-interval scale,* and there is no absolute zero, we cannot make comparisons using a ratio system. Therefore, an IQ of 100 is not twice as large as an IQ of 50. Many of the norm-referenced assessments of cognition described in this chapter are equal-interval scales; however, assessments that use an ordinal scale of measurement are becoming more widely used, especially for infants and young children with severe disabilities.

Quantification of Performance and Accompanying Cautions

It is difficult to accurately measure the behavioral and developmental status of infants and young children. Several assumptions must be recognized: (a) young children are bound more closely to biological development than are their older peers; (b) the limited communication abilities of young children may interfere with their ability to respond to or to understand verbal instruction; (c) distractibility and short attention span may compromise assessment outcomes; (d) separation issues occur throughout the preschool years; and (e) a lack of compliance or understanding of social relationships may also be evidenced (Lidz, 1991b).

When these problems are compounded by the presence of a disability, the examiner faces an especially challenging task in assessing a young child's cognitive ability.

Professionals must also be cautious in interpreting and ascribing an unwarranted level of confidence and meaning to the outcomes generated by evaluation or assessment tools. A test score tells only a small part of the story. For example, children can achieve the same score for entirely different reasons. Bobby might get all the items correct until a certain point and then miss them all; Joey, on the other hand, misses items throughout the test. Thus equivalent scores could result from very different responses. Closer examination may show that Joey missed only those items that required physical manipulation of objects or visual acuity. These tasks require a different and more difficult response if Joey has cerebral palsy or low vision. A discussion of various types of scores and accompanying information on validity and reliability is included in Chapter 2.

Stability of Early Development

Discontinuity, which is important to the issue of stability of cognitive development, characterizes the wide variety of behaviors in individual children and among children considered to be typically developing or "normal" (Neisworth & Bagnato, 1992). Young children display great variability in day-to-day performance; furthermore, their development is seldom parallel across developmental domains. Observations of young children and discussions with their parents suggest that development is often delayed in one area while the child uses his or her energies to master a behavior in another. Parents frequently describe a lapse in language development during the period when their children begin to walk and, similarly, a slower rate of motor development is reported when language development is expanding. This uneven pattern of development, which is normal for young children, cannot be accurately reflected in a single number.

The stability of cognitive development is even more important when considered in the context of transition periods—when a behavior is emerging but is not fully integrated in the child's repertoire. If assessment takes places during a developmental transition, the assessment may capture a less advanced version of the skill undergoing rapid change and progress. The more advanced skill may be displayed and preferred by the child within the next week (Neisworth & Bagnato, 1996). As children age, the rapid rate of development slows and the range of behaviors considered normal narrows (Bracken, 1991).

PROCEDURAL CONSIDERATIONS

Assumptions Underlying Assessment

In 1988 Salvia and Ysseldyke identified five assumptions that must be met for assessment information to be valid and reliable: the administrator is skilled; error will be present; acculturation is comparable; behavior sampling is adequate; and present behavior is observed, future behavior is inferred.

Administrator Is Skilled   When the behavior of children is measured by a test or measurement tool, at least three assumptions concerning the skills of the person administering the test are made: The person is (a) adequately trained, (b) proficient in establishing rapport, and (c) knowledgeable to administer the tool or test, score the responses, and interpret the outcomes (Salvia & Ysseldyke, 1988). These characteristics are critical in the assessment of infants and young children. Adequate training of personnel is a critical issue for many states that have not had a long history of providing services to infants, toddlers, and preschoolers with special needs. States must develop strategies that ensure appropriate licensure and certification for individ-

uals administering cognitive assessments or intelligence tests to young children. Decisions that affect the provision of services for children and their families must be made by individuals with adequate training. The establishment of rapport is equally important in the assessment of young children. Recommended practice requires the ability to observe children's behavior, respond, expand on their behavior, and elicit other behaviors in their repertoires. Rapport building and maintenance is a dynamic balance of interactions among the examiner, the child, and the family. As children age, this balance moves from observations of sensory, motor, and prelinguistic behaviors to those of concept development, language, and interaction with objects and social environments. The examiner must be able to adjust the rate of stimulus presentation, verbal input, and other variables that may affect the quality of the interaction between examiner and child and, therefore, the outcome of the assessment. The examiner must also be patient to increase the opportunities for observation and be skilled in eliciting information from caregivers and family members.

Administering, scoring, and interpreting standardized assessments are also skills the examiner must demonstrate. Proper administration and scoring ensure that the outcomes are an accurate measure of the child's performance against a norm group or criterion measure and provide useful information for programming. Assessments are continually being developed, revised, and restandardized. Individuals responsible for the administration of these assessments must maintain knowledge of current and available assessments and choose those most appropriate to the purpose of the assessment as well as to each child's characteristics. The interpretation of behaviors demonstrated by young children in a standardized assessment requires knowledge of both typical and atypical developmental patterns. The examiner must possess skill in evaluating a response within these parameters. In 1979 Cohen and Gross (1979a; 1979b) provided a useful guide for the identification of typical developmental sequences which is still relevant today; useful information regarding developmental sequences for children with disabilities can also be found in Wachs and Sheehan (1988).

Error Will Be Present Few psychological phenomena or constructs can be measured without error, either examiner error or instrument error. No matter how skilled and well trained, examiners will make some errors—in the administration of an item, the tabulation of the responses, or the scoring of the test. The amount of this deviance is reported as an error term. The size of this term is dependent on several factors, one of which is the age of the child being tested. For example, the error term for a 5-year-old on the *Kaufman Intelligence Test for Children* (Kaufman & Kaufman, 1983) is 8 points, while the error term for an 8-year-old is 5. The reported scores then might be 69 ± 8 and 69 ± 5. We can assume that the scores generated for 5-year-olds were less stable and therefore needed a wider band of error than those for 8-year-olds. Also important is the degree of certainty with which we want to treat the assigned score. For example, if we want to be right 99 times out of 100, the error term will be larger than if we widen our level of tolerance to 95 out of 100. Error can be systematic or random. The degree of systematic error indicates a bias that can be predicted; the degree of random error is less predictable and indicates the extent of the reliability of the outcome. Assessments demonstrate varying degrees of reliability. Reliability is also dependent on the age and characteristics of the child being assessed.

Acculturation Is Comparable The issue of comparable acculturation or experiences is possibly the most problematic assumption in the administration of norm-referenced tests of cognition or intelligence for young children with special needs. Simply stated, this assumption requires that the child being tested has participated in experiences similar to those of the group of children on which the assessment was normed;

this is questionable in a country with vast regional, cultural, linguistic, and social diversity. When children who learn in different ways and possess alternative strategies to process sensory, motor, or social information are included, the assumption may be stretched further than is reasonable. The assumption of comparable acculturation is even more tenuous when preschoolers are involved. Schooling provides somewhat common experiences in the 6-hour school day. As children proceed through these standard experiences, the appropriateness of comparisons increases, but for preschoolers this common experience is absent. The presence of a disability and potential differences in acculturation pose real problems in the assessment of children with disabilities. Therefore, many examiners and test developers are turning to assessments that allow for administration within the child's natural environment. Use of familiar toys, typical communication partners, and everyday environments may decrease this discrepancy. Professionals involved in the use of norm-referenced instruments must be cognizant of the issue of acculturation and explain possible problems when discussing assessment results with other professionals and parents.

Cultural uniqueness further complicates this assumption of comparable acculturation. Culture has a profound impact on every aspect of human development (Shonkoff & Phillips, 2000). In her classic work, Mercer (1979) suggests that intelligence tests used with children from culturally diverse backgrounds measure the level of acculturation rather than cognitive ability. The longer a family or a child has had to acquire behaviors valued by the dominant culture, the more valid the assessment will be. Limited experience in the dominant culture calls for considerable caution in the generation of indices of cognitive development.

Behavior Sampling Is Adequate Assessment must provide adequate opportunities for young children to demonstrate their unique abilities across multiple behaviors and response sets. For example, good cognitive assessments are neither completely verbal nor completely nonverbal in their makeup, but strive for adequate sampling of multiple behaviors indicative of cognitive development. Adequate behavioral sampling must, however, be balanced with efficiency. If five items provide equivalent information, test publishers will delete four, using only one, since the four are redundant. On the other hand, if each provides a unique opportunity for the child to demonstrate a particular skill, the inclusion of all five may be warranted. This balance is not an easy one and often is cause for caution when using assessments that attempt to measure abilities across a broad age range with few items.

The types of behavior that are sampled are important; the level of specificity of items is equally important. The sensitivity of an instrument to small differences in ability is indicated by the amount of change in a standard score when an additional item is passed or failed. Bracken (2000) uses the term *item-gradient* to describe this phenomenon. This difficulty is experienced frequently when norm-referenced instruments are used with young children. Examiners, early interventionists, teachers, and parents complain that a child "falls through the cracks" to describe a lack of item specificity or gradient. In other words, there are insufficient items to accurately reflect a child's ability. This problem is particularly evident with assessments such as the *Battelle Developmental Inventory* (BDI) (Newborg, Stock, Wnek, Guidubaldi, & Svinicki, 1984) that force scales downward with limited items to allow accurate discriminations between children at the younger ages.

Bracken (2000) also describes another important criterion related to behavioral sampling for preschool instruments. The term *floor* describes the degree to which a test discriminates among children at the lower range of ability. A test with a limited floor does not accurately sort children of differing ability levels who are functioning significantly below the mean (typically at least

2 standard deviations) or who are at the lowest age level. A parallel term, *ceiling*, applies to this problem at the upper end of ability or age levels. An inadequate floor is particularly troublesome in the assessment of preschoolers with disabilities, many of whom are performing significantly below the mean. The BDI again provides an excellent example of this problem. The lowest deviation quotient provided by the BDI is 65; therefore, many examiners assign this score to children who in fact demonstrate abilities far below this cutoff. Although this strategy is not inappropriate, it may be very misleading to parents and other team members. To remedy this difficulty, many examiners extrapolate raw scores below this cutoff for a more accurate reflection of the performance of the children tested (McLean, McCormick, Bruder, & Burdg, 1987). Extrapolation, however, does not produce normalized scores with equivalent psychometric characteristics. For assessments such as the Battelle, which can be used with children from birth to 8 years of age, we may assume that children in the middle of the age range (3 to 5 years) may experience the least difficulty with a floor or ceiling effect, while those at the extremes would be most affected.

Present Behavior Is Observed; Future Behavior Is Inferred It is this issue that appears to be the most difficult to address in the assessment of the cognitive development of preschoolers. The years between 3 and 5 provide a transition between poor and relatively good predictions of later cognitive development (Clark, 1982; Lidz, 1991a). Lidz states: "If preschool children were stable responders (which frequently they are not) and the assessment tools reliable and valid (which frequently they are not) diagnostic labels might at least be valid descriptors of the child's current levels of functioning, if not good predictors of future levels of functioning" (p. 20).

Factors Important in Assessment

Developmental History Preassessment strategies include good information gathering and discussion with parents, caregivers, day-care providers, and other team members. Parents and other caregivers can provide information concerning the acquisition of developmental milestones, medical history, names of family members, daily routines, occupations, and typical environments. This information is critical to the assessment process and provides the beginning building blocks for hypothesis generation and diagnostic planning. For children with motor or sensory disabilities, developmental histories can provide information to guide the selection of appropriate adaptations, aids, prosthetics, and assessment tools. Current medical and nutritional status as well as information regarding medications and daily schedules are also very important in guiding assessment planning.

Cultural Uniqueness Early intervention in the United States must respond to the increasing racial, ethnic, cultural, linguistic, urban/rural, socioeconomic, and educational diversity of infants, toddlers, and preschoolers with disabilities. Approximately one third of the U.S. population are people who define themselves as African American, Native American, Asian Pacific, Hispanic, or as other people of color, and diversity among young children is even greater (Chang, 1990, McAfee & Leong, 2002). Accurate and appropriate assessment of children from culturally diverse environments requires attention to the uniqueness of a child's culture and acknowledgment of the requirements of standardization. For example, attention to task or directions, solutions to social problems, and social interactions may be influenced by culture. Expressive skills and styles of interacting with adults are also influenced by cultural membership. Specific culturally dependent behaviors such as eye contact may carry distinctly different messages. These differences are closely associated with the issue of comparable acculturation mentioned previously. The reader is referred to Chapter 4 for more information on this topic.

Impact of Disability The greatest concern for the examiner testing children with motor or sensory impairments is that the assessment reflect the child's cognitive ability rather than the degree of disability. Neisworth and Bagnato (1992) suggest that most cognitive assessments "measure the child's disability rather than his ability" (p. 8). Professionals in the early intervention disciplines have historically been challenged to establish techniques and instruments that effectively evaluate a child's cognitive status without violating the principles of standardization (Fewell, 2000). The process of modifying materials and instruments for the purpose of gaining more information about the child's cognitive status without the impact of the disability is sometimes called "testing the limits." For example, for an infant who is slow to alert or attend, the examiner may first score the item under the standardized conditions and then attempt to gain the infant's attention through alternative alerting behaviors. At issue, especially for children with disabilities, is not whether the child can pass or fail the item attempted but whether the child truly has acquired the critical function of the item measured.

The question "What is this item really measuring?" will provide insight into the critical function of the item, although often multiple behaviors other than the critical function are also required to pass the item. For example, the task of picking up a cup to retrieve a hidden object involves multiple behaviors and abilities other than the critical function of object permanence. If the child has motor impairments, difficulties with grasp, reach, and upper body strength may prevent the demonstration of object permanence. The child with impaired vision may have the concept of object permanence but have difficulty locating the cup. Haring et al. (1981) described three techniques to modify test items in the *Uniform Performance*

Assessment System Support adaptations provide positional and physical support, prosthetic adaptations involve the use of equipment or aids, and general adaptations represent any change in the requirements of the task. Others, such as Thurlow, Ysseldyke, and Silverstein (1993) suggest modifications of materials, modifications of the manner in which the items are administered, and modifications in the response required by the child. If modifications are used, the examiner must be extremely careful to document them and should not assume that they do not alter the standardization process. Some test publishers have attempted to provide a standardized format for modifications. The BDI (Newborg et al., 1984) includes adaptations appropriate for children with hearing, vision, and motor impairments.

Examiners must also be cognizant of the unique influence that specific disability conditions may have on the young child's behavior. For example, fatigue may be exacerbated by the effort of the child to move, visually track, or auditorily localize. The effects of medication may further complicate readiness or desire to participate in social interaction or object play required during most assessments. In addition, disabilities may produce a differential developmental sequence for the acquisition of some cognitive skills. Robinson and Fieber (1988) suggest that limited motor behavior may constrain object exploration, which is typically believed to precede concept development, but that concept development may still be evidenced without the fine motor behavior necessary for object manipulation. In other words, some children may compensate through other developmental pathways for the missing information typically gained through motor behavior (McLean & McCormick, 1993). The limitations that a missing pathway of information place on a child's interpretation of his social and physical environment must be carefully considered when selecting assessment tools and interpreting their outcomes (Robinson & Fieber, p. 130).

In the evaluation of children with hearing impairments, examiners should present tasks in a consistent and organized manner in order to facilitate habituation and response expectations. It is also important to note that many children with hearing impairments have learned socially appropriate responses (such as nodding and smiling) to verbal directions that they do not hear or understand. Children with visual impairments often have developed abilities in using tactile cues in tandem with auditory cues. Older children with visual impairments often have visual aids or glasses that will facilitate the use of their vision during assessment. The skilled evaluator will question family members or caregivers concerning the use of these devices. Early childhood professionals who are remiss in this area can be faced with "Oh, I forgot to tell you, his glasses are in my purse" following a lengthy (and invalid) assessment. Examiners should make the best use of residual vision, using strategies such as high-contrast visual stimuli, materials of increased size, and ample time to explore materials (Fewell, 1983).

In evaluating children with physical impairments, the evaluator must first determine the extent to which the impairment interferes with the response demands of the evaluation. Issues of head control and postural stability are important in making children comfortable and enabling/preparing them to move. Alternative seating or support is encouraged, especially if the child has difficulty moving to midline or focusing his vision. Assessments with time limits are particularly problematic for children with motor difficulties. For children with physical impairments at least seven issues must be addressed: primary response mode, sensory input, degree of motor impairment, positioning, fatigue, medical problems, and signs of learning disabilities (Venn & Dykes, 1987).

Two additional factors, *family choice and preference* and *team membership* are also important factors in the assessment process. These are thoroughly reviewed in Chapter 3 of this text.

Approaches to Assessment

In the early 1990s researchers began to identify emerging trends in the evaluation and assessment of young children with disabilities: play-based assessment, ecological assessment, arena assessment, judgment-based assessment, and adaptive (sometimes called adaptive-to-handicap) assessment (Fewell, 1991; Neisworth & Bagnato, 1992). Common among many of these trends was the use of natural environments, community and home settings where children and their families could interact as active participants in familiar environments in preferred ways. More recent developments have encompassed strong family involvement and inclusive team membership (Woods & McCormick, 2002). Some of these trends are discussed in this section.

Free-Play, Elicited and Structured Play

Linder (1993a) provides an approach to using play as a medium for a more naturalistic and authentic evaluation of a child's developmental status through observation in the natural environment. Linder's model includes an adjustable six-phase process. The first phase is *unstructured facilitation,* lasting about 25 minutes, when the child takes the lead. The facilitator for the assessment interacts with the child, attempting to move him or her to higher skill levels through modeling. In the second phase, *structured facilitation,* cognitive and language behaviors that were not observed are elicited. In this phase the facilitator takes a direct approach, with specific requests made to the child, while maintaining play as the vehicle for assessment. *Child-to-child interaction* in an unstructured situation describes the third phase; the fourth phase is *parent-child interaction,* with some opportunity provided to observe separation and greeting behaviors. The fifth phase consists of *motor play,* and the sixth is *snack.* Intervention strategies and curriculum are also linked to this assessment in the accompanying curriculum by Linder (1993b).

The advantages of natural environments and behavioral response sets such as play in the assessment of cognition are obvious. Children are free to interact with objects and environments that are interesting and motivating to them. Examiners are free to observe, to model, and to expand infant and child behaviors to more accurately ascertain the child's level of engagement with and understanding of familiar and novel physical and social environments. However, examiners must be judicious in their choice of settings in which to conduct the evaluations and assessments. Paget (1991) suggests that the ideal setting for the assessment of young children is an area that is familiar to the child, where he or she is at ease, and where distractions are at a minimum. Natural environments meet the first two of these three requirements. Examiners must work with family members to meet the requirements of minimum distractions. As evaluations take place more and more frequently in the home and community, creative and family-centered decisions regarding the best environments for evaluation and assessment will be evidenced.

Traditional assessments remove children from the environments where they have learned and practiced behaviors. Natural environments - provide children with opportunities to display behaviors that have functional utility in their environments. Compensatory efforts and strategies can also be observed. The examiner has the opportunity to observe behaviors that are transitional or emerging in natural environments. Furthermore, the benefits of using family members and caregivers in providing assessment information and in active participation in the evaluation and assessment process cannot be overstated.

Dynamic Assessment

Assessment approaches that use a test–teach–test model hold tremendous promise in allowing teachers and interventionists to measure more accurately the cognitive ability of young children. This model, which Feuerstein (1979) describes as a *dynamic assessment,* determines a child's level of functioning, provides training, and then reevaluates the child in a structured situation. Proponents of this model believe that a more accurate measure of potential rather than performance can be obtained. An example of an instrument developed and now widely used by Feuerstein and his colleagues is the *Learning Potential Assessment Device* (LPAD) (Feuerstein, 1979). The LPAD is designed to estimate the child's cognitive deficits, preferred cognitive strategies and perceptual modalities, capacity for modifiability under optimal training conditions, and the generalizability of strategies to new tasks. Feuerstein's model is also referred to as an instrumental enrichment model.

Other researchers (Campione & Brown, 1985; Lidz, 1987) suggest that the second assessment in the test–teach–test paradigm provides a far more valid measure of children's cognitive abilities than the initial one, and they have attempted to quantify this change by identifying factors such as the level of prompts, the number of models needed to accomplish the task and meet criteria, and the child's ability to generalize this new information to similar tasks. Benner (1992) describes two assessments designed for preschoolers that use a test–teach–test model: the *Children's Analogical Thinking Modifiability* (CATM), which was developed by Tzuriel and Klein in 1987, and the *Preschool Learning Assessment Device*, developed in 1987 by Lidz and Thomas. Each uses a mediated learning experience task to evaluate the child's level of cognitive modifiability (the ability to improve performance). According to Benner (1992), kindergartners from low socioeconomic environments demonstrate high modifiability on the CATM using this model. Dynamic assessments often use a test–teach–test paradigm and emphasize the process a child uses to produce a response rather than the correctness of the product/response. These assessments also focus on the specification of conditions that produce effective performance and on obstacles to such performance.

Criterion-Referenced Assessment   Criterion-referenced tests measure a child's mastery or performance of a specific set of skill objectives and are interpreted in comparison to a predetermined criteria. Curriculum-based assessment (CBA) is one form of criterion-referenced measurement and is regarded as the most commonly utilized assessment approach in early intervention (Bagnato, Neisworth, & Munson, 1997). CBA refers to methods in which a child's performance of specific curricular objectives is assessed. CBA approaches provide a direct assessment of a child's skills upon entry into a curriculum; guide development of individual goals, interventions, and accommodations; and allow for continual monitoring of developmental progress. Bagnato et al. distinguish between two types of CBA instruments: curriculum-referenced scales and curriculum-embedded scales. Curriculum-referenced scales cover skills that are included in most preschool curricula but are not specific to the curriculum in which a particular child is being instructed. Such scales can be useful for identifying a child's strengths and weaknesses and making inferences about performance in a specific curriculum. Two examples are the *BRIGANCE Diagnostic Inventory of Early Development–Revised* (Brigance, 1991) and the BDI (Newborg et al., 1984). In contrast, curriculum-embedded scales assess the same skills that are specified in the child's curricular objectives. Thus, assessment items are drawn directly from a program's curriculum, which allows for goal development and progress monitoring. The *Hawaii Early Learning Profile* (HELP) (Parks, Furuno, O'Reilly, Inatsuka, Hoska, & Zeisloft-Falbey, 1994) is one of the most comprehensive and frequently utilized curriculum-embedded scales in early intervention programs.

The models of criterion-referenced testing discussed above reflect an approach, referred to as "critical skills mastery" by Deno (1997), that is characterized by the assessment of specific skills and subskills that are developmentally sequenced within domains. This approach has historically dominated assessment practices within early childhood education (McConnell, 2000). Critical skills mastery approaches are considered useful for describing a child's developmental status and planning interventions linked to assessment information. Measuring progress over time is a critical purpose for which assessment is often completed. Critical skills mastery approaches allow for the comparison of skills over time, addressing questions about the attainment of specific skills (McConnell, 2000). While such information is important, it is equally important that assessment methods also monitor progress toward long-term goals and rate of development. According to McConnell, critical skills mastery approaches do not adequately address this need and, thus, an alternative assessment paradigm is needed in early intervention; namely, general outcome measurement approaches.

General outcome measures sample a broad domain, or cluster, of skills through the assessment of indicators related to the broad domain and allow for the continual monitoring of progress toward goals as well as rate of progress over time (Deno, 1997). Standardized assessment measures can be administered repeatedly and are regarded as indicators of a particular domain but are not designed to comprehensively reflect a domain nor provide information about specific skills that a child may/may not demonstrate. One example of general outcome measures is curriculum-based measurement (Shinn, 1989) used for school-aged children. General outcome measurement techniques have recently emerged for use with infants and toddlers (Greenwood, Luze, & Carta, 2002), preschoolers (McConnell, Priest, Davis, & McEvoy, 2002), and early elementary (Good, Gruba, & Kaminski, 2002). As an example, *Individual Growth and Development Indicators* (IDGIs), will be discussed later in the chapter.

Norm-Referenced Assessment/Traditional Psychometric

The psychometric assessment of young children began with Binet and Simon in 1905 (Kelly & Surbeck, 2000). Under contract from the educational system in Paris, Binet and Simon developed a 30-item instrument to discrim-

inate between children who would benefit from instruction and those who would not. In 1908 these two pioneer psychometricians developed a second test, using the new concept of mental age. Binet continued this work while at Stanford University, established norms for the United States and named the subsequent tool the Stanford-Binet. In the following years, researchers such as Lucy Sprague Mitchell, John B. Watson, Robert Yerkes, and J. C. Foster were active in the study of intelligence, concentrating on the early years of children's development (Kelly & Surbeck). Instruments such as the *Merrill-Palmer Scale of Mental Tests* (Stutsman, 1931), the *Minnesota Preschool Scale* (Goodenough, 1926), the *Cattell Infant Intelligence Scale* (Cattell, 1940), the *Leiter International Performance Scale* (Leiter, 1948), and the *California First Year Mental Scales* (Bayley, 1933) were the precursors of many of the psychometric assessments used with young children today. Later, psychologists, statisticians, and test publishers sought to make these instruments more methodologically sound and to make measurement more precise. These efforts were prompted by the need for effective evaluation of early intervention projects receiving significant federal, state, and local funds, such as Project Head Start. Through legislative efforts, programs receiving federal monies were mandated to include an evaluation component with appropriate instrumentation. Institutes such as the Battelle Institute and other private and public corporations responded to the growing need for measures to evaluate the developmental progress of infants, toddlers, and preschoolers.

Developers of instruments to assess cognitive development have generally followed two theoretical models. The *global theory model* suggests that intelligence is best defined as the ability to think abstractly and to solve problems. Test authors include items that correlate with a large factor (typically referred to as "g"). This global factor is omnibus and encompasses many behaviors that are reflective of general intelligence. The earlier editions of the Stanford-Binet incorporated this model. However, the second model, the *factor analytic model*, currently has a greater number of proponents. Researchers postulate a general factor with specific factors related to specific tasks. The number of these specific factors ranges from 2 (Horn, 1968; Wechsler, 1974) to 120 (Guilford, 1967). Factor analytic models with multiple factors, however, appear to have limited value for preschoolers. Multiple factors are not evidenced beyond two general ones (mental and motor) for many infants and toddlers (Snyder, Lawson, Thompson, Stricklin, & Sexton, 1993; Sheehan & Snyder, 1989–1990). The psychometric approach emphasizes standardized procedures with item selection based on statistical criteria. Norm-referenced assessments are the best examples of assessments with a psychometric foundation.

Founded in a psychometric orientation, *neuropsychological* assessments of young children and preschoolers are conducted to provide information regarding diagnostic profiles, prognosis, treatment, and to advance the understanding of brain–behavior relationships. Typically conducted by neuropsychologists or psychologists with a strong background in neurodevelopment, neuropsychological assessment procedures include a) formal neuropsychological batteries such as the *Reitan-Indiana Neuropsychological Battery* (Reitan, 1969) and the *Developmental Neuropsychological Assessment* (NEPSY; Korkman, Kirk, & Kemp, 1998); b) intellectual batteries; and c) informal approaches such as those presented by Teeter and Semrud-Clikeman (1997) and Deysach (1986). Interested readers are directed to a more comprehensive discussion of neuropsychological assessment in Hooper (2000).

Considerations in Test Selection and Administration

Opportunity for Family Involvement and Participation In 1990 and again in 2000, the Division for Early Childhood (DEC) of the Council for Exceptional Children (CEC) invited families and professionals to identify recommended practices in assessment for early intervention and early childhood special education. Two broad concerns emerged. First, parents and family members are primary stakeholders and play a critical role in assessment throughout the process. The role of the family member as the child's first and most significant teacher has long been acknowledged. The team benefits from the family's "teaching experience when they inquire about the child's preferences for activities, materials, play partners, and schedules" (Woods & McCormick, 2002). Family members contribute in multiple ways to the assessment process. They inform team members about their child, enhance observations of professionals by describing performance in other settings, validate test results obtained by professionals, facilitate child engagement with team members, and interact with their child in play and caregiving routines. A family-centered approach provides opportunities for family members to identify their preferences for different roles and acknowledges their expertise and competence as team members throughout the assessment process. The reader is referred again to Chapter 3 of this text for a more thorough discussion of the collaborative role of the family in the assessment process.

Accommodations The second concern voiced was that assessment strategies and tools must accommodate the developmental and disability-specific characteristics of young children. Neisworth and Bagnato write, "The styles, methods, and content of assessment must become compatible with, rather than at odds with, the behavior and interests of young children. A fundamental precept of developmentally appropriate practice is that teaching and assessment must take place in the child's natural context—rather than decontextualized" (2000, p. 19). Keeping these concerns in mind, Neisworth and Bagnato (2000) identified seven critical qualities to guide professionals and family members in the evaluation of assessment procedures and instruments. These are included in Table 10.1. Bagnato et al. (1997)

TABLE 10.1
Critical Qualities for Assessment: Selection and Use

Quality	Descriptor
Utility	Assessment must be useful in identifying individual goals, program goals, and assessment of developmental competencies and status.
Acceptability	Families and professionals must consider the assessment methods, materials, and outcomes useful and acceptable. The assessment must have social validity.
Authenticity	Assessment occurs in familiar environments, with familiar materials, during typical routines and everyday tasks.
Collaboration	Family members and caregivers act as collaborative partners and team members with professionals and staff members from multiple disciplines.
Convergence	Multiple sources of information are used in understanding child behavior and assessment outcomes.
Equity	Use of materials and procedures to accommodate individual differences in child behavior (environment, culture, sensory, and behavior) facilitates assessment of what a child can do.
Sensitivity	Includes sufficient opportunities and items to detect small changes in child status and plan instruction.
Congruence	Developed and tested for use with children of varying levels of disabilities and development stages. Applicable in both home and early childhood center or school environment.

Note: Adapted from Neisworth, J. T. and Bagnato, S. J. (2000), Recommended Practices in Assessment. In S. Sandall, M. McLean, and B. J. Simth, *DEC Recommended Practices in Early Intervention/Early Childhood Special Education.* Longmont, CO: Sopris West.

use a similar set of attributes to evaluate assessment instruments that may be useful to the reader in test selection and administration.

Response Demands The response demands of an assessment instrument must be carefully analyzed prior to the evaluation and assessment of the cognitive abilities of children with disabilities. Some tests require verbal fluency and expressive communication; others place demands on the child's sensory and motor systems. Most will include items that require a broad range of behaviors across sensory, motor, and communication domains. Assessment instruments should

be chosen that will best reveal the child's cognitive ability while minimizing the impact of one or multiple disabilities (see previous section on Impact of Disability).

Representation of Children with Disabilities Norm-referenced testing assumes that development progresses in a predictable and orderly manner. For some children with disabilities, especially those with limited motor or sensory ability but adequate cognitive ability, this may be a faulty assumption. Historically, standardization samples for norm-referenced assessments have not included a "clinical" population, although there are some notable exceptions (see discussion of the Differential Abilities Scale, Elliott, 1990). The purpose of the test is to discriminate the "clinical" from the "norm." Therefore, there are few children who "match" the children with whom these tests are used. For this reason some psychologists and special educators have suggested that norm-referenced tests may not be valid for children with disabilities.

Assessments for children with specific disabilities are few and the majority of them are quite dated. Many have items that are obsolete and would not be understood by children today (Hoy & Gregg, 1994). Nonverbal measurements, which had previously been of some use in the assessment of children with limited motor and communication behavioral repertoires, are also out of date. Furthermore, older assessment tools, such as the *Columbia Mental Maturity Scale* (Burgemeister, Blum, & Lorge, 1972), and *French's Pictorial Test of Intelligence* (French, 1964), use black-and-white photographs or line drawings and provide little that is stimulating or motivating for the young child. The newer *Differential Abilities Scale* (Elliott, 1990) is a noteworthy exception and does include children with disabilities in the normative sample in sufficient numbers to represent special education categories present in the 1988 school population; however even this normative group is now more than 15 years old.

In summary, authentic child- and family-centered assessment practices put the child and family at the center of the process. An individualized approach focuses on child and family strengths and needs and provides a mechanism for relevant, meaningful information to be captured. The use of multiple methods that make sense and address family-identified strengths, needs, concerns, and questions provides a comprehensive and accurate reflection of child status in important and functional activities. Team members, including family members, have the opportunity to collaborate and work together to make decisions about eligibility for program services, placement options, and the identification of appropriate IEP

goals and instructional strategies (McCormick, Woods, & Hallam, 2002).

REPRESENTATIVE METHODS

As programs for infants, toddlers, and preschoolers with disabilities grow in number, test publishers and researchers respond to the demands for assessment tools to determine eligibility, to plan interventions, and to document progress. It must be remembered that few tests available can meet all three of these requirements. Included in this section are instruments available to the field. New instruments and revisions are constantly being marketed. Early intervention team members should be cautious in the selection and interpretation of tools to measure cognitive development. They must recognize the limitations of the instruments they use and share their cautions and concerns with all team members, especially family members, being ever-mindful of the power these assigned numbers take on. Children are not defined by the outcomes of assessments nor is their behavioral repertoire always accurately reflected. The use of a multimeasure, multisource, multisetting, and multisituation model alleviates some of the inherent difficulties in the assessment of young children. However, the dynamic nature of development during this period cannot be overstated. One should remember that children with disabilities are children first, and that their cognitive, language, or motor development is only a part of who they are within their families and culture.

Accurate evaluation and assessment of young children are critical to good interventions. While these terms are often used interchangeably, they connote two different processes. *Evaluation* may be defined as the procedures used to determine a child's initial and continued eligibility for services; *assessment* is the ongoing process used by qualified personnel throughout the period of a child's eligibility to identify the family's resources, priorities, and concerns as well as the child's unique needs (McLean & McCormick,

1993). The examiner must choose which instruments are appropriate to fulfill the requirements of each of these processes, which are thoroughly reviewed in Chapter 1 of this text.

Norm-Referenced Measures

Norm-referenced instruments have two attributes: They are based on the performance of a norming group, and they typically use a standardized score to report outcomes. They are most appropriately used as evaluation tools. The issues previously mentioned in the chapter are important in the selection of appropriate norm-referenced measures of cognitive development. Recommended practice would advocate instruments that provide the best match between the child and the requirements of the assessment or evaluation tool. Several measures are identified in this section. Examiners should choose the instrument that will yield the most reliable and valid information about the individual child, keeping in mind the assumptions underlying the test development, test characteristics (normative sample, adequate floor, predictive validity), and response requirements.

A note of caution is appropriate here in regard to the use of norm-referenced assessments for children with significant or multiple disabilities. Berdine and Meyer (1987) suggest that the use of norm-referenced assessments to label and classify children with severe or profound disabilities is gratuitous at best and potentially damaging in the worst case. The use of a comparison group of individuals who function within a normal range of abilities may be irrelevant to the assessment of the abilities of children with severe or profound disabilities. The unexamined use of norm-referenced assessments with this population, which leads to statements such as "this child is untestable," is indefensible. Informed examiners and team members recognize the limits of such assessments and will develop alternative and appropriate assessment models that can reflect accurately the ability levels of children with severe

or profound disabilities. A further caution relates to the use of items from norm-referenced instruments as instructional targets.

Battelle Developmental Inventory The Battelle Developmental Inventory (BDI) (Newborg et al., 1984) is a developmentally based norm-referenced assessment appropriate for measuring the development of children from birth to age 8. It consists of 341 items grouped within five domains and 22 subdomains, and provides a variety of standard scores including developmental quotients, percentile ranks, and age equivalents. Scores can be obtained for the full scale as well as domains and subdomains (10 summary scores). Additional materials include a materials kit and computerized scoring system available in an IBM DOS format. Bos, Vaughn, and Levine (1990) have developed curriculum materials based on the BDI domains and subdomains to provide a link from assessment to intervention. These materials are available from the publisher.

The normative sample consisted of 800 children selected by stratification variables based on 1980 census data. The BDI has four distinct advantages: first, it is a multidomain assessment (cognitive, communication, motor, personal-social, and adaptive); second, a 3-point scoring system is used that allows for the crediting of emerging abilities; third, three procedures for obtaining information (traditional administration, observation, and interview) provide an ecologically appropriate assessment using observations by parents and team members within naturally occurring routines and activities; and fourth, adaptations for item instruction, procedures, and materials are provided for specific disabilities.

Test authors suggest that the subtests/domains can be administered independently to measure independent traits or abilities; however, research suggests that for children with severe disabilities these domains are less independent and caution should be used, especially when interpreting domain scores in communication, cognition, and social-emotional development for this population (Snyder et al., 1993). Boyd (1989) has reported that age-related discontinuities could produce radically different scores on a child from one day to the next despite identical item performance, especially for infants and toddlers. He hypothesizes that this problem may be the result of an insufficient number of infants included in the normative sample. For example, *Bayley Scales of Infant Development* (Bayley, 1993) used 450 infants between the ages of birth and 6 months, while the BDI used only 50. "Depending upon whether the BDI is given prior to or after a particular cut-off point, BDI results can make the child appear relatively better or worse than a companion instrument" (Boyd, p. 118). Sheehan and Snyder (1989–1990) support Boyd's research and caution against the use of the BDI for all children below the age of 2 because of limited item sampling. Bagnato et al. (1997) suggest some problems with outcomes yielding an overestimation of children with development disabilities with the BDI but suggest that the 1988 recalibration of the norms may have addressed this issue. McLean, McCormick, Baird, and Mayfield (1987) found that use of the BDI screener did result in considerable overreferral for a population of 30 children.

Bailey, Vandiviere, Dellinger, and Munn (1987) identify three problems with the BDI. First, for 247 protocols scored by 76 teachers, only 20.2% were scored without errors; second, of 247 children, 174 (75%) required extrapolated scoring; and third, 49 children (20%) received negative developmental quotients as a result of extrapolation. Extrapolated scores are sometimes necessary evils when evaluating children with disabilities. However, two cautions are appropriate. First, these scores do not have the psychometric integrity of scores generated within standardization and norming procedures; they are only estimates of scores that might have been obtained. Second, logic would dictate that a minimal range of raw scores must be earned (Bailey & Wolery, 1989). It would be unreasonable

to extrapolate scores on the basis of multiple scores of zeros.

The BDI is an example of a unique hybrid of norm-referenced and developmental/criterion-based assessment. The distinction between criterion-based and norm-referenced is easily seen in school-age assessments. For example, the *Key Math–Revised* (Connolly, 1998) is readily identified as a criterion measure of mathematical ability; the *Wechsler Intelligence Scale for Children* (Wechsler, 1991) measures cognitive abilities. This distinction is less obvious in assessments for preschoolers, and the use of the generic term *developmental assessment* for both kinds of measures makes the distinction even more difficult. Furthermore, many of the items included in norm-referenced developmental assessments may be seen as intervention targets. The key to understanding this distinction is the way in which the outcomes/scores are generated. Norm-referenced outcomes are comparisons with the performance of the norm group; developmental/age equivalents from a non-norm-referenced developmental assessment are generated based on what we assume to be ages when these skills typically develop. Again, these arbitrarily assigned expectations or assumptions are problematic for children with disabilities. Critical to the appropriate use of age equivalents based on developmental milestones or schedules is a sound knowledge of child development. The BDI authors suggest that this assessment inventory can be used for the purposes of evaluation and assessment. In other words, it can be used for eligibility determination and for program planning. It is naive, however, to believe that the BDI can adequately fulfill both of these missions. Despite these difficulties, the Battelle Developmental Inventory continues to enjoy widespread usage and appears to meet psychometric standards for use with children age 2 and older with mild to moderate disabilities.

A revision of the BDI, the Battelle Developmental Inventory, 2nd Edition (BDI-2), will be available for publication in the Fall of 2004 with standardization trials for 3,000 children occurring in 2002 and 2003 (D. Madsen, personal communication, September 4, 2002). The BDI-2 differs from the first edition in three important ways. First, there are significantly more items to provide greater item specificity throughout the age ranges and to improve the floor for infants and toddlers at the lower end of the age range (birth to 2). The standardization sample will include approximately 150 additional new and/or revised items. Second, norms will not be provided for all subtests for the full age range in the second edition. For example, the Conceptual Development subdomain will not include items in the earliest age levels (i.e., will begin at 18 months). This change is anticipated to improve the authenticity of the outcomes. Third, test materials and protocols have been changed to facilitate ease of administration and scoring and to elicit greater child attention and engagement. The interview items will be more scripted, scoring rubrics will be presented in a chart format to facilitate easier scoring, more color has been added to the test stimuli, and test manipulatives have been improved. In addition to the Record Form, the BDI-2 will include a Subject Workbook for some of the items in the cognitive and motor domains for children in the upper age ranges. These are notable improvements and may correct some of the current problems in the use of this assessment tool.

Bayley Scales of Infant Development

The Bayley Scales of Infant Development II, the 1993 revision of the original Bayley Scales of Infant Development (Bayley, 1969), provides a comprehensive assessment of the development of children ages 1 month through 42 months. The second edition, similar to the first, contains three scales: (1) a mental scale includes the assessment of perceptual acuity, discrimination, object constancy and memory, learning and problem solving, verbal ability, generalization, and classification; (2) a motor scale assesses muscle control and coordination; and (3) a behavior rating scale contains four subscales: orientation/engagement, attention, motor quality, and emotional regulation.

The Bayley uses a two-tiered theoretical model and provides developmental age equivalents for motor, personal/social, language, and cognition. No studies have yet reported on the validity of this model, although reliability and validity studies reported by the publishers demonstrate adequacy. Scale scores are also provided for the mental and motor scales. The normative sample included 1,700 children stratified by race, gender, parental education level, and geographic region. A clinical sample was assessed to validate the normative sample. This sample included children with autism and developmental delay, as well as children who were premature, HIV positive, prenatally exposed to drugs, and asphyxiated at birth (Cohen & Spenciner, 1994).

Differential Ability Scales

The *Differential Ability Scales* (DAS) (Elliott, 1990) is a revision of the *British Ability Scales* (Elliott, Murray, & Pearson, 1979) for children ages 2 years 6 months through 17 years. The DAS contains two components: a cognitive battery with two levels, one for preschool and one for school-age children, and a set of academic achievement tests for school-age children. The cognitive battery provides a composite score (the General Conceptual Ability score), cluster ability scores, and individual subtest scores, similar to the three-tiered model used in the *Stanford-Binet, 4th Edition* (Thorndike, Hagen, & Sattler, 1996). The cognitive battery is composed of two types (core and diagnostic) of subtests. Only the core subtests are used in calculating the GCA composite (mean of 100 and standard deviation of 15). The authors of the DAS suggest that it provides greater subtest specificity than other cognitive measures due to an increased effort to design subtests that were "relatively pure" (Elliott, Daniel, & Guiton, 1991, p. 134). However, poor subtest specificity is still an issue in the assessment of preschoolers. According to Elliot et al., as children age and ability increases, the general factor underlying core subtests becomes more differentiated. For example, at the early level (2 years 6 months to 3 years 5 months) the four core tests measure a single factor. For ages 3 years 6 months to 5 years 11 months, the six core tests measure two factors, verbal and non-verbal. By age 6, three factors emerge: verbal, nonverbal, and spatial.

Test administration is somewhat different for the DAS. Rather than a basal and ceiling approach, starting and stopping points termed *decision points* are used in estimating the child's ability from the test results using a procedure based on the Rasch model of item response theory (Elliott et al., 1991). The aim is to administer items of moderate difficulty rather than working downward toward items that are "too easy" or upward until items become "too hard." DAS authors contend that the preschool level of the test is tailored for preschoolers rather than being a mere extension of school-age items. Brightly colored manipulatives and pictures are used to elicit and maintain the attention of young children. The DAS also provides sample items and allows for teaching following failure on initial items. Furthermore, the DAS provides a brief battery that can be used to obtain a special nonverbal composite score in place of the General Conceptual Ability (GCA) score. Directions for these items can be delivered through gestural communication and require only gestural responses from the child (pointing, drawing, and manipulating objects). In addition, the DAS makes use of extended norms that allow the calculation of GCAs as low as 25 (Platt, Kamphaus, Keltgen, & Gilliland, 1991) and provides for "out-of-level" testing when evaluating children who are performing considerably lower (or higher) than others of the same chronological age (Elliott et al., 1991).

The normative sample for the DAS included children who exhibited learning disabilities, speech and language impairments, mild mental retardation, emotional disturbance, and/or mild visual, hearing, or motor impairments. This produced a sample that closely matched the 1984 percentage for special education categories in the population and a percentage of other children

representative of the general population (Elliott et al., 1991). In all, 3,475 children, reflecting the population distribution of race, socioeconomic status, and region, as measured by 1988 U.S. census data, were included in the sample. Item bias ascribed to race or gender was analyzed, and items that were differentially difficult were excluded from the test.

Concurrent validity studies were conducted by the publisher using other cognitive measures such as the Wechsler Preschool and Primary Scales of Intelligence–Revised (Wechsler, 1989), the Kaufman Assessment Battery for Children (Kaufman & Kaufman, 1983), the Stanford-Binet, 4th Edition (Thorndike, Hagen, & Sattler, 1986), and the McCarthy Scales of Children's Abilities (McCarthy, 1972) as the criterion measures. Coefficients ranged from .68 to .89, indicating moderate to strong relationships (Elliott et al., 1991), however no independent validation studies are reported.

Kaufman Assessment Battery for Children

The Kaufman Assessment Battery for Children (K-ABC) (Kaufman & Kaufman, 1983) contains four scales: sequential processing, simultaneous processing, achievement, and nonverbal for children ages 2 years 6 months to 12 years 5 months. The authors used this four-factor model to minimize the effect of verbal processing, ethnic bias, and gender bias on the estimate of cognitive development. A mental processing composite of the sequential and simultaneous scales is produced with a mean of 100 and a standard deviation of 15. Subtest scaled scores have a mean of 10 and standard deviation of 3.

The normative sample consisted of 2,000 children chosen by a stratification procedure based on race and ethnicity, age, gender, geographic region, socioeconomic status as measured by parent education, and community size according to 1980 census data. However, African Americans from lower-socioeconomic environments and Hispanic Americans were underrepresented by 24% and 10% (Benner, 1992). Reliability and validity studies suggest moderate to strong correlations with other measures such as the WPPSI. However, there is some concern that the exclusion of verbal ability (to support a more culture-fair measure) severely limits the behavioral sampling of the mental processing composite. Furthermore, difficulties with an inadequate floor have also been cited when the test is used with preschoolers with below-average abilities (Bracken, 1987). As with other multiple-factor models, the factor structure for preschoolers is questionable. Gridley, Miller, Barke, Fischer, and Smith (1990) found no evidence of the two factors for a sample of preschoolers; Kaufman and Kamphaus (1984) report that the K-ABC produces two factors (sequential and simultaneous) for young children (ages 2 and 3) with a third (achievement) emerging at age 4.

The K-ABC was developed with great attention to the uniqueness of preschool assessment. Test materials are colorful and use colorful photographs rather than line drawings. The attentional demands of standardized assessments with young children are also accommodated by the use of only seven subtests for younger children. As children age and attention spans increase, the number of subtests increases. Instructions were simplified to remove any embedded concepts such as "middle" or "after." Sample and teaching items facilitate test administration and validity. Furthermore, the K-ABC Nonverbal Scale may provide examiners with supporting information about the cognitive abilities of children with limited English proficiency and children with language or hearing impairments. However, caution should be exercised when using the K-ABC with preschoolers with hearing impairments because of a limited number (three) of subtests (Telzrow, 1984). In summary, limitations for preschoolers include too few manipulative tasks; too few easy items (limited floor); a heavy emphasis on visual stimuli, making the test difficult for children with visual impairments; and too little opportunity to sample verbal reasoning and spontaneous expression (Kaufman, Kamphaus, & Kaufman, 1985).

The Learning Accomplishment Profile–Diagnostic Standardized Assessment (LAP–D)

The LAP–D (Nehring, Nehring, Bruni, & Randolph, 1992), an instrument with characteristics similar to the BDI, was originally developed as a criterion-referenced measure of developmental status. The *LAP–D Standardized Assessment*, according to the authors, may be used for educational decisions concerning placement and developmental profile. The LAP–D includes four domains: fine motor (writing and manipulation), cognitive (matching and counting), language (naming and comprehension), and gross motor (body movement and object movement). Like the BDI, each domain has its own manual with accompanying materials.

The LAP–D yields age equivalents, percentile ranks, and z and t scores. Normative data were generated for 792 children ages 30 to 72 months, stratified by gender and race. Stratification procedures did not include geographic region or the socioeconomic or educational status of parents. Subtest floors and total test floor appear to be adequate; however, item gradient problems were noted for the lowest age range (30 to 35 months). A concurrent validity study with 60 children ages 30 months to 72 months conducted by Mayfield, McCormick, and Cook (1993) suggests moderate to strong correlations between subtest age equivalents reported by the LAP–D and the BDI. McCormick, Mayfield, and Ridgley (2001) also reported on the relationship of eligibility outcomes for a sample of young children using the LAP–D and the BDI. Significant discrepancies for more than half of the children assessed were evidenced. A comprehensive review of the LAP-D by Sexton, Lobman, and Oremland (1999) suggests that the LAP-D be used primarily as a performance-based screening tool. The Learning Accomplishment Profile (LAP) (Sanford & Zelman, 1981) and the Early Learning Accomplishment Profile (ELAP; Glover, Preminger, & Sanford, 1978) have enjoyed a long history of use as assessments for program planning and measurement of child progress in many preschool programs, particularly in Head Start. Perhaps because of this previous familiarity with the instrument as a criterion-referenced assessment, its use as an evaluation for eligibility has not as yet become widespread. In conclusion, the merits of the LAP-D cannot be determined without a sufficient database from which to judge its psychometric and functional utility (Sexton et al., 1999).

Leiter International Performance Scale— Revised

The *Leiter International Performance Scale–Revised* (Roid & Miller, 1997) is the newest revision of the *Leiter International Performance Scale* (Leiter, 1948, 1979) and the *Arthur Adaptation of the Leiter International Performance Scale* (Arthur, 1949). The Leiter was one of the first nonverbal measures of cognitive abilities. It was first published in 1929 and renormed in 1949 without changing any of the items. The assessment has enjoyed a long history of use by school and clinical psychologists who were interested in better understanding the cognitive status of children with hearing, communication, or motor impairments. The Leiter-R includes four domains (reasoning, visualization, memory and attention) and 20 subtests. The test was standardized on 1,800 typically developing children, and 725 children whose development was atypical. The authors report moderate to high reliability coefficients for both internal consistency and test–retest. Salvia & Ysseldyke (2001) suggest that in addition to the populations mentioned previously (those with hearing, communication, or motor impairments) the nonverbal format of the Leiter-R also makes it popular for use with children whose acculturation is different from that of the dominant culture.

Merrill-Palmer Developmental Scales— Revised

The Merrill-Palmer Scales have a long history, beginning in 1931, in the assessment of young children with developmental delays. Last revised in 1959, the current revision authored by Roid and Sampers, is scheduled for publication in

Fall 2003 and is entering standardization (G. Roid, personal communication, March 13, 2002). The new Revised Merrill-Palmer (MP) was developed for use with children between the ages of 2 months and 6 years 6 months to address the five domains of early childhood assessment including cognition, language, motor, socio-emotional, and self-help (Roid & Sampers, 2000). In addition, the revision will provide an assessment of premature infants. Retaining the popular hands-on, toy-like materials of previous MP scales, the revision will feature updated artwork, diversity-sensitive materials, and child friendly tasks.

Based on the Cattell-Horn-Carroll hierarchical "g" model (Gf/Gc) of cognitive abilities, the revision of the Merrill-Palmer assesses cognitive skills such as fluid and crystallized abilities, visual-spatial ability, short-term memory, speed of processing, and fundamental quantitative reasoning. The main battery assesses cognition, receptive language, and fine motor skills and will be standardized to yield an overall Developmental Quotient and Verbal and Nonverbal Composite indexes all with a mean of 100 and standard deviation of 15. The main battery has two major sections, an Infant/Toddler section for children aged 1 month to 2 years 5 months; and a Preschool section for ages 2 years 6 months to 6 years 6 months. Self-help and socio-emotional domains are assessed using parent rating scales. A supplemental battery will be available to assess expressive language and gross motor abilities.

Extensive psychometric studies of reliability, validity, classification accuracy (e.g., for identifying children with developmental delays), and fairness-of-assessment will also be conducted (G. Roid, personal communication, March 13, 2002). Data for clinical samples of infants born prematurely (less than 37 weeks gestation age) will also be included. Items for the standardization edition were selected following extensive studies of the tryout edition conducted on 581 children ages 2 months to 6 years 11 months. Nationally-representative norms on a large sample are anticipated with clinical samples such as premature infants and young children with cognitive delay, motor delay, language/communication delays, hearing impairments, and gifted also included.

Mullen Scales of Early Learning, AGS Edition (MSEL-AGS), Mullen Scales of Early Learning (MSEL) and Infant Mullen Scales of Early Learning (IMSEL)

The Mullen Scales of Early Learning (Mullen, 1992) is a norm-referenced test to assess modality status and performance, and to identify learning ability, learning disability, and mental retardation of children between 21 and 63 months of age (Mullen, 1992). Four subtests are divided into 9 half-year age intervals. Basal and ceiling rules are used within each subtest: visual receptive organization scale, visual expressive organization scale, language receptive organization scale, and language expressive organization scale. A norming sample of 1,016 children was used to evaluate the 144 items. Sampling was adequate but limited information on factor independence (no total score is used) for the subtests is problematic. In addition, no information is provided on the identification of learning disability and mental retardation (Salvia & Ysseldyke, 2001). The Infant Mullen Scales of Early Learning (Mullen, 1989) is a norm-referenced assessment of mental and motor abilities of infants from birth to 36 months. The 37 items are included in five subtest scales: gross motor base scale (not included in the Mullen Scales of Early Learning), visual receptive organization abilities scale, visual expressive organization abilities scale, language receptive organization abilities scale, and language expressive organization abilities scale. A normative sample of 1,231 children was used in test development, however many of the norming age groups were based on fewer than 100 children. Technical information is incomplete for both the IMSEL and the MSEL (Salvia & Ysseldyke, 2001). Bracken (2000) reports that internal consistency reliability is appropriate for screening only.

The Mullen Scales were purchased by AGS in 1993 with subsequent publication of the Mullen Scales of Early Learning, AGS Edition in 1995. The AGS Edition includes reanalyzed norms and expanded scoring options. It is a comprehensive assessment for children ages birth to 5 years 8 months, combining the two previous scales into one. The AGS Edition has five scales: gross motor, visual reception, fine motor, expressive language, and receptive language. Computer software is available to convert raw scores and provide other scoring information. In addition, an optional intervention report links intervention activities and developmentally appropriate tasks to the assessment outcomes.

Pediatric Evaluation of Disability Inventory

The Pediatric Evaluation of Disability Inventory (PEDI) (Haley, Coster, Ludlow, Haltiwanger, & Andrellos, 1992) is a curriculum-compatible, standardized, norm-referenced instrument designed to measure pediatric functional capabilities and performance, and to detect and evaluate difficulties and delays important to individual and group rehabilitation of young children (6 months to 7 years) with physical, sensory, and neuromotor impairments (Bagnato et al., 1997). Content domains include adaptive, mobility, and social function. The PEDI was designed to be used to describe functional status, plan individualized instruction, and monitor child progress. Bagnato et al., describe the PEDI as follows: "It creatively combines the best of authentic, curriculum-based, adaptive, and norm-based assessment procedures in an easily used, accessible, practical format" (p. 266). The assessment has three scales: the Functional Skills Scales, the Caregiver Assistance Scales, which describe the extent of caregiver support in natural environments and routines, and the Modifications Scales, which describe the types and frequencies of modifications or adaptations used by the child. Scoring software is also available.

Stanford-Binet Intelligence Scales–5th Edition Continuing the work begun in 1905 by Binet and Simon, the newest revision of the Stanford-Binet will be published in 2003 as the Stanford-Binet Intelligence Scales, 5th Edition (SB5) (Roid, in press). While building upon the foundation of previous Binet scales, the SB5 was developed to assess individuals across the broad ability continuum, increase clinical utility, enhance child-friendly characteristics to address early childhood assessment, implement modern measurement, increase coverage of cognitive factors, and address the need for comprehensive nonverbal assessment methods (Roid, 2002). The SB5 was developed for use with individuals from 2 years to 90 years, which is an extended age range compared to previous editions. The theoretical model of the SB5 will consist of a general factor, followed by broad verbal and nonverbal factors. In addition, five cognitive domains (reasoning, knowledge, quantitative reasoning, visual-spatial processing, and working memory) are represented. Several subtests from previous editions were retained as was the routing procedure used to guide subsequent subtest administration based upon an individual's functioning as opposed to chronological age. The SB5 also features tasks/items within each cognitive domain that can provide a nonverbal assessment when needed. Although empirical evidence is still needed to support use of the SB5 with young children, the strong foundation upon which it was built and the many improvements featured indicate great promise for practitioners working with diverse children, adolescents, and adults.

Syracuse Scales of Infant and Toddler Development or Syracuse Assessments for Birth to Three The *Syracuse Assessments for Birth to Three* (Ensher et al., 1997) is a norm-based assessment appropriate for children birth to 36 months, which is organized so that multiple developmental domains can be evaluated from a common set of activities. Activities are play-based using new or novel toys and objects in structured and unstructured tasks. Opportunities such as those embedded in Linder's *Transdisciplinary Play-based Assessment* (1993a), are included for team members to observe children during snack and other typical activities. In addition, child-initiated and spontaneous behaviors may be documented without specific administration. The *Caregiver Report of Home and School Environment* facilitates parent participation.

Wechsler Preschool and Primary Scale of Intelligence–3rd Edition The third revision of the Wechsler Preschool and Primary Scale of Intelligence (WPPSI-III) was published in Fall, 2002. Preliminary information is presented here and is based upon Coalson, Weiss, Zhu, Spruill, and Crockett (2002). Goals for the revision included improved psychometric properties, stronger theoretical foundations, enhanced clinical utility, and making the test more user-friendly and age-appropriate for children. The WPPSI-III was normed for children ages 2 years 6 months to 7 years 3 months, which is an extension at the youngest end of the age range over the WPPSI-R. In the revision, 5 subtests (arithmetic, animal pegs, geometric design, sentences, and mazes) were eliminated; 7 subtests (information, similarities, vocabulary, coding, block design, object assembly, and picture completion) were modified; and 8 new subtests (picture naming, receptive vocabulary, word context, concept grouping, matrix reasoning, picture concepts, coding, and symbol search) were developed. In comparison to the WPPSI-R, subtests on the revision have practice or sample items and place less emphasis on verbal expression and speed.

A significant change in the WPSSI-III is that different core and supplemental subtests are recommended based upon a child's chronological age. For children ages 2 years 6 months to 4 years 11 months, 4 core subtests are recommended with an administration time of 30 to 45 minutes. Full, verbal, and performance scales, which are standardized to yield a mean of 100 with a standard deviation of 15.0, are available. Two supplemental subtests are also recommended for this youngest age group. For children ages 5 years to 7 years 3 months, 8 core subtests yield three factors: verbal, performance, and processing speed, which contribute to a full scale score. In addition, the verbal and performance composites form a general ability index. This core battery has an average administration time of 45 to 60 minutes. Six supplemental subtests are available for this age group.

Final analyses of the WPPSI-III are still being conducted, therefore it is premature to comment on the psychometric qualities of the revision. However, several features of the revision appear promising for improving the usefulness of the WPPSI-R for young children. Decreasing administration time, adding teaching items and subtests, and providing different batteries based on chronological age will likely make the test more interesting and enjoyable for children while also providing practitioners with developmentally appropriate and useful assessment data.

Woodcock-Johnson Psychoeducational Battery–3rd Edition

The Woodcock-Johnson (Woodcock, McGrew, & Mather, 2001) is a wide-range set of tests designed to measure cognitive abilities, scholastic aptitude, oral language, and achievement of children 2 years through adult. The cognitive assessment was based on the Cattell-Horn-Cattell (CHC) theory and measures a general intellectual ability (g) as well as specific cognitive abilities. The 3rd Edition includes 8 new subtests in the tests of cognitive abilities and 7 new subtests in the tests of achievement. Technical and normative data for 8,800 children and adults are included in the manual.

Additional Instruments

In addition to the assessment tools reviewed in the preceding sections, there are a number of assessment scales which have dated norms. A brief summary of some of these is provided here and may be useful to the reader. The *Cattell Infant Intelligence Scale* (Cattell, 1960, 1980) uses a single-factor model of intelligence and includes items from the Gesell schedules. The Cattell was initially designed as a downward extension of the Stanford-Binet and is very similar to the early Bayley Scales of Infant Development. Many of the items on the Cattell are almost identical to those on the Bayley; however, the number of items is less comprehensive. For many of the age levels, the Cattell contains two additional items to be used as substitutions if a previous item is spoiled during administration (Langley, 1989). The *Griffiths Mental Development Scales* (Griffiths, 1954, 1979), which includes five independent measures (locomotor, personal-social, hearing and speech, eye-hand coordination, and performance) was developed in post–World War II England and has not been standardized on an American population. Concurrent validity efforts, however, suggest that the Griffiths Scales are consistent with other multidomain measures typically used in the United States, such as the Bayley Scales of Infant Development and the BDI. Some research has also suggested that scores obtained on the Griffiths are somewhat inflated (McLean, McCormick, & Baird, 1991). The scales include The Abilities of Babies (birth to 24 months) and The Abilities of Young Children, expanding the scale to 8 years. Each of the scales produces a developmental quotient and a general intelligence quotient. The *McCarthy Scales of Children's Abilities* (McCarthy, 1972) contains five scales: verbal, perceptual-performance, quantitative, memory, and motor. Three of the five scales (verbal, perceptual-performance, and quantitative) are combined to form a composite score termed a general cognitive index (mean of 100 and standard deviation of 16). Profile subtest scaled scores (mean of 50 and standard deviations of 10) are also generated. Moderate reliability is reported; concurrent validity coefficients range from .45 to .91 (Sattler, 1990). Bracken (1991) points to the limited floor for young or developmentally delayed children for most of the subtests. However, the general cognitive index does provide an adequate floor and item gradation.

Assessment of Specific Disability Populations A number of norm-referenced assessment tools have been developed for specific disability populations. Many of these are quite dated and may no longer be available for purchase. Again, a brief description of these is included for the reader's reference. The *Hiskey-Nebraska Tests of Learning Aptitude* (Hiskey, 1966) provides assessment information for children ages 3 through 17 and includes deaf and hard-of-hearing norms. The Hiskey-Nebraska can be administered by pantomime or verbal directions. Other assessments for children with hearing impairments are the *Nonverbal Performance Scale* (Smith & Johnson, 1977) and the *Adaptation of WPPSI for Deaf Children* (Ray & Ulissi, 1982). The *Perkins-Binet Intelligence Scale* (Davis, 1980) was developed for children with visual impairments and provides two forms appropriate to the child's level of usable vision. Mental age and IQ scores are obtained, using a normative sample of visually impaired children. The *Reynell-Zinkin Developmental Scales for Young Visually Handicapped Children* (Reynell, 1983) provides six age scales to assess cognitive and linguistic development of children from birth to 5 years. The *Callier-Azusa Scale* (Stillman, 1978) was designed to assess the developmental status of children with dual sensory impairments and children with severe or profound disabilities, from birth through 9 years. The *Columbia Mental Maturity Scale* (Burgemeister et al., 1972) and The *Pictorial Test of Intelligence* (French, 1964) are tools developed for the assessment of children with motor and language deficits. Both require only a pointing response and can be used with a yes/no question-and-answer format. The *Detroit Tests of Learning Aptitude–Primary* (Hammill & Bryant, 1986, 1991) is also a norm-referenced cognitive assessment designed for use with a disability population.

Criterion-Referenced Instruments and Methods

Criterion-referenced and curriculum-based assessment are the most widely used of the assessment models in early intervention and early childhood special education and are designed to provide a direct link between assessment and intervention goals or outcomes. Their popularity is based on their ease of use and flexibility of standardization and administrative procedures. These qualities support a team approach and facilitate family participation. In addition, the items "make sense" and their significance is easily recognized and visible. Expertise and performance is direct rather than inferred. Some of these tools are reviewed in the following section.

Brigance Diagnostic Inventory of Early Development–Revised The Brigance Inventory of Early Development–Revised (Brigance, 1991) measures abilities in 11 areas and includes 84 skill sequences. Domains are preambulatory motor, gross motor, fine motor, self-help, speech and language, general knowledge and comprehension, social and emotional development, readiness, basic reading skills, manuscript writing, and basic math. Computer-based programs are available to link the assessment to the *Brigance Prescriptive Readiness; Strategies and Practice* (Brigance, 1990). Tasks, objectives, and activities are cross-referenced and cross-coded. Supplemental and comprehensive sequences are also available for 400 developmental and social behaviors, which are useful with children for whom more specific task analysis is needed; however, many still lack sufficient sensitivity for children with severe disabilities (Bagnato et al., 1997). Developmental age equivalents can be obtained; however, these are not norm-based and can be considered only as estimates of developmental status.

The Carolina Curriculum for Infants and Toddlers with Special Needs, 2nd Edition and The Carolina Curriculum for Preschoolers (Johnson-Martin, Jens, Attermeier, & Hacker, 1991; Johnson-Martin, Attermeier & Hacker, 1990) The Assessment Log and Developmental Progress Charts for children birth to 2 years is part of The Carolina Curriculum for

Infants and Toddlers with Special Needs and includes items in cognition, communication, social/adaptation, and fine and gross motor skills. More than 350 items are included, which are correlated with 26 curriculum sequences and presented in a checklist format. Cognition (using a Piagetian model), language/communication, fine and gross motor, and self-help/social skills are included. The Assessment Log and Developmental Progress Chart–Preschoolers (Johnson-Martin et al., 1990) measures 400 skills in five domains with 25 skill sequences. These assessments may be completed using observation and direct testing with corresponding program areas for intervention. Specific adaptations are provided for children with sensory or motor impairments. An assessment log also allows for documenting progress for children from 12 to 36 months, thereby overlapping the two assessments.

Developmental Observation Checklist System

The Developmental Observation Checklist System (DOCS) (Hresko, Miguel, Sherbenou & Burton, 1994) is a curriculum compatible norm-based screening assessment for children birth to 6 years. The DOCS uses real-life tasks in naturally occurring routines and activities in typical settings to score each of 475 developmental skills. Three components, Developmental Checklist, Adjustment Behavior Checklist and the Parental Stress and Support Checklist, are divided into four domains: language, social, motor, and cognition. The assessment uses parent response and observations. According to Bagnato et al. (1997), "The DOCS represents one of the first attempts to infuse authentic or naturally occurring developmental skills as content in a developmental measure . . . and is an exemplar of the new directions in authentic assessment with a clear curricular focus" (p. 153). Although it is a screening instrument, the DOCS provides a comprehensive assessment for observing and recording functional skills in naturally occurring activities and routines. Limited research is available on this instrument. Gilbert (1997) reported that outcomes were dif-

ferent based on the role/relationship of the raters. Specifically, among a sample of 100 sets of participants, mothers rated the child's skills highest, fathers next, and teachers last.

Gesell Developmental Schedules

The Gesell Developmental Schedules (revised by Knobloch & Pasamanick in 1974, and in 1980 by Knobloch, Stevens, & Malone) describe development across motor (gross and fine), communication, personal-social, and adaptive behavior for children between the ages of 4 weeks and 72 months. Gesell intended that the schedules be used as benchmarks, in the same manner as criterion-based instruments, to determine the current functioning of the child rather than to predict future status. A Developmental Quotient (DQ) can be derived from a ratio formula using the mental and chronological ages. A parent questionnaire can also be used to validate direct test administration (Gibbs, 1990).

Hawaii Early Learning Profiles for Birth to Three and Preschoolers (3-6)

The Hawaii Early Learning Profile (HELP) (Parks et al., 1994; VORT, 1995) provides an assessment of development in cognitive (which includes receptive language), expressive language, fine and gross motor, self-help/adaptive, and social domains through observations of young children engaged in typical activities in everyday settings. Specific guidelines for assessment of children with disabilities are also included. In addition to assessment information for more than 1300 skills, the HELP provides an authentic linkage to intervention planning through the inclusion of teaching activities for each of the test items. Furthermore, there appears to be an adequate number of items to assess the emergence of sensorimotor behavior in the young child, an important component of early cognition. In addition to the HELP, there is *HELP at HOME* (Furano et al., 1985), which provides information for parents and professionals in facilitating development within specific skill areas; the *HELP Checklist*; *HELP Family-Centered*

Interview; and HELP *Together*, a computer software package for reporting data and planning intervention. Some material is also available in Spanish.

High/Scope Child Observation Record (COR)

The High/Scope Child Observation Record (High/Scope, 1992) is an observational assessment of child behavior in six areas of development: initiative, social relations, creative representation, music and movement, language and literacy, and logic and mathematics. Although it does not specifically address cognition, items in the creative representation and logic and mathematics are closely tied to this domain. The COR is a highly systematized tool for the assessment of development for children 2 to 6 years of age. Assessment begins with observation and anecdotal recording of child behavior sufficient to provide evidence to complete 30 items in the six domains. Each item has five specifically described levels— ranging from easiest to hardest in a hierachial sequence. High/Scope suggests that the instrument is best used by team members after attending a 2-day workshop. High/Scope is currently preparing to expand the COR downward for infants and toddlers and upward for children in primary grades.

Infant-Toddler Developmental Assessment

The Infant Toddler Developmental Assessment (IDA) (Provence, Erikson, Vater, & Palmeri, 1995) consists of three instruments/forms: IDA/Provence Birth-to-Three Developmental Profile, IDA Parent Rapport, and IDA Health Recording Guide. The assessment focuses on motor, language, cognitive/adaptive, feelings, social adaptation, and personality trait domains. The scale items appear compatible with general curriculum goals (Bagnato et al., 1997). Authors describe the IDA as an integrated clinical process composed of six consecutive phases. Each phase is prerequisite to the next. Phases are (1) referral and pre-referral data gathering, (2) initial parent interview, (3) health review, (4) developmental observation

and assessment, (5) integration and synthesis, and (6) result sharing. Scale domains are gross motor, fine motor, relationship to inanimate objects, language/communication, self-help, relationship to people, emotions and feeling states, and coping behavior.

Vulpé Assessment Battery–Revised Edition

The Vulpé Assessment Battery, Revised Edition (VAB-R) (Vulpé, 1994), a developmental assessment of the behavior of children from birth to age 8, contains items across six domains: gross-motor, fine-motor, language, cognitive processes, adaptive behavior, and activities of daily living. The cognitive processes and specific concepts contain a number of Piagetian concepts as well as a number of items more typically found in assessments of information processing. The VAB-R uses a 7-point scoring system similar to a most-to-least prompt system. For example, the lowest score is a *no score* (if a child doesn't attend to the task) and proceeds through *attention, physical, socio-emotional,* and *verbal assistance* to *independent* and *transfer* (generalization) scores. Age equivalents are assigned to the items. Developmental sequences are of moderate density and also provide an assessment of the early intervention environment and caregiving styles of staff (Bagnato et al., 1997). The VAB-R allows a flexible format to combine observation, parent report, and direct assessment. Flexibility, team orientation, and use of modifications (sensory and response) and multiple and convergent data sources are noteworthy.

Work Sampling System

The Work Sampling System (WSS) (Meisels, Jablon, Marsden, Dichtelmiller, Dorfman, & Steele, 1994) focuses on developmental and curriculum tasks in the preschool (3 to 5 years old) and early elementary environments. Domains include personal and social, language and literacy, mathematical thinking, scientific thinking, social studies, the arts, and physical development. Children are rated "proficient," "in process," or "not yet" on performance indicators. A summary report rates overall child performance as "developing as expected" or "needs development." Assessment is based on work samples.

Ordinal Scales

Assessment in Infancy: Ordinal Scales of Psychological Development

Assessment in Infancy: Ordinal Scales of Psychological Development (Uzgiris & Hunt, 1975) is comprised of six scales: visual pursuit and permanence of objects, means for obtaining desired environmental events, imitation (vocal and gestural), operational causality, construction of object relations in space, and relation to objects. These scales are further broken into steps or test items. Items include an activity, directions for eliciting the response, and suggested location and materials. The criterion behavior is also included.

These scales are individually administered and may be presented in a single session or in multiple ones. No norms are provided; however, in 1980 Dunst assigned estimated developmental age placements for each of the scale steps that provided a reasonable estimate of current functioning and have demonstrated moderate to high correlations with norm-referenced instruments such as the Bayley Scales of Infant Development and the Griffiths Mental Development Scales (Dunst, Rheingrover, & Kistler, 1986). These scales are based primarily on Piaget's theory of intelligence, which suggests that the acquisition of competencies is dependent on the mastery of prior competencies at a lower level of functioning. Learning is hierarchical with increasing sophistication and expansion of previous learning. Dunst and Gallagher (1983) describe ordinal scales in this way: "The test items on ordinal assessment scales consist of eliciting situations designed to evoke a possible range of critical actions and behaviors from the infant" (p. 45). Developmental status is obtained by noting the highest item passed on each scale. Ordinal scales have a distinct advantage for testing children with disabilities. Test procedures are much more flexible and permit the examiner to vary materials and create situations that elicit the required response/behavior.

Although the Ordinal Scales were originally developed for use with infants functioning within the sensorimotor stage, they are also frequently used with older children, especially those with severe delays or disabilities. To provide greater specificity, Dunst (1980) developed a manual that offers additional items to make the scales more sensitive to the smaller changes in development often evidenced by children with severe or profound disabilities.

Observation of Behavior in Socially and Ecologically Relevant and Valid Environments

The Observation of Behavior in Socially and Ecologically Relevant and Valid Environments (OBSERVE) (Dunst & McWilliam, 1988) provides an observational method of evaluation based on Piagetian stage theory that is particularly useful for children with multiple disabilities (Benner, 1992). The OBSERVE assesses interactive competencies in social and nonsocial environments, using a hierarchical system comprised of five levels of behavioral capabilities: attentional interactions, contingency interactions, differentiated interactions, encoded interactions, and symbolic interactions. The assessment provides a mechanism for observing ongoing interactions of the child and the social and nonsocial environment, and a set of "eliciting" situations (Dunst, Holbert, & Wilson, 1990). Using five mutually exclusive levels of behavior capabilities (following Piaget's cognitive development sequence), the system provides a running record of behaviors demonstrated by the child in adapting to natural and elicited environmental demands in daily routines. These five levels and four transition levels/points provide a nine-level model to describe the capabilities of young children with or without disabilities. By closely matching learning conditions to the child's ability to interact with the environment and response capabilities, a more accurate measure of his ability to learn new behaviors may be obtained (Baird,

McCormick, McLean, Bruder, Dunst, 1991). In other words, the response demands of the assessment are designed to match the response capabilities of the child, rather than the reverse.

ASSESSMENT LINKED TO STANDARDS AND OUTCOMES

Assessment of young children must respond to the increasing validation of accountability and use of standards as educational outcomes by public, professional, and community stakeholders. Standards have been proposed by national organizations, federal and state agencies, and even legislators. For example, Kentucky carefully monitors and ranks schools based on performance of students on the Kentucky Commonwealth Accountability Testing Sytem (CATS). Accountability indices based on this data are published in local newspapers for public review and dissemination with incentives awarded to schools for achievement and progress toward identified goals. Standards have been established across content areas (mathematics, science, the arts, and physical education) and have also been developed for more general learning and knowledge. Necessary to the measurement of child progress in meeting the educational standards developed by professional organizations and agencies, has been the mandated assessment of the progress of children toward these standards (McAfee & Leong, 2002). According to Meisels (2000), every state has developed standards for K–12 education with mandated assessment systems to determine the progress of children in meeting state (and/or national) standards. Standardized assessments have been used to provide a level of accountability and to document that children meet state and national standards in reading/writing and math for children in the K–12 system, however, early childhood educators have been able to avoid the use of standardized assessment for accountability during the preschool years because of the lack of clear expectations for preschool children. However, this is changing. Early childhood education programs will soon be included in these high-profile and high-stakes assessments.

In 1998, the Head Start Act was amended to include the Head Start Performance Standards, closely coordinated with the Head Start Program Performance Measures in response to a specific legislative mandate and emphasis on accountability and results-oriented evaluation. Beginning January 1, 1998, the Head Start Program Performance Standards were effective for all children, birth to 5 years, enrolled in Head Start programs. Many of the Program Performance Measures are based on the Program Performance Standards. The Head Start Outcomes Framework is based on the Head Start Performance Standards and Performance Measures and includes 8 domains, 27 domain elements, and 100 indicators that are believed to be important for school success. The framework is intended to guide the selection or adaptation of available instruments or the development of instruments to measure child progress for children 3 to 5 years old. It is not intended to be used as a checklist; every Head Start program will have an assessment system aligned with its curriculum that gathers data on child progress in each of the eight domains of learning and development (Administration on Children, Youth and Families, 2000). Because four of the eight domains are legislatively mandated, programs must collect and analyze data on four domain elements and nine indicators in language, literacy, and numeracy skills. Assessment of child outcome is intended to be from multiple sources such as teacher observations, child work samples and performance, parent report, and direct assessment. The seventh domain, Approaches to Learning, includes three domain elements: initiative and curiosity, engagement and persistence, and reasoning and problem-solving, with accompanying indicators and is included in Table 10.2. The Head Start Child Outcomes Framework can be accessed at www.headstartinfo.org/pdf/im00_18a.pdf.

Concurrently with the development of the Program Performance Measures and Outcomes,

TABLE 10.2

Head Start Child Outcomes Framework, Domain 7 Approaches to Learning

Domain Elements	Indicators
Initiative and Curiosity	Chooses to participate in an increasing variety of tasks and activities.
	Develops increased ability to make independent choices.
	Approaches tasks and activities with increased flexibility, imagination, and inventiveness.
	Grows in eagerness to learn about and discuss a growing range of topics, ideas, and tasks.
Engagement and Persistence	Grows in abilities to persist in and complete a variety of tasks, activities, projects, and experiences.
	Demonstrates increasing ability to set goals and develop and follow through on plans.
	Shows growing capacity to maintain concentration over time on a task, question, set of directions or interactions, despite distractions and interruptions.
Reasoning and Problem Solving	Develops increasing ability to find more than one solution to a question, task, or problem.
	Grows in recognizing and solving problems through active exploration, including trial and error, and interactions and discussions with peers and adults.
	Develops increasing abilities to classify, compare and contrast objects, events, and experiences.

Note: From Administration on Children, Youth and Families (August 10, 2000). Head Start Child Outcomes Framework. In *Information Memorandum on Using Child Outcomes in Program Self-Assessment. IM-00-18.* Washington, DC: Administration on Children, Youth and Families.

Head Start began a national longitudinal study of the cognitive, social, emotional, and physical development of Head Start children, titled Head Start Family and Child Experiences Survey (FACES) as part of Head Start's Program Performance Measures Initiative to provide outcome-based information about the Head Start program to its stakeholders (Head Start Bureau, U.S. Department of Health and Human Services, local Head Start grantees, Congress, and the public) (McKey, Tarullo, & Doan, 1999). The study has five phases of data collection (from 1997 to 2000) and, in addition to program evaluation, will provide useful information to the field regarding the strengths of the selected assessment model.

Researchers combined a number of components from published assessment tools such as the Peabody Picture Vocabulary Test III (Dunn & Dunn, 1997) and the Woodcock-Johnson (Woodcock, McGrew, & Mather, 2001) in the child assessment battery designed to measure cognitive outcomes. In addition, researchers used assessment from the recently released Early Childhood Longitudinal Study in Reading and General Knowledge conducted by the National Center for Education Statistics (NCES). This study is a nationally representative sample of approximately 22,000 children from K– 5th grade. The study was commissioned by the U.S. Department of Education and other federal agencies in response to public awareness of the importance of early education, the National Education Goal for school readiness, and the apparent lack of information available regarding the status of kindergarten readiness of America's children. Information about the Early Childhood Longitudinal Study can be accessed at http://nces.ed.gov/ecls/. Information about the FACES can be found at http://www2.acf.dhhs.gov/programs/hsb/hsreac/faces/. The NCES has begun the study of 13,500 infants born in 2001 to provide a similar database for infants and toddlers. Head Start has begun similar efforts to expand FACES to Early Head Start.

A thorough review of the debate regarding the use of testing in the preschool classroom for accountability purposes is beyond the scope of this chapter. However, Meisels (2000) suggests that alternative strategies such as the testing of a random sample of children can provide an adequate representation of child learning and progress toward state and national standards sufficient to document program effectiveness and should be proposed and advocated by early childhood professionals.

Preschool Individual Growth and Development Indicators (IGDI) Preschool IGDIs (McConnell et al., 2002) are part of a decision-making model being developed by the Early Childhood Research Institute on Measuring Growth and Development (ECRI-MGD) to provide a framework for comprehensive assessment of growth and development within early intervention. The proposed model is designed to monitor development and provide intervention to children birth to age 8 (ECRI-MDI, Technical Report 6, 1998). This model is conceptually similar to databased problem-solving models currently being used in the disciplines of school psychology and special education. The model emphasizes outcomes, as opposed to problems, and consists of sequential steps to a) establish desired outcomes, b) identify developmental concerns relative to the desired outcome, c) validate concerns by describing cur-

rent level of performance on relevant indicators, d) explore strategies for achieving desired outcome, e) implement strategies and evaluate effectiveness, and f) determine whether intervention was sufficient and concern is no longer present.

An example of the general outcome measurement approach, Preschool IDGIs are designed for use with children ranging from 30 to 66 months of age and consist of a set of measures that allow for repeated assessment of a child's development over time in the developmental domains of language, cognition, social, motor, and self-help. Such measures of relevant indicators provide a sample of a child's performance on a broad domain, or terminal skill in a particular domain, and indicate when progression is occurring toward a specified goal or when intervention may be needed. As an example, the general outcome measure for expressive language is "The child uses gestures, sounds, and words to express wants and needs and convey meaning to others" with two promising indicators (picture naming and semi-structured play) currently identified (McConnell et al., 2002). The picture naming task requires a child to name as many pictured objects as possible in a 1-minute session. Concurrent validity using the Peabody Picture Vocabulary Test—Revised (Dunn & Dunn, 1997) and the Preschool Language Scale—3 (Zimmerman, Steiner, & Pond, 1992) has been investigated with a moderate relationship (correlation coefficients ranging from .47 to .69) reported. The semi-structured play indicator involves a 10-minute play session with a peer during which verbal behavior is observed using a 10-second partial-interval method (McConnell et al., 2002). The session is coded for two variables: the number of intervals in which an utterance of three or fewer words is made and the number of intervals in which an utterance of four or more words is made. McConnell and colleagues consider the observational measure of four or more word utterances a promising indicator of expressive language. Preschool IGDI's are currently being developed and evaluated to assess early literacy development, social interaction, motor, and adaptive domains.

The process and procedures for identifying general outcomes and corresponding indicators are thoroughly presented in several documents produced by the ECRI-MGD: ECRI-MGD Technical Report 2, Selection of General Growth Outcomes for Children between Birth to Age Eight; ECRI-MGD Technical Report 3, National Survey to Validate General Growth Outcomes for Children between Birth to Age Eight; and ECRI-MGD Technical Report 4, Research and Development of Individual Growth and Development Indicators: Children between Birth and to Age Eight. Preschool IDGI's are still in the process of being developed, researched, and evaluated; however, the approach appears promising as a useful tool in linking assessment with intervention for young children (Greenwood et al., 2002).

Assessment of Conceptual Development

Assessments that are primarily measures of concept development are also available for preschoolers; however, the National Association for the Education of Young Children (NAEYC) suggests caution in the use of such instruments to determine school readiness in their 1995 position statement on school readiness (NAEYC, 1995). A brief summary of three such instruments is provided. The *Basic School Skills Inventory–Diagnostic* (Hammill & Leigh, 1983) was designed to be used as both a norm-referenced and criterion-referenced assessment. The test includes 110 items in six areas: daily living skills, spoken language, reading, writing, math readiness, and classroom behavior. The *Boehm Test of Basic Concepts–Preschool Version* (Boehm, 1986a, 1986b) and the *Bracken Basic Concept Scale–Revised* (Bracken, 1998) also measure basic concept attainment for preschoolers and early elementary-age children. The Boehm Test of Basic Concepts–Preschool Version is a downward extension of the Boehm–R, an instrument that provides information regarding a child's mastery of concepts labeled important for suc-

cessful performance early in school by the author. This assessment surveys the child's understanding of 26 basic relational concepts that help children understand and describe the world around them. The results were intended to be used by teachers to plan interventions and as indicators of school readiness (Boehm, 2000), however Bracken (2000) suggests that use of the Boehm tests should be limited to screening alone because of poor reliability and inadequate norms. The Bracken Basic Concept Scale–Revised assesses 308 concepts in 11 areas: color, letter identification, numbers/counting, sizes, comparisons, shapes, direction/position, self/social awareness, textural/ material, quantity, and time/sequence. The test is divided into two instruments—a diagnostic full-scale instrument and an alternate form screening test—and can be used with children 2 years 6 months to 8 years. Adaptations of the response mode (verbal response, directed eye gaze) are permitted.

In addition to standardized tests of concept development are state and district-developed assessments and scales. For example, North Carolina has completed an extensive review of current assessment instruments and practices in preparation of a general policy statement to define school readiness, to develop a school readiness system to assess the conditions of children entering school, and to adopt a school readiness system to assess schools' readiness for children. Educators in North Carolina communicated to state policy makers and the public that (1) there is no widely accepted definition of school readiness, and (2) there is no national system for assessing school readiness. Most often, states define a child as ready for kindergarten when he or she reaches a certain age criterion (Saluja, Scott-Little, & Clifford, 2000). Based on recommendations from the National Education Goals Panel, North Carolina adopted five domains of children's early development and learning when defining school readiness; health and physical development, emotional well-being and social competence, approaches to learning, communicative skills, and cognition and general knowledge. North Carolina also will use a modified version of the Family and Child Experiences Survey (FACES) battery as its general outcome assessment tool. The cognition and general knowledge outcomes include basic knowledge about the world (e.g., knows own name, knows basic science concepts) and other cognitive competencies such as early mathematical skills (e.g., knowledge of numbers, shapes, and simple patterns), and basic problem-solving skills (e.g., similarities and differences).

The concerns of the early childhood community voiced by NAEYC regarding school readiness are particularly important for children at-risk for disabilities and school success. Three of these are fundamental. First, the concept of readiness doesn't account for the diversity of early life experiences. Many children lack access to opportunities that promote school success. It is unfair to penalize them for their lack of opportunity. Second, many of the criteria included in assessments of readiness are based on unsuitable expectations for populations of such diversity and variation in rate and nature of individual development. Third, school readiness connotes a misplaced focus. It is the school that must be ready to meet the needs of the child as he enters; not the child who must be ready to meet a predetermined set of capabilities required by school (NAEYC, 1995).

Assessment of Emergent Literacy

Most people, public and professional, would agree that reading is a critical skill that children must demonstrate for academic and life success. Traditionally, reading instruction is associated with formal instruction during the elementary years, and some concerns exist about an emphasis placed on formal instruction in reading during early childhood. Such concerns are based upon differing viewpoints about how reading skills develop and whether reading instruction can occur in developmentally appropriate ways for young children (Teale, 1995). Teale provides a comprehensive discussion of the issues related to reading within

early childhood and defines emergent literacy as a perspective that "recognizes the need to help children learn about phonemic awareness, letters, and sounds, but . . . sees these facets of reading within the broader context of functionality, purpose, and meaning" (p. 124). Teale further advocates for early childhood educators to assume a proactive approach to reading through the use of developmentally appropriate activities in ways that facilitate children's learning about important literacy concepts and skills in an enjoyable and meaningful fashion.

Three concepts or skill areas have been identified as necessary for the subsequent development of skilled reading: a) phonological awareness refers to the ability to hear and manipulate the sound structure of language, b) alphabetic principle includes the association of printed letters to speech and the phonological recoding of letter strings into corresponding sounds as well as blending sounds into words, and c) automaticity or fluency with connected text (Simmons & Kame'enui, 1998). These areas provide a framework for assessments designed to provide information about a child's skills related to reading skill development.

Assessment of early literacy skills can be conducted to identify children at-risk for reading difficulties and to monitor a child's progress in early literacy skills. Casey and Howe (2002) provide a review of best practices in early literacy assessment and address concepts/skill areas such as phonological awareness, letter recognition, rapid letter naming, letter-sound association, ability to manipulate speech sounds, and knowledge about print including identifying the front of the book, pointing to a word, and identifying where to begin reading. Casey and Howe describe the *Dynamic Indicators of Basic Early Literacy Skills* (DIBELS) (Good & Kaminski, 2001) as the most comprehensive measure currently available. A general outcome measurement approach to emergent literacy, DIBELS is designed for use with early elementary students and is composed of five tasks: a) letter naming fluency, b) initial sound fluency, c) phoneme segmentation fluency, d) nonsense word fluency, and e) oral reading fluency. Tasks are designed to represent the broad domain of reading and serve as indicators of a child's skills in specific areas predictive of later reading achievement. Research is underway that links DIBELS with the previously discussed Preschool IDGI's for younger children and with Curriculum Based Measurement (Shinn, 1989) procedures for older children in an effort to provide a set of measures within which to evaluate rate of growth and development across a larger age span (McConnell et al., 2002). For more information about DIBELS, refer to the home page at http://dibels.uoregon.edu/.

TRANSLATING ASSESSMENT INFORMATION INTO INSTRUCTIONAL GOALS

Linking Assessment to Intervention

The future of assessment instruments will depend on their usefulness in planning and evaluating programs for young children (Kelly & Surbeck, 2000). The use of norm-referenced assessments in isolation has been increasingly challenged (Neisworth & Bagnato, 1996). School psychologists and educational diagnosticians are using alternative assessment instruments more and more frequently to determine a child's abilities and to plan intervention (Neisworth & Bagnato, 1992). Alternative methods of assessment may include authentic, dynamic, portfolio, curriculum-based, process, and performance assessments as well as task analysis (Cohen & Spenciner, 1994). *Authentic* assessment reflects children's development and learning in daily activities and routines. Its primary purpose is to guide and support children's learning (McAfee & Leong, 2002). *Performance* assessment uses a systematic collection, synthesis, and analysis of data outcomes from multiple methods and products, such as observational techniques, anecdotal records, and video and audiotaping.

Photographs and work samples are also used in performance assessment. Losardo & Notari-Syverson (2001) define performance assessment as "systematically using children's behaviors and projects to make judgements for assessment purposes" (p. 72).

Bagnato and Neisworth (1991) describe a convergent assessment model which provides a link to intervention through the establishment of a developmental content, behavioral strategies hypothesized to be effective for intervention, and appropriate data-keeping methods. There is strong support for the use of a more convergent model in linking assessment and evaluation to intervention. Recommended practice suggests the use of multiple measures: (a) norm-referenced; (b) criterion-referenced; (c) judgment-based; and (d) ecological-based. Multiple sources such as parents and other family members, caregivers, and early care and education providers must also be used to gather information concerning the abilities of the child in multiple settings, for example, home, preschool, church, grandmother's house, and the grocery store. A convergent model of multiple measures for children ages 36 to 48 months is included in Table 10.3.

Convergent assessment refers to the synthesis of information gathered from several sources, instruments, settings, and occasions to produce the most valid appraisal of developmental status and to accomplish the related assessment purposes of identification, prescription, and progress evaluation (Bagnato & Neisworth, 1991). The convergent model establishes an organized context in which information from multiple sources may be used in a systematic way.

Bricker and her colleagues have also developed a system for linking assessment to program planning and progress evaluation. The *Assessment, Evaluation, and Programming System (AEPS) for Infants and Children* (Volumes 1–4) is a comprehensive system that encompasses the assessment, intervention, and evaluation process and provides strong linkages between a curriculum-referenced instrument and intervention planning

TABLE 10.3

Sample Assessment Battery for a Preschool Child (36 to 48 months)

Type	Example
Norm-based	Differential Ability Scales (Elliott, 1990)
Curriculum-based	Assessment, Evaluation, and Programming System (AEPS): Measurement for Three to Six Years (Bricker, 2002)
Judgment-based	Social Skills Rating System (Gresham & Elliott, 1990)
Eco-based	Early Childhood Environment Rating Scale–Revised Edition (Harms, Clifford, & Cryer, 1998)

Source: Adapted from Assessment for Early Intervention: Best Practices for Professionals (1991) by S. Bagnato and J. Neiswoth, London: Guilford Press.

and implementation. Bagnato et al., (1997) describe the AEPS as a "precise yet family friendly assessment" (p. 95). The system, which is described in four volumes (Bricker, 2002) includes (a) the AEPS Test for Birth to 3 years and 3 to 6 years; (b) a set of IEP/IFSP goals and objectives; (c) observation data recording forms; (d) the AEPS Family Report—an assessment designed to be completed by families; (e) the AEPS Child Progress Form; and (f) the AEPS Curriculum for Birth to Three Years and the AEPS Curriculum for Three to Six Years.

The AEPS, which is designed to measure functional abilities, is comprehensive (1 month to 6 years), uses observation as the primary method of obtaining information, and allows the examiner to adapt or modify the presentation format for children with motor or sensory impairments. In addition, a parallel form of the assessment may be used by family members to assist them in the identification of IEP/IFSP goals and objectives. Accompanying materials also include assessment activity plans that provide suggestions for the acquisition of assessment information in natural environments and during typical routines such as group play.

The activity-based assessments and materials developed by Bricker and her colleagues provide a comprehensive and unified approach to assessment, intervention, and program evaluation. The AEPS provides an opportunity to assess young children comprehensively within naturally occurring routines and environments with parents as partners. Materials provide opportunity for team members, including families, to identify priorities, interests and concerns for program planning and to jointly assess child progress during intervention.

The advantages of using ecological and curriculum-based tools such as the AEPS are many. First, a greater number of behaviors than typically are sampled in a norm-based assessment are identified, thereby providing greater specificity to more accurately reflect developmental status. Second, the items are typically more useful and relevant to family concerns. Additionally, these tools allow for multiple opportunities to demonstrate skills in multiple settings with preferred and multiple partners, objects, and materials. The observation and analysis of behaviors that are child initiated and use familiar materials from home, the child-care center, or preschool classroom provide more useful information for instruction because of their authenticity.

Assessments that are child-centered and interactive rather than those that simply enumerate or quantify the presence or absence of isolated skills generate a stronger base of knowledge to understand the child, his learning and knowing, and his ability to interact with the everyday environment. Assessments that yield information about child behavior and preferences with people, objects, events, and settings, together with information obtained from multiple and authentic sources provide a more accurate and holistic view of the child (McCormick et al., 2002). Fewell states: "The process, the products, and the procedures of assessment have changed dramatically, but the goals remain essentially the same: we want to gain valid, reliable, and useful information about children without penalizing them through the limits of our measurement system. Further we want information that can be translated quite easily into improved instruction and services for children with special needs" (Fewell, 2000, p. 42).

· · · · · · · ·
SUMMARY OF KEY CONCEPTS

- New methods of assessing and evaluating infants and young children with disabilities are being developed and used to capture reliable and realistic child and family information.
- An awareness of the theoretical issues in the assessment of cognitive development allows early interventionists to examine their philosophy and to become more knowledgeable consumers of instruments and tools.
- The assessment of cognition can be viewed from a number of perspectives, including traditional psychometrics, cognitive stage or Piagetian, information processing, social learning, maturational/developmental, and functional.
- If assessment information is to be valid and reliable, five important assumptions must be met: the administrator is skilled; error will be present; acculturation is comparable; behavior sampling is adequate; and present behavior is observed, future behavior is inferred.

- When assessing children, interventionists must attend to children's developmental histories, their cultural uniqueness, and the impact of their disabilities.
- Emerging trends in the evaluation and assessment of young children with disabilities include play-based assessment, ecological assessment, and judgment-based assessment. Common among these is the use of naturalistic environments, community and home settings, where children can interact and participate in preferred ways in familiar surroundings.
- Early interventionists should be familiar with representative norm-referenced instruments, developmental scales and checklists, ordinal scales and instruments, and tools designed for specific populations.
- Alternative methods of assessment such as curriculum-based, process, and performance assessments are increasingly becoming a part of the assessment battery.

· · · · · · · ·
REFERENCES

Administration on Children, Youth and Families (August 10, 2000). Head Start child outcomes framework. In *Information memorandum on using child outcomes in program self-assessment. IM-00-18*. Washington, DC: Administration on Children, Youth and Families.

Anastasiow, N. (1986). *Development and disability.* Baltimore: Paul H. Brookes.

Arthur, G. (1949). The Arthur adaptation of the Leiter International Performance Scale. *Journal of Clinical Psychology, 5,* 345–349.

Bagnato, S., & Neisworth, J. T. (1991). *Assessment for early intervention: Best practices for professionals.* London: Guilford Press.

Bagnato, S. J., Neisworth, J. T., & Munson, S.M. (1997). *LINKing assessment and early intervention: An authentic curriculum-based approach.* Baltimore: Paul H. Brookes.

Bailey, D. B., Bruer, J. T., Symons, F. J., & Lichtman, J. W. (2001). *Critical thinking about critical periods.* Baltimore: Paul H. Brookes.

Bailey, D. B., Vandiviere, P., Dellinger, J., & Munn, D. (1987). The Battelle Developmental Inventory: Teacher perceptions and implementation data. *Journal of Psychoeducational Assessment, 3,* 217–226.

Bailey, D., & Wolery, M. (1989). *Assessing infants and preschoolers with handicaps.* Upper Saddle River, NJ: Merrill/Prentice Hall.

Baird, S. M., McCormick, K., McLean, M., Bruder, M. B., & Dunst, C. J. (1991). Techniques for infants and toddlers with multiple or severe disabilities. In S. Raver (Ed.), *Intervention strategies for infants and toddlers with special needs: A team approach* (2nd ed, pp. 224–258). Upper Saddle River, NJ: Merrill/ Prentice Hall.

Bandura, A. (1978). The self system in reciprocal determinism. *American Psychologist, 33,* 344–358.

Bayley, N. (1933). *The California first year mental scale.* Berkeley, CA: University of California Press.

Bayley, N. (1969). *Bayley Scales of Infant Development.* San Antonio, TX: Psychological Corp.

Bayley, N. (1993). *Bayley Scales of Infant Development—II.* San Antonio, TX: Psychological Corp.

Benner, S. (1992). *Assessing young children with special needs: An ecological perspective.* New York: Longman.

Berdine, W. H., & Meyer, S. A. (Eds.). (1987). *Assessment in special education.* Boston: Little, Brown.

Boehm, A. E. (1986a). *Boehm Test of Basic Concepts–Preschool Version.* San Antonio, TX: Psychological Corp.

Boehm, A. E. (1986b). *Boehm Test of Basic Concepts–Revised.* San Antonio, TX: Psychological Corp.

Boehm, A. E. (2000). Assessment of basic relational concepts. In B. Bracken (Ed.), *The psychoeduca-tional assessment of preschool children* (3rd ed., pp. 186–203). Boston: Allyn and Bacon.

Bos, C. S., Vaughn, S., & Levine, L. M. (1990). *2 to 6: Instructional activities for children at risk.* Chicago: Riverside Corporation.

Boyd, R. D. (1989). What a difference a day makes: Age-related discontinuities and the Battelle Developmental Inventory. *Journal of Early Intervention, 13*(2), 114–119.

Bracken, B. A. (1987). Limitations of preschool instruments and standards for minimal levels of technical adequacy. *Journal of Psychoeducational Assessment, 5,* 313–326.

Bracken, B. (1991). The assessment of preschool children with the McCarthy Scales of Children's Abilities. In B. Bracken (Ed.), *The psychoeducational assessment of preschool children* (2nd ed., pp. 53–85). Boston: Allyn and Bacon.

Bracken, B. A. (1998). *Bracken Basic Concept Scale–Revised.* San Antonio, TX: Psychological Corp.

Bracken, B. (2000). The clinical observation of preschool assessment behavior. In B. Bracken (Ed.), *The psychoeducational assessment of preschool children* (3rd ed., pp. 45–56). Boston: Allyn and Bacon.

Bricker, D. (2002). *Assessment, evaluation, and programming system for infants and children:* Second Edition. Baltimore: Paul H. Brookes.

Brigance, A. H. (1990). *Brigance Prescriptive Readiness; Strategies and practice.* North Billerica, MA. Curriculum Associates.

Brigance, A. H. (1991). *Brigance Diagnostic Inventory of Early Development–Revised.* North Billerica, MA: Curriculum Associates.

Burgemeister, B., Blum, L., & Lorge, I. (1972). *Columbia Mental Maturity Scale.* San Antonio, TX: Psychological Corp.

Campione, J. C., & Brown, A. L. (1978). Toward a theory of intelligence: Contributions from research with retarded children. *Intelligence, 2,* 279–304.

Campione, J. C., & Brown, A. L. (1985). Linking dynamic assessment with school achievement. In C. S. Lidz (Ed.), *Dynamic assessment: An interactional approach to evaluating learning potential* (pp. 82–195). New York: Guilford Press.

Casey, A., & Howe, K. (2002). Best practices in early literacy skills. In A. Thomas & J. Grimes (Eds.), *Best practices in school psychology IV:* Vol. 1 (pp. 721–736). Bethesda, MD: National Association of School Psychologists.

Cattell, P. (1940). *The measurement of intelligence of infants and young children.* New York: Psychological Corp.

Cattell, P. (1960). *Cattell Infant Intelligence Scale.* San Antonio, TX: Psychological Corp.

Cattell, P. (1980). *The measurement of intelligence of infants and young children.* San Antonio, TX: Psychological Corp.

Chang, P. (1990). Early intervention with culturally diverse families of infants and toddlers with disabilities. *Infants and Young Children, 3*(2), 78–87.

Clark, A. M. (1982). Developmental discontinuities: An approach to assessing their nature. In L. A. Bond and J. M. Joffe (Eds.), *Facilitating infant and early childhood development* (pp. 58–77). Hanover, NH: University Press of New England.

Coalson, D., Weiss, L., Zhu, J. Spruill, J., & Crockett, D. (2002). *Development of the WPPSI-III.* Paper presented at National Association of School Psychologists Annual Conference, Chicago.

Cohen, L., & Spenciner, L. (1994). *Assessment of young children.* New York: Longman.

Cohen, M., & Gross, P. (1979a). *The developmental resource: Behavioral sequences for assessment and program planning* (Vol. 1). New York: Grune & Stratton.

Cohen, M., & Gross, P. (1979b). *The developmental resource: Behavioral sequences for assessment and program planning* (Vol. 2). New York: Grune & Stratton.

Connolly, A. J. (1998). *Key Math–Revised: A diagnostic inventory of essential Mathematics–Normative Update.* Circle Pines, MN: American Guidance Service.

Davis, C. (1980). *Perkins-Binet Test of Intelligence for the Blind.* Watertown, MA: Perkins School for the Blind.

Deno, S. L. (1997). Whether thoust goest. Perspectives on progress monitoring. In J. W. Lloyd, E. J. Kame'enui, & D. Chard (Eds.), *Issues in educating students with disabilities* (pp. 77–99). Mahwah, NJ: Lawrence Erlbaum Associates.

Deysach, R. E. (1986). The role of neuropsychological assessment in the comprehensive evaluation of preschool-age children. *School Psychology Review, 15,* 233–244.

Dunn, L. M., & Dunn, L. M. (1997). *Peabody Picture Vocabulary Test–III.* Circle Pines: MN: American Guidance Service.

Dunst, C. J. (1980). *A clinical and educational manual for use with the Uzgiris and Hunt scales of infant psychological development.* Austin, TX: PRO-ED.

Dunst, C. J., & Gallagher, J. (1983). Piagetian approaches to infant assessment. *Topics in Early Childhood Special Education, 3*(1), 44–62.

Dunst, C. J., Holbert, K. A., & Wilson, L. L. (1990). Strategies for assessing infant sensorimotor interactive competencies. In E. D. Gibbs & D. M. Teti (Eds.), *Interdisciplinary assessment of infants: A guide for early intervention professionals.* Baltimore: Paul H. Brookes.

Dunst, C. J., & McWilliam, R. A. (1988). Cognitive assessment and multiply handicapped young children. In T. D. Wachs & R. Sheehan (Eds.), *Assessment of developmentally disabled children* (pp. 213–238). New York: Plenum Press.

Dunst, C. J., Rheingrover, R. M., & Kistler, E. D. (1986). Concurrent validity of the Uzgiris-Hunt Scales: Relationship to Bayley Scales mental age. *Behavioral Science Documents, 16,* 65.

Early Childhood Research Institute on Measuring Growth and Development (1998). *Selection of general growth outcomes for children between birth to age eight* (Tech. Rep. No. 2). Minneapolis, MN: Center for Early Education and Development, University of Minnesota (available at http://ici2.umn.edu/ecri).

Early Childhood Research Institute on Measuring Growth and Development (1998). *National survey to validate general growth outcomes for children between birth to age eight* (Tech. Rep. No. 3). Minneapolis, MN: Center for Early Education and Development, University of Minnesota (available at http://ici2.umn.edu/ecri).

Early Childhood Research Institute on Measuring Growth and Development (1998). *Research and development of individual growth and development indicators for children between birth to age eight* (Tech. Rep. No. 4). Minneapolis, MN: Center for Early Education and Development, University of Minnesota (available at http://ici2.umn.edu/ecri).

Early Childhood Research Institute on Measuring Growth and Development (1998). *Theoretical foundations of the Early Childhood Research Institute on Measuring Growth and Development: An early childhood problem-solving model* (Tech. Rep. No. 6). Minneapolis, MN: Center for Early Education and Development, University of Minnesota (available at http://ici2.umn.edu/ecri).

Elliott, C. D. (1990). *The Differential Ability Scales*. San Antonio, TX: Psychological Corp.

Elliott, C. D., Daniel, M. H., & Guiton, G. W. (1991). Preschool cognitive assessment with the Differential Ability Scales. In B. Bracken (Ed.), *The psychoeducational assessment of preschool children* (2nd ed., pp. 133–153). Boston: Allyn and Bacon.

Elliott, C. D., Murray, D. J., & Pearson, L. S. (1979). *The British Ability Scales*. Windsor, England: National Foundation for Educational Research.

Ensher, G. L., Bobish, T. P., Gardner, E. F., Michaels, C. A., Butler, K. G., Foertsch, D., & Cooper, C. (1997) *The Syracuse Assessments for Birth to Three*. Syracuse, NY: Applied Symbolix.

Feuerstein, R. (1979). *The dynamic assessment of retarded performers*. Baltimore: University Park Press.

Fewell, R. (1983). Assessing handicapped infants. In G. Garwood & R. Fewell (Eds.), *Educating handicapped infants* (pp. 257–297). Rockville, MD: Aspen Systems.

Fewell, R. R. (1991). Some new directions in the assessment and education of young handicapped children. In J. M. Berg (Ed.), *Science and service in mental retardation* (pp. 179–188). London: Methuen.

Fewell, R. (2000). Assessment of young children with special needs: Foundation for tomorrow. *Topics in early childhood special education, 20*(1), 38–42.

French, J. L. (1964). *Pictorial Test of Intelligence*. Boston: Houghton Mifflin.

Furuno, S., O'Reilly, K., Hosaka, C. M., Inatsuka, T. T., Allman, T. L., Zeisloft, B. (1985). *Hawaii Early Learning Profile (HELP) at Home*. Palo Alto, CA: VORT Corp.

Gage, N. L., & Berliner, D. C. (1991). *Educational psychology*. Boston: Houghton Mifflin.

Gibbs, E. D. (1990). Cognitive language and developmental assessment. In E. D. Gibbs & D. M. Teti (Eds.), *Interdisciplinary assessment of infants: A guide for early intervention professionals* (pp. 77–91). Baltimore: Paul H. Brookes.

Gilbert, S. (1997). *Parent and teacher congruency on variations of a screening instrument: An examination*. East Lansing, MI: National Center for Research on Teaching and Learning. (ERIC Document Reproduction Service No. ED413726).

Glover, M. E., Preminger, J. L., & Sanford, A. R. (1978). *Early Learning Accomplishment Profile for Young Children (Early LAP)*. Lewisville, NC: Kaplan Press.

Good, R., Gruba, J., & Kaminski, R. (2002). Best practices in using Dynamic Indicators of Basic Early Literacy Skill (DIBELS) in an outcomes-based model. In A. Thomas & J. Grimes (Eds.), *Best Practices in School Psychology IV*: Vol. 1 (pp. 699–720). Bethesda, MD: National Association of School Psychologists.

Good, R. H., & Kaminski, R. A. (Eds.). (2001). *Dynamic Indicators of Basic Early Literacy Skills* (5th ed.). Eugene, OR: Institute for the Development of Educational Achievement. Available: http://dibels.uorgeon.edu/

Goodenough, F. L. (1926). *Measurement of intelligence by drawings*. Chicago: World Book.

Greenwood, C., Luze, G., & Carta, J. (2002). Best practices in assessment of intervention results with infants and toddlers. In A. Thomas & J. Grimes (Eds.), *Best Practices in School Psychology IV*: Vol. 2 (pp. 1219-1230). Bethesda, MD: National Association of School Psychologists.

Gresham, F. M., & Elliott, S. N. (1990). *Social Skills Rating System*. Circle Pines, MN: American Guidance Service.

Gridley, B., Miller, G., Barke, C., Fischer, W., & Smith, D. (1990). Construct validity of the K-ABC with an at-risk preschool population. *Journal of School Psychology, 28,* 39–49.

Griffiths, R. (1954). *The abilities of babies*. High Wycombe, United Kingdom: The Test Agency.

Griffiths, R. (1979). *The abilities of young children*. London: Child Development Research Center.

Guilford, J. P. (1967). *The nature of human intelligence*. New York: McGraw-Hill.

Haley, S. M., Coster, W. J., Ludlow, L. H., Haltiwanger, J. T., & Andrellos, P. J. (1992). *Pediatric Evaluation of Disability Inventory*. Boston, Massachusetts: PEDI Research Group.

Hammill, D. D., & Bryant, B. R. (1986). *Detroit Tests of Learning Aptitude–Primary*. Austin, TX: PRO-ED.

Hammill, D. D., & Bryant, B. R. (1991). *Detroit Tests of Learning Aptitude–Primary* (2nd ed.). Austin, TX: PRO-ED.

Hammill, D., & Leigh, J. (1983). *Basic School Skills Inventory–Diagnostic*. Austin, TX: PRO-ED.

Haring, N. G., White, O. R., Edgar, E. B., Affleck, J. Q., Hayden, A. H., Munson, R. G., & Bendersky, M. (Eds.). (1981). *Uniform Performance Assessment System*. Upper Saddle River, NJ: Merrill/Prentice Hall.

Harms, T., Clifford, R. M., & Cryer, D. (1998). *Early Childhood Environment Rating Scale–Revised Edition*. New York: Teachers College Press.

High/Scope (1992). *High/Scope Child Observation Record (COR)*. Ypsilanti, MI: High/Scope Press.

Hiskey, M. S. (1966). *Hiskey-Nebraska Test of Learning Aptitude*. Lincoln, NE: Author.

Hooper, S. R. (2000). Neuropsychological assessment of the preschool child. In B. Bracken (Ed.), *The psychoeducational assessment of preschool children* (3rd ed., pp. 383–398). Boston: Allyn and Bacon.

Horn, J. L. (1968). Organization of abilities and the development of intelligence. *Psychological Review, 75,* 242–259.

Hoy, C., & Gregg, N. (1994). *Assessment: The special educator's role*. Pacific Grove, CA: Brooks/Cole.

Hresko, W., Miguel, S., Sherbenou, R., & Burton, S. (1994). Developmental Observation Checklist System (DOCS). Austin, TX: PRO-ED.

Johnson, M. H. (1997). *Developmental cognitive neuroscience: An introduction*. Oxford, England: Basil Blackwell.

Johnson, M. H. (1999). Developmental Neuroscience. In M. H. Bornstein & M. E. Lamb, (Eds.)., *Developmental psychology: An advanced textbook* (4th ed., pp. 199–230). Mahwah, NJ: Lawrence Erlbaum Associates.

Johnson-Martin, N. M., Attermeier, S. M., & Hacker, B. J. (1990). *The Carolina Curriculum for Preschoolers with Special Needs* (2nd ed.). Baltimore: Paul H. Brookes.

Johnson-Martin, N. M., Jens, K. G., Attermeier, S. M., & Hacker, B. J. (1991). *The Carolina Curriculum for Infants and Toddlers with Special Needs* (2nd ed.). Baltimore: Paul H. Brookes.

Kaufman, A. S., Kamphaus, R. W., & Kaufman, N. L. (1985). The Kaufman assessment battery for children. In C. Newmark (Ed.), *Major psychological assessment instruments*. Boston: Allyn and Bacon.

Kaufman, A. S., & Kamphaus, R. W. (1984). Factor analysis of the Kaufman Assessment Battery for Children (K-ABC) for ages 2½ through 12½ years. *Journal of Educational Psychology, 76,* 623–637.

Kaufman, A. S., & Kaufman, N. L. (1983). *Kaufman Assessment Battery for Children*. Circle Pines, MN: American Guidance Service.

Kelly, M. F., & Surbeck, E. (2000). History of preschool assessment. In B. Bracken (Ed.), *The psychoeducational assessment of preschool children* (3rd ed., pp. 1–18). Boston: Allyn and Bacon.

Knobloch, H., & Pasamanick, B. (1974). *Gesell and Amatruda's Developmental Diagnosis: The evaluation and management of normal and abnormal neuropsychological development in infancy and early childhood* (3rd ed.). New York: Harper & Row.

Knobloch, H., Stevens, F., & Malone, A. F. (1980). *Manual of developmental diagnosis*. New York: Harper & Row.

Kolb, B., & Fantie, B. (1997). Development of the child's brain and behavior. In C. R. Reyonlds & E. Fletcher-Janzen (Eds.), *Handbook of clinical child neuropsychology* (2nd ed., pp. 17–41). New York: Plenum Press.

Korkman, M., Kirk, U., & Kemp, S. (1998). *NEPSY: A Developmental Neuropsychological Assessment*. San Antonio, TX: Psychological Corp.

Langley, M. B. (1989). Assessing infant cognitive development. In D. Bailey & M. Wolery (Eds.), *Assessing infants and preschoolers with handicaps* (pp. 249–274). Upper Saddle River, NJ: Merrill/Prentice Hall.

Lefrancois, G. R. (1995). *Theories of human learning*. Pacific Grove, CA: Brooks/Cole.

Leiter, R. G. (1948). *International Performance Scale*. Chicago: Stoelting.

Leiter, R. G. (1979). *Leiter International Performance Scale* (Rev. ed.). Wood Dale, IL: Stoelting.

Lidz, C. S. (Ed.). (1987). *Dynamic assessment: An interactional approach to evaluating learning potential*. New York: Guilford Press.

Lidz, C. S. (1991a). Issues in the assessment of preschool children. In B Bracken (Ed.), *The psychoeducational assessment of preschool children* (2nd ed., pp. 18–32). Boston: Allyn and Bacon.

Lidz, C., S. (1991b). *Practitioner's guide to dynamic assessment*. New York: Guilford Press.

Lidz, C. S., & Thomas, C. (1987). The Preschool Learning Assessment Device: Extension of a static approach. In C. S. Lidz (Ed.), *Dynamic assessment: An interactional approach to evaluating learning potential*. New York: Guilford Press.

Linder, T. (1993a). *Transdisciplinary play-based assessment: A functional approach to working with young children* (Rev. ed.). Baltimore: Paul H. Brookes.

Linder, T. (1993b). *Transdisciplinary play-based intervention: Guidelines for developing a meaningful curriculum for young children*. Baltimore: Paul H. Brookes.

Losardo, A., & Notari-Syverson, A. (2001). *Alternative approaches to assessing young children.* Baltimore: Paul H. Brookes.

Mayfield, P., McCormick, K., & Cook, M. (1993). *A comparison of the Battelle Developmental Inventory with the Learning Accomplishment Profile–Diagnostic Edition.* Unpublished manuscript. University of Alabama, Tuscaloosa, AL.

McAfee, O., & Leong, D. (2002). *Assessing and guiding young children's development and learning* (3rd Ed.). Boston, MA: Allyn & Bacon.

McCarthy, D. (1972). *Manual for the McCarthy Scales of Children's Abilities.* San Antonio, TX: Psychological Corp.

McConnell, S. R. (2000). Assessment in early intervention and early childhood special education: Building on the past to project into our future. *Topics in Early Childhood Special Education, 20*(1), 43–48.

McConnell, S., Priest, J., Davis, S., & McEvoy, M. (2002). Best practices in measuring growth and development for preschool children. In A. Thomas & J. Grimes (Eds.), *Best Practices in School Psychology IV:* Vol. 2 (pp. 1231–1246). Bethesda, MD: National Association of School Psychologists.

McCormick, K., Mayfield, P., & Ridgley, R. (2001, December). *Utility of the Learning Accomplishment Profile–Diagnostic Standardization Assessment.* Paper presented at the 17th Annual DEC International Early Childhood Conference on Children with Special Needs, Boston.

McCormick, K., Woods, J., & Hallam, R. (2002). Planning for success: Comprehensive preassessment planning for preschool children with disabilities. Unpublished manuscript. University of Kentucky, Lexington, KY.

McKey, R. H., Tarullo, L. B., Doan, H. M. (1999, April). *FACES: The Head Start Family and Child Experiences Survey.* Paper presented at the meeting of the Society for Research in Child Development Biennial Meeting, Albuquerque, NM.

McLean, M., & McCormick, K. (1993). Assessment and evaluation in early intervention. In W. Brown, S. K. Thurman, & L. F. Pearl (Eds.), *Family-centered early intervention with infants and toddlers: Innovative cross-disciplinary approaches* (pp. 43–81). Baltimore: Paul H. Brookes.

McLean, M., McCormick, K., & Baird, S. (1991). Concurrent validity of the Griffith's Mental Development Scales with a population of children under 24 months. *Journal of Early Intervention, 15*(4), 338–344.

McLean, M., McCormick, K., Baird, S., & Mayfield, P. (1987). Concurrent validity of the Battelle Developmental Inventory Screening Test. *Diagnostique, 13*(1), 10–20.

McLean, M., McCormick, K., Bruder, M. B., & Burdg, N. (1987). An investigation of the validity and reliability of the Battelle Developmental Inventory with a population of children younger than 30 months with identified handicapping conditions. *Journal of the Division for Early Childhood, 11*(3), 238–246.

Meisels, S. J. (2000). On the side of the child. *Young Children, 55*(6), 16–19.

Meisels, S. J., Jablon, J. R., Marsden, D. B., Dichtelmeiller, M. L., Dorfman, A. B., & Steele, D. M. (1994). *The work sampling system: An overview* (3rd ed.). Ann Arbor, MI: Rebus Planning Associations.

Mercer, J. R. (1979). *System of multicultural pluralistic assessment technical manual.* New York: Psychological Corp.

Mullen, E. M. (1989). *Infant Mullen Scales of Early Learning.* Circle Pines, MN: American Guidance Services.

Mullen, E. M. (1992). *Mullen Scales of Early Learning.* Circle Pines, MN, American Guidance Services.

Mullen, E. M. (1995). *Mullen Scales of Early Learning, AGS Edition.* Circle Pines, MN, American Guidance Services.

National Association for the Education of Young Children, (1995). *National Association for the Education of Young Children Position Statement on School Readiness.* Washington, DC: Author.

Nehring, A. D., Nehring, E. F., Bruni, J. R., & Randolph, P. L. (1992). *Learning Accomplishment Profile Diagnostic Standardized Assessment.* Lewisville, NC: Kaplan School Supply Corp.

Neisworth, J. T., & Bagnato, S. J. (1992). The case against intelligence testing in early intervention. *Topics in Early Childhood Special Education, 12*(1), 1–20.

Neisworth, J. T., & Bagnato, S. J. (1996). Assessment for early intervention: Emerging themes and practices. In S. Odom & M. McLean (Eds.), *Recommended practices in early intervention.* Austin, TX: PRO-ED.

Neisworth, J. T., & Bagnato, S. J. (2000). Recommended practices in assessment. In S. Sandall, M. McLean & B. J. Smith (Eds.), *DEC recommended practices in early intervention/early childhood special education.* Longmont, CO: Sopris West.

Newborg, J., Stock, J. R., Wnek, L., Guidubaldi, J., & Svinicki, J. (1984). *Battelle Developmental Inventory.* Allen, TX: DLM.

Paget, K. (1991). The individual assessment situation: Basic considerations for preschool-age children. In B. Bracken (Ed.), *The psychoeducational assessment of preschool children* (2nd ed., pp. 32–39). Boston: Allyn and Bacon.

Parks, S., Furuno, S., O'Reilly, K. A., Inatsuka, T. T., Hoska, C. M., & Zeisloft-Falbey, B., (1994). *Hawaii Early Learning Profile (HELP).* Palo Alto, CA: VORT.

Pelligrino, J. W., Chudowsky, N., & Glaser, R, (Eds.) (2001). *Knowing what students know: The science and design of educational assessment.* Washington, DC: The National Academy Press.

Peterson, N. (1987). *Early intervention for handicapped and at-risk children.* Denver: Love.

Platt, L., Kamphaus, R., Keltgen, J., & Gilliland, F. (1991). Overview of and review of the Differential Ability Scales: Initial and current research findings. *Journal of School Psychology, 29,* 271–278.

Provence, S., Erikson, J., Vater, S., & Palmeri, S. (1995). *Infant Toddler Developmental Assessment.* Chicago: Riverside.

Ray, S., & Ulissi, S. M. (1982). *Adaptation of the Wechsler Preschool and Primary Scales of Intelligence for Deaf Children.* Natchitoches, LA: Steven Ray.

Reitan, R. M. (1969). *Manual for administration of neuropsychological test batteries for adults and children.* Indianapolis, IN: Author.

Reynell, J. (1983). *Manual for the Reynell-Zinkin Developmental Scales for Young Visually Handicapped Children.* Windsor, Berks, UK: NFER-NELSON.

Robinson, C., & Fieber, N. (1988). Cognitive assessment of motorically impaired infants and preschoolers. In T. Wachs & R. Sheehan (Eds.), *Assessment of young developmentally disabled children* (pp. 127–162). New York: Plenum Press.

Roid, G., & Miller, N. (1997). *Leiter International Performance Scale–Revised.* Wood Dale, IL: Stoelting.

Roid, G. H. (2002). *The new Stanford-Binet Intelligence Scales–5th Edition: Author perspective.* Symposium presented at National Association of School Psychologists Annual Conference, Chicago.

Roid, G. H. (in press). *Stanford-Binet Intelligence Scales–5th Edition, Standardization Edition.* Itasca, IL: Riverside.

Roid, G. H., & Sampers, J. (2000). *Examiner training manual for the Tryout Edition of the Merrill-Palmer Developmental Scale–Revised.* Wood Dale, IL: Stoelting.

Saluja, G., Scott-Little, C., & Clifford, R. M. (2000). *Kindergarten, state characteristics.* Washington, DC: Education Commission of the States.

Salvia, J., & Ysseldyke, J. (1988). *Assessment in special and remedial education.* Boston: Houghton Mifflin.

Salvia, J., & Ysseldyke, J. (2001). *Assessment* (8th Ed.). Boston: Houghton Mifflin.

Sanford, A. R., & Zelman, J. G. (1981). *The Learning Accomplishment Profile.* Winston-Salem, NC: Kaplan School Supply.

Sattler, J. (1990). *Assessment of children* (3rd ed.). San Diego, CA: Jerome M. Sattler.

Sexton, D., Lobman M., & Oremland, J. (1998–1999). Learning Accomplishment Profile–Diagnostic Standardized Assessment. *Diagnostique 24*(1–4), 183–196.

Sheehan, R., & Snyder, S. (1989–1990). Battelle Developmental Inventory and the Battelle Developmental Inventory Screening Test. *Diagnostique, 15,* 16–30.

Shinn, M. R. (1989). *Curriculum-based assessment: Assessing special children.* New York: Guilford Press.

Shonkoff, J. P., & Phillips, D. A. (Eds.). (2000). *From neurons to neighborhoods: The science of early childhood development.* Washington, DC: National Academy Press.

Simmons, D. C., & Kame'enui, E. J. (Eds.). (1998). *What reading research tells us about children with diverse learning needs: Bases and basics.* Mahwah, NJ: Lawrence Erlbaum Associates.

Smith, A. J., & Johnson, R. E. (1977). *Smith-Johnson Nonverbal Performance Scale.* Los Angeles: Western Psychological Services.

Snyder, P., Lawson, S., Thompson, B., Stricklin, S., & Sexton, D. (1993). Evaluating the psychometric integrity of instruments used in early intervention research: The Battelle Developmental Inventory. *Topics in Early Childhood Special Education, 13*(2), 216–232.

Stillman, R. (1978). *The Callier-Azusa Scale.* Dallas, TX: South Central Regional Center for Services to Deaf-Blind Children.

Stutsman, R. (1931). *Mental measurement of preschool children.* New York: World Book.

Teale, W. H. (1995). Young children and reading: Trends across the twentieth century. *Journal of Education, 177,* 95–127.

Teeter, P. A., & Semrud-Clikeman, M. (1997). *Child neuropsychology. Assessment and interventions for neurodevelopmental disorders*. Boston, MA: Allyn and Bacon.

Telzrow, C. F. (1984). Practical applications of the K-ABC in the identification of handicapped preschoolers. *The Journal of Special Education, 18*, 311–324.

Thorndike, R. L., Hagen, E. P., & Sattler, J. M. (1986). *Guide for administering and scoring the Stanford-Binet Intelligence Scale (4th ed.)* Chicago: Riverside.

Thurlow, M. L., Ysseldyke, J. E., & Silverstein, B. (1993). *Testing accommodations for students with disabilities: A review of the literature (Synthesis Report 4)*. Minneapolis, MN: National Center on Educational Outcomes, University of Minnesota.

Tzuriel, D., & Klein, P. S. (1987). Assessing the young child: Children's analogical thinking modifiability. In C. S. Lidz (Ed.), *Dynamic assessment: An interactional approach to evaluating learning potential*. New York: Guilford Press.

Uzgiris, I., & Hunt, J. McV. (1975). *Assessment in infancy: Ordinal scales of psychological development*. Urbana, IL: University of Illinois Press.

Venn, J., & Dykes, M. K. (1987). Assessment of the physically handicapped. In W. H. Berdine & S. A. Meyer (Eds.), *Assessment in special education* (pp. 278–308). Boston: Little, Brown.

VORT, (1995). *Help for Preschoolers*. Palo Alto, CA: Author.

Vulpe, S. G. (1994). *Vulpé Assessment Battery–Revised*. East Aurora, NY: Slosson Educational Publications.

Vygotsky, L. S. (1978). *Mind in society: The development of higher psychological processes*. Cambridge, MA: Harvard University Press.

Wachs, T., & Sheehan, R. (1988). *Assessment of young developmentally disabled children*. New York: Plenum Press.

Wechsler, D. (1974). *Manual for the Wechsler Intelligence Scales for Children–Revised*. San Antonio, TX: Psychological Corp.

Wechsler, D. (1989). *Wechsler Preschool and Primary Scale of Intelligence–Revised*. San Antonio, TX: Psychological Corp.

Wechsler, D. (1991). *Wechsler Intelligence Scale for Children–III*. San Antonio, TX: Psychological Corp.

Witt, J. C., Elliott, S. N., Kramer, J. J., & Gresham, F. M. (1994). *Assessment of children: Fundamental methods and practices*. Dubuque, IA: Brown and Benchmark.

Woodcock, R. W., & McGrew, K. S., & Mather, N. (2001). *Woodcock-Johnson Psychoeducational Battery–3rd Edition*. Chicago: Riverside.

Woods, J., & McCormick, K. (2002). Toward an integration of child- and family-centered practices in the assessment of preschool children: Welcoming the family. *Young Exceptional Children. 5*(3), 2–11.

Zimmerman, I. L., Steiner, V. G., & Pond, R. E. (1992). *Preschool Language Scale–3*. San Antonio, TX: Psychological Corporation.

Assessing Motor Skills in Infants and Young Children

Martha J. Cook
University of Alabama
Jennifer Kilgo
University of Alabama-Birmingham

By definition, motor development is the gradual acquisition of control and/or use of the large and small muscles of the body. The acquisition of motor skills provides young children with the ability to interact with their environment. Thus, motor development is considered to be a central component of child development. Further, motor development is a generally recognized means of assessing the overall rate and level of development in infants and young children (Gesell, 1973; Illingworth, 1975). The focus of this chapter is on the assessment of motor skill development and movement in young children with special needs. The goal of this chapter is to provide an overview of the motor domain, as well as to describe current approaches and recommended practices to be used in conducting meaningful motor assessments of young children with known or suspected disabilities.

The chapter begins with a rationale for assessing motor skill development and movement in young children with known or suspected disabilities. Emphasized in this section is the interface of motor skills with other areas of development. The section that follows is a description of the motor domain and the various dimensions of a motor assessment including gross motor skills, muscle tone, reflexes, postural reactions, volitional movements, and fine motor skills. Procedural considerations and representative methods of motor assessment are presented next, including examples of standardized, norm-referenced tools designed to discriminate children with motor delays from those who are experiencing typical motor development, as well as instruments used for planning intervention and monitoring progress. The final section of the chapter illustrates how motor assessment information can be translated into functional goals and outcomes and intervention techniques that will enable young children with motor delays or disabilities to participate as fully as possible in a variety of natural environments.

RATIONALE FOR ASSESSING MOTOR SKILLS

In order to understand the importance of the assessment of movement and motor skill development in young children, a number of factors must be considered. First, during the early years of life, the major motor skills (e.g., rolling over, sitting independently, or walking) serve as important developmental landmarks. In fact, motor development milestones provide a clinical correlate for the underlying maturation of the *central nervous system* (CNS). Thus, delayed motor milestones may serve as an indicator of an existing developmental delay or as a predictor of later developmental differences in other developmental domains (e.g., cognitive, social, communication skills) (Batshaw, 1997).

Another reason for conducting motor assessments is that motor delays or differences are common in many types of disabilities. Motor problems may be caused by damage to the central nervous system (e.g., cerebral palsy) or chromosomal abnormalities (e.g., Down syndrome) or may be associated with other disabilities such as visual impairments or mental retardation. Not only do delays in the attainment of motor skills occur in children who have diagnosed conditions such as Down syndrome or cerebral palsy, but a possibility of motor delays exists in children with less prevalent and often difficult to diagnose disabilities as well (e.g., Duchenne muscular dystrophy) (Batshaw, 1997). Again, delayed attainment of motor milestones may serve as a discriminative index or as an initial screen to signal the need for conducting a more comprehensive assessment of a child's abilities.

Finally, the interrelationship of motor skills to other areas of development is another reason why it is important to assess a child's motor abilities. Movement has a strong influence on other aspects of development, particularly during the first few years of life and delayed development of motor skills can lead to other aspects of development being hindered. For children with motor disabilities or delays, movement and environmental exploration may be compromised, which can be a significant threat to the attainment of useful skills in other domains. Not only is it important to assess motor milestones, but functional motor skills and related skills in other domains should be assessed as well (e.g., eating and mobility skills in the natural environment) (Haley, Coster, Ludlow, Haltiwanger, & Andrellos, 1992).

DIMENSIONS AND DOMAIN CONTENT OF MOTOR ASSESSMENTS

For the reasons cited above, motor assessments are of critical importance for young children with known or suspected motor disabilities. A motor assessment is a multidimensional process that is conducted for a variety of purposes that range from detecting a motor disability, to establishing eligibility for services, to determining the functional implications of the disability within the context of the child's natural environment, and, finally, to monitoring progress over time (Gargiulo & Kilgo, 2000). Thus, appropriate information must be collected that yields data to make decisions in the aforementioned areas. The greater number of sources and types of information collected, the greater the potential for a well informed decision-making process.

Two areas typically emphasized in motor assessments are the *gross motor* and *fine motor* domains. Gross motor skills usually refer to activities that involve the large muscles of the body, including the neck and trunk muscles and the proximal muscles of the arms and legs. Gross motor milestones include basic body movements such as lifting the head, rolling, creeping, crawling, walking, running, jumping, and skipping. Strength and endurance of the large muscles are required for gross motor skills such as climbing,

lifting, or pushing. Examples of functional gross motor activities for children with physical disabilities might include, for example, transferring (e.g., from wheelchair to toilet) or using various methods of locomotion (e.g., using crutches, a walker, or a wheelchair).

Fine motor skills involve the use of smaller and more distal muscles, particularly the muscles of the arms and hands, to perform more precise movements. Fine motor developmental milestones include reaching, grasping, pinching, and releasing. The performance of many fine motor tasks requires the eyes to direct the hands (Bushnell & Boudreau, 1993). Examples of such tasks include cutting and copying. These are often referred to as tasks involving eye-hand coordination or perceptual-motor skills. Functional fine motor activities include eating, drinking, drawing, or writing. Although oral-motor skills often are addressed in a motor assessment, this area of development is included in another chapter of this text.

The assessment of motor skills often requires the involvement of a number of personnel from diverse backgrounds (e.g., educator, physical therapist, occupational therapist) depending on the purpose of the assessment and the child's individual needs. Often two important members of the assessment team for children with known or suspected motor delays or disabilities are occupational therapists and physical therapists. *Occupational therapists* tend to focus on the fine motor area while *physical therapists* focus on the gross motor area. For example, children who demonstrate muscle weakness, exhibit poor head control or sitting posture, have delays in the attainment of developmental milestones, or demonstrate poor balance may need a thorough motor assessment conducted by a physical therapist. Children who have difficulty in fine motor skills (e.g., grasping, using both hands, drawing, or writing) and activities of daily living (e.g., eating, drinking, dressing) may require the involvement of an occupational therapist in the assessment process.

Although team members usually rely on the expertise of physical and/or occupational therapists in conducting motor assessments, there are many reasons why other early childhood personnel should be knowledgeable of and involved in the process. With all disciplines having general knowledge and skills in motor assessment, each team member will be able to contribute to decisions regarding the diagnosis, eligibility for services, development of specific motor intervention plans, and progress monitoring. The family and the child's teacher will be able to contribute a broad understanding of the child's functional performance on everyday tasks and thus offer the team a unique frame of reference for viewing the child. With training and experience, all members of the team will be able to effectively blend their perspectives so that motor assessments are comprehensive and meaningful for children and families. Listed below are some of the necessary knowledge and skill areas:

1. Familiarity of terminology from relevant disciplines (e.g., physical therapy, occupational therapy, adaptive physical education) in order to communicate more effectively with members of those disciplines;

2. A clear understanding of typical motor development and screening methods used to identify children who need a thorough motor assessment;

3. Familiarity with the recommended motor assessment practices used to ensure the acquisition of quality motor assessments;

4. Familiarity with motor assessment instruments;

5. Ability to determine children's current motor ability and needs in motor functioning in order to plan and implement appropriate intervention programs;

6. Skills in identifying subtle changes in children's motor skills, monitoring intervention strategies, documenting progress, and evaluating effectiveness.

Movement Terminology Related to Motor Development

In order to participate in the assessment of motor skills, a thorough understanding of motor development is needed. Although it is not possible to include all relevant information within this chapter, the following section provides a brief description of some of the necessary movement terminology, normal gross and fine motor milestones, and the dimensions addressed in a motor assessment.

Some commonly used movement terms and definitions are contained in Table 11.1. Early childhood personnel should be familiar with these terms in order to facilitate communication among various members of the assessment team.

Principles of Typical Motor Development

In addition to being familiar with terminology, early childhood personnel should have an understanding of the principles of motor development. A child's movement competency develops in a sequential fashion of skill acquisition, which means that early motor skills form the basis for more advanced skills that develop later. Motor development proceeds in a manner described in these principles:

1. *Cephalo to caudal pattern.* Muscular development and movement proceed from the head down through the spine. That is, infants first learn to raise their heads, bear weight on their arms, gain trunk stability, and then gain control in their lower body.

2. *Proximal to distal pattern.* Muscles and muscle control tend to develop from the spine (proximal) to the extremities (distal). Trunk and shoulder stability develop before moving on to the elbows, wrists, hands, and fingers.

3. *Flexion to extension.* Infants are born with a predominantly flexed pattern, which allows for maximum stability and security. As infants develop, they gain skills that allow them to extend their bodies and maintain extension against gravity.

TABLE 11.1
Motor Assessment Terminology

Flexion	Curling up the body; bending a body part at a joint
Extension	Unfolding of the body; straightening a body part at the joint
Prone	Lying on the stomach; usually refers to the whole body but can refer to body parts
Supine	Lying on the back; usually refers to the whole body but can refer to body parts
Lateral	Pertaining to the side; can be a body part or the whole body
Symmetry	Equal development of both sides of the body in size and shape and/or same position of both sides of the body while assuming postures and performing movements
Asymmetry	Unequal development of one side of the body from the other in size or shape and/or different position of one side of the body from the other while assuming postures and performing movements
Rotation	Twisting of the body along the body axis or movement between the shoulders and pelvis (trunk rotation), needed in all volitional and transitional movements (moving from one posture to another)
Internal rotation	Rotation of a body joint that moves a body part toward the midline
Automatic reactions	Involuntary and unconscious responses of the body in relation in gravity and to changes in the alignment of body parts; needed to make postural adjustments and to maintain balance during movement; begin to be exhibited between 4 and 6 months of age and remain throughout
Volitional movements	Cognitively directed, intentional movements
Distal	Farthest away from the center of the body, such as the hand is distal to the elbow
Proximal	Nearest to the center of the body, such as the shoulder is proximal to the elbow
Postural control	Regulation of the body's position in space for stability and orientation

4. *Vertical to horizontal to diagonal movements.* This pattern refers to the development of movements in planes. Initially, children operate in vertical planes (moving arms up and down), then develop horizontal movement patterns, and finally develop diagonal or rotational movement patterns.

5. *Gross motor to fine motor movements.* Children gain control over larger movements before they perfect more controlled and subtle movements or fine motor skills. For example, children are able to make strokes with a crayon using full arm movement prior to making short, definitive lines with crayons.

6. *Reflexive to volitional movements.* Movement patterns are initially involuntary and are caused by external stimuli. As the central nervous system matures, movements controlled by thought processes become dominant.

7. *Undifferentiated to differentiated movements.* At birth, infants display seemingly random movements that involve the total body. As children mature, their movements become more refined and purposeful.

8. *Stabilizing to mobilizing movements.* As the central nervous system matures, children initially work to become stable in a variety of positions. Once stability has been mastered, children work to maintain various positions while moving.

9. *Bilateral to unilateral movements.* Initially, new movement patterns are exhibited symmetrically. As a movement pattern is mastered, children can exhibit the movement pattern in isolation with one side of their body.

Understanding these motor development principles is critical to understanding motor delays or disabilities in young children.

Developmental Milestones

In the first two years of life, gross and fine motor development is directly related to the developmental principles described above. Achievement of motor milestones proceeds in an orderly pattern in children without disabilities, although timing and rate of acquisition can vary tremendously from child to child depending on gender, genetics, and environmental factors (e.g., amount of stimulation, motivation). The motor milestones and general age levels for attaining them can provide a reference point to determine if delays are present (Bly, 1983). Table 11.2 presents the sequence of gross and fine motor development during the first two years of life (Molnar, 1992).

Although gross and fine motor milestones are described in this table, it is important to note that motor development should not be perceived as just the attainment of motor milestones. Instead, motor development should be seen as the process of acquiring the necessary postural control and movement components to perform purposeful movements. The achievement of each motor milestone is the end product of combining and recombining the components to produce a functional motor act (e.g., reaching, sitting, walking). When assessing motor skills, it is important to determine what components the child lacks or is performing abnormally in order to plan intervention programs to facilitate the acquisition of the missing components and attain functional motor skills. For example, the motor milestone of walking requires that the child use motor components such as balance and weight shift in order to walk.

Depending on the purpose of the assessment, various types of information will be gathered and used as part of a motor assessment. In most cases, a thorough motor assessment will address several dimensions including *muscle tone*, *primitive reflexes* and *automatic reactions*, *postural alignment*, and *functional abilities and limitations*. The following section describes the dimensions of motor assessment and discusses the assessment procedures commonly used for each.

Muscle Tone

Many children have motor disabilities that are related to atypical muscle tone. The term muscle tone refers to the degree of underlying tension or stiffness in the muscles as a result of insults to the CNS (Dunn, 1996). Muscle tone provides the basis for the development of normal background postures (positions) or stability against gravity to enable the acquisition of voluntary movements (Campbell, 1987a). As evidenced when a child's muscle tone is in the normal range, the tone must be high enough to hold the body upright against gravity, yet low enough to allow mobility in the joints for coordinated movements into and away from gravity. It is important to note that when muscle tone is in the normal range, it is evenly distributed throughout the body and remains fairly constant throughout life.

Assessment of Muscle Tone The assessment of muscle tone is a critical aspect of a thorough motor assessment. The process of assessing

TABLE 11.2

Gross and Fine Motor Development Milestones (Newborn to Age 2)

Age	Gross Motor	Fine Motor
Newborn to 1 month	• Flexor tone predominates (arms and legs are under body in prone). • Infant turns head to side in prone. • Infant turns head in supine due to ATNR. • Infant "walks" automatically (reflex walking) when suspended. • Infant's spine is rounded when held sitting.	• Hands are fisted. • Infant grasps reflectively. • Infant has state-dependent ability to fix and follow bright object.
2 to 3 months	*In prone:* • Infant can lift head against gravity due to labyrinthine righting reflex. • Head-raised position elicits neck righting reflex, stimulating upper part of the trunk to raise up. • Infant's arms and hands move in front of the shoulders. *In supine:* • The head begins to come to midline. • Infant tries to lift head when pulled to sitting.	• Eyes begin to converge. • Arms begin to come together in midline.
4 to 5 months	• The head is midline. • Infant holds head in midline when pulled to sitting. • Infant lifts head to 90° and lifts chest slightly in prone. • Infant turns from supine to side-lying. • In supine, infant can reach hands to knees. • In prone, infant "swims" in air.	• Hands are mostly open. • Midline hand play begins. • Crude palmar grasp appears. • Infant begins reaching.
5 to 6 months	• Strong optical righting develops, which facilitates head lifting. • Infant can bear weight on extended arms with hip extension in prone. • The equilibrium reaction in prone allows for control of flexion and extension against gravity. • Rolls from back to stomach.	• In supine, body can bear weight with one arm and reach with the other.
7 to 8 months	*In prone:* • Infant can lift stomach off the supporting surface.	• In prone, infant can bear weight with one arm and reach with the other.

Continued

TABLE 11.2

Continued

Age	Gross Motor	Fine Motor
	• Infant can shift weight between arms and legs in the quadruped position (hands and knees) and push back into a seated position. • Creeping may begin. • Infant begins to belly-crawl, with the arms doing most of the work. • Infant's arms are free in sitting to move and reach without loss of balance. *In supine:* • When pulled to sitting, infant flexes chain and pulls up. • Infant maintains sitting; may lean on arms. • Infant moves from sitting to prone. • Infant rolls to prone. • Infant bears all weight; bounces when held erect. • Infant may begin to cruise. • Infant may assume kneeling position.	• Intermediate grasp appears. • Infant transfers cube from hand to hand. • Infant hangs objects.
9 to 10 months	• Infant can push back into sitting with rotation from prone. • The presence of the righting reflex allows infant to get onto the knees from prone. • Infant may use half-kneeling to pull to stand. • Infant cruises forward.	• Pincer grasp, mature thumb-to-index grasp appears. • Infant bangs two cubes held in hand.
12 to 14 months	• Infant walks alone, arms in high guard or midguard. • Wide base, excessive knee and hip flexion. • Foot contact on entire sole.	• Infant piles two cubes. • Infant scribbles spontaneously. • Infant holds crayon, full length in palm. Infant combines objects.
18 months	• Arms are at low guard. • Mature supporting base and heel strike appear. • Infant seats self in chair. • Infant walks backwards.	• Hand dominance emerges. • Crude release appears. • Infant holds crayon, butt end in palm. • Infant dumps raisins from bottle spontaneously.
2 years	• Infant begins running. • Infant walks up and down stairs alone. • Infant jumps on both feet, in place.	• Hand dominance is usual. • Infant builds eight-cube tower.

Note: Based on *Pediatric Rehabilitation*, by G. E. Molnar. Copyright 1992, Williams & Wilkins. Used with permission.

muscle tone is generally subjective, and clinical observation is the most widely used method of assessing muscle tone. The examiner usually feels the amount of tension in the muscles and observes the child's movements while they are performing various motor tasks in functional activities. The assessment of muscle tone is done under both passive and active conditions to ensure reliability and accuracy. The distribution of tone throughout the body and the influences of other factors affecting muscle tone also are determined.

The presence of abnormal muscle tone usually results in delays in the achievement of motor milestones, atypical postures, and atypical movement patterns. Muscle tone can be lower or higher than the expected range and can be described using a continuum from severely reduced muscle tone (*hypotonia* or low muscle tone) to excessive muscle tone (*hypertonia* or *spasticity*). In some cases, children have *fluctuating muscle tone* (e.g., *athetosis*) that is present even when the child is at rest. Fluctuating muscle tone is not only abnormal but is constantly changing, and may occur in varying degrees from hypotonic to hypertonic. A summary of the results of the assessment of muscle tone (i.e., normal tone, hypertonia, hypotonia) using various methods is contained in Table 11.3.

Factors Influencing Muscle Tone Many factors can affect muscle tone, such as the child's position in relation to gravity. Observing a child's posture in various positions under both passive and active conditions determines gravitational influences. In general, higher antigravity postures (e.g., sitting, quadruped, kneeling, standing) tend to increase muscle tone more than do low anti-gravity postures (e.g., prone, supine, sidelying). This information is useful to the examiner in determining the positions that should be used to reduce or normalize hypertonicity, thus improving posture and motor functioning.

Other factors that can affect muscle tone are sensory stimuli, environmental influences, and the child's state. Auditory, visual, and tactile stimuli may cause changes in muscle tone and influence motor functioning. Children with hypertonia tend to have a low threshold for sensory input, meaning a small amount of sensory input can increase their muscle tone. On the other hand, many children with hypotonia have a much higher threshold; thus, large amounts of sensory stimuli are needed to produce a change in muscle tone. For example, loud or sudden noises may increase muscle tone, while soft or soothing sounds may have the opposite effect. Another example is that sudden, jerky movements that provide visual input may increase tone; conversely, slow, directed movements tend to reduce

TABLE 11.3
Results of Assessment of Underlying Muscle Tone Based on Types

Measure	Normal	Hypotonia	Hypertonia
Consistency	Firm	Soft, flabby	Hard, stony
Extensibility	Normal range of motion of joints	Exceeds normal range of motion of joints (hypermobility)	Joint tightness with limited range of motion (contractures)
Passivity	Attempt to control movement	No resistance to movement	Resistance to movement may increase, joint tightness
Posture	Symmetrical, weight evenly distributed on weight-bearing surface	No resistance to gravity, "molds" to support surface, arms and legs flaccid/passive	Too tightly flexed or extended

muscle tone. Information about the effects of sensory stimuli is gathered by observing children's reactions to various stimuli and by interviewing those who know them well. Environmental factors such as the type of activity that is going on, the child's level of motivation, or the child's mood or state can have a definite influence on muscle tone. Children who are uncooperative or crying usually exhibit muscle tone that is less consistent than children with more relaxed and responsive behavior.

Assessment of Muscle Tone *Underlying muscle tone* is assessed when a child is passive or at rest and is in various positions. Particular attention is given to the proximal parts of the body (e.g., the head and neck, shoulder girdle, trunk, and pelvis), which should be moved passively in order to determine the presence of muscle and joint tightness. It is important to note that children tend to develop increased muscle tone in proximal body parts (e.g., trunk, shoulders, hips) first, as they attempt to compensate for low muscle tone in attaining antigravity postures (e.g., sitting, standing). Again, it is important to remember that the degree of muscle tone may not be evenly distributed throughout the body. *Predominant muscle tone* is assessed when a child is actively involved in maintaining antigravity postures and moving through space. Information must be gathered related to changes in muscle tone as a result of the various postures, types of movements, and positions.

Distribution of Muscle Tone Diagnostic categories of muscle tone are based on the predominant type of muscle tone and the distribution throughout the body. Topographical classification systems based on the areas of the body involved are used to describe the distribution of abnormal tone. Minear (1956) developed the most well-known system, one in which physical impairments were classified according to limb involvement (presence of abnormal tone). The most common categories are: (a) *hemiplegia* (involvement of the trunk and one side of body); (b) *quadriplegia* (involvement of the trunk with equal involvement of upper and

lower extremities); and *diplegia* (involvement of the trunk and all four extremities, with greater involvement in the lower extremities).

Primitive Reflexes

In infancy, most movements are accomplished using the whole body and are controlled by primary or *primitive reflexes*. Reflexes are automatic, stereotypical, involuntary responses that are demonstrated spontaneously or elicited in response to specific environmental stimuli (Crutchfield & Barnes, 1993), such as a loud noise or sudden change of head position. Reflexes occur in the first months of life in typically developing infants but gradually disappear during the first year of life in most cases. They are controlled by lower centers of the brain and diminish or become inhibited by higher centers of the brain by 4 to 6 months of age. When reflexes are inhibited, this allows for the development of more sophisticated skills (e.g., righting and equilibrium reactions).

When brain damage has occurred, the higher centers of control in the brain may be incapable of inhibiting the primitive reflexes, such as is the case in children with cerebral palsy. Retention of primitive reflexes, such as the asymmetrical tonic neck reflex (ATNR), beyond the time when they should typically disappear can be important in the early diagnosis of some types of cerebral palsy, as well as in other disorders. Primitive reflexes are correlated with age ranges in which they appear and disappear or become inhibited. The age ranges should be used only as a general guide because individual differences in rate often will occur. An in-depth description of primitive reflexes is contained in Table 11.4, including the normal age ranges, the stimulus, response, and clinical significance of each primitive reflex (Molnar, 1992).

Assessment of Primitive Reflexes The process used in the assessment of reflexes involves presenting the required environmental stimulus and observing the resultant motor response. Contained in Table 11.4 are selected reflexes that are

TABLE 11.4

Infantile Reflex Development

Reflex	Stimulus	Response	Suppression	Clinical Significance
Primitive Reflexes: Present at Birth, Suppressed with Maturation				
Asymmetrical tonic neck	Head turning or tilting to the side	Extension of the extremities on the chin side; flexion on the occiput side	Suppressed by 6 to 7 months.	Obligatory abnormal at any age; persistent suspicious of CNS pathology
Symmetric tonic neck	Neck flexion Neck extension	Arm flexion, leg extension, arm extension, leg flexion	Suppressed by 6 to 7 months	Obligatory abnormal at any age; persistent suspicious of CNS pathology
Moro	Sudden neck extension	Arm extension; abduction followed by flexion-adduction	Suppressed by 4 to 6 months	Abnormal if persists
Tonic labyrinthine	Head position in space, strongest at 45° angle in horizontal; supine and prone	Predominant extensor tone; predominant flexor tone	Suppressed by 4 to 6 months	Abnormal at any age if hyperactive or if persistent
Positive supporting	Tactile contact and weight-bearing on the sole	Leg extension for supporting partial body weight	Suppressed by 3 to 7 months and replaced by volitional standing	Abnormal at any age; if obligatory or hyperactive, suggests spasticity of the legs
Rooting	Stroking the corner of mouth; upper or lower lip	Moving the tongue, mouth, and head toward the site of stimulus	Suppressed by 4 months	Searching for nipple; diminished in CNS depression obligatory; persistence may be immature CNS development.

Continued

TABLE 11.4
Continued

Reflex	Stimulus	Response	Suppression	Clinical Significance
Primitive Reflexes: Present at Birth, Suppressed with Maturation				
Palmar grasp	Pressure or touch on the palm; stretch of finger flexors.	Flexion of fingers.	Suppressed by 5 to 6 months.	Diminished in CNS depression; absent in lower motor neutron paralysis; persistence suggest spasticity, (i.e., cerebral palsy).
Plantar grasp	Pressure on sole just distal to metatarsal heads	Flexion of toes	Suppressed by 12 to 18 months	Absent in lower motor neutron paralysis; persists and hyperactive in spasticity (i.e., cerebral palsy)
Automatic neonatal walking	Contact of sole in vertical position tilting the body forward and from side to side	Automatic alternating steps	Suppressed by 3 to 4 months.	Variable activity in normal infants; absent in lower motor neutron paralysis of the legs
Placing	Placing tactile contact on dorsum of foot or hand	Flexion to place the leg or arm over the obstacle	Suppressed before end of first year	Absent in lower motor neutron paralysis or extensor spasticity of the legs

Note: Based on *Pediatric Rehabilitation*, by G. E. Molnar. Copyright 1992, Williams & Wilkins. Used with permission.

commonly persistent in children with neurological damage. When neurological damage is present, some primitive reflexes may be delayed in emergence (absent), delayed in integration (persistent), or abnormal in quality (tone). Assessment of primitive reflexes should not be limited to the presence or absence of the reflex. Instead, the focus should be on gathering qualitative information such as the consistency and intensity of the reflex and the impact it has on movement. Questions that should be answered when conducting assessments of reflexes include: (a) Does the reflex produce an excess of hypertonia? (b) Does the reflexive response to the stimulus occur consistently? and (c) Does the reflex control the child's movements; that is, can the child escape the static position caused by the reflex? Constant use of these primitive reflexes can prevent the development of more sophisticated motor skills and lead to structural deformities such as spinal curvatures or hip dislocations. The results of the reflex assessment will have implications for planning intervention, positioning, and handling of the child, and positioning objects and persons relative to the child.

Automatic Postural Reactions

Automatic reactions are postural responses of the body and limbs to changes in the body's center of gravity. These automatic reactions, of course, are not present at birth, but emerge in relationship to developmental milestones. As the central nervous system (CNS) matures, higher-level reactions take over from the early primitive reflexes to help regulate postural control against gravity. The postural reactions of righting, protective, and equilibrium reactions are established at this time, providing the subtle, postural adjust-

ments necessary to maintain balance while performing movements (Campbell, 1997).

Assessment of Automatic Postural Reactions

Similar to the assessment of primitive reflexes, automatic reactions are tested by presenting the environmental stimulus and observing the response. Table 11.5 provides a list of postural responses including the stimulus to elicit the reactions, a description of the response if the reaction is present, the age of emergence, and the clinical significance of a delay or absence of the response. Persistent primitive reflexes and abnormal tone usually interfere with the emergence of automatic reactions. The absence or delay of response indicates pathology or CNS immaturity.

The first of the postural reactions to be explained are **righting reactions,** which are automatic

TABLE 11.5
Postural Responses: Emerge with Maturation, Present Throughout Life, Modulated by Volition

Postural Response	Stimulus	Response	Emergence	Clinical Significance
Head righting	Visual and vestibular	Align face vertical, mouth horizontal; prone supine.	Emerge at 2 months, 3 to 4 months.	Delayed or absent in CNS immaturity or damage or motor unit disease
Body, head righting	Tactile, proprioceptive, vestibular	Align body parts	Emerge from 4 to 6 months.	Delayed or absent in CNS immaturity or damage or motor neuron disease
Protective extension or propping	Displacement of center of gravity outside or supporting surface	Extension-abduction of extremity toward the side of displacement to prevent falling	Emerge between 5 and 12 months	Delayed or absent in CNS immaturity or damage or motor unit disease
Equilibrium or tilting	Displacement of center of gravity	Adjustment of tone and trunk posture to maintain balance	Emerge between 6 and 14 months	Delayed or absent in CNS immaturity or damage or motor unit disease

Note: Based on *Pediatric Rehabilitation,* by G. E. Molnar. Copyright 1992, Williams & Wilkins. Used with permission.

reactions that position the head and trunk upright in space. Righting reactions interact with one another and work toward the establishment of a normal head and body relationship in space. They maintain the head in a vertical position relative to the midline of the body and keep the eyes horizontal to the vertical plane (midline). For example, when an infant briefly lifts his wobbly head off of his mother's shoulder, this is an example of a righting reaction. Righting reactions appear and then disappear (are inhibited) as higher postural reactions emerge (equilibrium and protective reactions). They are assessed by placing the child in various postures and situations that change the relationship of the position of the head and body. The initial purpose of these reactions is to facilitate rolling and rotation of the trunk (diagonal control).

Protective reactions are another type of postural reaction and can be described as movements of the extremities that assist in preventing the loss of balance or a fall. Protective extension is tested by rapidly shifting a child's weight while he is in a sitting position (to each side, front, and back). The normal response is extension and abduction of the arms (movement away from the midline) as he attempts to break the fall by supporting himself with an open hand. This response is also seen in the lower extremities when children are lowered rapidly to the floor feet first and the legs show signs of abduction (legs spread apart).

The third type of postural reactions are **equilibrium reactions,** which are compensatory movements of the trunk and limbs in response to changes in the body's center of gravity caused by displacement of the body or the body's supporting surface (Swanson, 1979). They result from "the interplay between stability [posture] and mobility [movement]" (Campbell, 1982, p. 6) and allow the body to maintain balance. In normal development, equilibrium reactions emerge between 5 and 18 months of age, depending on the position, and continue throughout life. Equilibrium reactions are elicited by creating a situation in which a child's body is displaced off its center of gravity. As a child loses his balance his attempts to regain and maintain balance are noted during an assessment.

Posture and Volitional Movements

Volitional movements are cognitively directed voluntary movements (e.g., reaching, walking, and grasping) and transitional movements (e.g., pulling to stand, sitting from standing, and rotation to sitting). Posture provides the antigravity background positions (stability) from which automatic and volitional movements occur. Most motor assessments have traditionally focused on the number of developmental milestones that have been attained by a particular child, giving little or no attention to the way in which postures and movements were performed. However, the current trend in assessing children with atypical muscle tone includes a description of the form or quality of posture and movement patterns, as well as the function or purpose of the movement (Campbell, 2000). For example, a child may be able to maintain a sitting position (function), but may be relying on increased muscle tone or proximal joint fixations in order to do so (quality). In order for children to make gains in motor development, posture and movement patterns that are of a normal quality are required. In working with children with motor disabilities, it is important to be concerned with the quality of the postural and movement patterns. These patterns must be analyzed with missing and/or atypical components identified in order to plan appropriate therapeutic intervention.

Assessment of Posture and Volitional Movements
When posture and movement are assessed, primary attention should be given to the way children use movement components to maintain antigravity postures and perform volitional movements (Campbell, 2000). Infants and young children with abnormal posture and movement are likely to demonstrate proximal fixations (e.g., increased muscle tightness in the trunk, hips, and shoulders) in order to compensate for the lack of normal muscle tone. Typical patterns that are demonstrated by children with cerebral palsy are contained in Table 11.6. This list should not be used to assess children for the presence of specific proximal adjustments, but instead should be used

TABLE 11.6

Examples of Typical Proximal Adjustments that Contribute to Abnormal Posture and Movement Patterns

Proximal Adjustment	Description	Compensatory Patterns	Consequences
Neck hyperextension	Absence of head/ neck flexion; cannot bring head to midline; does not tuck chin in supine or forearm propping; may push back with head	Relies on hyperextension of head/ neck to remain in prone; elevates shoulders to stabilize head in upright position in prone and from supine to sitting; prevents normal head and neck movements	Normal range of motion of scapula impaired, thus development of upper extremities is prevented; shortened neck extensors; lack of neck flexion (chin tuck); inability to close mouth, jaw juts forward
Head and neck asymmetry	No symmetrical use of head/neck flexors; results in inability to bring or maintain head in midline, which results in continued domination by ATNR	Due to domination by ATNR, must rely on unilateral upper extremities wiping/reaching on extension side; decreased bilateral upper extremities function; misses optical convergence and coordination that comes with midline orientation of head; forced to use lateral or uncoordinated ocular movements	Poor use of bilateral upper extremities resulting in lack of body exploration; poor hand-to-mouth play resulting in lack of normalization of oral sensitivity, and poor ocular control resulting in poor visual perception; continued ATNR sets stage for scoliosis and hip dislocation on flexed side due to constant rotation of pelvis in this position
Shoulders	Scapular instability; scapular winging while on forearms in prone position or inability to bear weight on forearms; lack of independent dissociated humeral movements	In prone position, uses scapular adduction and spinal extension to elevate trunk; stabilizes humerus close to sides of trunk and bears weight on pronated forearms	Scapular instability and tightness (muscle shortening); poor development of upper extremities (forearms will be pronated or internally rotated at elbows, feed into ulnar deviation of hand due to weight bearing in abnormal position); poor upper

Continued

TABLE 11.6

Continued

Proximal Adjustment	Description	Compensatory Patterns	Consequences
			extremity weight bearing in prone and creeping positions; poor protective extension; poorly coordinated reach, grasp, and manipulation patterns
Pelvis/Hips			
Anterior pelvic tilt	Anterior pelvic tilt is not balanced by flexion components (posterior pelvic tilt) due to abdominals not developing to posteriorly tilted pelvis and elongated lumbar extensors (lower back); prevents practice of lateral weight shifting in prone position and interferes with development of normal righting reactions.	Child maintains frog-legged position while prone to control or prevent lateral weight shifting when attempts are made to reach while lying prone.	Frog-legged position while prone increases flexion, abduction, and external rotation of hips; decreases extension, adduction and internal rotation of hips (reinforces total pattern & prevents development of complimentary movements patterns) when weight shifts in prone position; normal development of lower extremities is impeded in frog-legged position.
Posterior pelvic tilt	Presence of abnormally strong extension in lumbar with extension of hips and adduction of legs in prone position; limited hip mobility in flexion and abduction with inactive abdominals	Loss of function in lower extremities due to excessive extension; uses other available movements for mobility (usually upper extremities—diplegia).	Tight hip extensors prevent flexion at hips and subsequent rounding of lumbar spine and thoracic spine in sitting position; tight hip extensors also cause increased knee flexion.

as a guide in describing the typical proximal adjustments that may be observed and as an example of the application of movement terminology to specific problems of posture and movement that are frequently encountered.

Campbell (1985, 1987) suggests that an assessment of posture and movement should answer the following questions:

1. What are the child's areas of difficulty (typically proximal), such as the head/neck, shoulder, arm(s), pelvis, leg(s), and trunk, and under what gravitational conditions?

2. What are the compensatory patterns, caused by the proximal adjustments, used in postural alignment and movement patterns (e.g., automatic and volitional or goal-directed movements)?

3. What components of mature movement (e.g., extension, symmetry, independent movements, rotation) are missing that prevent optimal skill performance?

4. What muscular or orthopedic changes are present or may develop in the future due to continued use of compensatory patterns?

5. What are possible intervention strategies?

These questions can be answered through an analysis of the muscular components of postural and movement patterns with simultaneous observation of changes in muscle tone. These observations should take place in natural environments with familiar people (e.g., teacher, family members) assisting or acting as facilitators. The assessment should be conducted in the context of functional activities and play situations. Developmentally appropriate toys and objects should be used to facilitate a variety of postures and movements for analysis. Each child should be observed while moving on the floor, interacting with objects, moving from one place to another, moving from one posture to another (transitional movements), and while positioned using various types of adaptive equipment.

When assessing postural control and volitional movements, consideration should be given to the children's posture and the quality of their movement patterns. The components of mature movement (i.e., symmetry, extension, independent movements, rotation) should be used as a guide in describing movement patterns. The volitional movements to be observed are shown in Table 11.7 and are organized according to various positions. As observations are made of children in various positions, the focus should be on each body part, paying close attention to the position of the head. Observations of proximal body parts (e.g., shoulders, hips/pelvis) should occur prior to the observation of more distal body parts (e.g., arms/hands, legs/feet). Table 11.8 contains a list of questions, organized by areas of the body, which can serve as a guide in assessing posture. The results of an assessment of posture and movement should be descriptive in nature, addressing how the child uses movements to attain and maintain postures and accomplish goal-directed movements as well. For example, the assessment should address posture and movement in routine activities such as eating, dressing, and playing.

FINE MOTOR SKILLS

Often children with delayed gross motor development also experience delays in the development of fine motor skills. Children with abnormal muscle tone who exhibit atypical motor development often will have difficulties in performing fine motor tasks. In young children, emphasis is placed on those fine motor behaviors (e.g., grasp, release, reach) that comprise a variety of other useful tasks (e.g., turning book pages, buttoning, drawing, writing) that are developmentally appropriate (Case-Smith, 1993).

Assessment of Fine Motor Skills

An assessment of fine motor skills is generally conducted using developmental tests and checklists. Although this information is useful in determining children's proficiency level in fine motor skills, this type of assessment places little emphasis on the quality (form) of fine motor patterns. In addition, systematic observations

TABLE 11.7

Assessment Variables for Conducting Observations of Volitional Movements

Position	Variables
Supine	• What postural asymmetries are present during movement (head, trunk, pelvis, extremities)? • What is the posture and movement of the arms and legs? • Can the child raise her head? How does the child perform this movement? • Can the child roll to prone? How does the child perform this movement? • Can the child pull to a sitting position? How does the child perform this movement? • Does the child have adequate hand functions in this position? How does the child perform these movements?
Prone	• What postural asymmetries are present during active movement (i.e. head, trunk, pelvis, extremities)? • What is the posture and movement of the arms and legs? • Can the child raise his head? How does the child perform this movement? • Can the child use his forearms and/or extended arms for support? How does the child perform this movement? • Can the child reach out using weight shift and trunk rotation? How does the child perform this movement? • Can the child roll to supine? How does the child perform this movement? • What mode of mobility does the child use to progress on the floor? How does the child perform this movement? • Can the child assume an all-fours position (on hands and knees)? Can the child move from this position to sitting? How does the child perform these movements? • Does the child have adequate hand function in this position? How does the child perform these movements?
Sitting	• What is the position of the child's pelvis, trunk/spine, shoulders, head, arms, and legs in long sitting, side sitting (both sides), tailor sitting, and sitting in a chair (e.g., regular chair, highchair, adapted chair, wheelchair)?
Standing/Walking	• Can the child move from all fours to upright kneeling (on both knees), half kneeling (on one knee), then to standing? How does the child perform these movements (e.g., weight shifting)? • Can the child assume standing from the floor, squatting, chair/wheelchair? • What is the position of the pelvis, trunk, shoulders, head, arms, and legs while standing (e.g., equal weight bearing, body alignment)? • Can the child walk? How does the child perform this movement (e.g., weight shift, equal weight-bearing, trunk rotation, body alignment, posture)?

TABLE 11.8

Guiding Questions to Assess Posture in Various Positions

Body Areas	Observation Questions
Head	Positioned in midline? Positioned predominantly to one side?
Neck	Clearly visible, front and back? Hyperextended, visible just in front?
Shoulders	Elevated? Retracted? (pulled back) Protracted? (pushed forward)
Scapula	Stabilized? Hypermobile or unstable?
Arms	Internally rotated? Externally rotated?
Elbows	Flexed, extended?
Forearms	Pronated, supinated?
Wrists	Flexed, extended?
Hands	Open, fisted?
Trunk	Symmetrical? Asymmetrical? "Short" (laterally flexed) to which side? Does asymmetry change with positioning of the head?
Pelvis/Hips	Flexed? Extended? Dislocated? (ask therapist or parent) Pelvis tilted back? (posterior pelvic tilt) Pelvis tilted forward? (anterior pelvic tilt)
Legs	Internally rotated? (scissoring) Externally rotated (frogging)
Knees	Flexed? Extended?
Feet	Plantar flexion, neutral, dorsi-flexion?
Other	Contractures and deformities?

should be conducted in natural contexts on how well children use fine motor skills in functional tasks (e.g., eating/drinking, dressing, manipulating objects). Particular attention should be focused on foundational skills related to the development of fine motor skills including vision, head and truck control, and upper extremity function. Fine motor skills should be assessed concurrently with the assessment of posture and volitional movements. The child's posture and overall movement patterns will have direct bearing on the quality of hand function. In Tables 11.7 and 11.8, the portions of the observation methods that focus on the upper extremities should be used because they relate directly to the assessment of hand function.

The critical role that vision plays in the development of fine motor skills must be considered. Vision allows children to locate objects and provides vital information related to motivation to reach and grasp objects. Vision, however, is not a precursor to the development of fine motor skills as evidenced when children with visual impairments acquire fine motor skills. The process is facilitated, however, when vision is intact because a visual motivation to reach is provided. Children with specific motor disabilities may have adequate vision; however, they may be unable to use their vision functionally due to poor head control or the inability to coordinate their movements bilaterally due to muscle imbalance. This difficulty can have an impact on their ability to locate an object visually. Thus, the variables of head and ocular control should be assessed to determine the impact on fine motor development.

The ability to reach and transport objects (e.g., spoon, ball) is considered to be more of a gross motor skill of the upper extremities than a fine motor skill. However, it is important to understand that the development of hand functions, such as grasp and release, are dependent on the ability to reach and transport objects. As such, children must have the ability to maintain a stable background posture (e.g., using head control, trunk control, and symmetry), control leaning forward at the trunk, use weight shift and trunk rotation to free the reaching arm, and dissociate the humerus (upper arm) from the shoulder girdle.

Grasp and release are critical components of fine motor skills. As can be seen in Figure 11.1, there is a sequential development of various types of grasps (Erhardt, 1982). A description of each type of grasp is included to assist in the assessment of the components that comprise particular grasp patterns. Fine motor assessment instruments do not include variables related to reach and transport or quality indicators of grasp and release. The quality of grasp and release behaviors is directly related to (a) overall muscle tone in the body, (b) overall body position and control, (c) the position and function of the shoulder girdle, and (d) the position of the forearm (pronated or supinated). The results will have direct implications for how children should be handled and positioned in order to facil-

itate upper extremity and hand function, as well as the specific therapeutic techniques to be used in assisting with fine motor skill development. Observations should include such aspects as how well the child uses the fine motor components of extension, flexion, and dissociation of the wrist and fingers from the hand, and adduction and dissociation of the thumb from the hand.

From the results of the assessment of fine motor skills, therapeutic intervention can be formulated to improve hand function. However, if activities to develop fine motor skills are conducted in isolation with no attention given to the child's muscle tone and overall movement patterns, little success will be realized. In most cases, children with severe motor disabilities (e.g., severe hypertonia/spasticity) will have considerable deficits in the development of fine motor skills. As such, occupational therapists may recommend such adaptive equipment as hand splints to reduce tone and to keep the hands from being maintained in a fisted position. In addition, assistive devices may be recommended, such as adaptive switches used with battery operated toys or spoons with built-up handles to aid a child with a weak grasp (Case-Smith, 1993).

In summary, motor assessments should not be limited to the use of standardized measures designed to examine the attainment of motor milestones, but should include assessment of the children's abilities to move in their environment, to act on their environment, and to make meaningful use of information gained from their environmental interactions. With these different goals in mind, choices of procedural considerations will be discussed in the next section.

PROCEDURAL CONSIDERATIONS

Prior to a motor assessment, personnel must gather information that will guide the assessment process and give some indication of the individual needs of children and families. Essential information concerning the child's motor delays is

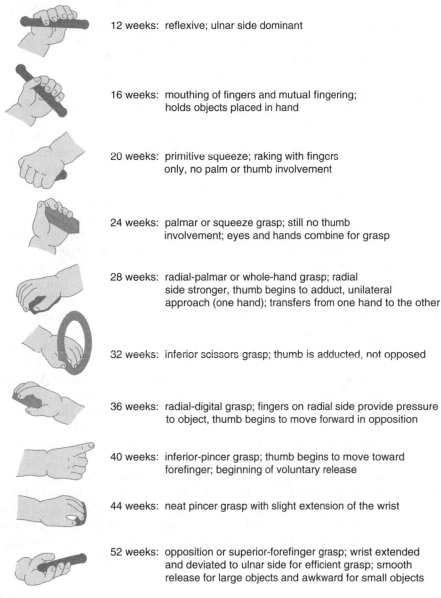

12 weeks: reflexive; ulnar side dominant

16 weeks: mouthing of fingers and mutual fingering;
holds objects placed in hand

20 weeks: primitive squeeze; raking with fingers
only, no palm or thumb involvement

24 weeks: palmar or squeeze grasp; still no thumb
involvement; eyes and hands combine for grasp

28 weeks: radial-palmar or whole-hand grasp; radial
side stronger, thumb begins to adduct, unilateral
approach (one hand); transfers from one hand to the other

32 weeks: inferior scissors grasp; thumb is adducted, not opposed

36 weeks: radial-digital grasp; fingers on radial side provide pressure
to object, thumb begins to move forward in opposition

40 weeks: inferior-pincer grasp; thumb begins to move toward
forefinger; beginning of voluntary release

44 weeks: neat pincer grasp with slight extension of the wrist

52 weeks: opposition or superior-forefinger grasp; wrist extended
and deviated to ulnar side for efficient grasp; smooth
release for large objects and awkward for small objects

FIGURE 11.1
Sequential development of grasp

summarized during this process. In general, motor skill assessment is conducted concurrently with the assessment of skills in other domains because (a) the results of the assessment of motor skills may provide information about the child's capabil- ities in other domains of development, and (b) the presence of abnormal muscle tone and movement patterns may influence how the child is handled and positioned when other skills are assessed. In determining the appropriate instruments or methods for assessing motor skills, a number of procedural considerations must be addressed, such as the level of the disability, the child's age and state, and the test location and environment.

When conducting motor assessments, several child characteristics may have an impact on the quality and validity of the results. These characteristics include the child's level of disability, the presence of sensory impairments, and associated conditions such as seizure or behavioral issues. For example, if a child has a seizure disorder requiring medication, the side effects of the medication may affect the child's behavioral state and, therefore, should be taken into consideration.

One of the most important procedural considerations in conducting an appropriate motor assessment is the child's age. Each of the published motor assessment instruments specifies the age range for which the instrument is recommended. Although a specific chronological age range is provided, many test developers encourage the use of the instrument for children whose developmental motor skills fall within the age range even if the children are chronologically older than the instrument's upper limit. In the *Bayley-II*, for example, an explanation is provided of how the instrument may be administered to children who are older than 42 months, providing that their developmental skills fall within the 1- to 42-month range. Although it is not possible to determine a developmental index for a child who falls outside the age range of children on whom the test was normed, it is possible to determine a mental or motor developmental age for that child (Bayley, 1993). Similarly, Haley and colleagues (1992) suggest that the *Pediatric Evaluation of Disability Inventory* can be used for the functional evaluation of children who are chronologically older than the 7.5-year upper limit (Haley et al., 1992).

The choice of the test environment depends in part on the purpose of the assessment. In attempting to discriminate the presence or degree of motor delays, it is most logical to use a standardized, norm-referenced instrument, such as the *Peabody Developmental Motor Scales* (Folio &

Fewell, 2000). When administering a standardized instrument, specific test materials must be used, and the assessment must be conducted in a standardized fashion. For such purposes, a clinical setting may be more satisfactory than the child's natural environment. When determining a child's functional mobility skills, as with the *Pediatric Evaluation of Disability Inventory*, the child's natural environment (e.g., home, child care, preschool classroom) is preferable. Assessments in the child's natural environment provide a more valid representation of general motor functioning.

Regardless of the purpose of the assessment, the environment should be set up to facilitate the child's optimal performance. Environmental factors such as time of day or difficulty of the task, as well as how the child is handled or positioned, may affect a child's motor functioning. In a standardized assessment situation, environmental distractions such as nonstandardized toys, unexpected noises or visual stimuli, and the presence of siblings or other children should be minimized. In a natural environment, such as the home, classroom, or playground, these types of distractions are a normal part of the environment and should be included. The child's functional motor capabilities are best assessed in a natural setting, complete with real-world environmental stimuli, noises, and activities of daily living. For example, a child who can ascend and descend stairs independently in a clinical setting but who is unable to climb the front porch steps at home will succeed in the clinical setting but not in the natural environment. Assessment of motor skills in both types of environments is important for gaining an overall, authentic representation of the child's true abilities.

REPRESENTATIVE PURPOSES AND METHODS OF MOTOR ASSESSMENT

Some children have diagnoses indicative of atypical motor development with the potential of resulting in delays. Usually diagnoses such as cerebral palsy, spina bifida, and Down syndrome indicate the presence of abnormal muscle tone, orthopedic problems (e.g., paralysis, contractures, hip dislocations), and associated health problems (e.g., seizure disorder, hydrocephalus) (Batshaw, 1997). Taken singly or in clusters, all of these characteristics should determine the selection of appropriate assessment instruments and procedures.

Some children have generalized delays in development that include delays in achieving motor milestones such as sitting, crawling, and walking, but not orthopedic or muscle tone problems. For children who have generalized delays in motor development and other areas, the selection of instruments and procedures may vary depending on information provided by the family. Instruments used may include an initial multidomain developmental test, a test of motor skills, and observational information that can be collected.

Initial assessments for eligibility may have "fixed" federal and state regulations; however, additional information may be gathered for children with motor delays from the family and various members of the assessment team. If the purpose of assessment is to establish eligibility, especially if the major area of suspected delay is in motor development, much information can be gained by doing a thorough review of existing information supplied by the family or permitted by the family. The collection of the child's medical history, developmental history, and the identification of existing assessments and service providers may greatly facilitate the assessment process. While standardized multidomain instruments are often required, the value of this assessment may be limited after eligibility is established and intervention goals are being formulated.

As described earlier, assessments of children with atypical or delayed motor development may be conducted for a variety of reasons, including screening, diagnosis or eligibility, program planning, and progress monitoring or evaluation (Gargiulo & Kilgo, 2000). Depending on the purpose of the assessment, several types of instru-

ments may be used during the motor assessment process including norm-referenced, criterion-referenced, and curriculum-referenced measures of motor skills. In addition, these measures will need to be supplemented with qualitative information derived from direct observations that have been discussed in previous sections.

Motor Assessment Purposes

Screening, the first step in the assessment process, is designed to identify young children who potentially have motor delays or disabilities and, therefore, need further assessment. Examples of screening instruments frequently used to determine motor skills are the *Denver II* (Frankenburg et al., 1992) and the *Milani-Comparetti Motor Development Screening Test* (Stuberg, Dehne, Miedaner, & White, 1987). Because the *Denver II* is a quick, inexpensive tool, it is widely used in the identification process. The *Milani-Comparetti* provides more qualitative information and is used to correlate functional motor achievement with underlying neurological functioning by assessing the maturity of neuromotor reflexes, automatic reactions, and protective and equilibrium reactions.

Diagnosis and/or **eligibility** comprise the second phase of the assessment process. Assessment tools designed for this purpose provide information regarding how a child compares with children of the same age and are used to establish eligibility for services. Many general diagnostic instruments provide information about motor development, as well as functioning in other developmental domains. Generally, standardized tools are used to determine whether a child has achieved specific motor milestones; however, they do not provide information about the quality of a child's movement. The *Peabody Developmental Motor Scales* (Folio & Fewell, 2000) is an example of a standardized tool often used by physical and occupational therapists to assess both fine and gross motor skills in children from birth through 7 years of age. A variety of normed scores can be derived including percentile rank, motor age equivalent, and a developmental motor quotient. A developmental profile can be generated that outlines the child's strengths and areas of need.

Program and intervention planning, the third phase of motor skill assessment, is used to develop goals and outcomes to be included in individual educational plans (IEPs) or individualized family service plans (IFSPs). This phase of the assessment process may involve information from norm-referenced, criterion-referenced, and/or ecological assessments conducted in the natural environment. It is important to note, however, that functional skills, rather than developmental milestones, are stressed during this phase of assessment. Some programs use the *AEPS* (Bricker, 2002) for program development because it addresses all developmental areas and is linked to programming and the evaluation of progress.

The final phase of the motor assessment process, **progress monitoring and evaluation,** is the point in which the purpose is to monitor change over time. Evaluative measures such as the *Gross Motor Function Measure* (Russell et al., 1990) or the *Pediatric Evaluation of Disability Inventory* (Haley et al., 1992) are appropriate, as well as other measures that link assessment, programming, and progress monitoring such as the *AEPS* (Bricker, 2002).

The assessment instrument selected for use should be based on the purpose of the assessment. Table 11.9 contains a list of the most widely used assessment instruments for assessing motor skills. The instruments are grouped according to their purpose with each purpose discussed in greater detail within the table.

In conducting motor assessments, it is crucial that assessment instruments be used only for their intended purpose (Rosenbaum et al., 1990). For example, the use of norm-referenced instruments to evaluate change in a child as a result of motor intervention, such as physical or occupational therapy, is not appropriate in that these measures are typically designed to be discriminative in nature. In assessing motor skills, examiners should be familiar with the instrument's purpose and should use it

only for that purpose to ensure that the test results are both meaningful and valid (Zittel, 1994).

Format and Methods Used in Motor Assessment

The format used in the assessment of motor skills may vary from separate individual assessments completed by therapists and educators separately in specific settings to an arena format where all participants assess motor skills together in a natural setting with the latter being recommended when possible.

Of the possible formats that can be used, an arena assessment provides optimal opportunities for families and professionals to cooperatively plan intervention goals from the same perspective using an appropriate assessment whose purpose is to link assessment with intervention (Foley, 1990). Curriculum-based assessment instruments, such as the *AEPS*, are designed to enhance the likelihood that all members will be working from the same document. These instruments are also designed to provide repeated measures of progress over time. The *AEPS* and the *Carolina Curriculum*, for example, can be used to accommodate quarterly administrations. Children with physical challenges often have a number of professionals who complete assessments and develop intervention goals and therefore, the level of collaboration must be high in order to meet the changing needs of children with motor delays or disabilities.

Methods and styles of assessment may vary from direct testing to observations. Direct testing of motor skills presents a challenge because it requires the child to have the prerequisite language and cognitive skills of understanding directions (e.g., stand on one foot), imitation, and copying a model. Direct testing also presumes that the child will be willing and motivated to perform skills out of context for personnel who may be unfamiliar to them. Observational information may be more acceptable and have more social validity due to the child's comfort level in performing skills in natural and familiar settings,

TABLE 11.9

Examples of Frequently Used Instruments to Assess Motor Skills

Purpose/Instruments	Age Range	Motor Areas Assessed	Unique Aspects
Screening Instruments:			
Denver Developmental Screening Test (DDST-II) (Frankenburg, et al., 1992)	Birth to 6 years	Gross motor; fine motor—adaptive	Norm-referenced; Uses observation or parent interview format; Good reliability but validity questioned; Profiles score normal, abnormal, questionable, untestable; Less reliable and sensitive for children birth to 30 months; Includes prescreening questionnaire.
Milani-Comparetti Motor Development Screening Test (Stuberg, Dehne, Miedaner, & White, 1987)	Birth to 2 years	Postural control; active movement; primitive reflexes; righting parachute and tilting reactions	Quick screening for motor delays and and disabilities; Intervals are provided for regular follow along; Administered by therapist or trained personnel.
Developmental Profile II (DP-II) (Alpern, Boll, & Shearer, 1980)	Birth to 9 1/2 years	Physical age: Gross and fine motor (coordination, strength, stamina, flexibility)	Standardized functional assessment for screening purposes; Interview or direct testing may be used; Good reliability and validity; Easily and accurately completed by parents.
Diagnostic/Eligibility Instruments:			
Battelle Developmental Inventory (BDI) (Newborg et al., 1984)	Birth to 8 years	Motor domain: Muscle control, body coordination, locomotion, fine motor, perceptual motor	Norm-referenced; Includes procedures for diagnostic testing; Interview and observational methods are

Continued

TABLE 11.9

Continued

Purpose/Instruments	Age Range	Motor Areas Assessed	Unique Aspects
Diagnostic/Eligibility Instruments:			
			included for many items; Easy-to-follow instructions; Includes adaptations for children with sensory and motor impairments; Includes screening test.
Bayley Scales of Infant Development (Bayley II) (Bayley, 1993)	Birth to 42 months	Gross and fine motor milestones	Norm-referenced; provides developmental motor age; norms established for 2 to 3 months; Widely used to determine developmental delays; Provides no information on quality of movement; Good reliability and validity; Requires training to administer.
Bruininks-Oseretsky Test of Motor Proficiency (Bruininks, 1978)	4 1/2 to 14 1/2 years	Gross and fine motor proficiency: Running speed and agility, balance, bilateral coordination, strength, upper limb coordination, response speed, visual-motor control, and upper limb speed and dexterity	Norm-referenced; well-standardized; Good reliability and validity; Difficult to administer to younger children and those with delays; Lengthy.
Early Learning Accomplishment Profile (ELAP) (Glover, Preminger, & Sanford, 1988)	Birth to 3 years	Gross and fine motor skills	Criterion-referenced; Indicates presence, absence, or emergence of skills; Widely used

TABLE 11.9

Continued

Purpose/Instruments	Age Range	Motor Areas Assessed	Unique Aspects
Diagnostic/Eligibility Instruments:			
			in interdisciplinary settings; Developmentally sequenced; Each item includes testing procedure and description of correct response.
Miller Assessment for Preschoolers (MAP) (Miller, 1988)	2.9 to 5.8 years	Sensory and motor abilities	Norm-referenced; Comprehensive; Recommended for identifying children with mild to moderate delays.
Movement Assessment of Infants (MAI) (Chandler, Andrews, Swanson, & Larson, 1980)	Birth to 1 year	Muscle tone; primitive reflexes; automatic reactions; volitional movements	Provides quantitative information on the degree of motor dysfunction related to test items; Used to identify infants with motor disabilities and those at risk; Includes step-by-step procedures for each item; Administered by therapist or trained personnel.
Programming Instruments:			
Assessment, Evaluation, and Programming System (Bricker, 2002)	Birth to 6 years	Gross and fine motor skills	Criterion-referenced; Links assessment, intervention, and evaluation; Involves families in the process.
Brigance Diagnostic Inventory of Early Development-R (Brigance, 1985)	Birth to 6 years	Preambulatory motor skills and behaviors; gross motor skills; fine motor skills	Criterion-referenced; Provisions for tracking progress; Skill sequences are task analyzed; Easily administered.

Continued

TABLE 11.9
Continued

Purpose/Instruments	Age Range	Motor Areas Assessed	Unique Aspects
Programming Instruments:			
Callier-Azusa Scale Stillman, 1978)	Birth to 6 years	Motor development; postural control; locomotion; fine motor; visual motor	Based on longitudinal observation of child behavior; Specifically for use with children who are deaf/blind and those with multiple disabilities; Criterion-referenced; Developmentally sequenced.
Carolina Curriculum Infants and Preschoolers, Second Edition (Johnson-Martin, Jens, & Attermeier 1991)	Birth to 5 years	Tactile integration and manipulation; feeding; reaching and grasping; object manipulation; bilateral hand activity; gross motor skills	Curriculum-referenced check sheet; Curriculum sequences provided for each skill; Good task analyses of skills arranged in developmental sequences.
Developmental Assessment of Young Children (Voress & Maddox, 1998)	Birth to 6 years	Physical; abilities; adaptive behavior.	Norm-referenced; Provides standard scores.
Hawaii Early Learning Profile (HELP) Furuno, O'Reilly, Hosaka, Inatsuka, Allman, & Zeisloft, 1992)	Birth to 5 years	Gross and fine motor skills.	Curriculum-referenced; Provides developmental milestones useful in program planning; Qualitative descriptions of items are provided as well as teaching activities.
Mullen Scales of Early Learning (Mullen, 1995)	Birth to 5 years	Gross and fine motor skills	Norm-referenced; Standardization and reliability data; Developmentally integrated and comprehensive.
Peabody Developmental Motor Scales II (PDMS-2) (Folio & Fewell, 2000)	Birth to 7 years	Gross and fine motor skills	Curriculum-referenced; Five criteria are used to indicate child's

TABLE 11.9

Continued

Purpose/Instruments	Age Range	Motor Areas Assessed	Unique Aspects
Programming Instruments:			
			performance on items (e.g., total dependence, complete independence); Provides developmental age for both gross and motor skills; Includes teaching activities and provides description of performance of each item.
Vulpé Assessment Battery (Vulpé, 1997)	Birth to 6 years	All developmental areas including tactile, vestibular, and/or proprioceptive functions	May be used with children with multiple disabilities.
Gross Motor Function Measures (GMFM) (Russell et al., 1993)	Children within gross motor developmental range of birth to 5 years	Quantifications of five dimensions of motor behavior (lying and rolling; sitting; crawling and kneeling; standing; walking, running, and jumping	Measures change over time in children with cerebral palsy; Measures the effects of treatment; Measures functional movements; Relatively new test; not normed.
Gross Motor Performance Measure (GMPM) (Boyce et al., 1991)	Children within gross motor developmental range of birth to 5 years or children with cerebral palsy from 5 months to 12 years	Measures gross motor movement quality (postural alignment, selective control, coordination, stabilization, and weight shift)	Measures quality of movement in children with motor disabilities; Measures the effects of treatment; Measures functional movements; Relatively new test; little supportive research.

often in the context of play. Further, assessment materials must be acceptable and adaptable for children with motor delays or disabilities.

TRANSLATING ASSESSMENT INFORMATION INTO INTERVENTION

The results of an assessment of motor skills should be used to develop goals and design intervention strategies. These goals and strategies should be determined and designed individually based on the family's preferences and children's particular motor needs. Following the assessment, the team should develop goals that originate from the family. Examples of these goals may be, "I want my child to walk" or "I want my child to write his name." With this information as a starting point, the team can then formulate an appropriate intervention plan that will address these general goals. Goals and strategies should be developed within the context of daily routines and purposeful activities and should be aimed at assisting children in experiencing movement that is as normal as possible and that allows them to participate fully in their natural environments (Campbell, 2000).

Intervention techniques can enhance a child's movement competence, thus increasing their participation in activities related to mobility, self-care, communication, play, socialization, and cognitive tasks. In addition, specific techniques may be designed to assist parents and caregivers in their interactions with and daily care of the child. Programming should include both direct instruction using specific therapeutic intervention strategies, which often includes using appropriate positioning and handling techniques and adaptive equipment (Breath, DeMauro, & Snyder, 1997).

Many variables must be considered before the assessment process begins: the setting, age of the child, degree of motor delay, composition of the assessment team, family preferences, and community options available. For example, the composition of the team should be determined

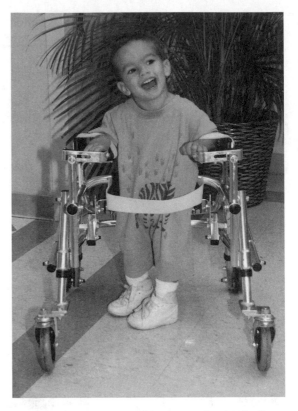

Goals and strategies should be designed individually based on the family's preferences and the child's motor needs

by the child's needs based on referral information, the accumulation of previous assessments information and the medical history of the child. The team may assess the child using a number of different approaches, which may range from discipline-specific, isolated assessments to arena assessments in natural settings. Using the arena assessment format, participants often gain a greater understanding of the child's developmental profile and the family's concerns across all areas of development and across all settings.

If a child has cerebral palsy, Down syndrome, or spina bifida, the team may consist of the family, an educator, service coordinator, speech-language pathologist, occupational therapist, physical therapist, and a nurse. The service coordinator may receive test results and recommendations from all of the disciplines, which is followed by the identification of team members who will have the opportunity to observe the child across different settings. The administration of a criterion-based or curriculum-based assessment is a practical procedure often used in the development of an intervention plan. An example of a frequently used assessment instrument is the *Assessment, Evaluation, and Programming for Infants and Children (AEPS)* (Bricker, 2002). The AEPS provides more discerning and practical information than standardized measures used to determine motor skills. An example of the fine motor section of the AEPS can be located in Table 11.10.

All assessment information should be reviewed by the team in order for them to gain the insight needed to develop appropriate goals that are generated from the families' preferences. The AEPS is organized in a goal/objective format making it simple for team members to use in determining goals. Goals and intervention strategies should be practical in order for them to be embedded into the ongoing routines and activities of the child.

The following examples illustrate the process that can be used to translate motor assessment information into intervention for children with various types of disabilities.

Anna Katherine *Anna Katherine is a 26-month-old child, who was diagnosed with cerebral palsy at 6 months of age. Her specific diagnosis was spastic diplegia, meaning that her leg muscles were hypertonic with functional use of her arms and hands. What follows is a summary of an assessment profile for Anna Katherine.*

Fine Motor Development
Peabody Motor Scales: 16 months age
   equivalent (AE)
Battelle Developmental Inventory (fine
   motor): 22 months (AE)

Gross Motor Development
Peabody Motor Scales: 6 months
Battelle Development Inventory (gross
   motor): 8 months (AE)

The physical therapist reported that Anna Katherine had made considerable progress, although there was no change in her gross motor assessment. She can sit independently and maintain that position. She can roll and scoot on her belly to get where she wants to go. Standing is not yet a functional position for her due to the muscle tightness throughout her legs and hips.

The occupational therapist reported that Anna Katherine is doing well with sitting in a chair with support for her feet and a seat belt to keep her hips bent. In this seat, she can use her hands well to eat, drink, and participate in group activities using paint, magic markers, glue, etc. Her grasping skills are becoming more and more sophisticated and consistent.

The family and the educator reiterated that Anna Katherine has made great strides in the area of fine motor development; however, they reported that her gross motor development has not changed for the past 6 months. Her mother stated that her greatest desire was for Anna Katherine to walk. The team started with this goal and developed objectives and strategies to address walking. After the initial assessment, the team determined that Anna Katherine needed a more efficient manner of moving from one place to another and that she may eventually walk with concerted effort on the part of all individuals who are responsible for the implementation of the plan.

Anna Katherine is attending a preschool program that has large classrooms. Within each classroom, children are required to move from center to center to engage in activities according to a classroom schedule. Anna Katherine is somewhat socially isolated because she crawls on the floor while everyone else walks from center to center, therefore it takes her longer to get from place to place. The team referred the family to an orthopedic clinic to determine the procedures that were needed to get Anna Katherine off the floor and walking. She was provided with a wheelchair to temporarily get her at the same eye level as all of the other children. This was beneficial to her socially because her peers could give her a push if she needed help and they could interact with her more appropriately. The chair also allowed her to move from center to center according to the schedule.

The second step was to assess her potential for using a walker for moving around in the room. The orthopedist performed surgical procedures

TABLE 11.10

Sample Items from the AEPS Fine Motor Domain, Birth to 3 Years

Strand A	Reach, Grasp, and Release
G1	Simultaneously brings hands to midline
	1.1 Makes directed batting and/or swiping movements with each hand
	1.2 Makes nondirected movements with each arm
G2	Brings two objects together at or near each arm
	2.1 Transfers object from one hand to another
	2.2 Holds an object in each hand
	2.3 Reaches toward and touches object with each hand
G3	Grasps hand-size object with either hand using ends of thumb, index, and second fingers
	3.1 Graphs hand-size object with either hand using the palm, with object placed toward the thumb and index finger
	3.2 Grasps cylindrical object with either hand by closing fingers around it
	3.3 Grasps hand-size object with either hand using whole hand
G4	Grasps pea-size object with either hand, using tip of the index finger and thumb with hand and/or arm not resting on surface for support
	4.1 Grasps pea-size object with either hand using tip of the index finger and thumb with hand and/or arm not resting on surface for support
	4.2 Grasps pea-size object with either hand using side of the index finger and thumb
	4.3 Grasps pea-size object with either hand using fingers in a raking and/or scratching movement
G5	Places and releases object balanced on top of another object with either hand
	5.1 Releases object onto and/or into a larger target with either hand
	5.2 Releases hand-held object with each hand

Strand B	Functional Use of Fine Motor Skills
G1	Rotates either wrist on horizontal plane
	1.1 Turns object over using wrist and arm rotation with each hand
G2	Assembles toy and/or object that requires putting pieces together
	2.1 Fits variety of shapes into corresponding spaces
	2.2 Fits object into defined space
G3	Uses either index finger to activate objects
	3.1 Uses either hand to activate objects
G4	Copies simple written shapes after demonstration
	4.1 Draws circles and lines
	4.2 Scribbles

Note: From Bricker, D. (2002). *Assessment, Evaluation, and Programming System for Infants and Children (AEPS)*™, Second edition: Volume 1: Administration Guide (pp. 164–165). Baltimore: Paul H. Brookes Publishing Co. Adapted by permission.

to release some of the tightness in her hips, legs, and feet. During this time, she continued to use the wheelchair, which allowed her to participate in the classroom without interruptions. The walker was ordered and the use of it in the classroom was closely monitored by the physical therapist, who also interacted with the family and visited the home. The intervention team provided continual and repeated assessments of the quality of Anna Katherine's use of the walker.

The team initially considered the quality of Anna Katherine's movements rather than the distance that she covered. That meant that the distance she needed to travel to engage in routine activities at school and at home called for the use of the walker. Her progress was noted in her AEPS with the teacher noting that she was walking with adaptations. Eventually Anna Katherine was able to move longer and longer distances. Her family wanted her to be able to use the walker at the shopping mall. The team also felt that it was important for Anna Katherine to walk into and out of the school building without help. As her confidence increased, she began to be able to cruise around the room without the walker and move from center to center by holding onto the furniture or the walls of the classroom. After learning to move more efficiently, she became more independent in the bathroom and at lunch. Becoming more independent also allowed her to interact more confidently with her peers and to initiate ideas during center play. These spin-off effects were noted in her portfolio.

Emma Grace: Emma Grace is a 3-year-old child who was born with spina bifida. She has paralysis beginning at her mid-chest area. In addition, she has hydrocephalus and a shunt. Emma Grace has no bowel and bladder control, which requires that she be catheterized several times a day. She attends a preschool program five days a week.

Emma Grace's performance on the Bayley and Peabody Motor Scales revealed scores estimating that Emma Grace was functioning on a level similar to that of a 6-month-old child in gross motor and a 20-month-old in fine motor. The report from the physical therapist follows:

"Emma Grace scoots on her stomach to get around, commonly referred to as "belly scooting." She loves to try to climb up the slide and go down on her stomach. As she scoots around on the floor, she is able to navigate around obstacles. Although her lower extremities are flaccid, she is able to

push up to sitting and adjust her legs with her hands. While in sitting, she can balance herself while reaching over her head for an object."

The following is a report from the occupational therapist:

After several observations in the classroom, it has been determined that Emma Grace is doing very well in the area of self-feeding. Fine motor skills continue to progress, which are evidenced as she shows interest in a variety of materials and activities. An area in which she does not enjoy participating is finger painting, although she will finger paint when prompted. Emma Grace is able to operate a variety of cause/effect toys appropriately. She can turn pages in books, as well as point to pictures. She is able to make large scribble marks and has begun to imitate drawing lines and circles.

In the small program where Emma Grace attends preschool, she is one of four children in the school with a disability. Her speech and cognitive skills are age-appropriate at this time. Emma Grace's mother wants her to be able to move around like the other children her age so that she will be able to play with her friends more easily. Her teacher reiterated these goals, indicating that Emma Grace has trouble joining in center activities and play groups because it takes her so long to get from one area of the room to another.

The motor delays have contributed to the lack of opportunity for Emma Grace to interact with other children. She initiates conversations with adults on a frequent basis but rarely with the other children. She is often adult-dependent because of her paralysis and medical needs. Therefore, the team developed an intervention plan to address all of these concerns.

The physical therapist recommended the use of a scooter board to help Emma Grace get from place to place quickly and to strengthen her arms and shoulders. She could not get on the scooter, however, without assistance. Another issue was that in the play areas, many materials were beyond her reach from the floor. Although she was taught to move from her scooter to sitting, the higher shelves were still inaccessible. She was measured for a wheelchair that would enable her to be on eye-level with the other children. After receiving the wheelchair, Emma Grace has begun to interact more with the other children and is beginning to move about the room very efficiently.

The physical therapist determined that Emma Grace should be in a standing position at times *and ordered a parapodium for her. Her teacher and parents were provided numerous opportunities to learn the basics of placing Emma Grace in and out of the equipment. They were also given a duration schedule so that the amount of time in the equipment could gradually be increased with a means for recording the progress. In addition, they were given a cautionary checklist to follow so that any problems could be reported immediately. The teacher planned time for center participation so that Emma Grace would be able to use the parapodium to stand in the house-keeping area and play with the sink, refrigerator, etc. at the same eye-level as the other children.*

During gross motor play in the gym or on the playground, the team decided that Emma Grace would not be strapped in to any equipment or chairs. Instead they wanted her to freely move about, going down the slide independently, crawling into the ball pit, and so on. They considered this to be the time that Emma Grace could be free to play and at the same time develop her upper body strength.

After all of these accommodations were in place, Emma Grace showed remarkable progress in social skills and in developing higher level play skills. She became more integrated into the classroom as a result of being able to be more independent and interactive with the other children and materials.

Walt *Walt is a 5-year-old boy who is currently attending a pre-K program and will be attending kindergarten next year. He has no medical problems and has been in early intervention since he was 6 months old. Walt received physical therapy until he was 3 years of age, at which time it was determined that he no longer needed extra help in developing gross motor skills. The physical therapist has continued to observe in his classroom and consults with the teacher as needed. Walt currently receives occupational therapy. An assessment of his motor skills yielded the profile that follows.*

> *Peabody Motor Scales:* 26 months (AE)
> *Battelle Developmental Inventory:*
> > Fine Motor Skills: 28 months
> > Adaptive Skills: 31 months

Walt's teacher and occupational therapist determined that his fine motor skills should be the focus of intervention and used a kindergarten checklist as their guide for constructing goals.

The teacher, parents, and occupational therapist have noted that his grasping and general hand usage are his greatest areas of strength. He is able to handle a variety of shapes and sizes of objects easily. He is beginning to show more of a left-hand preference, imitating and using his left hand more than his right. He does at times switch to his right. In prewriting, Walt is making more of an effort to color and cover areas with a more concentrated stroke, and he is beginning to imitate specific strokes (horizontal and vertical lines) as well. Walt has made progress with scissor skills. He can snip the edges of paper while an adult holds the paper. Adaptively, he has no problems handling a spoon and a fork, he attempts to open a milk carton, and he carries his tray to and from the kitchen at lunch. At snack, he pours his juice into his cup, selects the snack that he wants, and passes the tray to the next child at the table. In addition, he independently brushes his teeth.

Walt's family is very proud of his accomplishments. Their perception is that he will have no problems in kindergarten in most areas. The family, teacher, and occupational therapist met and developed the following goals:

1. Walt will print his name independently;
2. Walt will use paper, glue, crayons, pencils, and scissors appropriately; and
3. Walt will engage in sports activities (i.e., soccer and T-ball).

The team determined that a major problem existed in the classroom, which had become a barrier to fine motor skill development. Adults seemed to be giving Walt too much hand-over-hand assistance, and had become reluctant to develop other accommodations and adaptations. Further, there was no plan in place to diminish the amount of assistance provided to Walt. As a result, the team developed a checklist that showed the adults a sequence for providing less intensive assistance, as well as a list of modifications that could be made for the materials that he would need. The checklists follow:

Level of assistance
1. Hand-over-hand;
2. Hand on elbow to give a nudge toward materials;
3. No physical assistance, verbal reminders.

Modifications
1. Large crayons, pencils, markers, chalk;
2. Kindergarten paper to ready him for writing his name;

3. Tracing stencils;
4. Magnetic letters;
5. MagnaDoodle;
6. Uppercase letters first, then lower;
7. Repetition, name written on all products.

As Walt had the opportunity to practice his fine motor skills without adult assistance, his skills improved. Upon the family's request, the lists and materials were provided to them to use at home. Currently, Walt is approximating his first and last name using a large crayon on kindergarten paper. The entire class is participating in more cooperative games and is learning the prerequisite skills for participating in soccer and T-ball. Walt is able to kick the ball and attempts to hit the ball on the tee with some success.

These case studies have illustrated ways in which assessments and interventions can be linked. The following is a list of general guidelines that can be used by the team in developing appropriate goals for motor development:

1. Motor intervention should be provided within the context of the natural environment.
2. In centers, the major goal of motor intervention is to provide the child with more opportunities to use materials and interact with others.
3. The child's schedule should be reviewed to determine the optimal times for using any mobility equipment.
4. Equipment should not isolate the child from others.

5. Plans should be in place for diminishing assistance, giving the child opportunities to practice skills with less help or with no adapted materials.
6. Adapted materials should approximate those that other children use.
7. The development of fine motor skills will impact adaptive skills development, especially in the areas of feeding and dressing.
8. The development of gross motor skills or mobility can affect the child's independence and increase his/her interactions with other children.

As can be seen throughout these examples, the translation of motor assessment information to intervention optimally requires a team approach. The team should work together in the child's natural environment to ensure that the goals and intervention strategies are appropriate, functional, and practical in the home, group setting, or other important environments. Interventions should be compatible with the child's schedule and should enhance development in other areas such as adaptive and social skills. Modifications of materials should be a major strategy with less emphasis on adult assistance. Using these considerations as a guide, children's motor development will be enhanced which will ultimately have a positive impact on the lives of children and families.

· · · · · · · ·

SUMMARY OF KEY CONCEPTS

■ Movement competence and motor skills are integral to all other areas of development.

■ Delays and/or deviations in motor development are exhibited in infants and young children with various disabilities. Thus, motor assessment is a complex but critical component of the overall assessment process for young children with known or suspected motor delays or disabilities.

■ Dramatic changes have occurred over the past two decades in the assessment of motor skills in young children. Instead of working in isolation, families and service providers work together throughout the assessment process to gather authentic information about children's motor skills that can be used to fulfill a variety of purposes.

- Motor assessments usually are led by physical and occupational therapists and involve other team members as well. All team members should be knowledgeable of and have skills in the various dimensions of motor assessment.
- The dimensions of a motor assessment include gross motor skills, muscle tone, reflexes, postural reactions, volitional movements, and fine motor skills.
- Although there are no easy formulas for the selection of an appropriate assessment process, this chapter reviews procedural considerations and representative methods of motor assessment. Included are examples of standardized, norm-referenced tools designed to discriminate children with motor delays from those who are experiencing typical motor develop-

ment, as well as instruments and procedures that can be used for planning intervention and monitoring progress.

- Choosing assessment procedures and instruments should be based on the purpose of the assessment.
- Regardless of the instruments or procedures selected, the motor assessment process must provide a detailed description of a child's motor abilities to be used in designing appropriate goals and therapeutic interventions.
- Motor assessment information can be translated into functional goals and intervention techniques that will enable young children with motor delays or disabilities to participate as fully as possible in a variety of natural environments.

· · · · · · · ·

REFERENCES

Alpern, G., Boll, T., & Shearer, M. (1980). *Developmental Profile II*. Aspen, CO: Psychological Development Publications.

Batshaw, M. J. (1997). *Children with disabilities* (4th ed.). Baltimore: Paul H. Brookes.

Bayley, N. (1993). *Bayley Scales of Infant Development–2nd Edition*. San Antonio, TX: Psychological Corp.

Bly, L. (1983). *The components of normal movement during the first year of life and abnormal motor development*. Chicago: Neurodevelopmental Treatment Assn.

Boyce, W., Gowland, C., Rosenbaum, P., Lane, M., Plews, N., Goldsmith, C., et al. (1991). Gross motor performance measure: Validity and responsiveness of a measure of quality of movement. *Physical Therapy*, 75(5), 603–613.

Breath, D., DeMauro, G., & Snyder, P. (1997). Adapting seating for young children. *Young Exceptional Children*, 11(1), 10–16.

Bricker, D. (2002). *Assessment, evaluation, and programming system for infants and children*. (2nd ed.) Baltimore: Paul H. Brookes.

Brigance, A. H. (1985). *Brigance Diagnostic Inventory of Early Development*. North Billerica, MA: Curriculum Associates.

Bruininks, R. (1978). *Bruininks-Oseretsky Test of Motor Proficiency examiner's manual*. Circle Pines, MN: American Guidance Service.

Bushnell, E., & Boudreau, J. (1993). Motor development and the mind: The potential role of motor abilities as a determinant of aspects of perceptual development. *Child Development, 64*, 1005–1021.

Campbell, P. H. (1982). *Introduction to neurodevelopmental treatment*. Akron, OH: Children's Hospital Medical Center.

Campbell, P. H. (1985). *Assessment of posture and movement in children with severe movement dysfunction*. Akron, OH: Children's Hospital Medical Center.

Campbell, P. H. (1987a). Physical management and handling procedures with students with movement dysfunction. In M. E. Snell (Ed.), *Systematic instruction of persons with severe handicaps* (3rd ed., pp. 174–187). Columbus, OH: Merrill.

Campbell, P. H. (1987b). Programming for students with dysfunction in posture and movement. In M. E. Snell (Ed.), *Systematic instruction of persons with severe handicaps* (3rd ed., pp. 188–211). Upper Saddle River, NJ: Merrill/Prentice Hall.

Campbell, P. H. (2000). Promoting participation in natural environments by accommodating motor disabilities. In M. Snell & F. Brown (Eds.), *Instruction of students with severe disabilities* (5th ed., pp. 291–329). Upper Saddler River, NJ: Merrill/Prentice Hall.

Campbell, S. K. (1997). Therapy programs for children that last a lifetime. *Physical and Occupational Therapy in Pediatrics, 17*(1), 1–15.

Campbell, S., Kolobe, T., Osten, E., Lenke, M., & Girolani, G. (1995). Construct validity of the Test of Infant Motor Performance. *Physical Therapy, 75*(7), 585–596.

Case-Smith, J. (1993). *Pediatric occupational therapy and early intervention.* Stoneham, MA: Butterworth-Heinemann.

Chandler, L. S., Andrews, M. S., Swanson, M. W. & Larson (1980). *Movement assessment of infants: A manual.* Rolling Bay, WA: Infant Movement Research.

Crutchfield, C. A., & Barnes, M. R. (1993). *Motor control and motor learning in rehabilitation.* Atlanta, GA: Stokesville.

Dunn, W. (1996). The sensorimotor systems: A framework for assessment and intervention. In F. Orelove & D. Sobsey (Eds.), *Educating children with multiple disabilities* (3rd ed., pp. 35–78). Baltimore: Paul H. Brookes.

Erhardt, R. P. (1982). *Developmental hand dysfunction: Theory, assessment, and treatment.* Laurel, MO: RAMSCO.

Foley, G. M. (1990). Portrait of the arena evaluation: Assessment in the transdisciplinary approach. In E. D. Gibbs & D. M. Teti (Eds.), *Interdisciplinary assessment of infants: A guide for early intervention professionals* (pp. 271–286). Baltimore: Paul H. Brookes.

Folio, R. & Fewell, R. F. (2000). *Peabody Developmental Motor Scales* (2nd ed.). Allen, TX: Developmental Learning Materials Teaching Resources.

Frankenburg, W., Dodds, J., Archer, P., Bresnick, B. Maschka, P., Edelman, N., & Shapiro, H. (1992). *The Denver II* Denver: Denver Developmental Materials.

Furuno, S., O'Reilly, K. A., Hosaka, C. M., Inatsuka, T. T., Allman, T. L., & Zeisloft, B. (1992). *The Hawaii Early Learning Profile.* Palo Alto, CA: VORT.

Gargiulo, R. & Kilgo, J. (2000). Young children with special needs. Albany, NY: Delmar Publishers/An International Thomson Publishing Company.

Gesell, A. (1973). *The first five years of life: A guide to the study of the preschool child.* New York: Harper & Row.

Glover, M. E., Preminger, J. L., & Sanford, A. R. (1978). *Early learning accomplishment profile for developmentally young children.* Winston-Salem, NC: Kaplan.

Haley, S. M., Coster, W. J., Ludlow, L. H., Hakiwanger, J. T., & Andrellos, P. J. (1992). *Pediatric Evaluation of Disability Inventory (PEDI).* San Antonio, TX: Therapy Skill Builders.

Illingworth, R. S. (1975). *The development of the infant and young child: Normal and abnormal.* Edinburgh: Livingstone.

Johnson-Martin, N., Jens, K. G., & Attermeier, S. M. (1991). *The Carolina Curriculum for Handicapped Infants and Infants at Risk.* Baltimore: Paul Brookes.

Miller, L. (1988). *Miller Assessment for Preschoolers (MAP) manual revision.* San Antonio, TX: Harcourt Brace Jovanovich.

Minear, W. L. (1956). A classification of cerebral palsy. *Pediatrics, 18,* 841–852.

Molnar, G. E. (1992). *Pediatric rehabilitation.* Baltimore: Williams and Wilkins.

Mullen E. M. (1995). *Mullen Scales of Early Learning.* Circle Pines, MN: American Guidance Service.

Newborg, J., Stock, J. R., Wnek, L., Guidubaidi, J., & Svinicki, J. (1984). *Battelle Developmental Inventory.* Allen, TX: DLM Teaching Resources.

Rosenbaum, P. L., Russell, D. J., Cadman, D. T., Gowland, C., Jarvis, S., & Hardy, S. (1990). Issues in measuring change in children with cerebral palsy: A special communication. *Physical Therapy, 70,* 125–131.

Russell, D., Rosenbaum, P., Gowland, C., Hardy, S., Lane, M., Plews, N. et al. (1990). *Gross motor function measure manual.* Hamilton, Ontario: McMaster University.

Russell, D., Rosenbaum, P., Gowland, G., Hardy, S., Lane, M., Plews, N. et al. (1993). *The Gross motor function measure manual: 2nd Edition,* Hamilton, Canada: McMaster University.

Sandall, S., McLean, M., & Smith, B. (2000). *DEC recommended practices for early intervention/early childhood special education.* Longmont, CO: Sopris West.

Stillman, R. D. (1978). *Callier-Azusa Scale.* Reston, VA: Council for Exceptional Children.

Stuberg, W. A., Dehne, P., Miedaner, J., & White, P. (1987). *Miliani-Comparetti Motor Development Screening Test* (Rev. ed.) Omaha: Meyer Children's Rehabilitation Institute, University of Nebraska Medical Center.

Swanson, S. W. (1979). Early motor development: Assessment and intervention. In B. L. Darby & M. J. May (Eds.), *Infant assessment: Issues and application* (pp. 79–101). Seattle, WA: Western States Technical Assistance Resource.

Voress, J. & Maddox, T. (1998). *Developmental assessment of young children*. San Antonio, TX: Psychological Corp.

Vulpe, S. G. (1997). *Vulpe Assessment Battery*. Toronto Canada: National Institute on Mental Retardation.

Zittel, L. (1994). Gross motor assessment of preschool children with special needs: Instrument selection considerations. *Adapted Physical Activity Quarterly, 11*, 245–260.

Assessing Communication Skills

Elizabeth R. Crais
Joanne Erwick Roberts
The University of North Carolina at Chapel Hill

Communication is integral to everyday functioning; through it we exchange ideas, information, and feelings, achieve goals, share past events, and make plans for the future. Basic communication skills are critical for accessing and enjoying others and for managing everyday activities. For many young children with special needs, learning to communicate is not easy or natural; therefore, focusing on communication skills in assessment and intervention becomes an important component of the overall early intervention process.

The focus of this chapter is on the assessment of communication skills for the purpose of determining appropriate instructional goals for infants and preschool children with special needs. First, a rationale is provided for involvement across professionals in assessing and facilitating communication skills. Next, the dimensions and nature of communication development are presented. Finally, procedural considerations and representative methods of assessing communication are highlighted, along with suggestions for translating assessment information into instructional goals.

RATIONALE FOR ASSESSING COMMUNICATION

The recent shifts toward transdisciplinary or interdisciplinary service delivery models and assessing and intervening with children in their natural environments have challenged many professionals to gain new knowledge and skills for working with young children with special needs and their families (Davis, Thurman, & Mauro, 1995; Schwartz & Olswang, 1996; Stayton & Bruder, 1999; Whitehead, Jesien, & Ulanski, 1998). A critical component of all these interactions with children and their families is communication, including the ways the child communicates and the ways others communicate with the child and with each other. Of particular importance for the child is the enhancement of communicative and social interactions that are necessary for development across a variety of related areas (e.g., cognitive, affective,

academic). By attending to the child's and their own communication skills, professionals can influence development directly by working with the child and indirectly by working with the child's caregivers and each other.

To enhance the child's overall development, professionals should be familiar with communication concepts and assessment for a variety of reasons. First, because communication develops in accordance with a child's social, emotional, cognitive, and motor skills, professionals must look at communication in relation to the child's overall development and needs, as well as the intervention plans made for the child. For example, in the case of a young child with cerebral palsy who has difficulty communicating through pointing, professionals can work with the family and other caregivers (e.g., daycare providers, grandparents) to facilitate the child's overall development. The occupational therapist can provide ideas for developing the child's pointing response while the physical therapist helps with trunk stability to enable pointing. The speech-language pathologist can provide ideas to help combine pointing and vocalizing to request a desired object, whereas the early childhood special educator can focus on ideas for helping the child point to the object to indicate recognition of its name. As the family and professional team members work together, goals and activities can be coordinated to meet the child's overall needs and can be embedded within the child's natural routines and environments.

A second reason for understanding communication development and assessment is that all professionals and family members interact and intervene with the child through communication. Professionals should, therefore, be able to recognize the child's overall level of communication (e.g., both how the child communicates *with* and *understands* others) and modify their own communication and the task demands placed on the child. The closer the adult is to the child's level(s) of communicating (both receptively and expressively), the more likely it is that the child will be engaged in and gain from the interaction.

Third, a large number of preschool children have communication needs. Recent estimates indicate that close to 80% of children receiving special education services have primary or secondary communication deficits (U.S. Department of Education, 2000). In addition, children are often referred to early intervention programs based on delays in their communication or motor skills, thus awareness of typical and atypical communication skills is critical for all professionals who serve young children (Crais, 2001).

Fourth, children with language impairments in the preschool years often have later academic, emotional, and behavioral difficulties (Aram & Hall, 1989; Beitchman, Hood, & Inglis, 1990; Catts, 1993; Tomblin et al., 1997). Indeed, Aram and Hall (1989) reported that 60% of the children who exhibited language disorders in preschool received special education services during the school years. Moreover, for kindergarteners who continue to display language deficits, their likelihood of reading and/or learning disabilities is close to 85% (Larivee & Catts, 1992). Further, some findings indicate that negative effects of early communication deficits continue into adulthood, especially in regard to employment and income (Records, Tomblin, & Freese, 1992). Intervention to facilitate communication skills in the early years, however, may prevent or mitigate later learning, emotional, and behavioral difficulties (Baker & Cantwell, 1987; Prizant & Wetherby, 1993; Thal & Katich, 1996).

Finally, interventionists should be familiar with communication development and assessment because of the current focus on facilitating communication in natural settings such as the home and classroom. Moreover, unless the environment where communication skills are taught is similar to the environment where they are used, most children with special needs will not generalize the newly acquired skills (Cole, Mills, Dale, & Jenkins, 1996; Noonan & McCormick, 1993). Therefore, most communication assessment and teaching should be taken out of highly structured and isolated settings and moved to more natural communication environments where a child actually uses communication (Camarata, 1996; McWilliam, 2000; Notari-Syverson & Losardo, 1996; Warren & Kaiser, 1986). In the classroom, children have many opportunities to interact with their teachers and peers, as do children at home with their families. Thus, all early intervention professionals need to be familiar with communication development and assessment because they will be responsible for facilitating communication skills in children, helping caregivers recognize and use appropriate techniques, and knowing when to make referrals to and seek assistance from a speech-language pathologist.

DIMENSIONS OF COMMUNICATION ASSESSMENT

Definitions of Communication, Language, and Speech

Communication is a social act, the primary function of which is interaction with another living being. It is an active process with a sender who encodes or formulates a message and a receiver who decodes or comprehends the message. Communication can also occur, however, without the intent or the knowledge of the sender (e.g., a sender who inadvertently frowns may communicate displeasure). Communication can occur between and among many species (e.g., dogs, bees, humans); however, for it to be considered language, a mutually understood symbol system is necessary. Thus, language is a code of symbols and rules for combining those symbols. For example, English and Japanese are both languages with their own symbol and rule systems.

Communication and language also require a means for expression. Speech, the production of vocal sound patterns, is the most common means of human communication, although many other types exist, including gestures (e.g., pointing), facial expression (e.g., smiling), vocalizations (e.g., "baba"), nonspeech sounds (e.g., laughter, motorboat sound made with mouth), writing (e.g., "Dear Matthew"), signing (e.g., American Sign Language), and singing (e.g., "Rock-a-bye baby").

Components of Language

When acquiring any language, children must learn rules about its sounds, grammar, meanings, and uses. These rules are reflected in four components of language: phonology, syntax, semantics, and pragmatics. Phonology and syntax relate to the form of language, semantics to the meaning of language, and pragmatics to the use of language. *Phonology* refers to the rules for the formation of speech sounds, or phonemes, and how phonemes are joined together into words. Phonological rules govern what sounds can appear in various positions within a word (e.g., in English, *ft* can occur in the medial and final positions of words, but never in the initial position) and also in what sequences they can occur (e.g., *sl* is a permissible sequence, but *sd* is not). *Syntax* is the rule system for combining words into phrases and sentences. These rules specify parts of speech (e.g., noun, adjective, verb), word order, and sentence constituents (e.g., noun phrase, verb phrase). Someone who knows the syntax of a language can generate any number of sentences and identify those that are grammatically incorrect (e.g., The boy ball the threw). *Semantics* refers to the rules for meanings of words and their joint relationship to one another. A particular word has many characteristics that establish its meaning, and a child's task is to learn which factors are critical in acquiring the use of a word. Some words (e.g., *glasses*) take on very different meanings depending on the context in which they are uttered (eyeglasses, drinking glasses). Further, just as the words in the utterance "Johnny jumps" can be described as a noun and a verb in a syntactic approach, they can also be described as agent (Johnny) and action (jumps) in a semantic approach. See Table 12.1 for a list of common semantic relations.

Pragmatics refers to the rules that govern the use of language in social contexts and for the purpose of communication. Two different levels of pragmatics are commonly assessed: intentions and discourse. Communicative intentions are the reasons that someone talks (e.g., to request an object, to protest something, or to share information). Because intentions are expressed through a variety of means (e.g., vocal, gestural, verbal), even children who are not yet using words may be intentionally communicating. For example, when a child points to a truck on the floor, he could either be requesting the truck or commenting about it. When a child shakes her head and screams as a peer takes away a toy, she is clearly using the intention of protesting. Children who have not yet learned to indicate their needs in a consistent and "readable" manner are said to be at a "preintentional" stage. Once a child can communicate one intention consistently through any means available, he or she is said to be at an intentional stage. A second area of pragmatics is discourse, specifically, how to participate in interaction by taking turns. A conversation or interaction between two or more individuals is made up of turns, with each person taking the floor to communicate. To eventually become an effective conversationalist, a child must first learn how and when to begin, maintain, and end an interaction. The length of the turn, how to take a turn, when it is acceptable to take a turn, and when it is not acceptable for turn-taking are all examples of the rules for conversation (Keenan & Schieffelin, 1976).

Development of Communication and Language

The following sections briefly describe the development of the four language components. The area of pragmatics receives the most detail, because many have argued that it has the greatest implications for young children (Miller, 1981; McLean & Snyder-McLean, 1978).

Pragmatics Although infants do not typically produce meaningful words until the end of their

TABLE 12.1
Semantic Relations Expressed in Prelinguistic, One-Word, and Multiword Utterances

General Relationship	Function/Meaning	Child Behavior		
		Prelinguistic	One-Word	Multiword
Agent	The individual performing the action	Throws ball to teacher and smiles proudly	Throws ball and says "Me"	"Me throw."
Action	Requests action	Holds hands up to be picked up	"Up," to indicate "pick me up"	"Up Mommy."
Object	Comments on the object of action	Points to ball being pushed	"Ball," as ball is pushed	"Ball go."
Recurrence	Requests/comments on repetition of activity/object	Drinks milk and holds up empty bottle	"More," to indicate "more milk"	"Me more milk."
Disappearance	Comments on nonexistence/ disappearance of object or person	Points to missing wheel on car	"Wheel," while pointing to car	"No wheel."
Cessation	Comments on cessation of activity	Points to top that stopped spinning	"Stop," to indicate top is no longer spinning	"Top stop."
Rejection	Protests/comments on undesired action or something forbidden	Turns head away from food	"No," in response to peas	"No peas."
Location	Comments on spatial location	Holds truck and points to box	"Box," while pointing to toy box	"Put box."
Possession	Comments on possession of object	Reaches for own shoes among others' shoes and points	"Mine," while getting own shoes	"My shoes."
Agent action*	Comments on agent and action			"Boy hit."
Action object*	Comments on action and object			"Kick ball."
Agent action object*	Comments on agent, action, and object			"Mommy throw ball."
Action object location*	Comments on agent, action, and location			"Put ball chair."

*These are more commonly used examples of relational combinations; many possibilities exist.

349

first year, they become actively involved in interactions with people in their environment early in life. During the first few months, caregivers respond to infants' unintentional signals (e.g., eye gaze, facial expressions) as if they were purposeful. For example, infant crying or repetitive sucking appear to be reflexive reactions rather than intentional communication, but caregivers typically interpret these behaviors as purposeful expressions of hunger or of a desire to be picked up. As noted by Goldberg (1977), readability, or the ability of caregivers to recognize and respond to the infant's behaviors, is an important factor in the infant's ability to learn the effects these behaviors can have on others. These early nonverbal exchanges between child and caregiver form the basis for later conversational turn-taking (Bruner, 1978). From 3 to 8 months, there are dramatic increases in the child's interactions with caregivers, clarity of signals, and ability to participate in turn-taking sequences.

Between 8 and 12 months, children's gestures and sound vocalizations (e.g., extending arms to be picked up, saying "ah" while pointing to a desired object) begin to be used consistently and others begin to understand what the infant is intentionally communicating. Thus, the infant's communicative attempts begin to serve particular communicative functions. Wetherby and Prizant (1993), based on Bruner's (1981) work, describe three types of functions children use by the end of their first year: (a) behavior regulation serves to regulate the behavior of another individual to do something (e.g., child requests a ball on a shelf) or to stop doing something (e.g., while eating, the child pushes away offered food); (b) social interaction attracts and maintains attention to the child so an individual will look at or notice the child (e.g., waving bye-bye as father leaves); and (c) joint attention attracts and maintains attention of an individual to an object or event (e.g., the child points to a picture in a book). See Chapman (1981) and Roth and Spekman (1984) for a review of other taxonomies of communicative intentions.

Because it may be difficult at times to determine whether a young child is intentionally communicating, Wetherby and Prizant (1989) suggest using the following criteria: Does the child (a) alternate eye gaze between the listener and the goal; (b) persist in signaling or change the signal until a goal is accomplished; (c) use a conventional (e.g., waving bye) or ritualized (e.g., "woof" for dog) form of signal; (d) pause for a response from a listener; (e) terminate a signal and/or display satisfaction when a goal is met; and/or (f) display dissatisfaction when a goal is not met? Examples of communicative intentions expressed at the prelinguistic stage appear in Table 12.2.

At approximately 12 to 15 months, children begin to use words (e.g., *up, mama*) and word approximations (e.g., "ba" for *ball*) to indicate the same intentions expressed in the prelinguistic stage. Thus, when a child wants a cookie, in addition to (or instead of) putting the adult's hand on the jar to get it open, the child says "open" or "oh." The infant's signals are now easier to interpret, and if a signal is not understood, the infant can repeat and vary the communication.

At about 18 months, children begin to combine words and to indicate their communicative intentions with word combinations. Children also learn to use words to express intentions in relation to preceding utterances in conversation. As shown in Table 12.2, these discourse functions include requesting information (e.g., "What's that?"), answering (e.g., child says "juice" in response to "What do you want?"), and acknowledging (e.g., child says "okay" to a request to sit down). Although the ability to maintain a conversation is not typically established until the third year of life, children now show increasing ability to maintain a topic for a greater number of turns. Bloom, Rocissano, and Hood (1976) found that at 21 months, children maintained the topic approximately 50% of the time.

The 3- to 4-year-old shows increasing sophistication in discourse skills. Children can at this point maintain the topic of a conversation 75% of the time (Bloom et al., 1976) and can provide new

TABLE 12.2
Communicative Intentions Expressed in Prelinguistic, One-Word, and Multiword Utterances

Intention	Definition	Prelinguistic	One-Word	Multiword
Attention seeking	Solicits attention to self or aspects of the environment; has no other intent	Child tugs on her mother's skirt.	"Mommy," as she tugs on skirt	"You know what?"
Request object	Demands desired tangible object; includes requesting consumable and nonconsumable objects	Child points to a dog he wants.	"Dog"	"Give me dog."
Request action	Commands another to carry out an action; includes requesting assistance and other actions involving another person or between and an object	Child puts adult's hand on lid of jar while looking at the adult.	"Open," while giving jar to adult	"Mama, open bottle."
Request information	Finds out something about an object or event; includes *wh-* questions and other utterances having the intonation contour of an interrogative	Child points to animal and says "da?" with rising intonation.	"Shoe?" as he points to shoe box	"Where shoe?"
Protest	Commands another to cease an undesired action; includes resisting another's action and rejection of object that is offered	Child pushes the adult's hand away when an undesired food item is offered.	"No," in response to undesired food	"No peas, Mama."
Comment on object	Directs another's attention to an object; includes pointing, showing, describing, informing, and interactive labeling	Child holds up toy car toward the adult and says "da" while looking at the adult.	Child points to the car in his hand and says "Car"	"My car."
Comment on action	Calls listener's attention to the movement of some object or action of others or self	Child laughs and points at wind-up toy bear as it falls off table.	"Down," as wind-up toy falls	"Bear fall down."

Continued

TABLE 12.2
Continued

Intention	Definition	Prelinguistic	One-Word	Multiword
Greeting	Communicates salutation and offers conversational rituals "hi," "bye," "please," and "thank you"	Child waves as mother leaves.	"Bye"	"Bye, mom."
Answering	Responds to request for information	Child points to nose when asked "Where's your nose?"	Child says "nose"	"Here my nose."
Acknowledgement of other's speech	Acts or utterances used to indicate that the other's utterance was received, not in response to a question; includes repetition of an utterance	Child produces jabbering sounds after adult says name of favorite song.	Child says "Barney"	"Barney song."
Other	Teases, warns, alarms, exclaims, or conveys humor	Child says "ah" as she takes a turn in a tickle routine.	Child teases and says "no" as she sticks her tummy out to be tickled	"No tickle me" to invite tickling

Source: Adapted from "The Communication Intention Inventory: A System for Coding Children's Early Intentional Communication," by T. Coggins and R. Carpenter, 1981, *Applied Psycholinguistics, 2;* "A Pragmatic Description of Early Language Development," by J. Dore, 1974, *Journal of Psycholinguistic Research, 4;* and "Assessing the Pragmatic Abilities of Children: Part I, Organizational Framework and Assessment Parameters," by F. Roth & N. Spekman, 1984, *Journal of Speech and Hearing Disorders, 49.*

information on the topic. Their language use shifts from a focus on things in their environment to events and people more distant in time. They use language to report on present and past events, describe imaginative situations, identify their own and others' feelings, plan events, and anticipate what will happen in the future. They can also recognize and respond appropriately to a listener's request for clarification in conversations. Thus the 4-year-old has some awareness of the linguistic and cognitive abilities of the listener and can modify speech and language accordingly. The child can now tell jokes, tease, and provide warnings, and show increasing ability to use language for abstract purposes not tied to the present context. Five-year-olds continue to advance in their story-retelling skills, their use of elaborated play themes and "scripts" for what to say during play scenarios, and in their knowledge of their listener's needs in conversation.

Phonology During the first few months of life children coo and gurgle and produce some single syllables such as "na" and "ya." They use mostly vowels in their early sound making and later begin to add consonants to their inventory. Infants typically begin to babble, using consonant-vowel combinations such as "mama" or "baba" at around 6 to 8 months and produce different vocalizations that include both nonspeech (e.g., squeals) and speech sounds. Somewhere between 9 and 15 months, they begin to use wordlike sounds consistently (e.g., "ba" to indicate a desired object or "da" for *dog*). As children begin to use words, speech sounds generally develop in a predictable sequence at certain ages. For example, most children by 3 years of age produce many sounds, although the "r," "l," and "th" sounds are often not produced correctly until at least 4 years. By age 4, children can produce most sounds accurately, although continued refinements of words with multisyllables take place over the next few years. As children acquire adult speech, they often fail to produce sounds or sound sequences in accordance with the adult form. For example, a child may

consistently say "wabbit" for *rabbit* or "pusketti" for *spaghetti*. These errors have been described as resulting from phonological processes, which are patterns of simplifications that children use when learning words. For example, omitting the final "g" in "*dog*" and the "s" in "*house*" are instances of the phonological process of deletion of final consonants. Bernthal and Bankson (1998) provide further descriptions of sound development and phonological processes.

Syntax The rules of syntax are acquired gradually as children learn to put words together. One-word utterances are typically produced by 12 to 15 months, two-word utterances by 18 months, and three-word utterances by about 2 years. The 2- to 2 1/2-year-old may produce many two- and three-word utterances, but is also still producing one-word utterances and may occasionally use a five-word utterance. At this point, the child begins to use different types of sentences such as questions, negatives, and imperatives. At first, early forms are not grammatically correct. For example, negatives are formed by using *no* or *not* in utterances such as "No go eat" or "He not big." Early yes-no questions are signaled by a rising intonation (e.g., "Mommy going?" for "Is mommy going?"); *wh-* questions lack a copula or auxiliary verb (e.g., "Where my hat?" for "Where is my hat?"). At about age 3, children begin to learn complex sentence structures so that clauses can be joined and embedded in one another. Now sentences may sound like "Mommy says that baby's crying" and "Why you not like chocolate on it?" By the time children are 5, basic and complex syntactic structures are established, yet the refinement of complex sentence usage continues into the elementary school years.

A good estimate of young children's syntactic complexity is mean length of utterance (MLU) in words. MLU is computed by dividing the number of words in a sample of the child's language by the number of utterances in the sample (150 words/50 utterances = 3.0 MLU). MLU in words is a valid index of language development when the MLU is between 1.0 and 4.5 words (Miller, 1981). As children get beyond this MLU level, the complexity of their sentence structure should also be taken into account. Miller, Freiberg, Rolland, & Reeves (1992), however, suggest that MLU continues to be a valid developmental measure into the school years. See Miller (1981) and Paul (2001) for further discussion of the development of sentence structure.

Semantics Children's early words relate to the things that are most meaningful to them, such as the names of people and objects in their environment. For example, early words such as *mommy, daddy,* and *doggie* are common. Around 18 months, children may use about 50 words although they may comprehend as many as 300. At this time, children talk about things that exist (e.g., cat), disappear (e.g., "daddy?" while looking for daddy), recur (e.g., "more juice") and are rejected ("no" in response to bedtime). Around 18 months, children are also beginning to combine words into multiword utterances that consist of combinations of semantic categories such as agent-action ("Doggie bark"), and agent-action-object ("Mommy eat cookie"). Some of the common semantic categories children use in their prelinguistic communication and their one-word and multiword utterances are summarized in Table 12.1.

After 2 years of age, word knowledge increases dramatically. For example, a child can have a production vocabulary of 500 words at 2 1/2 to 3 years and can comprehend as many as 1,000. Children now learn about complex concepts such as color, quantity, and spatial and temporal relations; they also begin to talk about causality. At around 4 years, they begin to develop metalinguistic knowledge—how to use language as a tool to focus on language form and content. This includes the ability to identify grammatical versus ungrammatical utterances, segment words into phonemes and sentences into words, and to rhyme words.

Language Comprehension

The descriptions above focus primarily on the development of *language production* in young children. It is also important to identify the child's development of *comprehension* in these early stages, from both linguistic and nonlinguistic standpoints. Based on the work of Chapman (1978) and Edmonston and Thane (1992), Paul (2001) provides an excellent overview of young children's comprehension abilities and response strategies utilized in understanding the world around them. Children between 8 and 12 months can typically understand a few single words in routine contexts through the use of nonlinguistic strategies such as looking at objects looked at by another, acting on objects that are noticed, and imitating ongoing action. Children in the 12- to 18-month period, understand single words outside of the routines, but continue to need contextual support. At this age the comprehension strategies used are typically based on some linguistic element and include attending to an object mentioned, giving evidence of notice to objects or actions, and doing what is usually done in a situation (e.g., child puts on coat when others do). Children from 18 to 24 months can understand words for absent objects and some two-word combinations. In addition to the previous strategies, those used include acting on objects as the agent (e.g., child lies down when asked to "Put the baby to sleep") and using conventional behaviors (e.g., combing hair with a brush). Children in the 2- to 4-year period, understand three-word sentences through strategies such as using probable location (e.g., child puts things where they usually go) and probable event strategies (e.g., when asked to point to "boy bites dog," child selects picture of "dog bites boy"). At this stage, children can also give information in response to a question, although not always correctly. For example, to the question "How do you eat?" a young child may respond "cereal." Question comprehension often follows the same sequence as the production of questions in that "what," "what doing," and "where" questions are understood (and spoken) before "why," "who," "when," and "how" questions (Miller, 1981). Between 3 1⁄2 and 5, children begin to use word order ("boy bites dog") as a cue to sentences heard. For a more complete description of the development of comprehension skills, see Chapman (1978); Miller and Paul (1995); and Paul (2001).

Emergent Literacy

Emergent literacy includes the behaviors, knowledge, and attitudes that occur before a child learns to read and write and the environments that affect this process (Sulzby, 1989; Teale & Sulzby, 1986; Whitehurst & Lonigan, 1998). The skills of learning to read and write develop during the early childhood years through literacy socialization activities such as reading with a family member (Schieffelin & Gilmore, 1986; Snow, Barnes, Chandler, Goodman, & Hemphill, 1991). A child's emergent literacy development is affected by many factors which can be assessed. These include the child's language skills, in particular vocabulary, concepts, and syntax, and decontextualized language (that is, language about things or events not present in the immediate context such as describing a past event). Children's knowledge of the conventions of print (such as reading from left to right and how to open a book), the form of print (including identifying the name, sound, and print symbol of each alphabet letter), and children's phonemic awareness skills (the manipulation of sounds in words or syllables, such as rhyming or identifying initial sounds of a word) can also be assessed. It is well documented that reading and writing have strong linguistic bases. Children with language delays during the preschool years often have later delays in reading and writing (Catts, Fey, Zhang, & Tomblin, 2001; Johnson, Beitchman, Young, Escobar, Atkinson, & Wilson, 1999). See Newman & Dickinson (2001) and Catts and Kamhi (1999) for information about assessing children's emergent literacy skills.

Communication-Related Domains

Hearing Due to the impact that a hearing loss can have on speech and language development, it is important that all children suspected of developmental delays have their hearing checked periodically (American Speech-Language-Hearing Association, 1997). Hearing loss may be identified when an infant is in the newborn nursery, but only if the hospital employs screening procedures for neonates, and, in some instances, only if the neonate is at risk for a hearing loss. The hearing status of neonates can be screened by measuring the auditory brain stem response (ABR) evoked by electrodes placed on the child's scalp. By 6 months, infants can be tested with visual reinforcement audiometry (VRA), which involves sounds emitted from a loudspeaker and an animated, lighted toy that is turned on when the child looks in the direction of the sound signal. Children 2 years and older can be assessed using pure tone audiometry; the child wears earphones and is taught to drop a block or perform a similar task when a sound is heard. Although the hearing of older children can be screened by a health care professional, screening of children under the age of 3 should be performed by an audiologist. For more information about hearing testing, see the American Speech-Language-Hearing Association (ASHA) Guidelines (1997), Northern and Downs (2002), and Martin and Clark (2000). Chapter 6 includes more information on hearing screening and assessment.

Otitis media with effusion, which is one of the most common illnesses of early childhood (Stool et al., 1994), is of concern for children's language development because it is often accompanied by fluid in the middle ear, which can cause a mild to moderate fluctuating hearing loss (Roberts, Wallace, & Henderson, 1997; Ruben et al., 1998; Stool et al., 1994). Children who have or are suspected of having recurrent middle ear problems should be monitored by a physician to minimize the risk of hearing loss.

Symbolic Play   Increasingly, there is evidence that language and play skills are highly correlated and that during some stages of development, they reflect common underlying cognitive processes (Bloom, 1993; Kennedy, Sheridan, Radlinski, & Beeghly, 1991; Yoder, Warren, & Hull, 1995). For example, as first words are appearing along with more consistent communicative gestures (12 to 18 months), single pretend schemes (e.g., child feeds self with spoon) are emerging during play (Kennedy et al., 1991). As children begin to use language for interactional purposes, they also develop the ability to represent objects, actions, and feelings in symbolic play, using one object to stand for or represent an absent object during dramatic or make-believe play. As children begin to combine words (18 to 24 months), they also combine single pretend schemes (e.g., child stirs in empty bowl, then feeds self with spoon). By 28 months, children are learning the rules for syntax, producing ordered play sequences, and showing an increase in productivity in language and other symbolic domains (Kennedy et al., 1991; McCune, 1995). For typically developing children (Bates, Bretherton, & Snyder, 1988) and children with developmental delays (Kennedy et al., 1991; Thal, Tobias, & Morrison, 1991), higher levels of comprehension have been associated with higher levels of play maturity and gestural production. In addition, combinatorial play (e.g., stacking rings or cups) and symbolic play have been shown to predict language skills in both typically developing children (Bloom, 1993) and those with developmental disabilities (Mundy, Sigman, & Kasari, 1990; Thal et al., 1991). Westby (1988) has described seven stages of symbolic play that correspond to stages in children's language development. See Chapter 14 for a description of the assessment of play skills.

Social, Motor, and Cognitive Skills   When planning assessment and intervention for infants and young children, the interventionist should consider the mutual influences of social, motor, and cognitive development on the child's efforts to communicate and learn language. The infant's interactions with people and objects in the environment set the stage for the development of many nonverbal behaviors considered to be the antecedents of "language" (McCathren, Yoder, & Warren, 1999; Mundy, Kasari, Sigman, & Ruskin, 1995). Eye gaze, gestures, and joint attention are important components of social and communicative development in the first 2 years of life. Further, the ability to follow the gaze and point of others, the rate of early social interaction, and the use of joint attention in the second year of life are all predictive of later language development (Mundy et al., 1990, 1995). Indeed, these early prelinguistic behaviors have been shown to discriminate between children with and without developmental disabilities (Baranek, 1999; Mundy et al., 1990; Osterling & Dawson, 1994; Sigman & Kasari, 1995).

The development of communicative competence in the infant depends on the caregiver's social responsiveness, which in turn is influenced by the child's behaviors (Dunst, Lowe, & Bartholomew, 1990; Yoder & Munson, 1995). As suggested by Siegel-Causey, Ernst, and Guess (1987), contingency relationships between infants with special needs and their caregivers may be compromised by (a) the infant's medical involvement, which decreases the opportunity for social interaction; (b) parental attitudes and feelings that limit the parents' provision of associated events; (c) the limited response repertoire of the infant, which makes both social and object co-occurrences less likely; (d) the limited ability of some children to detect and remember co-occurrences; and (e) the complex interactions of the infant and the environment, which may reduce the frequency of social co-occurrences. Thus, infants with special needs may have difficulty integrating the social, cognitive, and motor components necessary to gain communicative competence. For more information on the development of social skills and their effect on development, see Chapter 13, Dunst et al. (1990), Prizant and Meyer (1993), and Wetherby and Prizant (1992).

Impairments in motor skills further compromise integration of cognitive, social, and communicative skills. In children with multiple special needs, it is difficult to differentiate the influence of the motor impairment from other factors (Nelson, 1998). For children with motor impairments, it is important to consider the effect of the motor impairment on both the conceptual development underlying their language and their speech production abilities. For more information on the effects of motor difficulties on communication, see the augmentative and alternative communication section in this chapter, Chapter 11 of this text, Beukelman and Mirenda (1998), and Glennen and DeCoste (1997).

A recent trend in assessment is to incorporate nonstandard measures of nonverbal cognitive skills such as those described by Piaget, as well as the scores of nonverbal (performance) mental ages on standardized intelligence tests (see Chapter 10). This practice typically allows for comparison between verbal and nonverbal skills and between cognitive and other developing skill areas. Although there is disagreement as to the exact relationship between language and cognitive development, the correlation between measures of cognition and language takes on particular importance when assessing children whose development is delayed (Paul, 2001). Although Paul does not recommend the use of mental age criteria for determining eligibility for speech-language services, she does suggest that contrasting a child's mental age and language age can be helpful, particularly in planning intervention. Indeed, Paul suggests that intralinguistic profiling (e.g., comparing the child's production, comprehension, phonology, syntax, pragmatic skills) may help identify target intervention goals and mental age may help set expectations for behaviors. For practical guides to cognitive development and assessment within the framework of an overall communication assessment, see Cole and Fey (1996) and Paul (2001); for general cognitive assessment, see Chapter 10.

PROCEDURAL CONSIDERATIONS IN ASSESSING COMMUNICATION SKILLS

During the past several years, assessment of infants and preschoolers with special needs has undergone substantial changes in the ways information is gathered and shared by family members and professionals. Several characteristics of assessing communication skills in young children reflect these trends, such as the current emphasis on ecological validity of assessment tools and practices, the ongoing nature of assessment, the increased emphasis on active participation of family members and other caregivers, and the collaborative nature of the assessment and intervention planning process. In addition, changes in assessment practices in the area of communication reflect the broadening view of what constitutes communication in young children. Moreover, the terms *evaluation* and *assessment* have come to have differing definitions according to IDEA legislation. Evaluation activities, which are defined as the procedures to determine a child's initial and continuing eligibility, include determining the child's status in each developmental area (McLean & McCormick, 1993). Assessment is defined as the ongoing procedures used to identify a child's strengths and needs; the family's resources, priorities, and concerns; and the intervention services necessary to the child and the family. In this chapter, the term *assessment* is defined broadly to include *all* types of activities used to gather information about the child and the family, whereas *evaluation* is used only to indicate the process of determining eligibility. The following sections first highlight concerns related to traditional approaches to assessment followed by a discussion of more recent trends in assessment practices.

Concerns Related to Traditional Assessment Approaches

Traditionally, the assessment of communication skills in young children included the primary use of standardized instruments with some observational information gathered. Coggins (1998) suggests that standardized measures can be useful when establishing eligibility, in comparing children with a normative group, and for providing a general index of change over time. Standardized measures, however, were not generally designed to provide information for intervention planning (Bricker, 1993). Indeed, these measures were developed to provide information under a "standard" set of conditions; therefore, an examination of a child's skills in contexts that represent his or her daily interactions is not fostered. Regarding communication assessment, standardized testing typically does not describe how the child actually communicates (verbally or nonverbally) in natural environments, nor are there any standardized tests available for examining all aspects of language. As suggested by Chapman (1992), qualitatively accurate assessment should try to capture everyday communication in all the diverse ways it occurs.

An additional area of concern with traditional assessment measures is their poor predictive validity (Coggins, 1998; McCathren, Warren, & Yoder, 1996; Neisworth & Bagnato, 1992), especially for infants and young children with delays and disabilities. Moreover, few standardized measures have included children with disabilities in the norming population (Fuchs, Fuchs, Benowitz, & Barringer, 1987; Neisworth & Bagnato, 1992); thus, the question of whether they are appropriate for *assessing* children with disabilities has not been adequately addressed.

A further problem arises for children with communication difficulties. As indicated by the work of Fuchs, Fuchs, Power, and Dailey (1985), although preschool children without disabilities performed equally well with familiar and unfamiliar examiners, children with communication difficulties performed more poorly with unfamiliar examiners. Moreover, for children with communication difficulties, professionals need to consider the child's level of comfort with the examiner and the assessment context, the response type expected from the child (pointing, answering), and the type of stimulus materials (pictures, objects) used for the assessment activities. Children, unlike most adults, may not be willing or capable of talking freely to an unfamiliar adult, and helping them feel comfortable in a new and possibly challenging setting is not always easy. Figure 12.1 provides a list of suggestions for engaging children in interaction. Some children may be more comfortable communicating nonverbally, although they are capable of speaking. In this case, the administration of nonverbal tasks first in the assessment process may be useful. Children's responses also may vary according to the type of stimuli used. For young children, objects may be more interesting and may elicit better responses than pictures. For all assessments, the type of stimuli used, the nature of the accompanying instructions, and the mode of communication should be noted in the protocol and report.

The final issue of concern with most traditional communication assessment measures is their limited profiling of the child's strengths and needs across and within domains related to communication (Wetherby & Prizant, 1992; Paul, 2001). Where once syntax and semantics were the primary areas of assessment, additional areas such as social-affect, communicative intent, gestures, play skills, turn-taking, eye contact, number and types of initiations, and level of overall communication skills have become increasingly important. As indicated by Wetherby and Prizant (1992) and McCathren et al. (1996), most of the traditional instruments used to assess the communication skills of newborns to 3-year-olds fail to provide a profile of the child's strengths and needs across these critical areas.

Sociocultural Awareness

In contrast to traditional assessment tools and approaches which take more of a "one size fits all" stance, there is increasing recognition that professionals should be sensitive to the social, cultural, linguistic, and ethnic characteristics of the children and families they serve. Increasingly, professionals are interacting with families of diverse backgrounds

1. Choose developmentally appropriate toys and materials. Use play and motor development scales to help in the selection.

2. Limit your own talking, especially questions. Pause often to encourage the child to initiate communication and take a turn.

3. Watch for and encourage any means of communication demonstrated by the child (e.g., eye gaze, point, reach, word approximation).

4. Parallel play with the child, mimicking his/her actions. Play animatedly with object or toy and occasionally comment on an object or action.

5. Place a few items within eye gaze but out of reach, as well as partially hide a few objects. If necessary, point to or comment on objects to encourage a comment or request by the child.

6. Let child choose objects and/or activities, particularly in the beginning (and throughout the interaction if possible). Be prepared to watch and interact/ comment when the child shows interest.

7. Include parent or another child to help "break the ice." Stay in the background and slowly get into the interaction.

8. Begin interaction with activities that require little or no talking and gradually move to more vocal or verbal tasks.

9. Be genuine in your questions and stay away from asking what is obvious to both you and the child.

10. Follow the child's lead in the interaction by maintaining the child's focus on particular objects or topics.

11. Show warmth and positive regard for the child and value his/her comments.

FIGURE 12.1

Guidelines for interactions with children

that often differ from their own. One of the challenges in considering a child's communication skills is the need to understand the effects of culture on communication. Sociocultural background influences many aspects of communication, including when and how a child interacts with adults or strangers, the dialect used, and the ways the child views the communication process. For example, Cheng (1987) noted that for children from Asian-American families, communication is to be carried out with the fewest words possible and nonverbal cues are critical to the accuracy of the message. A child's background also influences the types of materials and toys available and thus can influence early cognitive and literacy experiences.

For children with special needs who are non-English speaking or who have limited English proficiency, it is critical to determine whether communication difficulties occur in the primary language and specifically whether the child's own communicative behaviors differ substantially from the norms and expectations of the child's own language community (Battle, 2002; Gutierrez-Clellen, 1996; Nelson, 1998). In addition, there are many dialects in use in the United States (e.g., African-American Vernacular English, Hispanic English), and each represents a rule-based variant of Standard American English (SAE). Clearly, the results of tests based on standard English would provide an invalid picture of the communication skills of children who are used to speaking and hearing a dialect (Nelson, 1998).

In spite of the mandate that test materials and procedures be nondiscriminatory, few standardized communication assessment instruments are available that are dialectally or culturally sensitive (Battle, 2002; Craig & Washington, 2002). Some tests have alternative scoring protocols for syntax and phonology (for examples, see Table 12.3). Yet, test results must be interpreted carefully, because children may not have the same perspective or familiarity with taking tests. In contrast to standardized language tests, the language sampling methods described later in this chapter may be a good alternative. Whether using a standardized language test or language sampling methods, it is important to be familiar with the dialect and cultural expectations and behaviors of the child's community and family in order to determine if a child is having communication difficulties. Although it is possible to consult reference texts (e.g., Owens, 2001) to determine if a feature (e.g., omission of plural *s*) is characteristic of the child's community, the specific rules may not represent all individuals in the community or region. Determining the family's perspective of the child's communication skills is also essential if the child has language that is different from his or her own language community. Immersing oneself in the child's culture by observing other members of the cultural group, asking adults who use (or are familiar with) the dialect, using ethnographic observation, showing sensitivity to the family's style of communication, and using toys and other materials that are familiar and culturally appropriate should help to provide a nonbiased assessment (Nelson, 1998; Paul, 2001). In addition, Westby (1990) provides guidelines for using ethnographic interviewing to gather information from families about their concerns and priorities. For more information about culturally appropriate assessment, see Chapter 4 of this text, Battle (2002), Gutierrez-Clellen (1996), Paul (2001), and Craig and Washington (2002).

Family Priorities

As suggested in Chapters 3 and 8, it is critical that assessment activities be based on what the family wants and needs and would find useful. In this sense, the contexts of the family's concerns become the contexts for assessment. There are many reasons families want their child assessed; for example, some families may want to know why their child's communication skills are not developing typically and/or what they can do to help the child achieve. Others may want to know whether their child's language is delayed relative to other children. And still others may recognize their child's difficulties and simply want help in determining which preschool program is best for their child. Professionals perform assessments for varied reasons; for example, to meet the family's goals, ensure a child's eligibility, document progress in therapy, or seek information to facilitate intervention planning. Although some professionals may be constrained by meeting certain eligibility requirements (e.g., use of two standardized tests), careful selection and use of a variety of assessment measures and techniques can provide some flexibility.

Active Participation of Caregivers

A recent trend in assessment practices is the move toward greater reliance on and participation of caregivers (Crais & Belardi, 1999; Crais & Wilson, 1996; Mahoney & Filer, 1996; Roberts, Akers, & Behl, 1996). Within the area of communication skills, caregivers and others familiar with the child often have unique insights into the ways and reasons the child communicates and the best strategies to engage the child in interaction. In contrast, professionals are at a disadvantage in the assessment process because they typically have limited opportunities to see the child, may be strangers to the child, and may be unfamiliar with his or her behaviors. Increasingly, professionals across many disciplines are relying on caregivers to provide information that may not be easily observed or obtained in a brief assessment session. In addition, research has indicated that parents can be reliable when asked to indicate whether their child currently performs specific behaviors, for example, using forefinger and thumb to pick up food, or using particular words (Bricker & Squires, 1989;

TABLE 12.3
Summary of Speech and Language Instruments

A. Standardized Language Diagnostic Instruments

Test Name	Areas Assessed	Age Range	Format	Scores Obtained	Unique Aspects
Battelle Developmental Inventory (BDI) (Newborg, Stock, Wnek, Guidubaldi, & Svinicki, 1984)	personal-social, adaptive, motor, communication and cognitive	0–8:0	observation, structured interaction, and caregiver/ teacher interview	percentile, standard score, age equivalent	includes screening test
Carrow Elicited Language Inventory (Carrow, 1974)	grammatical form and structure	3:0–7:11	elicited imitation	percentile, stanine, age equivalent	
Clinical Evaluation of Language Fundamentals– Preschool (Wiig, Secord, & Semel, 1992)	expressive and receptive language skills	3:0–6:0	picture identification, sentence comprehension, grammatical completion, question answering, recalling sentences in context, comprehension of linguistic concepts	standard score, percentile, age equivalent, receptive, expressive, and total score	
Communication and Symbolic Behavior Scales (CSBS) (Wetherby & Prizant, 1993)	communication functions and means, comprehension, symbolic and constructive play, social-affective signaling, reciprocity	8–2:0	observation and elicited interaction	standard score, percentile, age equivalent	caregiver perception rating scale
CSBS–Developmental Profile (Wetherby & Prizant, 2001)	same areas as original (fewer items than original)	8–2:0	observation and elicited interaction	standard score, percentile, age equivalent	caregiver perception rating scale
Detroit Tests of Learning Aptitude–	cognitive, attention linguistic, and motor	3:0–9:0	picture identification, object identification,	percentile and standard score	

Continued

361

TABLE 12.3
Continued

Test Name	Areas Assessed	Age Range	Format	Scores Obtained	Unique Aspects
Primary: 2 (Hammill & Bryant, 1991)			object manipulation, observation, drawing	for general intelligence and specific skills, age equivalent	
Developmental Observation Checklist System (Hresko, Miguel, Sharbenou, & Burton, 1994)	motor, social, language, and cognition	0–6:11	parent/caregiver completed checklist	standard score, percentile rank	computer scoring available (IBM, Macintosh), linked with adjustment behavior checklist, and parental stress and support checklist Spanish version
Expressive One-Word Picture Vocabulary Test–2000 Edition (Brownell, 2000)	expressive vocabulary	2:0–11:11	picture naming	mental age, percentile, stanine, IQ, age equivalent, standard score, scaled score	
Mullen Scales of Early Learning (Mullen, 1997)	fine and gross motor; receptive and expressive language; visual-reception	0–3:0	picture identification, observation, labeling pictures, following directions, manipulation of objects, responses to questions	standard score, age score, T-score, percentile	
Kaufman Survey of Early Academic and Language Skills (Kaufman & Kaufman, 1993)	receptive and expressive vocabulary, some concepts (numbers, letters, words, counting), articulation survey	3:0–6:0	picture identification, labeling, pictures	standard score, percentile	

Test Name	Areas Assessed	Age Range	Format	Scores Obtained	Unique Aspects
MacArthur Communicative Development Inventories, Words & Gestures, Words and Sentences Versions (Fenson, Dale, Reznick, Bates, Thal, Hartung, & Reilly, 1992)	vocabulary comprehension and production, word endings and forms, syntactic development	8–3:0	parent-completed checklist	percentile, mean	evaluation by parent
Peabody Picture Vocabulary Test–Third Edition (Dunn & Dunn, 1997)	receptive vocabulary	2:5–adult	picture identification	receptive vocabulary age, standard score, percentile, stanine	adaptable for children with motor impairment, Spanish edition
Preschool Language Scale–4 (Zimmerman, Steiner & Pond, 1997)	developmental aspects of auditory comprehension, articulation, grammatical form and structure, basic concepts	0:1–6:0	responses to pictures, object manipulation, picture identification, following directions	total language, auditory comprehension expression scores, standard score, percentile, rank by age, language age equivalent	Spanish translation
Receptive One-Word Picture Vocabulary Test–2000 Edition (Brownell, 2000)	receptive vocabulary	2–11:11	picture identification	standard score, percentile, stanine, scaled score	Spanish version
Reynell Developmental Language Scales (Reynell & Gruber, 1990)	general expressive and receptive language skills	1:0–6:0	observation, picture identification, object identification, object manipulation	communication age equivalent, standard score, percentile, developmental age score	normed verbal comprehension version for children responding only by pointing

Continued

TABLE 12.3
Continued

Test Name	Areas Assessed	Age Range	Format	Scores Obtained	Unique Aspects
Sequenced Inventory of Communicative Development–Revised (Hedrick, Prather, & Tobin, 1984)	sound awareness and discrimination, comprehension of vocal, and verbal expressions	0:4–4:0	parent report, object manipulation, picture identification, following directions	receptive communication age, expressive communication age	assesses some prelinguistic skills, uses elicited and parent report information
Test for Auditory Comprehension of Language–3 (Carrow-Woolfolk, 1997)	comprehension of grammatical form and structure, content, and vocabulary	3:0–adult	picture identification, object manipulation, best choice	percentile rank, comprehension age equivalent, percentile ranks for grade equivalents	computer scoring available (Apple and IBM)
Test of Early Language Development–3 (Hresko, Reid, & Hammill, 1999)	receptive and expressive grammatical forms, content of language, and word knowledge	2:0–7:11	picture identification, answering questions, object manipulation, imitation, picture description, sentence completion, synonyms, sentence formulation, defining words	percentile, language age, language quotient, standard score, age equivalent	
Test of Language Development–Primary–3 (Newcomer & Hammill, 1997)	grammatical understanding, receptive and expressive vocabulary, expressive grammatical structure	3:0–8:11	picture identification, imitation, grammatical completion, defining words, word discrimination, word articulation	language ages for each subtest, standardized global index of language ability	computer scoring available (Apple and IBM)
Test of Pragmatic Skills–Revised (Shulman, 1986)	how children verbally adapt to various communicative contexts	3:0–8:11	four guided play interactions	means, percentile	computer scoring available (Apple)

Test Name	Areas Assessed	Age Range	Format	Scores Obtained	Unique Aspects
B. Standardized Language Screening Instruments					
Ages and Stages Questionnaires (ASQ): A Parent-Completed Child-Monitoring System (Bricker & Squires, 1999)	fine and gross motor, communication, problem solving, personal-social and overall	4–4:0	parent-completed checklist	pass/fail	evaluation by parent Spanish version
Bankson Language Screening Test–2 (Bankson, 1990)	vocabulary, grammatical form, content, visual and auditory perception, semantic knowledge, morphological and syntactic rules, pragmatic knowledge	3:0–8:0	picture identification, object identification, best choice, imitation, sequencing, matching	standard deviation scores, percentiles	
Birth to Three Assessment & Intervention System–2 (Ammer & Bangs, 2000)	problem solving, personal-social skills, motor skills, general receptive and expressive language	0–3:0	observation, following directions, motor and verbal imitation, picture identification, naming body parts, object identification, parental report	standard score, percentile rank, stanine	norm-referenced screening test, criterion-referenced checklist
Compton Speech and Language Evaluation (Compton, 1978)	articulation, vocabulary, colors, shapes, fluency, voice, oral mechanism, auditory-visual memory, expressive grammatical structure, and grammatical understanding	3:0–6:0	object identification, object labeling, oral mechanism exam	pass/fail	Spanish version

Continued

TABLE 12.3
Continued

Test Name	Areas Assessed	Age Range	Format	Scores Obtained	Unique Aspects
Fluharty Preschool Speech and Language Screening Test–Second Edition (Fluharty, 1999)	articulation, vocabulary, receptive and expressive language ability	2:0–6:0		object identification, picture identification, sentence repetition	cut-off scores for each age group
Northwestern Syntax Screening Test (Lee, 1971)	receptive and expressive grammatical form and structure	3:0–7:11	elicited productions	age equivalent	
Pragmatics Screening Test (Prinz & Weiner, 1987)	maintaining topic, formulating speech acts, politeness, establishing a referent for listener, narration, revising a directive when listener does not understand	3:5–8:5	gamelike tasks (ghost trick, absurd requests, referential communication)		
Receptive-Expressive Emergent Language Test (Bzoch & League, 2003)	prelinguistic skills	1–3:0	parent report interview	receptive and expressive communication age, quotients, combined language age	
C. Criterion Referenced Instruments					
Assessment, Evaluation, and Programming System for Infants and Children, 2nd ed. (Bricker, 2002)	fine and gross motor, adaptive, cognitive, social-communication, and social	0–6:0	observation and elicited interaction, parent evaluation	criterion-referenced age equivalents	parent and professional evaluation

Test Name	Areas Assessed	Age Range	Format	Scores Obtained	Unique Aspects
Carolina Curriculum for Infants and Toddlers with Special Needs (Johnson-Martin, Jens, Attermeier, & Hacker, 1991)	cognition, fine and gross motor, communication, social adaptation	0–2:0	observation and elicited interactions	criterion-referenced age equivalents	assessment log and curriculum guide for intervention
Carolina Curriculum for Preschoolers with Special Needs (Johnson-Martin, Attermeier, & Hacker, 1990)	cognition, communication, social adaptation, fine and gross motor	2:0–5:0	observation and elicited interactions	criterion-referenced age equivalents	assessment log and curriculum guide for intervention
Hawaii Early Learning Profile (HELP) (Furuno, O'Reilly, Inatsuka, Hosaka, Allman, & Zeisloft-Falbey, 1987)	cognition, receptive language, fine and gross motor, social, and self-help	0–3:0	checklist	criterion-referenced age equivalents	
HELP for Preschoolers Assessment & Curriculum Guide (1995)	self-help, motor, communication, social, and learning/cognitive	3.0–6.0	checklist	criterion-referenced age-equivalents	
Parent/Professional Preschool Performance Profile (Bloch, 1987)	social, motor, cognitive, self-help, language, and classroom adjustment	6 mos–6.0	parent and professional checklist	criterion-referenced age equivalents	parent and professional evaluation

Continued

TABLE 12.3
Continued

D. Nonstandardized Assessment Instruments

Test Name	Areas Assessed	Age Range	Format	Scores Obtained	Unique Aspects
Assessing Prelinguistic and Linguistic Behaviors (Olswang, Stoel-Gammon, Coggins, & Carpenter, 1987)	cognitive antecedents, play, communicative intention, language production and comprehension	0–2:0	observation, elicited interactions	criterion-referenced age equivalents	video training tapes available
Infant-Toddler Language Scale (Rossetti, 1990)	play, gesture, interaction-attachment, pragmatics, language comprehension and expression	0–3:0	observation, elicited interaction, and parent report	age equivalents	includes parent questionnaire
Preschool Language Assessment Instrument (Blank, Rose, & Berlin, 1978)	discourse, general language ability, language skills needed in teaching environment	3:0–5:11	responses to pictures, questions	profile of discourse skills, qualitative rating of language adequacy	can be used with children who have poor school performance and whose language skills are questionable (up to 10 years old), Spanish version
Pre-Speech Assessment Scale (Morris, 1982)	feeding, sucking, swallowing, biting and chewing, respiration-phonation, sound play		rating scale	levels of development	
Transdisciplinary Play-Based	cognitive, communication	6 mos–6:0	play-based arena	age equivalencies available from	includes observation of

Test Name	Areas Assessed	Age Range	Format	Scores Obtained	Unique Aspects
Assessment (Revised Edition) (Linder, 1993)	and language, sensory-motor, and social-emotional		assessment	developmental charts	peer play
E. Standardized Speech Diagnostic Instruments					
Arizona Articulation Proficiency Scale–Revised (Fudala & Reynolds, 1986)	determining misarticulations and total articulation proficiency	any age, norms for 1:5–13 years	picture identification	total score weighted for percent each error sound is used in English; intelligibility descriptions, developmental age equivalent, percentile, standard score	
Assessment of Phonological Processes–Revised (Hodson, 1986)	phonological processes	2:0–9:0	labeling objects	percentage of occurrence, phonological deviancy score, phonological process average	computer analysis available (Apple), Spanish version
Bankson-Bernthal Test of Phonology (BBTOP) (Bankson & Bernthal, 1990)	articulation and phonological processes	3:0–9:0	labeling pictures	standard scores, percentile ranks	
Compton-Hutton Phonological Assessment (Compton & Hutton, 1978)	broad patterns of articulation errors and linguistic analyses of misarticulations	any age	picture identification	summary of phonological pattern analysis, phonological rule analysis	

Continued

TABLE 12.3
Continued

Test Name	Areas Assessed	Age Range	Format	Scores Obtained	Unique Aspects
Goldman-Fristoe Test of Articulation, Second Edition (Goldman & Fristoe, 1999)	articulation errors and stimulability for correct production of error sounds	2:0–16:0+	picture identification, story retell, imitation	standard score, percent of speech in error	
Khan-Lewis Phonological Analysis, Second Edition (Khan & Lewis, 2002)	diagnosis and description of phonological processes	any age, norms for 2:0–5:11	uses stimulus material from *Goldman-Fristoe Test of Articulation,* test yields error scores, percentage ranks	developmental phonological process rating	

Dale, 1991, 1996). Caregivers are often indispensable in assessing a child's communication behaviors, which can be quite variable and/or limited in the presence of strangers.

In addition, it is helpful for the caregivers of young children to be physically present and to assist with the assessment itself. Caregivers are critical when the interventionist needs information on a child's level of mastery of communication skills as well as his or her likes, dislikes, and typical behaviors. Caregivers and others can be asked to play and interact with the child to allow the professional to view interactions with a familiar person. Parents and teachers can be asked to encourage the child's performance during a direct testing phase and to provide direct feedback on the representativeness of the child's performance. In later sections, tools and techniques that utilize parent report or evaluation of a child's behaviors (including communication skills) are highlighted (see Chapter 3 for a discussion of caregiver participation as well as Crais, 1996).

Collaborative Assessment and Intervention Planning

A further trend in assessment and intervention planning is the shift toward collaborative efforts among professionals and family members. Recent theoretical trends and legislative mandates have indicated the need for assessment and intervention planning to be a shared process that derives from the concerns and priorities of the family. In regard to communication skills, all caregivers and service providers who routinely interact with the child should be encouraged to participate in the assessment and intervention process because of the overriding importance of communication to the child's overall development. Instruments and techniques that encourage assessment and discussion by professionals *and* caregivers may enhance both the assessment and intervention planning components of the process. Although some caregivers may be quite willing to participate actively in assessment, others may be less comfortable in taking an active role. As suggested in Chapter 3,

professionals can describe various options for caregiver participation, but should always be respectful of caregivers' preferences.

Use of Augmentative and Alternative Communication (AAC)

Children with severe cognitive, neurological, structural, emotional, or sensory impairments may have difficulties using spoken and, later, written modes of communication (Consensus Statement, 1992). In assessing these children, alternate modes of communication such as gestures, signing, facial expressions, or communication systems may be necessary. The term *augmentative and alternative communication* refers to the use of any or all of these modes to supplement whatever communication skills an individual possesses (ASHA, 1991). AAC strategies have been implemented with infants as young as 4 to 6 months (Hanrahan, Ferrier, & Jolie, 1987), and for children with severe disabilities the use of an AAC system may be critical to development. An AAC system is "an integrated group of components, including the symbols, aids, strategies, and techniques used by individuals to enhance communication" (ASHA, 1991, p. 10). Typical skills and capabilities examined when considering an AAC system are cognitive and sensory functioning, fine and gross motor skills, history of natural speech use, oral and speech motor skills, language and imitation skills, therapy progress and prognosis, and caregivers' attitudes and beliefs. Because of the complex nature of the factors influencing the decision of whether and what type of system to use, an interdisciplinary team is necessary (ASHA, 1991). See Beukelman and Mirenda (1998), Consensus Statement (1992), and Glennen and DeCoste (1997) for criteria and guidelines for use of AAC.

OVERVIEW OF AREAS TO ASSESS
Preverbal Child

To gain information on a child's communication skills, the child's primary means (ways to communicate) and functions (reasons for communicating) need to be identified. Does the child primarily use nonverbal behaviors (e.g., body movements, grimaces) and vocalizations that may not be clear to caregivers what he or she is signaling? In such a case, the child may be preintentional; therefore, the assessment may focus on identifying any consistent communicative behaviors or those that could be used to develop a means of communication (Wilcox, 1992). As suggested by Wilcox, caregivers and professionals can work together to identify a single behavior to interpret as meaningful (e.g., using a particular vocalization), then systematically reinforce the behavior in a particular context (e.g., during mealtime) to help the child develop intentional behavior (e.g., requesting food). See Warren and Yoder (1998), Wilcox (1992), and Wilcox and Shannon (1998) for overviews of strategies for establishing and/or increasing productive use of intentional communication in young children with special needs.

For children in the early stages of intentionality, it is important to identify the range of communicative functions and means used. For those who are prelinguistic and using gestures and vocalizations meaningfully (e.g., pointing or vocalizing for something), expanding the child's means and functions of communication can increase overall communicative efficiency. For this to happen most effectively, however, caregivers and professionals must recognize the child's *existing* means and functions and expand them. For example, when a child vocalizes "uh" to request objects, the caregiver may model "uh" or "uhuh" when the child shakes her head to protest undesired foods or actions and may thereby prompt her to use "uh-uh" for protesting. A child who either points *or* vocalizes "da" to request an object may begin to use both *together* after caregivers model the vocalization "da" *while* pointing. In addition to functions and means, McCathren et al., (1996) also note that prelinguistically, babbling, vocabulary comprehension, and combinatorial and symbolic play skills are important predictors of later language skills. Thus getting an idea of the types of sounds

the child uses (e.g., consonants versus vowels and their combination as described in the Phonology section), the words/word combinations comprehended (as detailed in the Comprehension section), and play behaviors exhibited (as described under Symbolic Play) will provide an idea of the child's developmental level in other areas.

For children in the early intentional stage who are also using word approximations (e.g., "ba" for *ball*), the professionals and caregivers can identify the sounds, sound combinations, and word approximations attempted by the child. In recognizing that new skills are built from existing ones, professionals can help caregivers extend the child's existing repertoire by encouraging the sounds and word approximations that are already used and attempting to shape or add to them in a systematic way (e.g., "ba" for bottle becomes "baba"). For young children who do not yet use "words," it is critical to help caregivers recognize and reinforce the many ways the child already communicates (e.g., pointing, shaking his or her head, making sounds).

Verbal Child

For children in later stages of development who use primarily words and word combinations, it continues to be important to identify the *reasons* that they communicate as well as the words they use. The examiner should look for protests and requests for objects and actions in the early stages, comments and requests for social games later, and more sophisticated communicative functions such as requests for information and permission toward the end of the second year of life (Crais, Day, & Cox, in press). The child's conversational skills, such as whether they initiate conversational interactions, who they interact with, and in what contexts should be examined. The child's words can also be classified into semantic categories, such as animals, people, actions, and animal sounds to get an idea of the variety of categories used. Identifying the semantic relations expressed in a child's prelinguistic, one-word, and multiword utterances can also be beneficial (see Table 12.1). For the interventionist to be able to build from a child's existing verbal skills, it is important to recognize and make use of what the child is already producing. For example, if the child currently uses single words to express the semantic relations of agency *(baby)*, action *(eat)*, and object *(cup)*, it is natural that caregivers could model word combinations using two of these relational words together (e.g., "baby eat," "baby cup," "eat cup"). To further expand the child's use of semantic relations, possession may be introduced (e.g., "baby's cup," "mommy's cup").

As the child develops, it will be necessary to look at syntactic skills including morphological markers (e.g., *-ed*, plural *s*, *-ing*) and the complexity of sentences (e.g., simple versus complex) as well as phonological skills. At all levels, the child's comprehension abilities also need to be documented either through informal activities (e.g., "Which one is the cow?," "Show me the baby is drinking") or formal measures. In addition, skill areas related to communication, such as motor, play, social, cognitive skills, and emergent literacy should also be examined. See individual chapters in this text for extensive assessment information related to these areas.

Communication Partners

A necessary part of all assessment will include observation of children with their interactional partners in their daily environments. As suggested by McLean (1990), the nature of communication and communication development is transactional, and both partners influence the amount and type of interaction. The literature in adult/child interaction has indicated that behaviors that facilitate communication include following the child's attentional lead, providing contingent responses, providing positive models, imitating or expanding the child's actions or words, accepting the child's attempts, and arranging the environment to elicit child initiations (Dunst et al., 1990; Warren & Yoder, 1998). This is not to say, however, that there

is one best way to interact with a child or to encourage practitioners to judge caregivers by how they interact with the child. Rather, the focus in observing caregiver/child or teacher/child interactions is to identify the behaviors that may be facilitating interaction and communication and to encourage and refine those behaviors.

With the recent attention to the interplay of child and caregiver characteristics and the individual nature of caregiver/child interactions, however, practitioners should be careful in drawing conclusions and suggesting interventions. For example, parents may be controlling or directive in their interactions with their child because they have learned over time that this style is more effective in getting and keeping their child's attention and participation. In addition, Plapinger and Kretschmer (1991) have reported that some caregiver behaviors differ across contexts and are more a factor of the parents' expectations of their role in an activity (e.g., teacher or therapist) than of caregiver interactional style. Indeed, Sorsby and Martlew (1991) reported a low incidence of directive comments produced during bookreading versus play with toys. In addition, the fact that some children produce very few vocalizations may serve to limit the responsivity of their caregivers (Konstantareas, Zajdeman, Homatidis, & McCabe, 1988; Zirpoli & Bell, 1987). Speech intelligibility has also been shown to be a factor in responsivity as indicated by Conti-Ramsden (1990), who examined the contingency of responses of mothers of children with and without language impairments and revealed that the greater the child's intelligibility, the greater the likelihood that the mother used semantically contingent utterances. As suggested by Conti-Ramsden (1993), attempts to assess and modify parental conversational behaviors may carry the implication that the parents have somehow failed to provide what their child needed, or worse, that they may have somehow contributed to the "problem." Thus, as Conti-Ramsden suggests, it is necessary to share with families that their interactional behaviors are not wrong and to remind them that children with special needs most likely need special help in learning language. Indeed, the literature is quite clear about the kinds of strategies that can facilitate communication in children, and introducing caregivers to some of these strategies in culturally sensitive ways can be productive. Positive ideas for examining and influencing caregiver/child interactions can also be found in MacDonald (1989), McCollum and Yates (1994), Warren and Yoder (1998), Wilcox (1992), and Wilcox and Shannon (1998).

METHODS OF ASSESSMENT

A variety of methods are currently available for the assessment of communication skills, and professionals are encouraged to use multiple sources of information and multiple means to gather this information. This section begins by providing a list of commonly used standardized tests, followed by a discussion of alternative tools and techniques to broaden the scope of available methods of assessment. Finally, communication sampling and decision trees, and examples of how these two techniques might be used by professionals are provided.

Standardized Tests of Language and Communication

As noted previously, standardized testing is particularly useful for evaluation (e.g., identifying developmental levels and determining eligibility), although less useful for identifying instructional targets. Table 12.3 contains a list of representative standardized speech and language diagnostic and screening tests that can be used to evaluate the communication of infants and preschoolers. Indicated for each test are the areas assessed, age range, format of the test, type of score obtained, and unique aspects. In recent years, a number of professionals (Coggins, 1998; Crais, 1995; Paul, 2001) have argued against the sole use of standardized testing and suggest adding observational

and informal assessment measures. In particular, they suggest a blend of standardized testing and nonstandardized assessment, including direct observation, interaction with the child, and caregiver interviews and observations. For professionals to observe and informally assess children's communication skills in their natural environments, nonstandardized measures are particularly appropriate.

Two standardized tools, however, that have several characteristics of nonstandardized techniques in focusing on observations of children in more naturalistic activities are the *Communication and Symbolic Behavior Scales* (CSBS) (Wetherby & Prizant, 1993) and the MacArthur Communicative Development Inventories (CDI) (Fenson et al., 1993). The original *CSBS* and it's newer counterpart, the *CSBS-Developmental Profile (CSBS-DP)* (Wetherby & Prizant, 2001) are designed for use with preverbal and verbal children developmentally between the ages of 8 and 24 months. Caregivers are encouraged to be not only present, but to actively participate in the assessment. The tools are accompanied by a detailed parent interview form completed before the assessment and a caregiver perception rating form completed afterwards. Both the *CSBS* and *CSBS-DP* profile behaviors across several prelinguistic communication skills (gestures, affect, vocalizations, functions and means of communication, comprehension) as well as combinatorial and symbolic play. The format of the scales is to present naturalistic toys and activities and observe and assess the child's behaviors. Unlike the original *CSBS*, which requires videotaping for scoring, the *CSBS-DP* can be scored as the scales are administered. In both versions of the *CSBS*, Wetherby and Prizant have created child- and family-friendly tools that can be used in either a standardized or informal descriptive approach with information directly applicable for intervention planning.

In using parent report of a child's skills, the *CDI* (Fenson et al., 1993) also encourages observation of the child in the natural environment. The CDI is comprised of two levels focusing on children from 8 to 30 months. The younger level (Words and Gestures, 8 to 16 months) includes word comprehension and production, familiar phrase comprehension, gestures, social games, functional and symbolic play, and imitating an adult. The older level (Words and Sentences, 17 to 30 months) includes single word production, word combinations, and some grammatical forms. The *CDI* has shown good correlation with other standardized language tests and language sampling mean length of utterance (Dale, 1996). Advantages to using tools such as the *CSBS* and the *CDI* include those attributable to standardized tools (e.g., normative data, age-matched comparisons) as well as gaining active participation of the caregiver, allowing the professional time to gather observational and naturalistic data, the ability to gather information on a wide range of communication-related domains within one test, and perhaps most importantly to do so in a child- and family-friendly manner.

Criterion-Referenced and Nonstandardized Instruments

Criterion-referenced instruments and developmental scales are typically not standardized and are often developed by compiling information taken from standardized tests, other developmental charts and scales, and clinical experiences. This type of information can be particularly useful in assessment and later intervention planning, although care should be taken when using developmental scales as anything more than rough guidelines to development. Table 12.3 provides a list of commercially available criterion-referenced and nonstandardized speech and language instruments. In addition to assessing communication skills, many of these instruments also examine social, cognitive, play, and motor skills. Examples are the *Assessment, Evaluation, and Programming System* (Bricker, 2002), the *Hawaii Early Learning Profile* (Furuno, O'Reilly, Inatsuka, Hosaka, Allman, & Zeisloft-Falbey, 1987), the *Infant-Toddler Language Scale* (Rossetti, 1990), and the

Parent/Professional Preschool Performance Profile (Bloch, 1987). Some instruments, such as the *Battelle Developmental Inventory* (Newborg, Stock, Wnek, Guidubaldi, & Svinicki, 1984), are both standardized and criterion-referenced.

Ecological Approach to Assessment

As noted in previous chapters, when professionals talk about the ecology of the child, they often refer to Bronfenbrenner's (1977) concept of the child nested within the family, which is itself embedded in a larger community system. Taking an ecological perspective, Bronfenbrenner suggested that to understand human development, one must go beyond observation of one or two people in the same location. In considering the ecologies that surround the child (e.g., home, day-care, preschool), professionals are urged to take into account the child's interactions across multiple settings and the facilitators and constraints inherent in those settings. Thus our assessment approaches need to be broadened to include observing children in their natural environments with the people they interact with routinely.

In recent years a number of professionals have recognized the need to view assessment as ongoing rather than as a one-time set of activities. Due to the high variability shown by young children, the need to get a representative sample of behaviors, and the difficulty of seeing a child's best (or sometimes even typical) performance under testing conditions, assessment strategies need to be viewed as serial. In addition, a child's communication skills need to be examined across a variety of contexts and with multiple sources contributing to the information gained. The use of multiple methods of assessment (e.g., observation, naturalistic interaction, direct assessment by professionals and family members, communication sampling, discussions with caregivers) can both add to the information available and contribute to the overall reliability and validity of the process. Indeed, the move toward more naturalistic activities and settings can increase the ecological validity of assessment and intervention planning. The opportunity to view a child over time and to gather information under different conditions allows the team the chance to develop a more accurate picture of the child.

Communication Sampling

Collecting a communication sample is a frequently used method for obtaining information about a child's communication. This type of sample can provide a running record of communication efforts during a set period of time and can be collected in such natural settings as the child's home with the family or the child's classroom with peers. Communication samples are particularly useful for assessing the frequency and manner in which children communicate in their daily environments. The ultimate goal is to collect information that is representative of a child's communicative performance.

Several issues should be considered before collecting a communication sample. First, what is the purpose of the sample? Is it to identify the child's overall level of communication or primarily to pinpoint the use of specific communication behaviors? Second, how will the behaviors of interest be measured? That is, will all the occurrences of a behavior be counted or only those occurring during specific points in time? Third, how will the sample be collected? The context, participants, and nature of the interaction can all influence a child's communication. Fourth, how will the sample be recorded? Will online notes or transcription be performed or will video or audio recording be done? Finally, how will the information be analyzed? Will the target behaviors be totaled or will further analysis be necessary in the areas of communication or play, such as coding the type of communication attempts or play behaviors exhibited during play?

Identifying the Purpose of the Sample   The
sample can examine any area of communication that is of interest to the early interventionist and other team members. Sampling, for example, could determine how a child intentionally communicates (e.g., requests, protests), a child's typical form of communication (e.g., gesture, vocalization, or speech) or the diversity of communicative functions used. The sample can also address specific communication areas such as how the child responds to teacher requests or how he or she protests when a peer grabs a toy during playtime. Once the purpose of the sample is determined, the behaviors of interest should be behaviorally defined. For example, if the child's requesting behavior in the classroom is of interest, should the number of times he or she makes a request, the types of requests used (e.g., gestures versus speech), or the proportion of communication attempts that are requests be studied?

Collecting the Sample   Variables associated
with the collection of the sample are critical because the context of the interaction can influence the child's communication and thus the representativeness of the sample. The sample can be collected almost anywhere (e.g., classroom, home, playground), during any activity (free-play, block building, book-reading, diapering), and with any partners (peers, siblings, teachers, parents, other caregivers). Familiar contexts and activities that are both age-appropriate and interesting can increase the child's level and type of communication. Children tend to communicate more with conversational partners who follow their topic, respond to their communicative attempts, pause for the child to take a turn, and use open-ended rather than closed-ended questions (Girolametto, Verbey, & Tannock, 1994; Wilcox, 1992; Yoder, Warren, McCathren, & Leew, 1998). The suggestions in Figure 12.1 can be useful for engaging a child in interaction. Because context, activities, and partners influence a child's communication, it is advantageous, although not necessary, to sample more than one context in a setting, for example, by varying the setting as well as changing the communicative partner or activity. A further variable is how long the sample should last. The time can be as short as 5 minutes or as long as needed, depend-

ing on the sample's purpose. For a representative sample, Miller (1981) suggests at least two 15-minute sampling sessions with a minimum of 50 to 100 utterances recorded.

Once the context is selected, the technique for eliciting the sample should be identified. One technique available is naturalistic observation, in which the interventionist observes the child in a natural environment and does not actively engage the child. For example, the child may be observed during free-play in the classroom, during games such as peek-a-boo with a parent, or playtime with a sibling. The professional can provide a set of toys or the child can play with familiar toys available in the sampling context. With naturalistic observation, however, certain types of communicative behaviors (e.g., question asking) may occur infrequently or not at all (Coggins, Olswang, & Guthrie, 1987). In such cases, the professional might use a second technique, structured interaction, in which the situation is structured to increase the likelihood that particular types of behaviors will occur. This technique can be used to elicit behaviors such as the communication functions of requests or protests or specific language structures such as use of questions. For example, if the professional desires information about requesting behavior, the child can be given a tightly closed plastic jar with Cheerios inside to see if and how he or she requests assistance. Owens (1999) and Paul (2001) describe other procedures for eliciting communication in structured interactions.

Recording the Sample   Communication samples can be recorded online, with the observer writing down the information from the session or using a video or audio recorder. For online transcription, the professional can either note what the child says or does that relates to the target behaviors or code the target behaviors, using predetermined categories. If continuous sampling is used, the coder writes down everything that happens or codes every target event; if interval sampling is used, the examiner records whether a behavior occurred within

a set interval of time (e.g., during a 10-second time block). Audio or video recording can be used to supplement online transcription or for later analysis. Clearly, audio or video recording provides more accurate retrieval of the child's communicative interactions; however, it may not be necessary for the sample's purpose. Further, the difficulty of using recorders in natural settings and the time needed for transcription and/or coding may make their use impractical. A form for collecting a brief communication sample is shown in Figure 12.2. The form can help the observer identify the speaker, the communication itself, the type of turn, the communication function, and the means used to communicate. Nonverbal behaviors and other contextual information can be noted in parentheses; this is often necessary, because the meaning of an utterance may differ depending on the context.

Analyzing the Sample   For the professional who is primarily interested in an overview of a child's communicative behavior (e.g., whether a child communicates by vocalizing or gesturing), the collected sample itself may provide adequate and interpretable information. For some children, however, more detailed analyses are necessary in the areas of pragmatics, semantics, syntax, phonology, or play. Below are examples of the kinds of information that can be derived from a sample in each of these domains.

In analyzing pragmatic behavior, for example, children's communicative functions can be coded into specific categories, using Wetherby and Prizant's (1993) taxonomy outlined previously. The communication sample can then be examined for three indices: the frequency of communication (e.g., 5 times in 10 minutes), the diversity of communication functions expressed (e.g., 2 requests, 1 protest, 1 comment, 1 answer), and the diversity of means used to express the communicative functions (e.g., 2 vocalizations, 3 gestures). The sample can also be analyzed for discourse skills; for example, determining the percentage of the times a child responds or initiates and with whom the child communicates (e.g., adults only, never with

Instructions: Please check under level of use each communicative function and write in the communication mode.

Functions	Level of Use			Communication Mode Used*		Situations	
	Yes does this	Is learning this	Does not do this	Most often	Least often	In what situations?	Give example
1. *Requests objects*—Does child communicate that he wants an object that is out of reach? (e.g., pushes adult's hands toward a cookie or says "cookie")							
2. *Requests action*—Does child communicate that she wants help doing something? (e.g., hands adult a jar to open or says "open")							
3. *Attention seeking*—Does child communicate that he wants you to attend to him or to something in the environment? (e.g., tugs on mother's pants or says "mama")							
4. *Comment on object*—Does child communicate that she wants you to notice or comment on an object? (e.g., points to "dog" and smiles or says "dog")							
5. *Comment on action*—Does child communicate that he is interested in something another person or object has done or does he try to get you to notice? (e.g., flies plane in air and claps or says "up")							

FIGURE 12.2
Communication report form

Instructions: Please check under level of use each communicative function and write in the communication mode.

Functions	Level of Use			Communication Mode Used*		Situations	
	Yes does this	Is learning this	Does not do this	Most often	Least often	In what situations?	Give example
6. *Protests*—Does child communicate that she does not like or does not want something? (e.g., pushes your hand away or says "no")							
7. *Requests information*—Does child ask for names and locations of things, animals, or people? (e.g., points to picture in book and looks at adult or asks "what that?")							
8. *Answers*—Does child respond to your questions about name and locations of things, animals, or people? (e.g., when asked, "What do you want?" points to chocolate cookie or says "cookie")							
9. *Acknowledges*—Does child do something to indicate that he has heard you speaking to him? (e.g., nods his head or says "yes")							
10. *Social Routines*—Does child communicate routines such as "please," "thank you," "hi," and "bye" (e.g., to indicate "bye-bye" waves or says "bye")?							

* GE = gesture, SP = speech, SO = sounds, SI = signing

FIGURE 12.2
Continued

peers). The average number of turns that a child takes in routines such as patty-cake, in vocal play, or in conversational exchanges can also be useful. Table 12.4 shows how communicative functions and turn-taking can be coded in a communication sample. For additional information on coding pragmatic behaviors, see Paul (2001).

For semantic abilities, the analysis can include the total number of words used in the sample, the number of different words, and the number and type of semantic relations. Using Table 12.1, each utterance can be examined to determine the semantic categories used in prelinguistic, one-word, and multiword utterances, as well as whether a variety of semantic roles are used. If, for intervention purposes, the professional is interested in a specific category of words such as common foods or action words, these categories can also be included in the analysis. When analyzing the sample for syntax, the professional can look at both the child's overall utterance length or mean length of utterance (as described earlier) and the basic sentence structures used. For a child using only one- or two-word utterances, syntactic analysis is not necessary. For a child using three-word or multiword constructions, the analysis could include the use of grammatical morphemes (e.g., *ing, ed*), negatives, questions, and simple versus complex sentence structures, as described in Miller (1981).

In analyzing the sample for phonological skills, the professional can note both the sounds the child does and does not produce and the number of syllables generally used (e.g., two in *uh-oh*, one in *up*). An increase in the number of syllables used is an indication of advancing phonological skills. It is also helpful to note how often the child's speech is intelligible, that is, understandable (e.g., all, most, some, or none of the time) and whether it varies depending on the context (e.g., home versus school), conversational partner (e.g., parent versus peer), or utterance length (e.g., one-word versus multiword utterances). Although a communication sample can be analyzed for specific sounds and error patterns, a detailed analysis is generally performed by a

speech-language pathologist. Developmental information on phonology can be found in Bernthal and Bankson (1998).

Analyses Illustrated An example of how information from a communication sample can be analyzed is illustrated for a 4-year-old child, Bob, who has cerebral palsy. The communication sample was collected during two 10-minute classroom activities (e.g., snack time and free-play). A portion of the snack-time sample is shown in Table 12.4. Bob communicated 20 times during the two observations, using speech most frequently and gestures on occasion. His speech consisted primarily of one- and two-word utterances and an occasional three-word utterance. Except for very structured interactions, Bob infrequently initiated communication to his teacher and less frequently to peers. If an adult started and controlled the interaction, however, Bob responded by taking as many as five turns using speech. He often used repetition of the adult's utterance as a means for continuing the interaction. He responded appropriately to many adult requests by answering questions with words and gestures; however, he typically responded to peers nonverbally through smiling or gestures (especially grabbing), and when frustrated, cried rather than verbalized his desires.

The semantic analysis indicated that Bob used a total of 30 words and that there were 15 different words. His words included the names of people and common objects, actions, social words, and modifiers. Bob expressed a range of semantic relations at the two-word level, such as agent + object, action + object, and recurrence + object, and one at the three-word level (agent + action + object). The syntactic analysis of the 15 utterances indicated that during the sample Bob's mean length of utterance (MLU) in words was 1.75, although this figure should be interpreted cautiously. As recommended by Miller (1981), MLU should be based on at least 50 utterances. The phonological analysis indicated that Bob used age-appropriate initial and medial consonants but omitted most final consonants.

TABLE 12.4

Communication Sample Analysis

Child: Bob (B) Other participant: Teacher (T) Setting: Classroom Date: 5/7/02

Activity: Snack Length of observation: 10 minutes Observer: JR

Notes: Bob has a cold and an ear infection.

Speaker	Communication Behavior	Turn*	Function†	Mode‡
T	"It's snack time. Look." (teacher puts cookies on table out of reach of children)			
B	Reaches for cookie as looks at teacher.	I	RO	GE
T	"What do you wan:?"	R		
B	(points to package as looks at teacher)	R	RO	GE
T	"Cookie?"			
B	"Yeah, cookie."	R	AN	SP
T	"Do you want chocolate chip or sugar?"			
B	"Chocolate."	R	AN	SP
T	Gives Bob cookie			
B	"Cookie good."	I	CO	SP
T	"Yes. The cookie is good!"			
B	"More cookie." (pointing toward others on plate)	I	RO	SP

° Turn: I = Initiation, R = Response
† Function: RO = request for object, AN = answer, CO = comment on object
‡ Mode: GE = gesture, SP = speech

In summary, the information derived from a communication sample can provide important information about how a child communicates in everyday situations and can be a working basis for later intervention decisions. The following section provides an additional means for practitioners to gain information about a child's communication skills.

Decision Trees

Three decision trees developed by Crais and Roberts (1991) for children functioning at the prelinguistic, one-word, and multiword levels appear in Figures 12.3, 12.4, and 12.5. They incorporate questions to help identify a child's level of communication functioning, for the purpose of guiding intervention planning. The key points in assessing young children are *whether* a child communicates and *when, what,* and *how* information is transmitted. As noted for prelinguistic children, the focus is on early-developing social and interactive aspects of communication. For example, if a child uses only gestures and vocalizations, the focus in assessment would be primarily on determining whether those behaviors represent functional communication. For verbal children, although words are important, the focus still remains on functional and interactive aspects; therefore, assessments of semantics and pragmatics rather than phonology or syntax are highlighted. Furthermore, the decision trees were designed for use with children functioning *developmentally* between 6 months and 3 years of age. For children functioning at a higher level, the assessment tools in Table 12.3 can be utilized.

Each decision tree includes three major skill areas: social interaction, comprehension, and production. For practical purposes, production has been divided into two areas, spontaneous and imitation, although imitation crosses each of the other areas. Within each skill area is a list of behaviors that can be observed or elicited. The individual behaviors are generally listed in a developmental sequence from early- to later-

developing; however, since some behaviors develop simultaneously, the sequence may vary. Although each skill area is presented as discrete, any one behavior *within* a skill area may incorporate aspects of the other skill areas.

The professional should generally move vertically through each list of behaviors, stopping where the child either does not exhibit a few consecutive behaviors, or does so in a limited or inconsistent manner. Once this point, which is the child's current level of functioning, is established, the interventionist can then move through the other two areas of the decision tree. At any point in the process, further analysis in any of the areas can be initiated. Developmental charts and scales and interactive assessment techniques (described in the previous sections) can be used to identify additional behaviors between achieved and unachieved behaviors. Most of the behaviors can be elicited through interaction with the child or gained from discussion with parents and other caregivers.

When moving through the decision trees, the interventionist should remember that each child is unique and will therefore display some degree of individual variability. Thus the decision questions are basic guidelines and are not presented as hard-and-fast rules for each child's absolute progression of skills. Although the three decision trees are presented separately, interventionists may need to move back and forth between them to explore a child's full range of communication skills. It is also important to remember that opportunity plays a part in *which* skills will be exhibited by an individual child. The type and number of interactions that are initiated by, responded to, and encouraged by a child's caregivers or teachers can shape the kinds of behaviors displayed. It is often helpful to observe the caregiver(s) or teacher(s) interacting with the child to get an idea of the typical opportunities the child may have available.

An example of how one might use the decision trees to assess communicative behavior in a child at a prelinguistic level is described here for the

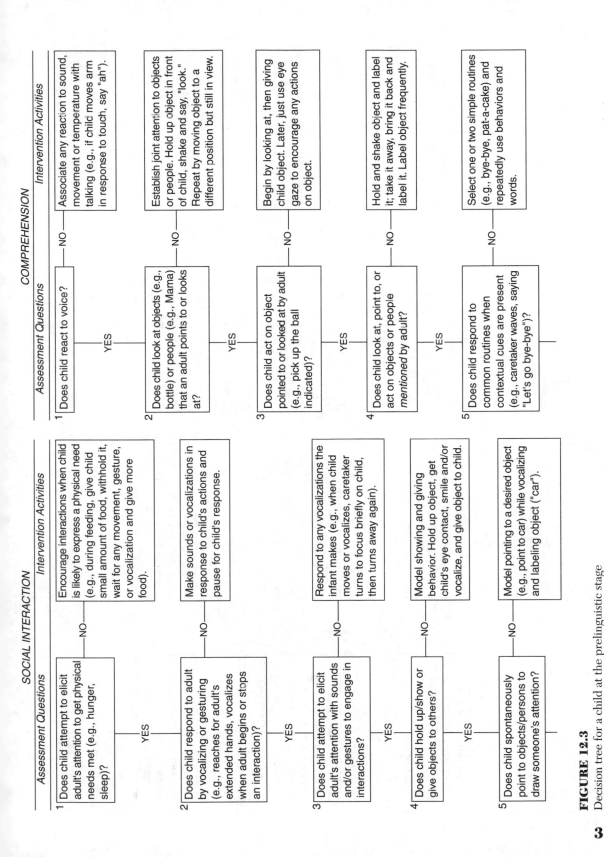

FIGURE 12.3

Decision tree for a child at the prelinguistic stage

Source: Adapted from "Decision Making in Assessment and Early Intervention" by E. Crais and J. Roberts, 1991, *Language, Speech, Hearing Services in Schools, 22,* pp. 25–30. Copyright 1991 by ASHA. Reprinted by permission.
^aFor children with severe motor, cognitive, and/or sensory impairments, alternative communication modes may be necessary.

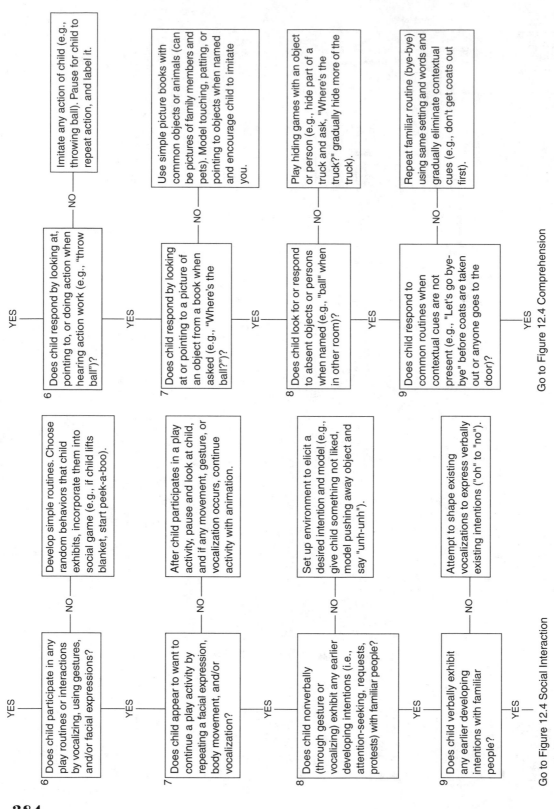

Go to Figure 12.4 Social Interaction

FIGURE 12.3
Continued

384

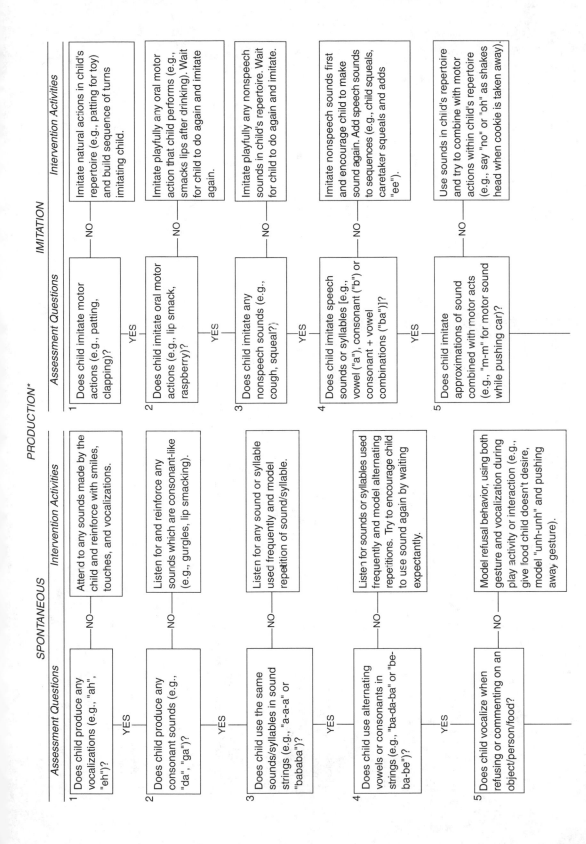

PRODUCTION*

SPONTANEOUS

IMITATION

Assessment Questions	Intervention Activities
1 Does child produce any vocalizations (e.g., "ah", "eh")?	Attend to any sounds made by the child and reinforce with smiles, touches, and vocalizations.
2 Does child produce any consonant sounds (e.g., "da", "ga")?	Listen for and reinforce any sounds which are consonant-like (e.g., gurgles, lip smacking).
3 Does child use the same sounds/syllables in sound strings (e.g., "a-a-a" or "bababa")?	Listen for any sound or syllable used frequently and model repetition of sound/syllable.
4 Does child use alternating vowels or consonants in strings (e.g., "ba-da-ba" or "be-ba-be")?	Listen for sounds or syllables used frequently and model alternating repetitions. Try to encourage child to use sound again by waiting expectantly.
5 Does child vocalize when refusing or commenting on an object/person/food?	Model refusal behavior, using both gesture and vocalization during play activity or interaction (e.g., give food child doesn't desire, model "unh-unh" and pushing away gesture).

Assessment Questions	Intervention Activities
1 Does child imitate motor actions (e.g., patting, clapping)?	Imitate natural actions in child's repertoire (e.g., patting for toy) and build sequence of turns imitating child.
2 Does child imitate oral motor actions (e.g., lip smack, raspberry)?	Imitate playfully any oral motor action that child performs (e.g., smacks lips after drinking). Wait for child to do again and imitate again.
3 Does child imitate any nonspeech sounds (e.g., cough, squeal?)	Imitate playfully any nonspeech sounds in child's repertoire. Wait for child to do again and imitate.
4 Does child imitate speech sounds or syllables [e.g., vowel ("a"), consonant ("b") or consonant + vowel combinations ("ba")]?	Imitate nonspeech sounds first and encourage child to make sound again. Add speech sounds to sequences (e.g., child squeals, caretaker squeals and adds "ee").
5 Does child imitate approximations of sound combined with motor acts (e.g., "m-m" for motor sound while pushing car)?	Use sounds in child's repertoire and try to combine with motor actions within child's repertoire (e.g., say "no" or "oh" as shakes head when cookie is taken away).

FIGURE 12.3
Continued

385

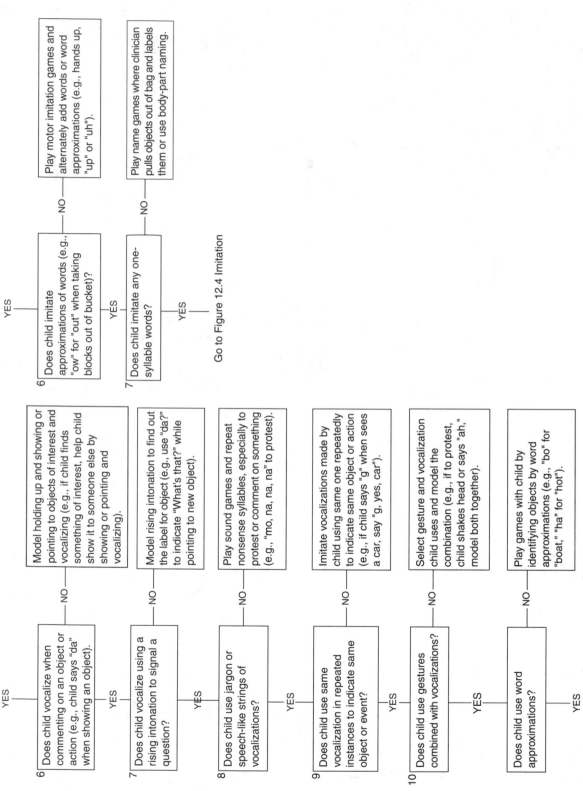

Play motor imitation games and alternately add words or word approximations (e.g., hands up, "up" or "uh").

Play name games where clinician pulls objects out of bag and labels them or use body-part naming.

6 Does child imitate approximations of words (e.g., "ow" for "out" when taking blocks out of bucket)?

7 Does child imitate any one-syllable words?

Go to Figure 12.4 Imitation

Model holding up and showing or pointing to objects of interest and vocalizing (e.g., if child finds something of interest, help child show it to someone else by showing or pointing and vocalizing).

Model rising intonation to find out the label for object (e.g., use "da?" to indicate "What's that?" while pointing to new object).

Play sound games and repeat nonsense syllables, especially to protest or comment on something (e.g., "mo, na, na, na" to protest).

Imitate vocalizations made by child using same one repeatedly to indicate same object or action (e.g., if child says "g" when sees a car, say "g, yes, car").

Select gesture and vocalization child uses and model the combination (e.g., if to protest, child shakes head or says "ah," model both together).

Play games with child by identifying objects by word approximations (e.g., "bo" for "boat," "ha" for "hot").

6 Does child vocalize when commenting on an object or action (e.g., child says "da" when showing an object).

7 Does child vocalize using a rising intonation to signal a question?

8 Does child use jargon or speech-like strings of vocalizations?

9 Does child use same vocalization in repeated instances to indicate same object or event?

10 Does child use gestures combined with vocalizations?

Does child use word approximations?

Go to Figure 12.4 Spontaneous Production

FIGURE 12.3
Continued

386

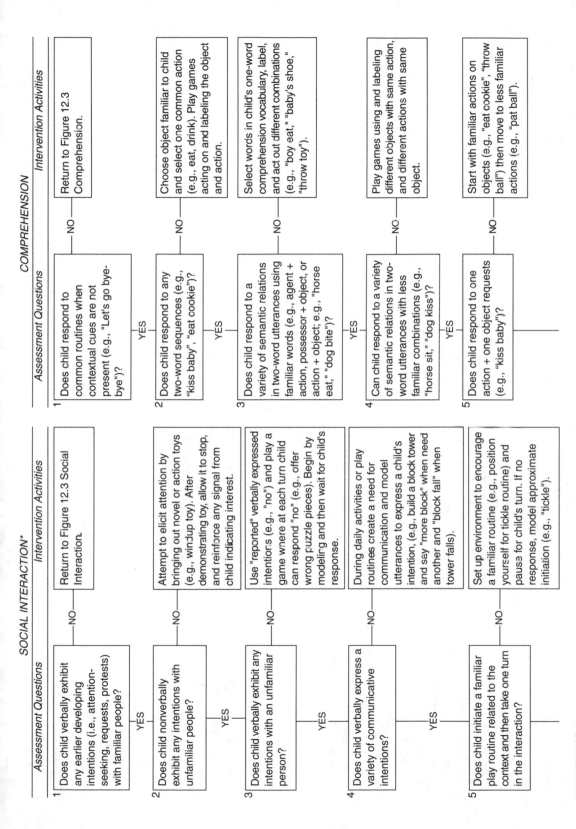

FIGURE 12.4

Decision tree for a child at the one-word utterance stage

Source: Adapted from "Decision Making in Assessment and Early Intervention" by E. Crais and J. Roberts, 1991, *Language, Speech, Hearing Services in Schools, 22,* pp. 25–30. Copyright 1991 by ASHA. Reprinted by permission.

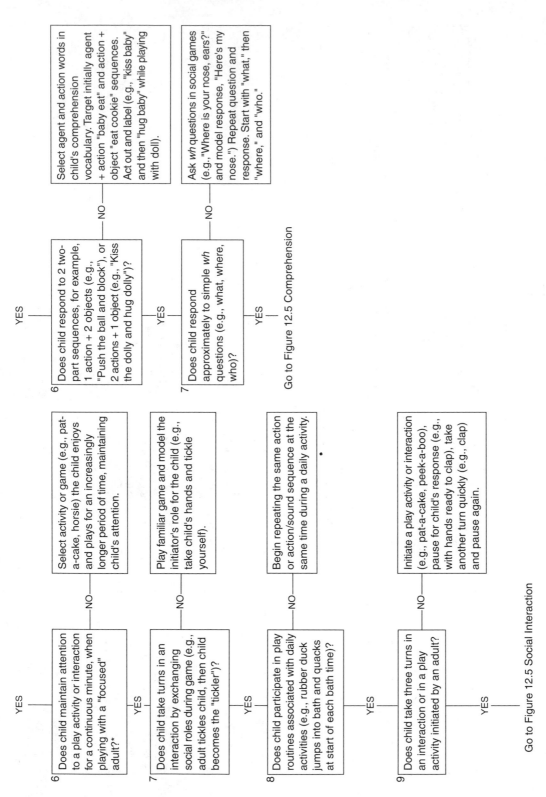

6 Does child maintain attention to a play activity or interaction for a continuous minute, when playing with a "focused" adult?*

— NO → Select activity or game (e.g., pat-a-cake, horsie) the child enjoys and plays for an increasingly longer period of time, maintaining child's attention.

YES
↓

7 Does child take turns in an interaction by exchanging social roles during game (e.g., adult tickles child, then child becomes the "tickler")?

— NO → Play familiar game and model the initiator's role for the child (e.g., take child's hands and tickle yourself).

YES
↓

8 Does child participate in play routines associated with daily activities (e.g., rubber duck jumps into bath and quacks at start of each bath time)?

— NO → Begin repeating the same action or action/sound sequence at the same time during a daily activity.

YES
↓

9 Does child take three turns in an interaction or in a play activity initiated by an adult?

— NO → Initiate a play activity or interaction (e.g., pat-a-cake, peek-a-boo), pause for child's response (e.g., with hands ready to clap), take another turn quickly (e.g., clap) and pause again.

YES
↓

Go to Figure 12.5 Social Interaction

6 Does child respond to 2 two-part sequences, for example, 1 action + 2 objects (e.g., "Push the ball and block"), or 2 actions + 1 object (e.g., "Kiss the dolly and hug dolly")?

— NO → Select agent and action words in child's comprehension vocabulary. Target initially agent + action "baby eat" and action + object "eat cookie" sequences. Act out and label (e.g., "kiss baby" and then "hug baby" while playing with doll).

YES
↓

7 Does child respond approximately to simple *wh* questions (e.g., what, where, who)?

— NO → Ask *wh* questions in social games (e.g., "Where is your nose, ears?" and model response, "Here's my nose.") Repeat question and response. Start with "what," then "where," and "who."

YES
↓

Go to Figure 12.5 Comprehension

FIGURE 12.4

Continued

*As the child's communicative skills improve, these turn-taking behaviors should first be seen vocally and later verbally.

388

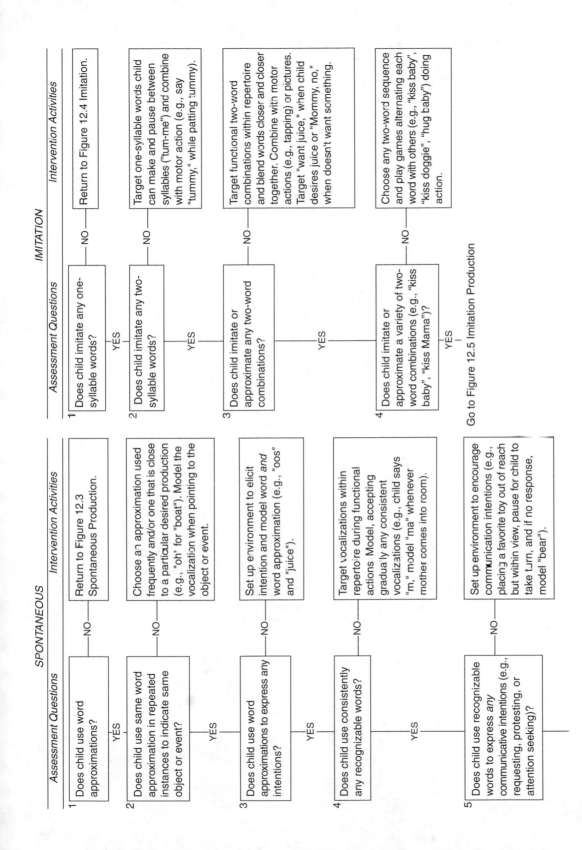

SPONTANEOUS

Assessment Questions

1 Does child use word approximations?

2 Does child use same word approximation in repeated instances to indicate same object or event?

3 Does child use word approximations to express any intentions?

4 Does child use consistently any recognizable words?

5 Does child use recognizable words to express *any* communicative intentions (e.g., requesting, protesting, or attention seeking)?

Intervention Activities

Return to Figure 12.3 Spontaneous Production.

Choose an approximation used frequently and/or one that is close to a particular desired production (e.g., "oh" for "boat"). Model the vocalization when pointing to the object or event.

Set up environment to elicit intention and model word *and* word approximation (e.g., "oos" and "juice").

Target vocalizations within repertoire during functional actions. Model, accepting gradually any consistent vocalizations (e.g., child says "m," model "ma" whenever mother comes into room).

Set up environment to encourage communication intentions (e.g., placing a favorite toy out of reach but within view, pause for child to take turn, and if no response, model "bear").

IMITATION

Assessment Questions

1 Does child imitate any one-syllable words?

2 Does child imitate any two-syllable words?

3 Does child imitate or approximate any two-word combinations?

4 Does child imitate or approximate a variety of two-word combinations (e.g., "kiss baby", "kiss Mama")?

Go to Figure 12.5 Imitation Production

Intervention Activities

Return to Figure 12.4 Imitation.

Target one-syllable words child can make and pause between syllables ("tum-me") and combine with motor action (e.g., say "tummy," while patting tummy).

Target functional two-word combinations within repertoire and blend words closer and closer together. Combine with motor actions (e.g., tapping) or pictures. Target "want juice," when child desires juice or "Mommy, no," when doesn't want something.

Choose any two-word sequence and play games alternating each word with others (e.g., "kiss baby", "kiss doggie", "hug baby") doing action.

FIGURE 12.4
Continued

389

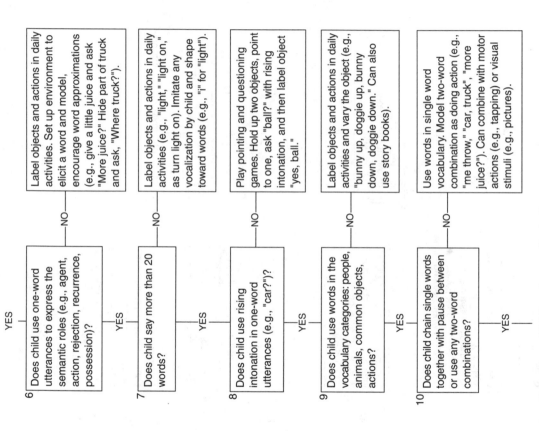

YES

6 Does child use one-word utterances to express the semantic roles (e.g., agent, action, rejection, recurrence, possession)?

NO — Label objects and actions in daily activities. Set up environment to elicit a word and model, encourage word approximations (e.g., give a little juice and ask "More juice?" Hide part of truck and ask, "Where truck?").

YES

7 Does child say more than 20 words?

NO — Label objects and actions in daily activities (e.g., "light," "light on," as turn light on). Imitate any vocalization by child and shape toward words (e.g., "I" for "light").

YES

8 Does child use rising intonation in one-word utterances (e.g., "car?")?

NO — Play pointing and questioning games. Hold up two objects, point to one, ask "ball?" with rising intonation, and then label object "yes, ball."

YES

9 Does child use words in the vocabulary categories: people, animals, common objects, actions?

NO — Label objects and actions in daily activities and vary the object (e.g., "bunny up, doggie up, bunny down, doggie down." Can also use story books).

YES

10 Does child chain single words together with pause between or use any two-word combinations?

NO — Use words in single word vocabulary. Model two-word combination as doing action (e.g., "me throw," "car, truck", "more juice?"). Can combine with motor actions (e.g., tapping) or visual stimuli (e.g., pictures).

YES

Go to Figure 12.5 Spontaneous Production

FIGURE 12.4
Continued

390

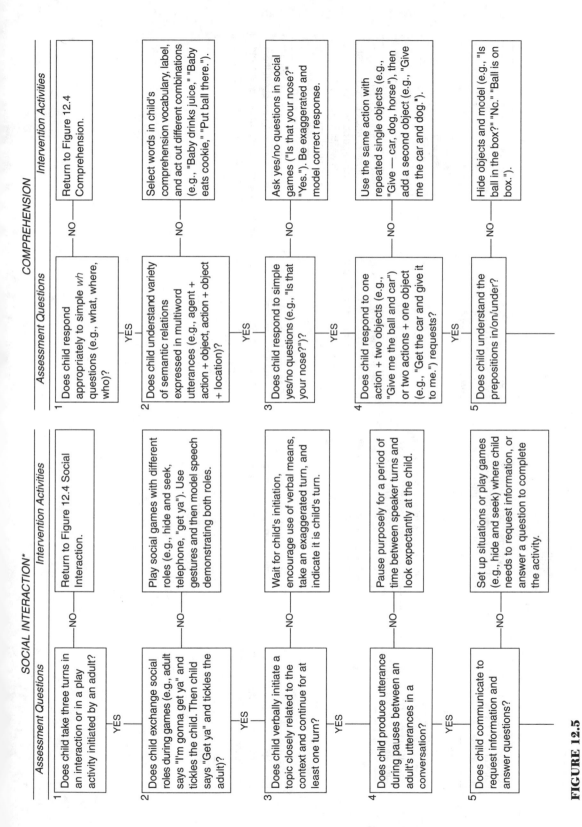

FIGURE 12.5

Decision tree for a child at the two-word utterance stage and above

Source: Adapted from "Decision Making in Assessment and Early Intervention" by E. Crais and J. Roberts, 1991, *Language, Speech, Hearing Services in Schools, 22,* pp. 25–30. Copyright 1991 by ASHA. Reprinted by permission.

*Imitation can be initially used for response development with prompts and later fading of imitation for spontaneous productions.

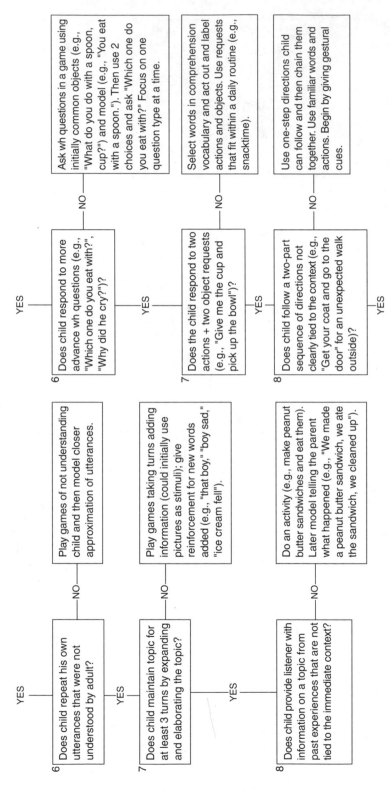

6 | Does child repeat his own utterances that were not understood by adult? — NO — Play games of not understanding child and then model closer approximation of utterances.

6 | Does child respond to more advance wh questions (e.g., "Which one do you eat with?", "Why did he cry?")? — NO — Ask wh questions in a game using initially common objects (e.g., "What do you do with a spoon, cup?") and model (e.g., "You eat with a spoon."). Then use 2 choices and ask "Which one do you eat with?" Focus on one question type at a time.

7 | Does child maintain topic for at least 3 turns by expanding and elaborating the topic? — NO — Play games taking turns adding information (could initially use pictures as stimuli); give reinforcement for new words added (e.g., "that boy," "boy sad," "ice cream fell").

7 | Does the child respond to two actions + two object requests (e.g., "Give me the cup and pick up the bowl")? — NO — Select words in comprehension vocabulary and act out and label actions and objects. Use requests that fit within a daily routine (e.g., snacktime).

8 | Does child provide listener with information on a topic from past experiences that are not tied to the immediate context? — NO — Do an activity (e.g., make peanut butter sandwiches and eat them). Later model telling the parent what happened (e.g., "We made a peanut butter sandwich, we ate the sandwich, we cleaned up").

8 | Does child follow a two-part sequence of directions not clearly tied to the context (e.g., "Get your coat and go to the door" for an unexpected walk outside)? — NO — Use one-step directions child can follow and then chain them together. Use familiar words and actions. Begin by giving gestural cues.

For higher level skills, see individual assessment instruments.

For higher level skills, see individual assessment instruments.

FIGURE 12.5
Continued

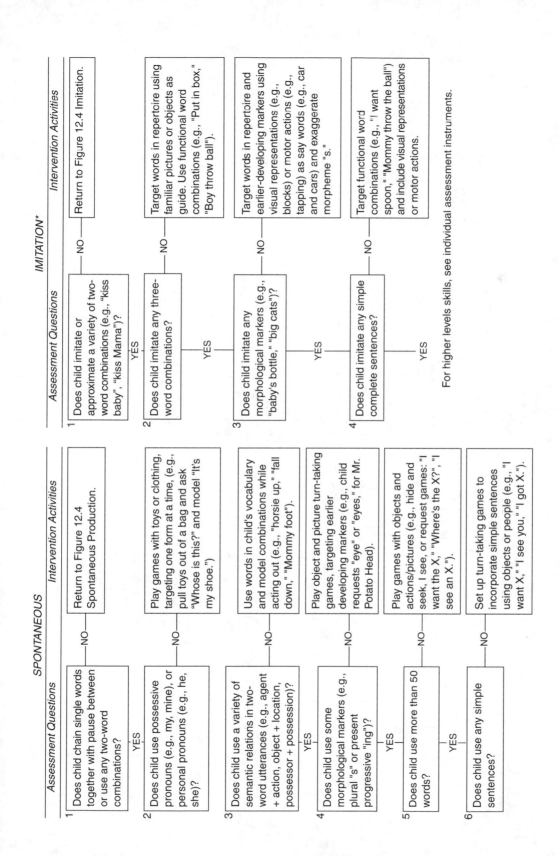

FIGURE 12.5
Continued

393

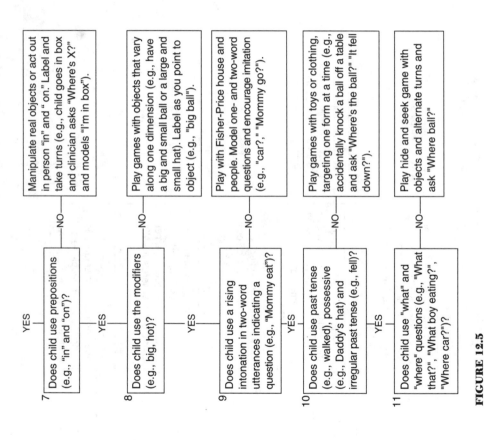

FIGURE 12.5
Continued

Social Interaction area. The interventionist could set up situations to elicit specific communicative means and functions, observe the means and functions that are readily used by the child, and look for evidence of those not yet developed. The interventionist could also rely on caregiver or teacher report through the use of a form like that shown in Figure 12.2. The interventionist can ask the caregiver or teacher to describe (a) *what reasons* (functions) the child does or does not communicate about (e.g., behavior regulation = requests for objects or actions, protests); (b) *what means* are used to express those functions: nonverbal (gesture, body movement, facial expression), verbal (speech, signing), or vocal (speech sounds, nonspeech sounds); and (c) in *what situations* the child expresses these functions.

Using the Decision Trees

To illustrate the use of the decision trees in identifying a child's current communicative means and functions, the process of observing and interacting with a 20-month-old child named Susan will be described. Because Susan's parents (Ella and Matt) reported that what they primarily wanted from the assessment was ideas for how they and their child-care provider (Terry) could work to improve Susan's communication skills at home, it was suggested that Susan be observed interacting with her parents, her 4-year-old sister, the child-care provider, and the examiners in free-play, and with her parents during mealtime and dressing. Once the professionals had offered various options of assessment tools and techniques, Ella and Matt noted they liked best the idea of using informal observations and the decision trees. Because they reported that Susan does not use any "words" and that she primarily gets her needs met by gesturing and vocalizing, the decision tree for a child at the prelinguistic stage (Figure 12.3) was selected. The professionals and caregivers briefly reviewed the decision tree and agreed that over the next few weeks they would each look for and identify the items Susan was able to do. Three observation and

interaction sessions were arranged over a 3-week period. Following the last observation, Ella, Matt, Terry, and the professionals discussed their observations. For each skill area and the items in each area, Susan's typical and observed behaviors were pinpointed and written directly on a copy of the decision tree.

In the Social Interaction skill area, the parents and the professionals were specifically looking for the means and functions Susan uses to communicate and the type of social games in which she participates. By caregiver report and observation, Susan elicited adult attention by vocalizing "ah," showed and gave objects to others, played two social interaction games (e.g., tickle and peek-a-boo), and used a vocalization ("ba") to protest when a favorite food was taken away and a pushing-away gesture when she did not want a cracker. She requested an object by vocalizing or gesturing, and once by vocalizing *and* gesturing. When Susan wanted an activity to continue (peek-a-boo) she held up the blanket to her mother. All observers agreed that she did not yet use any verbal means to get her needs met.

In the Comprehension area, Susan looked at objects mentioned, reacted to "bye-bye" when context cues were present (e.g., the examiner put on her coat and moved toward the door), and when her sister was not in the room, looked for her after hearing her name. All observers agreed that Susan did not respond to any action words or indicate a recognition of routines without the presence of contextual cues. In the Spontaneous Production area, Susan vocalized when refusing a cracker and when pointing to a new object held by the examiner, used a rising intonation when vocalizing to put a block in a box as if to ask "in here?," used speechlike strings of vowels and consonants, and on one occasion used a vocalization with a gesture (drinking gesture and "da" when requesting juice). She did not use consistent vocalizations or word approximations. In the Imitation area, Susan imitated motor and oral motor actions, some nonspeech sounds ("grr" for a tiger, buzzing sound for a bee) and a few speech sounds ("bu," "mu," "da") during a game with the examiner. She imitated two sounds combined with a motor act (buzzing "zz" while holding fingers together like a bee and "grr" while scratching like a tiger), but did not imitate any word approximations or words. Figure 12.6 provides a summary of Susan's observed and reported communicative behaviors.

After reviewing the behaviors Susan did and did not exhibit on the prelinguistic decision tree, the professionals and caregivers then began to evolve an intervention plan for Susan. They also discussed how Susan and her caregivers interacted (e.g., how she gained their attention, how they gained hers, how she responded to their initiations and they to hers, and the kinds of sounds and words they modeled for her). An example of goal planning with the information gained from using the prelinguistic decision tree with Susan is provided in the final section of the chapter. In regard to utilizing the decision trees, one additional comment should be made. As with most assessment tools and techniques, use of the decision trees often involves only brief interactions between a child and other individuals, and so the examiner and caregivers may need to gather further information. If developmental levels are desired by the family or needed by the professionals in terms of determining eligibility, standardized tests, developmental charts, and/or some of the alternative techniques suggested can be used in conjunction with the decision trees.

TRANSLATING ASSESSMENT INFORMATION INTO INSTRUCTIONAL GOALS

As with assessment planning, intervention planning must begin with the family's concerns and priorities. Once the assessment has been completed, Kjerland and Kovach (1990) suggest that the postassessment discussion include critiquing the assessment, describing the child (strengths and needs), drawing conclusions, and setting priorities. To help set priorities, the family may be asked questions such as "What seems most important to you at this point?" or "What would you like your child to learn or to change within the next few months?" The family and the professionals can then begin identifying the specific goals and strategies used to reach the broad goals. For each goal, the team first discusses the child's current behaviors and ideas for how change can be made and who will help facilitate that change (Kjerland & Kovach, 1990).

In the area of communication, as with many other areas, families typically have broad skills or achievements that they would like their child to attain. For example, they may say that they want their child to be able to "use words instead of all these sounds," "let us know what he wants," or "talk in a way that other people can understand her." They may not, however, know the discrete skills or the individual activities that could help their child achieve these broader outcomes. With the recent focus on providing family-centered services, professionals are often challenged to provide information and ideas and yet to do so in a way that is responsive to the concerns and priorities of the family. When considering the broad outcomes identified by the family, the following questions may help professionals and family members think about what subgoals might be identified to help the child attain the larger outcomes.

1. What outcomes are most important to accomplish first?
2. What modifications would have the most effect on communication?
3. What modification in behavior will have the greatest effect on other skill areas?
4. What skill areas or behaviors are being worked on by other professionals?
5. What behaviors have the best possibility of generalizing across contexts?
6. What ways can family members and other caregivers imagine working on these areas within the daily routines of the child?
7. Which behavior is the most easily modified?
8. On which outcome could the child and/or the family be most successful?

I. *SOCIAL INTERACTIONS*

Behavioral Regulation

Requests = vocalization "uh uh," gestures (e.g., pointing to objects and people)

vocalization + gesture (e.g., "da" + reach for cookie, "da" + "drinking" motion for juice)

Protests = vocalization (e.g., "uh" when food taken away, "ah" when refusing cracker), gestures (e.g., pushing away unwanted cracker)

Social Interaction

Calling attention = vocalization (squeals)

Social/Play Routines: peek-a-boo, tickle

Joint Attention

Comments = gesture (showing and giving an object)

vocalization + gesture (e.g., "ah" when pointing to new object)

Request Info = vocalization ("di?" rising intonation when putting block in box)

II. *COMPREHENSION*

Looked at objects mentioned (ball, juice)

Waved "bye-bye" with context cues

Looked for absent sister

Semantic relations observed:

4 agents = Mama, Daddy, doggie, baby

6 objects = ball, juice, cookie, car, cup, boat

FIGURE 12.6

Analysis of communication behaviors for Susan based on the decision tree

III. *PRODUCTION*
   Spontaneous

   Vocalizations   =   when refusing cracker
                         when pointing at object
                         when putting block in box
                         to get attention
                         speechlike string of vowels and consonants
                         vocalization + gesture (see above)

   Observed sound inventory = /m/, /b/, /g/, /d/ with some vowels
   Babbling of consonant-vowel combinations
   Nonspeech sounds = raspberries, play cough, tongue clicks, laugh

   Imitation

   Vocalizations   =   motor acts (clapping, swaying body)
                         oral motor acts (stick out tongue, open mouth)
                         nonspeech sounds ("grr" for tiger, "zz" for bee)
                         speech sounds (bu, mu, da)
                         sounds and motor acts ("zz" with fingers like bee, "grr" while
                         scratching like tiger)

FIGURE 12.6
Continued

9. What goal would be the most motivating for the child and/or the family?

In working closely together, the family and the professionals can identify the types of subgoals that will help the child achieve the broader outcomes and can bring together the expertise of both the family and the professionals.

Illustration of Goal Planning

When professionals and families are planning intervention, there are two alternative approaches. The first is to focus on the child's *needs* compared with children of the same chronological age level. In this method, the interventionist and family primarily examine standardized measures or developmental charts to identify the skills and behaviors that the child does not exhibit. Intervention planning then consists of working on teaching those deficient skills in order to get the child closer to age level.

The other, and preferable, approach to planning is to focus on what the child *can* do and then begin expanding the already available skills. The decision trees are one means to identify what the child can do. In this way the family and the interventionist start at the child's current level and build in a vertical and horizontal fashion from where the child is functioning. This latter method of planning instructional goals will be illustrated for the 20-month-old child, Susan, previously discussed (see "Using the Decision Trees").

To help begin the intervention planning process, the parents, the childcare provider, and the professionals discussed Susan's overall strengths, which included her ability to get some of her needs met by gesturing and vocalizing, her frequent and varied vocalizations, her positive social affect in interactions with adults and her sister, her interest in interacting with the professionals, her willingness to attempt to imitate sounds and motor acts, and her recognition of the names of people and objects around her. The professionals also pointed out her persistence in trying to gain others' attention and

her ability to use different means (e.g., gesture, vocalization) to get something she wanted. The group then discussed their perspectives on Susan's needs. Her parents noted that sometimes she has difficulty letting them know what she wants and they would like to be able to understand her better. They also reported that she is not able to imitate words they say and they felt that this was important to her development. The child-care provider suggested that she would like Susan to be able to play longer with toys and books and would like some suggestions for toys that might hold Susan's interest longer during play activities. In addition, they all discussed wanting to see continued growth in Susan's comprehension skills. The broad outcomes identified by the group are listed in Figure 12.7.

For each outcome identified, the caregivers and the professionals talked about strategies and activities that could help attain the outcome. Concerning Ella and Matt's desire to be able to better understand Susan, several ideas were generated by the group. First, everyone agreed that one way to understand Susan better was to get her to use the sounds and gestures she can already produce more frequently and consistently. Through discussion, the group agreed that everyone would encourage Susan to use more sounds by responding positively to her attempts and by imitating her sounds and gestures. When asked how Susan was progressing in her communication skills, Matt and Ella noted that she was just beginning to use sounds and gestures combined together (an item from the decision tree), and they felt that this improved their ability to understand her. They suggested that everyone also reinforce Susan's use of gestures and sounds together. When asked for ways that have helped Susan learn new things, both parents said she usually tries to imitate their actions. Thus they were encouraged to model the gestures Susan currently uses combined with some of her sounds and to model some new simple gestures that may help her communicate (e.g., shaking her head for "no," taking an adult's hand to indicate a need for help).

Outcome 1. Susan will use sounds and gestures more often and more consistently so that Matt, Ella, and Terry will be able to understand her needs throughout the day.

Strategies/Activities

a. Matt, Ella, and Terry will respond immediately and very positively to Susan whenever she uses any gesture or sound, or gesture-sound combination to communicate her needs.
b. Matt, Ella, and Terry will model some of Susan's familiar gestures and sounds combined together (e.g., "uh uh" while pointing to toy).
c. Matt, Ella, and Terry will model simple gestures for Susan (e.g., shaking head to mean "no").

Outcome 2. Susan will imitate sounds, actions, and words used by Ella, Matt, and Terry during play and social games.

Strategies/Activities

a. Matt, Ella, and Terry will imitate Susan's sounds and actions during play activities.
b. Matt, Ella, and Terry will make sounds to encourage Susan to imitate them, initially making sounds that Susan can already produce (e.g., "uh," "da," "di").
c. Matt, Ella, and Terry will use word approximations alternately when naming people and things in the home (e.g., "ba" and "bottle" for bottle, "di" and "diaper" for diaper).
d. Matt, Ella, and Terry will continue to expand Susan's social routines (e.g., this little piggie, "gotcha," bounce on knee for "horsie") and will use sounds and word approximations (e.g., "pee" and "boo" for peek-a-boo).

Outcome 3. Susan will play longer and interact more with others while playing with toys.

Strategies/Activities

a. Matt and Ella will bring some of Susan's toys and books to Terry's house for Susan.
b. Matt, Ella, and Terry will use simple words and gestures with Susan to encourage her participation in play activities and social games.
c. Matt, Ella, and Terry will encourage Susan to play in new ways with her existing toys.

Outcome 4. Susan will continue to develop her ability to understand words and word combinations.

Strategies/Activities

a. Matt, Ella, and Terry will name common objects and people in Susan's environment and will use repetition to highlight the names ("boat, there's the boat").
b. Matt, Ella, and Terry will play games with common objects such as hiding, putting them into other larger objects and naming the objects when hiding and finding them.
c. Matt, Ella, and Terry will encourage Susan to look at or point to objects named during play activities.
d. Matt, Ella, and Terry will act on and label their actions with objects (hug, kiss, pat doll).

FIGURE 12.7
Possible outcomes and strategies for intervention with Susan

In talking about why they think Susan does not imitate words, Matt and Ella suggested that maybe she did not want to or could not imitate words when asked. Given that she imitates some things, it was suggested that perhaps words were too hard for her at this time and that encouraging the imitation of any actions or sounds might be more useful. All three caregivers were encouraged to use play activities with familiar actions and sounds to encourage her to imitate them. For example, the caregivers can watch for naturally occurring motor acts such as patting, tapping, or nonspeech sounds (e.g., squeals, snorts), playfully and explicitly imitate the action or sound (e.g., tapping, giggling), and encourage Susan to repeat the behavior. In this way they can help Susan learn to take turns with them and to be more consistent in her use of some gestures and sounds. Social routines are perfect for motor and sound imitation; see Platt and Coggins (1990) and Warren and Yoder (1998) for ideas for developing infants' and young children's early social routines. The caregivers can also play sound games by performing an action (e.g., patting the floor, putting a ring on a ring stack, throwing blocks into a bucket) while vocalizing a sound from the child's repertoire. As the child does the motor action combined with vocalizations, the vocalizations can gradually be shaped to new sounds. In addition, the caregivers were encouraged to use both the name and a word approximation for simple objects and people in Susan's environment ("You want the milk," "Here's the mi") and then to encourage her for any attempt she makes to vocalize.

As for helping Susan play more with toys and books, Ella and Matt noted that they would lend some of Susan's favorite books and toys to Terry. The group also discussed ways to encourage Susan's participation by making activities simpler and looking at books that are closer to Susan's developmental level. Examples included simplifying what was said to her to include single words or short phrases (e.g., "boat," "look at the boat"), encouraging her to show or pat the object mentioned, using gestures and eye gaze to help her understand what was said

(e.g., pointing to the picture of the "dog" in the book), and using frequent repetition. In addition, the group thought of a few new ways that Susan could be encouraged to play with some of her toys (e.g., using the rings in her ring stacker for bracelets, to peek through, putting them in something and then getting them out).

The last area discussed was Susan's comprehension and ways to increase her ability to show what she understands as well as for her to learn new things. The group suggested hiding and finding games, labeling and getting her to pat or touch the object, giving her two choices and letting her point to one ("milk or juice"), and acting on objects with different actions and labeling the action ("hug the doll," "kiss the doll," "pat the doll") to help build her action word comprehension. Finally, Ella and Matt indicated an interest in having the speech-language pathologist, Barbara, continue to provide them with suggestions for ways to help her and to help them monitor Susan's progress over time.

To further the application of assessment information to intervention planning, the following section highlights several guidelines for use by professionals and families when developing communication goals and activities for intervention. Although many of the guidelines can be applied to any type of intervention, some are specific to communication abilities. It may be useful for both professionals and family members to read over the guidelines when developing intervention plans.

Intervention Guidelines

Start at the Child's Level Children cannot be expected to achieve skills beyond their cognitive, motor, social, play, or communicative levels, and sometimes it is hard for both professionals and caregivers to remember to focus on the child's current levels, particularly if they are below the child's chronological age. A concrete example of starting at a level that is too high is when the parent, teacher, or professional expects a child to use words when she typically only produces vocalizations (e.g., Susan in the previous example). Although modeling words or structures that are slightly beyond the child's current capabilities can be facilitative, it is also important to meet the child at his or her level of functioning and to provide a bridge to the next higher skill level. An example of bridging for this child would be to (a) model entire words ("boat"); (b) reduce the whole words to a shortened form ("bo" or "o"); (c) encourage and reinforce the child for *any* communication attempts; (d) playfully guide the child to make closer and closer approximations of words; and (e) not expect her to produce words or word approximations until she is able to consistently produce a variety of sounds and sound combinations. In essence, it is important to be aware of the child's overall developmental and communicative skills and balance instructional goals to encompass both the current level of functioning and behaviors at a slightly higher or more complex level.

Move Vertically and Horizontally When planning intervention, consider both vertical and horizontal movement in various skill areas. As the previous example illustrates, if the child is not ready or able to move vertically to the next level (from vocalization to verbalization), the adult can encourage either smaller vertical behaviors (e.g., any consistent vocalization, pairing vocalization with gesture, and then word approximations) or other horizontal skills (e.g., if the child requests objects or actions, caregivers can model protesting and can encourage the use of vocalizing to meet other needs). For practical guides to communication development, the interventionist can turn to the developmental scales listed in Table 12.3, the decision trees (Figures 12.3 through 12.5), Nelson (1998), and Wetherby (1992).

Watch the Child for Cues Readability, the ability of the parent or professional to recognize and respond to the child's behaviors, is an important part of the intervention process (Goldberg, 1977). The better the adult is at "reading" the infant, the more likely the adult's response is to get

or keep an interaction going. In addition, reading cues more accurately can help the family and professionals more accurately establish the child's level of communication functioning. Parents are often good at reading their child's cues, but with some infants (or for some parents) this may not be an easy task. Clearly, interventionists need to orient their own skills to reading infants and also, at times, to helping caregivers develop or expand their abilities. It is also important for all caregivers and interventionists to look for *all* means (e.g., nonverbal and vocalizations) used by the child to communicate and to take the focus off words as the *only* means. Refer to Dunst and Wortman-Lowe (1986), Wetherby and Prizant (1992), and Wilcox (1992) for ideas for recognizing communicative efforts in young children.

Be Functional Use naturalistic settings, materials, and procedures as often as possible. As described in earlier chapters, the acquisition and generalization of newly acquired skills are facilitated when the context for training is closest to the setting in which the behavior actually occurs. With communication skills, for example, the context for teaching a child to request an action should occur at the time when and in the place where the child actually needs someone to perform that action. Language is typically acquired in a context in which the child is motivated to communicate to achieve a desired response from others; therefore, always provide the child with a reason to communicate. In this way, the achievement of the desired response often becomes its own reinforcement. Bricker, Pretti-Frontczak, and McComas (1998), McWilliam (1992) and Nelson (1998) provide excellent guides to the use of naturalistic contexts for intervention.

Follow the Interests of the Child Use developmental and play scales as a guide to toys, materials, and activities that are of interest to children at different developmental levels. As noted previously, the closer the match between a child's cognitive and developmental level and the tasks and materials, the more likely it is that the child will succeed and enjoy the activity. A major tenet of incidental teaching—one that has considerable empirical support in facilitating children's communication (Warren & Kaiser, 1986; Hart & Risley, 1978)—is following a child's interests when selecting communication targets. Sources such as Bricker (2002); and Johnson-Martin, Jens, Attermeier, and Hacker (1991) are useful for guiding decisions about children's interests and developmental skills.

Target Behaviors for Success Target either frequently occurring behaviors that need modification, or desired but nonexisting behaviors that have many opportunities for practice and reinforcement. Clearly, new behaviors that can be used frequently and those that build from the child's existing repertoire are more likely to be acquired. For example, modeling vocalizations to request objects that the child likes and is exposed to frequently is an appropriate target for a child who uses vocalizations to protest but not to make requests. To facilitate success, the modeled vocalizations should at first be ones already used by the child for other purposes and can later be new ones created from the sounds the child produces.

Consider the Content of the Activities Keep in mind the developmental level and functionality of the topics chosen for intervention. Some preschool programs for children with special needs continue to focus on colors or shapes or the days of the week, when more functional skills such as requests for information or how to ask a peer for a toy could be more useful targets. In other words, when planning content for intervention, consider how and when that content could be used by the child. Choose topics that he or she can benefit from frequently in everyday life.

Be Efficient Plan goals that focus on more than one skill area or aspect of an area. For example, plan goals that focus on communication as well as cognitive skills and embed them both in a play activity, or, while focusing on word approxi-

mations and requests for objects, use words with sounds the child has already acquired to increase the likelihood that he or she will be able to produce the approximation.

Use Direct Training at Times Remember that many children with special needs have had difficulty learning some skills in an incidental manner, that is, through naturalistic interactions with people and objects in their environment. Therefore, it may be appropriate to teach some skills more directly. This may be true, for example, of articulation skills (correct production of *s*) or syntactic structures (use of *ed*) for some children. In addition, the use of imitation, particularly for sound, word, word approximation, phrase, or grammatical learning can be extremely productive. As noted previously, imitation is often used for items that the child is in the process of learning (Owens, 2001). Thus, the use of imitation training and later generalization to more natural and spontaneous contexts has empirical support from the language acquisition literature. An efficient strategy could be to target a particular behavior in a concentrated way. For example question asking (e.g., "What's that?") could be targeted first by having a bag with hidden objects. The professional or parent could model "what's that?" before pulling each object out of the bag. Later, new or unusual objects could be placed around the room where the child and an adult could "find" them to prompt the use of "what's that?" in a more natural context.

Be Facilitative To facilitate interaction, use techniques such as modeling desired verbal and nonverbal behaviors, describing your own or a child's actions, expanding communications used by the child, allowing the child time to take a turn, and revising a child's communication attempt in your next utterance. Nonverbal behaviors and vocalizations can be modeled as easily as verbalizations. For example, hold a toy to trade while vocalizing "uh?" and pointing to the desired toy, or model only what you want the child to *say*, such as

"That's mine," while demonstrating a gentle pulling-away gesture with the toy, rather than using, "Say, 'that's mine'." Remember, you are a model of communication for the child, so consider carefully *what* and *how* you communicate. As often as possible, use vocalizations, words, phrases, and sentences that children would be likely to use in their own interactions. Bricker et al. (1998) is an excellent source for a variety of facilitation techniques. For further information on intervention planning, see Kjerland and Kovach (1990), McWilliam (1992), McWilliam, Winton, and Crais (1996), and Norris (1992).

CONCLUSION

In this chapter, standard and nonstandard ways of looking at communication assessment and intervention planning have been presented with a few suggestions for going about these activities. In closing, there are a few final suggestions for the interventionist. First, use continuous reality checking to remember the real world. Keep asking (a) Is this outcome important to the child's develop-

ment? (b) Will it improve communication in a substantial manner? and, finally (c) Why should this outcome be selected for intervention above all others possible? If the answers are "yes," "yes," and a worthwhile "because . . . ," follow through with the outcome. If the answers are "no," "no," and "I'm not sure," rethink the implementation of this outcome.

Second, children will usually try to communicate the best way they know how. Interventionists, families, and other professionals need to be aware of the many and varied means through which children communicate. For children with communication difficulties, families and professionals must discover what the best means of communication are and then help the child expand and develop those communication means. Third, remember that you serve as a model for the child in an interaction, so think carefully about what you want to model and how you will do it. Finally, remember that you are an experienced communicator and therefore you can use your own knowledge of what promotes or hinders communication to guide the assessment and goal planning process.

• • • • • • • •
SUMMARY OF KEY CONCEPTS

- Communication is a social act, the primary function of which is interaction; language is the symbol system used in communication; and means of communication can include verbal, vocal, and nonverbal ways to communicate.

- Interventionists should be familiar with communication concepts and assessment because communication occurs within the context of other developmental domains; all professionals and families interact and intervene with the child through communication; a large number of preschool children have communication needs; children with language disorders often have later academic, emotional, and behavioral

difficulties; and the current focus in intervention is on facilitating communication in natural settings (e.g., classroom and home).

- Components of language include pragmatics, phonology, semantics, and syntax; pragmatics and semantics should receive the most attention in assessment and the greatest emphasis in intervention for many preschool children.

- With the current emphasis on ecologically valid assessment, issues related to sociocultural awareness, family priorities, active participation of caregivers, and collaborative assessment and intervention planning play greater roles than in more traditional assessment approaches.

- Professionals are encouraged to use multiple sources and multiple means for gathering assessment information, including standardized and nonstandardized activities. Recognizing the limitations to many standardized instruments, professionals are encouraged to seek alternative assessment strategies.
- Different areas of assessment are highlighted for children, depending on their existing level of communication (preverbal and verbal); a necessary part of assessment for all children is the observation of the child with his or her communication partners.
- Collection and analysis of communication samples is one of the more in-depth methods of assessing children's communication skills.

- Three separate decision trees were described for guiding assessment efforts and one was illustrated through a case example.
- Information gathered during the assessment of communication skills should be used for planning intervention. Guidelines for intervention are (a) start intervention at the child's level, (b) move vertically and horizontally in planning intervention targets, (c) watch the child for cues, (d) use functional goals and activities, (e) follow the child's interests, (f) target behaviors that will result in success, (g) consider the content of the activities, (h) use efficient strategies, (i) use direct teaching at times, and (j) use techniques that facilitate interaction and communication.

· · · · · · · ·

REFERENCES

American Speech-Language-Hearing Association. (1997). *Guidelines for audiological screening.* Rockville, MD.

American Speech-Language-Hearing Association. (1991). *Report: Augmentative and alternative communication. ASHA, 33* (Suppl. 5), 9–12.

Ammer, J. & Bangs, T. (2000). *Birth to Three Assessment and Intervention System, Second Edition.* Austin, TX: PRO-ED.

Aram, D., & Hall, N. (1989). Longitudinal follow-up of preschool communication disorders: Treatment implications. *School Psychology Review, 18,* 487–501.

Baker, L., & Cantwell, D. (1987). A prospective psychiatric follow-up of children with speech/language disorders. *Journal of the American Academy of Child and Adolescent Psychiatry, 26,* 546–553.

Bankson, N. (1990). *Bankson Language Screening Test–2.* Los Angeles, CA: Western Psychological Services.

Bankson, N., & Bernthal, J. (1990). *Bankson-Bernthal Test of Phonology (BBTOP).* Austin, TX: PRO-ED.

Baranek, G. (1999). Autism during infancy: a retrospective video analysis of sensory-motor and social behaviors at 9–12 months of age. *Journal of Autism & Developmental Disorders. 29*(3), 213–24, 1999.

Bates, E., Bretherton, I., & Snyder, L. (1988). *From first words to grammar: Individual differences and dissociable mechanisms.* New York: Cambridge University Press.

Battle, D. E. (2002). *Communication disorders in multicultural populations* (2nd ed.). Boston, MA: Butterworth Heinemann.

Beitchman, J. H., Hood, J., & Inglis, A. (1990). Psychiatric risk in children with speech and language disorders. *Journal of Abnormal Child Psychology, 18,* 283–296.

Bernthal, J. E., & Bankson, N. W. (1998). *Articulation and phonological disorders* (4th ed.). Boston, MA: Allyn and Bacon.

Beukelman, D., & Mirenda, P. (1998). *Augmentative and alternative communication* (2nd ed.). Baltimore: Paul H. Brookes.

Blank, M., Rose, S., & Berlin, L. (1978). *Preschool Language Assessment Instrument.* San Antonio, TX: Psychological Corp.

Bloch, J. (1987). *Parent/Professional Preschool Performance Profile (5Ps).* Syosset, NY: Variety Pre-Schooler's Workshop.

Bloom, L. (1993). Developments in cognition. In L. Bloom, *The transition from infancy to language: Acquiring the power of expression* (pp. 214–242). New York: Cambridge University Press.

Bloom, L., Rocissano, L., & Hood, L. (1976). Adult-child discourse: Developmental interaction between information processing and linguistic knowledge. *Cognitive Psychology, 8*, 521–552.

Bricker, D. (2002). *Assessment, evaluation and programming system for infants and children* 2nd ed. Baltimore: Paul H. Brookes.

Bricker, D., Pretti-Frontczak, K., & McComas, N. (1998). *An activity-based approach to early intervention* (2nd ed.). Baltimore: Paul H. Brookes.

Bricker, D., & Squires, J. (1989). The effectiveness of parental screening of at-risk infants: The infant monitoring questionnaires. *Topics in Early Childhood Special Education, 9*, 67–85.

Bricker, D., & Squires, J. (1999). *Ages and Stages Questionnaires (ASQ): A Parent-Completed Child-Monitoring System* (2nd ed). Baltimore: Paul H. Brookes.

Bronfenbrenner, U. (1977). Toward and experimental ecology of human development. *American Psychologist, 32*(7), 513–531.

Bronfenbrenner, U., & Morris, P. (1998). The ecology of developmental processes. In W. Damon & R. Lerner (Eds.), *Handbook of child psychology* (5th ed.) (pp. 993–1028). New York: Wiley.

Brownell, R. (2000). *Expressive One-Word Picture Vocabulary Test–2000 Edition*. Los Angeles: Western Psychological Services.

Brownell, R. (2000). *Receptive One-Word Picture Vocabulary Test–2000 Edition*. Los Angeles: Western Psychological Services.

Bruner, J. (1978). The role of dialogue in language acquisition. In A. Sinclair, R. J. Jarvella, & W. J. M. Leveit (Eds.), *The child's conception of language* (pp. 241–256). Berlin: Springer-Verlag.

Bruner, J. (1981). The social context of language acquisition. *Language Communication, 1*, 155–178.

Bzoch, K., & League, R. (1991). *Receptive-Expressive-Emergent Language Test–2*. Los Angeles: Western Psychological Services.

Camarata, S. (1996). A rationale for naturalistic speech intelligibility intervention. In M. Fey, J. Windsor, & S. Warren (Eds.), *Language intervention: Preschool through the elementary years* (pp. 63–84). Baltimore: Paul H. Brookes.

Carrow, E. (1974). *Carrow Elicited Language Inventory*. Chicago: Riverside.

Carrow-Woolfolk, E. (1997). *Test for Auditory Comprehension of Language–3*. Austin, TX: PRO-ED.

Catts, H. (1993). The relation between speech-language impairments and reading disabilities. *Journal of Speech and Hearing Research, 36*, 948–956.

Catts, H. W., Fey, M. E., Zhang, X., & Tomblin, J. B. (2001). Estimating the risk of future reading difficulties in kindergarten children: Research-based model and its clinical implementation. *Language, Speech, and Hearing Services in Schools, 32*, 38–50.

Catts, H. W., & Kamhi, A. G. (Eds.) (1999). *Language and reading disabilities*. Allyn & Bacon, Boston, MA.

Chapman, R. (1978). Comprehension strategies in children. In J. Kavanagh & P. Strange (Eds.), *Language and speech in the laboratory, school, and clinic* (pp. 308–327). Cambridge, MA: MIT Press.

Chapman, R. (1981). Exploring children's communicative intents. In J. F. Miller (Ed.), *Assessing language production in children* (pp. 111–136). Baltimore: University Park Press.

Chapman, R. (1992). Child talk: Assumptions of a development process model for early language learning. In R. Chapman (Eds.), *Processes in language acquisition and disorders* (pp. 3–17). St. Louis: Mosby.

Cheng, L. (1987). *Assessing Asian language performance: Guidelines for evaluating limited-English-proficient students*. Gaithersburg, MD: Aspen Publishers.

Coggins, T. (1998). Clinical assessment of emerging language: How to gather evidence and make informed decisions. In A. Wetherby, S. Warren, & J. Reichle (Eds.), *Transitions in prelinguistic communication* (pp. 233–259). Baltimore: Paul H. Brookes.

Coggins, T. E., Olswang, L. B., & Guthrie, J. (1987). Assessing communicative intents in young children: Low structured or observation tasks? *Journal of Speech and Hearing Disorders, 52*, 44–49.

Cole, K., & Fey, M. (1996). Cognitive referencing in language assessment. In K. Cole, P. Dale, & D. Thal (Eds.), *Assessment of communication and language*. Baltimore: Paul H. Brookes.

Cole, K., Mills, P., Dale, P., & Jenkins, J. (1996). Preschool language facilitation methods and child characteristics. *Journal of Early Intervention, 20*(2), 113–131.

Compton, A. (1978). *Compton Speech and Language Evaluation*. San Francisco, CA: Carousel House.

Compton, A., & Hutton, S. (1978). *Compton-Hutton Phonological Assessment*. San Francisco, CA: Carousel House.

Conti-Ramsden, G. (1990). Maternal recasts and other contingent replies to language-impaired children. *Journal of Speech and Hearing Disorders, 55,* 262–274.

Conti-Ramsden, G. (1993). Using parents to foster communicatively impaired children's language development. *Seminars in Speech and Language, 14,* 289–295.

Craig, H. K., & Washington, J. A. (2002). Oral language expectations for African American preschoolers and kindergartners. *American Journal of Speech-Language Pathology, 11*(1), 59–70.

Crais, E. (1993). Families and professionals as collaborators in assessment. *Topics in Language Disorders, 14*(1), 29–40.

Crais, E. (1995). Expanding the repertoire of tools and techniques for assessing the communication skills of infants and toddlers. *American Journal of Speech-Language Pathology, 4*(3), 47–59.

Crais, E. (1996). Applying family-centered principles to child assessment. In P. McWilliam, P. Winton, & E. Crais (Eds.), *Practical strategies for family-centered early intervention* (pp. 69–96). Baltimore: Paul H. Brookes.

Crais, E. (2001). Identifying communication and related developmental disabilities in young children. In J. Roush (Ed.), *Screening for hearing loss and otitis media in children*. San Diego, CA: Singular.

Crais, E. & Belardi, C. (1999). Family participation in child assessment: Perceptions of families and professionals. *Infant-Toddler Intervention, 9*(3), 209–238.

Crais, E., Day, D., & Cox, C. *The intersection of the development of gestures and intentionality*. Manuscript submitted.

Crais, E., & Roberts, J. (1991). Decision making in assessment and early intervention. *Language, Speech, Hearing Services in Schools, 22*(2), 19–30.

Crais, E., & Wilson, L. (1996). The role of parents in child assessment: Self-evaluation of practicing professionals. *Infant-Toddler Intervention, 6*(2), 125–143.

Dale, P. (1996). Parent report assessment of language and communication. In K. Cole, P. Dale, & D. Thal (Eds.), *Assessment of communication and language* (pp.161–182). Baltimore: Paul H. Brookes.

Dale, P. (1991). The validity of a parent report measure of vocabulary and syntax at 24 months. *Journal of Speech and Hearing Research, 34,* 565–571.

Davis, L., Thurman, K., & Mauro, L. (1995). Meeting the challenges of establishing interdisciplinary preservice preparation for infant personnel. *Infants and Young Children, 8*(2), 65–70

Dore, J. (1974). A pragmatic description of early language development. *Journal of Psycholinguistic Research, 4,* 343–350.

Dunn, L., & Dunn, L. (1997). *Peabody Picture Vocabulary Test–Third Edition*. Circle Pines, MN: American Guidance Service.

Dunst, C., Lowe, L., & Bartholomew, P. (1990). Contingent social responsiveness, family ecology, and infant communicative competence. *National Student Speech, Language, and Hearing Association Journal, 17,* 39–49.

Dunst, C., & Wortman-Lowe, L. (1986). From reflex to symbol: Describing, explaining, and fostering communicative competence. *Augmentative and Alternative Communication, 2,* 11–16.

Edmonston, N., & Thane, N. (1992). Children's use of comprehension strategies in response to relational words: Implications for assessment. *American Journal of Speech-Language Pathology, 1,* 30–35.

Fenson, L., Dale, P., Reznick, S., Thal, D., Bates, E., Hartung, J., Pethick, S., & Reilly, J. (1992). *MacArthur Communication Development Inventories*. San Diego, CA: Singular.

Fluharty, N. (1999). *Fluharty Preschool Speech and Language Screening Test–Second Edition*. Austin, TX: PRO-ED.

Fuchs, D., Fuchs, L., Benowitz, S., & Barringer, K. (1987). Norm-referenced tests: Are they valid for use with handicapped students? *Exceptional Children, 54,* 263–271.

Fuchs, D., Fuchs, L., Power, M., & Dailey, A. (1985). Bias in the assessment of handicapped children. *American Educational Research Journal, 22,* 185–197.

Fudala, J., & Reynolds, W. (1986). *Arizona Articulation Proficiency Scale–Revised*. Los Angeles: Western Psychological Services.

Furuno, S., O'Reilly, K., Inatsuka, T., Hosaka, C., Allman, T., & Zeisloft-Falbey, B. (1987). *Hawaii Early Learning Profile*. Palo Alto, CA: VORT Corp.

Girolametto, L., Verbey, M., & Tannock, R. (1994). Improving joint engagement in parent-child interaction: An intervention study. *Journal of Early Intervention, 18,* 155–167.

Glennen, S., & DeCoste, D. (1997). *Handbook of augmentative and alternative communication.* San Diego, CA: Singular.

Goldberg, S. (1977). Social competence in infancy: A model of parent-infant interaction. *Merrill-Palmer Quarterly, 23,* 163–177.

Goldman, R., & Fristoe, M. (1999). *Goldman-Fristoe Test of Articulation—Second Edition.* Circle Pines, MN: American Guidance Service.

Gutierrez-Clellen, V. (1996). Language diversity: Implications for assessment. In K. N. Cole, P. S. Dale, & D. J. Thal (Eds.), *Assessment of communication and language* (pp. 29–56). Baltimore: Paul H. Brookes.

Hammill, D., & Bryant, B. (1991). *Detroit Tests of Learning Aptitude–Primary:* 2. Austin, TX: PRO-ED.

Hanrahan, L., Ferrier, L., & Jolie, K. (1987, November). *Infants, caregivers and augmentative communication: We must intervene earlier.* Paper presented at the American Speech-Language Hearing Association Annual Convention, New Orleans.

Hart, B., & Risley, T. (1978). Promoting productive language through incidental teaching. *Educational Urban Society, 10,* 407–432.

Hedrick, D., Prather, E., & Tobin, A. (1984). *Sequenced Inventory of Communicative Development–Revised.* Los Angeles: Western Psychological Services.

HELP for Special Preschoolers. Santa Cruz County Office of Education. (1987). Palo Alto, CA: VORT Corp.

Hodson, B. (1986). *Assessment of Phonological Processes–Revised.* Danville, IL: Interstate Printers & Publishers.

Hresko, W., Miguel, S., Sharbenou, R., & Burton, S. (1994). *Developmental Observation Checklist System.* Austin, TX: PRO-ED.

Hresko, W., Reid, D., & Hammill, D. (1999). *Test of Early Language Development–3.* Austin, TX: PRO-ED.

Johnson-Martin, N., Attermeier, S., & Hacker, B. (1990). *Carolina Curriculum for Preschoolers with Special Needs.* Baltimore: Paul H. Brookes.

Johnson, D. J., Beitchman, J. H., Young, A., Escobar, M., Atkinson, L., & Wilson, B. (1999). Fourteen-year follow-up of children with and without speech/language impairments: Speech/language stability and outcomes. *Journal of Speech, Language, and Hearing Research, 42*(3), 744–760.

Johnson-Martin, N., Jens, K., Attermeier, S., & Hacker, B. (1991). *The Carolina Curriculum for Infants and Toddlers with Special Needs–Second edition.* Baltimore: Paul H. Brookes.

Kaufman, A., & Kaufman, P. (1993). *Kaufman Survey of Early Academic and Language Skills.* Circle Pines, MN: American Guidance Service.

Keenan, E., & Schieffelin, B. (1976). Topic as a discourse notion: A study of topic in the conversations of children and adults. In C. Li (Ed.), *Subject and topic* (pp. 337–384). New York: Academic Press.

Kennedy, M., Sheridan, M., Radlinski, S., & Beeghly, M. (1991). Play-language relationships in young children with developmental delays: Implications for assessment. *Journal of Speech and Hearing Research, 34,* 112–122.

Khan, L., & Lewis, N. (2002). *Khan-Lewis phonological analysis,* (2nd ed.). Circle Pines, MN: American Guidance Service.

Kjerland, L., & Kovach, J. (1990). Family-staff collaboration for tailored infant assessment. In E. Gibbs & D. Teti (Eds.), *Interdisciplinary assessment of infants: A guide for early intervention professionals.* Baltimore: Paul H. Brookes.

Konstantareas, M., Zajdeman, H., Homatidis, S., & McCabe, A. (1988). Maternal speech to verbal and high functioning versus nonverbal and lower functioning autistic children. *Journal of Autism and Developmental Disorders, 18,* 647–657.

Larrivee, L., & Catts, H. (1992). Kindergarten speech-language impairment-primary grade reading disability. Paper presented at the American Speech-Language-Hearing Association annual convention. San Antonio, TX.

Lee, L. (1971). *Northwestern Syntax Screening Test.* Evanston, IL: Northwestern University Press.

Linder, T. (1993). *Transdisciplinary Play-Based Assessment–Revised.* Baltimore: Paul H. Brookes.

MacDonald, J. (1989). *Becoming partners with children.* San Antonio, TX: Special Press.

Mahoney, G., & Filer, J. (1996). How responsive is early intervention to the priorities and needs of families? *Topics in Early Childhood Special Education, 16*(4), 437–57.

Martin, F.N., & Clark, J G. (2000). *Introduction to audiology.* Boston: Allyn & Bacon.

McCathren, R., Warren, S., & Yoder, P. (1996). Prelinguistic predictors of later language development. In K. Cole, P. Dale, & D. Thal (Eds.), *Assessment of communication and language* (pp. 57–76). Baltimore: Paul H. Brookes.

McCathren, R., Yoder, P., & Warren, S. (1999). Prelinguistic pragmatic functions as predictors of later expressive vocabulary. *Journal of Early Intervention, 22*(3), 205–216.

McCollum, J., & Yates, T. (1994). Dyad as focus, triad as means: A family-centered approach to supporting parent-child interactions. *Infants and Young Children, 6*(4), 54–63.

McCune (1995). A normative study of representational play at the transition to language. *Developmental Psychology, 31*(2), 198–206.

McLean, L. (1990). Communication development in the first two years of life: A transactional process. *Zero to Three, 11*, 13–19.

McLean, J., & Snyder-McLean, L. (1978). *A transactional approach to early language training.* Upper Saddle River, NJ: Merrill/Prentice Hall.

McLean, M., & McCormick, K. (1993). Assessment and evaluation in early intervention. In W. Brown, S. Thurman, & L. Pearl (Eds.), *Family-centered early intervention with infants and toddlers* (pp. 43–79). Baltimore: Paul H. Brookes.

McWilliam, P. J., Winton, P., & Crais, E. (1996). *Practical strategies for family-centered early intervention.* San Diego, CA: Singular.

McWilliam, R. (1992). *Family-centered intervention planning.* Tucson, AZ: Communication Skill Builders.

McWilliam, R. (2000). It's only natural to have early intervention in the environments where it's needed. In S. Sandall & M. Ostrosky (Eds.), *Young exceptional children monograph series no. 2: Natural environments and inclusion* (pp. 17–26). Denver, CO: The Division of Early Childhood of the Council for Exceptional Children.

Miller, J. (1981). *Assessing language production in children: Experimental procedures.* Baltimore: University Park Press.

Miller, J., Freiberg, C., Rolland, M., & Reeves, M. (1992). Implementing computerized language sample analysis in the public school. *Topics in Language Disorders, 12*(2), 69–82.

Miller, J., & Paul, R. (1995). *The clinical assessment of language comprehension.* Baltimore: Paul H. Brookes.

Morris, S. (1982). *Pre-speech Assessment Scale.* Clifton, NJ: Preston.

Mullen, E. (1995). *Mullen Scales of Early Learning.* Circle Pines, MN: American Guidance Service.

Mundy, P., Kasari, C., Sigman, M., & Ruskin, E. (1995). Nonverbal communication and language acquisition in children with Down syndrome and normally developing children. *Journal of Speech and Hearing Research, 38*, 157–167.

Mundy, P., Sigman, M., & Kasari, C. (1990). A longitudinal study of joint attention and language development in autistic children. *Journal of Autism and Developmental Disorders, 20*(1), 115–128.

National Institute on Disability and Rehabilitation Research. *Consensus statement on augmentative and alternative communication Intervention.* (1992). Washington, DC: Author.

Neisworth, J., & Bagnato, S. (1992). The case against intelligence testing in early intervention. *Topics in Early Childhood Special Education, 12*(1), 1–20.

Nelson, N. (1998). *Childhood language disorders in context,* (2nd ed.). Boston, MA: Allyn & Bacon.

Newborg, J., Stock, J. R., Wnek, L., Guidubaldi, J., & Svinicki, J. (1984). *The Battelle Developmental Inventory.* Allen, TX: DLM/Teaching Resources.

Newcomer, P., & Hammill, D. (1997). *Test of Language Development–Primary–3.* Austin, TX: PRO-ED.

Newman, S. B., & Dickinson, D. K. (Eds.) (2001). *Handbook of early literacy research* (pp. 232–241). NY: Guilford Press.

Noonan, M. & McCormick, L., (1993). *Early intervention in natural environments: Methods and procedures.* Pacific Grove, CA: Brooks/Cole.

Norris, J. (1992). Assessment of infants and toddlers in naturalistic contexts. *Best Practices in School Speech-Language Pathology, 2*, 21–31.

Northern, J., & Downs, M. (2002). *Hearing in children* (4th ed.). Philadelphia: Lippincott, Williams, & Wilkins.

Notari-Syverson & Losardo, A. (1996). Assessing children's language in meaningful contexts. In K. Cole, P. Dale, & D. Thal (Eds.), *Assessment of Communication and Language* (pp. 257–279). Baltimore: Paul H. Brookes.

Olswang, L., Stoel-Gammon, C., Coggins, T., & Carpenter, R. (1987). *Assessing Prelinguistic and Linguistic Behaviors.* Seattle, WA: University of Washington Press.

Osterling, J., & Dawson, G. (1994). Early recognition of children with autism: A study of first birthday home videotapes. *Journal of Autism and Developmental Disorders, 24*, 247–257.

Owens, R. (1999). *Language disorders: A functional approach to assessment and intervention* (3rd ed.). Needham Heights, MA: Allyn & Bacon.

Owens, R. (2001). *Language development: An introduction.* Upper Saddle River, NJ: Merrill/Prentice Hall.

Paul, R. (2001). *Language disorders from infancy through adolescence* (2nd ed.). St Louis, MO: Mosby.

Plapinger, D., & Kretschmer, R. (1991). The effect of context on the interactions between a normally-hearing mother and her hearing-impaired child. *Volta Review,* February/March, 75–87.

Platt, J., & Coggins, T. (1990). Comprehension of social-action games in prelinguistic children: Levels of participation and effect of adult structure. *Journal of Speech and Hearing Disorders, 55,* 315–326.

Prinz, P., & Weiner, F. (1987). *Pragmatics Screening Test.* Upper Saddle River, NJ: Merrill/Prentice Hall.

Prizant, B., & Meyer, E. (1993). Socioemotional aspects of language and social-communication disorders in young children and their families. *American Journal of Speech-Language Pathology, 2*(3), 56–71.

Prizant, B., & Wetherby, A. (1993). Communication and language assessment for young children. *Infants and Young Children, 5*(4), 20–34.

Records, N.L., Tomblin, J.B., & Freese, P.R. (1992). Quality of life in adults with histories of specific language impairment. *American Journal of Speech-Language Pathology, 1,* 44–53.

Reynell, J., & Gruber, C. (1990). *Reynell Developmental Language Scales–American Edition.* Los Angeles: Western Psychological Corporation.

Reynell, J., & Gruber, C. (1969). *Reynell Developmental Language Scales.* Los Angeles: Western Psychological Services.

Roberts, J. E., Wallace, I. F., & Henderson, F. (Eds.) (1997). *Otitis media in young children: Medical, developmental and educational considerations.* Baltimore: Paul H. Brookes.

Roberts, R., Akers, A., & Behl, D. (1996). Family-level service coordination within home visiting programs. *Topics in Early Childhood Special Education, 16*(3), 279–301.

Rossetti, L. (1990). *Infant-Toddler Language Scale.* East Moline, IL: LinguiSystems.

Roth, F., & Spekman, N. (1984). Assessing the pragmatic abilities of children: Part I. Organizational framework and assessment parameters. *Journal of Speech and Hearing Disorders, 49,* 2–11.

Ruben, R. J., Haggard, M. P., Bagger-Sjoback, D., Gravel, J. S., Morizono, T., Paparella, M. M., et al. (1998). Complications and sequelae. In D. J. Lim, C. D. Bluestone, & M. L. Casselbrant (Eds.), Recent advances in otitis media: Report of the sixth research conference. *Annals of Otology, Rhinology, and Laryngology.* Suppl. 174; *107*(10), Pt. 2, pp. 81–94.

Schieffelin, B., & Gilmore, P. (1986). *The acquisition of literacy: Ethnographic perspectives.* Norwood, NJ: Ablex.

Schwartz, I., & Olswang, L. (1996). Evaluating child behavior change in natural settings: Exploring alternative strategies for data collection. *Topics in Early Childhood Special Education, 16*(1), 82–101.

Shulman, B. (1986). *Test of Pragmatic Skills–Revised.* Tucson, AZ: Communication Skill Builders.

Siegel-Causey, E., Ernst, B., & Guess, D. (1987). Elements of nonsymbolic communication and early interactional processes. In M. Bollis (Ed.), *Communication development in young children with deafness/blindness: Literature review III* (pp. 57–102). Monmouth, OR: Oregon State System of Higher Education.

Sigman, M., & Kasari, C. (1995). Joint attention across contexts in normal and autistic children. In C. Moore & P. J. Dunham (Eds.), *Joint attention: Its origin and role in development* (pp. 189–203). Hillsdale, NJ: Lawrence Erlbaum.

Snow, C. E., Barnes, W. S., Chandler, J., Goodman, I. F., & Hemphill, L. (1991). *Unfulfilled expectations: Home and school influences on literacy.* Cambridge, MA: Harvard University Press.

Sorsby, A., & Martlew, M. (1991). Representational demands in mothers' talk to preschool children in two contexts: Picture book reading and a modeling task. *Journal of Child Language, 18,* 373–396.

Stayton, V., & Bruder, M. (1999). Early intervention personnel preparation for the new millennium: Early childhood special education. *Infants and Young Children, 12*(1), 59–69.

Stool, S. E., Berg, A. O., Berman, S., Carney, C. J., Cooley, J. R., Culpepper, et al. (1994). *Otitis media with effusion in young children. Clinical Practice Guideline,* Number 12. AHCPR Publication No. 94-0622. Rockville, MD: Agency for Health Care Policy and Research, Public Health Service, U.S. Department of Health and Human Services.

Sulzby, E. (1989). Assessment of writing and of children's language while writing. In L. Morrow & J. Smith (Eds.), *The role of assessment and measurement in early literacy instruction* (pp. 83–109). Upper Saddle River, NJ: Prentice Hall.

Teale, W., & Sulzby, E. (1986). Emergent literacy as a perspective for examining how young children become readers and writers. In W. H. Teale & E. Sulzby (Eds.), *Emergent literacy: Writing and reading* (pp. vii–xxv). Norwood, NJ: Ablex.

Thal, D., & Katich, J. (1996). Predicaments in early identification of specific language impairment. In K. Cole, P. Dale, & D. Thal (Eds.), *Assessment of communication and language* (pp. 1–28). Baltimore, MD: Paul H. Brookes.

Thal, D., Tobias, S., & Morrison, D. (1991). Language and gesture in late talkers: A 1-year follow-up. *Journal of Speech and Hearing Research, 34,* 604–612.

Tomblin, B., Records, N., Bukwalter, P., Zhang, X., Smith, E. & O'Brien, M. (1997). Prevalence of specific language impairment in kindergarten children. *Journal of Speech, Language, and Hearing Research, 40,* 1245–1260.

U.S. Department of Education. (2000). *Twenty-second annual report to Congress on the implementation of the Individuals with Disabilities Education Act. http://www.ed.gov/offices/OSERS/OSEP*

Warren, S., & Kaiser, A. (1986). Incidental language teaching: A critical review. *Journal of Speech and Hearing Disorders, 51*(4), 291–299.

Warren, S., & Yoder, P. (1998). Facilitating the transition from preintentional to intentional communication. In A. Wetherby, S. Warren, & J. Reichle (Eds.), *Transitions in prelinguistic communication* (pp. 365–384). Baltimore: Paul H. Brookes.

Westby, C. (1988). Children's play: Reflections of social competence. *Seminars in Speech and Language, 9,* 1–14.

Westby, C. (1990). Ethnographic interviewing: Asking the right questions to the right people in the right ways. *Journal of Childhood Communication Disorders, 13*(1), 101–111.

Wetherby, A. (1992). *Communication and language intervention for preschool children.* Manual for inservice workshop. Buffalo, NY: Educom Associates.

Wetherby A., & Prizant B. (1989). The expression of communication intent: Assessment guidelines. *Seminars in Speech and Language, 10,* 77–91.

Wetherby, A., & Prizant, B. (1992). Profiling young children's communicative competence. In S. Warren & J. Reichle (Eds.), *Causes and effects in communica-*

tion and language intervention (pp. 217–253). Baltimore: Paul H. Brookes.

Wetherby A., & Prizant, B. (1993). *Communication and Symbolic Behavior Scales.* Baltimore: Paul H. Brookes.

Wetherby, A., & Prizant B. (2001). *Communication and Symbolic Behavior Scales Developmental Profile.* Baltimore: Paul H. Brookes.

Whitehead, A., Jesien, & G., Ulanski, B. (1998). Weaving parents into the fabric of early intervention interagency training: How to integrate and sustain family involvement in training. *Infants and Young Children, 10*(3), 44–53.

Whitehurst, G. J., & Lonigan, C. J. (1998). Child development and emergent literacy. *Child Development, 69*(3), 848–872.

Wiig, E., Secord, W., & Semel, E. (1992). *Clinical Evaluation of Language Fundamentals–Preschool.* San Antonio, TX: Psychological Corp.

Wilcox, M. J. (1992). Enhancing initial communication skills in young children with developmental disabilities through partner programming. *Seminars in Speech and Language, 13,* 194–212.

Wilcox, M. J., & Shannon, M. (1998). Facilitating the transition from prelinguistic to linguistic communication. In A. Wetherby, S. Warren, & J. Reichle (Eds.), *Transitions in prelinguistic communication* (pp. 385–416). Baltimore: Paul H. Brookes.

Yoder, P., & Munson, L. (1995). The social correlates of coordinated attention to adult and objects in mother-infant interaction. *First Language, 15,* 219–230.

Yoder, P., Warren, & S., Hull, L. (1995). Predicting children's responses to prelinguistic communication intervention. *Journal of Early Intervention, 19,* 74–84.

Yoder, P., Warren, S., McCathren, R., & Leew, S. (1998). Does adult responsivity to child behavior facilitate communication development? In A. Wetherby, S. Warren, J. Reichle (Eds.), *Transitions in prelinguistic communication.* Baltimore: Paul H. Brookes.

Zimmerman, I., Steiner, V., & Pond, R. (1997). *Preschool Language Scale–3.* San Antonio, TX: Psychological Corp.

Zirpoli, T., & Bell, R. (1987). Unresponsiveness in children with severe disabilities: Potential effects on parent-child interactions. *The Exceptional Child, 34,* 31–40.

Assessing Social Competence

Samuel L. Odom
Indiana University
Hannah Schertz
Indiana University

Leslie J. Munson
Portland State University
William H. Brown
University of South Carolina

SCENE 1: *Anna was so pleased to bring her baby home. Nicole was born 12 weeks early and had had a hard time in the hospital. Nicole's fragile medical condition and Anna's own illness had prevented her from providing very much care. When Nicole first came home, she slept most of the time. Now she is 6 months old, and both she and Anna are having much difficulty. When Nicole cries, Anna attempts to soothe her by holding her, singing to her, and rocking her, but nothing seems to work. Medical routines and feeding take so much time that Anna has little time to play with the baby. When they do play, Nicole is sometimes unresponsive and often turns her gaze away. Even attempts to play peek-a-boo often end in tears for both of them (Odom & Munson, 1996).*

SCENE 2: *Kwesi was a 5-year-old child with Down syndrome. He began attending the Wesley Child Care Center in the fall of the year. In his class, there are 18 four-year-old children, with Kwesi having the only identifiable disability. Kwesi had a clear interest in his classmates. He would approach them and attempt to play, communicate with them using the few words in his limited expressive vocabulary, and smile at them when they played with him or held his hand when walking in line. However, when he tried to play with others, he did not seem to know what to do. For example, one day on a field trip to the park Kwesi was standing next Tommy, a boy in his class. Kwesi pulled some grass from the turf and sprinkled it over Tommy's head while smiling at him. The classmate said "Stop Kwesi." Kwesi got more grass and repeated his actions with Tommy again saying stop and then moving away. Kwesi was not malicious or aggressive, but his limited communication and social skills prevented him from being an attractive playmate for his peers and eventually lead to social rejection in the classroom (Odom, Zercher, Li, Marquart, Sandall, & Wolfberg, 2001).*

For infants and young children with disabilities, becoming an active and successful member of their social world is a major developmental achievement. Social competence in later childhood and on into adulthood is based on the skills learned through early interactions with caregivers and peers. However, for some infants and young children with disabilities, the developmental path-

way to social competence is neither direct nor clear of obstacles. For Nicole, in the scenario above, the predictable behaviors that signal when she is ready for playful social experiences are not clear, which leads to frustration for her and her mother. For Kwesi, the basic understanding of how to start a fun, playful, and mutually rewarding interaction with classmates was missing, which led to the peers avoiding and rejecting him. For both of these children, a breakdown in the social development process existed.

Infants and young children with disabilities often experience difficulty in interacting with others in a competent manner. Such interactions are the building blocks of social relationships with caregivers and peers and are necessary for social integration into typical group care and classroom settings. Across an extensive program of research, Guralnick (1999) has found that children with disabilities are often not well integrated in inclusive preschool settings. In their study of preschool children with disabilities in inclusive settings, Odom, Zercher, Li, Marquart, and Sandall (2002) found that about one third of the children in their sample were socially rejected by their peer group, although an equal number were socially accepted. This led the authors to propose that children having disabilities were at risk for social rejection and should be closely monitored. Given that social integration, social acceptance, and the development of friendships is a goal of inclusive programs (Guralnick, 2001; Odom, 2000) and the development of positive infant-parent and/or caregiver interactions is a goal of early intervention programs (Bromwich, 1997), then intervention to enhance social competence is important for many children. Systematic assessment of infants' and young children's competence in social interactions with caregivers and peers is an important first step in this process.

The purpose of this chapter is to describe assessment strategies and instruments that yield useful information about the social competence of infants and young children with disabilities. We will begin by describing the characteristics of social interaction and how it changes over the infant and preschool years. Information that assessments provide about the different dimensions of social competence as well as procedural considerations in conducting social assessments will be examined. A review of methods for assessing social performance appears as the central part of this chapter. We will conclude with a discussion of ways in which assessment information may be used in early intervention and early childhood special education programs.

A SKETCH OF EARLY SOCIAL DEVELOPMENT

During the early childhood years, interactions with caregivers and peers are two major influences on infants' and children's social development. These influences contribute to the acquisition of social skills and the development of social relationships. A brief description of caregiver-infant and peer-related social development appears in Table 13.1.

Parent-Infant Relationships

Social development begins with patterns of positive interaction that develop between infants and caregivers. These interactions are reciprocal and dynamic as the behavior of each member of the dyad influences the other (Bell, 1968; Lewis & Lee-Painter, 1974; Rothbart, 1996; Rochat, 2001; Zeanah & Zeanah, 2001). Early patterns of interaction develop into an *attachment* relationship during the last half of the first year. This relationship establishes a natural bond that assures survival, allows the infant the security to explore the environment, provides stimulation for learning, and supports the regulation of emotion (Ainsworth, Blehar, Waters, & Walls, 1978; Schore, 2000; Thompson, R. A., 2001). Early dyadic interaction patterns evolve into more sophisticated and interesting triadic patterns towards the end of the infant's first year with the development of joint attention—the mutual focus with a caregiver

around an object or event of common interest (Bates, 1976). In mutually supportive dyadic relationships, parent-infant interactions are characterized by positive affect, active participation, facilitative positioning (Clarke-Stewart, 1973; O'Connor, Sigman, & Kasari, 1992), verbal exchanges (Olson, Bates, & Bayles, 1984), responsivity (Bakeman & Brown, 1980; Kelly & Barnard, 2000), sensitivity (Barrera, Rosenbaum, & Cunningham, 1986; Hane, Feldstein, Morrison, & Loo, 1999), reciprocity (Rothbart, 1996; Osofsky & Thompson, 2000), and predictability (Goldberg, 1977).

Peer Relationships

Becoming an accepted member of a peer group and developing friendships are social developmental milestones for preschool and kindergarten children. Such relationships are built on a history of peer interaction. Although there is evidence of peer interaction and peer preference during the infant and toddler years (Brownell & Hazen, 1999), peer interactions increases in frequency or complexity during the preschool years (Rubin, Bukowski, & Parker, 1998). By 3 years of age, children begin to show a preference for playing with peers in a coordinated and cooperative way (Howes, 1992). By the time they are 5 years of age, most children are sophisticated social interactors. They know many social rules for interacting with a partner, although they may not be able to articulate them, and they can carry on sustained and reciprocal social interactions with their peers. The hallmark of this developmental period is social acceptance by peer groups and at least a small number of reciprocal friendships (Johnson, Ironsmith, Snow, & Poteat, 2000).

Social Development of Infants and Young Children with Disabilities

Some infants and preschool children with disabilities deviate from a typical development path. Infant/caregiver interaction may fail to develop as

TABLE 13.1
Development of Social Interaction in Infants and Young Children

Age	Social Development
Birth to 2 months	Infant shows a predisposition toward social behavior (attends selectively to faces, exhibits endogenous smiles, discriminates between self and others, attends to social play). State regulation is established.
2 months	Smiles in response to stimuli. Crying becomes more instrumental. Discerns perceptual cues from faces. Exhibits rudimentary imitation abilities (e.g., facial movements). Monitors and reciprocates with social partners.
3 months	Turns head to follow gaze. Discriminates between a normal adult gaze and a "still face." Expects people and objects to behave in different ways. Responds differentially to varying intensities of facial expression. Develops social smile.
6 months	Shows more interest in objects, less in people. Visual orienting begins. Focuses with a partner on an object of common interest (preliminary joint attention). Enjoys parent-initiated social play.
9 months	Uses adults for social reference, taking cues from their behavior. Actively imitates. Gestures to direct others' attention to objects (shows initiative in social relationship and uses the relationship as means to desired ends). Participates in social games with partner.
9–15 months	Joint attention skills are reliable and precise. Imitation skills are firmly established. Establishes and maintains proximity to caregiver via locomotion. Stranger anxiety appears.
15–24 months	Increasing language skills allow parent/infant interactions to become increasingly verbal and more sophisticated. Increasing cognitive skills allow child to represent attachment figures in their absence.
24–36 months	Interest in peers increases. Sociodramatic play skills become more refined, allowing inclusion of peers in symbolic play. Parent/child interactions maintained.
36–48 months	Children become frequent social interactors with peer group. Elaboration of sociodramatic play skills continues. Child moves to attachment relationship involving mutual understanding between child and attachment figure about his or her absence.
48–60 months	Children typically are competent social interactors with peers. They are learning to play positively with peers and negotiate conflicts and are beginning to learn responses to aggression.

expected. Preschoolers with disabilities may not engage in the types of social behavior, play, and communication that would lead to successful interaction with peers and acceptance within a peer group.

Parent-Infant Relationships Failure of either the infant or the caregiver to fully participate in early critical interactive interchanges may result in

less participation by the other member of the dyad. Infants show individual differences in the contribution they bring to the relationship based on factors related to temperament, medical status, or disability. Temperament characteristics include reactivity (positive or distress reactions) and self-regulation (Rothbart, 1996). The parent-infant relationship can also be disrupted by factors parents bring to the relationship such as a history of poor attachment during their own growing-up period, depression, inexperience, stress, substance abuse, family violence, or teenage parenthood (Barnard, 2000; Osofsky & Thompson, 2000; Shonkoff & Phillips, 2000). As the number of risk factors accrues, the infant's vulnerability for impaired social and emotional development increases (Zeanah & Zeanah, 2001). Fortuitously, infant resilience and environmental protective factors mediate the degree to which children's development is affected by risk factors (Osofsky & Thomson, 2000; Werner, 2000).

For some infants with disabilities, impairments or delays in development can compromise the quality of infant-caregiver interactions. Infant signals such as gazing, smiling, and reaching indicate to the caregiver that the infant is ready to interact. These signals engender feelings of excitement and affection in caregivers and encourage them to respond in kind, thus strengthening the attachment bond. When these infant abilities are diminished, delayed, or manifest in unusual ways, they are difficult for the adult to interpret, leaving both the adult and the infant without the benefit of satisfying patterns of reciprocal interaction.

For example, infants with autism are restricted in their ability to learn from natural experiences that usually evolve out of early language and social interaction. Autism is a significant threat to the development of an effective parent-infant social relationship because, the disorder may begin taking its toll in the early months (Schertz & Odom, 2002; Trapagnier, 1996). The social gaze, one important early contributor to the parent-infant relationship, may be disrupted in infants by autism or visual impairment (Trapagnier, 1996). Infants who are deaf may also be less active in their interactions with caregivers (Wedell-Monig & Lumley, 1980). Similarly, an infant who has a motor delay may provide signals that are unclear (Yoder, 1987). Infants with Down syndrome were found to smile later and less intensively, and to produce fewer vocal responses (Rothbart, 1996).

Infants with developmental delay tend to give cues less frequently and less clearly than do infants who are developing in a more typical pattern. Similarly, the muted smiles that infants who are blind develop and the absence of eye contact often prove distressful for their parents (Fraiberg, 1975). Mothers of children with delays tend to respond more directively and intrusively to their infants, and this may be a responsive adaptation to their infants' needs (Kelly & Barnard, 2000). These parents seem to work harder to make up for what the infant fails to bring to the relationship. For example, mothers of premature infants gaze at their babies for longer periods than do mothers of full-term infants (Field, 1983). While many infants with disabilities develop attachment relationships, a significant number are left with ambivalent or insecure attachments (Spieker, 1986). In one study of infants with developmental delay and their mothers, 55% of the dyads did not achieve a successful attachment relationship before the 15th month (Lee & Kahn, 2000).

The development of attachment does not follow a wholly deterministic pattern. Positive environmental influences can help to offset early negative experiences and inborn factors related to temperament or disability. For example, Pelaez-Nogueras, Field, Hossain, & Pickens (1996) found that depressed mothers who were trained to provide touch stimulation increased their infants' positive affect. Similarly, a relationship between touch and emotional attachment for preterm infants was demonstrated (Blackwell, 2000). Community social supports, temperamental resiliency, and bolstered family supports can buffer the negative impact for children deprived of an attachment bond in infancy (Thompson, 2001). The goal for interventionists is to support the development of protective factors such as these to offset potential harm from risk factors and disability.

Peer Relationships The social interactions of preschool-age children with disabilities differ in both quantity and quality from those of their more typically developing agemates. Research has repeatedly documented that preschoolers with disabilities interact with others less often than their nondisabled peers (Guralnick & Groom, 1987; Kopp, Baker, & Brown, 1992). In their study of integrated play groups, Guralnick and Groom (1988) found that the success in social interaction experienced by children with mild disabilities actually *decreased* across the time spent in the play group. This decrease suggests that as the group became more familiar with its members, deficits in social skills led to impaired interaction outcomes for the children with disabilities. To examine the social competence of preschool children with and without disabilities, McConnell and Odom (1999) used a multimethod approach to assess peer-related social competence. They found that the social performance of preschool children with disabilities was significantly lower on a central social competence factor than that of typically developing preschoolers. Researchers have noted both the unique competence (Salisbury, Britzman, & Kang, 1989; Wolfberg et al., 1999) and concerns related to social interaction for preschool children with a range of disabilities (Erwin, 1993; Roberts, Brown, & Rickards, 1995).

The development of peer relationships is undoubtedly based on participation in social interaction, as well as on other factors (e.g., appearance or attractiveness, reputation). In their study of social acceptance and rejection of children with disabilities in inclusive preschools, mentioned previously, Odom et al. (2002) used standard, multimeasure criteria to identify children who were socially accepted and rejected by typically developing peers. They found a number of behavior characteristics associated with acceptance and rejection. Across groups of children, it appeared that communication skills, social skills, and play skills differentiated the two groups. That is, children who were accepted tended to be competent, while children who were rejected had difficulties in these areas.

A *Note on Friendships* The development of friendships relates closely to the acquisition of social skills and social acceptance. Odom et al.

(2002) found that socially accepted children with disabilities tended to play more with friends, while this occurred less often for socially rejected children. It may be that friendship could serve as a mediating influence on the acquisition of social skills. Children with disabilities who have friends gain more opportunities for acquiring effective social skills. Conversely, when friendships do not develop, this valuable mediating influence may be missing. For teachers, parents, and service providers, the important implication is that when preschool-aged children do not play with other children and/or do not have friendships, this may serve as a red flag for future problems.

DIMENSIONS OF SOCIAL INTERACTION ASSESSMENT

Assessments of children's social interaction skills reflect different levels of analysis. Like viewing a mountainside through a telescope and adjusting the focus to get a clear picture of the landscape's details, one can adjust the focus of an assessment to provide different views of a child's social development. Assessments can provide information at the most detailed, microscopic level (e.g., individual social behavior), at a microscopic but dynamic level (e.g., social interactions), or at a more macroscopic level (e.g., relationship/social status) (Hundert, 1995). The assessor's choice of assessment will be determined by the purposes for which the information will be used. For example, a microscopic assessment approach might be used for planning or monitoring the immediate effects of intervention programs. More macroscopic approaches might be used for diagnostic or program evaluation purposes (Thompson, Symons, & Felce, 2000).

Individual Social Behaviors

When professionals assess the individual social behaviors of infants and children, they focus on several aspects of social behavior. Often, they count the *frequency* at which a social behavior occurs within a given time frame. Usually some judgment of a social behavior's *affective quality* (e.g., positive or negative) is made. Many assessments also indicate whether the child initiated an interaction or responded to the social behavior of another (Strain & Timm, 1974). Global (e.g., socially directed behavior) or specific (e.g., share/trade, leads peer) categories may be used. In their review of research from the 1980s, Odom and Ogawa (1992) found that over 240 behavioral categories of social behavior had been used by different researchers.

Interactional Level

Interaction refers to the dynamic interchanges among partners in a social interaction. At the interactional level, the concept of *social reciprocity* becomes significant. Social reciprocity has been defined in two ways. First, Strain and Shores (1977) referred to reciprocity as the immediate response of one child to the social behavior of another. In analyzing social behavior at this level, the *sequence* or *order* of behaviors in an interaction is most important. Social interaction may be viewed as a chain of social behavior directed back and forth between social partners. Social behaviors that produce a response from a peer (or adult) are reciprocal interactions. In their investigation of peer-related social behaviors, Tremblay, Strain, Hendrickson, and Shores (1981) identified social behaviors that were most likely to result in a positive response from a peer. Similarly, Bakeman and Brown (1977) examined conditional probabilities of mothers and infants responding to each other given a certain set of conditions.

A second type of reciprocity is assessed at a less microscopic level. Reciprocity defined in this way refers to the direction and frequency of social interactions with potentially available partners. Preschool-age children who direct positive social behaviors to peers receive positive social behavior from peers in return (Hartup, Glazer, & Charlesworth, 1967; Kohler & Fowler, 1985). To assess this type of reciprocity at the preschool

level, the assessor looks at the number of social behaviors that a child directs to his peers and the number directed to him from his peers. For example, Guralnick, Gottman, and Hammond (1996) defined a reciprocal friendship as one in which 33% of two children's social behavior was directed toward the other child. For infants and caregivers, Jaffe, Beebe, Felstein, Crown, and Jasnow (2001) documented coordinated vocalizations occurring at 4 months of age and showed that this reciprocal relationship was associated with attachment at 12 months.

The last dimension of the assessment of social behavior at the interaction level is *duration*. Like reciprocity, duration has also been interpreted in two slightly different ways. First, it may refer to the length of time an interaction continues. To measure duration in this way, a teacher might start a stopwatch when an interaction begins and stop it when the interaction ends. For example, Brown, Ragland, and Fox (1988) measured the number of seconds that children were engaged in interactions. Second, duration may also refer to the number of behaviors in a social interaction chain. For example, if a mother begins a social game with her infant, the infant responds, the mother makes another verbalization to the infant, and the infant responds again, a four-unit chain of interaction has occurred. To measure duration in this way, an assessor would record and then count the number of behaviors in each interaction. In their studies of peer interaction, Odom and Strain (1986) and Rubenstein and Howes (1979) assessed the duration of the interactions using this method.

Social Relationships

Assessment of the social relationships of infants and young children with disabilities occurs at a macroscopic level and measures the success with which children achieve the benchmark social developmental tasks of attachment and social acceptance within a peer group. As noted earlier, *attachment* refers to the relationship that develops between infants and their caregivers. The purpose of behaviors related to attachment (e.g., smiling, crying, locomotion to mother, talking to mother) is to ensure that the child stays in close proximity to the attachment figure, especially at times when the child feels insecure (Bowlby, 1969; Ainsworth et al., 1978). Assessment of attachment usually occurs through a laboratory procedure called the *Strange Situation*. In this assessment, the infant is exposed to various conditions in which the mother leaves him or her alone in a room and then returns to the room (Ainsworth & Bell, 1970). The critical indicator of the attachment relationship is the infant's behavior when mother and child are reunited. Research using the Strange Situation has revealed that different types of attachment relationships exist (e.g., secure, insecure, ambivalent) and are associated with interactions that occur between infants and mothers in naturalistic settings (Vondra & Barnett, 1999).

At the preschool level, social relationships with peers are most often measured by the use of a sociometric assessment. These assessments reveal the popularity of the child as well as the level of acceptance that the child has achieved in the peer group. Moreover, peer acceptance as measured by sociometrics has fairly substantial predictive validity (McConnell & Odom, 1986). A range of sociometric assessments, which are described in a later section, have been used with preschool-age children, and some evidence of reliability exists.

Social Competence versus Social Skill

Professionals have used the term *social competence* in many ways (Anderson & Messick, 1974; Zigler & Trickett, 1978; Shure, 1993). In this chapter, we follow the lead of Wright (1980) and Guralnick (1992a; 2001), who identified social competence as the use of social skills in ways that are appropriate for a specific context and effective in accomplishing social tasks (e.g., gain adult attention, enter play groups of peers). While their approach is compatible with the defining dimensions of appropriateness and effectiveness, McConnell and Odom (1999) also incorporated

McFall's (1982) concept of "performance" as a measure of competence. Performance is defined by social behaviors that are judged appropriate by significant social agents (e.g., teachers, parents) in the social environment (Odom & McConnell, 1985). Social competence is a summary dimension of social interaction skills, in that it incorporates information provided by multiple informants and collected through multiple methods.

PROCEDURAL CONSIDERATIONS IN ASSESSING SOCIAL INTERACTION

Assessment of children's social competence differs from assessment in most other developmental areas. The type of standardized assessment useful for measurement of cognitive or language development (e.g., individual administration of assessment, standard presentation of items) is neither available nor appropriate for assessing social interaction skills. Rather, these skills are usually observed in natural contexts and recorded by an observer or reported by a parent or teacher. The characteristics of the natural setting in which assessors observe infants and young children will affect the information obtained.

Setting of the Social Interaction

It is important to conduct observations in children's natural settings, where they are most comfortable and where the most typical patterns of behavior can be observed (Lynch, 1996). For infants, the natural setting is usually the home; however, for those receiving child care, observation in classroom settings can also provide important information.

When assessing infant and caregiver dyads, the "natural setting" can become unnatural with the intrusion of an unfamiliar observer, resulting in less valid measures of social interaction than would have occurred in the absence of the observer.

Therefore, it is important to allow adequate time for observers to establish rapport and for both members of the dyad to become accustomed to the presence of the observer.

Assessment of infant social development is an ongoing process and is conducted in the context of the relationship with the primary caregiver. Observing naturally occurring activities such as feeding, play, diapering, brief separations, and comforting patterns can provide meaningful contexts— venues in which typical behavior is most likely to be manifest. If assessment materials and specific tasks are introduced, it should be done in a minimally intrusive way, to preserve the likelihood of observing the dyad's most typical patterns of interaction.

When observing preschoolers' interactions with peers, similar issues exist. The most typical setting in which preschool social interaction is observed is free-play (Odom & Ogawa, 1992). The types of available toys and activities may well affect the nature and frequency of interaction. For example, children will be more likely to play with peers when "high social" versus "low social" toys or activities are available (Beckman & Kohl, 1984; Ivory & McCollum, 1999; McCabe, Jenkins, Mills, Dale, & Cole, 1999). Children tend to be more interactive during play activities that involve pretend play and when adults are not active participants in the play (Odom, Peterson, McConnell, & Ostrosky, 1990; Zercher, Brown, & Odom, 2002). In addition to the content of the activity, the structure of the activity (e.g., number in the group, definition of roles) will affect the level of interaction, with children being more interactive in high- versus low-structure activities (DeKlyen & Odom, 1989). The presence of unfamiliar observers may have immediate but transitory effects on peer social interaction; however, allowing time to establish familiarity can minimize these effects.

Participants in the Social Interaction

Because social interaction is a reciprocal process, children's behavior is affected by the partners with whom they interact as well as by the history of interaction between the partners. The social context of infant development is the relationship with the primary caregiver. A joint assessment process that integrally involves the parent can enrich the process, bringing out a depth of information that would otherwise not be accessible. Meaningful parent involvement in assessment of parent-infant interaction can also help to avoid cultural bias and mistaken assumptions (Kelly & Barnard, 2000).

For preschool children, the skills of the peer group may affect the degree and nature of interaction. For example, if the peer group consists only of children with disabilities, the child being assessed may not have the opportunity to engage in positive, reciprocal interactions because the peer group may be less responsive than a typically developing peer group (Brown, Odom, & Buysse, 2002). For example, Guralnick, Hammond, Gottman, and Kinnish (1996) found that children with disabilities interacted more frequently in inclusive play groups than in play groups consisting of only children with disabilities. Other researchers have found that interventions to promote social behavior are more likely to have a positive effect when typically developing children are present (Odom et al., 1999; Strain, 1983).

Use of Multiple Measures

As noted previously, McConnell and Odom (1999) and others (Gresham, 1986) have proposed that multiple sources of information and different informants (e.g., teachers, peers, caregivers) be used to assess children's social competence. If agreement exists across assessments, more confidence can be placed in the information obtained. For example, direct observation and teacher ratings of the child's social interactions might indicate the same performance level. However, it is possible that assessment information will not agree. For example, the teacher's ratings and the parents' ratings might differ substantially, due to the difference in behaviors exhibited by the child in the home and in the school setting or to different standards imposed by the raters. In either case, differences provide unique information about the child's social skills across settings, and a comprehensive evaluation should capture such information.

METHODS FOR ASSESSING SOCIAL PERFORMANCE

A variety of techniques exists for assessing the social performance of infants and young children with disabilities. Each provides slightly different information but all depend on some level of observation of children or caregiver/infant dyads. These observations may occur in single settings where the teacher or assessor steps away from the activity in which interaction may occur, watches the child, and records the information observed. Assessment information may be collected through (a) anecdotal notes; (b) questionnaires and checklists; (c) direct observation systems; (d) rating scales; (e) sociometric measures; (f) curriculum-based measures; or (g) norm-referenced assessments. Examples of each of these are provided in Table 13.2.

Anecdotal Data Collection

When observing infants and young children, teachers sometimes keep notes on infants' or children's social behavior. These anecdotal notes should describe the setting, activity, participants, and behaviors observed during the interaction. If possible, the teacher should write the notes while observing the interaction or immediately after the observation period. Parents can also use anecdotal reporting to describe interactive behaviors observed in the home. For some early childhood education curricula, anecdotal records serve as the primary assessment information collected (Beaty, 1998).

Questionnaires

Assessors sometimes use questionnaires to gather information from individuals who are knowledge-able about a child's behavior. These questionnaires differ from the rating scales discussed later in that they (a) do not require rating on a numeric scale; (b) usually do not have information related to reliability and validity; and (c) are sometimes used as clinical instruments for designing interventions. For example, to assess the friendships of young children with disabilities, Goldman and Buysee (2002) developed the *Playmates & Friends Questionnaire for Teachers*. An example of this form appears in Figure 13.1. The teacher provides information about children which whom a child plays occasionally or frequently as well as children who are the child's special friends. The teacher also provides information about strategies that she uses to promote friendships. Buysse, Goldman, and Skinner (2002) have used this questionnaire to examine the settings in preschool classes that promote friendship formation.

Direct Observation of Social Interaction

Observational systems that require the assessor to directly observe and immediately record infants' or children's social interaction provide detailed information. Direct observational systems are similar to anecdotal systems in that they depend on observation of the child in a social context, but are different in that the categories for observation are predetermined and the observations are made within a temporal frame (i.e., a specific point in time or within a time interval). In addition, assessors record ongoing entries they observe the social interaction.

Three types of direct observation systems exist for assessing children's social interactions. *Momentary time sampling* systems require that the observer record at a specific point in time whether the infant, the child, or the parent is engaged in a specific social behavior or interaction (Sackett, 1978). The use of many data points provides a representative picture of the social interaction in which the infant or child engages. In a momentary time sampling system called the

TABLE 13.2
Examples of Methods for Assessing Social Performance

Assessment Type	Title/Reference	Age Range	Description	Information Generated
Anecdotal	*Through the Looking Glass* (Nicholson & Shipstead, 1998)	Open	Narrative recording or report of infants'/children's participation in social interaction with peers or caregivers	Behaviors determined by teacher
Questionnaires	*Ages and Stages Questionnaire for Social-Emotional Behaviors* (Squires et al., 2000)	Infant through preschool	Set of screening questionnaires completed by caregivers periodically (from 6 months to 60 months)	Provides screening information on infants and children's personal-social behavior (self-regulation, compliance, communication, interaction with people
	Playmates and Friends (Goldman & Buysse, 2002)	Preschoolers	Teacher identifies children who are playmates and special friends, as well as strategies teachers use to promote friendships	Number of special friendships and playmates. Teachers' facilitation of friendships
Direct Observation	*Infant-Parent Social Interaction Code* (Baird et al., 1992)	Infant	Modified time sampling system	Parent behavior (contingent, responsivity directiveness, intrusiveness, facilitation) Infant behavior (initiation, participation, communication acts) Dyad (theme continuity)
	Early Coping Inventory (Zeitlin, Williamson, & Gzczepanski, 1988)	Infants and toddlers	Observational assessment of behavioral characteristics considered most relevant for effective coping	Sensorimotor organization, reactive behaviors, and self-initiated behaviors
	Parten/Smilansky Combined Scale (Rubin et al., 1976)	Preschoolers	Interval sampling system designed to measure cognitive play within a social context	See Figure 13.3 Interval sampling coding sheet

	Integrated Preschool Curriculum (Odom et al., 1988)	Preschoolers	Momentary time sampling system for scanning classrooms of children, designed to assess interactive play and social integration	Categories include: isolate/unoccupied, proximity, interactive, negative, teacher interaction
	Guralnick et al. (1996)	Preschoolers	Event recording for individual social behavior	34 categories of social behavior a) directed to peers (e.g., seeks attention, leads peers), b) in response to peers (e.g., following peers' lead, using peers as resource, and success
Rating Scales	*Parent-Child Observation Guide* (Bernstein et al., 1992)	Infants and toddlers	Binary rating of items at three age levels (birth–3 mos., 4–15 mos., 16–36 mos.)	Parent interaction (responsiveness to child's need and activity, positive feelings, helping)
	Infant-Caregiver Interaction Scale (Munson & Odom, 1994)	Infants and toddlers	Five-point Likert scale rating of parents' and infants/toddlers' behavior	Infant interaction (expression, using parent, involvement, positive feelings feelings, language) Environment (positioning, distractions, planning) Parent (participation, predictability, sensitivity/responsiveness/turn-taking, communicative intent, playful routines, imitation, affect) Infant (participation, predictability/consistency, sensitivity/responsiveness, communicative intent, playful routines, play behaviors, imitation, affect)
	Teacher Impressions scale in *Play Time/Social Time* (Vanderbilt-Minnesota Social Interaction Project, 1993)	Preschoolers	Five-point Likert scale rating completed after observing child in play	Rating on 16 behaviors, such as converses appropriately, takes turns plays cooperatively

Continued

TABLE 13.2
Continued

Assessment Type	Title/Reference	Age Range	Description	Information Generated
	Social Skills Rating System—Preschool Level (Gresham & Elliott, 1990)	Preschoolers	Three-point Likert ratings of how often behavior occurs and how important, for all items. Teacher and parent forms	Provides summary scores of social skills and problem behavior, with norms for interpreting scores. Subdomain scores available for Cooperation, Assertion, Responsibility, and Self Control
	Preschool and Kindergarten Behavior Scales 2nd ed. (Merrell, 2003)	Preschool and kindergarten	Likert ratings completed by teacher, parents, or other caregivers	Provides total rating scores on social skills and problem behaviors, as well as subscale scores. Norms are provided for interpreting scores
Sociometrics	*An Evaluation of Sociometric-Social Behavior Research with Preschool Children* Marshall (1957)	Preschool	Children select (nominate) photographs of peers who are their friends	Summary of scores of peer nominations as friends
	A Reliable Sociometric Measure for Preschool Children Asher et al. (1979)	Preschool	Children sort pictures of peers into three categories (plays with with a lot, plays with a little, does play with)	Average peer rating in individual children and ranking
Curriculum-based Assessment	*Hawaii Early Learning Profile* (Furuno et al., 1997)	Infants and toddlers	Social-emotional domain with five subdomains (Attachment, Development of Self, Expression of Emotion, Learning Rules, and Social Interaction and Play)	All of the curriculum-based assessments provide information about infants and children's performance on individual items. Each has an accompanying curriculum guide that contains teaching activities linked to specific items in the assessment

	Instrument	Population	Description	Scoring
	HELP for Preschoolers (Vort, 1995)	Preschoolers	Social Strand includes three subdomains (Social Manners, Social Language, and Personal Welfare)	
	AEPS (Bricker, 2002)	Infants and preschoolers	Three subdomains related to interaction with adults, environment, peers. Assessor determines child's performance on items through observation, direct assessment, interview	
	Transdisciplinary Play-Based Assessment (Linder, 1993a)	Preschoolers	Social emotional domain contains individual items related to children's play and development. Assessor collection information through observation of child in planned played activities with adults and peers	
Norm-referenced assessment	*Battelle Developmental Inventory* (Newborg et al., 1988)	Infants through preschoolers	Personal-social domains contains subdomains related to adult interaction, expression of feelings, affect, peer interaction, etc. Assessor collects information through observation, interview, and direct assessment	Provides standard scores and age-equivalence on social domain
	Vineland Adaptive Behavior Scale (Sparrow et al., 1984)	Infants through adults	Subdomain scores provided for social competence. Information collected through interview of parents, of form completed by teachers/caregivers	Provides percentile scores, age equivalents

Use a separate questionnaire to describe the playmates & friends of each selected child.

Playmates

1. Who does _____ play with? List as many or as few playmates as appropriate using first name and last initial. How often does **this child** play with each playmate? Check *occasionally* or *frequently*.

Playmate's Name	Occasionally	Frequently	Playmate's Name	Occasionally	Frequently
_____	❑	❑	_____	❑	❑
_____	❑	❑	_____	❑	❑
_____	❑	❑	_____	❑	❑
_____	❑	❑	_____	❑	❑
_____	❑	❑	_____	❑	❑

Special Friends

2. Who would you say are **this child's** special friends? List as many or as few playmates as appropriate.

Friend's Name	Friend's Age	(circle one) Male/Female	Is this friend a classmate?	How long have these two children been friends?	Does this friend have a disability (circle one)
_____	_____	male female	yes no	_____	yes no don't know
_____	_____	male female	yes no	_____	yes no don't know
_____	_____	male female	yes no	_____	yes no don't know
_____	_____	male female	yes no	_____	yes no don't know
_____	_____	male female	yes no	_____	yes no don't know
_____	_____	male female	yes no	_____	yes no don't know
_____	_____	male female	yes no	_____	yes no don't know
This child's age _____		male female	(circle one)	Does **this child** have a disability?	yes no don't know

FIGURE 13.1

Playmates and Friends Questionnaire for Teachers

Source: Goldman, B. O., and Buysse, V. (2002). *Playmates and Friends Questionnaire for Teachers, Revised.* Chapel Hill, NC: University of North Carolina, FPG Child Development Institute. Used with permission.

Social Interaction Scan (*SIS*) (Odom et al., 1988), the teacher observes a child for 2 seconds and in the subsequent 4 seconds records the behavior in which the child was engaged. As can be seen from the coding sheet in Figure 13.2, the observer circles one of the letters that indicates a category of play behavior. These categories include isolate/unoccupied (I/U), proximity (P), interactive play (I), negative interaction (N), and teacher interaction (T). For the I and N categories, superscripts and subscripts indicate whether the child was playing with a child with disabilities (H) or a nondisabled child (N). For the teacher category, the observer indicates whether the child was talking to the teacher (C) or the teacher was talking to the child (T).

This system is called a *scan* because after the observer records the behavior for one child, he or she moves on to the next child, and when the behavior of the final child on the list is recorded, the observer begins again with the first child. This technique provides a more representative picture of the children's social behavior across a play session than does a single block of observations. Alternatively, an assessor can observe a single child for a certain number of observations (e.g., 10) before moving on to the next child.

An advantage of time sampling is its relative ease of use compared to other observational methods. Using the SIS, one can collect information on frequency of interactive play, child attributes, and other factors (e.g., proximity, teacher interactions, etc.). In addition, information may be collected for the whole class in a short time. The SIS is a relatively simple scanning system, and more detailed and descriptive categories of social interaction could be developed.

Momentary time sampling systems do not allow the observer to collect information about the sequential nature of a child's social interaction (i.e., how many turns occurred in the interaction). Also, because the behavior is collected either instantaneously or within a very short interval, high-frequency behaviors tend to be overrepresented in the data and low-frequency behaviors tend to be underrepresented unless a substantial amount of data is collected for the assessment (Sackett, 1978). The authors of the SIS recommend that the teacher collect at least 100 to 150 data points per child to obtain a representative sample of children's behavior (Odom et al., 1988).

Interval sampling measures of social interaction require the observer to watch an infant or young child for a short period of time, usually between 6 and 15 seconds, and record whether the behavior occurred at all during the interval (i.e., partial interval sampling) or for the whole interval (i.e., whole interval sampling). In *discontinuous interval systems*, a short interval is provided after the observation interval to allow the observer to record the social behavior. In *continuous interval systems*, the observer records the behavior as it occurs and moves to the next observation interval without pausing. Usually an auditory tone (e.g., from an audiotape) cues the observer to change recording intervals.

An example of an interval sampling system for coding the social interactions of preschool children involved in a peer mediated intervention is provided in Figure 13.3 (Bevis & Odom, 2002). This system was used to assess the social orientation and social interactions of preschool children with autism, peers' interactions, and teachers' behavior. The behavior categories within variables were, for Target Child Orientation: Joint Attention (JA), Attention to Peer (AP), Stereotypic Behavior (SS), Not Applicable (NA), and for Target Child Behavior: Positive Initiation (PI), Positive Response (PR), Negative Initiation (NI), Negative Response (NR), with the PB indicating social behavior directed to a peer buddy and OP designating other peers in the class. Also, PB Behavior indicated Peer Buddies' social behavior directed toward the child with autism, and OP Behavior indicated Other Peers directing social behavior to the child. Adult Behaviors included Prompt to the Target Child (PTC), Prompt to the Peer Buddy (PPB), Prompt to Other Peer (POP), and Not Applicable (NA). Observers watched the target

Classroom/Teacher: _____   Time Started: _____

Observer: _____   Activity: _____

Date: _____

Child's Name	T^c_t I^h_n N^h_n P I/U	T^c_t I^h_n N^h_n P I/U	T^c_t I^h_n N^h_n P I/U	T^c_t I^h_n N^h_n P I/U	T^c_t I^h_n N^h_n P I/U	T^c_t I^h_n N^h_n P I/U	T^c_t I^h_n N^h_n P I/U	Child's Name	T^c_t I^h_n N^h_n P I/U	T^c_t I^h_n N^h_n P I/U	T^c_t I^h_n N^h_n P I/U	T^c_t I^h_n N^h_n P I/U	T^c_t I^h_n N^h_n P I/U	T^c_t I^h_n N^h_n P I/U	T^c_t I^h_n N^h_n P I/U
Child's Name								Child's Name							
Child's Name								Child's Name							
Child's Name								Child's Name							
Child's Name								Child's Name							
Child's Name								Child's Name							

FIGURE 13.2

Social interaction scan

Note: From *Integrated Preschool Curriculum* by S. L. Odom, M. Bender, M. Stein, L. Doran, P. Houden, M. McInnes, M. Deklyen, M. Speltz, and J. Jenkins, 1988, Seattle, WA: University of Washington Press. Copyright 1988 by University of Washington Press. Reprinted by permission.

Observer's Name: _____

Date: _____

Target Child (initials): _____

Peer Buddies: _____

Classroom: _____

Session: _____ a.m./p.m.

_____ Structured Play Group
_____ Free Choice Time
_____ Gross Motor/Recess
_____ Work Time
_____ Other

Intv	TC Orientation JA	AP	SS	NA	Target Child Behavior PI-PB	PR PB	NI PB	NR PB	PI-OP	PR OP	NI OP	NR OP	NA	PB Behavior PI	PR	NI	NR	NA	OP Behavior PI	PR	NI	NR	NA	Adult Behavior PTC	PPB	POP	NA
1																											
2																											
3																											
4																											
5																											
6																											
7																											
8																											
9																											
10																											

FIGURE 13.3

Interval sampling coding sheet for assessing attention, social behavior of focal child, social behavior of peers, and teacher behavior (Bevis & Odom, 2002).

child, peers, and adults for 10 seconds, and in the subsequent 5 seconds put a checkmark under the single category that occurred for each variable. For interval sampling systems such as this, Doll and Elliott (1994) recommend that at least four-10-minute sessions spread across 3 weeks be collected to provide a representative sample.

To assess parent interaction, Baird, Haas, McCormick, Carruth, and Turner (1992) developed an interval sampling observational system called the *Infant-Parent Social Interaction Code (IPSIC)*, which measured four parent behaviors (contingent responsivity, directiveness, intrusiveness, and facilitation), four infant behaviors (initiation, participation, signal clarity, and intentional communicative acts), and one dyadic behavior (theme continuity). The selection of behaviors was guided by theoretical and empirical evidence of their importance for development.

Interval sampling systems are less difficult to learn than the event recording systems noted below, although they are more difficult than momentary time sampling systems. Further, these systems provide more information about the reciprocal nature of social interactions than momentary time sampling systems, because the observer watches the interaction longer. However, interval sampling may be problematic when an interaction stretches across an interval, unless the code has a specific category for continuation.

An additional disadvantage for some interval sampling systems is that more than one behavior may occur in an interval. When this happens, the assessment data will actually underestimate the level of social interaction. Researchers sometimes limit the interval length (e.g., 6 seconds) to reduce the likelihood of more than one social interaction occurring per interval.

In *event recording systems* the observer records each instance of a social behavior or interaction. As in the other systems, these behaviors may be recorded within a specific time frame or interval, so that when interobserver agreement is collected, the teacher can determine the specific behaviors for which there is agreement or dis-

agreement. However, within the time frame, the assessor records all the behaviors that occur rather than just the fact that the behavior occurred (i.e., as in interval sampling).

To collect information about preschool children's social interaction and independent goal-oriented task behavior, Bronson (1994) developed an event recording system entitled the *Bronson Social and Task Skill Profile*. Observers collect six 10-minute samples of a child's behavior over a 1- to 3-week period. For the social interaction portion of this system, the observer records behavior grouped within a *planning and organizing dimension* (suggests direction for activity, assigns roles or resources, states rules) and an *accommodating strategies dimension* (helps, shares, trades, trades off, takes turns, combines resources, joint effort).

The relative accuracy of the event recording systems, as compared with time and interval sampling systems, is an advantage. By coding all behaviors (i.e., within the coding system) that occur, the teacher is likely to gain more accurate information about the child's social performance. Event recording systems are essential for coding the sequence of social behaviors that make up social interactions, because they allow the observer to record the behavior in real time. The disadvantage of event recording systems is that they are more difficult than the other systems to learn and use.

When collecting direct observation information, observers must be trained to an acceptable level of agreement, and interobserver agreement must be collected on 20% to 30% of the sample. Hartman and Wood (1990) provided clarity on issues related to measuring interobserver agreement and proposed a systematic plan for training observers.

In recent years, computer-based observational data collection systems have become much more accessible and feasible. Software systems are available for use on laptop and handheld computers (Tapp & Wehby, 2000). Systems such as the *MOOSES* (Tapp, Wehby, & Ellis, 1995), the *Observer* (Noldus Information System, 2000), and

SCOPES (Shores, 1997) have all been used to collect information on children's social interaction with adults and peers. Thompson, Felce, and Symons (2000) provide reviews of these and other observational assessment software tools.

The level of detail generated by direct observation systems (especially event systems) and the labor intensive nature of these systems may be more than is needed for designing and monitoring social interaction intervention programs for infants and young children with disabilities. More often, direct observation measures are applied in research or very systematic program evaluations.

A Note on a Classic Observational System

Any discussion of assessing children's social interaction would be incomplete without an acknowledgement of Mildred Parten's work. The *Parten Scale of Social Participation* (Parten, 1932) was one of the earliest social interaction observational assessments and has served as a basis for many other systems (e.g., the *SIS* scale described previously). The behavioral categories, presented in Table 13.3, denote the range of children's behavior from unoccupied to highly sophisticated cooperative play. In recent years, researchers have combined Parten's original social categories with Smilansky's (1968) measures of cognitive play to obtain an even more detailed description of the quality of children's social participation (Guralnick, Connor, Hammond, Gottman, & Kinnish, 1996; McCabe et al., 1999; Odom, 1981; Rubin, 1982; Rubin, Maioni, & Hornung, 1976).

Rating Scales

Rating scales require observers to make a judgment about the quality or quantity of social behaviors or interactions that occur over a longer period of time rather than to record behaviors as they occur (Cairns & Green, 1979). With this methodology, developers initially define the construct assessed by the rating scale and the behaviors that compose those constructs. Although Guilford (1954) noted that five types of rating scales exist (i.e., graphic, standard, cumulated

TABLE 13.3

Abbreviated Behavioral Categories of the Parten Scale of Social Participation and the Smilansky Scale, as Defined in Odom (1981)

Scale/Category	Definition
Parten Scale	
Unoccupied	Glancing around the room, but not focusing on an activity
Onlooker	Observing other children, but not interacting
Solitary	Playing alone with toys different from those being played with by children in the general proximity, not conversing
Parallel	Playing with toys similar to those used by children in the subject's vicinity
Associative	Playing with other children without role assignment, loosely organized
Cooperative	Playing with other children in an organized manner, roles assigned
Smilansky Scale	
Functional	Simple muscular activities, manipulating play objects
Constructive	Creative activities, appropriately manipulating academic materials
Dramatic	Manipulating objects in a symbolic manner
Games with rules	Playing games with prearranged rules

points, numerical, and forced-choice), numerical rating scales are used most frequently to assess children's social performance. Raters make judgments about the quantity or quality of behaviors represented in specific items by using a numerical scale, such as a Likert scale (Likert, 1932). Finn (1972) suggested that 5 and 7 numerical points were optimal for Likert-type scales and reliability decreased beyond seven levels. However, some 3-point and binary scales have also yielded reliable results (Rasmussen, 1989).

Behavioral anchors provide the rater with a definition or description of what each number represents. These behavioral anchors may be very general (e.g., 1 = rarely, 5 = frequently) or very specific (e.g., 1 = Parent shows pleasure in watching infant at least some of the time; 7 = Parent shows or reports pleasure in infant's enjoyment of his/her own activity). At a minimum, it is important that scale developers describe the behaviors at the low and high ends of the item ratings (Finn, 1972). Figure 13.4 provides an example of just such a rating scale of infant-caregiver interaction.

Raters may complete the scales immediately after observing the ratees for a specified time period, or judgments may be based on accumulated observations occurring over a longer period and many opportunities to observe behaviors. For example, in a rating scale developed by Crawley and Spiker (1982), observers must watch 10-minute segments of mother-infant interaction during free-play before rating the quality of the infant's social initiative on a 5-point Likert scale. For the *Social Skills Rating System (SSRS)* (Gresham & Elliott, 1990), raters make judgments based on multiple opportunities for observing the child.

Most rating scales include procedures for summarizing the ratings on individual items. A total score often consists of the sum of item ratings, or, if the individual items are designed to measure different behaviors or attributes, by calculating specific subscale scores. For example, on the *Parent-Infant Interaction Scale (PIIS)* (Clark & Seifer, 1986), a rating scale that measures the quality of mother-infant interaction, the

individual items are organized into three subsections: (1) interaction style, (2) social reference, and (3) assessment of context.

Ideally, a rating scale will provide information on the behaviors of both partners in a social interaction. The *Parent-Child Observation Guide (PCOG)* (Bernstein, Hans, & Percansky, 1992), *Infant-Caregiver Interaction Scale (ICIS)* (Munson & Odom, 1994), and the *PIIS* (Clark & Seifer, 1986) offer such systems. Each scale varies on the number of infant behaviors that are measured. Other systems, such as the *Maternal Behavior Rating Scale (MBRS)* (Mahoney, 1992), measure behaviors of only one member of the dyad (e.g., the mother). Through the use of interaction-based rating scales, some of the external influences on child and caregiver behavior are considered, acknowledging that behavior does not occur in a vacuum.

For assessing children's peer interactions, McConnell and Odom developed the *Teacher Impression Scales (TIS)* (Vanderbilt/Minnesota Social Interaction Project, 1993; McConnell & Odom, 1999) (see Figure 13.5). The *TIS* was designed to be completed immediately after observing a child in a play activity. The *Social Skills Rating System* (Gresham & Elliott, 1990) and the *Preschool and Kindergarten Behavior Scales (PKBS)* (Merrell, 2003) are rating scales that rely on a more cumulative impression of preschool children's interaction with peers and adults. The latter two scales provide norms for interpreting the scores that are generated.

The advantages of using rating scales to measure social interaction are that they usually (a) are easier to use than observational measures; (b) are relatively quick to administer; (c) are easy to score; (d) require less training for raters than observational measures; and (e) sometimes provide norms. Some scales are designed specifically to be completed by teachers or parents. Rating scales may be useful for practitioners in Early Childhood Special Education (ECSE) programs where time is an important consideration (McCloskey, 1990). In addition, for some behaviors, rating scales may

Infant's Name _____

Infant's Age (AA) _____ (CA) _____

Date of Interaction _____

Activity _____

Observer _____

Score _____

Directions: Mark 1–5 as appropriate.

PARTICIPATION

1. Infant participates in social interaction

| Infant never participates in social interaction. | 1 2 3 4 5 | Infant always participates in social interaction. |

2. Infant initiates interaction with caregiver.

| Infant never initiates. | 1 2 3 4 5 | Infant always initiates. |

Note how the infant initiates the inteaction.

PREDICTABILITY/CONSISTENCY

3. The infant's behaviors are consistent and identifiable.

| Infant's behaviors are never consistent. | 1 2 3 4 5 | Infant behaviors are consistent. |

SENSITIVITY/RESPONSIVENESS/TURN-TAKING

4. Infant attends to caregiver's presence.

| Infant never attends to caregiver. | 1 2 3 4 5 | Infant always attends to caregiver. |

5. Infant responds to caregiver's social initiations.

| Infant never responds to caregiver. | 1 2 3 4 5 | Infant always responds to caregiver. |

FIGURE 13.4

Infant-Caregiver Interaction Scale

Note: From *Infant-Caregiver Interaction Scale* by L. Munson and S. Odom, 1994. Unpublished manuscript. Reproduced by permission.

have higher predictive validity of later behavior than direct observation systems (Bakeman & Brown, 1980; Jay & Farran, 1981); some rating scales may have equal or higher stability over time (Schaefer, 1989; Clarke-Stewart & Hevey, 1981); and rating scales yield global information about the development of social interaction skills. As such, they may be useful for measuring general levels of social interaction, as the teacher might

need to do when screening children for possible problems, identifying current functioning level, or measuring change in behavior across the year.

Rating scales also have some disadvantages. They are more subjective than direct observation systems (Cairns & Green, 1979), and they provide less detailed information about specific behaviors, making them less useful for designing or monitoring interventions on specific behavior. Another

Child Name _____ Date _____

Teacher _____ Subject Number _____

Please read each item below and rate the degree to which it describes the child's behavior **in your classroom program.** If *you have not seen the child perform a particular skill or behavior, circle* **1,** *indicating* **Never.** If the child frequently performs the described skill or behavior, circle 5, indicating **Frequently.** If the child performs this behavior in between these two extremes, circle **2, 3,** or **4** indicating your best estimate of the rate of occurrence of the skill.

1 = Never Performs Skill   5 = Frequently Performs Skill

Circle only one number for each skill. Do not mark between numbers.

1 . . . 2 . . . 3 . . . 4 . . . 5	1. The child converses appropriately.
1 . . . 2 . . . 3 . . . 4 . . . 5	2. The child takes turns when playing.
1 . . . 2 . . . 3 . . . 4 . . . 5	3. The child plays cooperatively.
1 . . . 2 . . . 3 . . . 4 . . . 5	4. The child varies social behavior appropriately.
1 . . . 2 . . . 3 . . . 4 . . . 5	5. The child is persistent at social attempts.
1 . . . 2 . . . 3 . . . 4 . . . 5	6. The child spontaneously responds to peers.
1 . . . 2 . . . 3 . . . 4 . . . 5	7. The child appears to have fun.
1 . . . 2 . . . 3 . . . 4 . . . 5	8. Peers interacting with the child appear to have fun.
1 . . . 2 . . . 3 . . . 4 . . . 5	9. The child continues an interaction once it has begun.
1 . . . 2 . . . 3 . . . 4 . . . 5	10. Peers seek out the child for social play.
1 . . . 2 . . . 3 . . . 4 . . . 5	11. The child uses appropriate social behavior to begin an interaction.
1 . . . 2 . . . 3 . . . 4 . . . 5	12. The child enters play activities without disrupting the group.
1 . . . 2 . . . 3 . . . 4 . . . 5	13. The child suggests new play ideas for a play group.
1 . . . 2 . . . 3 . . . 4 . . . 5	14. The child smiles appropriately at peers during play.
1 . . . 2 . . . 3 . . . 4 . . . 5	15. The child shares play materials with peers.
1 . . . 2 . . . 3 . . . 4 . . . 5	16. The child engages in play activities where social interaction might occur.

FIGURE 13.5

Teacher Impression Scales

Note: From *Play Time/Social Time* by Vanderbilt/Minnesota Social Interaction Project. Copyright held by Odom and McConnell. Reproduced by permission of the authors.

disadvantage is the difficulty in finding complete validity and reliability data and training information (Munson & Odom, 1996).

Cautions When Assessing Parent-Infant Interactions The Zero to Three National Center for Infants, Toddlers, and Families (Greenspan & Meisels, 1996), in their recommendation for developmental assessment, and the CEC Division for Early Childhood in its statement of recommended assessment practices (Neisworth & Bagnato, 2000), propose that families always be included in the assessment of young children. Though it is possible to administer rating scales in collaboration with families, certain challenges are inherent to these judgment-based tools. Cautions about the use of rating scales to assess parent-infant interactions are raised by McCollum and McBride

(1997) based on concerns about cultural validity; by Mahoney, Spiker, and Boyce (1996) regarding concerns with reliability and validity, the need for more appropriate assessment instruments, and the need for extensive training; and by Munson and Odom (1996) regarding the subjective nature of rating scales, and measurement errors inherent in the these types of instruments. Therefore, if practitioners decide to use rating scales to assess parent-infant interaction, they should be careful to avoid violating the principles of family participation in assessment and cultural sensitivity. In fact, rating scales may be more useful for purposes of research and program evaluation than to guide intervention. Incorporating the family's vision of "good parenting" into the assessment process and providing interested families with information about child development implications of various parenting interaction styles are two approaches that can be used to involve families in the process of assessment (Baird & Peterson, 1997).

A variation on the rating scale is a checklist that requires the observer to determine whether a behavior or set of behaviors occurred during an observation or set of observations. Checklists typically require yes/no responses about a behavior's occurrence or nonoccurrence. They do not require finer judgments. The *Nursing Child Assessment Teaching Scale (NCATS)* (Barnard, 1978b) and *Nursing Child Assessment Feeding Scale (NCAFS)* (Barnard, 1978a) are examples of scales used with infants and caregivers. Both assessment scales measure parental behaviors during parent-infant interactions. To assess young children's social competence, McClellan and Katz (2001) developed the *Social Attributes Checklist*. The 24 items in the scale are grouped by individual, social skills, and relationship attributes. The scale is designed to assist early childhood teachers in monitoring the social development of children in their classes.

Sociometric Assessments

In *sociometric assessment* procedures, children provide general evaluations of the social acceptance,

social preference, or likability of other children. Typically, teachers gather sociometric information from intact groups of children, such as all the children enrolled in a particular class or all the children in a particular play group. As a result, sociometric measures cannot be used for children who are not enrolled in a child-care center. There are four general types of sociometric assessment instruments: (a) peer nominations; (b) peer ratings; (c) peer assessments; and (d) paired comparisons (McConnell & Odom, 1986). Given the level of resources needed and the limited scope of their application, peer assessments and paired comparisons have little relevance to work in applied settings and will not be discussed further in this section.

Peer Nominations Peer nominations are sociometric assessment procedures in which children are asked to identify classmates who meet general criterion. Children may be asked to identify classmates they consider their best friends, with whom they like to play or work, or who they like the least. Children may nominate a child or children who meet a criterion, select children from a list of classmates or, for preschoolers, select children from a set of pictures of classmates (Marshall, 1957). Peer nomination scores are calculated as the proportion of nominations a child receives from all peers in his or her class or play group.

By using both positive (e.g., "Name your three best friends") and negative (e.g., "Name three children you don't like") nomination criteria, children can be classified into sociometric groups. These groups typically include (a) "popular" children, who receive many positive and few or no negative nominations; (b) "neglected" children, who receive few positive or few negative nominations; (c) "rejected" children, who receive few positive and many negative nominations; and (d) "controversial" children, who receive high numbers of both positive and negative nominations (Coie, Dodge, & Copotelli, 1982).

It must be noted that the use of negative criteria in any sociometric assessment procedure may raise concerns from parents, teachers, and members of Human Subjects Review Committees. After administering peer nomination assessments with negative criteria to elementary-aged children, Hayvren and Hymel (1984) found no negative effects of the assessment on peer interactions of the children assessed. Nevertheless, users of negative nomination sociometric procedures should be attentive to concerns voiced about the assessments and to the possible effects of these assessment procedures on the behavior of young children.

Peer Ratings Unlike peer nominations, peer ratings require children to provide general qualitative ratings for each child in their classroom or play group. Like peer nominations, specific criteria vary as a function of the purpose of assessment; however, all ratings reflect general statements of preference (e.g., "How much do you like to play with ____?" or "How much do you like to talk with ____?"). These ratings typically employ a 3-point Likert-type scale (for preschool children) and provide average scores for each child in a particular group. Peer ratings provide one way to avoid the use of negative evaluations by children. All children in a group are rated on a common dimension; as a result, individual scores can be rank-ordered from most highly rated to least highly rated. However, as noted above, without negative nominations, specific sociometric subgroups cannot be formed.

Peer rating sociometrics also have been adapted for use with preschool children. Asher, Singleton, Tinsley, and Hymel (1979) developed and evaluated a picture rating procedure in which children sorted photographs of their individual classmates into marked boxes to indicate their relative ratings. This procedure proved to be quite useful and is now widely accepted as a standard procedure for collecting peer ratings among young children.

A Note on Reliability Preschool children are the informants for sociometric procedures and, given the complexity of the task, there may be some concern about the reliability or stability of these measures (McConnell & Odom, 1986). However, with suitable adaptations (e.g., training by rating pictures of foods and toys; the use of pictures of peers), it appears that these procedures generate reliable information. When examining peer nomination, Denham and McKinley (1993) found positive evidence for the stability and convergent validity of the measures. In their original adaptation of the peer rating methodology, Asher et al. (1979) found acceptable test-retest reliability coefficients for two groups of children. These findings were replicated by Poteat, Ironsmith, and Bullock (1986). However, with young children the assessor should still attempt to determine if the child raters understand the task before completing the assessment, especially if the children are below 4 years of age.

Curriculum-Based Assessment

Curriculum-based assessment instruments provide a useful link among assessment, intervention, and evaluation (Bagnato, Neisworth, & Munson, 1997). These instruments usually take a criterion-referenced form and provide assessment of skills across developmental domains (with "social" as one domain). Assessment items are usually ordered according to when they typically appear in a child's development (or ordered logically from simple to complex. The order, when supplemented by information from parents and teachers about functional skills, may assist in selecting skills for intervention (Bricker, 1989). In addition, some curriculum-based assessments include related curriculum activities that teachers can use to support the child's acquisition of identified skills.

A large number of curriculum-based assessment instruments and the related curricula are available (see Table 13.2). For example, the *Hawaii Early Learning Profile (HELP)* (Parks, 1997) is a curriculum-based developmental assessment for children from birth to 36 months. The social-emotional domain of the *HELP* includes the subdomains of attachment/separation/

autonomy, development of self, expression of emotions and feelings, learning rules and expectations, and social interactions and play. Additional materials that are available for use with *HELP* include *HELP at Home* (Parks & Furuno, 1997) and *HELP Activity Guide* (Furuno et al., 1997). The *HELP* has been extended through the preschool level (VORT, 1995), again with accompanying activities.

The *Assessment, Evaluation, and Programming System for Infants and Children (AEPS)* (Bricker, 2002) is a set of assessment and curriculum materials designed for infants and young children from birth through 6 years of age. The *AEPS* includes assessment manuals for birth to 3 years and 3 to 6 years, in which social development is one strand. Each assessment volume has an accompanying guide for designing intervention activities. An advantage of the *AEPS* is that it draws information on children's development from multiple sources (e.g., observation, direct testing, parents' report).

The *Transdisciplinary Play-Based Assessment, Revised Edition* (Linder, 1993a) assesses children's social skills in the subdomains of mastery motivation, attachment, separation and individuation, social relations with peers, and development of humor. Assessment information is obtained through observation of the child during standard play settings and activities. An accompanying curriculum, the *Transdisciplinary Play-Based Intervention* (Linder, 1993b) provides suggestions and guidelines for learning activities.

Although curriculum-based assessment can provide valuable information for identifying important goals for children's early intervention programs, McAllister (1991) has noted several inherent problems with this assessment approach. He proposes that the social skills domain is sometimes underrepresented in these assessments (i.e., merged with the adaptive behavior domain), may include too few items for a comprehensive assessment of social development, may not reflect the complexities inherent in social skills intervention (e.g., may not assess social performance across

settings and partners), and may not reflect adequately the social development of children with certain specific disabilities (e.g., infants with visual impairments, young children with autism). Curriculum-based assessment may be a necessary and important first step in identifying the social skills of young children with disabilities. Once those skills are identified, other assessment approaches described in this chapter might be more useful for monitoring children's actual performance in homes, classrooms, and communities.

Norm-Referenced Assessments

For certain purposes it is necessary to judge social behavior against established norms. In such situations the teacher is less concerned about specific interaction patterns or relationships than about the general performance of an infant or child. Rather than targeting specific skills for intervention, norm-referenced measures tend to describe social functioning across a broad spectrum. These measures compare the behavior, performance, or development of an individual child with the overall status of other children at similar ages, thus providing relative information regarding a child's current level of development. Typically, the norm-referenced assessment of social development and competence is seen as one part of a broader assessment of development of infants and preschool children with disabilities.

Norm-referenced measures of social development are included in several commonly used assessment instruments. For example, in the *Battelle Developmental Inventory (BDI)* (Newborg, Stock, Wnek, Guidubaldi, & Svinicki, 1988) social development is measured in the personal-social domain. The behaviors measured are adult interaction, expression of feelings/affect, self-concept, peer interaction, coping, and social role. Although these subdomains contain 85 items, with the exception of adult interaction, few items are included for developmental ages below 12 months. Administration of the *BDI* includes observation, parental and/or teacher interview, and structured tasks. In addition, specific adaptations are suggested for children with sensory or motoric disabilities. Scores in each of the six subdomains are summed to obtain a total personal-social domain score. Scores can be expressed in percentile ranks, standard score, or age equivalents. The *BDI* is unique in its dual role as a normed and criterion-referenced or curriculum-based assessment.

Norm-referenced assessments of adaptive behavior often include subsections related to social competence. *The Vineland Adaptive Behavior Scale (Vineland)* (Sparrow, Balla, & Cicchetti, 1984), one example of such a scale, is designed for use with individuals from birth to 18 years of age. It includes a survey form and an expanded edition that a parent or other informed adult completes through an interview. The socialization domain has three subdomains: (1) interpersonal relations, (2) play and leisure time, and (3) coping skills. Only interpersonal relations and play and leisure time include items beginning at birth. The *Vineland* offers age-level norms with raw scores converted to standard scores (mean of 100 and standard deviation of 15), percentile ranks, stanines, and age equivalents.

In addition to the *BDI* and general scales of adaptive behavior, several of the rating scales mentioned previously also contain norms. For example, the *SSRS* and the *PKBS-2* both yield standard scores and percentile ranks for general social skills as well as subscales.

USING SOCIAL INTERACTION ASSESSMENT INFORMATION

Information about children's social interaction is commonly used for screening, diagnosing social problems, designing instructional programs, monitoring instruction, program evaluation, and research. The assessment approaches discussed in this chapter are important for different purposes. Table 13.4 depicts the relationship between assessment approaches and purposes.

Screening

Professionals conduct screenings to identify infants and preschoolers who might be at risk for social interaction problems. When the teacher determines that a problem might exist, the infant or young child receives a more intensive assessment of social development. The information collected from a screening assessment is not sufficient for designing a social interaction intervention program; its use should be limited to determining the need for further assessment.

A parents' or caregivers' statements of concern about their infant's social interaction or responsiveness may be the most useful screening indicator for infants' social development. These concerns may be followed by an assessor's (e.g., early intervention specialist) observations and further anecdotal reports from parents and other caregivers. Formal screening tests might also be useful. For example, the *Ages and Stages Questionnaire: Social-Emotional* (Squires, Bricker, & Twombly, 2000) is a brief questionnaire that parents may complete to screen for possible delays in social development at eight points between the ages of 6 months and 60 months. In addition, two recently developed screening instruments addressing social skills of toddlers focus on identification of children at risk for autism. The *Checklist for Autism in Toddlers (CHAT)* assesses joint attention skills, especially "gaze monitoring" (turning to look in the same direction an adult partner is looking) (Baron-Cohen, 1999). The *Screening Tool for Autism in Two-Year-Olds (STAT)* assesses play, communication, and imitation skills and is an interactive measure (Stone & Ruble, 2002).

For preschool children, screening activities may differ depending on setting and child characteristics. First, general early childhood education teachers have the opportunity to observe preschool children with their peer group, and these teachers are often adept at picking up problems through observations. They may confirm their concerns for individual children by using a checklist or more formal screening measure. Second,

TABLE 13.4
Social Interaction, Assessment, Approaches, and Purposes

Purposes	Anecdotal	Direct Observation	Rating Scales	Sociometrics	Curriculum-based	Norm-referenced	Comments
Screening	X	X	X				
Diagnosis	X	X	X	X	X	X	Multimethod assessment important
Program Design	X	X	X		X		
Program Monitoring	X	X	X		X		
Program Evaluation		X	X	X		X	Multimethod assessment important
Research		X	X	X		X	Multimethod assessment important

teachers who work with a group of children for whom there is a risk of developmental or social problems (e.g., children who have been physically abused, children with prenatal exposure to cocaine or alcohol) might routinely collect screening information. Third, young children with disabilities who are poor communicators, have poor play skills, are aggressive or disruptive, and/or are socially isolated are often socially rejected by their peer group (Odom et al., 2002). Screening should occur for all of these children.

Teacher rating scales seem to be the most efficient assessment approach for screening preschool-age children. The *Social Attributes Checklist* (McClellan & Katz, 2001), the *Social Interaction Rating Scale* (Hops et al., 1979), the screening test of the *BDI* (Newborg et al., 1988), the overview section of the *Assessment of Peer Relations* (Guralnick, 1992b), and the *Teacher Impression Scales* (Vanderbilt/Minnesota Social Interaction Project, 1993) are examples of teacher rating measures that can be completed quickly and can screen for potential social problems.

Diagnosing Social Interaction Difficulties

Social interaction assessment information is often useful to document children's current skills and to diagnose a problem. To diagnose social interaction problems and to qualify children for special services, teachers often use norm-referenced assessments. For preschool-age children, assessments noted previously do include norms (e.g., *BDI*, *SSRS*, *Vineland*). Assessors should supplement this norm-referenced information by observing the child in the classroom or a play setting.

Few norm-referenced assessments are available for identifying social interaction problems for infants and their caregivers. Formally identifying social interaction as a concern will require the teacher to become familiar with the infant and the caregiver and to develop rapport before attempting any assessment. The teacher can interview the caregiver and observe the interactions, using instruments such as the rating scales or direct observation systems described previously. With this information, the teacher can document the discrepancy between normal and atypical development. Additional information may be gathered using a curriculum-based instrument. As with any assessment, infants should be alert and both caregiver and infant should be comfortable with their surroundings. As previously stated, the teacher should document the setting, the participants, and the activities of the interaction. In addition, he or she should observe interaction in more than one context and on more than one occasion.

Diagnostic assessment information on preschool children's social interactions with peers may be generated by rating scales, norm-referenced assessments, or direct observation. Most rating scales have specific instructions for collecting and interpreting the needed information. If an assessor is not the child's regular teacher and has not observed several free-play sessions, the regular teacher should complete the scale. If direct observation information is used, it should be collected over multiple play sessions that are at least 15 minutes in length, although the specific amount of information needed will depend on the observational instrument used. Usually norms for observational data are not available and the teacher may have difficulty interpreting the assessment information collected. A solution is to establish local norms by collecting identical assessment information on one or two children in the class who are competent social interactors. The referred child's data may then be compared with the data from the socially competent peers.

Designing Individual Intervention Services

A teacher may use assessment information to develop goals, objectives, and learning activities for individual children. Although normative data could be important for identifying general areas of need, information from other assessment approaches may be more useful in planning intervention.

When working with infants and caregivers, assessors must remember that there is no best way for caregivers to interact with infants (McCollum & McBride, 1997). Interventions should build on the positive patterns of interaction already existing in the parent-infant relationship (McCollum, Gooler, Appl, & Yates, 2001). Further, interventions must reflect cultural differences that influence the nature of infant-caregiver interactions (Chen & McCollum, 2000; McCollum, Ree, & Chen, 2000). One intervention, the *Mediational Intervention for Sensitizing Caregivers* approach, developed by Pnina Klein of Israel, teaches parents a responsive style of interaction that matches their infant's interests, drawing the infant into the interaction (Klein, in press). The "floor time" model developed by Greenspan and Weider (1999) also employs an intensive adult-child interactive component.

Teachers working with preschool-age children should follow a similar process of basing their intervention on assessment information. Direct observation of children in play settings may reveal valuable information about the nature of social exchanges and potential intervention targets. Rating scales based on these observations, such as the *Social Strategy Rating Scale* (Beckman & Lieber, 1994) or the *TIS* (Vanderbilt/Minnesota Social Interaction Project, 1993), may assist teachers in identifying intervention objectives.

Monitoring the Intervention Program

Social interaction assessment information that is useful for screening, diagnosing, and selecting objectives may not be as useful for monitoring the intervention program once it has been implemented. Monitoring information must relate directly to goals and objectives of the IFSPs and IEPs, must be collected efficiently and frequently (e.g., daily, weekly), and must be sensitive to changes in the behavior of infants/children, caregivers, and peers. The information must be in a form that teachers can use to make decisions about the child's intervention program (e.g., to continue the intervention, revise the program, determine that the child has met his or her objective).

For infants and their caregivers, the monitoring process must reflect the nature and quality of the interactive episodes. Direct observation, parent report, and rating scales can assist the teacher in monitoring an intervention program. For example, the *ICIS* (Munson & Odom, 1994) is completed periodically to provide consistent feedback on the progress of the intervention. In addition, following an intervention session, the teacher can record anecdotal information about the interactive behaviors that were observed.

Similarly, the teacher may observe preschool children with disabilities during play sessions with peers to note changes resulting (or not resulting) from the intervention sessions, then write anecdotal notes, record systematic direct observation data, or complete a rating scale like the *TIS* (Vanderbilt/Minnesota Social Interaction Project, 1993) or the *Social Strategy Rating System* (Beckman & Lieber, 1994). Although collecting this information on a daily basis would be ideal, it may not be practical. Instead, the teacher might set aside 1 day a week to collect such information and use it to make decisions about the child's program.

Program Evaluation

Program evaluation may be either formative or summative. In formative evaluation, assessment information is used to reorganize the program. The assessment information described above for monitoring intervention programs would also be appropriate for use in formative evaluations.

Summative program evaluations of early intervention programs often require that assessment information of children's social behavior be collected at the beginning and at the end of the year. Evaluators may compute the differences between the pretest and posttest assessments and then compare this information either with the changes that occurred for similar children who were not in the program, or to the expected changes (i.e., based on preprogram rate of development) that would have occurred if the infants or young children had not been enrolled in the program (Odom, 1988). To conduct this type of evaluation, assessment information must be quantifiable. Direct observational data summarized into one or a few scores, teacher rating scales that produce global scores, peer ratings scores, scores from norm-referenced assessments, and perhaps curriculum-based assessment information (i.e., number of criterion items passed) can be used to conduct summative evaluations for programs designed to teach social interaction skills. It should also be noted that naturalistic or ethnographic evaluation approaches may also be used in program evaluation (Guba & Lincoln, 1989). As we noted in Table 13.4, and as a number of leaders in program evaluation have noted (Snyder & Sheehan, 1996), collecting multiple sources of information is important.

Research

In conducting research on infants' social behavior, researchers have used rating scales (Lussier, Crimmins, & Alberti, 1994), direct observation (Garner & Landry, 1992), and a combination of methods (e.g., direct observation, rating scales, parent report) (Bakeman & Brown, 1980; O'Connor, Sigman, & Kasari, 1992). Many questions remain in the area of assessment of parent-infant interaction. To date, none of the available assessment methods is recognized as the standard method for research or for use in intervention programs. Rather, assessment methods are selected (or designed) to fit the research questions identified by the investigators. A wider range of assessment instruments (particularly

rating scales) is becoming available for use in research (Munson & Odom, 1996). Although these instruments are a valuable resource, they require that researchers continue to examine reliability and validity when the instruments are used in their studies.

For research with preschool-age children, assessment methods also continue to develop. Although the primary assessment methodology used in research with this group is direct observation of children's social behavior (Odom & Ogawa, 1992), other methodologies are also being employed to examine the nature of children's social relationships (Buysse et al., 2002) and the nature of social competence (Guralnick, 1992a). In addition, multiple methodologies are employed to examine convergence of judgments of social competence across multiple perspectives (McConnell & Odom, 1999) and to incorporate the qualitative technique of triangulation (Odom et al., 2002) across data sources when examining peer relationships.

CONCLUSION

A range of assessment methods exists for collecting information about the social interactions of infants and caregivers, and preschool children and peers. The methods vary in their precision, labor intensiveness, and psychometric quality. Also, the information generated by these assessments may be relevant for different purposes, so assessors must match their choice of assessment instrument to the questions they are trying to address about the infants' or children's participation in social interaction with caregivers or peers.

· · · · · · · ·
SUMMARY OF KEY CONCEPTS

- A primary task in social development is establishing positive styles of interaction and secure attachment relationships with caregivers.

- Some infants and young children with disabilities may experience difficulties in establishing positive styles of interaction with caregivers and peers or forming secure attachment relationships with parents.

- During the preschool years, acquiring skills for engaging in positive interactions and positive social relationships with peers is also an important developmental task.
- Assessment of children's social development may occur at the levels of individual social behavior, social interactions, or social relationships.
- Social competence is the effective and appropriate use of social behaviors, as judged by appropriate members of an individual's social ecology.
- The nature of the social setting and participants in the interaction affect substantially the social performance of infants and young children.
- Assessment techniques often use observation of children in naturalistic settings to provide information about infants, children, and their social partners; these assessment techniques range from less formal anecdotal recordings to more formal structured direct observation measures.

- Sociometric assessments that employ photographs of classmates have often been used to assess social status of preschool-age children.
- Curriculum-based assessments may generate information about children's social performance that is useful for designing intervention programs.
- Norm-referenced instruments may provide information about children's social development that is useful for diagnosis, program evaluation, and research.
- Assessors must match their choice of assessment instruments to the questions they are trying to address about the infants' or children's participation in social interaction with caregivers or peers.
- Comprehensive assessments of children's social competence should include information provided by multiple sources and informants.

· · · · · · · ·

REFERENCES

Ainsworth, M. D., & Bell, S. M. (1970). Attachment, exploration, and separation: Illustrated by behavior of one year olds in a strange situation. *Child Development, 41,* 49–67.

Ainsworth, M. D., Blehar, M. C., Waters, E., & Walls, S. (1978). *Patterns of attachment: A psychological study of the strange situation.* Hillsdale, NJ: Lawrence Erlbaum.

Anderson, S., & Messick, S. (1974). Social competency in young children. *Developmental Psychology, 15,* 443–444.

Asher, S. R., Singleton, L. C., Tinsley, B. R., & Hymel, S. (1979). A reliable sociometric measure for preschool children. *Developmental Psychology, 15,* 443–444.

Bagnato, S., Neisworth, J. T., & Munson, S. M. (1997). *LINKing assessment and early intervention.* Baltimore: Paul H. Brookes.

Baird, S., Haas, L., McCormick, K., Carruth, C., & Turner, K. (1992). Approaching an objective system for observation and measurement: Infant-parent social interaction code. *Topics in Special Education, 12,* 544–571.

Baird, S., & Peterson, J. (1997). Seeking a comfortable fit between family-centered philosophy and infant-parent interaction in early intervention: Time for a paradigm shift? *Topics in Early Childhood Special Education, 97,* 139–165.

Bakeman, R., & Brown, J. (1980). Early interaction: Consequences for social and mental development at three years. *Child Development, 51,* 437–447.

Bakeman, R., & Brown, J. V. (1977). Behavioral dialogues: An approach to assessment of mother-infant interaction. *Child Development, 49,* 195–203.

Barnard, K. (1978a). *Nursing Child Assessment Feeding Scale.* Seattle, WA: University of Washington.

Barnard, K. (1978b). *Nursing Child Assessment Teaching Scale.* Seattle, WA: University of Washington.

Barnard, K. (2000). High-risk families: The emotionally unavailable parent and the child. In Wattenberg, E. (Ed.), *The fragile early years: Assessing the mental health of infants and toddlers.* (pp. 8–13) A summary of proceedings of the symposium held at the University of Minnesota, September 1999. (ERIC Document Reproduction Service No. ED439832)

Baron-Cohen, S., Cox, A., Baird, G., Swettenham, J., Nightingale, K. M., Drew, A., & Charman, T. (1999). Psychological markers in the detection of autism in infancy in a large population. *British Journal of Psychiatry, 168,* 158–163.

Barrera, M., Rosenbaum, P., & Cunningham, C. (1986). Early home intervention with low-birthweight infants and their parents. *Child Development, 57,* 20–33.

Bates, E. (1976). *Language and context: The acquisition of pragmatics.* New York: Academic Press.

Beaty, J. J. (1998). Observing development of the young child (4th ed). Upper Saddle River, NJ: Merrill/ Prentice Hall.

Beckman, P. J., & Kohl, F. L. (1984). The effects of social and isolate toys on the interactions and play of integrated and nonintegrated groups of preschoolers. *Education and Training of the Mentally Retarded, 18,* 169–174.

Beckman, P. J., & Lieber, J. (1994). The Social Strategy Rating Scale: An approach to evaluating social competence. *Journal of Early Intervention, 18,* 1–11.

Bell, R. (1968). A reinterpretation of the direction of effects in studies of socialization. *Psychological Review, 75,* 81–95.

Bernstein, V., Hans, S., & Percansky, C. (1992). *Parent-child observation guide.* (Available from Victor J. Bernstein, Department of Psychiatry, Box 411, The University of Chicago, Chicago, IL 60637.)

Bevis, K., & Odom, S. L. (2002). *Peer-buddy intervention to promote joint attention and social engagement of preschool children with autism.* Unpublished doctoral dissertation.

Blackwell, P. L. (2000). The influence of touch on child development: Implications for intervention. *Infants and Young Children, 13*(1), 25–39.

Bowlby, J. (1969). *Attachment and loss: Attachment* (Vol. 1). New York: Basic Books.

Bricker, D. (1989). *Early intervention for at-risk and handicapped infants, toddlers, and preschool children* (2nd ed.). Palo Alto, CA: VORT.

Bricker, D. (Ed.). (2002). *Assessment, evaluation, and programming systems (AEPS) for infants and children, Second edition.* Baltimore: Paul H. Brookes.

Bromwich, R. (1997). *Working with parents and their infants at risk.* Austin, TX: PRO-ED.

Bronson, M. B. (1994). The usefulness of an observational measure of young children's social and mastery behaviors in early childhood classrooms. *Early Childhood Research Quarterly, 9,* 19–43.

Brown, W. H., Odom, S. L., & Buysse, V. (2002). Assessment of preschool children's peer-related social competence. *Assessment for Effective Intervention, 27*(4), 61–71.

Brown, W. H., Ragland, E. U., & Fox, J. J. (1988). Effects of group socialization procedures on the social interactions of preschool children. *Research in Developmental Disabilities, 9,* 359–376.

Brownell, C. A., & Hazen, N. (1999). Early peer interaction: A research agenda. *Early Education and Development, 10,* 403–413.

Buysse, V., Goldman, B. D., & Skinner, M. L. (2002). Setting effects on friendship formation among young children with and without disabilities. *Exceptional Children, 68,* 503–517.

Cairns, R., & Green, J. (1979). How to assess personality and social patterns: Observations or ratings? In R. Cairns (Ed.), *The analysis of social interactions: Methods, issues, and illustrations* (pp. 209–226). Hillsdale, NJ: Lawrence Erlbaum.

Chen, Y., & McCollum, J. A. (2000). Taiwanese mothers' perceptions of the relationship between interactions with their infants and the development of social competence. *Early Child Development and Care, 162,* 25–40.

Clark, G., & Seifer, R. (1986). *Parent-Infant Interaction Scale, a manual for analysis of videotapes of unstructured play.* (Available from Ronald Seifer, Institute for the Study of Developmental Disabilities, University of Illinois at Chicago, 1640 West Roosevelt Road, Chicago, IL 60680.)

Clarke-Stewart, K. (1973). *Interactions between mothers and their young children: Characteristics and consequences.* Monographs of the Society for Research in Child Development, 38(6–7, Serial No. 153).

Clarke-Stewart, K., & Hevey, C. (1981). Longitudinal relations in repeated observations of mother-child interactions from 1 to 2 1/2 years. *Developmental Psychology, 17,* 127–145.

Coie, J. D., Dodge, K. A., & Copotelli, H. (1982). Dimensions and types of social status: A cross-age perspective. *Developmental Psychology, 18,* 557–570.

Crawley, S., & Spiker, D. (1982). *Mother-child Rating Scale.* Chicago, IL: University of Illinois. (ERIC Document Reproduction Service No. ED221978)

DeKlyen, M., & Odom, S. L. (1989). Activity structure and social interaction with peers in developmentally integrated play groups. *Journal of Early Intervention, 13,* 342–351.

Denham, S. A., & McKinley, M. (1993). Sociometric nominations for preschoolers: A psychometric analysis. *Early Education and Development, 4,* 109–122.

Doll, B., & Elliott, S. N. (1994). Representativeness of observed preschool social behaviors: How many data points are enough? *Journal of Early Intervention, 18,* 227–238.

Erwin, E. J. (1993). Social participation of young children with visual impairment in specialized and integrated environments. *Journal of Visual Impairments and Blindness, 87,* 138–142.

Field, T. (1983). High-risk infants "have less fun" during early interactions. *Topics of Early Childhood Special Education, 3*(1), 77–87.

Finn, R. (1972). Effects of some characteristics in rating scale characteristics on the means and reliabilities of ratings. *Educational and Psychological Measurement, 32,* 255–265.

Fraiberg, S. (1975). The development of human attachments in infants blind from birth. *Merrill-Palmer Quarterly, 21,* 315–324.

Furuno, S., O'Reilly, K., Hosaka, C., Inatsuka, T., Zeisloft-Falbey, B., & Allman, T. (1997). *Hawaii Early Learning Profile (HELP) activity guide.* Palo Alto, CA: VORT.

Garner, P., & Landry, S. (1992). Preterm infants' affective responses in independent versus toy-centered play with their mothers. *Infant Mental Health Journal, 13,* 219–230.

Goldberg, S. (1977). Social competence in infancy: A model of parent-infant interaction. *Merrill-Palmer Quarterly, 23,* 163–177.

Goldman, B. D., & Buysse, V. (2002). *Playmates and friends questionnaire for teachers—Revised.* Chapel Hill, NC: The University of North Carolina, FPG Child Development Institute.

Greenspan, S. I. & Meisels, S. J., (1996). Toward a new vision for the developmental assessment of infants and young children. In S. J. Meisels, & E. Fenichel (Eds.), *New visions for the developmental assessment of infants and young children* (pp. 11–26). Washington, DC: Zero to Three: National Center for Infants, Toddlers, and Families.

Greenspan, S. I., & Wieder, S. (1999). A functional developmental approach to autism spectrum disorder. *Journal of the Association for Persons with Severe Handicaps, 24,* 147–161.

Gresham, F. M. (1986). Conceptual issues in the assessment of social competence in children. In P. S. Strain, M. J. Guralnick, & H. Walker (Eds.), *Children's social behavior: Development, assessment, and modification* (pp. 143–176). New York: Academic Press.

Gresham, F., & Elliott, S. (1990). *Social Skills Rating System.* Circle Pines, MN: American Guidance Service.

Guba, E. G., & Lincoln, Y. S. (1989). *Fourth generation evaluation.* Newbury Park, CA: Sage.

Guilford, J. (1954). *Psychometric methods.* New York: McGraw-Hill.

Guralnick, M. J. (1992a). A hierarchical model for understanding children's peer-related social competence. In S. Odom, S. McConnell, & M. McEvoy (Eds.), *Social competence of young children with disabilities* (pp. 37–64). Baltimore: Paul H. Brookes.

Guralnick, M. J. (1992b). *Assessment of peer relations.* Seattle, WA: Child Development and Mental Retardation Center, University of Washington.

Guralnick, M. J. (1999). The nature and meaning of social integration for young children with mild developmental delays in inclusive settings. *Journal of Early Intervention, 22,* 70–86.

Guralnick, M. J. (2001). Social competence with peers and early childhood inclusion: Need for alternative approaches. In M. Guralnick (Ed.), *Early childhood inclusion: Focus on change* (pp. 481–503). Baltimore: Paul H. Brookes.

Guralnick, M. J., Connor, R. T., Hammond, M. A., Gottman, J. M., & Kinnish, K. (1996). Immediate effects of mainstreamed settings on the social interactions and social integration of preschool children. *American Journal on Mental Retardation, 100,* 359–377.

Guralnick, M. J., Gottman, J. M., & Hammond, M. A. (1996). Effects of social setting on the friendship formation of young children differing in developmental status. *Journal of Applied Developmental Psychology, 17,* 625–651.

Guralnick, M. J., & Groom, J. M. (1987). The peer relations of mildly delayed and nonhandicapped preschool children in mainstreamed playgroups. *Child Development, 58,* 1556–1572.

Guralnick, M. J., & Groom, J. M. (1988). Friendships of preschool children in mainstream playgroups. *Developmental Psychology, 24,* 595–604.

Hane, A. A., Feldstein, S., Morrison, B. M., & Loo, S. (1999). *The relation between coordinated interpersonal timing and maternal sensitivity in four-month-old infants.* Paper presented at the Meeting of the Society for Research in Child Development, Albuquerque, NM. (ERIC Document Reproduction Service No. ED429693)

Hartman, D. P., & Wood, D. D. (1990). Observational methods. In A. Bellack, M. Hersen, & A. Kazdin (Eds.), *International handbook of behavior modification and therapy* (pp. 107–138). New York: Plenum Press.

Hartup, W. W., Glazer, J., & Charlesworth, R. (1967). Peer reinforcement and sociometric status. *Child Development, 38,* 1017–1024.

Hayvren, M., & Hymel, S. (1984). Ethical issues in sociometric testing: Impact of sociometric measures on interaction behavior. *Developmental Psychology, 20,* 844–849.

Hops, H., Guild, J., Fleishman, D. H., Paine, S., Street, A., Walker, H., & Greenwood, C. (1979). *Peers: Procedures for establishing effective relationship skills.* Eugene, OR: CORBEH.

Howes, C. (1992). *Collaborative construction of pretend play.* Albany, NY: State University of New York Press.

Hundert, J. (1995). *Enhancing social competence in young students: School-based approaches.* Austin, TX: PRO-ED.

Ivory, J. J., & McCollum, J. A. (1999). Effects of social and isolate toys on social play in an inclusive setting. *Journal of Special Education, 32,* 238–243.

Jaffe, J., Beebe, B., Feldstein, S., Crown, C. L., & Jasnow, M. D. (2001). Rhythms of dialogue in infancy. *Monographs of the Society for Research in Child Development, 66* (2, Serial No. 265).

Jay, S., & Farran, D. (1981). The relative efficacy of predicting IQ from mother-child interactions using ratings versus behavioral count measures. *Journal of Applied Developmental Psychology, 2,* 165–177.

Johnson, C., Ironsmith, M., Snow, C. W., & Poteat, G. M. (2000). Peer acceptance and social adjustment in preschool and kindergarten. *Early Childhood Education Journal, 27,* 207–12.

Kelly, J. F., & Barnard, K. E. (2000). Assessment of parent-child interaction: Implications for early intervention. In J. P. Shonkoff & S. J. Meisels (Eds.), *Handbook of early childhood intervention* (2nd ed., pp. 258–289). Cambridge, UK: Cambridge University Press.

Klein, P. S. (in press). A mediational approach to early intervention in Israel. In S. Odom, M. Hanson, J. Blackman, & S. Kaul (Eds.), *Early intervention practices from around the world.* Baltimore: Paul H. Brookes.

Kohler, F. W., & Fowler, S. A. (1985). Training prosocial behaviors to young children: An analysis of reciprocity with untrained peers. *Journal of Applied Behavior Analysis, 18,* 187–200.

Kopp, C. B., Baker, B. L., & Brown, K. W. (1992). Social skills and their correlates: Preschoolers with developmental delays. *American Journal on Mental Retardation, 96,* 357–367.

Lee, S., & Kahn, J. V. (2000). A survival analysis of parent-child interaction in early intervention. *Infant-Toddler Intervention, 10,* 137–156.

Lewis, M., & Lee-Painter, S. (1974). An interactional approach to the mother-infant dyad. In M. Lewis & L. Rosenblum (Eds.), *The effect of the infant on its caregiver* (pp. 21–48). New York: John Wiley.

Likert, R. (1932). A technique for the measurement of attitudes. *Archives of Psychology, 22*(140), 1–52.

Linder, T. (1993a). *The Transdisciplinary Play-Based Assessment-Revised,* Baltimore: Paul H. Brookes.

Linder, T. (1993b). *The Transdisciplinary Play-Based Intervention.* Baltimore: Paul H. Brookes.

Lussier, B., Crimmins, D., & Alberti, D. (1994). Effect of three adult interaction styles on infant engagement. *Journal of Early Intervention, 18,* 12–24.

Lynch, E. (1996). Assessing infants: Child and family issues and approaches. In M. Hanson (Ed.), *Atypical infant development* (2nd ed., pp. 115–146). Austin, TX: PRO-ED.

Mahoney, G. (1992). *Maternal Behavior Rating Scale-Revised.* (Available from Family Child Learning Center, 143 Northwest Avenue, Bldg. A, Tallmadge, OH 44278).

Mahoney, G., Spiker, D., and Boyce, G. (1996). Clinical assessment of parent-child interaction: Are professionals ready to implement this practice? *Topics in Early Childhood Special Education, 16,* 26–50.

Marshall, H. R. (1957). An evaluation of sociometric-social behavior research with preschool children. *Child Development, 28,* 131–137.

McAllister, J. R. (1991). Curriculum-based behavioral intervention for preschool children with handicaps. *Topics in Early Childhood Special Education, 11*(2), 48–58.

McCloskey, G. (1990). Selecting and using early childhood rating scales. *Topics in Early Childhood Special Education, 10,* 39–64.

McCabe, J. R., Jenkins, J. R., Mills, P. E., Dale, P. S., & Cole, K. N. (1999). Effects of group composition, materials, and developmental level on play in preschool children with disabilities. *Journal of Early Intervention, 22,* 164–178.

McClellan, D. E., & Katz, L. G. (2001). Assessing young children's social competence. *ERIC Digests.* Champaign, IL: ERIC Clearinghouse of Elementary and Early Childhood Education. (ERIC Document Reproduction Service No. ED450953)

McCollum, J. A., Gooler, F., Appl, D. J., & Yates, T. J. (2001). PIWI: Enhancing parent-child interaction as a foundation for early intervention. *Infants and Young Children, 14*(1), 34–45.

McCollum, J. A., & McBride, S. L. (1997). Ratings of parent-infant interaction: Raising questions of cultural validity. *Topics in Early Childhood Special Education, 17,* 494–519.

McCollum, J., Ree, Y., & Chen, U. (2000). Interpreting parent-infant interactions: Cross-cultural lesions. *Infants and Young Children, 12*(4), 22–33.

McConnell, S. R., & Odom, S. L. (1986). Sociometrics: Peer-referenced measures and the assessment of social competence. In P. Strain, M. Guralnick, & H. Walker (Eds.), *Children's social behavior: Development, assessment, and modification* (pp. 215–286). New York: Academic Press.

McConnell, S. R., & Odom, S. L. (1999). Performance-based assessment of social competence for young children with disabilities. Development and initial evaluation of a multi-measure model. *Topics in Early Childhood Special Education, 19,* 67–74.

McFall, R. M. (1982). A reformulation of the concept of social skill. *Behavioral Assessment, 4,* 1–33.

Merrell, K. W. (2003). *Preschool and kindergarten behavior scales, Second edition.* Austin, TX: PRO-ED.

Munson, L., & Odom, S. (1994). *Infant-Caregiver Interaction Scale (ICIS) Manual.* Unpublished observer training manual, Portland, OR: Portland State University, Department of Special Education.

Munson, L., & Odom, S.L. (1996). Review of rating scales that measure parent-infant interaction. *Topics in Early Childhood Special Education, 16,* 1–26.

Neisworth, J. T., & Bagnato, S. J. (2000). Recommended practices in assessment. In S. Sandall, M. McLean, & B. Smith, *DEC recommended practices in early intervention/early childhood special education* (pp. 17–27). Denver, CO: Sopris West.

Newborg, J., Stock, J. R., Wnek, L., Guidubaldi, J., & Svinicki, J. (1988). *Battelle Developmental Inventory with Recalibrated Technical Data and Norms.* Allen, TX: DLM.

Nicholson, S., & Shipstead, S. G. (1998). *Through the looking glass: Observations in the early childhood classroom* (2nd ed.) Upper Saddle River, NJ: Merrill/Prentice Hall.

Noldus Information System. (2000). *The Observer.* Sterling, VA: Author.

O'Connor, M., Sigman, M., & Kasari, C. (1992). Attachment behavior of infants exposed prenatally to alcohol: Mediating effects of infant affect and mother-infant interaction. *Development and Psychopathology, 4,* 243–256.

Odom, S. L. (1981). The relationship of play to developmental level in mentally retarded children. *Education and Training of the Mentally Retarded, 16,* 136–142.

Odom, S. L. (1988). Research in early childhood special education: Methodologies and paradigms. In S. Odom & M. Karnes (Eds.), *Early intervention for infants and young children with handicaps: An empirical base* (pp. 1–21). Baltimore: Paul H. Brookes.

Odom, S. L. (2000). Preschool inclusion: What we know and where we go from here. *Topics in Early Childhood Special Education, 20,* 20–28.

Odom, S. L., Bender, M., Doran, L., Houden, P., McInnes, M., DeKlyen, M., Speltz, M., & Jenkins, J. (1988). *Integrated preschool curriculum.* Seattle, WA: University of Washington Press.

Odom, S. L., & McConnell, S. R. (1985). A performance-based conceptualization of social competence of handicapped preschool children: *Implications for assessment. Topics in Early Childhood Special Education, 4*(4), 1–19.

Odom, S. L., McConnell, S. R., McEvoy, M. A., Peterson, C., Ostrosky, M., Chandler, et al. (1999). Relative effects of interventions for supporting the social competence of young children with disabilities. *Topics in Early Childhood Special Education, 19,* 75–91.

Odom, S. L., & Munson, L. J. (1996). Assessing social performance. In M. McLean, D. Bailey & M. Wolery (Eds). *Assessing infants and preschoolers with special needs.* Upper Saddle River, NJ: Merrill/Prentice Hall, 398–434.

Odom, S. L., & Ogawa, O. (1992). Direct observation of young children's social interaction with peers: A review of methodology. *Behavioral Assessment, 14,* 407–441.

Odom, S. L., Peterson, C., McConnell, S. R., & Ostrosky, M. M. (1990). Ecobehavioral analysis of early education/specialized classroom settings and peer social interaction. *Education and Training of Children, 13,* 316–330.

Odom, S. L., & Strain, P. S. (1986). Using teacher antecedents and peer initiations to increase reciprocal social interactions of autistic children: A comparative treatment study. *Journal of Applied Behavior Analysis, 19,* 59–71.

Odom, S. L., Zercher, C., Marquart, J., Li, S., Sandall, S., & Wolfberg, P. (2001). Social relationships of children with disabilities and their peers in inclusive preschool classrooms. In S. Odom (Ed.), *Widening the circle: Including children with disabilities in preschool programs* (pp. 61–80). New York: Teachers College Press.

Odom, S. L., Zercher, C., Li, S., Marquart, J., & Sandall, S. (2002). *Social acceptance and social rejection of children with disabilities in inclusive preschools.* Manuscript submitted for publication.

Olson, S., Bates, J., & Bayles, K. (1984). Mother-infant interaction and the development of individual differences in children's cognitive competence. *Developmental Psychology, 50,* 166–179.

Osofsky, J. D., & Thompson, M. D. (2000). Adaptive and maladaptive parenting: Perspectives on risk and protective factors. In J. P. Shonkoff & S. J. Meisels (Eds.), *Handbook of early childhood intervention* (2nd ed., pp. 54–75). Cambridge, UK: Cambridge University Press.

Parks, S., & Furuno, S. (Ed.). (1997). *HELP at home.* Palo Alto, CA: VORT.

Parks, S. (1997). *Inside HELP: Administration and reference manual for the Hawaii Early Learning Profile (HELP).* Palo Alto, CA: VORT.

Parten, M. B. (1932). Social participation among preschool children. *Journal of Abnormal and Social Psychology, 27,* 243–269.

Pelaez-Nogueras, M., Field, T. M., Hossain, Z., & Pickens, J. (1996). Depressed mothers' touching increases infants' positive affect and attention in still-face interactions. *Child Development, 67,* 1780–1792.

Poteat, G. M., Ironsmith, M., & Bullock, J. (1986). The classification of preschool children's social status. *Early Childhood Research Quarterly, 1,* 349–360.

Rasmussen, J. (1989). Analysis of Likert-scale data: A reinterpretation of Gregoire and Driver. *Psychological Bulletin, 105,* 167–170.

Roberts, S. B., Brown, P. M., & Rickards, F. W. (1995). Social pretend play entry behaviors of preschoolers with and without impaired hearing. *Journal of Early Intervention, 20,* 52–83.

Rochat, P. R. (2001). Social contingency detection and infant development. *Bulletin of the Mellinger Clinic, 65,* 347–361.

Rothbart, M. K. (1996). Social development. In M. J. Hanson (Ed.), *Atypical infant development* (2nd ed., pp. 273–310). Austin, TX: PRO-ED.

Rubenstein, J. L., & Howes, C. (1979). Caregiving and infant behavior in day care and in homes. *Developmental Psychology, 15,* 1–24.

Rubin, K. (1982). Nonsocial play in preschoolers: Necessarily evil? *Child Development, 53,* 651–657.

Rubin, K. H., Bukowski, W., & Parker, J. G. (1998). Peer interactions, relationships, and groups. In N. Eisenberg (Ed.), *Handbook of child psychology* (5th ed.), Vol. 3: Social, emotional, and personality development (pp. 619–700). New York: John Wiley & Sons.

Rubin, K. H., Maioni, T. L., & Hornung, M. (1976). Freeplay behaviors in middle- and lower-class preschoolers: Parten and Piaget revisited. *Child Development, 47,* 414–419.

Sackett, G. P. (1978). Measurement in observational research. In G. Sackett (Ed.), *Observing behavior: Data collection and analysis methods,* Vol. II (pp. 25–44). Baltimore: University Park Press.

Salisbury, C., Britzman, D., & Kang, J. (1989). Using qualitative methods to assess the social-communicative competence of young handicapped children. *Journal of Early Intervention, 13,* 153–165.

Schaefer, E. (1989). Dimensions of mother-infant interaction: Measurement, stability, and predictive validity. *Infant Behavior and Development, 12,* 379–393.

Schertz, H., & Odom, S.L. (2002). *Early diagnosis and intervention in autism: The role of joint attention.* Manuscript submitted for publication.

Schore, A. N. (2000). *Parent-infant communication and the neurobiology of emotional development.* Paper presented at the Head Start National Research Conference, Washington, DC, 2000. (ERIC Document Reproduction Service No. ED443546)

Shonkoff, J. P., & Phillips, D. A. (Eds.) (2000). *From neurons to neighborhoods: The science of early childhood development*. Washington, DC: National Academy Press.

Shores, R. (1997). *Social interaction continuous observation program for experimental studies (SCOPES)*. Parsons, KS: University of Kansas.

Shure, M. B. (1993). I can problem solve (ICPS): Interpersonal cognitive problem solving for young children. *Early Child Development and Care, 96*, 49–64.

Smilansky, S. (1968). *The effects of sociodramatic play on disadvantaged preschool children*. New York: John Wiley & Sons.

Snyder, S., & Sheehan, R. (1996). Program evaluation in early childhood special education. In S. L. Odom & M. E. McLean (Eds.), *Early intervention for infants and young children with disabilities and their families: Recommended practices* (pp. 359–378). Austin, TX: PRO-ED.

Sparrow, S., Balla, D., & Cicchetti, D. (1984). *Vineland Adaptive Behavior Scales*. Circle Pines, MN: American Guidance Service.

Spieker, S. J. (1986). Pattern of very insecure attachment found in samples of high-risk infants and toddlers. *Topics in Early Childhood Special Education, 6*(3), 86–99.

Squires, J., Bricker, D., & Twombly, M. S. (2000). *Ages and Stages Questionnaires: Social-Emotional (ASQ:SE)*. Baltimore: Paul H. Brookes.

Stone, W. L., & Ruble, L. A. (2002, July). *Development of the STAT for early autism screening*. Poster presented at the 2002 OSEP Research Project Directors Conference, Crystal City, VA.

Strain, P. S. (1983). Generalization of autistic children's social behavior change: Effects of developmentally integrated and segregated settings. *Analysis and Intervention in Developmental Disabilities, 3*, 23–34.

Strain, P. S., & Shores, R. E. (1977). Social reciprocity: A review of research and educational implications. *Exceptional Children, 43*, 526–530.

Strain, P. S., & Timm, M. A. (1974). An experimental analysis of social interaction between a behaviorally disordered preschool child and her classroom peers. *Journal of Applied Behavior Analysis, 7*, 583–590.

Tapp, J., Wehby, J. H., & Ellis, D. (1995). A multiple option observation system for experimental studies: MOOSES. *Behavior Research Methods, Instruments, and Computers, 27*, 25–31.

Tapp, J., & Wehby, J. H. (2000). Observational software for laptop computers and optical bar code readers. In T. Thompson, D. Felce, & F. Symons (Eds.), *Behavioral observation: Technology and applications in developmental disabilities* (pp. 71–82). Baltimore: Paul H. Brookes.

Thompson, R. A. (2001). Sensitive periods in attachment? In D. B. Bailey, J. T. Bruer, F. J. Symons, & J. W. Lichtman, *Critical thinking about critical periods* (pp. 83–106). Baltimore: Paul H. Brookes.

Thompson, T., Felce, D., & Symons, F. J. (Eds.). (2000). *Behavioral observations: Technology and applications in developmental disabilities*. Baltimore: Paul H. Brookes.

Thompson, T., Symons, F. J., & Felce, D. (2000). Principles of behavioral observation. In T. Thompson, D. Felce, & F. J. Symons (Eds.), *Behavioral observations: Technology and applications in developmental disabilities* (pp. 3 16). Baltimore: Paul H. Brookes.

Tremblay, A., Strain, P. S., Hendrickson, J. M., & Shores, R. E. (1981). Social interactions of normally developing preschool children: Using normative data for subject selection and target behavior selection. *Behavior Modification, 5*, 237–253.

Trepagnier, C. (1996). A possible origin for the social and communicative deficits of autism. *Focus on Autism and Other Developmental Disabilities, 11*, 170–183.

Vanderbilt/Minnesota Social Interaction Project (S. Odom and S. McConnell, Eds.) (1993). *Play time/social time: Organizing your classroom to build interaction skills*. Minneapolis, MN: University of Minnesota, Institute on Community Integration.

Vondra, J. I., & Barnett, D. (1999). Atypical attachment in infancy and early childhood among children at developmental risk. *Monographs of the Society for Research in Child Development, 64* (3, Serial No. 258).

VORT Corporation. (1995). *HELP for preschoolers: Assessment and curriculum guide*. Palo Alto, CA: Author.

Wedell-Monig, J., & Lumley, J. (1980). Child deafness and mother-child interaction. *Child Development, 51*, 766–774.

Werner, E. E. (2000). Protective factors and individual resilience. In J. P. Shonkoff & S. J. Meisels (Eds.), *Handbook of early childhood intervention* (2nd ed., pp. 115–132). Cambridge, UK: Cambridge University Press.

Wolfberg, P., Zercher, P., Lieber, J., Capell, K., Matias, S., Hanson, M., & Odom, S. L. (1999). "Can I play with you?" Peer culture in inclusive preschool programs. *Journal of the Association for Persons with Severe Disabilities, 24,* 69–84.

Wright, M. J. (1980). Measuring social competence of preschool children. *Canadian Journal of Behavioral Science, 12,* 17–32.

Yoder, P. (1987). Relationship between degree of infant handicap and clarity of infant cues. *American Journal of Mental Deficiency, 91,* 639–641.

Zeanah, C. H., & Zeanah, P. D. (2001). Towards a definition of infant mental health. *Zero to Three, 22,* 13–20.

Zeitlin, S., Williamson, G. G., & Gzczepanski, M. (1988). *Early Coping Inventory.* Bensenville, IL: Scholastic Testing Service.

Zercher, C., Brown, W. H., & Odom, S. L. (2002, February). Ecobehavioral analysis of children's social interaction in inclusive preschool settings. Presentation at the Conference on Research Innovations in Early Intervention, San Diego, CA.

Zigler, E., & Trickett, P. K. (1978). IQ, social competence, and evaluation of early childhood intervention programs. *American Psychologist, 33,* 789–798.

Assessing Play Skills

Ann N. Garfinkle
Vanderbilt University

Play is an important activity for young children with and without disabilities. In fact, the right of children to engage in play is recognized by the United Nations (United Nations High Commission for Human Rights, 1990). Developmentally Appropriate Practices (Bredekamp & Copple, 1997), which are often translated into recommended practices or curricula for early childhood education classrooms, are predicated on play. Likewise, play is the context for activity-based intervention (Bricker, Pretti-Frontczak, & McComas, 1998) and embedded learning opportunities (Sandall & Schwartz, 2002), which are recommended practices for young children with disabilities (Sandall, McLean, & Smith, 2000). This chapter addresses issues related to the assessment of play skills. Specifically, the chapter (a) provides a rationale for assessing play skills; (b) presents an overview of the characteristics of play; (c) describes several taxonomies of play; (d) describes methods for assessing play; (e) specifies guidelines for assessing play; (f) offers suggestions for using information from play assessments for establishing goals and objectives for young children with developmental disabilities; (g) includes suggestions for using information from play assessments for planning interventions; and (h) provides an overview of monitoring children's growth in play skills over time.

RATIONALE FOR ASSESSING PLAY

There is wide agreement that young children spend large amounts of time playing. Children played in ancient times, as evidenced by Egyptian wall paintings that depict children playing with balls and dolls and jumping rope (French, 1977). Children play in all cultures (Hughes, 1991). Interestingly, the type of play that children engage in, varies according to cultural norms and mores. For example, the play of children in technologically advanced affluent societies is characterized by high levels of competition, whereas communities that survive in a subsistence economy are less tolerant of such competition (Sutton-Smith, 1980). The reason children play, however, is not widely agreed upon. Early play theories suggested that children engaged in play to: discharge pent-up or surplus energy (Spencer, 1873); renew the body's energy (Patrick, 1916); retrace the evolutionary history of the species (Hull, 1943); or, prepare the child for the tasks of adulthood (Groos, 1901). Contemporary theories are as varied as these early theories: psychoanalytic theory suggests that children play to reduce anxiety (Freud, 1974); cognitive–developmental theory suggests play helps children learn to solve a variety of cognitive problems (Bruner, 1972) or to consolidate newly learned behaviors (Piaget, 1962).

Despite this array of theoretical rationales and explanations for play, there is agreement across contemporary theorists and researchers that through play, children exhibit skills they have already mastered and learn new skills (Malone, 1999). Social and communication skills are the most often sited examples of skills that children learn or exhibit while playing. It is also widely suggested that children develop cognitive skills through play. Some authors also suggest that children learn creativity and affective skills through play (Sherratt & Peter, 2002).

There is, however, little empirical support for these claims and the evidence that is available does not explain the relationship of play to skills in other developmental domains. For example, Eisert and Lamorrey (1996) found that for children younger than 20 months, play skills were correlated with adaptive and language skills, but that in children older than 20 months of age, play skills were correlated only with language skills. This lack of correlation between play skills and other adaptive behaviors has been replicated in other studies (e.g., Sigafoos, Roberts-Pennell, & Grave, 1999). Similarly, Kennedy, Sherida, Radlinski & Beeghly (1991) identified a relationship between complexity of play and complexity and length of verbal utterances. Interesting as these data may be, the data do not provide information to explain a causal connection between the skills in the two domains. One should keep in mind that these studies are correlational, and thus causation cannot be inferred. Further, there is always a possibility that a relationship like the one discussed here may be the result of the development of a skill, or skills, that is neither a language nor play skill, but affects development in both domains. Thus, although growth in play is theoretically linked to growth in skills in other developmental domains, more studies are needed to bring clarity and precision to describing the nature of the relationship.

While there is still much for researchers to learn about play, play is a valued activity and is a legitimate curricular domain for infants and young children with and without disabilities (Sherratt & Peter, 2000; Wolery, 1989). As in other areas of development, young children with disabilities may exhibit deficits or delays in play skills (Sigafoos, Roberts-Pennell, & Grave, 1999). The nature of these skill deficits is not well understood. In some cases, children's play skills may differ from same-aged peers but be similar to the skills exhibited by a child of comparable developmental status (Malone, Stoneman, & Langone, 1994) or with similar expressive language scores (Eisert & Lamorrey, 1996).

No disability is diagnosed due to deficits in play skills, but children with specific disabilities may have predictable deficits in play skills. The best example of this is in children with autism. Children with autism are believed to have deficits in symbolic and pretend play (Wing, Gould, Yeates, & Brierley, 1977). Researchers are currently working to determine if (a) these play skill deficits exist when developmental age is considered and (b) these measured deficits are pathogenetic in autism. There is evidence that children with other disabilities also have deficits in play skills. For example, the play of children with mental retardation may be characterized by a restricted repertoire of skills, reduced language during play, less sophisticated representational play, and limited selection of materials (Li, 1981). The play of children with severe disabilities may be characterized as consisting largely of stereotypic behaviors (Thompson & Berkson, 1985). Children with physical disabilities may have problems participating in play due to manipulative and mobility issues (Linder, 1994). Children with visual impairments may exhibit fewer social play exchanges and more time in solitary play than typically developing peers (Fewell & Kaminski, 1988). Children with language delays engage in less symbolic play, make fewer social contacts and have less organized play than typically developing peers (Lovell, Hoyle, & Siddall, 1968). Children with attention deficit/hyperactivity disorder (ADHD) seem to engage in less symbolic play and social play and more repetitive movements than typically developing peers (Allesandri, 1992). As with autism, it is not clear if these documented differences in play exist when the child's developmental age is considered.

The value placed on play by society and the likelihood that children with disabilities will have deficits or delays in play skills (when compared to same-aged peers) are two important reasons for assessing play. Researchers who study young children from a developmental perspective also suggest that the play of young children with disabilities should be assessed for the following reasons: play facilitates learning in other important developmental domains; play is an activity in which children learn self-respect; and play is an enjoyable activity. Researchers who approach the study of young children from an eco/behavioral perspective suggest the following rationales for assessing the play of young children: play is the context for implementing interventions; play increases opportunities for normative activities; play has a practical value; and play is a functional skill. The majority of these reasons have been discussed above or are straightforward. Three of these reasons—play increases opportunities for normative activities, play has a practical value, and play is a functional skill—need further explanation and are discussed here.

Play Increases Opportunities for Normative Activities

Parents believe that part of their job is to play with their child. This play may be social (as in tickle or patty-cake games) or involve objects (like rolling a ball back and forth). Thus, in order for parents to feel as if they are parenting their child, as opposed to being the child's therapist, parents and children need to spend time in playful and play-based interactions.

Likewise, young typically developing children interact with one another through play. In other words, play is the milieu in which peer social interactions take place. These social interactions then form the basis for social relationships. Thus, play is a foundation skill for the formation of social relationships. Relationships are a valued outcome for young children with disabilities (Schwartz, Garfinkle, & Davis, 2002).

Play Has a Practical Value

As stated in the beginning of this chapter, recommended practices for both early childhood education and early childhood special education consider play to be fundamental. Increasingly, intervention for young children with disabilities are embedded into the context of play or play-based activities. Thus, if young children with disabilities are going to participate in these programs, play skills are important. Similarly, because children are thought to engage naturally in play, play is often used as a context to assess developmental performance (Linder, 1993). Thus, play is the milieu in which important childhood activities take place.

Play Is a Functional Skill

There are many demands on the time of parents, especially parents of infants and young children with disabilities. If children have limited or inadequate play skills, parents must spend more time providing care for the child. If, however, the child can play independently, the parents can participate in other important tasks of daily living such as showering, cleaning, or preparing meals. Secondly, play is a lifelong skill. As the child ages, play activities develop into leisure skills. This is particularly important when one realizes that lack of leisure skills is problematic among secondary-aged students and adults with disabilities.

CHARACTERISTICS OF PLAY

Play is multifaceted and changes constantly (Fromberg, 2002). Play does not use a specific form; for example, no specific behaviors would always and only be considered play. Play is not conducted in a specific setting; it can happen almost anywhere. The behaviors that constitute play at one time may not constitute play at another time. Play is not unique to a specific age or specific skill level or a specific skill set. Play can be a solitary or social experience. Play is a word that is used as both a noun and a verb (Fromberg, 1999). Play can be the action, the process, and the product of children's behavior (Sherratt & Peter, 2002).

Because play is unspecified and is represented by such a broad array of behaviors, providing a single operational definition seems almost impossible (Wolery, 1989). Instead, researchers have chosen to either describe play or define the characteristics of play (Fewell & Kaminski, 1988). Fromberg (2002) characterizes play as voluntary, meaningful, symbolic, rule-governed, pleasurable, and episodic. Hughes (1991) characterizes play as intrinsically motivated, freely chosen, pleasurable, nonliteral, and actively engaged. In addition, Smith and Vollstedt (1985) also characterize play as being self-generated, flexible, and involving means more than ends—focused on the doing, not on reaching a particular goal.

Some authors differentiate play from exploration (Hughes, 1991). Exploration is commonly thought of as manipulating an object, sometimes in a stereotypical way, to learn about the properties of the object. The assumption is that once children learn about the object, then it can be used in play. This division is difficult to see in practice, however, particularly when considering the play behaviors of very young children or children without sophisticated play skills. Other authors differentiate play from work. Although some (e.g., Montessori) have described play as the work of the child, the distinction between work and play is meant to underscore that play is intrinsically motivated, freely chosen, pleasurable and nonliteral; whereas, for many, these traits would not characterize work. Thus even though play can be characterized and distinguished from seemingly similar behaviors, it is difficult to capture the essential qualities defining play.

The view that play is self-generated may lead some to conclude that play is innate. Due to a paucity of data, the question of innateness cannot be empirically answered. Regardless of whether or not play is innate, it should be noted that environmental variables affect children's play. For example, Malone, Stoneman and Langone (1994) reported systematic differences in the play behaviors of young children with disabilities when assessed at home and at school. Similarly, the presence of familiar peers and the gender of those peers influences play behaviors (Freeman & Kasari, 2002; Simpkins & Parker, 2002).

The view that play is intrinsically motivated, freely chosen, and pleasureable may suggest to some that play should not be taught. Of course, when instruction involves choice and is reinforcing, these statements may not be at odds. Regardless, some young children, especially those with severe disabilities, may have restricted play interests and spend little time independently and appropriately engaged with toys or other play materials. It is important to keep in mind that just because a child does not spontaneously play does not mean that the child is choosing not to play. There are multiple reasons a child may not spontaneously play (e.g., lack of skills, lack of experience, lack of play initiation skills). Thus, just because a child does not engage in spontaneous play does not mean that the child does not want to play.

Finally, it is clear that children learn play skills. For example, children learn to play with new toys, learn to use familiar toys in novel ways, learn games, and become more skilled players over time. Thus, the question of whether or not play is innate is an open question. The question of whether or not play should be taught is, however, answerable: play is and should be taught.

TAXONOMIES OF PLAY

Describing play through characteristics helps to describe what play is and what it is not. Description alone, however, does not provide enough specificity to aid with the measurement or assessment of play. Researchers have found that developing and using taxonomies is an effective way to help in the measurement of play. This measurement is possible because a taxonomy is a classification system. Each category in the taxonomy can then be defined by specifying behaviors that are discrete and observable. This specification of behaviors is the key that makes measurement and assessment possible.

A common but simplistic categorization of play is that play can be social or nonsocial. While this separation helps to make the point that play can be solitary with objects or social without objects, the dichotomy is too gross to provide information that is useful for assessing play when planning intervention. Also, this separation is artificial. That is, when describing the categories of non-social play, the more developmentally advanced categories tend to include descriptions of social play, which is counterintuitive for a nonsocial classification system. Many other taxonomies of play, however, have been developed.

Piaget (1962) provided an initial taxonomy with three major categories of play and subtypes within each category. He described practice play, symbolic play, and games with rules. Practice play involves repetitive motor actions on objects. Symbolic play involves the use of objects, real or imagined, to stand for a different object. Games with rules is play in which participants act in specific, predetermined ways. Children in the sensorimotor period of development engage in practice play. Children in the preoperational stage can participate in symbolic play. Children in the concrete operations period can participate in games with rules. However, this is not a lock-step sequence. Children in the concrete operations stage may participate in practice play, symbolic play, and in games with rules all in a short period of time. It is unlikely, however, that a child in the sensorimotor stage could be seen participating in either symbolic play, or games with rules.

Since Piaget, numerous authors have developed other taxonomies of play. Traditional taxonomies of play, such as Smilansky (1968), Chance (1979), Wehman (1977), and Sutton-Smith (1970) all share some features with Piaget's original description. See Table 14.1 for a description of each author's play taxonomy. Each of these taxonomies has been used in studies measuring children's play; none of these taxonomies, however, is preferred over another. In a 1995 review of methodological issues in studying toy play, Malone and Stoneman reported that over half of the studies they reviewed used a unique coding system. Where a common code was used across studies, it was most likely that a researcher or research team used the same coding system (e.g., Guralnick, 1981; Guralnick & Weinhouse, 1984). Few attempts have been made to validate the play taxonomies empirically (Malone & Stoneman, 1995). Thus, there is little empirical guidance for teachers in choosing one of these traditional play taxonomies.

Sherratt and Peter (2002), however, used the common features of the taxonomies to create a contemporary, general taxonomy that they use in their classroom-based work to teach play skills to children with autism. This general taxonomy includes sensorimotor play, relational play, functional play, symbolic play, and themed fantasy. A description of each of these categories is found in Table 14.2. One strength of this contemporary taxonomy is the range of play categories. The

categories range from sensorimotor play, the most basic play behaviors, to themed fantasy, which is elaborate, sophisticated, play. The advantage of this range is that teachers can learn and use one taxonomy for multiple children who exhibit a wide range of skills, such as the range of behaviors a teacher may experience in an inclusive classroom. Another advantage is that teachers can use this coding schema to monitor children's progress over time. That is, children will not quickly reach the ceiling of the taxonomy.

In addition to the Sherratt and Peter taxonomy, there are two other measurement systems that may be of particular interest to those who work with young children in classroom contexts. The first was developed by Parten (1932). Parten's work is classic and foundational but still relevant today. Unlike the taxonomies described above, which are based on the notion that the development of play parallels cognitive development, the focus of Parten's taxonomy is on the social aspects of play. Parten developed a seven category taxonomy of social play. Table 14.3 describes each of these seven categories.

Second and more recently, Malone has suggested that play level (as described in the Parten taxonomies) is insufficient to characterize the nature of children's play. Malone and colleagues (Malone, Stoneman & Langone, 1994) suggest play sequences must be measured to get a real sense about children's play skills. Malone has devised a three category, mutually exclusive and exhaustive code for coding play sequences. The categories are single scheme, unordered multischeme, and ordered multischeme. A *single scheme* is when a child uses a single action repeatedly. For example, a child pounds a drum with a stick. An *unordered multischeme* is when two or more unrelated actions are combined but there appears to be no plan for the object. For example, a child stacks a block on top of another block and rolls a car on the block. An *ordered multischeme* is when distinct actions are related in a sequential manner and there seems to be a logical progression to the actions. For example, a child pretends

TABLE 14.1
Traditional Taxonomies of Play

Author and Play Types (categories)	Description
Smilansky (1968)	
Functional play	Repetitive movements that appear playful and frequently involve objects
Constructive play	Use of objects to make or create something
Dramatic play	Use of pretend play with or without objects, frequently involving the child assuming a given role
Games with rules	Engagement in activities that involve compliance with the conventions and requirements of games and may involve competition with others
Chance (1979)	
Physical play	Action that is frequently social, may be competitive, and includes rough-and-tumble activities
Manipulative play	Actions on objects, designed to gain control of those objects
Symbolic play	Pretend play that may include objects being used to represent other objects
Games	Engagement in activities that involves compliance with the conventions and requirements of games and may involve competition with others
Wehman (1977)[a]	
Exploration	
Level I—Orientational responses	Relatively abrupt behavioral changes that occur as a result of external stimulation and appear to redirect the child's attention
Level II—Locomotor exploration	Movement about an environment that produces sensory feedback
Level III—Perceptual investigation and manipulation	Movements on objects that appear to provide the child with information about the characteristics of the object
Level IV— Searching	Seeking a new stimulus for exploration
Toy Play	
Level I—Repetitive manual manipulation/ oral contacts	Repetitive actions on objects with attention to sensory consequences
Level II—Pounding, throwing, pushing/ pulling	Repetitive actions on objects that frequently involve gross motor movements and a beginning awareness of cause/effect relationships
Level III—Personalized toy use	Use of toys to perform actions on the child's body, frequently uses miniatures of real objects to imitate common routines
Level IV—Manipulation of movable parts of toys	Movements on movable parts of objects: objects are viewed as having parts rather than being a whole

Continued

TABLE 14.1
Continued

Author and Play Types (categories)	Description
Level V—Separation of parts of toys	Movements on objects that result in separation of parts or of taking things out of containers
Level VI— Combinational use of toys	Movements on toys where two or more different objects are used together or where parts of objects are put back together
Sutton-Smith (1970)[b]	
Imitation	Copying the motor and/or verbal behavior of others
Exploration	Investigating what can be done with objects, and how they work
Prediction	Testing the effects of various actions on objects and the effects of different behaviors
Construction	Movements on objects to make or create something

[a]This classification is based on an adaptation of Wehman's (1977) hierarchies by Bailey and Wolery (1984).
[b]This categorization of play describes common modes of play seen throughout early childhood.
Note: From *Assessing Infants and Preschoolers with Handicaps* (pp. 433–4), by D. B. Bailey and M. Wolery, 1989, Upper Saddle River, NJ: Merrill/Prentice Hall. Reprinted with permission.

TABLE 14.2
Sherratt and Peter's Contemporary Play Taxonomy

Play Category	Description
Sensorimotor play	Exploring the world by acting on it through touching, mouthing, biting, smelling, tasting, hitting, kicking
Relational play	Exploring the relationship between properties of selected objects by inserting, building, grouping, or associating them in different ways
Functional play	Gaining pleasure from using objects in the way they are supposed to be used, like making a toy dog bark, pretending to drink from a cup
Symbolic play	Using object substitution, attributing false properties to an object; imagining an object; or, consciously acting out social interactions in a sequence of actions that form a simple story based on everyday occurrence
Themed fantasy	Highly imaginative and creative pretense within a dynamic narrative

to pour a drink into a cup and gives the baby doll a sip from the cup. The importance of this measurement system is that it yields information about the complexity and fluency of the child's play in a way that play level alone does not.

METHODS OF ASSESSING PLAY

In order to best assess play, one needs to understand play as a construct and the developmental characteristics of the young children who will be assessed. While the descriptions and taxonomies

TABLE 14.3
Parten's Social-Play Taxonomy

Category	Definition
Unoccupied behavior	Child does not play but is occupied with watching things of momentary interest
Solitary play	Child plays alone and with different toys from those children in close proximity
Onlooker	Child watches other children at play, stands or sits within speaking distance, and often talks to children being observed
Parallel activity	Child plays independently but with toys that will bring him or her closer to others; child plays beside but not with other children
Associative play	Children exchange materials and conversation about the common activity, and bring other children into the activity, but each child engages in what he or she wishes
Cooperative or organized supplementary play	One or two children direct the activities of the others and organize the group for some purposes, necessitating a division of labor and an organization of roles; accordingly, children either belong or do not belong to the group

Note: From Lifter, K. (1996). Assessing play skills. In M. McLean, D. B. Bailey, & M. Wolery (Eds.)., *Assessing Infants and Preschoolers with Special Needs,* 2nd ed. Upper Saddle River, NJ: Merrill/Prentice Hall.

just described give a sense of and structure to play, they may be insufficient to help conceptualize play as a unified construct. Figure 14.1 is a conceptual model of play. As indicated by the figure, in order to play, children must first be meaningfully engaged. That is, children need to be attending to and participating with materials or others in ways that are appropriate and meaningful. Play often, but not always, takes place in the context of social or communicative interactions. This idea is represented by the combination of the inner circle and the dashed line of the chevron. Play can be broadly conceptualized as involving objects or symbol use. Play in each of these categories ranges from simple to complex. When play is simple, object play and symbolic play are distinct from one another, but as play becomes more advanced, object play and symbolic play begin to merge. The most sophisticated play involves the full integration of object and symbolic play. This is represented by the way

that object/toy and symbolic play are placed within the chevron. The solid line that becomes dashed between the play types, the long upward arrows, and the inclusion of the two taxonomies (O1-O5 and S1-S5) is meant to represent this relationship as well as capture the developmental aspects of play. Layered on top of the object/toy and symbolic play chevron are Parten's categories of social play. The placement of these categories on the chevron is meant to illustrate the relationship between those social categories and the development of object/toy and symbolic play skills. Finally, even when young children can engage in this integrated, sophisticated play, play skills continue to develop. This is represented by the two small upward arrows that surround sophisticated play. This conceptual model, along with the information about children's play behaviors presented in Table 14.4, can guide one's understanding and assessment of young children's play.

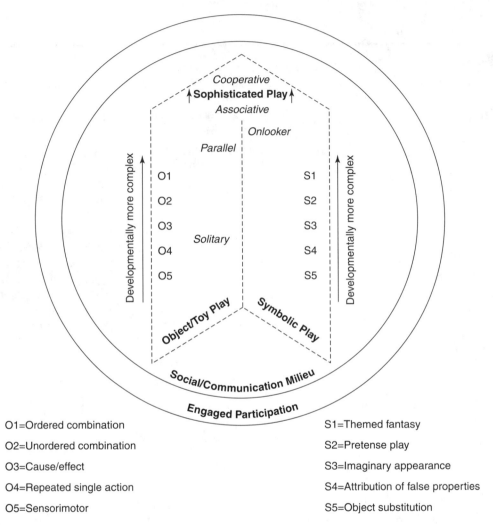

O1=Ordered combination
O2=Unordered combination
O3=Cause/effect
O4=Repeated single action
O5=Sensorimotor

S1=Themed fantasy
S2=Pretense play
S3=Imaginary appearance
S4=Attribution of false properties
S5=Object substitution

FIGURE 14.1
A conceptual model of play

Play is often used as a medium in which to measure other skills (e.g., communication, cognition). While this is a legitimate activity, often referred to as play-based assessment (Linder, 1993), the focus of this chapter is on assessing play by measuring play behaviors. Compared with the number of scales and inventories developed to measure other developmental domains, there are very few scales for measuring play.

With few exceptions (e.g., Moore-Taylor, Menarchek-Fetkovich, & Day, 2000; Mulhern, Fairclough, Friedman, & Leigh, 1990), the primary method for assessing play involves the direct observation of play. Table 14.5 provides an overview of selected instruments that have been developed to assess play as well as a brief description of how the assessment is conducted and scored.

TABLE 14.4

Examples of Developmental Sequences for Four Types of Play

Age (months)	Exploration/ Manipulation	Construction	Dramatics	Games
12–24	Sensorimotor/perceptual examination of objects; modes of exploration include banging, inserting and pulling out, tasting, creeping and crawling through, emptying and filling, tasting and scribbling	Simple towers with blocks, primarily exploration and manipulation	Imitates own behavior but in different situations; themes center on simple adult routines; late in this year child begins to perform activities with doll	Appearance/ disappearance (peek-a-boo); strange appearance, chase and capture
24–36	Exploration becomes integrated with other types of play such as construction and dramatics; child can manipulate and observe the results of behavior at the same time	Block building, painting, pasting, clay, puzzles; child is pleased with whatever she makes	Assumes more complete adult roles, usually pretending to be adult doing things to other children; a toy can symbolize another object	Participation in story telling; rhyme games
36–48	Becomes very interested in exploring new places, although usually prefers to have an adult companion; field trips begin to be meaningful and exciting experiences	Drawing, cutting, advanced puzzles, coloring, various structures with blocks	Increased variety of themes, creation of imaginary characters; wants some outstanding prop (shoes, hat) to aid in role play; enjoys puppet play	Imaginary monsters, friends and enemies; singing and chanting
48–60	Enjoys exploring increasingly greater range of experiences and places	Collages, painting, complex puzzles; child begins to be critical of own workmanship	Dramatic play becomes very social and at times cooperative; more advanced themes; child is more likely to want more than one prop or piece of clothing to aid in role play	Simple board games; hunts for hidden treasures; prisoners; hide-and-seek

From *Teaching Infants and Preschoolers with Handicaps* (p. 212), by D. B. Bailey and M. Wolery, 1984. Copyright 1984 by Merrill, Upper Saddle River, NJ: Merrill/Prentice Hall. Reprinted with permission.

TABLE 14.5
Overview of Selected Observational Play Assessments

Scale	Description	Structured Setting	Unstructured Setting	With Adult	Uses Specified Toys	Spontaneous Play	Modeled Play	Elicited Play
Atlas, J. A. (1990). Play in Assessment and Intervention in Childhood Psychoses. *Child Psychiatry and Human Development, 21*(2), 119–133.	Children interact with a specified set of 10 toys. Play is then rated as not symbolic play, stereotyped play, or pretend play.	X			X	X		
Belsky, J., Garduque, L., & Hrncir, E. (1984). Assessing Performance, Competence, and Executive Capacity in Infant Play: Relations to Home Environment and Security of Attachment. *Developmental Psychology, 20*, 406–417.	10-minute observation of free-play followed by a competence examination where the examiner attempts to engage the child in more sophisticated play.	X		X		X	X	X
Belsky, J., & Most, R. K. (1981). From Exploration to Play: A Cross-Sectional Study of Infant Free Play Behavior. *Developmental Psychology, 17*(5), 630–639	A 12-step sequence of developmental exploration and play that begins with infant explorations, and concludes with pretend substitutions. A set of toys is specified.	X		X	X			
Bromwich, R. M., Fust, S., Khokha, E., & Walden, M. H. (1981). *Play Assessment Checklist for Infants.* Unpublished document. Northridge, CA: California State University.	An observation instrument to be used in free-play situations. A checklist is used in conjunction with a specified toy set.		X		X	X		

TABLE 14.5

Continued

Scale	Description	Structured Setting	Unstructured Setting	With Adult	Uses Specified Toys	Spontaneous Play	Modeled Play	Elicited Play
Dixon, W. E., & Shore, C. (1990). Measuring Symbolic Play Style in Infancy: A Methodological Approach. *The Journal of Genetic Psychology, 152*(2), 191–205.	Provides three scenarios (breakfast, bath, and bed) under three conditions (spontaneous, modeled, and modeled with inappropriate object). Evaluates child's competence in symbolic play.	X		X	X	X	X	X
Fewell, R. (1986). *Play Assessment Scale (5th revision).* Unpublished manuscript, University of Washington, Seattle.	45 developmentally sequenced items. The child is observed playing with toys under spontaneous and elicited conditions.	X		X	X	X		X
Fewell, R., & Rich, J. S. (1987). Play assessment as a procedure for examining cognitive, communication, and social skills in multihandicapped children. *Journal of Psychoeducational Assessment, 5,* 107–118.	Children interact with specified toy sets. The scale looks at sequences of play behaviors and produces a play age.		X	X	X	X	X	
Flannery, K. A., & Watson, M. W. (1992). Are individual differences in fantasy play related to peer acceptance level? *Journal of Genetic Psychology, 54*(3), 407–416.	Codes child's free-play behaviors for frequency of fantasy play and nonfantasy play, and for the unreality level and unfamiliar level of the fantasy play.		X			X		
Gowan, J. W., & Schoen, D. (1984). *Levels of Child Object Play.* Unpublished	Observational study of play using content, signifiers, and modes of representational		X			X		

Continued

TABLE 14.5

Continued

Scale	Description	Structured Setting	Unstructured Setting	With Adult	Uses Specified Toys	Spontaneous Play	Modeled Play	Elicited Play
coding scheme manuscript. Chapel Hill, NC: Carolina Institute for Research on Early Education of the Handicapped, Frank Porter Graham Child Development Center.	analysis. The child is evaluated in an unstructured free-play situation.							
Kearsley, R. B. (1984). *The Systematic Observation of Children's Play.* Unpublished scoring manual. (Available from author, Child Health Services, Manchester, NH).	Standardized procedure of introducing the child to six sets of prearranged toys. Mother and child are observed for 10 minutes for four categories of play: stereotypical, relational, functional, and functional/symbolic	X		X	X	X	X	
Largo, R. H., & Howard, J. A. (1979). Developmental Progression in Play Behavior of Children Between Nine and Thirty Months. *Developmental Medicine and Child Neurology, 21,* 299–310.	Using a specified toy set, the tool accesses play behavior in the categories of exploratory functional, spatial, and nonspecific play behavior.	X			X	X		
Lifter, K., Sulzer-Azaroff, B., Cowdery, G., Avery, D., & Anderson, S. R. (1994). The Developmental Play Assessment (DPA) Instrument (2nd Rev.). Unpublished	Progress through a sequence of 14 play categories determined from a quantitative analysis of a 30-minute sample of unstructured play activities. Useful for identifying goals for interventions	X			X	X		

TABLE 14.5
Continued

Scale	Description	Structured Setting	Unstructured Setting	With Adult	Uses Specified Toys	Spontaneous Play	Modeled Play	Elicited Play
manuscript. Boston, MA: Northeastern University.	in play.							
Lowe, M., & Costello, A. J. (1976). The *Symbolic Play Test.* Windsor, England: NFR-Nelson Publishing Co.	An evaluation of children's spontaneous, nonverbal play activities with four specified sets of miniature objects.	X			X	X		
Lunzer, E. A. (1958). A scale of the organization of behavior for use in the study of play. *Educational Review, 11,* 205–217.	An abstract instrument that provides a 9-point developmental scale of the complexity play, of play emphasizing adaptiveness and the use/integration of materials.		X			X		
Mayes, S. D. (1991). Play assessment of preschool hyperactivity. In C. E. Schaefer, K. P. Gitlin, & A. Sandgrund (Eds.), *Play Diagnosis Assessment,* (pp. 249–281). New York: Wiley.	A small area is arranged with 7 manipulative toys. While the child is exploring the toys, the child's behavior is being coded by the examiner for level of activity.	X		X		X		
McCune-Nicolich, L. (1983). *A Manual for Analyzing Free Play.* New Brunswick, NJ: Department of Educational Psychology, Rutgers University.	An organized format for analyzing children's symbolic play according to Piagetian stages. A specified toy set is used.	X			X	X		
Morgan, G. A., Harmon, R. J., & Bennett, C. A. (1976). A System for Coding and Scoring Infants' Spontaneous Play	A free-play assessment for 8-to 24-month-olds. 40-minute observation of free-play with standardized set of		X		X	X		

Continued

TABLE 14.5

Continued

Scale	Description	Structured Setting	Unstructured Setting	With Adult	Uses Specified Toys	Spontaneous Play	Modeled Play	Elicited Play
with Objects. *JSAS Catalog of Selected Documents in Psychology, 6*, 105 (Ms. No. 1355).	toys to distinguish between exploratory and cognitively mature play							
Rogers, S. J. (1984). *Play Observation Scale.* Denver: University of Colorado Health Sciences Center.	Assesses sensorimotor and symbolic stages of play and includes a set of items on social/communicative behavior.	X			X	X		X
Rubenstein, J., & Howes, C. (1976). The Effects of Peers on Toddler Interactions with Mothers and Toys. *Child Development, 47,* 597–605.	Play is coded on a 5-point scale: oral contact, passive tactile contact, active manipulation, exploiting unique properties of an object, and creative or imaginative play. Compares solitary free-play with play with peer or mother.		X	X		X		X
Rubin, K. H. (1989). *Play Observation Scale.* Ontario, Canada: University of Waterloo.	Assesses play and non-play categories in an unstructured environment.		X			X		
Ruff, H. A., & Lawson, K. R. (1990). The development of sustained, focused, attention during free play in young children. *Developmental Psychology, 26*, 85–93.	Involves recording the amount of time the infant plays with and deliberately manipulates three to four objects.	X			X	X		
Watson, M. W., & Fischer, K. W. (1977). A Developmental Sequence of Agent	Four-phased play procedure: familiarization, modeling, free-play, and requested-	X			X	X	X	X

TABLE 14.5

Continued

Scale	Description	Structured Setting	Unstructured Setting	With Adult	Uses Specified Toys	Spontaneous Play	Modeled Play	Elicited Play
Use in Late Infancy. *Child Development, 48,* 828–836.	imitation. Coded by four types of agents: self, passive other, passive substitute, and active agent. Designed to capture Piaget's decentration notion.							
Westby, C. E. (1980). Symbolic Play Checklist: Assessment of Cognitive and Language Abilities Through Play. *Language, Speech, and Hearing Services in the Schools, 11,* 154–168.	Integrates language, cognitive, and social aspects of play in a 10-step hierarchy. Includes 9- to 60-month-olds.	X			X	X		X
Yarrow, L. J., McQuiston, S., MacTurk, R. H., McCarthy, M., Klein, R. P., & Vietze, P. M. (1983). Assessment of Mastery Motivation During the First Year of Life: Contemporaneous and Cross-Aged Relationships. *Developmental Psychology, 19,* 159–171.	A number of tasks are modeled, one at a time. The child is then presented with the objects and observed in undisturbed, free-play. Behaviors coded included: nontask, visual attention, task-directed, and success or solution of task/ problem.	X		X	X	X	X	

Note: Adapted from Linder, Holm, & Walsh (1999), Transdisciplinary Play-Based Assessment. In E. V. Nuttall, I. Romero, & J. Kalesnik (Eds.), *Assessing and Screening Preschoolers: Psychological and Educational Dimensions* (2nd ed.). Boston: Allyn and Bacon. Copyright 1999 by Pearson Education. Adapted by permission of the publisher.

In general, scales designed to assess play should specify which materials should be used, describe the context for the assessment, as well as describe what the adult's behavior should be during the assessment. The most common outcome measure of these scales is play level, but other dimensions such as length of play are sometimes measured. The *Play Assessment Scale* (Fewell, 1986) yields a play age. None of the measures is norm-referenced. While norm-referenced measures of toy play do not exist, there is one norm-referenced scale, the *Communication and Symbolic Behavior Scales (CSBS)* (Wetherby & Prizant, 1993), that codes play behaviors, along with gestures and facial expressions to yield a symbolic development score. While information from any of these scales and assessments may be helpful for establishing the child's current level of performance and monitoring children's growth over time, the information is less useful for determining intervention goals for young children with disabilities.

Researchers have found the same methods (e.g., frequency recording, interval recording, time sampling, event recording, duration recording, and running record) for recording observational data on skills in domains other than play are useful for measuring play (Malone & Stoneman, 1995). These methods and the criteria for their proper use are discussed in other chapters of this book. It may be instructive, however, to see how these tools can be used to assess play level. In particular, when assessing play for the purpose of planning intervention, it may be important to assess the following dimensions: (a) children's general contact with toys; (b) children's preference for specific toys; and, (c) children's level and types of play in the settings where the instruction will occur.

General Contact with Toys

General contact with toys can be determined by measuring the number of toys contacted, the types of toy contacted, and the duration of each contact.

The number of toys contacted and the types of toys contacted can be gathered by using the *Toy Inventory* (Garfinkle & Neitzel, 2000). The Toy Inventory was developed for use by teachers in preschool classrooms during unstructured play times. The toy inventory, seen in Figure 14.2, can be adapted for use in a particular classroom by changing the names of the toys to match those found in that setting. The interval in which teachers record data can vary based on the purpose of data collection, but taking data once every 5 minutes throughout the entire free-play session is recommended. A variety of mechanisms can be used to cue the teacher to the 5-minute intervals. A practical strategy is wearing a watch that can be programmed to ring its alarm every 5 minutes. When cued, the teacher looks at the target child and determines whether or not the child is engaged in toy play. If the child is engaged, the teacher marks a number to the right of the corresponding toy. The first time the child plays with the toy the teacher marks the 1, the second time the 2, and so on. A new data sheet is used for each data collection day. Once the data have been collected, a number of different calculations can be made. Specifically, the number of intervals the child was engaged with toys, the number of different toys, the percentage of intervals the child played with each toy, the percentage of intervals the child played with each toy type, and a rank order of toys.

The toy inventory does not calculate the duration of toy use. To do so, the teacher needs to operationally define the beginning and ending of play. Then a stopwatch can be used to time the length of actual toy play. Time per toy and total time playing may both be useful pieces of information.

Toy Preferences

For instructional purposes, understanding a child's toy preference is important. Preference, however, can be difficult to determine. The Toy Inventory, described above, records the number of times that the child engaged with each toy. This

Toy Inventory

Date:

Child:		Child:	
Unengaged	1 2 3 4 5 6 7 8 9 10 11 12 13 14 15 16 17 18	Unengaged	1 2 3 4 5 6 7 8 9 10 11 12 13 14 15 16 17 18
Prompted	1 2 3 4 5 6 7 8 9 10 11 12 13 14 15 16 17 18	Prompted	1 2 3 4 5 6 7 8 9 10 11 12 13 14 15 16 17 18
Manipulatives		**Manipulatives**	
Garage	1 2 3 4 5 6 7 8 9 10 11 12 13 14 15 16 17 18	Garage	1 2 3 4 5 6 7 8 9 10 11 12 13 14 15 16 17 18
Large Trucks	1 2 3 4 5 6 7 8 9 10 11 12 13 14 15 16 17 18	Large Trucks	1 2 3 4 5 6 7 8 9 10 11 12 13 14 15 16 17 18
Magnet Blocks	1 2 3 4 5 6 7 8 9 10 11 12 13 14 15 16 17 18	Magnet Blocks	1 2 3 4 5 6 7 0 9 10 11 12 13 14 15 16 17 18
Pegs	1 2 3 4 5 6 7 8 9 10 11 12 13 14 15 16 17 18	Pegs	1 2 3 4 5 6 7 8 9 10 11 12 13 14 15 16 17 18
Pop Beads	1 2 3 4 5 6 7 8 9 10 11 12 13 14 15 16 17 18	Pop Beads	1 2 3 4 5 6 7 8 9 10 11 12 13 14 15 16 17 18
Puzzle Blocks	1 2 3 4 5 6 7 8 9 10 11 12 13 14 15 16 17 18	Puzzle Blocks	1 2 3 4 5 6 7 8 9 10 11 12 13 14 15 16 17 18
Rabbit Builders	1 2 3 4 5 6 7 8 9 10 11 12 13 14 15 16 17 18	Rabbit Builders	1 2 3 4 5 6 7 8 9 10 11 12 13 14 15 16 17 18
Rolling Racer	1 2 3 4 5 6 7 8 9 10 11 12 13 14 15 16 17 18	Rolling Racer	1 2 3 4 5 6 7 8 9 10 11 12 13 14 15 16 17 18
Small Vehicles	1 2 3 4 5 6 7 8 9 10 11 12 13 14 15 16 17 18	Small Vehicles	1 2 3 4 5 6 7 8 9 10 11 12 13 14 15 16 17 18
Star Builders	1 2 3 4 5 6 7 8 9 10 11 12 13 14 15 16 17 18	Star Builders	1 2 3 4 5 6 7 8 9 10 11 12 13 14 15 16 17 18
Tool Bench	1 2 3 4 5 6 7 8 9 10 11 12 13 14 15 16 17 18	Tool Bench	1 2 3 4 5 6 7 8 9 10 11 12 13 14 15 16 17 18
Other:	1 2 3 4 5 6 7 8 9 10 11 12 13 14 15 16 17 18	Other:	1 2 3 4 5 6 7 8 9 10 11 12 13 14 15 16 17 18
Dramatic Play		**Dramatic Play**	
Appliances	1 2 3 4 5 6 7 8 9 10 11 12 13 14 15 16 17 18	Appliances	1 2 3 4 5 6 7 8 9 10 11 12 13 14 15 16 17 18
Babies	1 2 3 4 5 6 7 8 9 10 11 12 13 14 15 16 17 18	Babies	1 2 3 4 5 6 7 8 9 10 11 12 13 14 15 16 17 18
Baby Bottles	1 2 3 4 5 6 7 8 9 10 11 12 13 14 15 16 17 18	Baby Bottles	1 2 3 4 5 6 7 8 9 10 11 12 13 14 15 16 17 18
Camera	1 2 3 4 5 6 7 8 9 10 11 12 13 14 15 16 17 18	Camera	1 2 3 4 5 6 7 8 9 10 11 12 13 14 15 16 17 18
Cart	1 2 3 4 5 6 7 8 9 10 11 12 13 14 15 16 17 18	Cart	1 2 3 4 5 6 7 8 9 10 11 12 13 14 15 16 17 18
Dishes	1 2 3 4 5 6 7 8 9 10 11 12 13 14 15 16 17 18	Dishes	1 2 3 4 5 6 7 8 9 10 11 12 13 14 15 16 17 18
Mirror	1 2 3 4 5 6 7 8 9 10 11 12 13 14 15 16 17 18	Mirror	1 2 3 4 5 6 7 8 9 10 11 12 13 14 15 16 17 18
Phone	1 2 3 4 5 6 7 8 9 10 11 12 13 14 15 16 17 18	Phone	1 2 3 4 5 6 7 8 9 10 11 12 13 14 15 16 17 18
Plastic Food	1 2 3 4 5 6 7 8 9 10 11 12 13 14 15 16 17 18	Plastic Food	1 2 3 4 5 6 7 8 9 10 11 12 13 14 15 16 17 18
Pots and Pans	1 2 3 4 5 6 7 8 9 10 11 12 13 14 15 16 17 18	Pots and Pans	1 2 3 4 5 6 7 8 9 10 11 12 13 14 15 16 17 18
Purse	1 2 3 4 5 6 7 8 9 10 11 12 13 14 15 16 17 18	Purse	1 2 3 4 5 6 7 8 9 10 11 12 13 14 15 16 17 18
Stroller	1 2 3 4 5 6 7 8 9 10 11 12 13 14 15 16 17 18	Stroller	1 2 3 4 5 6 7 8 9 10 11 12 13 14 15 16 17 18
Velcro Fruit	1 2 3 4 5 6 7 8 9 10 11 12 13 14 15 16 17 18	Velcro Fruit	1 2 3 4 5 6 7 8 9 10 11 12 13 14 15 16 17 18
Other:	1 2 3 4 5 6 7 8 9 10 11 12 13 14 15 16 17 18	Other:	1 2 3 4 5 6 7 8 9 10 11 12 13 14 15 16 17 18
Art		**Art**	
Crayon	1 2 3 4 5 6 7 8 9 10 11 12 13 14 15 16 17 18	Crayon	1 2 3 4 5 6 7 8 9 10 11 12 13 14 15 16 17 18
Easel	1 2 3 4 5 6 7 8 9 10 11 12 13 14 15 16 17 18	Easel	1 2 3 4 5 6 7 8 9 10 11 12 13 14 15 16 17 18
Markers	1 2 3 4 5 6 7 8 9 10 11 12 13 14 15 16 17 18	Markers	1 2 3 4 5 6 7 8 9 10 11 12 13 14 15 16 17 18
Scissors	1 2 3 4 5 6 7 8 9 10 11 12 13 14 15 16 17 18	Scissors	1 2 3 4 5 6 7 8 9 10 11 12 13 14 15 16 17 18
Stamps	1 2 3 4 5 6 7 8 9 10 11 12 13 14 15 16 17 18	Stamps	1 2 3 4 5 6 7 8 9 10 11 12 13 14 15 16 17 18
Stickers	1 2 3 4 5 6 7 8 9 10 11 12 13 14 15 16 17 18	Stickers	1 2 3 4 5 6 7 8 9 10 11 12 13 14 15 16 17 18
Comments:			

FIGURE 14.2

The toy inventory
Source: Reprinted from Garfinkle and Neitzel (2000) with permission

data, however, does not necessarily constitute a preference for one toy over another or indicate which toy a child would like to play with at a particular time. Similarly, toys the child is never seen playing with should not be thought of as nonpreferred. There are many reasons why children may not play with a toy (e.g., lack of experience, toy was unnoticed). Thus, to determine a toy preference, a systematic preference assessment must be conducted.

A systematic preference assessment is conducted by presenting children with a number of toys. After children have played with the individual toys, the toys are presented in groups. The toy the child selects should be recorded. The toys should each be presented in several different groupings, and data should be recorded after each toy selection. Toys that the child consistently selects are potentially preferred toys. A short version of this assessment can be conducted quickly each day before the start of a play period to help ensure the child will be interested in the toy.

Children's Play Level

A child's play level can be determined by using any one of the play taxonomies described above. Figure 14.3 is an example of a data sheet that can be used in conjunction with a play taxonomy to help determine a child's play level. This data sheet uses interval recording, but other types of data collection systems (e.g., event, running record) can be used to record the child's play level. To use the data sheet in Figure 14.3, the teacher defines the length of an interval and the length of the observation session. Ten-second intervals for a 10-minute observation session is reasonable. At the end of each 10-second interval, the teacher looks at the target child, determines and records by the child's play level, the amount of adult support provided and if peers were present by circling the categories on the data sheet. The raw data can then be analyzed one of several ways to

determine play level. The most basic analysis strategy is to determine the percentage of time the child spends in each category of play, with the largest percentage representing the child's typical play level.

Malone (1997) suggests that to get a more complete view of a child's play level, global play sophistication and peak play type also be determined. *Global play sophistication* is determined by assigning weighted values to play categories (higher numbers for more developmentally advanced play) and multiplying that number by the total number of intervals the child spent in that play category. Figure 14.4 provides a data sheet for helping to determine the global play sophistication score. This data sheet also uses an interval recording system, but other ways to record the data may also be used. To use the data sheet in Figure 14.4, the observer determines the category that corresponds with the child's behavior and writes a brief description of the play (categories are defined on p. 456). The number of times a brief description has been recorded in each play type category is then calculated. This total is then weighted (by multiplying by the assigned number) and summed across types to yield one score that represents the child's global play sophistication.

Peak play type is a measure that determines the child's best performance, regardless of fluency or frequency. Peak play type is determined by identifying the most developmentally sophisticated play behavior the child was observed performing within each play level. Figure 14.5 shows one way to determine peak play type. Using a combination of an interval recording method and narrative, data can be recorded on play level and the level of adult assistance provided. After the data collection period, the observer reads the descriptions of the play by play type/level. Within each category, each play behavior or sequence of play behaviors is rank ordered by developmental sophistication. The most sophisticated play of each type is the peak play type.

Child: _____   Date: _____

Activity: _____   Materials: _____

Observer: _____   Observation start time: _____

Observation stop time: _____

Total observation time: _____

Interval	Play level					Adult Support				Peers present		
1.	Sen.	Rel.	Fun.	Sym.	Thm.F.	Pr	Verb	Phys.	Full	T	DD	N
2.	Sen.	Rel.	Fun.	Sym.	Thm.F.	Pr	Verb	Phys.	Full	T	DD	N
3.	Sen.	Rel.	Fun.	Sym.	Thm.F.	Pr	Verb	Phys.	Full	T	DD	N
4.	Sen.	Rel.	Fun.	Sym.	Thm.F.	Pr	Verb	Phys.	Full	T	DD	N
5.	Sen.	Rel.	Fun.	Sym.	Thm.F.	Pr	Verb	Phys.	Full	T	DD	N
6.	Sen.	Rel.	Fun.	Sym.	Thm.F.	Pr	Verb	Phys.	Full	T	DD	N
7.	Sen.	Rel.	Fun.	Sym.	Thm.F.	Pr	Verb	Phys.	Full	T	DD	N
8.	Sen.	Rel.	Fun.	Sym.	Thm.F.	Pr	Verb	Phys.	Full	T	DD	N
9.	Sen.	Rel.	Fun.	Sym.	Thm.F.	Pr	Verb	Phys.	Full	T	DD	N
10.	Sen.	Rel.	Fun.	Sym.	Thm.F.	Pr	Verb	Phys.	Full	T	DD	N

Key

Play Level:

Sen. = Sensorimotor play

Rel. = Relational play

Fun. = Functional play

Sym. = Symbolic play

Thm.F. = Themed fantasy

Adult Support:

Pr. = Proximal, within 3 feet

Verb = Verbal prompt

Phys. = Partial physical prompt

Full = Full physical prompt

Peers Present:

T = Typical

DD = With disabilities

N = Not present

Comments:

FIGURE 14.3
Interval-based data sheet for determining play level

An additional method for assessing the complexity of a child's play is by assessing the play on more than one scale simultaneously. Figure 14.6 illustrates how Sherratt and Peter's taxonomy can by recorded at the same time as Parten's social play. To use this data sheet, the observer makes a mark in the cell that corresponds to the child's play behavior. For example, if a child were banging a rattle by himself, the upper left square would be marked. If a child were pretending to be the mommy and were

Global play sophistication data sheet

Child: _____   Date: _____

Activity: _____   Materials: _____

Observer: _____   Observation start time: _____

                                             Observation stop time: _____

                                             Total observation time: _____

Trial	Single Action (Brief Description)	Unordered Multischeme (Brief Description)	Ordered Multischeme (Brief Description)
1.			
2.			
3.			
4.			
5.			
6.			
7.			
8.			
9.			
10.			

After observation computation:

	Single action	Unordered Multischeme	Ordered Multischeme
Total Trials:			
Multipled by:	1	2	3
Equals:	+	+	=

Global Play Sophistication Score

Comments:

FIGURE 14.4
Data sheet for determining the global play sophistication score

using props to cook dinner while another child, the daddy, helped, the bottom right square would be marked. Some cells are marked NA. These designations are in place where the definition of one category precludes it from being coded in the other category. For example, if the child is engaged in solitary play, by definition he cannot be also engaged in themed fantasy, or vice versa.

Taken together the information on children's general contact with toys, toy preferences, and

Peak play type

Child: _____

Activity: _____

Observer: _____

Date: _____

Materials: _____

Observation start time: _____

Observation stop time: _____

Total observation time: _____

Narrative Description of Play by Sequence	Adult Support	Type/Level	Rank in Type (complete after observation section)
1.	Proximal Verbal Partial Physical Full Physical	Sen. Rel. Fun. Sym. Thm.F.	
2.	Proximal Verbal Partial Physical Full Physical	Sen. Rel. Fun. Sym. Thm.F.	
3.	Proximal Verbal Partial Physical Full Physical	Sen. Rel. Fun. Sym. Thm.F.	

Key Play level:

Sen.　=Sensorimotor play

Rel.　=Relational play

Sym.　=Symbolic play

Thm.F.=Themed fantasy

Comments:

FIGURE 14.5
Peak play type data sheet

play level can be used, in conjunction with other assessment information (e.g., parent input) to determine children's play goals and objectives. In general, the assessment information should help determine what the child can do independently, what skills are emerging, what the child can do with assistance, and what the child cannot do. Goals and objectives should target emerging skills and skills that children need assistance to complete. This process is discussed more in the establishing goals and objective section of this chapter.

	Solitary	Onlooker	Parallel	Associative	Cooperative
Sensorimotor Play				NA	NA
Relational Play					NA
Functional Play					
Symbolic Play					
Themed Fantasy	NA	NA	NA	NA	

Child: _____   Date: _____

Activity: _____   Materials: _____

Observer: _____   Observation start time: _____

                                      Observation stop time: _____

                                      Total observation time: _____

Unoccupied:

Other, not play:

Comments:

FIGURE 14.6
Data sheet for combining the Sherratt and Peter Taxonomy with Parten's Social Play Levels

GUIDELINES FOR ASSESSING PLAY

The same guidelines that exist for assessing other developmental domains also hold true for assessing play. Thus, play assessment should be conducted on multiple days in multiple settings and involve multiple informants (Neisworth & Bagnato, 2000). Assessments also need to be conducted in the environment where the intervention will take place. There are several aspects of assessing play that are particular to play and should be taken into consideration when assessing play and analyzing play assessment data. These dimensions are: the length of the assessment, the toys used, the context and play format, the presence of peers, and the adults' behaviors.

Length of Assessment

The length of the assessment should vary as a function of the purpose of the assessment, the number of toys presented, the context, and child characteristics. However, empirical evidence suggests that the minimum observation length for meaningful data is 5 minutes (McCune-Nicolich & Fenson, 1984). For children with few interests or play skills a longer time period may be warranted. And, it should be kept in mind that often, the child's more advanced play skills are exhibited after an initial warm-up period.

Toy/Material Used

The characteristics of toys used during the assessment will impact the types of play that children exhibit (Elder & Pederson, 1978). For example, toys typically found in pretend play areas (e.g., dress-up clothes, miniature plastic replicas of food and kitchen ware) may increase the amount of time children spend in pretend play. Construction toys (e.g., blocks) are not, however, conducive to pretend play. Social toys (e.g., a teeter totter) result in different social play behaviors than do isolate toys (e.g., puzzles) (Beckman & Kohl, 1984). In general, the number, complexity, familiarity, and manipulability of the toys affect play behaviors (Feitelson & Ross, 1973; Few & Nunnelly, 1968; Granmza, 1976; Tizard, 1977).

Context/Play Format

Children's play varies across contexts and thus it is important to take into consideration when assessing play (Malone, Stoneman, & Langone, 1994). For example, children may play with toys in a relatively sophisticated way at home, but at school the child uses the toys in a less sophisticated manner. Similarly, the child may appear to have an artificially high play level if the assessment is conducted in a controlled setting when play is structured (e.g., elicited, modeled, prompted, facilitated) rather than assessing in an uncontrolled or free-play setting. Malone and Stoneman (1995) suggest that when play is assessed in a controlled, structured setting, the

play behavior may be more a function of the adult's behavior than that of the child.

Presence of Peers

The presence of peers affects play performance and is important to attend to when assessing play. Predictably, the presence of familiar peers generally increases the amount of time that children spend in social play (Johnson, Christie, & Yawkey, 1987), particularly if the peer is the same gender as the target child (Rubin & Howe, 1985). Interestingly, the presence of peers can also lower the child's nonsocial play level (Malone, Stoneman, & Langone, 1994). Thus, there is an unclear relationship between children's play performance and the presence of peers. This ambiguity only serves to highlight the need to note the presence of peers during a play assessment.

Adults' Behavior

As mentioned above, the presence of an adult and the adult's specific behavior may influence the results of a play assessment. This is not necessarily negative, rather the adult's behaviors and level of assistance should be noted in addition to the child's performance. This information may be of particular importance when developing goals and objectives.

USING ASSESSMENT INFORMATION FOR ESTABLISHING GOALS AND OBJECTIVES

The information obtained from assessing children playing in context can and should be used to determine appropriate play goals and objectives. In general, play goals for young children with disabilities should help children move from less sophisticated play to more sophisticated play. More sophisticated play is more social, more symbolic, and more thematic than the play was previously.

Sophisticated play involves using multiple toys in multiple ways for increasingly longer periods of time. Finally, sophisticated play involves the combination of individual play behaviors in coherent and intentional ways.

To determine appropriate intervention targets, the information gathered about the child's play level and length of play should be analyzed to determine the child's current level of performance. Play objectives should then be set to move the child toward more sophisticated play. There are two general strategies for insuring that the goals are appropriate for the child: 1) consider the child's "zone of proximal development" (Vygotsky, 1987) and 2) insure that play goals are functional.

Consider the Child's Zone of Proximal Development

By recording what play behaviors the children exhibit in an unstructured setting and the play skills the children exhibit when adults provide assistance (e.g., model, prompting, or facilitating), the child's zone of proximal development can be determined. The zone of proximal development is the difference between what the child can do independently and what the child can do with adult assistance. Good targets for intervention are the behaviors the child cannot do independently but can perform with adult assistance. For example, a child may be able to stack two blocks independently, but can stack five blocks only if an adult helps to hold the block base steady and helps align the blocks as they are stacked. Thus, an intervention target may be to stack 5 blocks independently.

Ensure Functional Play Goals

Functional play goals are those that are likely to be used by the child. That is, the targets of intervention need to fit the context of the intervention and be of interest to the child. By insuring that play goals are functional, the child is more likely to learn generalized play skills.

USING ASSESSMENT INFORMATION FOR PLANNING INTERVENTION

Once play assessment data has been collected and analyzed, and goals and objectives have been determined, specific interventions can be planned. Information that was collected during the play assessment can be helpful when planning interventions. Specifically, variables in the environment and the nature of play need to be considered when planning interventions.

Consider the Environment

Just as the toys, the context, and the presence of others (adults and peers) affect the validity and reliability of assessment data, these variables must also be considered when determining intervention strategies. Interventions should be conducted with toys that are safe, age-appropriate, and likely to be of interest to the child. The context for the intervention should be carefully determined. The role that adults and peers play in the intervention should be well thought out.

Consider the Nature of Play

Beyond the developmental nature of the play taxonomies, there are few guidelines about the sequence in which play should be taught. For example, there is no empirical evidence that suggests whether a child should first learn to play with multiple toys in multiple ways or learn to play with a more limited repertoire of toys but do so in more social ways. Until there is empirical guidance for these instructional decisions, teachers of young children with disabilities need to have a well-developed understanding of play and intervention strategies that teach play skills.

Sherratt and Peter (2002) have developed intervention suggestions that map onto their play taxonomy. The model, pictured in Figure 14.7, illustrates the general play taxonomy and six

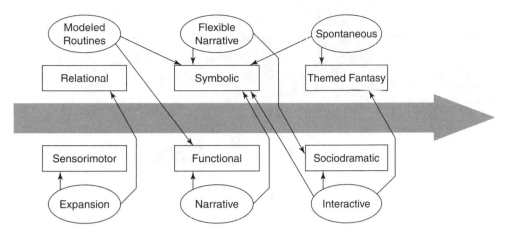

FIGURE 14.7
Sherratt and Peter's model of intervention strategies and play
Note: From *Developing Play and Drama in Children with Autistic Spectrum Disorders,* by H.D. Sherratt and M. Peter, 2002, London: David Fulton Publishers. Reprinted with permission.

intervention strategies that they have found useful for teaching each type of play. The six intervention strategies are: 1) expansions (adding one behavior to the child's play); 2) modeled routines (the adult shows the child how to combine play behaviors that the child does independently); 3) narrative (the teacher provides a structure for more symbolic play by providing a story line); 4) flexible narrative (the teacher provides less of a story line, but supports children to generate their own story line); 5) interactive (the teacher supports children in developing a story line together); and 6) spontaneous (the child generates a story line that is carried out with peers). Because the focus of this chapter is on assessment, not intervention, these intervention strategies will not be explained. The point of this model in the context of this chapter is to illustrate that teachers can use the play assessment data they have collected and this model to have a starting point for planning play interventions. Modifications and adaptations will be needed for individual children, but the model may provide guidance until there is empirical evidence to help with this type of decision making.

MONITORING PLAY OVER TIME

Because of the observational methods used, all of the assessments described in the previous section that determine the child's general contact with toys, toy preferences, and play level can be used repeatedly and over time without undue stress on the child and without compromising the psychometric properties of the instruments. Thus, any of these instruments can be used to monitor children's response to intervention and learning over time. These instruments, however, may not provide enough discrete categories to effectively assess children's growth and learning. For gathering information that is more specific than play level, measurement within play level is warranted. Methods for assessing each play level in the Sherratt and Peter general taxonomy are presented below.

Sensorimotor Play

Sensorimotor play is exploration of objects in the world through basic actions. Figure 14.8 gives an example of how one may assess behaviors within

Within level play assessment: Sensorimotor

Child: _____   Date: _____

Activity: _____   Observation start time: _____

Observer: _____   Observation stop time: _____

                                      Total observation time: _____

Toy/Material	Touching	Mouthing	Biting	Smelling	Tasting	Hitting	Kicking	Other	Social
1.									
2.									
3.									
4.									
5.									
6.									
7.									
8.									
9.									
10.									

Comments:

FIGURE 14.8
Within play level data sheet: Sensorimotor play

the sensorimotor category. This recording system uses event recording. When the observer sees the child interact with a toy, the name of the toy is written down and a mark is placed under the behavior that the child exhibited. Toys need to be listed only once, as each subsequent behavior can be recorded by an additional mark.

Relational Play

Relational play is when children explore the relationship between the properties of different objects. Figure 14.9 shows a data sheet that can be used to record the play behaviors of children who are exhibiting relational play. This data sheet can be used with event recording. The data sheet is

Within level play assessment: Relational play

Child: _____   Date: _____

Activity: _____   Materials:_____

Observer: _____   Observation start time: _____

Observation stop time: _____

Total observation time: _____

Toy	Insert	Build	Group							
1.										
2.										
3.										
4.										
5.										
6.										
7.										
8.										
9.										
10.										

Comments:

FIGURE 14.9
Within play level data sheet: Relational play

similar to the one described for sensorimotor play in that the observer records the toy the child was playing with and the relationship that the child was describing. Blank columns are provided so the observer can add the specific relationships that the specific child is exhibiting.

Functional Play

Functional play is using materials in the ways that they are supposed to be used. Figure 14.10 shows a data sheet that can be used to assess functional play behaviors. This data sheet uses event recording and has a similar layout to the sensorimotor and

Within play level assessment:

Child: _____   Date: _____

Activity: _____   Materials: _____

Observer: _____   Observation start time: _____

                                      Observation stop time: _____

                                      Total observation time: _____

Toy	Way toy was used								
1.									
2.									
3.									
4.									
5.									
6.									
7.									
8.									
9.									
10.									

Comments:

FIGURE 14.10
Within play level data sheet: Functional play

relational play data sheets. Specifically, the observer records the toy the child is using and then specifies the way the toy was used. For sensorimotor play, relational play, and functional play the data sheets presented will yield information about the number of toys played with and the number of ways the child played with the toys. In general, as children become more sophisticated players, they will use more toys in more different ways.

Symbolic Play

As illustrated in Figure 14.11, there is a developmental sequence for symbolic play. The sequence

Within play level assessment: Symbolic play

Child: _____

Activity: _____

Observer: _____

Date: _____

Observation start time: _____

Observation stop time: _____

Total observation time: _____

Toy	Use	Object substitution	Attribution of false property	Imagining an object	Acting out a sequence to tell a story	Other
1.						
2.						
3.						
4.						
5.						
6.						
7.						
8.						
9.						
10.						

Peers present:

Comments:

FIGURE 14.11
Within play level data sheet: Symbolic play

ranges from using objects to stand for other objects to acting out a series of play behaviors that tell a story. Figure 14.11 shows a data sheet that will facilitate recording symbolic play behaviors. This data collection system uses event recording.

The observer records the toy or material the child was using and the way the child used the toy. Based on that information, the recorder checks the type of symbolic play in which the child was engaged.

Within level play assessment: Themed fantasy

Child: _____   Date: _____

Activity: _____   Materials: _____

Observer: _____   Observation start time: _____

Observation stop time: _____

Total observation time: _____

Narrative description of play, by sequence	Familiar theme?	Role in play	Adult support level	Peers present (list by name)
1.	Y N	L RC E P	Proximal Verbal Partial Physical Full Physical	1. 2. 3. 4. 5.
2.	Y N	L RC E P	Proximal Verbal Partial Physical Full Physical	1. 2. 3. 4. 5.
3.	Y N	L RC E P	Proximal Verbal Partial Physical Full Physical	1. 2. 3. 4. 5.

Key:
L   = Leader in play—deciding actions, direction of play, assigning roles
RC = Responds to change—adapts behavior to fit them or new idea suggested for play
E   = Expander—suggests ideas and helps develop play theme, but does not make decisions for the group
P   = Passive—plays in role assigned to others but does not suggest ideas or extend play

Comments:

FIGURE 14.12
Within play level data sheet: Themed fantasy

Themed Fantasy

Fantasy play is imaginative play that includes the use of pretense and a narrative. Figure 14.12 shows an example of a data sheet that could be used to assess themed fantasy. This system uses event recording, when an event is defined as an imaginative play sequence. The observer records the play sequence, uses knowledge of the child and the child's experience to determine if the theme of the play is familiar or novel, records the target child's role in the play, the level of adult assistance, and the peers the child is playing with. The *role in play* refers to the way in which the child functions in the group. The child may be the leader in play. This position is characterized by making decisions about the direction of the play and by assigning other children roles to play or actions to perform. The child may be a player who responds to the changes suggested by the leader, or the child may expand on the ideas presented by the leader (which would be coded as an expander).

Finally, the child may play a passive role in the play, not suggesting his own idea but not greatly changing his behavior to accommodate the suggestions of the leader or the expander.

Figures 14.8 through 14.12 are designed to measure play within a category. These data collection systems are limited in that data on only one play category is being recorded at one time. Within-category codings, however, are designed to record information that is precise. This precision may be of help when establishing children's goals and objectives and is likely to be of great value when measuring children's progress on their goals and objects over time. The data collection systems presented are useful examples, but the teacher may find other methods and formats that assist in within-category play assessment. Whichever system a teacher chooses, the system must be well defined and provide the information the teacher most needs to facilitate the acquisition of play skills in young children with disabilities.

· · · · · · · ·
SUMMARY OF KEY CONCEPTS

- Play is an important developmental domain because it is valued by society and because of its role in the facilitation of learning in many domains.
- Play is easier to describe than to define, but the use of play taxonomies helps to articulate play behaviors in a way that makes them measurable. However, teachers who are going to measure play need to have a conceptual understanding of the construct of play as well as a framework for the child's development of play skills and how those are expressed in play behaviors.

- No one taxonomy is preferred over another, but many contextual variables (e.g., toy or material, setting, structure, presence of others) should be considered when assessing play and planning interventions for play skills.
- Global measures of play, measures of play level, and measures of skills within play level should all be assessed and should guide the establishment of goals and objectives as well as aid in monitoring children's learning of play skills over time.

· · · · · · · ·
REFERENCES

Allessandri, S. M. (1992). Attention, play, and social behavior in ADHD preschoolers. *Journal of Abnormal Child Psychology, 20,* 289–302.

Bailey, D. B., & Wolery, M. (1984). *Teaching infants and preschoolers with handicaps.* Upper Saddle River, NJ: Merrill/Prentice Hall.

Beckman, P. J., & Kohl, F. L. (1984). The effects of social and isolate toys on the interactions and play of integrated and nonintegrated groups of preschoolers. *Education and Training of the Mentally Retarded, 19,* 169–174.

Bredekamp, S. & Copple, C. (1997). *Appropriate practice in early childhood programs* (Rev. ed.) Washington, DC: National Association for the Education of Young Children.

Bricker, D., Pretti-Frontczak, K., & McComas, N. R. (1998). *An activity-based approach to early intervention* (2nd ed.) Baltimore: Paul H. Brookes.

Bruner, J. S. (1972). The nature and uses of immaturity. *American Psychologist, 27,* 687–708.

Chance, P. (1979). *Learning through play.* New York: Gardner.

Eisert, D. & Lamorrey, S. (1996). Play as a window on child development: The relationship between play and other developmental domains. *Early Education and Development, 7,* 221–235.

Elder, J. C., & Pederson, D. R. (1978). Preschool children's use of objects in symbolic play. *Child Development, 49,* 500–504.

Feitelson, D., & Ross, G. S. (1973). The neglected factor-play. *Human Development, 16,* 202–223.

Few, T. T. & Nunnelly, T. C. (1968). The influence of stimulus complexity novelty, and affective value on children's visual fixations. *Journal of Experimental Child Psychology, 6,* 141–153.

Fewell, R. (1986). *Play assessment scale* (5th ed.). Unpublished manuscript, University of Washington, Seattle.

Fewell, R. R., & Kaminski, R. (1988). Play skills development and instruction for young children with handicaps. In S. L. Odom & M. B. Karnes (Eds.), *Early intervention for infants and children with handicaps: An empirical base* (pp. 145–158). Baltimore: Paul H. Brookes.

Freeman, S. & Kasari, C. (2002). Characteristics and qualities of the play dates of Children with Down Syndrome: Emerging of true friendships. *American Journal on Mental Retardation, 107,* 16–31.

French, V. (1977). History of the child's influence: Ancient Mediterranean civilizations.In R. Q. Bell & L. V. Harper (Eds.), *Child effects on adults.* Hillsdale, NJ: Lawrence Erlbaum.

Freud, S. (1974). *The ego and the mechanisms of defense.* New York: International Universities Press.

Fromberg, D. P. (1999). A review of research on play. In C. Seefeldt (Ed.), *The early childhood curriculum: Current findings in theory and practice* (3rd ed.). New York: Teachers College Press.

Fromberg, D. P. (2002). *Play and meaning in early childhood education.* Boston: Allyn and Bacon.

Garfinkle, A. N. & Neitzel, J. (2000). *The toy inventory.* Unpublished manuscript. University of North Carolina.

Granmza, A. F. (1976). Responses to manipulability of a play object. *Psychological Reports, 38,* 1109–1110.

Groos, K. (1901). *The play of man.* New York: Appleton.

Guralnick, M. J. (1981). The social behavior of preschool children at different developmental levels: Effects of group composition. *Journal of Experimental Child Psychology, 31,* 115–130.

Guralnick, M. J., & Weinhouse, E. M. (1984). Peer-related social interactions of developmentally delayed young children: Development and characteristics. *Developmental Psychology, 20,* 815–827.

Hughes, F. P. (1991). *Children, play and development.* Boston: Allyn and Bacon.

Hull, C. L. (1943). *Principles of behavior.* New York: Appleton-Century-Crofts.

Johnson, J. W., Christine, J. F., & Yawkey, T. D. (1987). *Play and early childhood development.* Glenview, IL: Scott, Foresman and Company.

Kennedy, M. D., Sheridan, M. K., Radlinski, S. H., & Beeghly, M. (1991). Play-language relationships in young children with developmental delays: Implications for assessment. *Journal of Speech & Hearing Research, 34,* 112–122.

Li, A. K. F. (1981). Play and the mentally retarded child. *Mental Retardation, 19,* 121–126.

Linder, T. W. (1993). *Transdisciplanary play-based assessment: A functional approach to working with young children* (Rev. ed.). Baltimore: Paul H. Brookes.

Linder, T. W. (1994). The role of play in early childhood special education. In R. L. Safford, B. Spodek, & O. N. Saracho (Eds.), *Yearbook in early childhood education: Early childhood special education,* (Vol. 5). New York: Teachers College Press, Columbia University.

Linder, T. W., Holm, C. B., & Walsh, K. A. (1999). Transdisciplinary play-based assessment. In E. V. Nuttall, I. Romero & J. Kalesnik (Eds.), *Assessing and screening preschoolers: Psychological and educational dimensions* (2nd ed.). Boston: Allyn & Bacon.

Lifter, K. (1996). Assessing play skills. In M. McLean, D. B. Bailey, & M. Wolery (Eds.), *Assessing infants and preschoolers with special needs* (2nd ed.). Upper Saddle River, NJ: Merrill/Prentice Hall.

Lovell, K., Hoyle, H. W., & Siddall, N. C. (1968). A study of some aspects of the play and language of young children in delayed speech. *Journal of Child Psychology and Psychiatry*, 9, 41–50.

Malone, D. M. (1997). Preschoolers' categorical and sequential toy play: Change over time. *Journal of Early Intervention, 21*, 45–61.

Malone, D. M. (1999). Contextual factors informing play-based program planning. *International Journal of Disability, Development and Education, 46*, 307–324.

Malone, D. M. & Stoneman, Z. (1995). Methodological issues in studying the toy play of young children with mental retardation. *Topics in Early Childhood Special Education, 15*, 459–487.

Malone, D. M., Stoneman, Z., & Langone, J. (1994). Contextual variation of correspondences among measures of play and developmental level of preschool children. *Journal of Early Intervention, 18*, 199–215.

Montessori, M. (1967). *The absorbent mind.* New York: Dell.

McCune-Nicolich, L. & Fenson, L. (1984). Methodological issues in studying early pretend play. In T. D. Yawkey & A. D. Pellegrini (Eds.), *Child's play: Developmental and applied.* Hillsdale, NJ: Lawrence Erlbaum.

Moore-Taylor, K., Menarchek-Fetkovich, M. & Day, C. (2000). The play history interview. In K. Gitlin-Werner & A. Sandgrund (Eds.), *Play diagnosis and assessment* (2nd ed.). New York: John Wiley & Sons.

Mulhern, R. K., Fairclough, D. L., Friedman, A. G., & Leigh, L. D. P. (1990). Play performance scale as an index of quality of life of children with cancer. *Psychological Assessment, 2*, 149–155.

Neisworth, J. T., & Bagnato, S. J. (2000). Recommended practices in assessments. In S. Sandall, M. E., McLean, & B. T. Smith (Eds.), *DEC Recommended practices in early intervention/early childhood special education.* Longmont, CO: Sopris West.

Parten, M. (1932). Social participation among preschool children. *Journal of Abnormal & Social Psychology, 27*, 243–269.

Patrick, G. T. W. (1916). *The psychology of relaxation.* Boston: Houghton Mifflin.

Piaget, J. (1962). *Play, dreams, and imitation.* New York: Norton.

Rubin, K. H. & Howe, N. (1985). Toys and play behaviors: An overview. *Topics in Early Childhood Special Education, 5*, 1–10.

Sandall, S., McLean, M. E., & Smith, B. J. (2002). *DEC recommended practices in early intervention/early childhood special education.* Longmont, CO: Sopris West.

Sandall, S. R., & Schwartz, I. S. (2002). *Building blocks: A comprehensive approach for supporting young children in inclusive placements.* Baltimore: Paul H. Brookes.

Schwartz, I. S., Garfinkle, A. N. & Davis, C. A. (2002). Arranging preschool environments to facilitate valued social and educational outcomes. In M. R. Shinn, H. M. Walker, G. Stoner (Eds.), *Interventions for academic and behavior problems II: Prevention and remedial approaches.* Bethesda, MD: NASP Publications.

Sherratt, H. D. & Peter, M. (2002). *Developing play and drama in children with autistic spectrum disorders.* London: David Fulton Publishers.

Sigafoos, J., Roberts-Pennell, D., Grave, D. (1999). Longitudinal assessment of play and adaptive behavior in young children with developmental disabilities. *Research in Developmental Disabilities, 20*, 147–161.

Simpkins, S. D. & Parker, R. D. (2002). Do friends and non-friends behave differently? A social relations analysis of children's behavior. *Merrill Palmer Quarterly, 48*, 263–283.

Smilansky, S. (1968). Sociodramatic play: Its relevance to behavior and achievement in school. In E. Klugman & S. Smilansky (Eds.), *Children's play and learning: Perspectives and policy implications* (pp. 18–42). New York: Teachers College Press.

Smith, P. K., & Vollstedt, R. (1985). On defining play: An empirical study of the relationship between play and various play criteria. *Child Development, 56*, 1042–1050.

Spencer, H. (1873). *Principles of psychology.* New York: Appleton-Century-Crofts.

Sutton-Smith, B. (1970). *A descriptive account of four modes of children's play between one and five years.* New York: Columbia University Teachers College.

Sutton-Smith, B. (1980). Children's play: Some sources of play theorizing. In K. H. Rubin (Ed.), *Children's play*. San Francisco: Jossey-Bass.

Thompson, T. & Berkson, G. (1985). Stereotyped behavior of severely disabled children in classroom and freeplay settings. *American Journal of Mental Deficiency, 89,* 580–586.

Tizard, B. (1977). Play: A child's way of learning? In B. Tizant & D. Harvey (Eds.), *Biology of play*. London: Heinemann.

United Nations High Commission for Human Rights (1990). *Declaration of the rights of the child*, Principle 7.

Vygotsky, L. S. (1987). *The collected works of L.S.Vygotsky*. New York: Plenum Press.

Wehman, P. (1977). Establishing play behaviors in mentally retarded youth. *Rehabilitation Literature, 36,* 238–246.

Wehman, P. (1978). Play skills development. In N. H. Fallen & G. E. McGovern (Eds.), *Young children with special needs*. Upper Saddle River, NJ: Merrill/Prentice Hall.

Wetherby, A. M. & Prizant, B. M. (1993). *Communication and symbolic behavior scales*. Baltimore: Paul H. Brookes.

Wing, L., Gould, J., Yeates, S. R. & Brierley, L. M. (1977). Symbolic play in severely mental retarded and in autistic children. *Journal of Child Psychology and Psychiatry and Allied Disciplines, 18,* 167–178.

Wolery, M. (1989). Assessing play skills. In D. B. Bailey, Jr. & M. Wolery (Eds.), *Assessing infants and preschoolers with handicaps*. Upper Saddle River, NJ: Merrill/Prentice Hall.

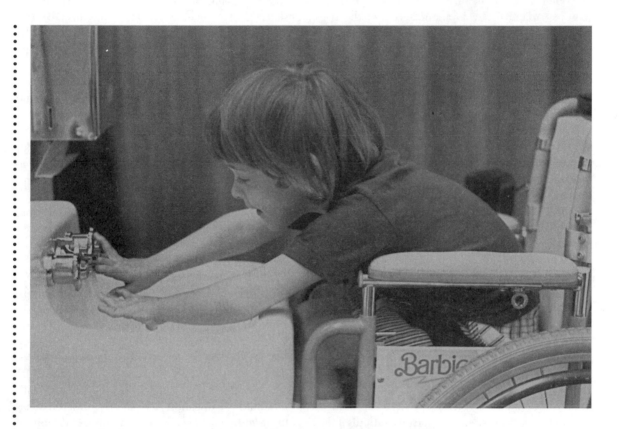

Assessing Adaptive Behavior

Eva Horn
University of Kansas
Amy Childre
Georgia College and State University

The ways in which young children complete everyday functional tasks that reflect chronological-age group expectations for independence can be broadly conceptualized as *adaptive behavior*. Identification of levels of adaptive development in young children is important for two distinct reasons. Adaptive development is one of the five areas used to determine if a child can be labeled developmentally delayed (the other four are cognitive, physical, communication, and social-emotional developmental) (Individuals with Disabilities Education Amendment [IDEA], 1997). Second, identification of specific strengths and needs as well as a comprehensive view of the child's status in adaptive development can help to guide program planning. This chapter describes (a) the rationale for assessing development in this domain; (b) critical dimensions of adaptive development in the early childhood years, including a definition and subdomains representative of the area; (c) procedural considerations in identifying the child's developmental status in terms of adaptive behavior; (d) methods of assessment; and (e) information on using assessment data for planning instruction.

RATIONALE FOR INCLUSION OF ADAPTIVE BEHAVIOR ASSESSMENT

Adaptive behavior is a concept that has held a critical role in assessment of persons with disabilities for many years (Harrison, 1987). This role is particularly evident in the area of eligibility evaluation. Beginning in 1984, (Frankenberger,1984) and continuing with the most recent edition, the American Association on Mental Retardation (AAMR) definition of mental retardation has included limitations in adaptive behavior (Luckasson et. al., 2002). The inclusion of adaptive behavior as a criterion for defining developmental disability marked a pronounced shift in societal attitudes and values concerning mental impairment (Brown & Snell, 2000). This perspective requires assessments to include measures that give a clearer view

of an individual's capabilities by including functioning under realistic situational demands. The shift reflects a more practical approach to the education of persons with disabilities. Further, the current recommended practice in the assessment of adaptive behavior emphasizes the performance of skills (Luckasson et. al., 2002). From this performance perspective, assessment data must note the "skill level a person typically displays when responding to challenges in his or her environment" (Widman & McGrew, 1996, p. 98). In addition, the reason for failure to respond appropriately must be determined and may include any of the following: (a) not knowing how to complete the skill or task; (b) not knowing under which contexts to use the skill; or (c) other motivational issues that may prevent the child from completing the task (Luckasson et. al, 2002).

In the field of early childhood special education, the broader concept of adaptive behavior has been less evident, particularly in intervention planning. Narrower definitions and terms like *self-care* or *self-help skills* were initially used (Johnson-Martin, Attermeier, & Hacker, 1990; Johnson-Martin, Jens, Attermeier, & Hacker, 1991; Umansky & Hooper, 1998; VORT Corporation, 1995). Originally in the IDEA, Part C, Infant/Toddler Program, self-help was included as an area of development for both assessment and intervention. With the 1991 amendments (P.L. 102-119, Individuals with Disabilities Education Act), the term was changed to *adaptive development*. A broad definition should be applied. Adaptive behavior as a curriculum domain should include skills that reflect chronologically age-appropriate skills for meeting the demands of the child's multiple unique environments.

Several rationales for including adaptive behavior in early childhood curricula can be offered. First and foremost, independent participation in normal environments is an anticipated outcome of early intervention (Sandall, McLean, & Smith, 2000). Children who can dress, feed, and toilet themselves are obviously more independent than children who cannot. Similarly, children's acquisition of these skills should decrease caregiving demands. All children require care, but a child with disabilities may have more intense and enduring needs (Dyson & Fewell, 1986). Furthermore, many of the behaviors defined as adaptive, such as social adjustment and personal/social responsibility, address important socially acceptable behaviors. Acquisition of these skills results in a child appearing more normal, thus promoting meaningful inclusion in community settings.

Some characteristics of adaptive behaviors also provide logical support for their place in early childhood curricula. Many adaptive behaviors are acquired during early childhood; mastery of these skills is part of daily routines for all children. In addition, the development of these skills takes a long time and reflects a hierarchical sequence of simple to complex. For example, the skill area of eating may proceed as follows: smoothly sucks from nipple, pulls food off spoon with lips; feeds self finger foods, scoops food from dish with spoon, and, finally, uses appropriate mealtime behaviors, including social graces.

Many adaptive behaviors are visible skills (e.g., putting on clothing, using the toilet, occupying oneself) and their acquisition is obvious. Attainment of these adaptive behaviors may have an immediate, concrete impact, particularly from the family's perspective. Other skills are related to safety issues, such as appropriate behaviors on trips into the community with family or other adults (e.g., holding the adult's hand when walking across the street). A few skills may even have an immediate economic benefit. For example, toileting and eating regular food eliminates the need for the more expensive infant diapers and food.

A final rationale for the inclusion of the adaptive behavior domain is the impact of independent functioning on the child's self-concept and sense of competence. Consider the sense of personal accomplishment embodied by a toddler proudly proclaiming, "I did it!" upon pulling off his or her shirt or other article of clothing. This image illustrates the tremendous impact mastery of these skills can have on a child's sense of self-worth. Conversely, lack of independence may lead to learned helplessness and passivity (Seligman, 1992).

CRITICAL DIMENSIONS OF ADAPTIVE BEHAVIOR DEVELOPMENT

Adaptive behavior is a dynamic construct, influenced by cultural norms and age-related expectations (Horn & Fuchs, 1987). The construct emphasizes the capacity to respond to demands of the immediate environment and the community. A person judged as "adaptive" in one setting (community) may not necessarily be evaluated similarly in another place. The nature of these demands also changes as an individual progresses through the life cycle. For the young child, adaptive behavior encompasses skills such as walking, talking, and basic self-care. For the school-age child, it reflects the capacity to understand and respond appropriately to the social rules of various settings, including school, community, and home. For the adult, adaptive behavior includes the ability to hold a job, maintain a residence, contribute to family life, and so forth. Adaptive behaviors at one developmental level are qualitatively different from those at another level. In short, adaptive behavior is relative and dynamic, rather than absolute and static.

Defining Adaptive Behavior for the Early Childhood Years

The AAMR Ad Hoc Committee on Terminology and Classification in 2002 revised its definition of adaptive behavior to: "Adaptive behavior is the collection of conceptual, social and practical skills that have been learned by people in order to function in their everyday lives" (Luckasson et. al. 2002, p. 73). This revised definition with its three broad domains of adaptive behavior (i.e., conceptual, social, and practical) represents a shift from earlier definitions in which 10 specific skill areas were identified (Luckasson et. al., 1992). While the new three domain approach is less differentiated than the 10 skill domains that were listed in the 1992 definition, it is more consistent with the conceptual models in the literature that describe major domains of personal competence (Greenspan, 1999; Greenspan & Driscoll, 1997; Gresham & Elliot, 1987; Thompson, McGrew, & Bruininks, 1999). As we look to define the skills and expectations within each of these broad subdomains we must acknowledge the importance of the developmental relevance of each skill within these adaptive areas. The Task Force on Recommended Practices of the Division for Early Childhood (DEC) of the Council for Exceptional Children (CEC) in 1993 provided the following definition of adaptive behavior from an early childhood perspective:

> Adaptive behavior consists of changes in children's behavior as a consequence of maturation, development and learning to meet increasing demands of multiple environments. Independent functioning in these environments is the long-term goal. Instruction requires accommodating and adapting to support the specific strengths of individual children. Comprehensive interventions should address the following subdomains: self-care, community self-sufficiency, personal-social responsibility, and social adjustment. (DEC Task Force on Recommended Practices, 1993 p.89)

Using the new three subdomains from AAMR the final sentence could be updated to read, "Comprehensive interventions should address the following subdomains: *practical* (replacing self-care and community self-sufficiency), *conceptual* (replacing personal-social responsibility), *and social* (replacing social adjustment)." Each of these subdomains can be further specified, in terms of the expectations in the early childhood years. In early childhood, the practical subdomain addresses personal care skills such as dressing/undressing, eating/feeding, toileting, and grooming (e.g., hand washing, face washing, toothbrushing). These personal care skills make up the abilities needed for independent functioning in relation to basic needs such as food and warmth. The practical subdomain also addresses community self-sufficiency skills that promote age and culturally appropriate functioning with adult

supervision in community environments such as restaurants, neighborhoods, and recreational areas. For example, the child might sit quietly through a religious service, occupying herself in a quiet activity and requesting only minimal attention from her parents. Basic skills in the conceptual domain include basic environmental interactions, self-directed behaviors, independent play/self-occupation, peer cooperation and interaction, and the assumption of responsibility (e.g., demonstrates caution, avoids dangers). Finally, the social subdomain includes behaviors such as the ability to adjust to new situations, regularity of behavior patterns (e.g., eating, sleeping), general disposition, tendency to stick to tasks despite obstacles, attention span and degree of distractibility, and amount of stimulation necessary to evoke a response.

Although this chapter focuses on the assessment of adaptive skills, it is clear that these skills are highly related to other areas of development. For example, acceptable eating behaviors include a variety of social and communication skills as well as the more obvious gross and fine motor skills. Further, critical skills of several of the subdomains are directly addressed in other developmental domains. For example, peer cooperation and interaction, a component of the personal/social responsibility subdomain, is clearly an important skill area in the social development domain. An implication of this overlap is not to remove it from consideration in adaptive behavior assessment but rather to highlight the importance of conducting comprehensive assessments that do not artificially splinter skills into measurable units. In beginning the assessment process with any child, the whole child perspective must always be kept at the forefront of our efforts.

Characteristics and Implications for Assessment

Certain characteristics of adaptive behavior have implications for the assessment process. Since adaptive behaviors are tied to the context in which they are used and focused on performance over time rather than one-time performance, more indirect measurement methods are used. Unlike standardized tests that an evaluator conducts in a test session with a child, many adaptive behavior assessments rely on information from an informant, usually a primary adult or caregiver who is familiar with the child's typical behaviors in multiple real-life settings (Sattler, 1992).

With adaptive behavior, a child's ability to perform a particular skill is insufficient if he or she fails to use the skill as needed. For example, the preschool child may be able to furnish his or her first and last name and street address in opening circle, but, when lost, may not be able to respond to the question "Where do you live?" To detect this an evaluator might need to directly observe the child for an extended period of time. Therefore, in place of direct observation in every setting, evaluators rely on multiple methods and multiple informants in a true team effort. The following sections provide more detailed examples of the link between adaptive behavior characteristics and assessment.

Contextual Nature of Adaptive Behaviors
As previously stated, adaptive behavior relates to the "fit" of the child within and across settings. That is, can the child meet the demands of the many current and future settings he or she encounters? The behaviors used to assess competence in adaptive behavior at a specific chronological age are identified from an analysis of the unique needs and lifestyles of the child and his or her family, peers, and community. Similarly, adaptive behaviors are typically a part of regularly occurring events that focus on socially prescribed habitual behaviors (e.g., which food requires the use of utensils in eating and which utensil). This requires that the child learn the cultural expectations of self-care and self-sufficiency necessary in group settings inside and outside the home. Exactly what skills are learned is determined by the culture of the subsettings in which the family and the child participate on a regular basis. Finally, there is significant variance in normal

development sequences with heavy cultural influence (e.g., movement from breast milk or formula to solid food has varied across generations, regions, and/or nationalities from as early as 6 weeks to as late as 2 years).

An implication of the contextual nature of adaptive behaviors is that the members of the assessment team must develop a broad picture of the child's everyday contexts, including specific family, cultural, and community expectations for adaptive competence for his or her chronological age group. Families tend to be the primary facilitators of learning in many environments and activities in which young children participate on a daily basis (e.g., home, community, mealtimes, bathing, dressing) (Turnbull & Turnbull, 2001). The young child's acquisition of adaptive behaviors is embedded in the family's routines and their expectations. Further, since family members usually provide the most consistent support over time and have the broadest and most continuous picture, it follows that they should best know their child's strengths and needs that impact his or her fit in and across settings. In addition to providing valuable information, they can validate information collected from other sources. Interviews and discussions with the family can be particularly valuable, in that they provide an opportunity for parents to indicate the adaptive behaviors they consider to be instructional priorities. Thus, they should be the primary source for identification of skills, priorities, and contexts for assessment and subsequent intervention.

Adaptive Development in the Early Childhood Years
As noted earlier, adaptive behaviors are acquired throughout the early childhood years. Within each of the subdomains, acquisition represents a hierarchical sequence from simple to complex. This sequence typically reflects changes in the amount of adult support needed and the efficiency of completing the task. For example, in feeding, initially the infant is totally dependent on the adult to obtain nutrition and is relatively slow in sucking the liquid from the nipple; they rapidly gain independence in latching onto the nipple and

more efficiently sucking while maintaining a faster pace and losing less liquid. This development of greater independence continues, with the preschooler being able to pour milk from a pitcher (as long as it is not too full) with minimal spillage.

Overlap with Other Domains of Development   As with most areas of development considerable overlap between adaptive behavior and the other domains occurs across skill areas. Further, in order for the child to successfully and competently participate in many adaptive tasks, skill development in the areas of communication, cognition, fine and gross motor, and socialization is critical. Take for example the act of enjoying a carton of chocolate milk at snack time. Gross motor skills are required to travel to the snack area and sit comfortably and safely at the table. Communication skills are required in order to request the chocolate milk rather than the plain milk and other items needed, such as a straw and napkin. Fine motor skills must be quite refined in order to manipulate the opening of the carton. Problem-solving strategies are particularly useful as the child works on getting the opening started and asking for assistance if needed. And finally, the satisfaction of sharing the wonders of chocolate milk bubbles created by blowing into your straw with your peers is a classic preschool social event. The implication for assessment is that a comprehensive view of assessment that addresses the whole child is essential. Further, interdisciplinary involvement is critical.

Low-Frequency Behaviors   Some important adaptive behavior skills are used with relatively low frequency; nevertheless, these skills must become habitual to be truly functional. That is, they must be performed fluently in response to natural cues, maintained by natural consequences, and performed in varied settings and circumstances. This implies that the early childhood professional may need to change the traditional assessment and instruction contexts to reflect the diversity of settings in which the skills naturally occur (e.g., home, community, preschool). In addition, the assessment team may need to adapt their schedules in order to increase the opportunities for observing these skills within the context of routines. Children must be given real-life opportunities to demonstrate habitual, generalized responses to natural cues provided across multiple current and future environments. The assessment team must not only assess presence or absence of the adaptive behavior skill but also fluency, generalization, and maintenance. This characteristic highlights the importance of eliciting input from the family since they can provide information that cannot be collected easily through direct observation or testing (Turnbull & Turnbull, 2001).

Chains of Physiological and Learned Behaviors   Many adaptive behaviors require physiological maturity and learned behavior (e.g., feeding skills, toileting). These skills are not discrete behaviors but rather a sequence of behaviors the result in a complex function (e.g., toileting requires the physiological ability to hold and release urine, going to the toilet, removing clothing, sitting, etc.). The assessment team must be skilled in analyzing the component parts of complex skills and appropriately assessing the child's current developmental and physiological status in relation to each of these component parts. They must first determine if the required physiological components are present (e.g., equilibrium responses to maintain relaxed sitting on the toilet seat). If they are absent, the team should determine if adaptations can be provided that will bypass the component (e.g., adaptive positioning device) or if strategies can be developed to allow the child to learn to perform the component (e.g., intervention for teaching equilibrium responses).

Summary   Adaptive behaviors are important skills for children to learn. The specific characteristics of these skills require consideration in the assessment of current functioning and future needs (Luckasson et al., 2002). In sum:

- Skill levels should be determined in the context of natural environments typical of the individual's age group.

- Assessment must consider and make necessary adaptations for diversity in language or culture and for limitations and/or challenges.
- Strengths and limitations may coexist even within a single adaptive area for the young child.
- Gains in quality of life and independence in functioning generally occur for persons with disabilities when they are provided with appropriate supports over time.

PROCEDURES FOR ASSESSING ADAPTIVE BEHAVIOR DEVELOPMENT

This section includes the following segments: (a) discussion of multiple data collection methods; (b) summary of specific instruments available for assessing adaptive behaviors; and (c) specific assessment issues relevant to each of the subdomains. Examples of the range of skills within each subdomain as well as specific recommended practices for assessing these subdomains are also included in the last segment.

Data Collection Methods

As mentioned earlier, more indirect strategies are used as the primary method of data collection in assessing adaptive behavior development. Rather than conducting direct testing, observations in natural contexts and interviews with significant adults are the primary sources of information. There are several approaches to determining what to ask or what to look for, including developmental scales, criterion-referenced lists, and ecological inventory methods.

Developmental Scales Developmental scales are based on the normal sequence of development. Skills are sequenced according to the age at which they are acquired by typically developing children. There are several advantages to using these scales for assessing adaptive development in young children. Developmental test items are written in observable terms, aiding in the reliable determination of the presence or absence of the skill. The scales can also be re-administered periodically as a measure of child change.

Since skills are listed in chronological order, they may provide information for determining the next skill to teach. For many children the item following the last item passed in a subdomain may become a target for instruction. These scales also provide extensive listings of skills within the various subdomains, reducing the risk of overlooking an important skill. The developmental age equivalents provided for clusters of skills assist teachers in determining whether skills targeted for intervention are developmentally appropriate given the child's chronological age. For example, the teacher of an 18-month-old toddler would recognize that it is not developmentally appropriate to expect the child to eat her peas with a fork. Finally, because developmental sequences across various domains are familiar to many disciplines, they may facilitate communication between disciplines.

There are, however, some potential problems associated with using developmental scales, particularly in the area of adaptive development. An obvious one that has already been noted is the significant variation in developmental sequelae of some skills due to the current consideration of viewing child rearing from a cultural, geographic, and generational perspective. Further, some adaptive behaviors appearing on developmental scales may be irrelevant in certain populations. An obvious example would be the use of forks and knives for a child whose family meals are primarily eaten without utensils (e.g., sandwiches, tacos, burritos, pita bread) or other types of utensils such as chopsticks. For a child with specific sensory or motor disabilities, developmental items may need to be adapted so that the disability does not prevent assessment of the specific skill of interest. For example, a child who is blind may be able to eat fully independently with a fork once he is told the location of and types of food on his plate.

Other disadvantages relate to the use of the information obtained. Skills within and across subdomains may be seen in isolation. For example, the visual skill "tracks objects," which is often assessed using the "red ring," takes on more meaning in the context of tracking the movement of the bottle or spoon in one's mother's hand during feeding. Similarly, the purpose for including certain elements may not be obvious. Some items are listed on developmental scales because of their high reliability at certain ages (White, 1985). For example, the item "separates easily from caregiver," which is often included in the social adjustment subdomain, is not intended to address a lack of attachment by the child but rather the child's ability to handle transitions and to self-regulate. Further, the assumption is often made that if the item is on an assessment it must be meaningful for instruction. For example, the 3-month item "roots toward food or object infrequently" (Johnson-Martin, Jens, Attermeier, & Hacker, 1991) does not readily translate into an objective. The sequences of items on many scales may not be the best teaching sequences, especially for children with sensory and motor disabilities. For example, a child with a vision impairment would not necessarily go from "chews with a rotary/side-to-side action" (9-month item in feeding) to working on "feeds self with fingers" (the next item in feeding) (items from Johnson-Martin et al., 1991). The child may be able to chew food for quite some time before he or she is able to handle the visual-motor task of finding the food, picking it up, taking it to his or her mouth, and biting off a piece. Further, many sequences have large gaps between items (e.g., "identifies familiar objects by their use" and "identifies big and small") (Newborg, Stock, Wnek, Guidubaldi, & Svinicki, 1988). With each of these examples, misinterpretations could lead to an inaccurate picture of the child's abilities and to inappropriate instruction.

Developmental scales can serve an important role in the assessment process; however, the members of the assessment team must carefully evaluate the relevance of particular items for each child

and each family. The child's age, interest, motor or sensory disabilities, and home and community environments must be considered in the assessment process and in the interpretation and use of results.

Criterion-Referenced Lists of Adaptive Behavior Criterion-referenced assessments measure a child's performance as compared with a predetermined level of mastery, or criterion. Items are drawn from an analysis of functional skills thought to be essential for young children to function independently and to cope with environmental demands. The focus on functional skills and abilities enhances the likelihood that each test item is an appropriate intervention target (Salvia & Ysseldyke, 2001).

Several important advantages to criterion-referenced tests enhance their appropriateness in the adaptive behavior domain. The preferred method of collecting assessment data is through observation of the child in familiar and typical settings, which allows the assessment team to collect critical information about the responses the child uses in a functional manner and when and how they are used. In addition, most lists provide multiple-level scoring to reflect different levels of proficiency in using the skill. Since a standard presentation format does not have to be maintained, the evaluators are encouraged to find and use adaptations to assist the child in accomplishing the functional outcome. Freedom and flexibility in modifying the criteria for "correct" are acceptable because the assessment results are not for comparative purposes, but instead are used to generate appropriate interventions (Berk, 1988).

Another distinction between norm-referenced and criterion-referenced assessments is the breadth of the domain that is covered (Hopkins, 1998). The former typically survey broader domains and age spans, providing a sampling of skills within each. Criterion-referenced lists have fewer domains and/or age ranges but attempt to provide a comprehensive listing of skills with smaller increments to allow small changes to be reflected. Further, some criterion-referenced tests present items reflecting conceptual or response classes instead of singular, specific exemplar skills (Bricker, 2002); for example, an item might ask about adjustment to transitions, rather than "separates easily from caregiver."

The primary disadvantage of most criterion-referenced lists is that they do not provide norms for the test outcomes, which may be necessary for some aspects of eligibility determination, program evaluation, or progress monitoring. They also do not completely address the issue of contextually specific skills, which is often the case for adaptive behavior development. Skills on the lists may still not be relevant to the individual child and family contexts because they are generated to reflect the skills of large population groups and geographic areas.

Ecological Inventories Like criterion-referenced tests, ecological inventories examine the environment to determine needed skills; rather than using commercially available lists of skills, the current and future environments relevant to the particular child are analyzed (Brown et al., 1979). Consequently, the process is completely individualized. The purposes are to identify functional routines and activities across germane settings, such as home, preschool, and community. Subsequently, measures are taken to estimate the child's abilities to participate in specific routines and activities in those settings. Assessment and curricular content are identified by assessing the skill requirements of relevant environments. Thus, the environment is the source of the skills listed, as well as the assessment site.

The information to identify and analyze routines and activities is collected by direct observation and interviews with significant individuals in the child's life, including the family, who can describe the child's present level of participation in daily routines and activities. The ecological inventory process is child-, family-, and culture-specific. The routines, activities, and skills identified reflect a child's capabilities, interests, and temperament. The uniqueness of each family and child is reflected. The routines and activities will vary from

one child to another depending on such characteristics as family members present in the home, work and/or school responsibilities, social/recreational interests and preferences, interpersonal needs and strengths, and so on. Finally, cultural diversity will be reflected in the family's lifestyle and similarly seen in the daily routines from which the assessment content is drawn. For example, family culture will influence family members' roles (who does which chores), routines (in terms of meals and sleeping), and extent and type of participation in social and/or religious events.

The ecological inventory strategy first discussed by Brown and his colleagues (Brown et al., 1979) is comprised of five phases. The purpose of the first phase is to associate current level of functioning with major activities or settings, such as home living, leisure activities, and community life. In the second phase, current and future places where the child might participate (living, learning, and playing) are identified. For example, the child might currently attend a parents-day-out program three days a week but next year will be attending a five-day-a-week preschool program. The changes in expectation for participation in this program would need to be addressed.

The third phase of the ecological inventory involves identification of subsettings in which the child currently participates or may in the future. The family's home, for example, can be divided into bedroom, bathroom, kitchen, and living room; skills necessary for adaptive functioning in each of these subsettings can then be identified. The fourth phase requires an inventory of each subsetting. Examples of important activities for a bathroom subsetting include bathing, tooth-brushing, toileting, and picking up towels, toys, and so forth. Following identification of important activities with subsettings, the activities must be translated into teachable units or task-analyzed into precise sequences of behaviors. The fifth and final phase is to assess the child's performance of these sequences of behaviors. Based on the results of this assessment, an instructional program is designed and implemented. Using an ecological inventory approach and a "current versus subsequent" setting orientation helps members of the team identify skills that are most functional and relevant to the child and the family.

The primary disadvantages of ecological inventories relate directly to their primary advantages, that is, to their flexibility and individualization. This assessment process does not offer structure or specific guidelines for the identification of skills. Although the process ensures identification of skills relevant to the individual, the skill sequences identified by two teams may be very different. For example, a team led by a speech therapist or someone with extensive training in communication might identify many communication opportunities in their inventory. A second team, led by a physical therapist or someone with extensive training in working with children with physical disabilities, might focus on challenges of the physical environment and issues of access and control.

Furthermore, teams need to be sure that ecological inventories identify not only the observable activities and skills that are associated with competent performance in natural environments, but also related skills that may not be so apparent. For example, in addition to communication and motor skills used at mealtime, more subtle social skills, such as smiling at the waitress and making eye contact with your companions at a restaurant, may not be identified. These skills are not critical to the performance of the activity but nonetheless are important to a socially appropriate performance. Similarly, some skills may not be identified because they do not occur at the same time and place as the actual activity. Telling your parents about all the fun things that happened at your friend's birthday party or planning your own party based on your friend's party might not be identified in an ecological inventory. Providing more structure and systemization to guide the identification of skills by the team would begin to address some of these concerns.

Summary of Data Collection   At best, our assessment results are educated guesses based on

as much data as can be collected in the available time (Wortham, 2001). They give an idea of what the child can and cannot do and what seem to be the child's most critical needs in order to participate in current and future environments. If this information is generated from a developmental scale or set of predetermined criterion-referenced lists, the goals will typically be the next skills in whatever sequence is used. If, on the other hand, we use an ecological inventory process, goals will be based on their relevance to the child's daily activities and settings and will be directed at maximizing participation in ongoing tasks.

Used alone, either approach leaves us short of important information; used together they complement one another. For example, the ecological inventory could be used to identify the activities and routines (e.g., mealtimes, free-play, community trips) the child needs to learn in order to participate in important natural environments such as home or preschool. A developmental list or criterion-referenced list could be used to identify the specific skills across domains that are naturally embedded in these routines and that the child needs for successful, appropriate participation. Next, these skill lists could be validated by checking their appropriateness in the multiple natural settings in which they will be applied. Finally, the lists could be used to assess the child's status and needs for instruction.

Instruments for Assessing Adaptive Development

Assessment instruments including norm-referenced, developmental, and/or criterion-referenced scales for evaluating a young child's adaptive development are available commercially. As indicated earlier, in terms of early childhood curricula and texts, assessment tools in early childhood also use a variety of terms for skills that relate to adaptive behavior development (e.g., self-help, self-care, coping, personal/social responsibility). Measures of adaptive behavior development are also included as domains within multidomain assessment instruments (e.g., *Battelle Development Inventory*) or as instruments developed specifically to measure adaptive behavior (e.g., *Vineland Adaptive Behavior Scales*).

Global Assessments Embedding Adaptive Development Measures

Several multidomain assessments address adaptive behavior development. Although the goal of assessment is to gain a better understanding of the whole child, it is necessary to break the task into manageable pieces. Many global assessments offer subtests that are defined by the domains each attempts to measure. For example, the *Assessment, Evaluation, and Programming System* (AEPS) *for Infants and Children, Second Edition* (Bricker, 2002) includes fine motor, gross motor, adaptive, cognitive, social-communication, and social skills, whereas the *Learning Accomplishment Profile-Revised (LAP-R)* (Nehring, Nehring, Bruni, & Randolph, 1995) includes fine and gross motor, language, self-help, and social-cognitive skills. These instruments do not necessarily include the same domains nor do they necessarily define the domains in the same way. For example, the *AEPS* measures feeding, personal hygiene, and undressing as strands in the adaptive behavior domain. The *Battelle Developmental Inventory* (Newborg et al., 1988), on the other hand, includes attention, eating, dressing, personal responsibility, and toileting in the adaptive behavior domain.

Some of the available multidomain assessments for young children that include adaptive behavior strands are presented in Table 15.1. Also included in this table is the terminology used by that instrument to label the domains relevant to adaptive behavior.

Specific Measures of Adaptive Behavior

A number of instruments that are specifically focused on adaptive behavior development in young children are available. A brief listing appears in Table 15.2. More detailed reviews of four representative scales of adaptive behavior development in young children (birth to 8 years) follow.

The *AAMR Adaptive Behavior Scales: School and Community Version (ABS-S:2)* (Lambert, Leland, & Nihira, 1993) is intended for school-age children from 3 to 21. It is divided into two parts. Part One focuses on personal independence, coping skills, and daily living skills by assessing the following nine domains: (a) independent functioning (e.g., self-care, using transportation and other public facilities); (b) physical development (i.e., physical and motor abilities); (c) economic activity (i.e., managing money and being a consumer); (d) language development (i.e., receptive and expressive language in social situations); (e) numbers and time (i.e., basic mathematical skills); (f) prevocational/vocational activity (i.e., skills related to school and job performance); (g) responsibility (i.e., accountability for actions, belongings, and duties); (h) self-direction; and (i) socialization. Part Two focuses on problem behavior. The behaviors that are examined are divided into seven domains: (a) violent and antisocial behavior; (b) rebellious behavior; (c) untrustworthy behavior (i.e., stealing, lying, cheating, showing disrespect for public and private property); (d) stereotyped and hyperactive behavior; (e) eccentric behavior; (f) withdrawn behavior; and (g) disturbed behavior. The *ABS-S:2* is administered as an interview. Raw scores are converted to standard scores with a mean of 10 and a standard score of 3. Scores are converted to quotients that have a mean of 100 and standard deviation of 15. Percentiles are also available.

The *Checklist of Adaptive Living Skills (CALS)* (Moreau & Bruininks 1991), a criterion-referenced checklist of approximately 800 items, was developed to measure the adaptive behavior development of infants through adults. The *CALS* is divided into four domains: (a) personal living skills; (b) home living skills; (c) community living skills; and (d) employment skills. Each of these domains is organized into 24 specific skill strands. Each item covers a range of behaviors; items are arranged in order of difficulty. The scale is administered as an interview and takes approximately

TABLE 15.1
Multidomain Assessments That Include an Adaptive Behavior Domain

Title	Source	Age Range	Type	Adaptive Domain Addressed
Assessment, Evaluation, and Programming System (AEPS) for Infants and Children, Second Ed. (2002)	Paul H. Brookes Publishing Co., P.O. Box 10624, Baltimore, MD 21285-0624	birth to 6 years	criterion-referenced, developmental	adaptive: feeding/dining, personal hygiene, dressing/undressing
Battelle Developmental Inventory (BDI) (1988)	Riverside Publishing, 425 Spring Lake Drive, Chicago, IL 60143-2079	birth to 8 years	norm-referenced	adaptive: attention, eating, dressing, personal responsibility, toileting
Brigance Inventory of Early Development-Revised (1991)	Curriculum Associates, 153 Rangeway Rd. North Billerica, MA 01862	birth to 7 years	criterion-referenced	adaptive (self-help)
Carolina Curriculum for Infants and Toddlers with Special Needs (1991)	Paul H. Brookes Publishing Co., P.O. Box 10624, Baltimore, MD 21285-0624	birth to 24 months	developmental, criterion-referenced	self-help: eating, grooming, dressing, self-direction
Carolina Curriculum for Preschoolers with Special Needs (CCPSN) (1990)	Paul H. Brookes Publishing Co., P.O. Box 10624, Baltimore, MD 21285-0624	2 to 5 years	developmental, criterion-referenced	self-help: eating, dressing, grooming, toileting; responsibility, self-concept
Child Development Inventory (CDI) (1991)	Behavior Science Systems, P.O. Box 580274, Minneapolis, MN 55458	15 to 72 months	norm-referenced	self-help
Denver Developmental Screening Test II (DDST-II) (1990)	Denver Developmental Materials, P.O. Box 371075, Denver, CO 80237-5075	birth to 6 years	screening	personal-social abilities

Instrument	Publisher/Address	Age Range	Type	Domain
Developmental Assessment for Students with Severe Disabilities (DASH-2) (1999)	PRO-ED, 8700 Shoal Creek Blvd., Austin TX 78738-6897	birth to 6 years	criterion-referenced	activities of daily living
Developmental Profile II (DP-II) (1986)	Western Psychological Services, 12031 Wilshire Blvd; Los Angeles CA 90025-1251	birth to 9 years	norm-referenced, screening	self-help:eating, dressing, self-care, work
Diagnostic Inventory for Screening Children, 2nd Ed. (DISC) (1988)	Kitchener Waterloo Hospital, 835 King St. West, Kitchener, Ontario N2g 1G3	birth to 5 years	norm-referenced, screening	self-help
Early Learning Accomplishment Profile (Early-LAP) (1993)	Chapel Hill Training-Outreach Project, Kaplan Companies, P.O. Box 609, Lewisville, NC 27023-2014	birth to 36 months	criterion-referenced	self-help
Early Screening Profiles (ESP) (1990)	American Guidance Service, 4201 Woodland Road, P.O.Box 99, Circle Pines, MN 55014-1796	2 to 6 years	norm-referenced, screening	self-help
HELP for Special Preschoolers (HELP: 3–6) (1987)	VORT, P.O. Box 60132-TX, Palo Alto, CA 94306	3 to 6 years	criterion-referenced	self-help
Hawaii Early Learning Profile (HELP: 0–3) (1988)	VORT, P.O. Box 60132-TX, Palo Alto, CA 94306	birth to 36 months	criterion-referenced	self-help
Infant Development Inventory (IDI) (1994)	Behavior Science Systems, P.O. Box 580274, Minneapolis, MN 55458	birth to 18 months	developmental	self-help
Kent Inventory of Developmental Skills (KIDS) (2001)	Western Psychological Services, 12031 Wilshire Blvd., Los Angeles,CA 90025-1251	birth to 15 months	norm-referenced	self-help

Continued

TABLE 15.1
Continued

Title	Source	Age Range	Type	Adaptive Domain Addressed
Learning Accomplishment Profile-Diagnostic Edition (LAP-D) (1978)	Kaplan School Supply Corp., 1310 Lewis-Clemmons Rd., Lewisville, NC 27023	birth to 6 years	developmental, criterion-referenced	self-help
Learning Accomplishment Profile-Revised (LAP-R) (1995)	Kaplan School Supply Corp., 1310 Lewis-Clemmons Rd., Lewisville, NC 27023	32 to 72 months	criterion-referenced	
Preschool Evaluation Scales (PES) (1991)	Hawthorne Educational Services, 800 Gray Oak Drive, Columbia, MO 65201	birth to 6 years	norm-referenced, screening	self-help
Vineland SEEC: Social-Emotional Early Childhood Scales (1998)	American Guidance Service, 4201 Woodland Road, Circle Pines, MN 55014-1796	birth to 5 years	norm-referenced	coping

TABLE 15.2

Adaptive Behavior Scales for Young Children

Title	Source	Age Range	Subtests
AAMR Adaptive Behavior Scale–School and Community Edition (ABS-S:2) (1993)	PRO-ED, 8700 Shoal Creek Blvd., Austin TX 78758-6897	3 to 18 years	A norm-referenced scale that evaluates personal independence: independent functioning, physical development, language development, economic activity, language development, numbers and time, prevocational-vocational activity, responsibility, self-direction, socialization, social maladaptation: violent and antisocial, rebellious, untrustworthy, stereotyped and hyperactive, eccentric, withdrawal, disturbed behavior
Adaptive Behavior Assessment System (ABAS) (2000)	Psychological Corporation, P.O.Box 708906, San Antonio, TX 78270-8906	5 years to adult	A norm-referenced instrument that assesses adaptive behavior across the ten categories identified by AAMR
Adaptive Behavior Assessment System-Infant and Preschool (2002)	Psychological Corporation, P.O.Box 708906, San Antonio, TX 78270-8906	birth to 5 years	A norm-referenced scale that assesses adaptive skill functioning across skill areas specified by AAMR and DSM-IV
Adaptive Behavior Inventory for Children (ABIC) (1982)	Psychological Corporation, P.O.Box 708906, San Antonio, TX 78270-8906	5 to 11 years	A norm-referenced inventory measuring student role performance in the family, the community, the peer group, nonacademic school settings, earner/consumer activities, and self-maintenance
Adaptive Behavior Inventory (ABI) (1986)	PRO-ED, 8700 Shoal Creek Blvd., Austin TX 78758-6897	6 to 18 years	A norm-referenced inventory with subscales in self-care, communication, social skills, academic skills, and occupational skills
Checklist of Adaptive Living Skills (CAL) (1991)	Riverside Publishing, 425 Spring Lake Drive, Itasca, IL 60143-2079	Infants to adult	A criterion-referenced checklist divided into four domains: personal living skills, home living skills, community living skills, and employment skills
Early Coping Inventory (ECI) (1988)	Scholastic Testing Service, 480 Meyer Rd., Bensenville, IL 60106	4 to 36 months	A criterion-referenced scale covering the domains of sensorimotor organization, reactive behavior, and self-initiated behavior

Continued

501

TABLE 15.2
Continued

Title	Source	Age Range	Subtests
Inventory for Client and Agency Planning (ICAP) (1986)	Riverside Publishing, 425 Spring Lake Drive, Itasca, IL 60143-2079	Infants to adult	A norm-referenced inventory that yields a score of adaptive and maladaptive behavior that indicates need for care, supervision, and education
Scales of Independent Behavior-Revised (SIB-R) (1996)	Riverside Publishing, 425 Spring Lake Drive, Itasca, IL 60143-2079	Infants to adult	A norm-referenced scale of skills needed to function independently in home, social, and community settings
Vineland Adaptive Behavior Scales (1984)	American Guidance Service, P.O. Box 190, Circle Pines, MN 55014-1796	birth to 18 years	A norm-referenced scale with subtests in communication, daily living skills, socialization, and motor skills.

60 minutes to complete. Because it is a criterion-referenced checklist, the scale may be readministered periodically. Scoring requires simply checking items the child can perform independently according to the criterion.

The *Early Coping Inventory (ECI)* (Zeitlin, Williamson, & Szczepanski, 1988), which assesses the coping and adaptive development of young children between the ages of 4 and 36 months, contains 48 items that are divided into three major categories: (a) sensorimotor organization (i.e., regulation of psychophysiological functions and integration of sensory and motor processes); (b) reactive behaviors (i.e., responses to the demands of the physical and social environment); and (c) self-initiated behavior (i.e., self-directed behaviors intended to meet personal needs and to interact with objects and people). The inventory is completed through direct observation of the child. The evaluator rates the child on a 5-point scale according to the level of effectiveness, ranging from 1 (the behavior is not effective) to 5 (the behavior is consistently effective across situations). Raw scores on each of the categories are converted to effectiveness scores, which are used to compute the adaptive behavior index. A coping profile for the child can also be developed. The *Coping Inventory* (Zeitlin, 1985) is available for children 3 through 16 years of age and is similar in organization and administration to the *ECI.*

The *Vineland Adaptive Behavior Scales* (Sparrow, Balla, & Cicchetti, 1984) is one of the most widely used instruments for evaluating adaptive behavior. There are three separate versions of the scales: a survey form, an expanded form, and a classroom edition. The survey form is designed to obtain an overview of adaptive behavior and covers the age range of birth through 18 years. The expanded form is a comprehensive diagnostic instrument that provides in-depth information across a large sample of behaviors (577 items) and also covers the birth through 18 years age range. The classroom edition addresses adaptive behaviors in classroom and school settings for children 3 through 12 years of age.

All of the *Vineland* scales cover four adaptive behavior domains: (a) communication (i.e., receptive, expressive, written); (b) daily living skills (i.e., personal, domestic, community); (c) socialization (i.e., interpersonal relationships, play and leisure time, coping skills); and (d) motor skills (i.e., gross and fine). The scales are conducted as a general interview with a primary caregiver who knows the child well. The survey form and classroom edition take from 20 to 60 minutes; the expanded form takes from 60 to 90 minutes. Scoring procedures take 10 to 15 minutes and yield a standard score for each domain and a composite score. The scales also include an optional maladaptive behavior scale.

ASSESSMENT ISSUES WITHIN EACH SUBDOMAIN

In the last section concerning procedures for assessment of adaptive development, some attention will be given to each of the subdomains of adaptive behavior as presented earlier (i.e., practical, conceptual, and social. Specifically, examples of the range of skills within each subdomain will be provided as well as recommended practices in conducting assessments in these subdomains.

Practical

In early childhood, the two primary areas of the practical domain are personal care and community self-sufficiency.

Personal Care

Personal care includes such developmentally appropriate skills as dressing/undressing, eating/feeding, toileting, and grooming (e.g., hand-washing, face-washing, toothbrushing). By the age of 5, most children have learned basic personal-care skills (Johnson-Martin et al., 1990). All of the discrete behaviors in this subdomain are related to other areas of development. For example, dressing is more than putting on a shirt. It requires discriminating the front from the back, determining the appropriateness of the shirt for the weather, and control over a range of refined motor abilities.

Personal-care skills involve a number of discrete behaviors tied together (e.g., putting on pants requires a sequence of placing the pants, putting one leg in, the other leg, pulling them up, fastening, and zipping). Many assessments provide lists of skills (e.g., takes off shirt, puts on shirt, fastens shirt) and provide a binary system (yes/no) to record whether the child can or cannot do the behavior. The problem is that this gives very little information as to why the child is unable to complete the skill. Additionally, even if the child can accomplish the task, no information is gained as to the fluency of the child's response. Furthermore, many lists provide only one sequence of steps, although many personal-care skills can be accomplished using a variety of sequences (e.g., taking off a T-shirt can be done by one arm at a time; crossing the arms, grasping the bottom edge of the shirt and pulling it over your head; or using one arm over the back and pulling it over the head). Because all of these approaches have the same end result, none is right or wrong. Some, however, may be easier for an individual child at a particular point in time. Using predetermined lists does not allow the assessment team to address these issues. Lists can serve as guides but should be individualized to address the abilities and disabilities of the child in order to provide the information needed to develop an appropriate intervention. Table 15.3 provides a list of potential skills and suggested sequences across the major areas of personal-care. This list is not intended to be comprehensive nor does it break the skills down into their smallest components.

Dressing/Undressing and Grooming The assessment of behaviors in this strand requires flexibility by the assessment team. Direct observation should be conducted at natural times when the skill is needed (e.g., removing shoes to settle down for naptime), in natural contexts (e.g.,

brushing teeth at the bathroom sink, not at a water fountain), and using real materials (e.g., shirt or jacket rather than a buttoning board). After completing the assessment, the team should have answers to the following questions: (1) Can the child perform the task (e.g., take T-shirt off)? (2) If yes, can the child do this fluently and across multiple settings and materials? (3) If no, why not? What piece is missing from the sequence or chain of behaviors? and (4) What adaptations either in materials or strategy could correct this? A decision tree that provides a sequence of questions to be addressed, strategies for getting those answers, and subsequent questions to ask dependent on the initial answer could help to guide the assessment process of these chained behaviors. Table 15.4 provides such a decision tree or assessment heuristic for dressing/undressing and grooming, but could easily be applied to the assessment of other chained behaviors.

Toileting The typical timeline for accomplished toilet training is highly variable, with some children being trained well before 2 years while others are 3 or even 4 years old. Muscle control is obviously needed to control elimination. In addition, the behavioral control to stop an interesting activity to attend to toileting needs may be difficult for the young child. Snell and Brown (2000) suggest the following three criteria for initiating toilet training: (a) the child has a relatively stable pattern of urination and bowel elimination rather than a random pattern throughout the day; (b) the child has periods of $1\frac{1}{2}$-to-2 hours of dryness; and (c) the child is chronologically 2.5 years old or older. As with many other adaptive behaviors, toileting is learned in a logical developmental sequence, building on certain earlier skills. Assessment for readiness may begin with determining if the child has an awareness of wet or soiled pants, by observing whether he or she shows discomfort or somehow indicates that he or she wants clean clothing.

As the child matures, the time between elimination increases, and the child can begin to learn to "hold it" between adult-initiated trips. The best way

TABLE 15.3
Example Skills Across Major Personal-Care Skill Areas

Skill Area	Examples
Dressing/undressing	Cooperates in dressing/undressing (e.g., holds arm out for sleeve, foot out for shoe) Removes loose clothing (e.g., mitten, hat, untied shoes) Unfastens clothing zipper that has a large pull tab Puts on sock, loose shoes, and "stretch pants" Puts on all clothes unaided, except for fasteners Undoes fasteners (e.g., large buttons, snaps, shoelaces) Zips front-opening clothing such as jacket Selects and matches clothing appropriate for weather conditions and specific activities
Grooming	Enjoys playing in water Cooperates in hand-washing and drying Wipes nose, if given tissues Washes and dries hands and face without assistance Brushes teeth Runs brush or comb through hair Bathes self
Toileting	Usually indicates need to toilet, rarely has bowel accident Urinates in toilet Has bowel movement in toilet Anticipates need to toilet Cares for self at toilet (may need assistance wiping after bowel movement) Wipes and flushes after toileting Cares for clothing before and after toileting
Eating/feeding	Smoothly sucks from nipple Munches food, chewing up and down Pulls food off spoon with lips Chews with rotary/side-to-side action Feeds self with fingers Brings spoon to mouth and eats food off of it Holds and drinks from cup Scoops food from dish with spoon Uses fork Gets drink unassisted (e.g. turns tap on and off) Spreads with knife Uses napkin to wipe fingers and mouth Uses appropriate mealtime behaviors, including social graces

to determine whether this is occurring is to collect data on the child's elimination patterns. Probably one of the more common methods for doing this is to use a time-sampling recording system. The child is checked periodically, every 20 or 30 minutes. This information is recorded across several days to determine the child's usual pattern. It is important at this time of "training" for the adult to be aware of

TABLE 15.4
Heuristic for Assessing Chained Dressing/Undressing and Grooming Skills

Step	Assessment Task	Question Being Asked	Dimension Being Measured	Result	Next Step in Process
1	Teacher gives child opportunity to do entire task without assistance and in any sequence that will result in desired effect (e.g., take off or put on garment).	Can child complete the entire task? (i.e., take off or put on specific garment)	Accuracy	*No.* Child cannot complete entire task correctly.	Go to Step 2.
				Yes. Child completes task accurately.	Go to Step 7.
2	Teacher determines whether child has prerequisite skills to do task.	Does child have prerequisite skills?	Presence of prerequisite behaviors and their adequacy	*No.* Prerequisite skills not adequate.	Go to Step 3.
				Yes. Prerequisite behaviors present and adequate.	Go to Step 4.
3	Teacher searches and tests for task-modifications that will eliminate need for standard prerequisite behaviors.	Can task-modifications be found to eliminate need for standard prerequisite behaviors?	Accuracy with task-modifications being used	*No.* Task modifications not found.	Teach prerequisite skills
				Yes. Need for prerequisite behavior is eliminated, but child does not do skill accurately.	Go to Step 4.
				Yes. Need for prerequisite behaviors is eliminated and child does skill accurately.	Go to Step 7.
4	Teacher observes child attempt behavior and notes what type of error keeps child from	What type of error is occurring?	Type of error	Latency error—child can do steps but latency between responses is too long/short.	Identify the level of assistance needed and initiate teaching to eliminate errors

	completing entire task.			Topographical error—child incorrectly does specific responses in chain.	Go to Step 5.
5	Teacher lists topographical errors and searches for and tests adaptations that will eliminate errors.	Can adaptations eliminate topographical errors?	Accuracy with adaptations being used	*No.* Adaptations cannot be found to eliminate topographical errors. *Yes.* Adaptations eliminate topographical errors.	Go to Step 6. Go to Step 7.
6	Teacher searches for and tests sequences to eliminate topographical errors	Can a different sequence eliminate topographical errors?	Accuracy with different sequence of steps	*No.* Different sequences do not eliminate errors. Yes. Different sequences eliminate topographical errors.	Identify level of assistance needed and teach responses where errors occur. Go to Step 7.
7	Teacher observes child do skill to determine whether it is done quickly enough.	Is child fluent in doing the skill (i.e., can child do it quickly)?	Duration or rate of skill completion	*No.* Child does skill too slowly. *Yes.* Child does skill quickly.	Teach to increase fluency. Go to Step 8.
8	Teacher interviews parents or observes in generalization situations.	Does child perform the skill across needed situations?	Accuracy and fluency	*No.* Child does not do skill quickly in generalization settings. *Yes.* Child does skill in generalization situations.	Teach to facilitate generalization. Monitor for maintenance.

subtle signals that the child needs to void and to take him or her to the toilet at these times. He or she will soon begin to associate the physical sensation with the need to use the toilet.

Training can be viewed as a three-level process: (a) when taken to the toilet the child will urinate and/or have a bowel movement; (b) the child indicates the need to void and requests assistance or goes independently to the toilet; and (c) the child recognizes the need to void, goes alone, removes and replaces clothing, cleans self, and flushes the toilet. Although the third level is the ultimate goal, each level represents a number of complex skills, and success depends on the child's physical and social maturity.

Eating   Eating is much more than a means of ingesting adequate nutrition in a safe manner; it can be a pleasant and naturally reinforcing event. Ultimately, children should be able to eat unassisted in a range of settings (e.g., home, a school cafeteria, restaurants). Eating skills assessment should address: a) adequate nutritional intake; b) skill level related to food and liquid intake; c) skill level in feeding independently; d) eating preparation; e) table manners; f) maintaining conversations; and g) clean-up activities (e.g., cleaning one's plate, wiping the table clean).

Feeding   Adequate nutritional intake can be problematic for young children with disabilities, particularly those with physical disabilities or other chronic health impairments (Eicher, 2002). These potential problems may be related to the child's particular diagnosis (e.g., metabolic disorders, inadequate food intake due to oral motor impairments), the side effect of medication, specialized diets, or behavioral factors (Lowman & Murphy, 1998). These threats to nutritional intake can lead to malnutrition, obesity, constipation, aspiration, and other problems. Professionals should be aware of nutritional screening procedures and be able to recognize indications of need for further nutritional assessment. Helpful guides and questionnaires are available for collecting relevant dietary information and determining feeding needs (Arvedson, 2000; Brizee, Sophos, & McLaughlin, 1990). Information germane to nutritional screening includes (a) interviews with caregivers; (b) recordings of changes in height or weight and in appearance of gums, teeth, hair, and skin; and (c) reviews of health and medical records. Before beginning eating or feeding programming, young children should be seen by a physician to rule out possible organic causes for the eating problems (Lowman & Murphy, 1998). Medical diagnostic tests are available, which provide information to clearly define certain feeding difficulties (Eicher, 2002). Further, if there are any indicators of threats to the child's nutritional status, a nutritionist should be included on the team.

Effective eating depends on the following steps: (a) the ability to take in food, form a bolus, and swallow; (b) the absence of aspiration into the airway; (c) the lack of reflux of food once it enters the stomach; and (d) the normal digestion and movement of food through the intestines (Eicher, 2002). Problems can occur at one or more of these steps.

Transdisciplinary teamwork is required to assess and plan for interventions. Professionals from different disciplines (e.g., educators, occupational therapists, physical therapists, speech pathologists, and nurses) have expertise that should be considered in mealtime assessment and planning. Parents and other primary caregivers must be included, since they typically know the child and the history of interventions better than any other team member, and since they generally participate in feeding the child most of the time. Early attention to feeding difficulties by trained professionals (e.g. nurses, occupational therapists, and speech and language pathologists) can prevent the development of dysfunctional feeding patterns (Pridham, 1998).

Assessment requires both a determination of the child's current skills and the skills critical to improving the child's oral motor functioning. Several assessments of oral motor development and early feeding skills are available (e.g., Lowman & Murphy, 1998; Jelm, 1990; Morris & Klein, 1987). Assessment and subsequent intervention planning must address the following general categories: (a) positioning of the child; (b) food type and texture; (c) utensils; (d) feeding schedule; (e) feeding environment; (f) food presentation; (g) amount of physical assistance needed; (h) sensory sensitivity; (i) oral-motor status; (j) activities preceding meals; and (k) feeder-child interactions (Eicher, 2002; Kedesdy & Budd, 1998; Morris & Klein, 1987; Orelove & Sobsey, 1996).

Programs to promote feeding for a young child with a disability may often require a number of creative approaches and the involvement of several different professionals and family members. When effective, these methods enable the child to receive the necessary combination of nutrients, fluids, and oral-motor stimulation to help them grow, remain healthy, and develop new skills.

Self-Feeding More has been written about the specialized training of oral-motor skills in feeding than self-feeding skills (Orelove & Sobsey, 1996). Basic self-feeding includes handling finger foods, drinking from a self-held cup, and eating with a spoon. Each of these skills involves a fairly long chain of discrete responses by the child. A task analysis may be useful in assessing exactly what step in the sequence needs work and support. (See Chapter 16 for more information on task analysis.)

The first level in moving to independence in self-feeding is the predictably messy stage of eating finger foods. It provides opportunities to practice skills necessary for utensil use and to simultaneously continue to refine oral-motor skills. The young child picks up food and thus practices and refines his or her grasp and hand-to-mouth movement in combination with gumming, sucking, chewing, and swallowing of many soft foods. In planning assessment of current skill levels, a teacher or caregiver must determine which piece of the "eating finger-food chain" is missing or weak—finding the food, grasping, lifting to mouth, opening mouth at the appropriate time, leaving food in mouth, chewing, and/or swallowing. Furthermore, the teacher or caregiver may determine how the child handles larger food (tears it into smaller bites or bites off smaller pieces); how messy the child is; and what causes the messiness (e.g., too much food in the mouth). The determination of missing or weak skills/links in the chain allows the identification of skills for training.

Once the child can move food from the table to the mouth, the teacher or caregiver can provide self-feeding or drinking opportunities with utensils and a cup. Coordinating arm, hand, head, and mouth movements can be a challenge. Spoon use is the simplest of the utensil skills, followed in difficulty by eating with a fork, using a knife for spreading, and using a knife and fork for cutting. Spilling and messiness are typical well into the latter part of early childhood. If excessive spilling and messiness continue as the child becomes more proficient in eating, observation can assist in determining when the "error" occurs (e.g., while scooping something out of the bowl) and why (e.g., poor lip closure around the spoon in removing food). Once the problem is identified, adjustments in the equipment or instruction can be made.

Eating and mealtimes, as previously noted, involve more than just getting the food to one's mouth and consuming it. Preschool children can participate in mealtime preparation (e.g., serving one's plate), using appropriate table manners (e.g., discriminating between finger food and utensil food, using a napkin), maintaining a conversation (e.g., turn-taking, appropriate volume, not talking with food in the mouth), and clean-up activities (e.g., clearing one's plate, wiping the table clean). These activities are best assessed and taught within the natural flow of the mealtime settings in which the child participates (e.g., home, visiting relatives or friends, preschool, restaurant, fast food).

Community Self-Sufficiency

In early childhood, community self-sufficiency includes skills that promote age and culturally appropriate functioning *with adult supervision* in community environments such as restaurants, neighborhoods, and recreational areas. Specific skills could include:

- Traveling in the community
- Grocery and general shopping at stores
- Obtaining services from community businesses such as doctors and dentists, clinics, restaurants, and repair shops
- Using public transportation
- Using public facilities such as schools, libraries, post offices, and recreational areas
- Attending church or synagogue
- Attending theatre and recreational events

Related skills include communication of choices and needs, social interaction and behavior in the community, and the use of functional academics (Ford et al., 1989). The degree of independence, the range of settings, and the complexity (e.g., purchasing may involve making a choice between chicken nuggets and a hamburger) is adjusted to reflect developmental age and cultural expectations.

Skills related to "use of the community" overlap with other subdomains of adaptive behavior (e.g., eating, toileting) as well as with other domains such as cognitive (e.g., problem solving), motor (e.g., mobility), social, and communication. While this overlap is obvious, distinguishing community self-sufficiency as a subdomain is important in terms of measuring competency in a given skill based on the demands of the setting (e.g., eating in a restaurant). Competence requires the ability to change behavior to suit the demands of the setting (Evans, 1991). Thus content must be determined by evaluating the community environments of the young child, the child's access to them, and the demands for appropriate participation.

The actual as well as the future community environments that the infant/toddler or preschooler is apt to encounter must first be indexed. Then specific areas of each environment, the age-appropriate activities that occur there, and the specific skills needed to participate in those activities must be outlined (Brown et al., 1979). For example, eating is an activity in which an infant regularly engages at home and in the community. While at home or in the community with the mother, the

infant may be breast-fed, but at the child-care center he or she might be fed from a bottle. The component motor movements required to suck from a bottle constitute an important instructional objective because the skill is immediately useful. Drinking from a bottle might take place in multiple community environments (e.g., doctor's office, grocery store, riding in the car); thus, bottle drinking might be considered an adaptive community activity. This approach is highly individualized and specific to each child and each family. It requires establishing goals through consensus of the family and the interventionists, not by referring solely to a developmental list. However, normative comparisons can assist in assessing mastery of goals by noting if the child performs the skill in a manner that is developmentally appropriate for a chronologically same-age peer.

Conceptual

The conceptual domain includes basic environmental interactions, self-directed behaviors, independent play/self-occupation, peer cooperation and interaction, and the assumption of responsibility. More specifically, self-directed behaviors include skills such as making choices, learning and following a schedule, initiating context-appropriate activities, completing necessary or required tasks, seeking assistance as needed, problem solving in familiar and novel situations, demonstrating appropriate assertive and self-advocacy skills, and exercising judgment concerning health and safety. It becomes increasingly important to children between 12 and 24 months to be allowed to initiate and direct activities. They move away from the primary caregiver and initiate an interaction with another adult or child. They explore their immediate environments and begin to resist having things done for them (e.g., resist attempts by others to feed them and attempt to do it alone). They begin to make simple choices (e.g., have preferred toys, foods, clothes, books).

Independent play/self-occupation is related to the long-range goal of developing a variety of leisure and recreational interests that reflect individual preferences and choices, and, if applicable, are appropriate to age and cultural norms. Skills include choosing and self-initiating interests and using and enjoying home and community play activities. Children must learn to extend their participation in play activities and expand their repertoire of interests, awareness, and skills. For young children, these skills are directly related to the concept of engagement or the amount of time spent appropriately interacting with the environment (McWilliam, 1991). Strategies for assessing engagement are described by others (e.g., Jones & Warren, 1991; McGee, Daly, Izeman, Mann, & Risley, 1991; McWilliam & Bailey, 1992; Whaley & Bennett, 1991).

Peer cooperation and interaction involves knowing how to join, share, help, and negotiate. It also involves recognition of the rights, feelings, and needs of others. Specifically, peer cooperation and interaction include such social play skills as initiating a social interchange, learning to take turns, learning to end an interaction appropriately, increasing the duration of social interaction, and appropriately refusing a social interchange. Assessment strategies for these behaviors are discussed at length in Chapter 13.

An important part of growing up is assuming responsibility for one's own behaviors and actions. In fact, many children demand the right to take responsibility (e.g., "I want to do it myself!"). Skills assessment in this area addresses controlling one's behavior, learning the rules of safety, caring for property, and functioning in the community. Given the number of accidental injuries reported in children, safety skills are increasingly recognized as a critical area for young children. Beginning safety assessment and training during the preschool years can increase child awareness of their surroundings and support their well-being (Timko & Sainato, 1999). The amount of responsibility one gives to a child depends on his or her understanding of the potential consequences of various actions and the potential for physical or emotional harm. However, it is very important to avoid limiting the child by overprotecting rather than teaching.

Direct observation across multiple natural contexts is the primary data collection strategy for this subdomain. Documentation of the use of skills and level of independence across different settings, materials, and people is critical; in addition, it should include the consistency of a response across places and times. Can the child flexibly apply the skill or strategy, making appropriate adjustment to fit the circumstance? An example might be that the child understands that the rule of holding an adult's hand to cross a street also applies to large store parking lots but not necessarily to one's own driveway. A final important piece of information to collect is the degree to which the child's environments support the learning and demonstration of these behaviors. If a child, for example, never has regular opportunities to interact and play cooperatively with peers, cooperative play will probably not be a skill in his or her repertoire. This information has important implications for how interventions are designed.

Social

The social subdomain includes such social adjustment behaviors as the ability to adjust to new situations, regularity of behavior patterns, general disposition, tendency to stick to tasks despite obstacles, attention span and degree of distractibility, and amount of stimulation necessary to evoke a response. Positive adjustment reflects an integration and display of these attributes as well as other developmental skills in the context of the demands of the environment and personal needs (Zeitlin & Williamson, 1994). Effective adjustment fosters the acquisition of developmental skills, the development of a positive self-concept, and the ability to develop meaningful social relationships (Williamson, 1994).

For young children, coping behaviors focus on nutrition, security, and a combination of activity and rest, combined with an opportunity to pursue interests and motivations and to satisfy the drive to achieve mastery. Coping behaviors do not occur in isolation, but instead are a component of social responsibility that can influence all aspects of adaptive functioning. For assessment purposes the cluster of attributes, skills, and behaviors identified with coping in infants and toddlers can be divided into three descriptive categories: sensorimotor organization, reactive behaviors, and self-initiated behaviors (Zeitlin et al., 1988).

Sensorimotor organization behaviors, which reflect to some degree the neurobiological state of the child, include the child's ability to attend, to self-comfort, to control activity level, to manage the intensity and variety of sensory stimuli, and to adapt to handling. Reactive behaviors, which are responses to external demands from the physical and social environment, include the ability to adjust to daily routines, to accept warmth and comfort from a familiar person, to respond to vocal and gestural directions, and to adjust to changes in the environment. Self-initiated behaviors, which are more spontaneous and intrinsically motivated, include the ability to express likes and dislikes, to initiate action for communicating a need, to persist during activities, and to generalize skills to new situations.

A thorough understanding of the child's current coping style and strategies is necessary before initiating intervention. Observing the child in a variety of situations is the most effective assessment strategy (Zeitlin & Williamson, 1994) and may include identifying behaviors across the three areas of sensorimotor organization, reactive behaviors, and self-initiated behaviors (all noted previously). In addition, the assessor must note flexibility in the use of the behaviors, circumstances under which they are applied, their success in managing specific stressors, and how the child appears to feel about the effectiveness of his or her efforts. Based on this information, interventions can be planned to enhance the effectiveness of the child's coping strategies.

Summary of Assessment Issues in Subdomains

The conceptual framework that drives assessment across the subdomains of adaptive behavior (i.e., practical, conceptual, and social) is a functional ecological approach (DeStefano, Howe, Horn, & Smith, 1991; McDonnell & Hardman, 1988). Several common themes are identified with this approach:

- Assessment items are referenced to the unique needs and lifestyle of the child, family, peers, and community.
- Assessment emphasizes skills that reflect increases in the child's ability to interact with the world.
- Assessment emphasizes skills that are useful immediately and in the future.
- Assessment is conducted in multiple daily family and child routines and activities.

The characteristics of the skills in these subdomains readily allow the application of this model. However, there are many differences among cultures as to the value placed on these skills and expectations for when they should be acquired (Lynch & Hanson, 1998). How important these skills are at different ages and how they are supported varies among families within and across cultures. The acquisition of these skills is deeply embedded in the family's unique preferences and expectations. Thus, the specific behaviors at any given developmental stage that determine competence in adaptive behavior should be identified from an analysis of the unique needs and lifestyles of the child, family, peers, and community.

USE OF ASSESSMENT INFORMATION

One of the most challenging tasks facing the assessment team is drafting goals/outcomes for intervention. First, all of the assessment information must be assembled, summarized, and interpreted. The focus is not on the scores or developmental age equivalent, but on what the child knows and can do and how the child interacts with his or her environment. For young children, assessments should yield: a) the specific skills the child has mastered in the relevant subdomains; b) skills that are in the process of being acquired; c) skills needed to meet the demands of current environments; d) the environments/settings that provide sufficient opportunity and support for learning the skills; and e) related services, equipment, and aids that will facilitate the child's learning of the skill. The goal is to select adaptive behaviors for instruction that increase the young child's participation and independence. Even if the child is taught an alternative way of completing the task (e.g., self-catheterization for toileting), the outcome should address maximizing independence.

To establish goals in the adaptive behavior domain, the team must first summarizes the skills the child currently demonstrates in relation to the level of proficiency and the demands of the environments in which he or she participates. In addition, members of the team should consider the child's chronological age, the manner in which peers perform the task, and the settings in which the skills will be used. Goals should reflect typical expectations for the child's chronological age. Independent toileting in the community, for example, is not considered developmentally appropriate for a young child. Children in this age group usually receive help from their parents in public toilets, from getting the door open and locked, to getting on and off the toilet, and reaching the soap and hand dryer.

As teachers begin implementing instruction it becomes important that opportunities are presented to learn and master skills that meet social expectations. While adaptive behavior skills are critical and should be taught when they are needed, they are used at a relatively low frequency. Related to this characteristic is the fact that skills must become habitual to be truly functional. They must be performed fluently in response to natural cues, maintained by natural consequences, and performed in varied settings and circumstances. This implies that the interventionist may need to change the traditional instructional settings to reflect the diversity of settings in which the skills naturally occur (e.g., home, community, preschool). In addition, the team may need to make adaptations in schedules to increase the opportunities for practicing skills within the context of routines. Children must be given opportunities to practice and thus establish habitual responses to natural cues provided across multiple current and future environments.

In conclusion, the adaptive behavior domain is an important part of the early intervention endeavor. Providing instruction requires that professionals and/or caregivers accommodate and adapt to support the specific strengths of individual children and their families. Competent independent functioning is the long-term goal.

· · · · · · · ·

SUMMARY OF KEY CONCEPTS

- Adaptive behavior as a curriculum domain should include skills that reflect chronologically age-appropriate behaviors for meeting the demands of the child's multiple unique environments.

- Children's acquisition of adaptive skills leads to: a) increased independence in everyday environments; b) decreased caregiving demands; c) meaningful inclusion in community settings because the child may appear more "typical" and less different; and d) positive impacts on the child's self-concept and sense of competence.

- Any definition of adaptive behavior must take the perspective of not considering it a single entity but a composite of a wide range of abilities that are dependent on one's age, environment, and cultural group at any moment.

- Comprehensive assessment and intervention in the adaptive behavior domain should address the following subdomains: practical, conceptual, and social.

- The personal-care strand addresses dressing/undressing, eating/feeding, toileting, and grooming (e.g., hand-washing, face-washing, and tooth-brushing).

- Community self-sufficiency refers to skills that promote age and culturally appropriate functioning with adult supervision in community environments such as restaurants, neighborhoods, and recreational areas.

- Basic skills in the conceptual domain include basic environmental interactions, self-directed behaviors, independent play/self-occupation, peer cooperation and interaction, and the assumption of responsibility (e.g., demonstrates caution, avoids dangers).

- The social subdomain includes the ability to adjust to new situations, regularity of behavior patterns (e.g., eating, sleeping), general disposition, tendency to stick to tasks despite obstacles, attention span and degree of distractibility, and amount of stimulation necessary to evoke a response.

- The conceptual framework that should drive assessment across the domains of adaptive behavior should address the following themes: (a) assessment items are referenced to the unique needs and lifestyle of the child, family, peers, and community; (b) skills that reflect increases in the child's ability to interact with the world are emphasized; (c) skills that are useful immediately and in the future are stressed; and (d) assessment is conducted in multiple daily family-and-child routines and activities.

· · · · · · · ·

REFERENCES

Arvedson, J. C. (2000). Evaluation of children with feeding and swallowing problems. *Language, Speech, and Hearing Services in Schools, 31,* 28–41.

Berk, R. A. (1988). Criterion-referenced tests. In J. P. Keeves (Ed.), *Educational research methodology and measurement: An international handbook* (pp. 365–370). Oxford: Pergamon Press.

Brizee, L. S., Sophos, C. M., & McLaughlin, J. F. (1990). Nutrition issues in developmental disabilities. *Infants and Young Children, 2*(3), 10–21.

Bricker, D. (Series Ed.) (2002). *Assessment, Evaluation, and Programming System (AEPS) for Infants and Children,* Second Edition. Baltimore: Paul H. Brookes.

Brown, L., Branston, M. B., Hamre-Nietupski, S., Pumpian, I., Certo, N., & Gruenwald, L. (1979). A strategy for developing chronological-age-appropriate and functional curricular content for severely handicapped adolescents and young adults. *Journal of Special Education, 13*(1), 81–90.

Brown, F., & Snell, M. (2000). Meaningful assessment. In M. Snell & F. Brown (Eds.), *Instruction of students with severe disabilities* (5th ed., pp. 61–98). Upper Saddle River, NJ: Merrill/Prentice Hall.

DEC Task Force on Recommended Practices. (1993). *DEC recommended practices: Indicators of quality in programs for infants and young children with special needs and their families.* Reston, VA: Council for Exceptional Children.

DeStefano, D. M., Howe, A. G., Horn, E. M., & Smith, B. A. (1991). *Best practices: Evaluating early childhood special education programs.* Tucson, AZ: Communication Skill Builders.

Dyson, L., & Fewell, R. R. (1986). Stress and adaptation in parents of young handicapped and nonhandicapped children: A comparative study. *Journal of the Division of Early Childhood, 10*(1), 25–34.

Eicher, P. S. (2002). Feeding. In M. L. Batshaw (Ed.), *Children with disabilities* (5th ed.). Baltimore: Paul H. Brookes.

Evans, I. M. (1991). Testing and diagnosis: A review and evaluation. In L. H. Meyers, C. A. Peck, & L. Brown (Eds.), *Critical issues in the lives of people with severe disabilities* (pp. 25–44). Baltimore: Paul H. Brookes.

Ford, A., Schnorr, R., Meyer, L., Davern, L., Black, J., & Dempsey, P. (1989). *The Syracuse community-referenced curriculum guide.* Baltimore: Paul H. Brookes.

Frankenberger, W. (1984). A survey of state guidelines for identification of mental retardation. *Mental Retardation, 22,* 17–20.

Greenspan, S. (1999). A contextual perspective on adaptive behavior. In R. L. Schalock (Ed.), *Adaptive behavior and its measurements: Implications for the field of mental retardation* (pp. 61–80). Washington, DC: American Association on Mental Retardation.

Greenspan, S., & Driscoll, J. (1997). The role of intelligence in a broad model of personal competence. In D. P. Flanagan, G. Genshaft, & P. L. Harrison (Eds.), *Contemporary intellectual assessment: Theories, tests, and issues* (pp. 131–150). New York: Guilford Press.

Gresham, F. M. & Elliot, S. N. (1987). The relationship between adaptive behavior and social skills: Issues in definition and assessment. *Journal of Special Education, 21,* 167–181.

Harrison, P. L. (1987). Research with adaptive behavior scales. *Journal of Special Education, 21*(1), 11–26.

Hopkins, K. D. (1998). *Educational and psychological measurement and evaluation* (8th ed.). Boston: Allyn & Bacon.

Horn, E., & Fuchs, D. (1987). Using adaptive behavior in assessment and intervention: An overview. *Journal of Special Education, 21*(1), 11–26.

Jelm, J. M. (1990). *Oral-Motor/Feeding Rating Scale.* Tucson, AZ: Therapy Skill Builders.

Johnson-Martin, N. M., Attermeier, S. M., & Hacker, B. (1990). *The Carolina curriculum for preschoolers with special needs.* Baltimore: Paul H. Brookes.

Johnson-Martin, N. M., Jens, K. G., Attermeier, S. M., & Hacker, B. (1991). *The Carolina curriculum for infants and toddlers with special needs* (2nd ed.). Baltimore: Paul H. Brookes.

Jones, H. A., & Warren, S. F. (1991). Enhancing engagement in early language teaching. *Teaching Exceptional Children, 23*(4), 48–50.

Kedesdy, J. H., & Budd, K. S. (1998). *Childhood feeding disorders: Biobehavioral assessment and intervention.* Baltimore: Paul H. Brookes.

Lambert, N. M., Leland, H., & Nihira, K. (1993). *Adaptive Behavior Scales–School Edition: 2.* Austin, TX: PRO-ED.

Lowman, D. K., & Murphy, S. M. (1998). *The educator's guide to feeding children with disabilities.* Baltimore: Paul H. Brookes.

Luckasson, R., Borthwick-Duffy, S., Buntinx, W., Coulter, D.L., Craig, E. M., Reeve, A., et al. (2002). *Mental retardation: Definition, classification, and systems of support* (10th ed.). Washington, DC: American Association on Mental Retardation.

Luckasson, R., Schalock, R. L., Coulter, D. L., Snell, M. E., Polloway, E. A., Spitalnik, D. M., et al. (1992). *Mental Retardation: Definition, classification, and systems of support* (9th ed.). Washington, DC: American Association on Mental Retardation.

Lynch, E. W. & Hanson, M. J. (1998). *Developing cross-cultural competence: A guide for working with children and their families* (2nd ed.). Baltimore: Paul H. Brookes.

McDonnell, A., & Hardman, M. (1988). A synthesis of "best practice" guidelines for early childhood services. *Journal of the Division for Early Childhood, 12,* 328–341.

McGee, G. G., Daly, T., Izeman, S. G., Mann, L. H., & Risley, T. R. (1991). Use of classroom materials to promote preschool engagement. *Teaching Exceptional Children, 23*(4), 42–43.

McWilliam, R. A., (1991). Targeting teaching at children's use of time: Perspectives on preschoolers' engagement. *Teaching Exceptional Children, 23*(4), 42–43.

McWilliam, R. A., & Bailey, D. (1992). Promoting engagement and mastery. In D. B. Bailey & M. Wolery (Eds.), *Teaching infants and preschoolers with disabilities* (2nd ed., pp. 229–255). Upper Saddle River, NJ: Merrill/Prentice Hall.

Moreau, L. E., & Bruininks, R. H. (1991). *Checklist of adaptive living skills.* Allen, TX: DLM Teaching Resource.

Morris, S. E., & Klein, M. D. (1987). *Pre-feeding skills.* Tucson, AZ: Therapy Skill Builders.

Nehring, A. D., Nehring, E. F., Bruni, J. R., & Randolph, P. L. (1995). *Learning Accomplishment Profile-Diagnostic Standardized Assessment.* Lewisville, NC: Kaplan School Supply.

Newborg, J., Stock, J., Wnek, L., Guidubaldi, J., & Svinicki, J. (1988). *Battelle Developmental Inventory (BDI)*. Allen, TX: DLM Teaching Resources.

Orelove, F. P., & Sobsey, D. (1996). *Educating children with multiple disabilities: A transdisciplinary approach* (3rd ed.). Baltimore: Paul H. Brookes.

Pridham, K. (1998). Feeding support for infants and young children. *Exceptional Parent, 28,* 58-65.

Salvia, J., & Ysseldyke, J. (2001). *Assessment* (8th ed.). Boston: Houghton Mifflin.

Sandall, S., McLean, M., & Smith, B. J. (2000). *DEC recommended practices in early intervention/Early childhood special education*. Longmont, CO: Sopris West.

Sattler, J. M., (1992). *Assessment of children* (3rd ed.). San Diego: Author.

Seligman, M. E. (1992). *Helplessness: On depression, death and development* (2nd ed.). San Francisco: W. H. Freeman.

Snell, M. E. & Brown, F. (2000). *Instruction of students with severe disabilities* (5th ed.). Upper Saddle River, NJ: Merrill/Prentice Hall.

Sparrow, S. S., Balla, D. A., & Cicchetti, D. V. (1984). *Vineland Adaptive Behavior Scales, Interview Edition*. Circle Pines, MN: American Guidance Service.

Timko, T. C., & Sainato, D. M. (1999). Effects of first aid training using small group instruction with young children with disabilities, *Journal of Early Intervention, 22,* 323–336.

Thompson, J. R., McGrew, K. S., & Bruininks, R. H. (1999). Adaptive and maladaptive behavior: Functional and structural characteristics. In R. L. Schalock (Ed.), *Adaptive behavior and its measurement: Implications for the field of mental retardation* (pp. 15–42). Washington, DC: American Association on Mental Retardation.

Turnbull, A. P., & Turnbull, H. R. (2001). *Families, professionals, and exceptionality: Collaborating for empowerment* (4th ed.). Upper Saddle River, NJ: Merrill/Prentice Hall.

Umansky, W., & Hooper, S. R. (1998). *Young children with special needs* (3rd ed.). Upper Saddle River, NJ: Merrill/Prentice Hall.

VORT Corporation, (1995). *HELP for Preschoolers*. Palo Alto: Author.

Whaley, K. T., & Bennett, T. C. (1991). Promoting engagement in early childhood special education. *Teaching Exceptional Children, 23*(4), 51–54.

Widman, K. F., & McGrew, K. S. (1996). The structure of adaptive behavior. In J. W. Jacobson & J. A. Mulick (Eds.), *Manual of diagnosis and professional practice in mental retardation* (pp. 97–110). Washington, DC: American Psychological Association.

Williamson, G. (1994). Assessment of adaptive competence. *Zero to Three, 14*(6), 28–33.

White, O. R. (1985). The evaluation of severely mentally retarded individuals. In D. Bricker & J. Filler (Eds.), *Severe mental retardation: From theory to practice* (pp. 161–184). Reston, VA: Council for Exceptional Children.

Wortham, S. C. (2001). *Assessment in early childhood education* (3rd ed.). Upper Saddle River, NJ: Merrill/Prentice Hall.

Zeitlin, S. (1985). *Coping Inventory*. Bensenville, IL: Scholastic Testing Service.

Zeitlin, S., & Williamson, G. G. (1994). *Coping in young children: Early intervention practices to enhance adaptive behavior and resilience*. Baltimore: Paul H. Brookes.

Zeitlin, S., Williamson, G. G., & Szczepanski, M. (1988). *Early Coping Inventory*. Bensenville, IL: Scholastic Testing Service.

Using Assessment Information to Plan Intervention Programs

Mark Wolery
Vanderbilt University

Assessments are systematic efforts to gather information to make decisions. Thus, assessment activities are means to ends—making decisions. When doing assessments to plan children's intervention programs, the decisions to be made involve identifying individualized and personalized goals and outcomes, identifying the locations (e.g., settings, activities) for ensuring learning opportunities occur to meet the goals and outcomes, selecting intervention approaches, and devising a plan for integrating those interventions into children's current environments and ongoing activities to promote development and learning. Thus, activities for intervention planning assessments are not completed until these decisions are made. Much of this text has focused on how to gather and summarize information related to children's behavior and development. In this chapter, we focus on using assessment information to plan children's intervention programs. The chapter has four major sections. In the first, information is provided on how to describe assessments in written form. In the second section, the types of information needed to plan meaningful intervention programs are described. The third section describes considerations and guidelines for translating assessment information into intervention plans. The final section describes guidelines for implementing plans into children's days.

WRITING REPORTS FROM INTERVENTION PLANNING ASSESSMENTS

Writing assessment reports for intervention planning is a skill that requires considerable work and practice. The written assessment report is a document from which intervention programs are derived, but it also serves other functions, such as communicating with other team members and professionals, specifying the best estimation of a child's abilities at a given point in time, and as a record against which later performance can be compared. The report should be accurate, clear, objective, and detailed. Although numerous formats exist for writ-

ing assessment reports, some types of information are critical. (It should be noted that the information that follows is designed for instructional program planning assessments and not for screening reports, which would be briefer, or diagnostic reports, which have a different purpose.) Instructional program planning assessment reports should include identifying information about the child and the assessment, background information, methods of assessment, results of the assessment, and conclusions and recommendations.

Identifying Information

This section of the written report includes information about who was assessed, who conducted the assessment, and when and where it occurred. It should appear first in the written report and include the child's full name; agency/client number, if applicable; important demographic information (e.g., age; gender, date of birth; current placement, if any; diagnosis); the child's current living situation (e.g., with family, with foster care provider), and the names and addresses of family members. The person who initiated the referral and the reason for the referral should be noted, as well as the assessors' name and titles, the settings in which the assessment occurred, and dates of the assessment activities.

Background Information

This section provides historical information about the child; it should be a relatively brief narrative summary. For diagnostic assessment reports, this section may be much more comprehensive. Three things should be addressed: the child's birth and medical history, developmental history, and educational and therapeutic experiences. The source of the information also should be noted in this section; for example, parental interviews or review of records. The birth and medical history section should identify whether the pregnancy was difficult and what complications, if any, occurred; whether the birth was full-term or premature; whether it was characterized by any unusual events and what they were; and whether the child has a history of any medical treatment and the nature of that treatment. The developmental history should describe the age at which the child achieved important developmental milestones, and, if appropriate, when the parents suspected that difficulties might exist. The educational history section should be a record of the child's intervention contacts since birth and should include a listing and brief description of the services he or she has received.

Methods

This section should be written in narrative form and should include several subsections. The *tests* and *scales* used during the assessment should be listed, when and by whom they were administered should be recorded, and the purpose of each should be noted, as should the appropriate reference citations. The *observational procedures* should be described in terms of who conducted observations, purposes of the observations, when and where they occurred, and what types of behaviors were observed. When the setting for the observation is described, it should include a brief description of how many children were present, and so on, to give a flavor for the context in which it took place. *Interviews* with others should be described in terms of who was interviewed and their relationship to the child, who conducted the interview, and the topic or purpose of the interview. Finally, *environmental assessments* should be described, including which environments were assessed, what measures were used, when they occurred, who conducted them, and the purpose of using those measures. In short, the methods section provides a reader with a description of the measures and intentions of the assessors on which the results of the assessment are based.

Results of Assessment Activities

This section can be the most difficult to write, and considerable care should be taken to describe the following information: skills the child does independently and the conditions under which those

skills are used; skills the child does with support, adaptation, and/or assistance; the type of assistance, support, and/or adaptation needed; skills the child does not have but needs to function more adaptively or in more developmentally advanced ways; variables that may influence how intervention is designed (e.g., child's usual interaction style, interests, preferences); stimuli that appear to hold reinforcing value; and results of using, even briefly, any instructional or therapeutic strategies. When describing the child's performance, the conditions under which it occurred or did not occur should be included. For example, saying the "child requested cookies" is inadequate because several questions remain. What was occurring when she requested the cookies? Had she already eaten a cookie? Were cookies visible? Describing the conditions presents a more complete and meaningful picture of the child's performance.

Three formats for organizing this section can be used: by measure, developmental or curricular domain, or children's current environments. These organizational formats require different levels of integration of the results. When organized by measure, the results are described separately for each measure listed in the methods section. This format requires little integration; thus, is not recommended. When organized by developmental or curricular domain, the results for each domain (e.g., communication, physical) are described separately, but the findings from all measures related to each domain are integrated. For example, if a language test was used, observations of communicative behavior occurred, a language sample was collected, and parents were interviewed about the child's language and communication skills, then the findings of these different measures would be integrated rather than described separately. When organized by children's current environments, the results of all measures from each environment would be integrated and sometimes presented in order of the child's day across environments. This requires integration of information across domains to describe behaviors in context. The last two formats (by domain or by environments) are recommended, and these can be combined by presenting information by domain across environments, or by each environment across domains. When presenting results by domain or by environments, tables are sometimes useful that describe (a) the conditions under which the skill was assessed, and (b) three levels of skill: independent, supported, and did not do. Knowing the conditions provides more precise information for setting goals and outcomes, identifying learning opportunities, and selecting intervention strategies. Of course, to be useful, the information must be accurate and described in observable terms so that inferences are not included—or if included are identified as such.

Conclusions and Recommendations

This section of the assessment report summarizes the primary abilities of the child and the areas of need. Describing the conditions or situations under which those abilities are seen as independent and in need of intervention also is appropriate, because it informs planning the intervention strategies. It also should include suggestions about (a) the need for additional assessment activities; (b) potential long-term goals or outcomes; (c) potential settings in which learning activities could occur; and (d) potential intervention strategies, as well as a listing of any variables that would influence how the intervention should be implemented.

When writing assessment reports, interventionists should write to communicate with multiple audiences, including their team members, children's families, professionals to whom children might be referred, and future caregivers. This requires use of clear, objective, jargon-free prose. Further, reports should be written sensitively, because they will be available to family members. This does not mean that the hard issues should be ignored but that the conclusions should be described, qualified, and supported by the information gathered in the assessment activities. Finally, clear delineation of facts from assump-

tions should be made. Both may be included, but assumptions and inferences should be labeled as such.

INFORMATION NEEDED TO PLAN MEANINGFUL INTERVENTION PROGRAMS

The amount and types of contacts professionals have with children and the location of those contacts are different across localities and states. Some children attend full-day child-care classes, some attend part-day classes, some go to clinics for weekly visits with specialists, some have regular but intermittent (e.g., weekly) home visits, and some have different combinations of these (Wolery, McWilliam, & Bailey, in press). However, even in the most intense programs, nearly all children spend a majority of each day or week outside of "formal" intervention time or direct contacts with professionals. Nonetheless, when professionals are not with them, they continue to interact with their social and physical environments and to learn from those experiences. This fact holds two major implications for planning interventions. First, adults and settings in which children regularly spend time are the "true" or actual interventionists and intervention contexts, whether planned or not. Young children's learning is not restricted to contacts with teachers and therapists in centers or in their homes; it potentially occurs whenever a child interacts with the environment. The "interventions" children experience are beyond their contacts with professionals (McWilliam, 2000) and many everyday activities at home and in the community can positively affect children's learning (Dunst et al., 2001). Thus, a variety of individuals may need to know children's goals and outcomes and be able, when necessary, to use intervention procedures associated with those goals and outcomes. Second, the intervention plan should be designed to address children's full day in whatever settings they regularly spend time. Hobbs (1967) states, "We start with the assumption that each day, that every hour in every day, is of great importance to a child, and that when an hour is neglected, allowed to pass without reason and intent, teaching and learning go on nonetheless and the child may be the loser" (p. 1109). This does not mean active programming occurs for all of the child's waking day; rather, it means intervention strategies and practices should be appropriate for use in any context in which children regularly spend time. It also means children should have interesting and engaging events or activities with which to interact (Dunst et al., 2001), and children should not have extended time in the day in which they can learn to be passive or maladaptive. Finally, plans should be designed with knowledge of, and accommodation to, the activities, routines, and resources (human and otherwise) that are in children's regular settings.

To plan interventions that will address these realities, teams need four broad types of information. These are information about (a) children's functioning (abilities and needs) and their interactions with the environment; (b) the setting in which children spend time and their current schedules; (c) dimensions of the settings that are selected as intervention sites; and (d) families' concerns and priorities for their child. Information from these four broad areas helps in developing successful intervention plans and increasing the likelihood of consistent implementation. Specific types of information in the four broad areas are identified in the following paragraphs.

Information About the Child

Throughout this text, measurement strategies are described for gathering information on infants and young children, including rating scales, checklists, observational procedures and systems, interview protocols, and direct testing. When planning intervention programs, this information should be organized into meaningful categories to inform the planning process. Three categories are (a) developmental and functional *abilities* and *needs*; (b) usual

interaction patterns with the animate (social) and inanimate (physical) environment; and (c) effects of various supports, assistance, and intervention strategies. The team, including children's families, gathers this information over time, using multiple measurement strategies in all relevant and natural settings, using authentic materials, and with input from all relevant caregivers (Bagnato, Neisworth, & Munson, 1997).

Developmental and Functional Goals Specific types of developmental abilities and needs that should be identified and procedures for identifying them are described in Chapters 10 through 15. Many of these procedures also are useful in identifying a child's functional abilities and needs in terms of independence and mastery of environments. Direct observation (Chapter 17) also is useful. This information should be summarized to guide the team in identifying goals for intervention and for capitalizing on children's abilities when addressing their needs. In short, teams must have information about what children can do and about what they need to learn to do.

Usual Patterns of Interacting The information on children's usual patterns of interacting with the social and physical environments involves a number of issues. Teams need information on children's interaction patterns with peers and with adults (Chapter 13) and on how they play with toys and others (Chapter 14). Teams also need information about children's interaction styles and levels of activity. Style deals with constructs such as persistence, problem solving, sustained attention to toys and other objects in the environment, ability to shift attention, and nature of engagement with the environment, extent to which children are easily distracted, whether they imitate adults and peers, and compliance with routines and adult requests. This information is best gathered though interviews with adults who supervise the child regularly and through direct observation in children's environments. The ecological congruence assessment process (Wolery, Brashers, & Neitzel, 2002) described in Chapter 8 is a method for doing this. This process is a judgment-based assessment allowing teams to make decisions about whether children's behavior in classroom activities and routines is similar or different from peers, whether any identified differences are acceptable, and what types of help children need in those activities and routines. This information is useful for identifying new environment-specific goals, modifications of existing goals, development of new intervention practices, or refinement of existing practices.

For infants and children with significant disabilities their usual styles of interaction may involve measurement of their behavioral states to identify the stability and shifts between states (Guess, Roberts, Siegel-Causey, & Ault, 1993). Ault, Guy, Guess, Bashinski, and Roberts (1995) described a model for measuring children's states as well as environmental conditions that might interact with those states. The states include both inactive and active sleep states, as well as inactive and active awake states and transition states between sleep and alertness. Their system also includes a crying or agitated state and an awake state in which stereotypic behavior is common. The environmental conditions measured in this conceptualization include sensory input the child receives (across all sensory systems), movement, and issues related to the quality of the immediate environment (e.g., noise, interactions with others, activity levels). Through considerable training, teachers were able to measure states and environmental conditions, and with assistance develop and implement plans resulting in more stable time in desired states (Ault et al., 1995).

Another issue related to children's styles of interacting deals with their interests, preferences, choices, and reinforcers. Interests are those themes, objects, or persons for which children repeatedly show some preference by talking about them, integrating them into their play, or choosing them when given the option. Preferences are objects, people, and activities "the individual has selected in the past from among several

options," and choice is "the act of selecting an activity [object or person] from among several familiar options at a particular moment in time" (Romaniuk & Miltenberger, 2001, p. 152, words in brackets added). Knowing or identifying children's interests, preferences, and giving them choices are important from at least three perspectives. First, a fairly consistent finding is that incorporating children's preferences into activities and giving them choices is associated with reductions in problematic behaviors (Carter, 2001; Kern et al., 1998). Second, incorporating preferences into activities and providing choices may be associated with increases in adaptive behavior in those settings (Dunlap et al, 1994; Kern et al., 1998). Third, identifying preferences and providing choices is a means of identifying reinforcers that can be used during activities and routines (Logan & Gast, 2001). Reinforcers, of course, are consequent events that when applied contingently to a behavior results in an increase in the frequency with which that behavior occurs. Interests, preferences, and reinforcers can be identified in a variety of ways. Common methods include, interviewing families and others who know the child well; observing children and identifying (a) what activities and objects capture their attention; (b) what they do frequently; and (c) what activities and objects they choose when given choices (Wolery, 1994a). Although interviewing others to identify preferences and reinforcers is recommended, it sometimes does not work when children have significant disabilities (Reid, Everson, & Green, 1999). When necessary, reinforcer preference assessments can be done. These are done by providing a child with a series of choices between objects (e.g., toys, food) presented as pairs (DeLeon & Iwata, 1996) or as several at one time (Graff & Ciccone, 2002) and recording the children's selections. Another alternative is to present objects one at a time and record how long children are engaged with each (Hagopian, Rush, Lewin, & Long, 2001). Finally, because children's preferences change (Logan & Gast, 2001), one option is to present children with choices of objects before instructional sessions or activities and then using their selections as reinforcers in that activity (Gast, Jacobs, Murray, Holloway, & Long, 2000). Knowing children's interests and preferences, giving them choices, and identifying reinforcers assists in a number of important decisions in planning interventions including selecting materials, structuring activities, and using reinforcement-based procedures.

Effects of Supports, Assistance, and Instructional Strategies Teams need information about the effects of assistance, support, and intervention strategies. The assessment activities should result in information about what the child does under usual conditions and what he or she can do when assistance or support is provided. Vygotsky (1978) referred to this as the "zone of proximal development." The assistance and support may take a variety of forms such as adaptive devices and adult help, which includes such things as verbal prompts, gestural prompts, models, and physical assistance (Wolery, McWilliam, & Bailey, in press). Knowing the amount and type of assistance needed by a child to perform a given skill provides information about (a) whether that skill is a legitimate goal for intervention *and* (b) what strategies may be successful during intervention. For example, two children may not be able to put on their coats. One child can do it successfully if she is given a small amount of physical assistance with getting her arm through the second sleeve, but the second child requires substantial physical assistance on all steps. Knowing this information is likely to lead the team to conclude that putting on a coat is a legitimate goal for the first child but not for the second. Further, they may conclude that the strategy for teaching the first child to put on her coat should involve partial physical prompts.

Information About Environments and Schedules

When teams plan interventions that are relevant to a child's entire day, they need information about the settings in which the child spends time

and about when time is spent in those settings. Tremendous variability exists in terms of the environments in which young children spend time due to the structure of families (e.g., single parents), employment demands (e.g., families in which all adults work outside of the home), and informal supports (extended family member or friend helps care for the child). Also, the variability sometimes is due to the nature of the intervention program (e.g., half-day center-based programs or programs that offer services on selected days of the week). Some children spend nearly all of their time in a single home environment; for others, the major environments may be a classroom-based program and their homes. Many children, however, spend time in their homes, in a classroom-based program (e.g., half-day kindergarten), and in a child-care program or family day-care arrangement. Some children may have two home environments that are important; for example, when parents are separated and have joint custody, or when grandparents or other relatives care for the child. As a result, teams cannot assume children have one or two critical environments such as a home and an early childhood program; they should identify all of the settings in which children regularly spend substantial amounts of time during most weeks. In most cases, this information can be collected through interviews with the family.

In addition, teams need to get information on children's schedules. This should include the time spent in each setting from morning until bedtime. When collecting this information, the team should identify (a) the amount of time spent in each environment; (b) the times when the child goes from one setting to another; and (c) the general and usual activities and routines that occur in each setting. These activities and routines include such things as meals, dressing/undressing, taking naps, play time, and so on. For example, some children sleep at home, awake, get dressed, eat breakfast, and then go to a classroom program; however, other children may sleep at home, be awakened and taken to a grandmother's house for breakfast and dressing before going to a classroom program. Knowing when various routines occur gives the team information that is useful for (a) deciding whether an environment should be selected as an intervention site; (b) planning when particular goals can be addressed in context; and (c) identifying who will need to use the intervention practices and strategies. Sometimes the most difficult part of intervention planning is not identifying the important goals or the desirable intervention strategies, but determining how so many different adults can be encouraged and supported in carrying out interventions (i.e., working together rather than working at cross-purposes). Identifying the settings in which a child spends time, the amount of time spent in each setting, the times when children move from one setting to another, and the routines in each setting are critical information in planning intervention programs. As with identifying children's current settings, identifying children's schedules is best collected through interviews with families. Checklists and routine-based interviews should be used to collect information about specific aspects of routines and activities that are problematic and thus should be the focus of interventions (McWilliam, 1992).

Information About Specific Dimensions of Intervention Environments

After identifying the settings in which the child spends time, the daily schedule (which may vary from day to day), and the routines in each setting, the team can determine which settings can be selected as intervention sites. In settings where the team decides intervention is possible, they should gather information about (a) the physical dimensions and organization of the settings; (b) the sequence of activities and routines in each setting; (c) the usual roles of adults in those activities and routines; and (d) the structure of the activities and routines. Sample questions the team should ask about each of these dimensions are presented

in Table 16.1. This information is needed for selecting times and instances when learning opportunities are possible for various goals. It also is useful for identifying which intervention practices and strategies are most likely to be used, determining who needs to use those strategies, and what assistance they need to use them.

The primary means of collecting information to answer the questions in Table 16.1 are interviewing the family (and other caregivers as appropriate) and direct observation in the selected settings. The ecological congruence assessment process is appropriate in classroom placements (Wolery, Brashers, & Neitzel, 2002). Both interviews and observations probably should be used. Interviewing family members will secure their perspective of the settings, and direct observation will likely result in unique conclusions that are useful for planning interventions. For example, after observation, the team may conclude that the family day-care setting is not a desirable context for promoting acquisition of particular skills but may be an ideal context for promoting generalization of skills learned in the home or classroom.

Information About Family Concerns and Priorities

Practices for identifying family concerns and priorities are described in Chapter 7; they are not reiterated here. Further, as noted throughout the other chapters, families often have key information about children's abilities and needs. Family participation in intervention planning is critical for three decisions that must be made: determining the goals of intervention, selecting the intervention strategies and practices, and determining when and where selected interventions should be used for the identified goals. Families are likely to participate more in these decisions when they participate in earlier assessment activities. In seeking family participation in these decisions, teams need to be sensitive to cultural and linguistic

TABLE 16.1
Sample Questions About Dimensions of Potential Intervention Settings

Dimension
Question

Physical Dimension and Organization
- What materials and toys are in each environment?
- How are those toys and materials organized and placed about the room?
- Can the child access all areas and materials and if so, how?
- How much space is available, and how many children and adults are in it?
- What adaptations of equipment and materials, if any, are needed?
- Are there elements of the physical environment that are unsafe for this child?

Temporal Organization of Activities and Routines
- How are activities and routines scheduled within the setting?
- How long does each activity/routine last?
- What basic care routines (meals, toileting, dressing) occur in the setting?
- How much control does the child have over the sequence of activities/routines?

Adults' Roles in Activities/Routines
- For each activity/routine, what do adults do in relation to the child/children?
- When do adults observe children, interact directly with them, and take care of other tasks (e.g., material preparation, planning, meal preparation, etc.)?
- When, if ever, do adults lead activities (e.g., read a story, circle time)?
- How do adults interact with children (e.g., tend to direct child's play, respond to child's play, play with the child)?
- What types of verbal exchanges (e.g., questions, commands, comments, conversations) do adults have with the child/children?

Activity/Routine Structure
- How does the child get into and out of each activity/routine?
- How does the child know what is expected in each activity/routine?
- What is the child expected to do in each activity/routine?
- How many other children participate in each activity/routine?
- What toys/materials, if any, are used in each activity/routine?

Source: From "Implementing Instruction for Young Children with Special Needs in Early Childhood Classrooms" (p. 153) by M. Wolery, in M. Wolery and J. Wilbers (Eds.) *Including Young Children with Special Needs in Early Childhood Programs,* 1994, Washington, DC: National Association for the Education of Young Children. Copyright 1994 by the National Association for the Education of Young Children. Reprinted by permission.

differences (Lynch & Hanson, 1998; see also Chapter 4).

Summary

Teams need a great deal of information when developing intervention plans. This includes children's developmental and functional abilities as well as their developmental and functional needs. Information is needed on children's patterns of interacting with their social and physical environments, including their social interactions with others and their play with objects. Information is needed on their behavioral states (when appropriate) and the environmental factors that appear to influence state stability; their interests, preferences, and reinforcers; and the effects of supports on their performance. Finally, information is needed on the settings in which they are involved, the schedules in those settings, and variations in the key dimensions of those settings. When gathering this information, perspectives of children's families should be solicited and considered. This information is used to specify goals, select intervention sites, and identify intervention practices and strategies.

TRANSLATING ASSESSMENT RESULTS INTO INTERVENTION PLANS

In the following sections, guidelines for developing intervention plans are presented, and procedures and issues are discussed for three planning activities: identifying intervention goals, translating those goals into intervention objectives, and selecting potential intervention strategies.

General Guidelines

Involve Families in Preparing the Plan
Parents should be involved in preparing intervention plans because they have a large stake in the outcome of the plan (see Chapter 7). They may have unique information about what is possible in some of the environments, and they are likely to have information about children that is unknown to professionals. Involving families in assessment activities provides them with opportunities to help solve problems with professionals as interventions are selected and carried out. Family members can play several roles during the assessment process. Potential roles and examples of them are provided in Table 16.2. In the planning process, three roles are particularly critical: providing information, validating professionals' conclusions and interpretations of the child skills, and making decisions on the assessment information. Involving families in the assessment process and particularly in the planning process communicates to families that family-centered services and parental decision-making are not just platitudes

repeated by professionals but are the manner in which professionals interact with families. Of course, this involves scheduling planning meetings at times and in locations convenient for them, being flexible in terms of modes of communication (e.g., telephone, e-mail, meetings), listening to and addressing their concerns, presenting them with choices when open-ended questions result in deferral to professionals, providing them with information about the content and procedures of meetings well before the meetings occur, using jargon-free language, conducting meetings in an informal but efficient manner rather than in an officious manner, limiting the number of professionals at meetings to avoid overwhelming families with large numbers, and being prepared for meetings (Trivette & Dunst, 2000). Professionals should attend to the manner in which these activities are carried out, not simply ensuring that the activities occur; the manner in which professionals interact with families influences their perceptions of the helpfulness of those professionals (Dunst, 2000). Implicit in these strategies is the assumption that developing an intervention plan is not an activity that occurs in one meeting around a table with multiple assessment reports. Rather, it involves an ongoing dialogue among the members of the team, including the family.

Involve the Entire Team in Preparing the Plan
In addition to family members, all team members should be involved in the process of developing the intervention plan (Bruder, 1996). It is especially critical that the individuals who will be expected to implement the plan are involved in its development. For example, if parts of the intervention will occur in a child-care program, the child's teacher in that program should be involved in developing the plan. Bruder (1996) describes strategies for promoting teamwork among groups of professionals.

Comply with Legal Guidelines for Preparing the Plan
An individualized family service plan (IFSP) is required for infants and toddlers

TABLE 16.2
Potential Roles of Families in the Assessment Process

Role Description

Assisting in planning assessment activities
- Help in planning who should be interviewed and identifying times for such interviews
- Help in where and when the child could be observed for specific types of skills
- Help in identifying appropriate times and places for testing

Assisting in gathering information
- Help administer tests or parts of tests to ensure evaluator familiarity and to increase children's likelihood of responding
- Collect observational data in the home
- Complete checklists and rating scales about difficult to test domains

Providing needed information
- Respond to other team members' questions about the child's skills and behaviors as well as interventions that are likely to be successful
- Give information about the child's interests, preferences, and potential reinforcers
- Give information about the child's settings and schedule
- Give information about key dimensions of the child's current settings

Observing assessment activities
- Observe assessment activities (e.g., testing, direct observation in natural environment) to understand other team members' views of the child's skills and behaviors
- Observe and make judgments about whether the child's skills and behaviors in the assessment contexts are typical of the child's performance in other settings

Validating assessment information collected by other team members
- Confirm professionals' conclusions about the child's skills and needs
- Qualify, modify, or expand professionals' conclusions about the child's skills and needs
- Refute professionals' conclusions about the child's skills

Making decisions based on assessment results
- Rank which goals or outcomes are most important
- Select goals that should be addressed
- Match goals to specific settings and activities or routines
- Help decide whether given intervention strategies are acceptable and feasible in given settings
- Suggest intervention strategies and practices that are likely to work with the child

who receive early intervention services, and an individualized educational program (IEP) is required for preschoolers with disabilities who receive special education and related services. Families should be informed of the content of these plans, of their rights surrounding assessments and of their rights and options related to the implementation of intervention plans (Neisworth & Bagnato, 2000). Even if these formalized plans were not required, analyzing assessment information to form intervention plans is a defensible professional practice. The IFSP and IEP have specific requirements about the types of information that should be included on them, and professional team members should be familiar with this information. Likewise, IFSPs and IEPs have general procedures that should be followed in their development, including basing goals on assessment information, involving families, attending to linguistic and cultural differences, and attending to due process procedures. Also, some states or local agencies may have specific procedures that must be followed. The team needs to become familiar with these processes and comply with them, communicate them to families, or work to change processes that are not conducive to developing meaningful intervention plans. Unfortunately, the requirement to develop individualized plans does not guarantee that those plans will be carried out.

Consider the Veracity of the Assessment Results   The assessment results are the foundation on which the intervention plan is developed. Faulty assessment data will likely result in a faulty intervention plan. Faulty assessment results can occur for a number of reasons, for example, assessment information may be incomplete. When conducting an assessment, the team must balance the need for more information against the time and effort required to secure that information. As decisions are made, the team should be extremely aware of how complete their information is. If they realize their information is incomplete, two strategies are defensible. First, they can postpone making decisions and conduct more assessment activities. Second, they can make an initial decision, but also decide that as intervention is implemented additional information should be collected to evaluate that decision. For example, Kristen's assessment of her levels of social play showed she engaged primarily in solitary or parallel play. Her team decides to identify social play as an intervention goal. However, they may have little information on Kristen's sharing and social exchanges during play. By intervening to promote social play, they can monitor the effects of the intervention and decide whether the goal is appropriate or whether other goals should be established on related skills.

Sometimes the findings from different assessment activities may produce apparently contradictory conclusions. For example, in the home, the child may be engaged with toys at appropriate levels and for extended periods of time; however, observations in the child-care class may indicate engagement is intermittent and fleeting. This apparent contradiction may be a result of a number of factors, such as the materials/toys available, the child's familiarity with the settings, or differences in how engagement was measured in the two contexts. When contradictory findings arise, the team needs to determine if defensible explanations exist for those differences and whether those explanations lead to intervention goals or additional assessment activities. In the example noted above, the team may decide that the low levels of engagement in the child-care class are due to lack of familiarity with the setting. In such cases, the team may decide to monitor the child's engagement, and if it does not change as she becomes more familiar with the classroom materials and routines, a goal could be written and an intervention initiated.

Some assessment reports include statements about children's abilities or needs, but do not describe the conditions from which the findings were derived. For example, a report might say Taylor cannot put on his shoes. However, the type of shoes, the stability of his sitting position when he was trying to put on his shoes, and the assistance he received should be described. If such information is not included, then the conclusion that Taylor cannot put on his shoes does not lead to intervention planning. The conditions under which such summary statements are made must be described to plan meaningful intervention programs.

Some assessment information may be faulty because of lack of reliability. Such problems can occur in nearly every stage of the assessment process, including the measure itself, the manner in which the measure is used, and the way the results are scored (Barnett, Bell, & Carey, 1999). If reliability problems are apparent, they should be corrected. Data collected from unreliable measurement should not be used in making decisions about intervention programs.

In addition, some information may come from assessments that have validity problems. In general, the most important validity issue with instructional program planning assessments is construct validity (i.e., the degree to which the measurement procedures assess the phenomenon that is intended). Lack of construct validity can occur with observational measurement as well as with tests. For example, if a team was concerned about whether Anthony initiated social interactions to peers, this skill could be assessed through direct observation in a play setting. If initiations were defined only as speaking to other children (e.g., asking questions, suggesting play themes), the observation may not be valid, because initiations can occur in many different ways, such as giving a peer a toy, touching the peer, looking at the peer and smiling, gesturing, and so forth. A nonverbal child could engage in frequent initiations, but a definition of initiations that included only verbal behavior would lead to the conclusion that the child was not initiating interactions. Thus, all conclusions about children's performance should be analyzed for the degree to which the measure on which it is based is indeed a valid indication of the presumed skill.

View the Plan as a Tentative Guide for Intervention   Although a great deal of effort goes into developing an IFSP or IEP, it should be viewed with a healthy degree of skepticism. Children's development is complex, and a range of factors (including disabilities) can influence it substantially. Thus, despite the best efforts of team members to conduct a thorough assessment, intervention plans may require adjustment as they are implemented. In Chapter 17, issues related to monitoring the effects of intervention plans are described. The plan should not be viewed as a rigid and unchangeable document; it is a dynamic document that helps guide the intervention efforts. Teams should expect to make modifications and adjustments as the plan is implemented.

Identifying Intervention Goals

Developing intervention plans requires teams to summarize the assessment results into goal statements, determine the intent of each goal, and make decisions about the relative value or priority of the identified goals. These three tasks are described below.

Summarizing Assessment Results into Goal Statements   Goal statements are short sentences identifying the desired result of intervention. Examples are "Ashton will play independently with toys," "Juana will feed herself with a spoon," and "Kenton will carry on conversations with his peers." Teams can use three strategies to summarize assessment results into broad goal and outcome statements: developmental approach, functional approach, and ecological/person-centered approach. Perhaps the most frequently used in early intervention is the *developmental approach*. This approach is based on the assumption that children with developmental delays and disabilities acquire skills in sequences similar to children without disabilities, but often at a slower rate. With this approach, teams assess children's abilities in all relevant developmental domains, and then draw conclusions about their current level of development. Two types of information are used to devise the intervention goals. First, most children will be less developmentally advanced in some areas or domains than others, and goals are written for the areas in which they are less advanced. Second, the next skills in the sequence of development across all domains may be identified as intervention goals. The developmental approach has some inherent appeal. If used appropriately, broad developmental goals can be identified, and developmental gains can be demonstrated.

The developmental approach has been criticized, however, on many grounds, especially that teams tend to identify the "next items on the test" as the goals of intervention (Goodman, 1992). This practice raises the question "Should we teach to the test?" In the case of screening and diagnostic tests, the answer is definitely "No." In the case of other tests (e.g., criterion- and curriculum-referenced tests), the question is stated inappropriately and should be "Should we teach from test results?" The answer to this question is "Yes, *but* . . ." "Yes," because there is no other reason to conduct assessments for intervention planning than to use the results to plan the targets and methods of intervention. The answer is "Yes, *but* . . ." because there are many inappropriate ways to use test results. For example, a common practice is to assess children with criterion- or curriculum-referenced tests, identify all the skills the child can do in each domain, and then target the first items the child failed as the primary intervention goals or objectives. This practice is inappropriate for several reasons: (a) many of these measures have items that were not developed as instructional goals; (b) adjacent items on many tests are not necessarily related to the same skill; (c) the sequences of items on many tests may not be the best teaching sequences, especially for children with sensory and physical disabilities; and (d) many of the sequences may have large gaps between items. This practice also does not take into account prerequisite skills needed for some skills and the relationships of skills across developmental domains.

In addition, the answer to the question is "Yes, but . . . " because a child's failure on an item from criterion- and curriculum-referenced tests simply serves as a prompt to ask a series of additional questions:

1. What is the intent of the items the child failed, or what are these items designed to measure?
2. Are those intents important developmental constructs and skills the child should acquire?
3. Is this item a proxy for other important skills? Does this item represent a class of important behaviors?
4. Why did the child fail these items, and what does that say about the child's overall competence in this and other areas?
5. Why are these skills important to this individual infant or child?

6. Does the infant or child need this skill to function more adaptively in the settings in which he or she currently spends time or will spend time in the near future?
7. What are the prerequisite behaviors for performing this skill, and does the child have those prerequisite abilities?
8. How does performance on this skill relate to other skills in this domain or other developmental areas?
9. Is this skill an important prerequisite to other skills?
10. Should the focus of this skill be on acquisition, fluency, maintenance, or generalization?

Answers to these and related questions allow teams to make appropriate decisions based on testing and assessment results. Clearly, the process is much more complex than teaching the next item on a test. Test results should be supplemented with information taken from other measurement strategies such as direct observation and interviews.

Another approach to summarizing assessment information is called the *functional approach*. The assessment results with this approach are summarized around two basic themes: age-appropriateness and independence (Rainforth, York, & Macdonald, 1992). The individual items on developmental scales are not seen as critical, but the data are organized around major developmental skills (e.g., achieving mobility, establishing sustained attention and interaction with objects, imitating peers). Emphasis is placed on ensuring children are engaged in chronologically ageappropriate activities. The skills needed for participation and independence in those activities often become the goals of intervention. The assessment results also are organized around independence on basic skills, particularly those focusing on activities of daily living, independent living (for older children), and leisure or recreational skills. Examples of such skills are playing with toys independently, feeding oneself with utensils, being toilet trained, putting on and taking off one's clothing, and so on.

The functional approach also has some appeal. If used appropriately, it allows the team to identify goals that are developmentally useful, are age-appropriate, and may have immediate benefits for children and children's families and caregivers. That is, if the goals are met, children should become more independent and competent in the settings in which they live and spend time. The primary disadvantage is the lack of an adequate framework for conceptualizing goals for infants and toddlers with special needs.

The third approach, which is a variation and an extension of the functional model, is called the *ecological/person-centered approach* (Browder, 2001). This approach uses five steps: (1) summarize information known about the child; (2) meet with the family prior to an IEP meeting to use person-centered planning procedures; (3) facilitate the child's involvement in the process; (4) specify curricular goals for the child; and (5) develop the IEP (Browder, 2001). Within special education, person-centered planning is used primarily with older children and adolescents who have significant disabilities; the process with adaptations has applications for preschoolers as well. The second step (using person-centered planning) usually involves a meeting with the family and others they designate as important to answer a series of questions. Examples of those questions are what things does the child like/dislike, what experiences with intervention has the child and family had, what significant events have happened in the child's life, what in general is most valued by the family, what "hopes and dreams" (p.43) does the family have for the child, what goals are of the highest priority now, what has to happen to get those goals met and a plan established (Browder, 2001). The intent of these questions is to focus decision-making on children's abilities and preferences and on a hopeful vision of the future for the child. A key element of person-centered planning is helping students to participate in the decisions about the intervention

plan; that is, promoting self-determination. Young preschoolers' participation in decision making about goals and intervention practices is likely to be perceived by most individuals as being inappropriate. However, practices such as identifying their interests and preferences and providing frequent choices about activities and materials are ways to facilitate their self-determination. Also, helping families understand the value of promoting self-determination is a relevant outcome of early intervention.

Goals that are identified through the ecological/person-centered planning approach should include facilitating children's independence and mastery of specific tasks in their current settings, providing them with more control of their environments, developing social relationships with others, and fitting more appropriately in their current environments (Thurman, 1997). Rather than analyzing the assessment results by developmental domains as in the developmental approach, or age-appropriateness as in the functional model, results are analyzed by each environment and the activities and routines in those environments. For example, the home environment may be divided into the dining area, the bathroom, the area of the house where leisure activities occur (e.g., family room), the child's sleeping area, the yard, and any other area of the home in which the child might spend time. The activities and demands occurring in those areas are identified. For example, in the child's sleeping area, the activities might be dressing, going to bed at night, a story-time routine, and so forth. Other environments in which the child spends time also are analyzed in this manner. If the child is transported a great deal from setting to setting, the team might even analyze this "environment." For example, what can be done to help the child be more content in his car seat? This approach also is useful in helping children function in integrated classes where the expectations are designed for children without disabilities (Wolery, Brashers, & Neitzel, in 2002).

Two variations of the ecological model deserve mention: the PASSKey model (Barnett, Ehrhardt, Stollar, & Bauer, 1994) and variations of that model (Barnett, Bell, & Carey, 1999; Barnett, Bell, Gilkey et al., 1999) and template matching (Ager & Shapiro, 1995; McConnell, 2000). The PASSKey model is based on ecobehavioral analysis and on ecobehavioral consultation. It involves using interviews to identify important planned activities. Those activities are then observed through systematic sampling. Keystone behaviors (skills that serve as prerequisites to other skills or skills on which other important skills depend) are selected from observations, the research literature, and consultation with the caregivers. Scripts are devised to assist caregivers in implementing intervention plans, the implementation of the interventions is measured, adjustments are made, and finally the interventions are evaluated. The PASSKey model is particularly useful for addressing problems teachers, family members, and others might encounter with the child (Barnett, Bell, & Carey, 1999).

Template matching involves using ecobehavioral assessment procedures (Greenwood, Carta, & Dawson, 2000) to measure the performance of successful children in important settings and identify relationships between their behavior and various environmental events and variables. The environments and environment-behaviors relationships of the target child also are assessed with the same ecobehavioral procedures. The two sets of data are then compared to identify discrepancies in the environmental variables and events across settings. Based on these differences, adjustments are made in the child's environment. The primary utility of template matching may be in preparing children for new settings (Ager & Shapiro, 1995).

As with the other approaches, the ecological approach has considerable merit. It allows teams to develop goals that should produce immediate and long-term benefits for children and their families. It involves planning for children in their current situations as well as in the future. A potential weakness of the approach is that important developmental skills may be overlooked.

Each of these three approaches (developmental, functional, and ecological/person-centered) has advantages and disadvantages. They are not mutually exclusive; for example, combinations of the developmental and ecological approaches can be used. Regardless of the approach or combination of approaches used, the team should identify all relevant intervention goals for the child.

Determining the Intent of Each Goal   Once goals have been identified, teams should analyze each to determine its purpose or intent. For many important skills (especially cognitive, communication, and social skills), infants and young children can use many different behaviors to show evidence of that skill. For other important skills (e.g., self-care skills), a small number of behaviors can be used. For example, initiating social interactions can be performed by speaking to other people, touching them, giving them a toy, or making eye contact with them and looking expectantly at them. Each of the behaviors separately and in combination may result in starting an interaction. In many cases, having a way to start interactions is more important than the precise behaviors children use to start those interactions. Similarly, a child may request a drink of water in a number of ways, such as using a full sentence ("Please give me a glass of water"), using two words ("Want wawa"), using one word ("Wa-wa"), pointing at the sink without speaking, taking an adult's hand and leading him or her to the sink, and so forth. In each case, the child may be successful in getting a drink. Other skills, however, can be done by few behaviors or a small range of acceptable behaviors. For example, a child could use her fingers or a spoon to feed herself. She also could get the food in her mouth by lifting the plate and letting it slide in, or by putting her face down into the plate. However, the most acceptable behavior usually is using utensils, or for infants and young toddlers, finger feeding is appropriate.

In all three of these examples (initiating social interactions, requesting a drink, and self-feeding) there is a behavior and an effect of the behavior. White (1980) referred to this relationship as the *form versus function* issue. The form is the behavior; the function is the effect of the behavior. Each behavior is thought to produce an effect, and each effect is actualized by a behavior. For some goals, the form (behavior) is important, as in the case of self-feeding; for other goals, the effect is more important, as in the case of initiating social interactions with peers or requesting a drink. Neel and Billingsley (1989) suggest that assessment information should address form and function and that the results should be analyzed in terms of both. They present several potential combinations that would lead to different goals for the child. A child could have multiple behaviors that can be used for multiple functions, adequate behaviors but limited functions, limited behaviors that are used for multiple functions, limited behaviors and limited functions, and no identifiable behaviors or functions (Neel & Billingsley, 1989). For example, if a child's social interaction skills were analyzed, two important functions could be initiating interactions and responding to others' initiations. A child may have multiple and adequate behaviors for initiating interactions and limited forms for responding to others' initiations. In such a case, an appropriate goal would be to increase the number of behaviors (forms) for responding to initiations by peers. On the other hand, the child who requested a drink by using one word ("Wa wa") has a function (requesting drinks) but has limited forms. The goal of intervention would be to increase the number of forms or to teach more advanced and socially accepted forms. However, if requesting was the only function, then expanding the number of different functions would be an appropriate goal.

Analyzing each goal in terms of its behavior and effect (i.e., form and function) holds important implications for planning interventions. It provides guidance on how instructional objectives should be written (i.e., with prescribed behaviors or with a range of acceptable behaviors); it helps ensure that the objectives will result in more adaptive performance in naturalistic contexts; and it helps focus the team on relevant intervention strategies. A list of sample functions (effects) in several developmental domains is presented in Table 16.3. Others could be identified and these could be broken down to specific settings or smaller functions. When attending to the effects or functions, the goals that are written may be more generative. Generative behaviors are those that allow children to adapt their skills to changes in the environment that have not been encountered during instruction (Bricker, Pretti-Frontczak, & McComas, 1998).

Making Decisions About the Relative Priority of Each Goal

If the assessment activities are thorough and comprehensive, teams are likely to identify more goals than it is possible to address. Further, intervention appears to be more appropriate when a smaller number of goals or outcomes are established (McWilliam, 1996). To deal with this situation, goals can be categorized by their relative importance. Although no firm and hard categories exist, three appear useful: critical goals, valuable goals, and desirable goals. Different members of the team could sort each goal into one of these three categories, and then consensus could be established where disagreements occur. Although this three-tier hierarchy seems relatively straightforward, teams may find that it takes considerable discussion and judgment to place each goal into one of these categories.

The judgments of family members should carry substantial weight in categorizing the relative value of goals, but other factors also should be considered. Generally, goals should be given more importance if they allow children to gain access to or be maintained in inclusive settings. Likewise, goals should be given more importance if they allow children to learn skills that will result in learning other skills. For example, learning to imitate one's peers allows children to learn from observing the behavior of others; learning to initiate social exchanges sets children up to learn many different skills; learning to play with toys increases

TABLE 16.3
Examples of Functions (Effects) of Behavior by Developmental Domains

Developmental Domain Potential Function	Description
Gross Motor or Physical Development	
Maintenance of position in space	Ability to remain in a position without falling
Shifting positions in space	Ability to change the position of one's body without losing balance
Locomotion	Ability to move from one location to another
Fine Motor Development	
Object procurement	Ability to get an object
Manipulation of objects	Ability to move objects from one location to another or from one orientation in space to another
Social Development	
Maintaining proximity	Ability to stay near another person without distress
Initiating proximity	Ability to change location to be near another person
Initiating interactions	Ability to start an interaction with another person
Responding to others' initiations	Ability to perceive an initiation by another and respond so that the partner perceives the response
Sustaining interactions	Ability to continue interactions beyond two turns
Terminating interactions	Ability to stop interactions in mutually satisfying manner
Shared problem solving	Ability to be involved with others that leads to a common goal
Communication Development	
Requesting	Ability to communicate a desire for an object, action, information, permission, etc.
Commenting	Ability to direct another's attention to an object or action and provide information about it
Protesting	Ability to communicate the desire for something to stop
Greeting	Ability to acknowledge the presence of another person
Acknowledging	Ability to communicate that a message from another has been received
Answering	Ability to provide information to another who has posed a question
Cognitive Development	
Solving problems	Ability to generate and carry out solutions to problems that are encountered
Using symbols	Ability to use mental representations in objects and events
Imitating others	Ability to match the behavior of others with one's own behavior
Classification	Ability to place objects, actions, and attributes into common categories

children's opportunities for learning other important skills. Goals should be given more importance if they reduce the possibility of the child being stigmatized. For example, if a child is not toilet trained but is moving into a kindergarten placement, goals related to toilet training may take on added value. Frequently, goals that increase the ease with which children can be cared for also deserve higher status. For example, if a child is extremely fussy and cries a great deal, a legitimate goal is to assist the child in quieting more quickly, and finding interventions to promote consoling become important. Finally, goals should be given more value if they are useful (functional) across multiple settings—current and future (Neel & Billingsley, 1989).

Identifying the relative value of goals will assist teams in making decisions about how their time and effort should be distributed. Teams also can use this classification to ensure that high-priority goals are addressed at multiple points throughout each day (Bricker et al., 1998). This categorization of goals also provides guidance to team members in terms of which goals require more extensive monitoring as the intervention plan is implemented.

Translating Goals into Intervention Objectives

After goals are identified by summarizing the assessment results, analyzing the intent of the goals, and determining their relative priority, instructional objectives for each goal or outcome should be developed. A common procedure for doing this is task analysis. In this section, the steps for conducting task analyses are described, and then issues around writing instructional objectives are discussed.

Task Analysis

Task analysis is a *process* by which large goals are broken into smaller objectives and sequenced for instruction. Task analysis also is a *product;* the written result from conducting a task analysis is a product called a task analysis. This product is a list of short-term objectives that lead directly from the child's current level of performance to the long-term objective. It is not a set of teaching procedures or set of activities; rather it is a list of child behaviors that lead to the more advanced behavior in the long-term goals or outcomes.

Task analysis is a fundamental means of analyzing (into smaller units) curriculum content that is too large to be learned at once. Conducting task analyses is an important teacher competency. The steps for conducting task analyses are straightforward; Wolery, Bailey, and Sugai (1988) present five.

Step 1: Specify the long-term objective and look for related sources. The objective to be task analyzed should be specified precisely. The teacher should then look to various curricular guides for information concerning this objective. Over the past 20 years, hundreds of task analyses have been written, and many of them are found in curricula and other texts on teaching children with disabilities. While task analysis is a method for individualizing curriculum content, there is little need to write new task analyses for skills that already have been analyzed by someone else. However, teachers need the skill of analyzing objectives because published task analyses may not be available or may not be successful with a particular child for an important objective. In most cases, skills can be analyzed in a number of sequences. No single task analysis is necessarily correct, and the interventionist should attempt to find the one best suited to the child's learning patterns and current environment. Thiagarajan (1980) described a procedure for adapting previously written task analyses for individual children. This involves making adjustments in the entry point into a sequence of steps, adjusting the size of the steps (making them larger or smaller), adjusting the help children need to perform different steps, and adjusting the behaviors by which children show they have acquired the content of the task analysis.

Step 2: Break the long-term objective into steps or break the behavior into smaller behaviors. At this point in the process, the teacher is not concerned with how to teach the skill or how many steps are involved in the task analysis. Rather, he or she should attempt to break the skill into a few meaningful behaviors. Several means exist for doing this.

First, find a person who can do the skill competently, watch her do it, and write down the behaviors she does. Depending on the complexity of the task being analyzed, the teacher may have to watch the person do the skill several times to identify all of the small subtle behaviors involved. Competent performers do skills quickly, and the teacher may have to ask the person to do the behavior more slowly. Second, the teacher can do the behavior himself and write down the steps as they are done. Again, several repetitions may be needed, and doing the task slowly may be of benefit. These two methods are particularly useful for task analyzing skills that are composed of chains of motor responses, such as playing with certain toys, dressing/undressing, self-feeding, and riding a tricycle.

The two methods just described are not very useful for analyzing skills such as making a greeting response, matching shapes, or naming the letters of the alphabet. For such skills, teachers should use a third method: logical analysis. With logical analysis, teachers "think through tasks" to identify the behaviors and discriminations needed to perform the skill correctly. For example, a logical analysis of naming objectives would involve visual discrimination of the target objects from other similar objects, "matching" the object to the correct name from the infinite number of possible names, and then accurately saying the name.

Fourth, teachers can identify and use the sequences through which typical children acquire a given skill. The assumption of this method is that children learn complex behaviors sequentially, starting with the simplest behaviors and progressively moving toward more difficult responses. Thus, teachers merely determine the course through which a skill is acquired normally and write down the steps. Cohen and Gross (1979a, 1979b) described numerous sequences using this method across a number of different curricular domains. This method is inappropriate when the identified sequences are impossible for the child to do because of a disability. Also, in some skill sequences the behaviors are markers or representatives of competence rather than being useful or important skills in and of themselves (Wolery, McWilliam, & Bailey, in press).

Fifth, teachers can use a levels-of-assistance approach to break skills into steps. The process involves specifying the different amounts of help that a child might need at various points in learning a specific skill. For example, if a child can perform the target skill only when given a physical prompt, the steps of the task analysis might include doing it in response to partial physical prompts, a full model, a partial model, and without assistance. A similar approach is to increase the complexity of the conditions in which a child performs the skill. For example, if a child currently will greet one teacher, the steps of the task analysis might specify a number of different people and situations in which a greeting response is appropriate. When using this method, which is particularly useful when analyzing generalization tasks, all the possible situations in which the behavior might be needed should be listed.

Step 3: Eliminate unnecessary and redundant behaviors. When skills are task analyzed, unnecessary steps may be listed and should be eliminated in the written task analysis. Likewise, if the same behavior occurs several times, it should be listed only once.

Step 4: Sequence the steps for teaching. After behaviors have been listed and unnecessary and redundant steps have been eliminated, the remaining behaviors should be sequenced for teaching. The two primary methods for sequencing skills for teaching include sequencing by temporal order and sequencing by difficulty. *Temporal order* involves listing the steps in the sequence in which they will be performed when the skill is completely learned. This is a particularly useful method for chained skills (e.g., putting on clothing, brushing teeth) or for behaviors that occur during large routines (e.g., preparing to go home, mealtime routines). Because it is desirable to teach such skills during naturally occurring routines, specifying the skills to be learned in temporal order is helpful. *Sequencing by difficulty* is more useful with responses that do not occur in chains or larger routines. Teachers must consider the difficulty in actually producing each response and the difficulty of the discriminations associated with those responses. When skills are broken into different behaviors, using the levels-of-assistance method, sequencing by difficulty can be easily accomplished.

Step 5: Specify prerequisite behaviors. Most task analyses include some behaviors that must be acquired before the easiest step of the task analysis can be performed. If the target child cannot perform the prerequisite behaviors, instruction should be delayed on the task analysis until the prerequisite behaviors are acquired.

These five steps have been used repeatedly and successfully to develop task analyses of skills across different types of content. To decrease the effort expended in teaching, teams should retain copies of successful task analyses. If a task analysis was successful with one child, it may well apply to another. Therefore, teams should compile a task-analysis "bank." Also, teams who use task analysis frequently accumulate several different task analysis patterns into which they can fit similar content. For example, to name pictures of common objects, the steps of the task analysis might be (a) to imitate verbally the name of the picture; (b) to match the picture to an identical picture in the presence of three different pictures; (c) to

identify receptively the picture when given the name; and (d) to identify the picture verbally. This structure of verbal imitation, matching, receptive identification, and expressive labeling could fit other areas, such as naming objects, naming letters of the alphabet, reading sight words, and naming numerals. When teachers are aware of these task-analysis patterns, writing new task analyses can be done quickly.

Writing Instructional Objectives

Several sources have described procedures for writing instructional objectives (Mager, 1962; Wolery et al., 1988), which involves specifying the behaviors to be performed, identifying the conditions under which performance will be measured, and identifying the level (criterion) at which the behavior must be performed before it is said to have been learned. Objectives should be written because they focus instruction and are an individualized standard against which progress can be monitored. Also, they can be used to communicate to others precisely.

A *behavior* is a movement, has a beginning and an end, is repeatable, and can be measured reliably by two or more individuals. Further, behaviors have a variety of dimensions, such as their accuracy, rate, latency, duration, and intensity (see Chapter 17). Teams must identify the most appropriate dimension when writing objectives. In addition, they must identify whether the function (effect) or the form (behavior) of the skill is more important. As described earlier, the behavior may be important with some objectives, but function may be more important with others. When function is identified, then a list of appropriate behaviors should be made.

Conditions in instructional objectives refer to the materials, task directions, and situations in which the behavior must be performed. Careful specification of the conditions allows for consistent measurement of the effects of the instruction. When specifying conditions, those that will exist in generalization settings should appear in the objective, or separate generalization objectives should be written.

Criterion statements in objectives tell how well the child must perform the skill. Criterion statements serve several functions: (a) They set a goal toward which teachers, families, and children can work; (b) they tell the team when to move on to other skills; and (c) they provide a standard against which progress can be monitored. Too often the criterion portion of objectives is written without sufficient thought. Because of the important functions criterion statements serve, they should be written with care. Consideration should be given to several issues. The dimension (e.g., accuracy, rate, combination of accuracy and rate, duration) of behavior that is most important should be measured. This may change as instruction progresses. For example, initial focus may be on accuracy, and as it is established, the focus may switch to a combination of rate and accuracy. Consideration also should be given to how well the behavior must be performed before it will be useful to the child. This ability can be determined by measuring how well children who competently perform the behavior do it. An average of this measurement can then be used in the criterion statement. For example, the teacher could measure how long it takes typically developing children to brush their teeth, calculate an average time, and use that interval in the criterion statement for a target child. Consideration should be given to identifying the minimum level that will result in enjoyment of the skill or the minimum level needed to move on to the next skill or environment. Consideration also should be given to the form in which the criterion is written. If percentage is written into the criterion statement, then the number of opportunities on which the percentage is calculated also should be listed. For example, 100% could be one correct response out of one opportunity, or 10 out of 10, or 100 out of 100. When writing the criterion statements, teachers should always check them by asking, "What does this really mean?"

In addition to these considerations, the team should ensure that objectives exist for all phases of instruction (Kozloff, 1994). Children's performance can be conceptualized as progressing through five phases: acquisition, fluency, maintenance, generalization, and adaptation. Acquisition, the first phase, refers to learning the basic requirements of a skill. Objectives that target acquisition frequently focus on the accuracy of a response. The second phase of learning, fluency (or proficiency), refers to how quickly or smoothly the child performs skills. Fluency objectives frequently have rate or duration-per-occurrence measures in the criterion statements. Maintenance refers to continued performance of a skill in conditions similar to training; generalization refers to performance of acquired skills in situations other than the instructional conditions. For example, children need to apply and use skills when other people are present, in other settings, and with other materials. Billingsley (1984) analyzed IEPs of students with severe disabilities and found that few objectives targeted generalization of skills. Adaptation refers to the child's ability to modify the skill to perform it when the conditions in which it is needed change. A good rule of thumb is that no objective should be considered mastered until (a) it is performed fluently and over time for the persons who taught it in the situations in which it was learned, (b) it is performed for some other individual at a needed time in a situation different from the instructional setting, and (c) it is performed spontaneously when needed in a situation other than the instructional environment.

Selecting Potential Intervention Strategies

In addition to identifying the intervention goals and translating them into instructional objectives, teams must select from the wide range of intervention practices and strategies that can be used to address the goals of infants, toddlers, and preschoolers with special needs. These include the guidelines for developmentally appropriate practices (Bredekamp & Copple, 1997) and the recommended practices by the Division for Early Childhood of the Council for Exceptional Children (Sandall, McLean, & Smith, 2000). Other sources include Barnett, Bell, and Carey (1999); Bricker et al. (1998); Odom and McLean (1996); Wolery, McWilliam, and Bailey (in press). When selecting interventions, three general guidelines should be followed. First, the practices and strategies that are selected should be likely to be effective; they should result in children learning the goals and outcomes the team has specified on the intervention plan. Second, they should be likely to be used. The ideal strategy or practice requires minimal adaptations of ongoing activities and routines and minimal changes in the styles of interacting and roles that adults assume in those activities. When more than one strategy will be effective, the persons who will be using the strategy should be given choices about which one they prefer. Usually, they are more likely to use practices they have chosen over those that are imposed on them. Third, the selected practices and strategies should be as naturalistic as possible. When several strategies may be effective in helping a child achieve a goal, the strategy that seems most like what occurs in the natural environment should be used.

IMPLEMENTING INTERVENTION PLANS

General Guidelines for Implementing Interventions

After instructional objectives have been written, the team needs to schedule when and in which contexts intervention should be implemented. Six general guidelines should be followed in scheduling the instruction. Implicit in these guidelines is the fundamental assumption that intervention for infants and young children with special needs should be integrated into their daily activities. The intervention strategies should not, in most cases, be implemented at separate and specialized times; rather they should be embedded into the naturally occurring interactions with adults and peers and the ongoing daily activities and routines (Bricker et al., 1998). Another implicit assumption is that children's environments should be responsive to their behavior and should be designed to promote child-initiated activities by providing interesting activities that capture children's engagement (Dunst et al., 2001). Ensuring that children's social and physical environments are responsive means that some adjustments may be necessary in adults' interaction patterns, the physical environment, and the daily schedule. Adults must know children's goals, observe their activities, and take advantage of all the opportunities that naturally occur to support and reinforce their performance and use of targeted goals.

Promote Both Participation and Independence When implementing intervention, the team needs to establish a balance between two foundational assumptions. First, children should participate in the activities and routines that are planned for their peers (e.g., siblings, classmates at a child-care program). Second, teams should promote children's independence and mastery of their environments. In many cases, meeting both assumptions can be achieved without difficulty, and participation in regularly planned and ongoing activities and routines provides multiple opportunities to promote independence. When a child's disabilities may preclude participation, the team should seek to identify and use adaptations in the activities to ensure that the child with special needs is supported while participating (Baumgart et al., 1982; Ferguson & Baumgart, 1991). Children should not be excluded from activities and routines because of their ability levels, and they should not be put into situations in which they fail and their inabilities are highlighted to their peers. Thus, careful planning is needed to adapt activities and routines or to provide direct assistance at key times to ensure active participation.

Address Each Goal Multiple Times Throughout the Day Unlike instruction for older elementary school children, intervention on critical goals for infants, toddlers, and preschoolers with special needs must be addressed at multiple occasions throughout the day (Bricker et al., 1998). This guideline has two direct implications for planning instruction. First, planned opportunities for acquiring each critical goal should be interspersed throughout the child's day; the team should devise intervention plans for times outside of their own direct contacts with the child. Second, the persons who interact and care for the child must be cognizant of critical goals and take advantage of each teachable moment or opportunity to support the child's learning and development—even when that opportunity was not scheduled or planned.

Address Multiple Goals Within the Same Activity Because intervention strategies and practices are, for the most part, embedded into ongoing activities and routines, each activity and routine may provide opportunities to address mul-tiple goals almost simultaneously (Bricker et al., 1998). For example, snack time provides opportunities to practice drinking from a cup; it can also provide opportunities to use requesting skills, conversational skills with peers, and motor skills during snack preparation or cleanup. Ideally, each activity and routine would set the occasion to address multiple goals.

Use an Activity/Routine-by-Goal Matrix To accomplish the previous two recommendations (promote use of each important goal in multiple activities throughout the day, and promote use of multiple goals in each activity and routine), the use of an activities/routines-by-goal matrix is recommended (Bricker et al., 1998). This matrix is an organizational tool to assist teams in planning when each goal will be addressed throughout the day, ensuring that each activity and routine is used to address goals, and identifying times for monitoring children's progress. Guidelines for using the matrix are presented in Table 16.4.

TABLE 16.4
Steps for Completing Goal-by-Activity Matrices

---

1. Down the left-hand column of the matrix, list the events (e.g., activities) in which the child will participate during the day. The events should be listed in the order in which they occur daily.
2. Below each listing in the left-hand column of the matrix, list the location of each event. The listing should include the entire day. The purpose is to provide instruction in all relevant locations.
3. Also in the left-hand column of the matrix, list the time that each activity will start and its expected duration each day.
4. Also in the left-hand column of the matrix, list the name of the adult who is responsible for implementing the instruction; if peers also are used, then they should be listed here as well.
5. Across the top of the matrix list all of the skills that have been identified for instruction. Each column should include one behavior.
6. In the cells of the matrix, list the materials and specialized instructional strategies that will be used. If a skill is not addressed during a given event or time, then that cell should be left blank.
7. Check the matrix to ensure that skills will be taught by different adults using a variety of materials and settings to facilitate generalization.

Note: Adapted from "Application of the Individualized Curriculum Sequencing Model to Learners with Severe Sensory Impairments" (pp. 260–266) by E. Helmstetter and D. Guess, in L. Goetz, D.Guess, and K.Stremel-Campbell (Eds.) *Innovative Program Design for Individuals with Dual Sensory Impairments,* 1987, Baltimore, MD: Paul H. Brookes.

Adapt Ongoing Activities/Routines as Necessary Often, but not always, participation in ongoing activities and routines with attention to children's goals will be sufficient to allow children to acquire and use the skills the team has decided are important. However, in many cases, the activities and routines will need to be adapted. These adaptations or modifications are designed to increase the likelihood that children will acquire and use the skills the team has determined are critical. Several potential guidelines are possible. These include embedding instructional strategies within and across activities (Wolery, 2001); adjusting activities by changing what children do within those activities (Wolery, 1994b); adapting materials and adjusting rules of access to those materials (Ostrosky & Kaiser, 1991); adjust activities by increasing opportunities to respond, using responsive interaction styles, and using specialized reinforcement proce-

dures (Wolery, 2000); and using peer-mediated procedures (Kohler & Strain, 1999).

Monitor the Implementation and Effects of Intervention As noted previously, the intervention plan should be viewed as a tentative guide for designing intervention strategies and practices. Adjustments to the goals are likely as the plan is validated through implementation and as children make progress. Thus, regular monitoring of the effects of intervention is required. (A detailed discussion is presented in Chapter 17.) Because interventions are implemented during ongoing interactions, activities, and routines, the possibility is high that intervention practices and strategies will be used incorrectly or inconsistently. Thus, implementation of the intervention practices and strategies should be monitored (Barnett et al., 1994).

· · · · · · · ·

SUMMARY OF KEY CONCEPTS

- Assessment information should be collected to make specific decisions, and the decisions that need to be made influence how the information is collected and how it is used.

- Written reports of assessment activities should include the identifying information, background information, methods used in the assessment, results of the assessment, and recommendations and conclusions.

- To plan interventions, teams need information on children's developmental and functional abilities and needs, their usual interaction patterns, and the effects of various supports.

- To plan interventions, teams need information about children's current environments, including the schedule of activities and the social and physical structure of those settings.

- To plan useful interventions, teams need information about families' priorities and concerns.

- When planning interventions, all team members (including families) should be involved, be aware of and comply with relevant legal guidelines, evaluate the trustworthiness of the assessment information, and view the plan as tentative.

- Teams, in conjunction with families, should identify goals and outcomes, conduct task analyses, write instructional objectives, and devise plans for implementing intervention to accomplish the goals and objectives.

- When planning implementation of intervention, teams should promote both participation and independence, address each goal multiple times throughout the day, address multiple goals within the same activity, and use an activity-by-skill matrix to organize instruction.

- Intervention to address children's goals should be embedded into the ongoing daily routines and activities children experience.

········
REFERENCES

Ager, C. L., & Shapiro, E. S. (1995). Template matching as a strategy for assessment of and intervention for preschool students with disabilities. *Topics in Early Childhood Special Education, 15,* 187–218.

Ault, M. M., Guy, B., Guess, D., Bashinski, S., & Roberts, S. (1995). Analyzing behavior state and learning environments: Application in instructional settings. *Mental Retardation, 33,* 304–316.

Bagnato, S. J., Neisworth, J. T., & Munson, S. M. (1997). *Linking assessment and early intervention: An authentic curriculum-based approach.* Baltimore: Paul H. Brookes.

Barnett, D. W., Bell, S. H., & Carey, K. T. (1999). *Designing preschool interventions: A practitioner's guide.* New York: Guilford Press.

Barnett, D. W., Bell, S. H., Gilkey, C. M., Lentz, F. E., Graden, J. L., Stone, C. M., et al. (1999). The promise of meaningful eligibility determination: Functional intervention-based multifactored preschool evaluation. *Journal of Special Education, 33,* 112–124.

Barnett, D. W., Ehrhardt, K. E., Stollar, S. A., & Bauer, A. M. (1994). PASSKey: A model for naturalistic assessment and intervention design. *Topics in Early Childhood Special Education, 14,* 350–373.

Baumgart, D., Brown, L., Pumpian, I., Nisbet, J., Ford, A., Sweet, M., et al. (1982). Principle of partial participation and individualized adaptations in educational programs for severely handicapped students. *Journal of the Association for the Severely Handicapped, 7*(2), 17–22.

Billingsley, F. F. (1984). Where are the generalization outcomes? (an examination of instructional objectives). *Journal of the Association for the Severely Handicapped, 9,* 186–200.

Bredekamp, S., & Copple, C. (1997). *Developmentally appropriate practice in early childhood programs* (Rev. ed.). Washington, DC: National Association for the Education of Young Children.

Bricker, D. D., Pretti-Frontczak, K. L., & McComas, N. R. (1998). *An activity-based approach to early intervention* (2nd ed.). Baltimore, MD: Paul Brookes.

Browder, D. M. (2001). *Curriculum and assessment for students with moderate and severe disabilities.* New York: Guilford Press.

Bruder, M. B. (1996). Interdisciplinary collaboration in service delivery. In R. A. McWilliam (Ed.), *Rethinking pull-out services in early intervention: A professional resource* (pp. 27–48). Baltimore: Paul H. Brookes.

Carter, C. M. (2001). Using choice with game play to increase language skills and interactive behaviors in children with autism. *Journal of Positive Behavior Interventions, 3,* 131–151.

Cohen, M., & Gross, P. (1979a). *The developmental resources: Behavioral sequences for assessment and program planning* (Vol. 1). New York: Grune & Stratton.

Cohen, M., & Gross, P. (1979b). *The developmental resources: Behavioral sequences for assessment and program planning* (Vol. 2). New York: Grune & Stratton.

DeLeon, I. G., & Iwata, B. A. (1996). Evaluation of a multiple-stimulus presentation format for assessing reinforcer preferences. *Journal of Applied Behavior Analysis, 29,* 519–533.

Dunlap, G., dePerczel, M., Clarke, S., Wilson, D., Wright, S., White, R., et al. (1994). Choice making to promote adaptive behavior for students with emotional and behavioral challenges. *Journal of Applied Behavior Analysis, 27,* 505–518.

Dunst, C. J. (2000). Revisiting "rethinking early intervention." *Topics in Early Childhood Special Education, 20,* 95–104.

Dunst, C. J., Bruder, M. B., Trivette, C. M., Hamby, D., Raab, M., & McLean, M. E. (2001). Characteristics and consequences of everyday natural learning opportunities. *Topics in Early Childhood Special Education, 21,* 68–92.

Ferguson, D., & Baumgart, D. (1991). Partial participation revisited. *Journal of the Association for Persons with Severe Handicaps, 16,* 218–227.

Gast, D. L., Jacobs, H. A., Murray, A. S., Holloway, A., & Long, L. (2000). Pre-session assessment of preferences for students with profound multiple disabilities. *Education and Training in Mental Retardation and Developmental Disabilities, 35,* 393–405.

Goodman, J. F. (1992). *When slow is fast enough: Educating the delayed preschool child.* New York: Guilford Press.

Graff, R. B., & Ciccone, F. J. (2002). A post hoc analysis of multiple-stimulus preference assessment results. *Behavioral Interventions, 17*, 85–92.

Greenwood, C. R., Carta, J. J., & Dawson, H. (2000). Ecobehavioral assessment systems for software (EBASS). In T. Thompson, D. Felce, & F. J. Symons (Eds.), *Behavioral observation: Technology and applications in developmental disabilities* (pp. 229–251). Baltimore: Paul H. Brookes.

Guess, D., Roberts, S., Siegel-Causey, E., & Ault, M. M. (1993). Analysis of behavior state conditions and associated environmental variables among students with profound handicaps. *American Journal on Mental Retardation, 97*, 634–653.

Hagopian, L. P., Rush, K. S., Lewin, A. B., & Long, E. S. (2001). Evaluating the predictive validity of a single stimulus engagement preference assessment. *Journal of Applied Behavior Analysis, 34*, 475–485.

Hobbs, N. (1967). Helping disturbed children: Psychological and ecological strategies. *American Psychologist, 22*, 1105–1115.

Kern, L., Vorndran, C. M., Hilt, A., Ringdahl, J. E., Adelman, B. E., & Dunlap, G. (1998). Choice as an intervention to improve behavior: A review of the literature. *Journal of Behavioral Education, 8*, 151–170.

Kohler, F. W., & Strain, P. S. (1999). Maximizing peer-mediated resources in integrated preschool classrooms. *Topics in Early Childhood Special Education, 19*, 92–102.

Kozloff, M. A. (1994). *Improving educational outcomes for children with disabilities: Principles for assessment, program planning, and evaluation*. Baltimore: Paul H. Brookes.

Logan, K. R., & Gast, D. L. (2001). Conducting preference assessments and reinforcer testing for individuals with profound multiple disabilities: Issues and procedures. *Exceptionality, 9*, 123–134.

Lynch, E. W., & Hanson, M. J. (1998). *Developing cross-cultural competence: A guide for working with children and their families* (2nd ed.). Baltimore: Paul H. Brookes.

Mager, R. (1962). *Preparing instructional objectives*. Belmont, CA: Fearon.

McConnell, S. R. (2000). Assessment in early intervention and early childhood special education: Building on the past to project into our future. *Topics in Early Childhood Special Education, 20*, 43–48.

McWilliam, R. A. (1992). *Family-centered intervention planning: A routines-based approach*. Tucson, AZ: Communication Skill Builders.

McWilliam, R. A. (1996). Service delivery issues in center-based early intervention. In R. A. McWilliam (Ed.), *Rethinking pull-out services in early intervention: A professional resource* (pp. 3–25). Baltimore: Paul H. Brookes.

McWilliam, R. A. (2000). It's only natural . . . to have early intervention in the environments where it's needed. *Young Exceptional Children Monograph, 2*, 17–26.

Neel, R. S., & Billingsley, F. F. (1989). *IMPACT: A functional curriculum handbook for student with moderate to severe disabilities*. Baltimore: Paul H. Brookes.

Neisworth, J. T., & Bagnato, S. J. (2000). Recommended practices in assessment. In S. Sandall, M. E. McLean, & B. J. Smith (Eds.), *DEC recommended practices in early intervention/early childhood special education* (pp. 17–27). Longmont, CO: Sopris West.

Odom, S. L., & McLean, M. E. (Eds.) (1996). *Early intervention/early childhood special education: Recommended practices*. Austin, TX: PRO-ED.

Ostrosky, M. M., & Kaiser, A. P. (1991). Preschool classroom environments that promote communication. *Teaching Exceptional Children, 23*(4), 6–10.

Rainforth, B., York, J., & Macdonald, C. (1992). *Collaborative teams for students with severe disabilities: Integrating therapy and educational services*. Baltimore: Paul H. Brookes.

Reid, D. H., Everson, J. M., & Green, C. W. (1999). A systematic evaluation of preferences identified through person-centered planning for people with profound multiple disabilities. *Journal of Applied Behavior Analysis, 32*, 467–477.

Romaniuk, C., & Miltenberger, R. G. (2001). The influence of preference and choice of activity on problem behavior. *Journal of Positive Behavior Interventions, 3*, 152–159.

Sandall, S., McLean, M. E., & Smith, B. J. (2000). *DEC recommended practices in early intervention/early childhood special education*. Longmont, CO: Sopris West.

Thiagarajan, S. (1980). Individualizing instructional objectives. *Teaching Exceptional Children, 12*, 126–127.

Thurman, S. K. (1997). Systems, ecologies, and the context of early intervention. In S. Thurman, J. Cornwell, & S. Gottwald (Eds.), *Contexts of early intervention: Systems and settings* (pp. 3–19). Baltimore: Paul H. Brookes.

Trivette, C. M., & Dunst, C. J. (2000). Recommended practices in family-based practices. In S. Sandall, M. E. McLean, & B. J. Smith (Eds.), *DEC recommended practices in early intervention/early childhood special education* (pp. 39–46). Longmont, CO: Sopris West.

Vygotsky, L. S. (1978). *Mind and society*. Cambridge, MA: Harvard University Press.

White, O. R. (1980). Adaptive performance objectives: Form versus function. In W. Sailor, B. Wilcox, & L. Brown (Eds.), *Methods of instruction for severely handicapped students* (pp. 47–69). Baltimore: Paul H. Brookes.

Wolery, M. (1994a). Instructional strategies for teaching young children with special needs. In M. Wolery & J. S. Wilbers (Eds.), *Including children with special needs in early childhood programs* (pp. 119–150). Washington, DC: National Association for the Education of Young Children.

Wolery, M. (1994b). Implementing instruction for young children with special needs in early childhood classrooms. In M. Wolery & J. Wilbers (Eds.), *Including children with special needs in early childhood programs* (pp. 154–166). Washington, DC: National Association for the Education of Young Children.

Wolery, M. (2000). Recommended practices in child-focused interventions. In S. Sandall, M. E. McLean, & B. J. Smith (Eds.), *DEC recommended practices in early intervention/early childhood special education* (pp. 29–37). Longmont, CO: Sopris West.

Wolery, M. (2001). Embedding constant time delay in classroom activities. *Young Exceptional Children Monograph, 3,* 81–90.

Wolery, M., Bailey, D. B., & Sugai, G. M. (1988). *Effective teaching: Principles and procedures of applied behavior analysis with exceptional students*. Boston: Allyn & Bacon.

Wolery, M., Brashers, M. S., & Neitzel, J. C. (2002). Ecological congruence assessment for classroom activities and routines: Identifying goals and intervention practices in childcare. *Topics in Early Childhood Special Education. 22,* 131–142.

Wolery, M., McWilliam, R. A., & Bailey, D. B. (in press). *Teaching infants and preschoolers with disabilities* (3rd ed.). Upper Saddle River, NJ: Merrill/ Prentice Hall.

Monitoring Children's Progress and Intervention Implementation

Mark Wolery
Vanderbilt University

In this text, considerations, methods, and instruments are described for assessing infants and young children with developmental delays and disabilities to plan their intervention programs. Does assessment stop when a plan is developed? No, more emphasis is put on intervention activities, but assessment is never really completed. Each interaction with children provides opportunities to gather information for making decisions about their progress and intervention programs. In this chapter, such assessment is called *monitoring*. The purposes of monitoring are described, and then general considerations for doing monitoring assessments are presented. The next section describes data gathering methods for monitoring children's progress, and the final section focuses on monitoring the implementation of intervention.

PURPOSES OF MONITORING

Three broad purposes of monitoring children's progress are proposed: To (a) validate conclusions from an initial assessment; (b) develop a record of progress over time; and (c) determine whether to modify or revise intervention plans. Emphasis is placed on monitoring as an ongoing activity rather than as a periodic event (e.g., every six months or annually).

Validate Conclusions from Initial Assessment

To plan intervention—to develop individualized family service plans (IFSPs) and individualized educational programs (IEPs)—information often is gathered from multiple sources using multiple measurement strategies (testing, interviews, checklists, observations, judgment-based measures) (Neisworth & Bagnato, 2000). Teams then analyze the collected information and integrate the findings, draw conclusions, specify goals/outcomes, and select intervention practices. However, conclusions and decisions based on assessment

information may be faulty. Development is complex, it is further complicated by disabilities, children's settings are diverse and varied, and children change over time. Children's behavior also can vary considerably, depending on the social and physical contexts in which it occurs. Thus, information gathered during IFSP and IEP planning assessments may lead to conclusions that do not reflect children's behavior in other situations. For example, children's social and communicative behavior often is different when they are in familiar as compared with unfamiliar situations. Conducting assessments in natural settings and seeking parents' validation during the assessment process may minimize but not completely control for variations caused by different contexts. Finally, despite progress, our measurement methods and instruments are imperfect. Thus, decisions about goals and outcomes may be based on incomplete or faulty conclusions about children's abilities. To identify faulty conclusions, teams can monitor children's progress and use the collected data to make judgments about the adequacy of the initial plan; and, when indicated, the plan should be revised. Such monitoring should occur when the plan is first implemented.

Faulty conclusions and decisions about goals and outcomes occur on a continuum. At one extreme, goals are established for skills children already have in their repertoires—children can do the goal behavior but the assessment process indicated they did not. At the other extreme, goals and outcomes may be inappropriate because they are beyond children's capabilities or are inappropriate for children's current environments. Faulty conclusions and decisions also occur between these two extremes. Nonetheless, the time and energy of children and families should not be wasted on goals they have achieved, are impossible, or are not needed in their current settings. Whether the plan needs formal revision is a decision the entire team should make through formal or informal discussions.

Decisions about selected intervention practices also may be faulty. A solid foundation for intervention practices is emerging, but it is not yet complete (e.g., for summaries, see Barnett, Bell, & Carey, 1999; Guralnick, 1997; Odom & McLean, 1996; Sandall, McLean, & Smith, 2000; Wolery, Bailey, & McWilliam, in press). We often do not have information about (a) the conditions that help intervention practices "work;" (b) the prerequisite skills children need to benefit from practices and strategies; (c) the frequency with which they must be used; and (d) the levels of correct implementation needed for practices to produce maximal benefits. As a result, less than complete information is available for selecting interventions, which leads to the possibility that some practices may not work. Monitoring children's progress early in the implementation of interventions may identify ineffective practices.

Develop a Record of Progress

Another reason for monitoring is to develop a record describing children's progress and achievements. This record is important for several reasons. It provides a level of accountability for the team. It can alert the team to the need for a new plan when children achieve their goals or outcomes. The record can provide teams, including families, with concrete evidence that progress is being made, achievements exist, and celebration of accomplishments is in order. The record of progress also can alert teams when progress is not occurring as anticipated—leading the team to refocus efforts to address high-priority concerns. This may involve collecting more precise information about children's progress and practice implementation. Finally, the record of progress can be used to make predictions about future progress. A well known principle of human behavior is that current performance is a useful predictor of future performance; given, of course, situations in which it occurs remain relatively unchanged (White & Haring, 1980). Having information about how children currently function allows us to make informed assumptions about how they will function in the immediate future. Such information

may be useful in making decisions about changes in programs and placements.

Determine Whether to Adjust Intervention Practices

A primary function of monitoring is to make adjustments in intervention practices and strategies. To fulfill this function, teams must address two issues: deciding whether changes are needed, and deciding what changes to make. Ongoing monitoring information often is useful for making these decisions.

Deciding Whether Changes Are Needed

Monitoring children's progress provides information about their usual patterns of performance, and four major patterns are possible. First: *Children may be making steady to rapid progress.* In such cases, teams should probably conclude all is well and no adjustments are needed to the intervention plan. When steady progress is occurring, the team should systematically monitor whether children generalize (transfer, use) the skill when and wherever it is appropriate and needed. If such generalization does not occur, then goals and procedures for promoting generalization should be developed (Billingsley, Burgess, Lynch, & Matlock, 1991). The second pattern in the monitoring data may be: *No changes are occurring in children's performance.* If the family and other team members believe the goal or outcome is critical or desirable, then the intervention strategies and practices or the context in which they are being applied should be changed. The nature of the change depends upon whether those practices and strategies are used often enough and with adequate accuracy.

The third and fourth patterns of performance call for careful deliberation by the team. In some cases, the monitoring data will indicate: *Progress is being made, but it is slow or changing only slightly.* In other instances, the data may indicate: *Performance is highly variable.* On some days, progress seems to be occurring; but on other days, no progress or even regression is seen. For these patterns (slow change and variable performance), teams must decide whether to make changes in the intervention. They need to take into account children's previous learning or developmental patterns, contextual factors potentially affecting performance (particularly if performance is variable), and any other information that is relevant. Once a decision is made to change the intervention, then they must decide what to change.

Deciding How to Modify Interventions It is easy to see how monitoring children's progress leads to conclusions about whether changes are needed, but it is less obvious to see how that information can be used to make decisions about what to change. In context, however, such potential may be more obvious; consider the following examples.

> *Hoi's intervention team identified using two- and three-word statements with agent-action and agent-action-object structures as an intervention goal. They decided to use incidental teaching (Kaiser, Hancock, & Nietfeld, 2000) as an intervention strategy during free-play time in the classroom to teach this goal. The incidental teaching procedure involves the adult responding to Hoi's initiations and providing a request for more elaborate language (and assistance, if necessary) after each initiation. Over a couple of weeks, they monitored his use of the identified language forms and saw no increases. However, they also noticed on several days he made no initiations and on the remaining days he made only one initiation. Since the procedure is used only after initiations, the monitoring data suggest they need to restructure the free-play to increase his initiations. Thus, the monitoring data showed he was not making progress (indicated a change was needed); and the monitoring data showed the intervention, incidental teaching, was not being used frequently because Hoi was not initiating (it identified the change that was needed in the intervention plan). Thus, they could restructure the free-play session to provide more opportunities for Hoi to initiate and thereby experience the intervention procedure.*

> *Latasha's intervention team set playing with classmates as an intervention goal. As strategies,* *they decided to ensure that she was in play areas with socially responsive and playful peers with "social" as compared with "isolate" toys available (Odom & Strain, 1984; Ivory & McCollum, 1999). Over a couple of weeks, the team collected monitoring information and found Latasha had many opportunities to play with peers, but she rarely did so. They also noted she frequently took toys from peers and never offered them toys. Thus, they determined that teaching her to share would assist her in playing with others, and they decided to use a peer-assisted intervention (Kohler & Strain, 1999; Kohler, Strain, Hoyson, & Jamieson, 1997) to help her learn to share. In this case, monitoring data indicated a change was needed and another intervention also was needed to increase Latasha's likelihood of playing with her peers.*

> *The intervention team for Jorge and Emily identified peer imitation as a goal for both children. They decided to use time delay in the context of art activities to teach peer imitation (Venn et al., 1993). Time delay involves providing children with opportunities to do the target behavior (in this case, imitate a peer) and then provides them with the assistance (prompts) needed. Over repeated opportunities, the assistance is delayed for a few seconds after the opportunity is provided (Wolery, Ault, & Doyle, 1992). When the teacher noted a peer doing a distinct behavior during art activities, she said to Jorge or Emily, "See what (peer's name) is doing; you do it." She then assisted one of them in doing what the peer was doing. Over days she removed her assistance by delaying it in time. After a couple of weeks, the monitoring data indicated that neither Jorge nor Emily was imitating their peers independently. For Jorge, the monitoring information indicated he rarely looked at the peer when the teacher asked him to; clearly, he could not learn to imitate his peer if he did not see what they did. As a result, the intervention team decided to have the peer call Jorge's name and prompt imitation only after Jorge looked at the peer. Because Emily looked at the peer, but consistently responded incorrectly (did not imitate) before the teacher provided assistance, the team decided to provide the assistance more quickly and to remove it more slowly. In both cases, the monitoring information suggested a change was needed and provided guidance in what changes were potentially useful.*

Carie's intervention team identified increasing her engagement during story time as an intervention goal. The interventions they identified for promoting engagement were reading storybooks that had repetitive language and reading with animation and active participation by the children (Wolery & Wolery, 1992). After a couple of weeks of monitoring, it appeared that Carie was engaged for about half the time, and her levels of engagement were not increasing. Thus, a change was needed. Two other conclusions were drawn from the data. When the teacher asked a question about the story or encouraged them to say some of the repetitive words in the story, Carie was more attentive for a few seconds. In addition, she was more engaged at the beginning than end of each story. The teacher decided to read shorter stories and to increase gradually the length and to add more questions and opportunities for children to respond toward the end of those stories.

In these examples, monitoring data indicated a change was needed. Furthermore, it provided guidance in deciding what changes were needed in the intervention strategies and practices. In Hoi's case, the intervention was not being used because he did not initiate, so the team restructured the context to increase his initiations. In Latasha's case, she needed to learn a new behavior (sharing) to increase her chances of playing with peers; another intervention was needed for this skill. With Jorge, a change was made to increase his attention to peer's behavior; with Emily a need existed to remove the teacher assistance more slowly. With Carie, the teacher needed shorter stories and more opportunities for active participation toward the end of stories. Monitoring information is useful in making two decisions: deciding whether a change is needed, and if so, deciding what type of change to make in the intervention. In each case, information about the context was important in deciding which changes were indicated in the intervention. Some intervention strategies, particularly prompting procedures, have well-developed data-decision rules to guide teams' changes when given data patterns appear (Wolery et al., 1992).

In addition, some general data-decision rules have been proposed and found useful (Haring & Liberty, 1990; Liberty & Haring, 1990). These are discussed later in the chapter.

Summary

Collecting information on children's progress (monitoring) is useful for three reasons. It provides a check on the extent to which intervention plans (goals and strategies) are adequate. It allows teams to develop a record of children's progress and thereby identify when new plans are needed and to help in making decisions about the future. Finally, monitoring can help teams decide whether to make changes in intervention practices, and, if so, what changes are needed.

GENERAL CONSIDERATIONS/ GUIDELINES FOR MONITORING PROGRESS

Although the value of monitoring is apparent, actually conducting monitoring activities is challenging. The following guidelines are presented to assist teams in organizing and carrying out their monitoring activities and responsibilities.

Monitoring Activities Should Be Based on the Intervention Plan

The intent of IEPs and IFSPs is that they will guide intervention. Such plans are designed to identify important goals and outcomes, thus, monitoring progress on them is important. Ideally, each goal or outcome on a young child's plan should be monitored on some schedule. When developing a monitoring system, the intervention plan serves as a starting point—it identifies, in large part, what should be monitored. Monitoring systems will vary from infant to infant and from child to child, reflecting the unique aspects of their plans. The law requires regular reports of children's progress be given to their families. One option for doing this is to use a three-column table. In the first column, each goal is listed in a separate row. In the second column, a check is provided for each goal that is currently being addressed. In the third column, a summary of current progress is provided either in the form of summarized data and/or a narrative description. This type of summary provides a quick check for teams of children's progress as well as serving as a document for discussions with families.

Monitoring Activities Should Address Global Indices of Children's Behavior

In addition to children's intervention plans, monitoring should address broad aspects of children's behavior. For young children in group-care situations, their participation and engagement in activities should be monitored regularly (Barnett et al., 1999), as should how much time they are unoccupied or waiting for materials or help. Although children may not have goals related to engagement, regularly assessing levels of engagement and of waiting time provides information about how children's time is spent and identifies needed changes in the classroom ecology (Raspa, McWilliam, & Ridley, 2001). Also, children's levels of social contact and social play should be monitored even when their plans do not contain specific goals in these areas (see Chapter 13 for methods). Such information may identify children who have minimal social contact or negative interactions and thus need goals in these areas, as well as identifying factors to change and enhance the social climate of the setting (Odom & Bailey, 2001). The general levels of problem or maladaptive behavior also should be monitored on a regular basis (Kozloff, 1994). When monitoring global factors, it is desirable to document children's change over time on the same measures such as developmental tools. Traditionally, such data collection has been time consuming and cumbersome. Recent advances in developing general growth outcomes may solve this issue and lead to

meaningful measures of children's progress (Priest et al., 2001).

The Quality of Children's Classroom Environments Should Be Monitored

Children in high-quality classes appear to have better outcomes than children in low-quality classes (Bowman, Donovan, & Burns, 2001). Variables such as the classroom e.g., space, schedule, materials and social ecology (Odom & Bailey, 2001) should be monitored. Procedures for measuring the quality environments are described in Chapter 8. The rationale for regular monitoring is twofold: First, to identify deficits that can be corrected, and second to determine whether actions designed to correct such deficits were successful.

Monitoring Activities Should Be Planned

Because monitoring is important and is easy to forget, it must be planned. Planning monitoring activities includes: (a) identifying what information will be collected, (b) deciding who is responsible for collecting it, (c) selecting situations in which the information will be collected, (d) deciding how often it will be collected, and (e) deciding who is responsible for analyzing the collected information. As noted above, monitoring should include children's progress on their individualized goals/outcomes and their global behavior. The validity with which goals and outcomes are assessed is an important consideration (Barnett et al., 1999). For example, if a goal is to increase Max's conversations with peers, several measures may be appropriate: how often Max talks with peers, percentage of peers' communicative initiations Max responds to, number of communicative initiations Max makes to peers, percentage of the communicative initiations to which peers respond, number of turns per conversation, and number of peers with whom Max has conversations. Each of these will provide information about Max's conversations with peers. If the goal has a criterion statement, then that statement can be used in developing the monitoring system. The intent of the goal also should be considered. If the goal was written because Max engaged in few conversations, measuring the frequency of conversations may be a relevant measure; if the goal was established because Max had frequent but short conversations, the number of turns per conversation may be a more important measure; if the goal was established because Max rarely responded to peers' communicative initiations, the percentage of responses to peers' initiations is a relevant measure. If the monitoring system does not measure the intent of the goal/outcome, then it will be invalid and of limited usefulness in making decisions about intervention effectiveness.

Determining who should collect the information varies greatly depending upon the goal, type of services (e.g., home or classroom based), families' views and desires, resources of the program, and many other factors. Generally, adults who spend large amounts of time with the child are key candidates for monitoring progress; thus, teachers, child-care workers, and family members are potential candidates. However, individuals who see the child regularly but not daily (e.g., a therapist who sees the child weekly) also can monitor progress. The plan should specify who is responsible for monitoring each goal/outcome.

The plan also should specify the situations in which monitoring will occur. While this must include the setting, it should also include other important aspects. For example, to monitor children's self-feeding behaviors, mealtimes are appropriate settings. Whether the child is hungry and has preferred food available, however, also are relevant factors that would influence self-feeding behavior. When possible, such conditions should be part of the monitoring plan.

The frequency with which monitoring is needed varies from goal to goal. A general rule is: Monitoring should occur regularly and often enough to have sufficient information for making decisions, but no more often than necessary. This

issue is discussed in more detail in the next subsection, however, a general schedule for monitoring (e.g., weekly) should be established.

We monitor children's progress to make decisions, thus, analysis of the collected information is important. While a variety of individuals may monitor progress, someone should be responsible for reviewing and summarizing the information. For example, teachers and parents may collect information on a child's communication goals, and the speech-language pathologist could review the information and summarize it. Decisions about changes in programs, however, are team decisions.

Monitoring Activities Should Consider Contextual Factors

To be meaningful, monitoring activities should occur in authentic, realistic situations in which the behaviors of the goals and outcomes are relevant and needed (Neisworth & Bagnato, 2000), and factors that may influence the occurrence of the behavior should be recognized. For example, communicative skills are likely to be dependent on the responsiveness of partners and interesting events; play skills are likely to vary by the availability and novelty of toys; social interactions are likely to vary by the availability and responsiveness of interactive partners. Thus, identifying situations in which monitoring occurs is an important decision. Also, when interpreting monitoring information, variations in relevant factors and their influence on children's behavior should be considered.

Monitoring Should Address Multiple Persons' Perspectives of Progress

Because children's skills are meaningful only in context and because most skills are needed in multiple situations, input is needed from different individuals. Families, teachers, and therapists who work with the child each have unique and important information to contribute to decision-making. Thus, a well-developed monitoring system seeks input from multiple people who interact and observe the child in different situations and settings.

Monitoring Should Occur Regularly and Frequently

As noted, monitoring should occur regularly and often enough to get the information needed to make valid decisions, but no more often than is necessary. Often, but not always, more accurate decisions are made when more information is available (Munger, Snell, & Loyd, 1989); however, a balance is needed between the demands of monitoring multiple goals and providing high-quality care and early intervention. For some goals, daily monitoring may be needed; for others, weekly monitoring is adequate; for still others, monitoring every two weeks is sufficient. The frequency of monitoring depends on many factors, such as the importance of the goal, extent to which progress is being made, and other demands on caregivers.

More Frequent Monitoring Should Occur for High-Priority Goals   Goals are not equal; some goals are more important than others. Because more monitoring information often results in more accurate decisions, important goals should be monitored more often. For example, in describing interventions for moving children who are dependent on gastrostomy-tube feeding to oral feeding, Luiselli and Luiselli (1995) recommend collecting data each time the child is fed orally. Less frequent monitoring, however, can be used with less important goals. Families' views are particularly critical when deciding which goals are most important.

More Frequent Monitoring Should Occur for Goals on Which Decisions Are Needed
When children's progress is not occurring, or is slow or variable, then changes are needed and information is needed to make the correct decisions. Thus, more frequent monitoring is neces-

sary when children's progress is questionable. Also, after modifying an intervention, more frequent monitoring should occur to evaluate the effects of those changes.

Monitoring Should Be Purposeful

Monitoring is done for three purposes: to validate the initial assessment, to develop a record of progress over time, and to make decisions about whether and what modifications are needed in intervention strategies and practices. These purposes should be kept in mind when planning and carrying out monitoring activities. Collecting volumes of information but not using it to make decisions is no more defensible than not collecting data. The information that is collected should be used. To be useful, however, monitoring is like other assessment practices: The measurement procedures must be both reliable and valid. Reliability refers to the consistency of the information that is collected. With direct observational data, estimates of reliability are usually obtained by having two or more persons observe and record the same events simultaneously but independently. Interobserver agreement percentages are then calculated (Tawney & Gast, 1984). To increase the probability of agreement (reliability), the behavior being observed must be defined precisely, the data collection procedures should be simple to use, and the conditions under which data are collected should be free of major distractions. As a rule, it is better to have less data that are reliable than to have volumes of unreliable data. Validity, as discussed above, deals with the extent to which the measurement procedures match the intent of the goals or outcomes and the extent to which the measurement occurs in authentic contexts.

Summary

When monitoring children's progress, several guidelines are important. The outcomes and goals are the basis for developing a valid monitoring plan, but certain general aspects of children's behavior (e.g., engagement and social contact) also should be monitored. A monitoring plan should be developed and implemented in authentic contexts, using the input of multiple individuals, and occurring regularly and frequently. The information should be analyzed, because the purpose of monitoring is to get information to make decisions.

APPROACHES TO MONITORING

Three broad approaches are used to monitor children's progress: narrative descriptions and judgment-based assessments, work samples, and direct observation. Emphasis is placed in this section on direct observation because of its utility; however, each approach is defensible and useful to early intervention personnel.

Narrative Descriptions and Judgment-Based Monitoring

Narrative descriptions technically are a type of direct observation, and many judgment-based measures are based on observations. However, these approaches are discussed separately from direct behavioral observation because of the type of information gathered and differences in recording procedures. A complete monitoring system may use narrative descriptions, judgment-based measures, and direct observation in conjunction with clinical judgment.

Narrative Descriptions   Narrative descriptions include three types of observational recording systems: anecdotal records, running records, and specimen descriptions (Thurman & Widerstrom, 1990). Anecdotal records—often called progress notes—are used frequently in many professions to record observations of various kinds. They are written descriptions of events containing relevant clinical information. Such notes can be written for each goal on a regular basis and thereby provide a summary of children's progress over time. In fact, having a list of children's goals to use at the end of the day, and writing notes about each goal helps build a record of progress. Progress notes also are useful when making decisions about how to change interventions. Notes can provide information about the context in which the intervention is used, children's reaction to the intervention, and the accuracy with which the intervention is used. Notes should be written soon after the event occurs and should describe the situation e.g., setting, time as well as the sequence of things observed (i.e., the beginning, middle, and end) of the event (Thurman & Widerstrom, 1990). Notes should describe children's behavior in context, but qualitative information, inferences, and hypotheses may be included if identified as such. Progress notes can be collected efficiently, but are open to bias, inaccurate inferences, and the writer's memory and focus of attention.

Running records involve recording (usually writing down) all of the child's behavior and the relevant events for a period of time. When using running records, the times and places of observations should be selected purposefully, and the setting and situation should be described. The primary body of running records is a thorough description of what the child does, how he or she does it, and the events that may be related to the behavior (e.g., the behavior of others directed to the child). When completing a running record, emphasis is on describing behaviors and events; inferences and interpretation should be minimal. When running records are used, they must be transcribed soon after the observation. Transcripts are sometimes organized by placing events and behavior into three columns: antecedent events, child behavior, and consequent events. In monitoring, the primary function of running records is to collect information for solving specific problems. For example, if other methods indicate a child is not making progress and little information explains the lack of progress, collecting a running record may be illuminating. Running records are less useful in routine monitoring, because of the extensive time commitments involved in collecting and analyzing the data.

Specimen descriptions are similar to running records and use similar procedures. However, specimen descriptions are designed to portray specific episodes or a series of episodes. Thus, data collection is tied more to a given event than to all of the behavior that may occur. For example, if a child had frequent negative interactions with peers during transitions, a specimen description might provide a hypothesis about why this was occurring. Data would be collected only during transitions. The advantage of specimen descriptions is information can be collected on specific events or episodes; the disadvantages are similar to those of running records.

Judgment-Based Assessment Judgment-based assessment refers to "the formal use of structured, quantified judgment to (a) complement norm- and curriculum-based measures; (b) measure ambiguous child characteristics; and (c) serve as a vehicle for team decision making" (Neisworth & Fewell, 1990, p. ix). Judgment-based assessments can involve rating almost an endless array of factors, including children's developmental skills, their interests, their temperament, their progress on goals, and many others. Rating scales are used to quantify information about respondents' perceptions. Issues to consider in developing and evaluating rating scales are described by Spector (1992). As noted earlier, monitoring systems should include input from all individuals who have sustained contact with the child. Judgment-based measures can be used to collect such perceptions. The purpose, of course, is not to determine who is correct but to obtain a broad picture of the child's progress in different contexts. Judgment-based measures also allow assessment of important qualities, which may be difficult to measure; examples are persistence, flexibility, happiness, anxiousness, and so forth.

Work Sampling System

Meisels (1993) describes a performance assessment system for use in early childhood and early elementary grades. This system, called the Work Sampling System™ (WSS), contains three components: "(1) developmental checklists, (2) portfolios, and (3) summary reports" (Meisels, 1993, p. 36). The checklists are completed by teachers based on their observations and knowledge of each child and are not designed to be used as tests. The portfolios include "core" items and "other" items. The core items are products of the child's work that are collected in several areas at least three times each year. Other items vary by child and by date of collection. Because many young children's key activities do not result in permanent products, photographs of achievements are recommended (Hanline, Milton, & Phelps, 2001); of course, video or audio recordings also can be used. The summary reports are written narratives completed by the teacher (based on observations) and describe the child's performance in each domain. The summary reports are conducted three times a year.

The WSS appears to be a reliable and valid indication of children's progress, at least for kindergarten age children (Meisels, Liaw, Dorfman, & Nelson, 1995). Further, parents who received reports based on the WSS indicated the system was beneficial for their children and reported liking the system better than standard report cards (Meisels, Xue, Bickel, Nicholson, & Atkins-Burnett, 2001). Some attempts have been made to use the system with young children with disabilities, and in general it is thought to provide useful information when integrated with other monitoring systems (Schwartz & Olswang, 1996).

Direct Behavioral Observation

Direct observation as a means to monitor children's progress has a rich history in the science of human behavior (Bijou, Peterson, Harris, Allen, & Johnston, 1969). It involves observing and counting behavior; for complete discussions, see Cooper

(1980); Tawney and Gast (1984); Thompson, Felce, and Symons (2000); and White and Haring (1980). Journals publishing studies with single subject designs (e.g., *Journal of Applied Behavior Analysis, Journal of Behavioral Education, Journal of Positive Behavior Interventions,* and many others) include examples of using direct observation to measure children's behavior over time. Five steps are involved in using direct observation in monitoring: (1) defining behaviors and identifying relevant dimensions, (2) selecting data collection systems and data sheets, (3) selecting observation situations and times, (4) checking data collection accuracy, and (5) analyzing data and making decisions.

Defining Behaviors and Identifying Their Relevant Dimensions

Intervention outcomes and goals are the base from which monitoring systems are developed, but goals are often written in a general sense and do not define precisely the behaviors children are to perform. When using direct observation, teams must decide if the behavior or the behavior's effect is the intent of the goal (White, 1980). For example, if the goal is to increase a child's social interactions, the behaviors might be giving an object to peers or speaking to peers; the effect (also called *function*) is the fact that an interaction is started. A behavior, of course, is a movement with a definite beginning and end that can be performed repeatedly and measured reliability. The effect or function is the result of doing the behavior. For some goals, the effect may be critical and the behavior used to cause the effect will be less important, as in the goal of initiating interactions. In other cases, the behaviors used may be more important. For example, in self-feeding, a child who uses finger feeding has the effect (getting food to his mouth); however, using a spoon (specific behavior) may be an appropriate goal. In this case the behavior rather than the effect is important. In fact, in such situations, the goal is to replace an old behavior (finger feeding) that accomplishes the effect with a new behavior (using a spoon) that has the same effect. Thus, the team must decide whether the behavior or its effect will

be measured. If it is the effect, then that effect must be defined precisely and examples of behaviors used to cause the effect should be listed. If the behavior is to be measured, the behavior's dimension should be identified. Each behavior has several potential dimensions or characteristics: frequency, intensity, duration, latency, endurance, and accuracy.

Frequency (or *rate*) refers to how often a behavior occurs; more technically it refers to how often a behavior occurs in a given time period. *Intensity* refers to the amount of force with which the behavior occurs. *Duration* refers to the length of time a given behavior lasts. *Latency* refers to how long it takes a child to initiate a behavior once a cue has occurred. *Endurance* refers to the length of time a given behavior can be performed repeatedly with a rest period. *Accuracy* refers to whether a child's behavior conforms to a specific definition describing that behavior. When defining a behavior for monitoring intervention effectiveness, the most appropriate dimension should be selected. Two questions are relevant. First, if the child is to be more developmentally advanced, independent, or socially acceptable, which dimension(s) of the behavior should be changed? Second, which dimension can be measured most accurately and easily? For example, if one of Liam's goals is to name common objects, the accuracy of naming is more important than the frequency, intensity, latency, duration, or endurance. Accuracy will make him more advanced, and it can be measured accurately. However, Lynette hits others often and hurts them, so the frequency and intensity of her hitting should be changed to increase her social acceptability. The duration of the hits, latency from some cue, endurance, and accuracy of hits are less important dimensions. When frequency and intensity are applied to the second question, frequency can be measured more easily and accurately than intensity. The important dimension will vary from behavior to behavior and goal to goal. Accuracy may be important with a naming task, frequency with an aggressive behavior, intensity with a behavior such as speaking loudly enough, duration with behaviors such as holding up one's head or playing, latency with behaviors such as responding to others' initiations, and endurance with behaviors such as walking.

Selecting Data-Collection Systems and Designing Data-Collection Sheets Data collection systems used to monitor children's progress are event sampling, time sampling, category sampling, levels of assistance recording, and task-analytic recording. These systems are described below.

Event Sampling *Event sampling* refers to counting behaviors as they occur. The onset of the behavior cues the observer to record its occurrence. The simplest event sampling occurs when an adult tallies each time a behavior occurs; examples are counting the number of toys with which a child plays, correct responses, peers to whom a child speaks, steps taken, and many others. Event recording is best used with behaviors that have definite beginnings and ends and are relatively brief (have a consistent and short duration). The behaviors are recorded or counted as they occur. Some behaviors produce permanent products, which can be counted after the behavior occurs. Examples are art work (e.g., painted or drawn pictures), soiled diapers, toys put on shelves during cleanup, and number of pieces put in a puzzle.

To use event recording, several issues should be considered. The behavior should be defined precisely so no questions exist about when to record and what is being measured. As noted above, the team must select the dimension of behavior (accuracy, frequency, duration, latency, intensity, endurance) that is most relevant and easily recorded. The dimension selected influences how data are collected and interpreted. Accuracy data frequently are collected during instructional sessions when children have opportunities to respond to target stimuli. In such cases, responses are recorded as correct or incorrect based on specific definitions, and data are analyzed in terms of percentage correct and incorrect. Percentage is calculated by dividing the number

of each type of response by the number of opportunities provided.

Percentage data have distinct advantages. They are easy to calculate, especially when the number of opportunities are 10, 20, or 25. People readily understand percentages so the results are easily communicated to others. Percentage data also have limitations; a major one is an artificial ceiling is placed on performance. For example, two children could be at 100% correct, but one could have performed the same number of responses in half the time required by the other child. Many behaviors must be performed quickly to be useful, and percentage data do not give information about response speed. To deal with this problem, the rate of responding can be calculated with accuracy data. *Rate* refers to the number of responses occurring in a given time period, for example, a week, a day, or a minute. Using a minute as the time unit is useful because it is sensitive to change and can be recorded quickly; however, any standard time period can be used if data are collected for the entire observation and the behavior can occur at any time during the entire period. Rate is calculated by dividing the number of responses (e.g., number correct) by the number of time units (e.g., minutes). Thus, with accuracy data, correct and error rates can be calculated as well as percentages. Another disadvantage of using percentage data is they may be insensitive measures unless a large number of opportunities are provided. For example, if only five opportunities are provided, each response is worth 20 percentage points. A rule of thumb is that percentage should not be used unless there are at least 20 opportunities. However, many examples exist in which as few as 10 opportunities were provided, yet the data were useful for making decisions.

Frequency data can be collected on almost any behavior that has a short and consistent duration. For example, frequency data could be collected on the number of Daron's crying episodes, but the duration of episodes could vary considerably. On one day he might cry three times and each episode may last 30 to 40 minutes; on another day, Daron may cry six times, but each episode lasts 2 minutes. Although he had more episodes of crying on the second day, the crying would be a greater problem on the first. Frequency data can be recorded in a number of ways, including putting a tally mark on a data-collection sheet, using a golf counter or other counting device, or putting a bean in a jar on the shelf. The number of ways to record frequency data is limited only by an interventionist's creativity. The rule is to get an accurate count with a minimum of effort and time. When frequency data are being collected, the length of the observation period should be recorded. To say Lisa displayed three peer imitations on one day and six on another is not useful unless the time observed on both days is equal. By recording the length of the observation, frequency data can be interpreted meaningfully even when the lengths of observations vary, because frequency data can be converted to rate. Further, dividing the observation into several intervals will help in interpreting the data. For example, if you are counting the number of words said during a 20-minute play period, the observation could be divided into ten 2-minute intervals, allowing you to determine when during the 20 minutes the child spoke or spoke most often.

Duration data can be collected on behaviors lasting longer than a couple seconds. Each response is timed to get duration data. Although any clock can be used, stopwatches increase the precision of data collection. Duration data can be analyzed in three ways: total duration, average duration per occurrence, and percent of time. *Total duration* refers to the total amount of time the child does the target behavior during the observation session. Some stopwatches are designed to start and stop and start again without being reset and are useful for collecting total duration. The teacher simply starts and stops the watch each time the behavior occurs and then reads the time at the end of the session. *Duration per occurrence* refers to the average length of time the child does the behavior. This requires the observer to record the duration of behavior

each time it occurs and then involves dividing by the number of occurrences. *Percent of time* refers to the percentage of a session the child does the behavior. When data are collected so that the average duration per occurrence is recorded and the length of the observation session also is recorded, then each of the three calculations can be made. Duration data can be combined with frequency data, and this is called "real time" data (Thompson et al., 2000).

Latency data also require observers to time events, and stopwatches should be used. The timing should occur from the end of a cue until the start of the response. As with duration, the total latency for a session or the average latency per cue can be calculated. Generally, the average latency is more meaningful because the measure is tied to the number of cues provided.

Intensity or magnitude of a response is relatively difficult to measure for most behaviors. Exceptions include such things as how high or how far a child can jump. In most cases, however, measurement of intensity requires special instrumentation such as noise or pressure gauges. As a result, intensity is rarely measured to monitor progress. Similarly, endurance data is rarely collected but may be useful for some behaviors. For example, a teacher could time how long a child can repeatedly perform a discrete behavior such as walking or running, or how long a child will play beside others before moving away.

In addition to defining the behavior and selecting the relevant behavioral dimension, event sampling systems should be well calibrated (White & Haring, 1980). A *well-calibrated system* is one in which each occurrence of the behavior represents relatively equal amounts of behavior. For example, if the teacher is monitoring a child's ability to work puzzles, the number of pieces inserted or number of puzzles completed could be counted. Number of pieces would be better, because one puzzle might have four pieces and another sixteen. If number of puzzles completed were counted, the two puzzles would represent very different amounts of the behavior. A well-calibrated system also is sensitive to change—allows small changes to be detected. Finally, teams should select behaviors that are relatively easy to record. If the requirements of monitoring are too costly in terms of time and effort, less monitoring is likely to occur. As a result, ineffective interventions will be used longer than they should be.

Data-collection sheets are forms on which the record of the observation is written. Tawney and Gast (1984) recommend having three types of information on each data collection sheet: situational, performance, and summary. *Situational information* tells who was observed, who did the observing, what behavior was recorded, and when the observation occurred. Data sheets may also include the activity, beginning and ending times of the observation, and the strategies being used. *Performance information* is the actual record of behavior coming from the observation. This section of the data sheet varies depending on the type of data being recorded. For example, if data are being collected to monitor the effects of a direct instruction program, correct, error, and no responses may be counted. The data collection sheet could have a column for each of these types of responses, and when one of them occurred, a check can be placed in the appropriate column. However, if data are being collected on how often an infant spits up, a space for tally marks may be sufficient. The third component of data sheets is *summary information.* This section should include the total observation time, totals for the data recorded (by type, if used), and anecdotal notes made by the observer to explain the data or to describe a related event or issue. Summary data are used to reduce the time required to analyze performance across days and are useful for transferring the data to graphs. Examples of event sampling data collection sheets for frequency and accuracy data are shown in Figure 17.1, data sheets for duration are shown in Figure 17.2, and data sheets for latency are shown in Figure 17.3. These data sheets are samples; teams should design their own to match their situation, but be sure to include the three components (situational, performance, and summary information). Many different sample data sheets also are available in *Show Me the Data!* (Experimental Education Unit, 2001), which also is available on CD-ROM to down load the sheets for use in classrooms.

Time Sampling   *Time sampling* involves recording the occurrence of a behavior at a given time or time interval. Unlike event sampling in which the occurrence of the behavior cues the observer to record, in time sampling, time cues the observer to record. Time-sampling procedures can be used with discrete behaviors (those with relatively short durations) or behaviors of longer and more variable duration. Time sampling also can be used with categories of behaviors. In its simplest form, time sampling involves observers recording at prespecified times whether a behavior is occurring. For example, a teacher may check an infant at 9:00 and every 10 minutes thereafter and record whether she is sleeping or may see which toddlers are playing with toys every 5 minutes. Time sampling can be used with difficult-to-count behaviors and can be used to measure several children simultaneously. Using time-sampling procedures has some of the same considerations as event sampling; behaviors must be defined and relevant dimensions must be selected, but it also has some special considerations.

The type of time-sampling procedure must be selected. At least three types have been described: momentary, partial-interval, and whole-interval time sampling. With all three types, the observational session is divided into intervals. With *momentary* time sampling, the observer records whether the behavior is occurring at a specific time. For example, the 5-hour day may be divided into twenty 15-minute intervals. If the day began at 8:00, the observer would check the target child at 8:00, 8:15, 8:30, 8:45, 9:00, and so on. At each time (e.g., 8:15), the observer would record whether the behavior was occurring *at that instant*. With the *partial-interval*

Form A

Name: _____ Date: _____ Observer : _____

Behavior/objective: _____

Time: _____ to _____ Total time: _____

Trial	C	E	NR
1			
2			
3			
4			
5			
6			
7			
8			
9			
10			
Total #			
Total %			

Comments: _____

Form B

Name: _____ Date: _____ Observer: _____

Behavior/objective: _____

Time: _____ to _____ Total time: _____

Trial	Response		
1	C	E	NR
2	C	E	NR
3	C	E	NR
4	C	E	NR
5	C	E	NR
6	C	E	NR
7	C	E	NH
8	C	E	NR
9	C	E	NR
10	C	E	NR
Total #			
Total %			

Comments: _____

FIGURE 17.1

Examples of event recording data collection sheets for frequency and accuracy data

Note: Form A is used to record the accuracy of children's responses (C=correct, E=error, NR=no response); the observer would put a check mark in the appropriate column for each trial. *Form B* also is to record accuracy data; the teacher would circle or slash the letter in the appropriate column for each trial. *Form C* (next page) is for frequency (rate) data collection for use for an entire week. The observer would place a tally mark each time the behavior occurred in the column titled "Record of Behav." *Form D* also is for frequency (rate) data; the observer simply puts tally marks in the column each time a behavior occurs. *Form E* also is for frequency (rate) data; the observer circles or puts a slash mark in a consecutively higher number each time the behavior occurs. *Form F* is for frequency (rate) data that is broken into 2-minute intervals, allowing analysis of when behaviors occurred.

Form C

Name: _____ Date: _____ Observer: _____

Behavior/objective: _____

Day	# min Observ.	Record of Behav.	Total #	Rate
Mon				
Tues				
Wed				
Thur				
Fri				

Comments: _____

Form D

Name: _____ Date: _____ Observer: _____

Behavior/objective: _____

Time: ____ to _____ Total time: _____

Occurrences

Comments: _____

Total # of occurences: _____

Rate of occurences: _____

Form E

Name: _____ Date: _____ Observer: _____

Behavior/objective: _____

Time: ____ to _____ Total time: _____

Occurrences

1	2	3	4	5
6	7	8	9	10
11	12	13	14	15
16	17	18	19	20

Comments: _____

Total # of occurences: _____ .

Rate of occurences: _____

Form F

Name: _____ Date: _____ Observer: _____

Behavior/objective: _____

Time: ____ to _____ Total time: _____

2-min. intervals	# of behaviors
Total # occurences	
Total Rate	

Comments: _____

FIGURE 17.1

Continued

Form A

Name: _____ Date: _____ Observer: _____
Behavior/objective: _____
Time: _____ to _____ Total time: _____

Start time	Stop time	Total
Total # of occurences		
Total duration		
Average duration per occurrence		

Comments: _____

Form B

Name: _____ Date: _____ Observer: _____
Behavior/objective: _____
Time: _____ to _____ Total time: _____

Occurrence	Time
# of occurences	
Total duration	
Average duration per occurrence	

Comments: _____

FIGURE 17.2

Examples of data collection sheets for duration data
Note: Form A allows the observer to record the start time of each behavior and the end time of each behavior. *Form B* allows the observer to record how long each behavior occurred, but not the specific start and stop time.

method, the observation period would be broken into intervals, and the observer would observe for the entire interval (e.g., from 8:00 to 8:15 and from 8:30 to 8:45). If the behavior occurs during the interval, it is scored as having occurred. With the *whole-interval* method, the observation period also is divided into intervals, and the observer must watch for the entire interval. How-ever, for a behavior to be scored as occurring, it must occur for the *entire* interval. The whole-interval method tends to underestimate the true occurrence of a behavior, and the partial-interval method tends to overestimate the occurrence (Barnett et al., 1999). Both of these procedures are quite demanding on teachers' time because the teacher must observe for the entire interval.

Form A

Name: _____ Date: _____ Observer: _____
Cue: _____
Behavior/objective: _____

Time Cue Ended	Time Behavior Started	Latency

Comments: _____
Total # of cues: _____
Total latency: _____
Average length of latency: _____

Form B

Name: _____ Date: _____ Observer: _____
Cue: _____
Behavior/objective: _____

Cue Number	Latency
1	
2	
3	
4	
5	

Comments: _____
Total # of cues: _____
Total latency: _____
Average length of latency: _____

FIGURE 17.3

Sample data sheets for recording latency data

Note: Form A allows the observer to record the time the cue was given and how long until the behavior was initiated. *Form B* allows the observer to simply record the latency after each cue.

However, when observation sessions are short (e.g., 10 minutes), these methods can be used. Momentary time sample is probably the easiest and most useful to teachers, because they can be involved in other activities between observation points. This method, however, is not sensitive to behaviors that last for relatively short durations or occur infrequently. With each method, the percentage of intervals in which the behavior is recorded as occurring is calculated.

Selecting a time-sampling procedure requires consideration of the duration and frequency of the behavior. This information is used to set the length of the observation interval. If a behavior is of short duration, the partial-interval method should be used, although long intervals will overestimate the behavior's occurrence. With partial-interval recording, "the interval length should be less than the shortest bout [duration] and also less than half the shortest" time between behaviors (Barnett et al., 1999, p. 56; word in brackets added). If the behavior is of long duration, momentary time sampling or the whole-interval method should be used. For whole-interval systems, the interval length should be "less than half of the shortest bout and also less than the shortest" time between behaviors (Barnett et al., 1999, p. 56). For frequently occurring behaviors of moderate or variable duration, the momentary method is better than the others because less observation time is required. For behaviors that occur infrequently (e.g., less than once every 15 or 20 minutes), time-sampling procedures may not be appropriate. Finally, integrating the method into a teacher's other activities must be considered.

Data sheets for time-sampling procedures vary depending on the specific system being used. A sample data collection sheet for a momentary time sample is shown in Figure 17.4. The behaviors *or* the children being measured are listed on the top, and the times are listed in the first column. When the time arrives, the teacher simply notes the occurrence or nonoccurrence of the behavior. In Figure 17.5, a data-collection sheet for partial-interval and whole-interval methods is shown. As with event sampling, numerous variations of recording sheets exist, and teams should design sheets appropriate to their situations. With time-sampling procedures, observers need a signal to cue them to record. Some naturally occurring

events (e.g., transitions) are sufficient. However, many important behaviors either occur between transitions or require more frequent observation. Timers, digital watches, and some stopwatches have quiet beeps that can be used. Tape recorders with tapes specifically made to signal observers also could be used.

Category Sampling   Category-sampling procedures involve collecting data on categories of behaviors. The categories are defined, and frequently, several different behaviors could fit into each category. Category-sampling procedures can be used in an event-sampling format or in a time-sampling format, although time sampling is more common. For example, a team could measure an infant's interactive behavior with the following categories: initiating interactions, responding to others' initiations, and terminating interactions. These categories are not behaviors; they are descriptions of the effects of a variety of behaviors. The infant could use eye gaze, cooing and vocalizations, movement of the limbs, smiles, and other behaviors separately and in combination to initiate interactions. Looking away, making fussy noises, and decreasing activity might be used to terminate interactions. If a time-sampling procedure were used, a 6-second, partial-interval recording technique could be employed during a play session with the infant's father. The observer would look at the infant for 6 seconds and score any categories for which the defined behaviors occurred. An advantage of category systems is that a variety of behaviors serving the same effects can be measured. Further, a number of different but related categories of responses can be recorded.

Several factors are important when constructing a category-sampling recording system. The categories and behaviors must be defined clearly. The coding system should be *exhaustive,* meaning any behavior observed should fit into one of the categories. Because it is nearly impossible to anticipate all behaviors, many category-sampling systems have a category called "other." In some

Form A

Observer: _____ Behavior: _____ Date: _____

Children: _____

Names of children or of behaviors being recorded

Time						
9:00						
9:10						
9:20						
9:30						
9:40						
9:50						
10:00						
Total						
% of intervals						

Comments: _____

Form B

Observer: _____ Date: _____

Children: _____

Names of children being observed

Time									
9:00	E	NE	W	E	NE	W	E	NE	W
9:10	E	NE	W	E	NE	W	E	NE	W
9:20	E	NE	W	E	NE	W	E	NE	W
9:30	E	NE	W	E	NE	W	E	NE	W
9:40	E	NE	W	E	NE	W	E	NE	W
9:50	E	NE	W	E	NE	W	E	NE	W
10:00	E	NE	W	E	NE	W	E	NE	W
Total	E	NE	W	E	NE	W	E	NE	W
% of intervals									

Comments: _____

FIGURE 17.4

Sample data collection sheets for momentary time sampling data

Note: Form A can be used with multiple behaviors of a single child or a single behavior of multiple children; the observer places a plus (+) in the column if the behavior occurs and a minus (−) if the behavior does not occur. *Form B* is for recording engagement (E), non-engagement (NE), and waiting (W) for three children; the observer circles or places a slash through the appropriate letter for each child.

cases, interventionists may be interested only in a certain type of response (e.g., communicative behaviors), and other behaviors such as play would simply be noted as "play" or "other." However, if the "other" category constitutes the majority of the record, a revision of the categories may be necessary. In addition to being exhaustive, the categories should be *mutually exclusive*, meaning

Name: _____ Date: _____ Observer: _____

Behavior: _____

Objective: _____

Observation time: _____to_____Total: _____

Observation	Intervals					
Minutes	1	2	3	4	5	6
Minute 1						
Minute 2						
Minute 3						
Minute 4						
Minute 5						
Minute 6						
Minute 7						
Minute 8						
MInute 9						
Minute 10						
Total						

Comments: _____

FIGURE 17.5

Sample data collection sheet for partial- or whole-interval recording
Note: Each minute of a 10-minute observation is divided into six 10-second intervals. The observer records whether the behavior occurred or did not occur in each interval.

no behavior could fit into more than one category. If behaviors fit into more than one category, then errors in recording will occur, and the data will be useless for making decisions. To save time, teachers should consider using existing category-sampling systems, some examples of which are presented in earlier chapters; others can be found in the research literature.

Category-sampling systems should include only the number of categories needed to make the decision being considered. If irrelevant categories are included, the accuracy of recording may be affected and interpretation complicated. An advantage of category sampling is that covariation between different classes of behavior can be detected. For example, George's aggressive behavior may vary with his play behavior. When he is playing he appears to be less aggressive and when he is not playing, his aggressions increase. Ellie, on the other hand, appears to be more

aggressive when the frequency of social initiations from other children increases. Category-sampling procedures allow teams to identify such relationships, develop relevant intervention plans, and monitor the effects of the intervention. For example, with George, the team should develop a plan to increase his toy play rather than use a procedure to decrease his aggression. Similarly, Ellie's teacher should teach her to respond positively to peers' initiations. Category-sampling procedures also allow teams to measure the effects of one person's behavior on another. For example, in parent-infant interactions, the behaviors of the parent and the infant each may influence the behavior of the other. An interventionist may have a hypothesis that an infant is fussier and less playful when the parent is more directive. The interventionist could measure four categories of behavior: parental directiveness, parental responsiveness, child play behavior, and fussiness. Such data may indicate whether an association between fussiness and parental directiveness appears to be true; if so, an intervention could be developed.

When category systems are used, teams must choose between event- or time-sampling procedures. Time-sampling methods are used more frequently, but exceptions occur. Category sampling may be used in an event-sampling format when a child behavior requires careful measurement, occurs infrequently, and when multiple behaviors appear to produce the same effect. For example, a child may hit, bite, and pull the hair of other children and may use these actions to express frustration. To ensure that every instance of these behaviors is noted, the team could define each and record them in a category called "aggressive behavior." Similarly, children may be learning specific communicative functions (e.g., requesting), and the team may want to record each instance of requesting throughout the day. The nature of the request or the object being requested may be unimportant. In both of these examples, the behavior (aggressive behavior or requests) would prompt the teacher to record.

Usually, however, category sampling uses a time-sampling format. For example, the team may want to record children's play behaviors. Different categories of play could be developed, and a momentary time-sampling procedure could be used to record which categories were observed. When time-sampling procedures are used, at least one category should be recorded in each interval. When the categories represent a subset of the total possible behaviors, the team can devise a separate category representing the absence of those behaviors. For example, if solitary, on-looker, parallel, and cooperative play were being measured, it is possible that none of these categories would be observed in a given interval. In such cases, a category called "nonplay" behaviors could be added. The percentage of intervals in which this category is marked can be used to calculate the amount of time the child is not playing. With category sampling, the data sheets can vary from

relatively simple to quite complex. Two simple data collection sheets for recording aggressive and disruptive behaviors are shown in Figure 17.6. A time-sampling data sheet for measuring levels of social play is shown in Figure 17.7. Sometimes data are collected simultaneously on several children and for several behaviors.

Care should be taken when interpreting data from category-sampling procedures. The percentage of intervals the behavior occurred in each category is calculated and compared across categories. Few norms exist, however, telling how frequently different categories of behavior should occur. It is unlikely that each category will occur at the same proportions. For example, it would be undesirable to have children waiting the same percentage of time that they are engaged in activities; it is also unlikely that all children would be engaged 100% of the time. Thus, professional judgment is required in interpreting the results of category-sampling procedures. As noted earlier, covariation of different behaviors can be detected. Many times this covariation cannot be noted by analyzing the totals of the observation session but by analyzing the patterns of behavior within the observation. If one category frequently is recorded after another, then some sequential pattern may be present.

Levels-of-Assistance Recording   *Levels-of-assistance recording* is a variation of event sampling and involves recording the occurrence of a behavior at different levels of help. This type of data collection is useful for goals in which children require adult assistance to do the skill. The goal generally is to increase independence, and this system allows teachers to determine the extent of independence being demonstrated. Support or assistance can take many forms, such as adaptive devices or direct assistance from an adult. Some common types of teacher assistance are verbal cues, gestural prompts, models, partial physical prompts, and full physical manipulations (Wolery et al., 1992). Verbal cues may include specific instruction on how to do the

Form A

Name: _____ Date: _____ Observer: _____
Aggressive behaviors: _____
Disruptive behaviors: _____
Observation time: _____to_____Total: _____

Activity	Aggression	Disruption
Total		

Comments: _____

Form B

Name: _____ Date: _____ Observer: _____
Aggressive behaviors: _____
Disruptive behaviors: _____
Observation time: _____to_____Total: _____

Time	Activity	Aggression	Disruption	Other
9:00-9:05				
9:05-9:10				
9:10-9:15				
9:15-9:20				
9:20-9:25				
Total				

Comments: _____

FIGURE 17.6

Sample data collection sheets for category sampling

Note: Form A is used for event-based category sampling; the observer would record the activity in which the child was involved and place a tally mark each time an aggressive or disruptive behavior occurred in that activity. *Form B* is used for time-based category sampling. The observer would check during each time interval whether aggression, disruption, or other behavior occurred.

behavior, instruction on how to do part of a behavior, rules that help the child do the behavior, and indirect verbal cues such as hints. Gestural prompts are hand movements such as pointing that tell children how to do the behavior. Models are demonstrations of the behavior to be performed and may be motor or verbal. Partial physical prompts are nudges, pushes, and

taps that help the child to do the behavior, and full physical manipulations involve the adult moving the child's hands and putting him or her through the desired actions.

When monitoring a skill through levels of assistance recording, the amount of help required is usually recorded. For example, Deon is learning to put on his coat. When he is getting ready to go

Name: _____ Date: _____ Observer: _____
Area: _____ Activity: _____

Names of children or of behaviors being recorded

Time	Solitary	Onlooking	Parallel	Associative	Cooperative	None
0:30						
1:00						
1:30						
2:00						
2:30						
3:00						
3:30						
4:00						
4:30						
5:00						
5:30						
% of Interv.						

Comments: _____

FIGURE 17.7

Sample data sheet for category sampling (types of play) using a time-sampling procedure to determine the proportion of intervals the child spent in each type of play

out to play, the adult could monitor the amount of help required to allow him to do each step of putting on his coat. His teacher could record whether she used a verbal prompt ("Push your arm all the way out") or physical assistance (physically helping him get his arm through the sleeve). An advantage of such systems is that a record of the amount of adult help needed is obtained. In some cases, more assistance is needed; in other cases too much help is provided and independence is preempted. Also, some instructional procedures such as the system of least prompts (Filla, Wolery, & Anthony, 1999) and graduated guidance (Bryan & Gast, 2000) rely on providing different levels of help. Thus, levels-of-assistance recording is useful in monitoring skills being taught with these procedures. Three recording forms for levels-of-assistance data are presented in Figure 17.8. Data Sheet A has space to write down the type of assistance needed across trials. Data Sheet B includes a list of assistance types, ordered from no assis-

tance to the most intrusive level of assistance, and a row of numbers representing trials. The teacher circles the number that corresponds to the level of assistance needed by the child on that trial. Data Sheet C is similar, but the levels of assistance are presented in columns across the top. The number of trials is listed on the left-hand side, and the teacher places a check mark in the level of assistance presented and another symbol in the level at which the child was correct.

Task-Analytic Recording   Task analysis is a process of breaking a skill into teachable parts, and *task-analytic recording* involves recording children's performance on each step (part) of the skill. Task analysis is often used to develop a hierarchy of skills by difficulty. One or two skills on the hierarchy are initially taught. When they are mastered, the next most difficult skills are taught. Some skills, however, are chains or sequences of responses—a series of behaviors sequenced together to form

Form A

Name: _____ Date: _____ Observer: _____

Behavior/objective: _____

Observation time: _____ to _____ Total: _____

Trial	Record level of assistance needed
1	
2	
3	
4	
5	

Comments: _____

Form B

Name: _____ Date: _____ Observer: _____

Behavior/objective: _____

Observation time: _____ to _____ Total: _____

Level of Assistance Needed	Trial
Independent	1 2 3 4 5
Verbal prompt	1 2 3 4 5
Model	1 2 3 4 5
Partial physical prompt	1 2 3 4 5
Full physical manipulation	1 2 3 4 5

Comments: _____

Form C

Name: _____ Date: _____ Observer: _____

Behavior/objective: _____

Observation time: _____ to _____ Total: _____

Trial	Independent	Verbal Prompt	Model	Partial Physical	Full Physical Manipulation
1					
2					
3					
4					
5					
Total					

Comments: _____

FIGURE 17.8

Sample data collection sheets for levels of assistance data

Note: Form A has space for the teacher to write in the level of help needed on each trial. *Form B* has a list of types of assistance, and a row of numbers representing each trial; the teacher circles the number that corresponds to the level of assistance needed on each trial. *Form C* has the levels of assistance noted by columns, and the teacher checks which of these columns represents the level of assistance needed for each trial.

a complex skill, such as putting on and taking off clothing, using utensils for eating, putting toys away after play, and transitioning from one play area to the next. Response chains are highly useful skills and are goals or outcomes on many intervention plans. Chained skills should be taught (a) using total-task instruction (all steps taught simultaneously) rather than using backward (Kayser, Billingsley, & Neel, 1986) or forward chaining (McDonnell & McFarland, 1988); (b) when and where they are needed (Griffen, Wolery, & Schuster, 1992); (c) using flexible and functional step sequences rather than rigid step sequences (Wright & Schuster, 1994); and (d) in small groups (two or three children) whose members can observe one another learn the chain (Griffen et al., 1992; Hall, Schuster, Wolery, Gast, & Doyle, 1992) or taught with typically developing children as models (Werts, Caldwell, & Wolery, 1996). Data are collected on the accuracy of each step in a functional sequence in a natural situation.

In the simplest form, steps of the response chain (task analysis) are recorded as occurring or not occurring. Unfortunately, failure to do one step of the chain may preclude doing the other steps. For example, failing to put the arm through the sleeve of a coat keeps other steps from occurring. Two solutions to this problem are used. First, the teacher completes the step for the child and the step is scored as incorrect. Second, the teacher provides a prompt to help the child do the step and that step is recorded as occurring with assistance and then the child is given the opportunity to do the next step independently. Because functional rather than rigid step sequences should be used in most cases, the order in which children complete steps can be recorded by simply numbering the steps on the data sheet as children complete them. Examples of data sheets for task-analytic recording are shown in Figure 17.9.

Summary of Recording Procedures Five types of recording systems are used to monitor children's performance on goals and outcomes: event recording, time-sampling, category-sampling,

levels-of-assistance recording, and task-analytic recording. Each is useful for different types of skills, and none will be useful for all skills. Thus, teams need to be fluent in using each type of recording system when monitoring children's progress.

Selecting Times and Situations for Monitoring Usually monitoring should occur in children's natural environments. It should be done when children need the behavior or are likely to use the behaviors (Barnett et al., 1999). The frequency of monitoring should be often enough to get adequate information for making decisions, but not so often that it becomes difficult for the team to collect and analyze. Different goals and outcomes will require different observational places and observational times.

Checking the Accuracy of Data Collection A pervasive characteristic of the human condition is the tendency to make mistakes; in fact, we are familiar with the saying that "to err is human." Because humans use recording systems, errors are likely. Kazdin (1977) described two major types of errors: observer bias or expectations and observer drift. *Observer bias* refers to changes in data occurring because of the observer's expectations, feelings, and so on rather than because of actual changes in the behaviors being recorded. Observer bias is particularly likely to occur when monitoring children's progress, because the persons doing the monitoring also are the persons doing the intervention, and they are likely to expect positive effects from their work. *Observer drift* refers to unspecified changes in the definitions observers apply during data collection over time. Drift also is a particular problem with monitoring, because information is collected over many days and weeks.

To detect these problems, reliability checks can be conducted in which two or more individuals independently but simultaneously collect data on the same behaviors using the same methods. Their data are then compared and a percentage of agreement is calculated.

Form A

Name: _____ Date: _____ Observer: _____
Behavior/objective: _____
Observation time: _____ to _____ Total: _____

Steps of Task Analysis	Response	
	Correct	Error

Comments: _____
Total steps correct: _____

Form B

Name: _____ Date: _____ Observer: _____
Behavior/objective: _____
Observation time: _____ to _____ Total: _____

Steps of Task Analysis	Write order child did steps (1=1st, 2=2nd, 3=3rd, etc.)

Comments: _____

Form C

Name: _____ Date: _____ Observer: _____
Behavior/objective: _____
Observation time: _____ to _____ Total: _____

Steps of Task Analysis	Response		
	Correct	Error	Prompted

Comments: _____
Total steps correct: _____

FIGURE 17.9

Sample data collection sheets for task analytic recording

Note: Form A has spaces to write the steps of the task analysis; the teacher checks whether the child performed each step correctly or incorrectly. Form B has spaces to write the steps of the task analysis; the teacher records the order in which the child did the steps. Form C has spaces to write the steps of the task analysis; the teacher records whether the child did each step correctly, incorrectly, or needed a prompt. Form D (next page) has spaces to write the steps of the task analysis, and the teacher circles or slashes the levels of assistance the child needed for each step on each of five trials.

Form D

Name: _____ Date: _____ Observer: _____

Behavior/objective: _____

Observation time: _____ to _____ Total: _____

Steps of Task Analysis	Trials				
	1	**2**	**3**	**4**	**5**
	I V M PP FM	I V M PP FM	I V M PP FM	I V M PP FM	I V M PP FM
	I V M PP FM	I V M PP FM	I V M PP FM	I V M PP FM	I V M PP FM
	I V M PP FM	I V M PP FM	I V M PP FM	I V M PP FM	I V M PP FM
	I V M PP FM	I V M PP FM	I V M PP FM	I V M PP FM	I V M PP FM
	I V M PP FM	I V M PP FM	I V M PP FM	I V M PP FM	I V M PP FM

I = Independent, V = verbal prompt, M = model, PP = partial physical prompt, and FM = full physical manipulation

Comments: _____

FIGURE 17.9
Continued

Calculating agreement percentages for event sampling data involves dividing the smaller score by the larger and multiplying by 100. With time-sampling data, the records of both observers should be compared at each interval and their responses should be scored as agreements or disagreements. The number of agreements are then divided by the number of agreements plus the number of disagreements and multiplied by 100. Tawney and Gast (1984) and Suen and Ary (1989) describe procedures for collecting and calculating reliability estimates. Conducting reliability checks is difficult and time consuming in some early childhood settings, but it is possible. In part, if the decisions based on the data are critical and if there is a suspicion that bias or drift may be occurring, then reliability checks should be done. Faulty decisions may arise from unreliable data. Retraining observers, clarifying the definitions, simplifying the recording procedures, and giving observers practice in data collection frequently are sufficient strategies for correcting disagreements.

Using Data to Make Decisions A primary function of monitoring is to make decisions about children's progress and their intervention programs. The major decisions are whether a change is needed, and if so, what changes should be made. Interestingly, some research indicates teachers who frequently collect monitoring data have difficulty knowing how to use that data to make decisions (Farlow & Snell, 1989). Three practices may lend assistance: summarizing data, graphing data, and applying data-decision rules.

Summarizing Raw Data Summarizing data can be quite simple and may involve totaling the results of each observation; calculating the percentage, rate, or total time; and ordering the data in the sequence in which they were collected by date. When categories of behavior are measured, summary calculations should be made for each category. When changes in the situations under which the data were collected are known, they should be identified and the resulting data should be marked to aid in the interpretation.

Task-analytic data present particular problems in data summary (Haring & Kennedy, 1988). If one calculates only the percentage of correctly completed steps, that information does not indicate which steps are problematic and what types of decisions need to be made to correct the problem. As a result, the summary of task-analytic data should retain data on each step of the response chain. A format that preserves and summarizes such data is presented in Figure 17.10. This format allows the team to collect the data, summarize them, and graph them on the same sheet. Also, the types of errors that occurred can be recorded and analyzed (Ault, Gast, Wolery, & Doyle, 1992).

Graphing Data to Assist in Making Decisions Some research indicates experienced teachers can analyze data and make decisions based on graphed and ungraphed data (Snell & Loyd, 1991). However, other research indicates children may make more progress when their teachers graph the monitoring data rather than simply collecting and recording it (Fuchs & Fuchs, 1986). Tawney and Gast (1984) and Parsonson and Baer (1992) provide extensive information on how to graph data. Graphs are helpful in communicating with team members. In general, graphing data requires little time and the potential benefits are well worth the effort—especially when important decisions are being made about children's intervention programs.

Data Decision Rules Although some experienced teachers use rules to make decisions from their data, they tend to use fewer rules and have fewer rules available when their children are not making progress (Farlow & Snell, 1989). To assist teams in making consistent decisions based on their monitoring data, sets of data decision rules have been developed (Haring & Liberty, 1990; Liberty & Haring, 1990). Data decision rules exist for promoting initial learning of skills (acquisition) and for promoting fluent performance (Liberty & Haring, 1990); these are shown in Figure 17.11. Some research indicates when teachers use decision rules, their

students evidence additional achievement (Browder, Demchak, Heller, & King, 1989).

Data decision rules also have been developed for promoting generalization of skills across a number of relevant dimensions such as settings, people, objects and materials, and time (Haring & Liberty, 1990). These rules are shown in Table 17.1. The research also supports the use of these rules; more generalization occurs when the rules are applied (Liberty, Haring, White, & Billingsley, 1988). Belfiore and Browder (1992) found that if teachers were taught to monitor their own instructional decisions, they were more consistent in using the data decision rules. As a whole, these studies argue for the regular monitoring of children's progress, summarizing the data, graphing it, and applying rules to the patterns existing in the data. Two qualifications, however, should be noted. First, research on teachers' interpretation of monitoring data and on teachers' use of data decision rules has occurred with older students; it has not been well studied in early childhood contexts. Second, teams should bring all the knowledge they have about children and about how children are performing to the issues of interpretation and analysis of monitoring data.

INTERVENTION MONITORING

Previous sections discussed monitoring children's progress to evaluate its adequacy and determine whether and what changes are needed in their intervention plans. Such monitoring assumes intervention practices and strategies are being used as planned. In the Division for Early Childhood (DEC) recommended practices document (Sandall et al., 2000), the following recommendation is found: "Recommended instructional strategies are used with sufficient fidelity, consistency, frequency, and intensity to ensure high levels of behavior occurring frequently" (Wolery, 2000, p. 37). Unfortunately, this may not always be the case; and children's lack of progress may be due to infrequent,

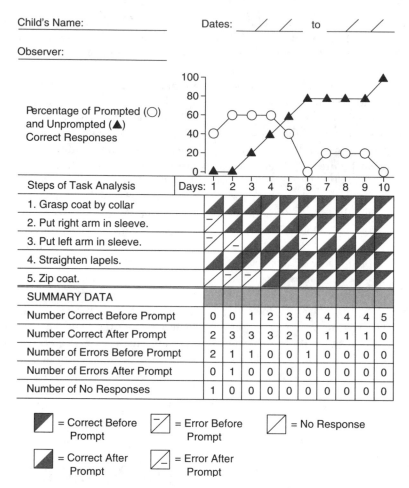

FIGURE 17.10

Sample data sheet and graph for task-analytic data

Note: The top portion is a line graph of the data; the middle portion is the data-collection sheet with symbols provided for recording the child's data; the lower portion is a summary of the data.

inaccurate, or inconsistent use of interventions. The practice of monitoring intervention use is known as *intervention integrity, treatment integrity, procedural fidelity,* and *procedural reliability;* in short, it involves collecting data on the degree to which intervention strategies and practices are used as planned (Gresham, 1996). The rationale for monitoring intervention integrity is relatively straightforward: If the intervention strategy is being monitored and slippage or incorrect implementation begins to

occur, that slippage can be detected and corrected. The foundational assumption is that high levels of accurate use will be associated with better child outcomes than will low levels of correct implementation.

In addition to detecting incorrect use, other advantages exist for monitoring intervention integrity. To measure the integrity with which a practice is used, the components of the practice (often adult behaviors) must be identified, described, and defined. This process can help

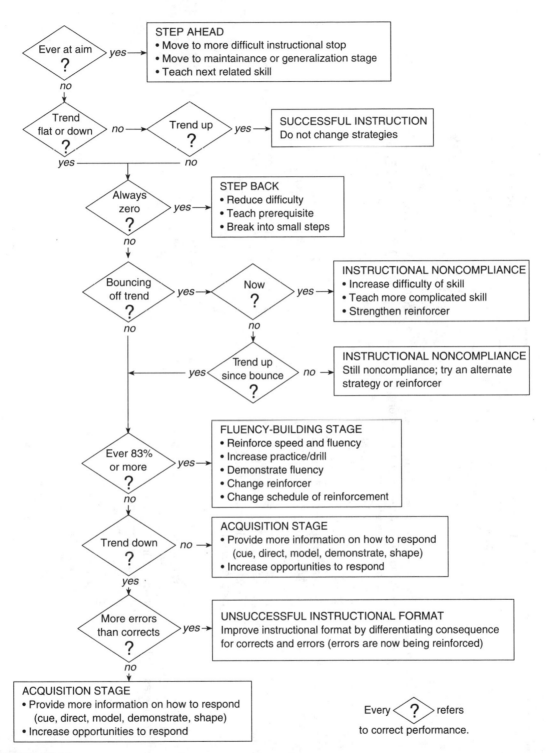

FIGURE 17.11

Data decision rules for analyzing data on acquisition and fluency programs

Note: From "Introduction to Decision Rule Systems" by K. A. Liberty and N. G. Haring, 1990, *Remedial and Special Education,* *11*(1), pp. 32–41. Copyright 1990 by PRO-ED, Inc. Reprinted by permission.

TABLE 17.1
Data Decision Rules for Generalization

Question	Procedures	Answer	Next Step/Decision
A. Has skill generalized at the desired level in all target situations?	Probe for generalization in all desired situations, then compare performance with criteria (IEP objective).	Yes	1. SUCCESSFUL INSTRUCTION • Step ahead to a more difficult level of skill • Choose a new skill to teach EXIT sequence
B. Has skill been acquired?	Compare performance in instructional situation with criteria for acquisition or performance levels specified in IEP objective. Answer yes if student has met performance levels in training situation but not in generalization.	No Yes No	CONTINUE with question B. CONTINUE with question C. 2. SKILL MASTERY PROBLEM • Continue Instruction EXIT sequence
C. Is generalization desired to only a few situations?	Analyze function of skill in current and future environments available to student.	Yes No	CONTINUE with question D. CONTINUE with question E.
D. Is it possible to train directly in those situations?	Are all situations frequently accessible for training so that training time is likely to be adequate to meet aim date in IEP objective?	Yes No	3. LIMITED GENERALIZATION SITUATIONS • Train in desired situation • Train sequentially in all situations (i.e., sequential modification) EXIT sequence CONTINUE with question E.
E. Is the student reinforced even though he/she does not do the largest skill?	Observe student behavior during probes and note events which follow appropriate, inappropriate, target, and nontarget skills. Determine if those events which should follow the target skills, or have been shown to reinforce other skills, are presented to the student, or available even if he does not respond, or if he does the skill incorrectly, or if he misbehaves.	No Yes No	CONTINUE with question E. CONTINUE with question F. CONTINUE with question H.
F. Does the student fail to respond and is reinforced?	Answer yes only if the student is reinforced for doing nothing (i.e.,	Yes	4. NONCONTINGENT REINFORCER PROBLEM

accesses reinforcers for "no response").

- Alter generalization contingencies

CONTINUE with question G.

G. Is the behavior reinforced by the same reinforcers as the target skill?

If misbehavior or other behavior accesses same reinforcer available for target skill, answer yes.

No

Yes → 5. COMPETING BEHAVIOR PROBLEM
- Increase proficiency
- Amplify instructed behavior
- Alter generalization contingencies

EXIT sequence

No → 6. COMPETING REINFORCER PROBLEM
- Alter generalization contingencies

EXIT sequence

H. Did the student generalize once at or close to criterion performance levels and then not as well on other opportunities?

Consider performance in current and past probes. Compare student performance for each response opportunity with performance level specified in objective. If near criterion performance occurred on the first response opportunity, and performance was poor or nonexistent after that, answer yes.

Yes → 7. REINFORCING FUNCTION PROBLEM
- Program natural reinforcers
- Eliminate training reinforcers
- Use natural schedules
- Use natural consequences
- Teach self-reinforcement
- Teach to solicit reinforcement
- Reinforce generalized behavior
- Alter generalization contingencies

EXIT sequence

No

CONTINUE with question I.

Yes → 8. DISCRIMINATION FUNCTION PROBLEM

Vary stimuli:
- Use all stimuli
- Use frequent stimuli
- Use multiple exemplars

EXIT sequence

I. Did the student respond partially correctly during at least one response opportunity?

Analyze anecdotal data and observation notes from probe.

No

CONTINUE with question J.

Yes → 9. GENERALIZATION TRAINING FORMAT
- Increase proficiency
- Program natural reinforcers
- Use natural schedules
- Use appropriate natural stimuli
- Eliminate training stimuli

EXIT sequence

J. Did the student fail to perform any part of the target skill?

Analyze student performance during probe situation.

No → STOP. You have made an error in sequence. Begin again at Question A.

Note: From "Decision Rules and Procedures for Generalization" by K. Liberty, in N. G. Haring (Ed.) *Generalization for Students with Severe Handicaps: Strategies and Solutions*, 1988, Seattle, WA: University of Washington Press. Copyright 1988 by Washington Research Organization. Reprinted by permission.

577

team members know what to do and can be used to identify training needs team members have before they try to apply the intervention. Further, defining the components of practice can assist in communicating with others what practices are being used. A common assumption is that practices adults find acceptable will be used more correctly; however, this is not necessarily the case. Ratings of practice acceptability do not appear to predict correct use of those practices (Peterson & McConnell, 1996; Sterling-Turner & Watson, 2002).

There is growing evidence in education suggesting the levels of correct implementation of intervention practices are associated with children's outcomes (Noell, Gresham, & Gansle, 2002). Some research with young children who have disabilities also supports the assumption that children's outcomes are associated with intervention integrity. For example, Holcombe, Wolery, and Snyder (1994) found high levels of correct use of prompt delivery with the constant time delay procedure was associated with rapid learning, whereas low levels of correct use of prompt delivery were associated with slower learning or actual failure to learn. Peterson and McConnell (1996) evaluated teachers' use of social skills interventions. They found: (a) teachers who used the interventions correctly tended to use the interventions more, and (b) both correct use and more use were associated with increases in children's scores on a social competence measure. However, in some cases, failure to use interventions as planned is not associated with less desirable child outcomes. For example, Wilbers (1990) found both high and low levels of correct implementation for the length of the delay interval with the constant time delay strategy produced similar learning. In the context of wraparound services, Toffalo (2000) studied whether different outcomes occurred when children received the number of hours of services prescribed on their intervention plans. No relationships were found between outcomes and the extent to which the number of hours of planned services were actually received. Thus, correct implementation appears to influence children's outcomes when critical as compared to non-critical components of intervention practices are used as planned.

Two broad issues are relevant in monitoring intervention integrity: (a) how often the practice is used, and (b) how accurately or consistently the practice is used. Logically, a practice must be used at some level (amount) before it can influence children's outcomes—a practice that is not used cannot be responsible for children's progress or lack thereof. Peterson and McConnell (1996) found more use of social skills interventions was related to children's social outcomes. However, measuring how often intervention practices are used is not straightforward. As Toffalo (2000) indicates, simply counting the number of hours of services is probably not a sensitive measure of intervention integrity or of practice usage. To further illustrate the complexity, two instructional studies are relevant. For preschoolers who attended a class every day, Venn, Wolery, and Greco (1996) compared two schedules of providing direct instructional sessions: daily and every other day. The every-other-day sessions produced more rapid learning (e.g., fewer minutes of instruction to criterion) than daily instructional sessions. A potential explanation was the every-other-day sessions provided more variety to children's days, and task variation is known to be associated with better outcomes (Dunlap, 1984). Similarly, in teaching preschoolers with autism to transition between classroom activities, Venn, Wolery, Morris, DeCesare, and Cuffs (2002) found independence did not occur based on the amount of prompts provided to children but on whether teachers systematically used and removed those prompts. These studies suggest more practice use is not necessarily better. Thus, in monitoring intervention integrity, amount is important (Peterson & McConnell, 1996), but amount may interact with other variables such as unrelated factors known to influence children's learning (Venn et al., 1996) and correct use of the actual practice (Venn et al., 2002).

Deciding what to measure in monitoring intervention integrity is influenced by the nature of the planned interventions. A variety of effective early intervention practices have been described and can be categorized as: (a) manipulations of the physical (e.g., space, materials), temporal (e.g., schedule), and social (e.g., group composition, proximity to peers) dimensions of children's environments; (b) modifications of regularly occurring routines; (c) use of planned group and play activities; (d) adult interactive behavior; (e) use of reinforcement and reinforcement-based procedures; (f) peer-mediated intervention strategies; and (g) use of instructional strategies (e.g., naturalistic teaching and response prompting procedures) (Wolery, 2000). Some of these practices require different types of monitoring than others. For example, documenting that a given arrangement of play areas in a classroom was "implemented" is different from monitoring whether a teacher was responsive to a child during play. Four guidelines are recommended for monitoring intervention integrity.

First, *general use of recommended intervention practices should be monitored.* Programs should on a regular basis determine whether their practices are in compliance with recommended practices. In the case of early intervention programs, the assessment system accompanying the DEC recommended practices document could be used (Hemmeter, Joseph, Smith, & Sandall, 2001). This system uses ratings as well as direct observations to determine whether programs are using recommended practices. Such measurement should be done in conjunction with other measures of the quality of children's ecology discussed in Chapter 8.

Second, *when children are not making progress, teams should examine the integrity of the intervention practices.* Regularly measuring intervention integrity of all of the practices teams use would be unrealistic and may not lead to better child outcomes; however, failure to measure intervention integrity of some practices is likely to lead to poor child outcomes. The question becomes, which practices should be measured? In this

guideline, we suggest measuring intervention integrity when children's progress is slow, variable, or is not occurring.

Third, *develop a method of measuring intervention practice integrity.* At least three types of measures are used to assess intervention integrity: rating scales, checklists, and direct recording systems. When devising measures of intervention integrity, it is often useful to task analyze the components of the practice. In short this means breaking the practice into the behaviors adults should do when using the practice. A method is then developed for measuring each of the adult behaviors.

Rating scales and other judgment-based procedures should be used when intervention practices are difficult to measure precisely such as being responsive to children's play and social-communicative attempts, and reading books interactively. Peterson and McConnell (1996) used a rating scale to assess teachers' use of social skill interventions. The intervention components were defined, and each was scored on a continuum of correct use with a 5-point scale from "very much like procedure specified in the intervention manual . . . to not at all like specified procedures" (p. 149). Checklists are useful when a practice is complex and involves several steps; for example, setting up and using a specific feeding regime with a child or using alternative and augmentative communication interventions (Schlosser, 2002). Sometimes fidelity checklists can be used to guide implementation and to monitor it. Checklists also have been used to monitor training and consultation sessions focused on helping teachers use specific procedures (Filla et al., 1999). These focus on whether the consultant addressed all the points and used the methods that represented the consultative approach.

Direct observation with a systematic recording system is useful when intervention practices involve sequences of adult and child behaviors. Examples of such practices are routines-based intervention strategies (e.g., interrupted chain procedure or transition-based teaching), milieu teaching procedures (e.g., incidental teaching, mand-model procedure), and response prompting procedures (e.g., time delay, simultaneous prompting) (Wolery, 2000). These procedures are often characterized as having antecedents (something that starts the learning opportunity), an interval for the child to use the behavior in the goal and for the teacher to provide assistance, and consequent events. Observing and measuring whether these elements occur as planned is recommended. Such measures can also include monitoring data on children's performance (e.g., Holcombe et al., 1994).

Fourth, *share the results of monitoring with the implementers.* In some cases, monitoring intervention integrity will involve one team member measuring another team member's practice. When intervention integrity is low, discussions with the person using the practice may assist in increasing correct usage (Noell et al., 2000); and in other cases, provision of performance feedback is necessary (Jones, Wickstrom, & Friman, 1997; Noell et al, 2000; Witt, Noell, LaFleur, & Mortenson, 1997). When intervention integrity is high, feedback and praise for correct usage also is appropriate.

SUMMARY

Monitoring children's progress is done to validate the results of initial assessments, develop a record of child progress, and determine whether interventions should be changed. When conducting monitoring assessments, goals and outcomes in intervention plans and selected global aspects of child behavior should be measured, as should the quality of children's environments. Monitoring plans should identify what will be measured, who will do it, and the contexts in which it will occur. The perspectives of families and team members who spend time with children should be solicited. Monitoring should occur in authentic naturalistic settings, occur regularly and frequently, and be summarized for decision making. Monitoring methods include narrative descriptions, judgment-based assessments, work samples, and direct observation. A variety of direct observation procedures are available and should be used. The collected data should be summarized and graphed, and data decision rules should be applied. Finally, intervention strategies and practices should be monitored for frequent and accurate use.

· · · · · · · ·

SUMMARY OF KEY CONCEPTS

- Monitoring children's performance should occur to validate the initial assessment conclusions, develop a record of progress, and make decisions about whether *and* what changes, if any, should be made.
- Children's progress on the individualized goals and objectives should be monitored as well as important indices of child behavior such as engagement, interactions with others, and maladaptive behaviors.
- Monitoring plans should identify the information to be collected, who will collect it, the situations in which it will be collected, how frequently it will be collected, and who will be responsible for analyzing it.

- Monitoring should occur in authentic contexts, include the perspectives of relevant individuals, and occur frequently—more frequently on important goals and on goals for which progress is questionable and decisions are needed.
- Broad approaches to monitoring children's progress are narrative descriptions, judgment-based assessments, work samples, and direct observation.
- Narrative descriptions include anecdotal records, running records, and specimen descriptions.
- Judgment-based assessments often involve ratings of children's performance and qualities; they are useful in securing multiple perspectives of children's behavior.

- Work samples are compilations (portfolios) of children's products over time that show progress and the richness of children's behavior.
- Using direct observation to monitor children's progress requires teams to define the behaviors being measured, select relevant data collection systems, select times and situations for observation, check the accuracy of the data collection, and summarize and make decisions based on the data.

- Direct observation methods include event sampling, time sampling, category sampling, level-of-assistance recording, and task-analytic recording.
- Collected data should be summarized and graphed and data decision rules should be consulted.
- Teams also should monitor the integrity with which intervention practices are implemented and use that information to correct implementation problems.

· · · · · · · ·

REFERENCES

Ault, M. J., Gast, D. L., Wolery, M., & Doyle, P. M. (1992). Data collection and graphing method for teaching chained tasks with the constant time delay procedure. *Teaching Exceptional Children, 24*(2), 28–33.

Barnett, D. W., Bell, S. H., & Carey, K. T. (1999). *Designing preschool interventions: A practitioner's guide.* New York: Guilford Press.

Belfiore, P. J., & Browder, D. M. (1992). The effects of self-monitoring on teachers' data-based decisions and on the progress of adults with severe mental retardation. *Education and Training in Mental Retardation, 27,* 60–67.

Bijou, S. W., Peterson, R. F., Harris, F. R., Allen, K. E., & Johnston, M. S. (1969). Methodology of experimental studies of young children in natural settings. *Psychological Reports, 19,* 177–210.

Billingsley, F. F., Burgess, D., Lynch, V. W., & Matlock, B. L. (1991). Toward generalized outcomes: Considerations and guidelines for writing instructional objectives. *Education and Training in Mental Retardation, 26,* 351–360.

Bowman, B. T., Donovan, M. S., & Burns, M. S. (2001). *Eager to learn: Educating our preschoolers.* Washington, DC: National Academy Press.

Browder, D. M., Demchak, M. A., Heller, M., & King, D. (1989). An in vivo evaluation of the use of data-based rules to guide instructional decisions. *Journal of the Association for Persons with Severe Handicaps, 14,* 234–240.

Bryan, L. C., & Gast, D. L. (2000). Teaching on-task and on-schedule behaviors to high-functioning children with autism via picture activity schedules. *Journal of Autism and Developmental Disorders, 30,* 553–567.

Cooper, J. O. (1980). *Measuring behavior* (2nd ed.). Champaign, IL: Research Press.

Dunlap, G. (1984). The influence of task variation and maintenance tasks on the learning and affect of autistic children. *Journal of Experimental Child Psychology, 37,* 41–64.

Experimental Education Unit (2001). *Show me the data!* Seattle, WA: Experimental Education Unit, University of Washington.

Farlow, L. J., & Snell, M. E. (1989). Teacher use of student performance data to make instructional decisions: Practices in programs for students with moderate to profound disabilities. *Journal of the Association for Persons with Severe Handicaps, 14,* 13–22.

Filla, A., Wolery, M., & Anthony, L. (1999). Promoting children's conversations during play with adult prompts. *Journal of Early Intervention, 22,* 93–108.

Fuchs, L. S., & Fuchs, D. (1986). Effects of systematic formative evaluation: A meta analysis. *Exceptional Children, 53,* 199–208.

Gresham, F. M. (1996). Treatment integrity in single-subject research. In R. D. Franklin, D. B. Allison, & B. S. Gorman (Eds.), *Design and analysis of single-case research* (pp. 93–117). Mahwah, NJ: Lawrence Erlbaum.

Griffen, A. K., Wolery, M., & Schuster, J. W. (1992). Triadic instruction of chained food preparation responses: Acquisition and observational learning. *Journal of Applied Behavior Analysis, 25,* 193–204.

Guralnick, M. J. (1997). *The effectiveness of early intervention*. Baltimore: Paul H. Brookes.

Hall, M. G., Schuster, J. W., Wolery, M., Gast, D. L., & Doyle, P. M. (1992). Teaching cooking skills to students with moderate handicaps in a small group instructional format using constant time delay. *Journal of Behavioral Education, 2,* 257–279.

Hanline, M. F., Milton, S., & Phelps, P. (2001). Young children's block construction activities: Findings from 3 years of observation. *Journal of Early Intervention, 24,* 224–237.

Haring, N. G., & Liberty, K. A. (1990). Matching strategies with performance in facilitating generalization. *Focus on Exceptional Children, 22*(8), 1–16.

Haring, T. G., & Kennedy, C. H. (1988). Units of analysis in task-analytic research. *Journal of Applied Behavior Analysis, 21,* 207–215.

Hemmeter, M. L., Joseph, G. E., Smith, B. J., & Sandall, S. (2001). *DEC recommended practices program assessment: Improving practices for young children with special needs and their families.* Longmont, CO: Sopris West.

Holcombe, A., Wolery, M., & Snyder, E. (1994). Effects of two levels of procedural fidelity with constant time delay on children's learning. *Journal of Behavioral Education, 4,* 49–73.

Ivory, J. J., & McCollum, J. A. (1999). Effects of social and isolate toys on social play in an inclusive setting. *Journal of Special Education, 32,* 238–243.

Jones, K. M., Wickstrom, K. F., & Friman, P. C. (1997). The effects of observational feedback on treatment integrity in school-based behavioral consultation. *School Psychology Quarterly, 12,* 316–326.

Kaiser, A. P., Hancock, T. B., & Nietfeld, J. P. (2000). The effects of parent-implemented enhanced milieu teaching on the social communication of young children who have autism. *Early Education and Development, 11,* 423–446.

Kayser, J. E., Billingsley, F. F., & Neel, R. S. (1986). A comparison of in-context and traditional instructional approaches: Total task, single trial versus backward chaining multiple trials. *Journal of the Association for Persons with Severe Handicaps, 11,* 28–38.

Kazdin, A. E. (1977). Artifact, bias, and complexity of assessment: The ABCs of reliability. *Journal of Applied Behavior Analysis, 10,* 141–150.

Kohler, F. W, & Strain, P. S. (1999). Maximizing peer-mediated resources in integrated preschool classrooms. *Topics in Early Childhood Special Education, 19,* 92–102.

Kohler, F. W., Strain, P. S., Hoyson, M., & Jamieson, B. (1997). Merging naturalistic teaching and peer-based strategies to address the IEP objectives of preschoolers with autism: An examination of structural and child behavior outcomes. *Focus on Autism and Other Developmental Disabilities, 12,* 196–206.

Kozloff, M. (1994). *Improving educational outcomes for children with disabilities: Principles for assessment, program planning, and evaluation.* Baltimore: Paul H. Brookes.

Liberty, K. A., & Haring, N. G. (1990). Introduction to decision rule systems. *Remedial and Special Education, 11,* 32–41.

Liberty, K. A., Haring, N. G., White, O. R., & Billingsley, F. F. (1988). A technology for the future: Decision rules for generalization. *Education and Training in Mental Retardation, 23,* 315–326.

Luiselli, J. K., & Luiselli, T. E. (1995). A behavior analysis approach toward chronic food refusal in children with gastrostomy-tube dependency. *Topics in Early Childhood Special Education, 15,* 1–18.

McDonnell, J., & McFarland, S. (1988). Comparison of forward and concurrent chaining strategies in teaching laundromat skills to students with severe handicaps. *Research in Developmental Disabilities, 9,* 177–194.

Meisels, S. J. (1993). Remaking classroom assessment with the work sampling system. *Young Children, 49,* 34–40.

Meisels, S. J., Liaw, F., Dorfman, A., & Nelson, R. F. (1995). The Work Sampling System: Reliability and validity of a performance assessment for young children. *Early Childhood Research Quarterly, 10,* 277–296.

Meisels, S. J., Xue, Y., Bickel, D. D., Nicholson, J., & Atkins-Burnett, S. (2001). Parental reactions to authentic performance assessment. *Educational Assessment, 7,* 61–85.

Munger, G. F., Snell, M. E., & Loyd, B. H. (1989). A study of the effects of frequency of probe data collection and graph characteristics on teachers' visual analysis. *Research in Developmental Disabilities, 10,* 109–127.

Neisworth, J. T., & Bagnato, S. J. (2000). Recommended practices in assessment. In S. Sandall, M. E. McLean, & B. J. Smith (Eds.), *DEC recommended practices in early intervention/early childhood special education* (pp. 17–27). Longmont, CO: Sopris West.

Neisworth, J. T., & Fewell, R. R. (1990). Foreword. *Topics in Early Childhood Special Education, 10,* ix–xi.

Noell, G. H., Gresham, F. M., & Gansle, K. A. (2002). Does treatment integrity matter? A preliminary investigation of instructional implementation and mathematics performance. *Journal of Behavioral Education, 11,* 51–67.

Noell, G. H., Witt, J. C., LaFleur, L. H., Mortenson, B. P., Rainer, D. D., & LeVelle, J. (2000). Increasing intervention implementation in general education following consultation: A comparison of two follow-up strategies. *Journal of Applied Behavior Analysis, 33,* 271–284.

Odom, S. L., & Bailey, D. B. (2001). Inclusive preschool programs: Classroom ecology and child outcomes. In M. J. Gurlanick (Ed.), *Early childhood inclusion: Focus on change.* (pp. 253–276). Baltimore: Paul H. Brookes.

Odom, S. L., & McLean, M. E. (Eds.) (1996). *Early intervention/early childhood special education: Recommended practices.* Austin, TX: PRO-ED.

Odom, S. L., & Strain, P. S. (1984). Classroom-based social skills instruction for severely handicapped preschool children. *Topics in Early Childhood Special Education, 4,* 97–116.

Parsonson, B. S., & Baer, D. M. (1992). The visual analysis of data, and current research into the stimuli controlling it. In T. R. Kratochwill & J. R. Levin (Eds.), *Single-case research design and analysis: New directions for psychology and education.* Hillsdale, NJ: Lawrence Erlbaum.

Peterson, C. A., & McConnell, S. R. (1996). Factors related to intervention integrity and child outcome in social skills interventions. *Journal of Early Intervention, 20,* 146–164.

Priest, J. S., McConnell, S. R., Walker, D., Carta, J. J., Kaminski, R. A., McEvoy, et al. (2001). General growth outcomes for young children: Developing a foundation for continuous progress measurement. *Journal of Early Intervention, 24,* 163–180.

Raspa, M. J., McWilliam, R. A., & Ridley, S. M. (2001). Child care quality and children's engagement. *Early Education and Development, 12,* 209–224.

Sandall, S., McLean, M. E., & Smith, B. J. (2000). *DEC recommended practices in early intervention/early childhood special education.* Longmont, CO: Sopris West.

Schlosser, R. W. (2002). On the importance of being earnest about treatment integrity. *Augmentative and Alternative Communication, 18,* 36–44.

Schwartz, I., & Olswang, L. B. (1996). Evaluating child behavior change in natural settings: Exploring alternative strategies for data collection. *Topics in Early Childhood Special Education, 16,* 82–101.

Snell, M. E., & Loyd, B. H. (1991). A study of the effects of trend, variability, frequency, and form of data on teachers' judgments about progress and their decisions about program change. *Research in Developmental Disabilities, 12,* 41–61.

Spector, P. E. (1992). *Summated rating scale construction: An introduction.* Sage University Paper Series on Quantitative Applications in the Social Sciences, 07-082. Newbury Park, CA: Sage.

Sterling-Turner, H. E., & Watson, T. S. (2002). An analog investigation of the relationship between treatment acceptability and treatment integrity. *Journal of Behavioral Education, 11,* 39–50.

Suen, H. K., & Ary, D. (1989). *Analyzing quantitative behavioral observation data.* Hillsdale, NJ: Lawrence Erlbaum.

Tawney, J. W., & Gast, D. L. (1984). *Single subject research in special education.* Upper Saddle River, NJ: Merrill/Prentice Hall.

Thompson, T., Felce, D., & Symons, F. J., (2000). *Behavioral observation: Technology and applications in developmental disabilities.* Baltimore: Paul H. Brookes.

Thurman, S. K., & Widerstrom, A. H. (1990). *Infants and young children with special needs: A developmental and ecological approach* (2nd ed.). Baltimore: Paul H. Brookes.

Toffalo, D. (2000). An investigation of treatment integrity and outcomes in wraparound services. *Journal of Child and Family Studies, 9,* 351–361.

Venn, M. L., Wolery, M., & Greco, M. (1996). Effects of every-day and every-other-day instruction. *Journal of Autism and Other Developmental Disabilities, 11,* 15–28.

Venn, M. L., Wolery, M., Morris, A., DeCesare, L. D., & Cuffs, M. S. (2002). *Use of progressive time delay and reinforcement to teach in-class transitions to preschoolers with autism.* Manuscript submitted for publication.

Venn, M. L., Wolery, M., Werts, M. G., Morris, A., DeCesare, L. D., & Cuffs, M. S. (1993). Embedding instruction in art activities to teach preschoolers with disabilities to imitate their peers. *Early Childhood Research Quarterly, 8,* 277–294.

Werts, M. G., Caldwell, N. K., & Wolery, M. (1996). Peer modeling of response chains: Observational learning by students with disabilities. *Journal of Applied Behavior Analysis, 29,* 53–66.

White, O. R. (1980). Adaptive performance objectives: Form versus function. In W. Sailor, B. Wilcox, & L. Brown (Eds.), *Methods of instruction for severely handicapped students* (pp. 47–70). Baltimore: Paul H. Brookes.

White, O. R., & Haring, N. G. (1980). *Exceptional teaching.* Upper Saddle River, NJ: Merrill/Prentice Hall.

Wilbers, J. S. (1990). *Effects of procedural fidelity in constant time delay procedures used to teach letter names to preschoolers.* Unpublished master's degree thesis, University of Kentucky, Lexington.

Witt, J. C., Noell, G. H., LaFleur, L. H., & Mortenson, B. P. (1997). Teacher use of interventions in general education settings: Measurement and analysis of the independent variable. *Journal of Applied Behavior Analysis, 30,* 693–696.

Wolery, M. (2000). Recommended practices in child-focused interventions. In S. Sandall, M. E. McLean, & B. J. Smith (Eds.), *DEC Recommended practices in early intervention/early childhood special education* (pp. 29–37). Longmont, CO: Sopris West.

Wolery, M., Ault, M. J., & Doyle, P. M. (1992). *Teaching students with moderate and severe disabilities: Use of response prompting strategies.* White Plains, NY: Longman.

Wolery, M., Bailey, D. B., & McWilliam, R. A. (in press). *Teaching infants and preschoolers with disabilities* (3rd ed.). Upper Saddle River, NJ: Merrill/Prentice Hall.

Wolery, M., & Wolery, R. A. (1992). Promoting functional cognitive skills. In D. B. Bailey & M. Wolery (Eds.), *Teaching infants and preschoolers with disabilities* (2nd ed.) (pp. 521–572). Upper Saddle River, NJ: Merrill/Prentice Hall.

Wright, C. W., & Schuster, J. W. (1994). Accepting specific versus functional student responses when training chained tasks. *Education and Training in Mental Retardation and Developmental Disabilities, 29,* 43–56.